understanding
DEVIANCE

understanding DEVIANCE

CANADIAN EDITION

David Downes

Paul Rock

Chris McCormick

OXFORD
UNIVERSITY PRESS

OXFORD
UNIVERSITY PRESS

70 Wynford Drive, Don Mills, Ontario M3C 1J9
www.oupcanada.com

Oxford University Press is a department of the University of Oxford.
It furthers the University's objective of excellence in research, scholarship,
and education by publishing worldwide in

Oxford   New York

Auckland   Cape Town   Dar es Salaam   Hong Kong   Karachi
Kuala Lumpur   Madrid   Melbourne   Mexico City   Nairobi
New Delhi   Shanghai   Taipei   Toronto

With offices in

Argentina   Austria   Brazil   Chile   Czech Republic   France   Greece
Guatemala   Hungary   Italy   Japan   Poland   Portugal   Singapore
South Korea   Switzerland   Thailand   Turkey   Ukraine   Vietnam

Oxford is a trade mark of Oxford University Press
in the UK and in certain other countries

Published in Canada by Oxford University Press

Library and Archives Canada Cataloguing in Publication

Downes, David M.

Understanding deviance / David Downes, Paul Rock, Chris McCormick.
—1st Canadian ed.

Includes bibliographical references and index.
ISBN 978-0-19-542567-3

1. Deviant behavior—Textbooks. 2. Crime—Sociological aspects
—Textbooks. I. Rock, Paul Elliott, 1956–
II. McCormick, Christopher Ray III. Title

HM811.D69 2008   302.5'42   C2008-903806-1

Cover Image: iStock photo
This book is printed on permanent (acid-free) paper ∞.

Printed and bound in Canada

1 2 3 4 – 12 11 10 09

Contents

Preface and Acknowledgements

When the opportunity came along to work on the first Canadian edition of Downes and Rock's *Understanding Deviance*, I knew it was too good to pass up. *Understanding Deviance* has long been a classic compendium of theorizing in the sociology of deviance. Its review of theories and its understanding of the deeper issues behind the standard interpretations have educated students now for almost three decades.

At the same time, an adaptation of a well-known classic has to tread a fine line between revising the text to fit a new context without altering it beyond recognition or comfort. What I particularly wished to retain was Downes and Rock's narrative style of comparing theories to one another.

The interest in studying theories of the past is more than an exercise in intellectual archaeology. Studying Durkheim, Merton, and Thrasher shows us the early roots of our discipline, while reading Cicourel, Matza, and Garland reveals the interest in revising those early approaches for present-day analysis. The work of theorizing is a discussion about social conditions and a conversation with other theorists.

Going back and reviewing the roots of present-day deviance studies for this work has reminded me of texts I have long forgotten. I would recommend theorists go back and read the original publications in such journals as the *Canadian Review of Sociology and Anthropology* (since 1964), the *Canadian Journal of Sociology* (since 1975), the *American Journal of Sociology* (since 1895), the *American Sociological Review* (since 1936), *Social Problems* (since 1953), and the *Journal of Educational Sociology* (since 1927).

In this exercise it is possible to glimpse lesser-known work not seen before. To a theorist, it was exciting to find an article by Frederic Thrasher from the 1920s on his research with gangs that I had never seen referred to; a piece by Carl Dawson from the 1920s concerning an address he gave in Montreal on his kidney-zone model of social development, a model which is significant for its contribution to a Canadian sociology; and references to the work of Shutz preceding what has been thought to be the beginning of his influence on sociology. Rereading these pieces reminded me of how theorists talk about one another's work in an interest to make their work practical and of relevance to current social conditions.

For this Canadian edition the original text has been updated and revised to make it more relevant to the Canadian context. Dozens of new studies have been included, historical references to Canadian cases are referred to, and newspapers are used as a source of information on how deviance was handled in Halifax, Montreal, Vancouver, and Toronto.

However, it should also be added that while this was originally a British text, many of the trends in deviance and control it describes have been found to be applicable to many Western countries. One trend we have noted is the shift toward the political right, to a law-and-order approach to deviance and control. Because the sociology of deviance has traditionally maintained itself distinct from criminology, we try to avoid veering into a discussion of crime and prevention. The two fields are very different, but we also adopt a new term, 'deviantology', to describe more easily our interest in the scientific study of deviance and control.

In addition to the revisions described above, various pedagogical features have been added to the book to enhance its value for students and teachers alike. They are meant to be a springboard for exploration. Every chapter has a discussion feature called Deviance and Culture and another called Deviance Explorations. In each of these sections an interesting and critical issue is explored more fully to illustrate the complex character of deviance in the modern world and to relate deviance issues to topics in our culture, literature, and news. Each chapter has a case study and discussion questions, and copious references; many chapters also refer the reader to relevant websites and to recent or well-known films. I have also added a glossary at the end that defines almost a hundred of the terms used throughout the book.

I want to thank the people at Oxford for proposing this project and for working to bring it to fruition, especially developmental editor Jennifer Charlton and copy editor Freya Godard. I would also like to thank the anonymous reviewers who evaluated the proposal and manuscript; and, of course, David Downes and Paul Rock for being open to these changes in the first place.

And finally, here is a note on how to read this book. It is not only a summary of different theoretical approaches, but also an argument that theorizing is an activity, and that its reflection on the developing character of deviance in research has direct relevance to our daily lives in society.

Chris McCormick, 2008
St. Thomas University

Chapter One

Confusion and Diversity

Chapter Overview

In this chapter we comment on the apparent diversity in the sociology of deviance and on why there are so many divergent perspectives on what should be a study of the same thing—deviant behaviour. Not only are there different ways of seeing one specific type of deviance, such as witchcraft, but there are also different philosophical perspectives on deviance in general. For example, some see deviance as opposition against the social order, whereas others see it as the result of the organization of society. There is often a reluctance to consider behaviour as deviant until all other explanations are exhausted.

Some ways of looking at deviance are quite abstract, and others stress practical crime-fighting techniques. Each is based on different assumptions, and each yields different conclusions. We give a brief overview some of the major areas within the sociology of deviance and explain how politics, institutional traditions, and even human nature can influence the field. We argue that the apparent confusion and diversity are a characteristic of deviance in the world, as well as a feature of the sociology of deviance itself.

■ Introduction

The very name of the discipline, 'the sociology of crime and deviance', is a little misleading. A singular noun and a hint of science seem to promise a unified body of knowledge and an agreed-upon set of procedures for resolving analytic difficulties. It suggests that the curious and troubled may secure sure answers to practical, political, moral, and intellectual problems. And, of all branches of applied sociology, the demands placed on the sociology of crime and deviance are probably the most urgent. Deviance is upsetting and perplexing, and it confronts people in many settings, but in turning to sociology, inquirers are more likely to encounter something akin to the Tower of Babel. They are offered, not one answer, but a series of different, sometimes competing and contradictory visions of the nature of people, deviation, and the social order. Very often, their questions cannot even be discussed until they are rephrased so that they can be analyzed in the context of one of the master theories of crime and deviance.

> The study of deviance is a collection of different versions of sociology.

The sociology of crime and deviance is not one coherent discipline at all but a collection of relatively independent versions of sociology. What has given a tenuous unity to the enterprise is a common subject, not a common approach. At different times, people with different backgrounds and different purposes have argued about rule breaking. The outcome has been an accumulation of theories that only occasionally mesh, but which resemble a conversation. Since deviance is crucial to all ideas of morality and politics, the explanation of it has been championed with great fervour. After all, substantial consequences can flow from the acceptance of a particular argument. The reader will be bombarded by magisterial claims and criticisms and propelled toward final solutions and definitive approaches. Few authors have attempted to reveal all the uncertainties and complexities of their stance, many have simply avoided controversy or criticism, and others are openly partisan. And the result has been that textbooks are often poor guides. After a while, the reader is prone to become giddy, defeated, or prematurely committed to one position above others.

Novices in the reading of theory are evidently vulnerable. It is only through prolonged exposure to a mass of conflicting ideas that they can stand back and understand what has been omitted, what evidence has not been examined, and which assertions have not been challenged. However, at the outset, they are ill-equipped to judge the merits of an apparently persuasive work.

Understanding Deviance was written to answer some of these difficulties. We have prepared it as an intellectual framework in which the various theories of deviance can be set and assessed. It cannot be regarded as an entirely satisfactory substitute for the reader's own analysis. Yet it may provide a rough map for someone who enters the labyrinth of 'deviantology' for the first time.

We shall not pretend that the very diverse perspectives on deviance can be reduced to a fundamental harmony. Admittedly there *are* common preoccupations and methods that lend the sociology of deviance a loose working consensus. Despite their disagreements, one sociologist can still recognize and talk to another. But the consensus is rudimentary, and it is sensible to acknowledge disunity by examining the differences of opinion that mark the discipline. Accordingly, in this book we undertake a survey of each of the major schools of thought, not pretending that they can be easily reconciled. We state those schools' assumptions in a straightforward manner, marshal the doubts that others have voiced, and repeat or invent the replies of the schools' champions. Instead of protecting one or other fragment of the discipline, we simply parade various alternatives so that the whole may be appreciated and organized by the reader. The reader, in turn, would do well to suspend judgment about the worth of particular ideas until the whole conflicting array has been examined.

■ The Character and Sources of Ambiguity

We have observed that the sociology of deviance contains, not one vision, but many. It is a collection of different and rather independent theories. Each theory has its own history; it is supported by a long train of arguments that reach into the foundational ideas of philosophy and politics; it discloses a number of distinct opportunities for explaining and manipulating deviant behaviour; and in the main, its assertions will be put in such a distinctive terminology that they resist immediate comparison with rival arguments. Thus, one intellectual faction, radical sociology, may speak of the oppression and alienation caused by the institutions of capitalist society. It will call deviance liberation and conformity collusion. It will point to endemic contradictions and crises that will culminate, perhaps, in a society rid of all deviance.[1] Another faction, control theory, will depict institutional restraints as indispensable to a properly conducted society. Deviance is seen as a regression to a wilder state of man (or, less commonly, woman). Conformity is a laudable achievement.[2] Yet another faction, functionalist sociology, portrays deviance as an unrecognized and unintended buttress of social order. The claim is made that seemingly harmful conduct really underpins the conventional order. The work of prostitutes, for instance, is held to preserve marriage, as in Davis's observation, writing in 1937: 'Enabling a small number of women to take care of the needs of a large number of men, [prostitution] is the most convenient sexual outlet for an army, and for the legions of strangers, perverts, and physically repulsive in our midst. It performs a function, apparently, which no other institution fully performs.'[3]

Similarly, organized crime can be said to undermine social inequality,[4] while heresy may be used to defend religious orthodoxy.[5] These theories cannot be reconciled or matched because they are embedded in opposing metaphysical beliefs that can be neither proved nor disproved. One theory can hold an image of people corrupted by society, while another retains the doctrine of original sin.

The apparent disagreements should not be regarded as a failing that ought to be remedied. Indeed, it is not obvious what the benefit would be from an attempt to reconcile such disparate ideas. In fact, it can be instructive to explore a diversity of intellectual positions, because the existence of confusion can emphasize special properties of deviance. Deviance would be a rather different process if people *did* agree on its constitution and significance. But people do not agree, and deviation may not be susceptible to a single definition and a single explanation.

On one level, it is our position that ambiguity and uncertainty are 'integral' characteristics of deviance itself. While some of the phenomena of everyday life can be neatly arranged and classified, others cannot. Sociologists do not always accept common-sense classifications as binding: they may wish to impose their own schemes and categories. But the sociological task is complicated if problems and processes are already murky and elusive before the intervention of any sociologist.

Ambiguity does seem to be a crucial facet of rule breaking. People are frequently undecided whether a particular episode *is* truly deviant or what true deviance is. Their judgment depends on circumstances, biography, and purpose. Certain behaviour can cause discomfort in those who witness it, but they may hesitate to define it as wrong, sinful, or harmful. Many are prepared, for example, to tolerate *some* pilfering (but from institutions and not an excessive amount),[6] *some* sexual misconduct (if it is discreet and does not impinge on others),[7] or *some* rudeness (if it takes place in a place where liquor is sold).[8]

As further evidence of ambiguity, there is often a reluctance to categorize an activity as deviant until other explanations are exhausted. In this way, deviance is a *residual category*, that is, a label of last resort. Thus, in one study, wives preferred to attribute their husbands' misbehaviour to tiredness or strain. There was an initial unwillingness to accept a diagnosis of mental illness.[9]

In a similar study, husbands showed a similar inclination to consider their wives' behaviour, such as hearing voices, as normal. The wife of the man quoted here is later committed after she breaks all the dishes and burns the house down:

Mr. Urey: We'd moved into an old house, I was working late hours. My wife couldn't sleep at night. There was an attic there, the house made noises, the way old houses do. She was frightened, she used to think there was someone in the house with the kids.
Interviewer: What did you make of that?
Mr. Urey: I just thought it was that.
Interviewer: What?
Mr. Urey: The way the house was situated—old and creaky. A person can think a lotta things.[10]

If 'pluralism' and 'shifting standards'[11] work on deviant behaviour to render it ambiguous and fluid, no coherent and definitive argument can ever completely capture it. Sociologists may have to reconcile themselves to the fact that logical and systematic schemes are not invariably mirrored in the 'structure' of the social world.

That structure contains what seems to be a necessary measure of contradiction, contingency, paradox, and absurdity, and some have even tried to develop a 'sociology of the absurd'.[12] But social life often defies precise description. Something will always have to be left out. The analytic possibilities of sociology can be

---

Ambiguity is a central feature of deviance.

Deviance is a residual category.

realized only when there is an abundance of discrepant theories that stress the anomalous ideas that no one theory can contain. The contrasting features of deviance may find adequate expression only in contrasting theories. Even so, difficulties will remain because deviance probably eludes final definition. Deviance stems from the construction and application of moral rules, and as Bittner argues, it is impossible to predict and control all its implications: 'If we consider that for every maxim of conduct we can think of a situation to which it does not apply or in which it can be overruled by a superior maxim . . . then it is clear that all efforts to live by an internally consistent scheme of interpretation are necessarily doomed to fail.'[13]

In this view, deviance will always be messier than science. To be sure, sociologists may argue that the appearances of everyday life are deceptive and that an internally consistent scheme could be found with the proper methodology. Scientific reason might illuminate deeper principles of organization that hide beneath the muddle of ordinary thinking about deviance. Yet, as we have observed, there actually appears to be little agreement among the sociologists themselves. It's almost like Harding's classic comment:

> The social scientists tend obediently to accept their place in the hierarchy without dispute. They say that human beings and animals are different from metals and muscles and are most incalculable. They say you very well know what will happen when you put two chemicals together, but that there is no way on earth of telling what may happen when you put two human beings together. . . . [However] the social sciences tend to be more complex, more inclusive, and more exact, in the sense with making contact with life at more points than the physical sciences.[14]

Each sociologist may be decisive individually, but collectively there is great indecision and many academic disputes. Of course, it is conceivable that the claims of one school *are* valid and that deviance is actually unambiguous when it is properly interpreted. However, just as an addict, a judge, a psychiatrist, and a policeman may share no one perspective on the use of opiates, so different sociologists face deviation in numerous guises and situations. Psychiatric knowledge may be adequate enough, but it may not solve all the practical problems of policing and justice.[15] It would become the sole truth only if psychiatric issues were alone important. Similarly, functionalists' problems may not be the same as those of radical sociologists. Radicals might state that the problems *should* be the same, but functionalists are unlikely to be instantly persuaded. They could retort that the radicals are themselves misguided. More prosaically, sociologists interested in the effects of store design on theft or of policing patterns on vandalism might find radical sociology less helpful than other approaches. There might be questions about whether they *should* investigate those effects, but again, those questions would remove one from a consideration of the immediate effects of control and into the metaphysical and ethical foundations of control policies. A settlement of the argument would have to take the form of a conversion that would be more metaphysical than rational. Moreover, theorists and theories shape their own materials. It is not as if difficulties arose simply because radical and functionalist move about the same world with different problems. In some significant measure, they seem to act as if they do not live in the same world at all.

And matters are yet further complicated because the sociology of deviance itself does not and cannot house all that may be said about its subject, and those who search within it alone for answers to problems may find that they have missed much of value that lies outside. There are the necessary simplifications imposed by focusing on a few variables or ideas abstracted from a larger mass, but also the simplification of relying just on sociology itself. Sociology proper—and political science, economics, law, anthropology, psychology, and psychiatry—also have much that is useful to say about how deviance and control arise,[16] and the search for an answer can acquire indefinite proportions. And when we try to find the answer to moral questions, as the following discussion on polygamy shows, things can become even more confused.

> **The study of deviance is interdisciplinary.**

In short, there may be no still, perfect, and absolute centre from which deviance may be surveyed as it really is. Neither need there be a simple test for discovering the superiority of one approach. The members of each intellectual position may hold that that they alone can see what is true and real. But not all those claims can be valid: there are many centres, and it is not our intention to ally ourselves with any one position for very long.

Discussion: Deviance and Culture—Polygamy

Polygamy is the practice of being married to more than one person at the same time. This contrasts with the more usual practice of monogamy, in which a person has only one spouse at a time. Polygamy is illegal in Canada; however the government seems to be taking a hands-off approach, despite allegations of child brides, statutory rape, sexual assault, sexual exploitation, human trafficking, and immigration scams.

At different historical times, and in different cultures, polygamy has been practised for social and economic reasons, such as among Muslims in Pakistan and Bangladesh, Afghanistan, Singapore, and some African countries.

In North America, polygamy has been associated with Mormonism, whose founder, Joseph Smith, claimed in 1831 to have received a revelation from God allowing polygamy. A Mormon leader, Brigham Young, was arrested for polygamy in 1871, and the US Supreme Court ruled against polygamy in 1878. Even though Utah outlawed polygamy in 1890 under the threat that it would be denied statehood, perhaps 40,000 people still practise polygamy in Utah and nearby states today.

Various individuals and groups have spoken out against polygamy have included Joseph Smith himself in 1893, the Women's Christian

Temperance Union in 1902, the National Council of Women in 1905, and the Moral and Social Reform Council of Canada at its annual meeting in 1912.

Some members of the church came to Canada to set up new communities, such as the one in Cardston, Alberta, where they could practise their religion freely. When the Mormons negotiated for the right to settle in Canada, a condition attached was that they abandon polygamy. However, this particular Mormon sect believes that polygamy is necessary for entrance into heaven. In 2006, a number of children of polygamist families spoke at a rally in Utah, saying that they felt their families were misunderstood.

In the news now is Bountiful, a small town in southeastern British Columbia that has caused legal and political controversy. In the sect that lives in Bountiful, older men often have many, usually younger wives. Despite allegations of child abuse and sexual exploitation, charges have not been laid. In fact it seems that polygamy has never been prosecuted in Canada.

The community has split into two factions, one of which is loyal to Warren Jeffs, who was arrested in the United States and has been convicted of arranging under-age marriages and thus being an accomplice to rape. The other faction is led by Winston Blackmore, who has over twenty wives and more than 100 children. The teen pregnancy rate in Bountiful is much higher than the provincial average, as are the rates of childhood injury.

In 1990 the Creston rcmp announced that they were recommending polygamy charges. A woman willing to testify against Jeffs in Utah said she was forced into a religious marriage when she was fourteen and that everyone made her feel as if she was defying God and would never go to Heaven. Under Utah law it is illegal to have sex with anyone aged fourteen to eighteen unless the two people are within three years of each other in age.

A 2005 study commissioned by the federal government actually recommended that Canada decriminalize polygamy. The authors argue that the law would not survive a Charter challenge under religious freedom. It echoes a 1985 Law Commission study which recommended that traditional marriages be equated with alternative forms of relationships.

However, in 2006, Status of Women Canada said that polygamy has negative consequences for both women and children. And a new report commissioned by the federal justice department said Canada is violating international agreements regarding women and children. Now, in the face of increasing attention, concerns have risen that the colony of Bountiful will simply sell its properties and move out, which given the practice of non-prosecution might not be a bad thing.

A majority of Canadians surveyed for the Institute of Canadian Values believed that polygamy should remain illegal and that governments should intervene more aggressively to protect children in polygamous communities. One said, 'We have moved to a pluralistic acceptance of almost everything.'

In British Columbia, the Attorney General is now considering laying charges against a fundamentalist Mormon sect under Section 293 of the Criminal Code, which makes polygamy illegal in Canada, or under Section 153, which prohibits underage marriages.

On the surface the debate is over how much allowance should be made for religious differences. More deeply, it has to do with whose interests are served under the law.

Source: Based on Chris McCormick, 'Polygamy: Whose Interests Are Being Served?' (Crime Matters column), *Fredericton Daily Gleaner*, 7 June 2007.

Deviance Is Not a Single Problem with a Single Solution

Indeed, it seems as if almost all the contrasting styles of argument that abound in the larger world have been turned on deviance at some point, and each has imposed its own distinctive gloss. Each represents a separate way of seeing such conduct, and as Kenneth Burke would argue,[17] each is a separate way of not seeing such conduct. Together, they compose a great kaleidoscope of theorems. An examination of even one small part of that kaleidoscope can be illuminating. It should demonstrate how deviance reflects the ambitions and visions of those who probe it, laying itself open to an extraordinary range of interpretations.

Some sociologists would assert that deviance is a political phenomenon.[18] After all, it is intimately connected with the exercise of power and the application of rules.[19] To others, deviance poses a series of questions about the practical management of social pathology. Useful knowledge would then be generated by the need to formulate policy. Thus, Clarke and Cornish and James Wilson dismissed all those theories that made no contribution to the business of controlling crime. They took much deviance to be distressing and disruptive action that inflicted pain and subverted trust and community. Theorizing that offers no assistance to the legislator and administrator is cast as fanciful and irrelevant, mere speculation without apparent purpose, utility, or responsibility.[20]

Others also think the study of deviance should be a repository of practical information and advice, as does Morris and Hawkins's *The Honest Politician's Guide to Crime Control*, which urges policy-makers to appreciate the unintended and undesired consequences of their actions. It advocates caution in the construction of schemes for the suppression of law breaking. There are also those who focus on specific problems and their solution, such as the design of public vehicles and its effects on vandalism;[21] the design of public space and how it effects the monitoring of deviance;[22] the organization of social life and the supervision of the young.[23]

But there is a different position. Some have held that the unrecognized consequences of control are so grave and diffuse that they have moved towards a flirtation with anarchism, libertarianism, or extreme conservatism. Arguing with

Deviance is political and is based on the exercise of power.

Herbert Spencer that rule enforcement tends only to make social problems worse, they preach a politics of laissez-faire, or 'anything goes'. Schur contends that almost any interference with juvenile delinquency amplifies deviance, formal regulation acting merely to confirm the deviant in an outcast status.[24] John Braithwaite's reply would be to ensure that the juvenile is reintegrated into the community.[25] On a different note, Becker and Horowitz extol the virtues of San Francisco, which they describe it as a civilized compact between peaceable deviant groups free of undue control.[26] Szasz, too, castigated the intervention of the State, arguing that it has no business managing the private moral problems of its citizens: 'In the animal kingdom, the rule is, eat or be eaten; in the human kingdom, define or be defined.'[27]

More skeptically still, it has been concluded that the supposedly 'unintended' consequences of control are actually intended. Politicians are said to require the presence of a deviant population. The visible lawbreaker is 'manufactured' in large numbers to perform the role of scapegoat for the ills of society. In this way, the deviant deflects outrage away from the evils committed by the powerful elites.[28] The State has a designated pool of deviants who are exploited for dramatic purposes.[29] Foucault, for example, observes that it has long been apparent that prisons generate criminality. It is not neglect or ignorance that prevents the abolition of imprisonment. On the contrary, the penal system is deliberately tended as a deviant preserve.[30]

Pursuing that vision of oppression yet further, some argue that deviants may be put to work in the service of revolution. For instance, Thomas Mathiesen took a leading part in the Scandinavian prisoners' unions, trying to bring about changes that would have led to an unspecified but profound upheaval in penal policy. Maintaining that participation in rational negotiations would only strengthen the grip of officials and domesticate the unions, he was deliberately irrational and non-conciliatory.[31] The political domination of analysis can thereby turn sociology into a combatant in class, gender, or race wars, where its ideas are judged by their impact on conflict.

It may be that the sociology of deviance cannot maintain a scholarly objectivity. Quinney[32] and Platt[33] proclaimed that it must be surrendered to the demands of ideological struggle and must promote only those truths that fuel the revolution. However, there has been a new twist in the argument as a later generation of radical 'left realists', in response to victimization surveys and feminism, argue for the control of deviance with all the excitement of the 'administrative criminologists' they once criticized.

Marxist historians claim that deviance may provide a 'history from below', an unofficial commentary of the dispossessed on their own past. Rulebreaking discloses the suppressed under-life of society; it documents the stirrings of the illiterate, voiceless, and dominated, delineating patterns of communal opposition to the State and its masters. For example, poachers and smugglers can be used to illustrate the hostility that attended the emergence of class society in England.[34] Attempts to enclose land were met by demands based on the traditional rights of people to use pastures, commons, and forests.[35] Efforts to mechanize agriculture or assert the supremacy of the market were stalled by 'collective bargaining by

> The criminal justice system creates criminals because it needs a client population.

riot'.[36] The very attempt to reduce poachers, smugglers, rioters, and rick burners to 'criminals' may there be read as an aspect of the politics of naming.[37] Naming deviance becomes political, and the deviant is a prologue to conscious and articulate resistance by those without property or voice.[38]

The Luddites protested against the introduction of steam technology in the early 1800s.

On occasion, deviance can take expressly political directions Thus certain homosexuals organized to become the Gay Liberation Front[39] and later Outrage, and prisoners adopted the tactics of student demonstrators.[40] On occasion, politics can take a deviant path The early Bolsheviks, the Irish Republican Army, and the Baader-Meinhof gang[41] robbed banks, and Eldridge Cleaver raped to revenge himself on the white world.[42] On occasion, however, matters are not at all clear and the deviant and the political can merge into a definitional fog. Argument can turn on whether people are 'really' freedom fighters, guerrillas, or terrorists. There may be debate about whether a riot is 'really' a political event or 'mere' lawlessness. Description becomes even more difficult because there can sometimes be political consequences from the acts of deviants who are not overtly committed to a political stance. Conversely, political motives can be claimed by those who seek an acceptable front for predatory activity.[43] All these shifts, pronouncements, and conflicts require delicate analysis.

Discussion: Deviance Exploration—The Relativity of Deviance

There are many forms of behaviour that are not criminal but that are considered odd. These forms of deviance range from such things as dressing in an unusual way to mildly eccentric forms of behaviour, such as talking to oneself. However, what is considered deviant in this culture at this time might not be considered deviant in another culture at another time. This means that deviance is relative. Sociology illustrates how deviance is relative rather than absolute by making cross-cultural and historical comparisons.

For example, as we saw earlier, one of the founding fathers of Mormonism espoused polygamy and had fifty wives. A third of Mormons practised multiple marriages in the eighteenth century. Polygamy is illegal in Canada, but the authorities tend not to take action. It is estimated that many cultures in the world still practise polygyamy today, either for purposes of ensuring survival or for displaying wealth and status.

Cross-cultural comparisons are 'synchronic', which means that we compare cultures at the same time. In Islamic countries, for example, the use of alcohol is prohibited and the penalties for using it are quite severe. Foreign workers in Saudi Arabia have to be careful not to violate this standard. Similarly, in recent memory, a youth was threatened with the traditional punishment of a public caning in Singapore for a crime that probably would have been punished by a community sentence in Canada.

Singapore is notorious for its strict rules about behaviour in public places; for example, it is illegal to chew gum in public.

In comparison to the prohibition on alcohol in those countries, Western countries permit and regulate the sale of alcohol, sometimes dispensing it at government-run stores. Even though the long-term cost of alcohol to society is high, because the short-term profit is also high, it is attractive to governments as a source of revenue. In Western culture, then, alcohol is associated with sociability—getting together with friends and living the good life—and with the rewards of hard work.

Historical comparisons are '*diachronic*', which means that we look at social standards across time. Here we can make an interesting parallel to the topic of alcohol. In the nineteenth century none of the narcotics prohibited in Canada today were illegal. Cocaine and opium were widely available and were found in prescription medicines, toothache remedies, hair tonics, and digestives and other tonics. It is not that these substances were suddenly discovered to be dangerous or that their use and effect on the user's mind and body changed. It was social issues and standards that changed. We can look at the criminalization of cocaine, opium, and marijuana and see how there were specific social reasons for their criminalization that were separate from the substance and its use.

Not all deviance, however, is considered relative. Some is universally held in contempt. However, most forms of deviance are culturally and historically variant. This is what it means to say that deviance is relative.

■ Sources of Diversity

It is apparent that the sociology of deviance can encompass many ideologies and ambitions, and part of our task must be to recount how such diversity arose and how the separate explanations attained plausibility.

•*Sociology is not enclosed or sealed against arguments that exist in the wider world.* Just as intellectual variety is a simple product of exposure to diverse ideas, sociology is heir to a long tradition of brooding about deviance and sin, politics being but one strand of that tradition. Lawyers, psychiatrists, theologians, moralists, anthropologists, philosophers, statisticians, social reformers, historians, and psychologists have laid claim to the problems of deviance and tried to impose their own stamp on current thinking. Each has had a stake in the outcome because the acceptance of a particular view confirms a system of morals, law, or politics and has implications for the rise and fall of policies and occupations.[44] Thus the right to manage the mad was claimed by clergymen, magistrates, and doctors. The prize was the administration of asylums.[45] Similarly, juvenile delinquents were fought over by social workers, psychiatrists, and lawyers; the prize was power over juvenile courts and reformatories.[46]

•*Sociology has its own language, and techniques, but it has also fed on ideas that have originated in other fields.* In this sense, it lends a special form and focus to familiar arguments. Thinking about social problems cannot be insulated against what has gone before. The reworking of old conceptions need not be conscious or deliberate: after all, few sociologists are fully versed in the history of ideas. Yet earlier thought shapes the environment in which all speculation takes place. The disputes of the medieval schoolmen and eighteenth-century pamphleteers have been handed on to acquire new shapes in the university of the twenty-first century. For example, radical sociology can trace its lineage back to such thinkers as Plato, Kant, Hegel, Rousseau, and Marx. Control theory incorporates the political philosophy of Hobbes, the psychiatry of Eysenck and Freud, and the sociology of Durkheim. Functionalists may be clustered with the biologist Cannon, the political economist Petty, the philosopher Plato, and the anthropologists Malinowski and Radcliffe-Brown. The sociology of deviance is simply another opportunity to organize all that has passed for relevant intellectual work in the West. It gives another life to the principal ideas of the principal schools. Just as those schools were varied in their thinking, so the sociology of deviance is varied. Just as those schools' disputes have never been conclusively settled, so the internal debates of the sociology of deviance remain unresolved.

The different debates can set very different goals for the study of deviance. Sociologists may be required to control or exploit deviance, undertake dispassionate analysis, provide moral commentaries, design, criticize, or close prisons, study the past, or predict the future. They may, indeed, have no great interest in deviance but be searching for answers to analytic puzzles: thus Cicourel explored probation and police practices in order to illuminate some general properties of social interaction;[47] Durkheim treated deviance and law as an indicator of social cohesion;[48] and Merton took deviance to be a demonstration of the processes by which a society maintains itself.[49]

•*Such an interplay of projects and thoughts becomes more complicated as the minds of different sociologists work on the materials offered them.* There is an ever increasing body of arguments, criticisms, and studies, and no sociologist is capable of mastering, reading, or remembering all that is produced. Scholars will acquire a selective experience of the sociology of deviance, an experience shaped by contingency, knowledge, choice, fashion, and practical objectives. They may consider a work important, although few of their colleagues may have read it. They may combine its arguments with those of other writings, generating a new personal synthesis. What is held to be fascinating and provocative now may later be seen as dull. The intellectual significance of a theory or idea is consequently unstable: it will depend on the circumstances of those who encounter it and on its place in a sequence of thoughts. Ideas therefore reflect the biographies and preoccupations of particular people at particular points of time.

•*The sociology of deviance has thereby accumulated a vast number of nuances.* These nuances can become exaggerated and publicized as sociologists, often working in a university, pursue the new and the original. The university is more than a mere vehicle for transmitting received truths, because faculty submit doctoral

theses before or during their period of appointment and one of the chief criteria
for the acceptance of a thesis is its originality. Promotions hinge on successful
publication, and publishers are not anxious to print the simple parrotings of other
people's ideas. Sometimes sociological works are recognizably and novel and
important, but often they are not. Sociologists frequently strive for the identifi-
ably new, the special emphasis that will set him or her apart as an original thinker
who deserves honour and reward. That result can be a proliferation of attempts
at intellectual revolution, and almost every published work will carry the assertion that it constitutes a major revision, synthesis, or formulation of ideas.[50]
Hence the freedom of the academy has resulted in a diversity of thought.

•*Product differentiation has inevitably been accompanied by the making of pro-
prietorial claims.* People tend to acquire very real stakes in their ideas. They 'possess' them, are reluctant to share authorship or ownership, and may strive to
conserve and guard them against adulteration. The attraction in the logic of a
simplified argument is that excessive complexity can render analysis unmanageable, so that slight initial divergences can result in radically different conclusions.
Douglas once complained of this drift towards the artificial segregation of arguments: 'Most . . . theories are right to some degree about some part of the things
they are studying, but they almost all deal with small parts—as if the parts were
the whole thing—and the theories wind up being distortions of the vastly complex realm of human life.'[51]

•*Then there is the impact of the academy that both spurs and limits the growth of
intellectual variety.* Universities and disciplines enforce their own special controls,
which is what they were devised to do. Ideas will be scanned in reviews, lectures,
and seminars; sociologists and other academics dissect their colleagues' work; and
arguments are examined for their logic, methodology, and coherence. The routine activities of university work resemble a process of natural selection that condemns some arguments and upholds others. Reputations have been lost
irrevocably, but what passes for damning critical criteria is itself variable, enjoy-
ing a history of fashion and the popularity of schools. Thus, interesting developments in the social geography of deviance in the mid-nineteenth century were
suppressed by the end of the century, only to be revived in the 1930s[52] and again
in the 1990s.

•*The matter is yet further complicated by the very different traditions that are borne
by the university departments and schools in which 'deviantology' is studied and taught.*
Processes of natural selection may be inhibited because institutions of learning are
so numerous and the sociological profession is so large that antagonists need never
confront one another. The advocates of a particular theory can surround themselves with their own circle of followers and their own network of journals and
publishers. It is quite possible for one intellectual faction to create, examine, and
extend its ideas without much interference from outsiders. Like middle-class neighbours who prefer simply to avoid one another rather than quarrel,[53] sociological
challenges can simply be ignored. For example, radical analysis did not dominate
the sociology of deviance, as most sociologists did not hold its assumptions, and
it was simply neglected by those who were not its adherents. In this fashion,

phenomenology, interactionism, structuralism, functionalism, femininism, and the other major schools can flourish independently and unmolested, constituting a number of parallel intellectual universes that need never intersect.

•*Such insulation can be further reinforced by the division of intellectual labour within universities.* Students require schooling in a collection of specialist areas, universities recruit appropriate staff to teach them, and there is a consequent weakening of the ability to monitor and judge the works of one's colleagues in the same institution. Sociologists of religion or development may not believe themselves equipped to assess the competence and range of a deviance scholarship. There is an attendant reduction of discipline: sociologists of deviance (like any other sociologist) have acquired a charter to issue almost any argument provided a publisher will broadcast it and some colleagues somewhere will endorse it.

■ The Social Contexts of Differentiation

One of the chief constraints on intellectual production is the place in which it takes place. The sociology of deviance is practised in different situations, which frame what may be said and the manner of its expression. We can give only a few scattered examples of those situations, but our illustrations should highlight the part played by environment.

Perhaps the largest single setting is the State, and the State can dramatically affect creativity. We have claimed that the sociology of deviance may have implications for moral and political reasoning. Particular conceptions of deviance are capable of subverting the absolute authority of the State and may require censorship. One important example is the position of sociology in the former Soviet Union, a government that was based on Marxism. Deviance is held to stem from the defects of capitalism, that is, the moral disorganization, inequalities, and possessive individualism of a society based on social classes. Having become classless, it was argued, a truly Marxist society could not engender crime. As the director of the Moscow Institute of Criminology pronounced, 'socialism does not give birth to crime, . . . the regularities immanent in socialism do not give birth to crime.'[54] A non-Marxist sociology would have located some of the sources of deviance in Soviet social organization, but it would have upset Soviet Marxism and the claims of the Soviet Union to be a Marxist society, and it was not allowed to develop. In Soviet sociology, deviance was presented as a consequence of foreign influence, capitalist survivals, or personal, organic, or psychological disturbance. In the Soviet Union and in the People's Republic of China, sociology, for very political reasons, became politically neutral, a kind of technical instrument that abstained from criticism in the service of the State.[55]

Within societies, too, there are quite disparate contexts for the pursuit of 'deviantology' because it can be put to very different uses, and its practitioners may be discovered in a host of different organizations. Institutionally, the demands of government research agencies like Statistics Canada; the Canadian Centre for Justice Statistics; or the British Home Office Research, Development, and Statistics Directorate (RDS) are most dissimilar to those imposed by universities. There is a clear stipulation that ideas be presented in a form useful to policy and action, that arguments be put in a fashion intelligible to the administrator, and that there be little flirtation with the metaphysics of deviance. Paul Wiles, a leading researcher, having become head of the RDS, said that in its business plan, 'work will play a key role in supporting all seven Home Office aims, providing measurement for Public Service Agreement targets. . . . Also included are . . . a comprehensive programme of policy evaluation and appraisal and a statistical work programme [on] key regular statistics.' So defined, research tends towards a model of natural science, employing statistical methods in practical projects designed to support government policy. It tends characteristically to lean towards rational choice theory, the vision of men and women as people bent on increasing rewards and averting pain in a context riddled with risk. Clarke and Cornish said of rational choice theory that its focus is 'on offenders as rational decision-makers calculating where their self-interest lies.'[56] It can map events and relationships that escape others, but it is not calculated to feed a radical consciousness or explore questions simply because they are intriguing. It is constrained by rules that need not restrain a university lecturer. People working in official agencies are expected primarily to be reliable, not original. To be sure, agencies constantly hanker after new programs and policies—there is a perennial hunt for the obviously efficient reform. But organization is imposed by the disciplines and discourses of political rationality and practicability. Someone who worked in a British justice policy-planning unit declared: 'It is perhaps not a particularly difficult task to formulate the objectives of policy-oriented research. They might be stated as being to assist and contribute to the formulation and development of policy and to evaluate the effects of its implementation.'[57]

However, in an excellent examination of the Canadian Centre for Justice Statistics, Kevin Haggerty (of the University of Alberta) criticizes the organizational politics involved in studying and producing statistics. In one example he discusses how the Centre began and then abandoned an examination of the relationship between race and crime because of the political ramifications. He also criticizes the uses to which justice statistics are put:

> Historically, it has been presumed that rhetoric would ultimately be thwarted by truth, as represented by the rational use of criminal-justice statistics. However, the trends . . . might be shifting. . . . Although there will undoubtedly continue to be a role for agencies such as the Canadian Centre for Justice Statistics, it is possible that they will increasingly be approached not as resources for data that can assist rational policy development, but as sources for data to be invoked in support of narrowly technicist crime-fighting endeavours or as a justification for broadly symbolic or even reactionary politics.[58]

In contrast, the academic has a licence to produce new ideas. Many academics *do* busy themselves with moral and political concerns, but they are not obliged to do so and they are as often devoted to a kind of boundless speculation.

Consider the scale and character of the task described in the preface to one book on the sociology of deviance:

> This book is the product of my own search for a coherent view of the relationship between persons and institutions. . . . Seeking theoretical continuity, I discovered that discontinuity characterized explanations of social order and change. Reviewing these historical perspectives and issues, I found that, rather than clarifying ambiguities, deviance theories illustrate how scholarly controversies over styles of reasoning and world views produce radically different versions of social reality.[59]

Those rather different definitions of the criminological task extend outwards to affect the network of institutions that train and house sociologists of deviance.

On the one hand, the work of the academic sociologist of deviance is subordinate to particular demands, and frequently he or she is but one sociologist among many contributing to the general education of students. Such sociologists will certainly be required to know more than the research on deviance alone, and their sociology may be little more than yet another perspective on broad intellectual and social problems. In this sense, their attachment to deviance is somewhat arbitrary. They could ask much the same questions of innumerable other areas.

On the other hand, sociologists of deviance may be discovered in special institutes or schools whose goal is not the promotion of a general theoretical competence. Throughout the world, institutes have been established to produce professionals dedicated to the exploration of the substance of deviance. And they are often designed to meet the requirements of organizations in government and applied research that employ such professionals. In the pursuit of these ends, they often achieve vastly more than the preparation of technicians.

The appointments secured by sociologists who study deviance depend on the vagaries of the market and personal history. Fortunately, the formal charters of institutions rarely describe the exact activities that take place, and so there are many departures from official goals, and many opportunities to explore the difference between 'pure' and 'applied' sociology.

There is perhaps one further source of differentiation. Universities and university departments have histories that are shaped by national, local, and intellectual influences. Since the study of deviance has only recently become a professional pursuit, its adherents have had to find a place for themselves in long-established organizations. Sociology has been grafted onto institutions whose structure defines its character and evolution. In South America, for example, many sociologists have had to associate themselves with physical anthropology: their quest has been the detection of organic sources of deviance. In Germany, the sociology of deviance has been adopted by many law departments. In the United States, deviancy study is largely identified with sociology. In Britain and Canada, scholars who study deviance are usually scattered among departments of sociology, psychology, law, and social administration.[60] The outcome has been the introduction of complexity and greater diversity.

Criminology is influenced by the cultural context.

A department or university does require certain teaching and academic duties of its members. Thus, sociologists in a law department must follow a distinct syllabus and a distinct set of aims. Their students will not be versed in sociology. Whatever their interests may be, sociologists so placed will find that their thoughts are focused on special problems and a special body of writing. Theirs will still be the sociology of deviance, but it will have acquired a particular complexion.

■ Implications

It is clear that the sociology of deviance is diverse, and to a great extent, such diversity is useful. Sociologists cannot impose a single orthodoxy upon their readers or one another because their arguments can always be compared to those of their competitors and critics, revealing not only their strengths but their limitations. Sociology has a self-relativizing strain that can chasten people who seek immediate and unambiguous answers to moral and intellectual problems.

•*Readers at the beginning of their study of deviance should be open-minded, skeptical, and charitable.* It would be immature to make up your mind before you know more about the available intellectual choices. Eventually, to be sure, there will be a need to prefer a certain theory, but it would be unwise to do so without having first considered the others that are likely to have some merit. And no theory can be assessed intelligently until it has been regarded with sympathy. Ideas can be appreciated only if there is some willingness to take their authors' assumptions and preoccupations seriously. The early stages of understanding deviance are most fruitful when one tries to grasp the opportunities presented by very different systems of thought, the problems that confronted their authors, and the doubts they may cast on favourite arguments.

Wary disinterest is also to be commended because it is very easy to condemn and lose what may actually be quite valuable. We shall enlarge on the problems of sociological methods in the next chapter. Nevertheless, it is apparent that those methods revolve around the difficulties of knowing and describing individual deviants and groups that have little to gain from becoming known. The world of deviance and social control is riddled with discredited information and secrecy. Even though research is sometimes flawed, it is an achievement to bring it to a conclusion. Critics are sometimes too prone to dismiss the whole because of the deficiencies of a few of its parts. When ideas and information can be extracted only with great effort, it is sensible to examine the work for what it may offer instead of stalking its failings.

•*Only rarely will a single study exhaust all the interesting possibilities of a problem.* When observation is hindered, perspectives will be partial and inferences incomplete. Few instances of deviance are paraded before a sociologist in their entirety, and a consequence of such restricted vision is the inevitable relativism of argument. With great good fortune, social anthropologists like the Iannis might obtain access to a family of organized criminals.[61] It would have been impossible to examine all such families or even every aspect of one single family. And it follows that such methodological considerations invite one to treat the sociology of deviance as a series of what may be little more than tenuously connected glimpses of the world. Much would be sacrificed by the assumption that each work must be approached as if it were complete in itself. One should not forget that we can treat sociology as a reservoir of different, sometimes contradictory arguments that can be dismantled and reassembled with some freedom.

Work on juvenile delinquency provides a useful example. Delinquency has worried and intrigued criminologists and others for decades, and there has been a continuous stream of writing from different sources, times, and places. Thrasher observed Chicago gangs in the 1920s,[62] William Foot Whyte discussed Boston delinquency in the 1930s,[63] Matza argued about New Yorkers in the 1960s,[64] Parker the Liverpool of the 1970s,[65] Foster the delinquents of South East London in the 1980s,[66] Anderson the delinquents of Philadelphia,[67] Alexander the Asian gangs of London in the 1990s,[68] and Joan Sangster (of Trent University) Canadian juvenile delinquency at various stages in the twentieth century.[69]

Yet there has been a curious tendency in sociology to proceed as if all these random sightings should be treated as attempts to confront an identical problem with identical data.[70] One study has been played off against another as if only one explanation should be allowed to survive. There is no good reason to suppose that delinquency in the 1920s was the 'same' as delinquency in the 1970s.[71] Neither is there cause to assume that the events of Chicago must be reproduced in Liverpool. It is not necessary to try to resolve all differences between various studies. It is much better to give some social context to delinquency, for example, and see it as evolving historically, within a spatial and economic context.

> **Deviance theories are extensions of common-sense arguments.**

•*Sociological theories of deviance tend to represent the most articulate versions of arguments that have currency in everyday life.* Almost every major common-sense explanation of deviance has a modified sociological expression. In this sense, sociology exposes ideas that elsewhere may be examined only dimly. The conventions of ordinary conversation do not really allow one to inspect the weaknesses and opportunities of argument in any detail. Commonplace theorizing about deviance touches on delicate moral and social matters, and it is difficult, often subversive, to challenge it. It would be a breach of good manners to offer certain arguments about motives and behaviour although they can receive prolonged attention in the university. It would also be considered tedious and rude to

> **Sociology requires proof often missing in everyday talk.**

demand a defence of every statement. Yet, sociology rests on canons of proof, presentation, and evidence that are largely foreign to everyday talk. It permits one to be banal, boring, naïve, or outrageous, suspending some of the inhibitions that restrict discussion outside the university. If the sociology of deviance is sometimes accused of merely repeating common-sense observations, it does work on those observations in an unusual, taxing, and rather exhaustive fashion. It probably represents the only important means of dismantling commonplace explanation and gauging its worth. What emerges is usually a significant advance on the thinking that occurs elsewhere. Even the most ordinary examples of the sociology of deviance will continue to be justified so long as they are more methodical, rigorous, and reflective than their alternatives. They are supported by the conscious deployment of techniques and critical procedures not in common use. They subject their ideas to an organized scrutiny. And they are supported by a substantial body of fieldwork and research. Whatever its faults may be, the sociology of deviance is a relatively orderly, disciplined, searching, public, and cumulative process of enquiry. Even when it is flawed, and it *is* often flawed, a confrontation with its obvious defects can force the reader to think usefully and perhaps for the first time about criticisms, contrasts, and alternatives.

•*Sociologists often display a willingness to become closely involved with matters that most people shun*. In this, they are unusual and perhaps a little deviant themselves. Not only may it be considered eccentric or even shocking to defend certain arguments about deviance, but it is also sometimes discreditable to associate with deviants without good purpose. There are very few who have an occupational mandate to be publicly curious and adventurous in deviant regions. Yet sociologists have come to know poolroom hustlers,[72] drug users,[73] homosexuals,[74] receivers of stolen goods,[75] armed robbers,[76] and child molesters.[77] They are also more likely to know politicians, lawyers, and police officers. Not infrequently, the result has been a breaking down of barriers and an extraordinary knowledge that may be compared advantageously with the lay, political, and journalistic theorizing about deviance that all too frequently is second-hand, lazy, and speculative and based upon imagination, others' reports, and hostile encounters. As Christopher Jencks once said in a rather different context, 'In self-defense, we can only say that the magnitude of [our] errors is almost certainly less than if we had simply consulted our prejudices, which seems to be the usual alternative.'[78]

The judgment of theory and research should not therefore be rushed, for it is an intellectual approach that puts arguments in their most solid form. Only in this way will the reader actually have the possibility of learning and synthesizing ideas. Few systems are so barren that something cannot be retained. By crediting other sociologists' work with intelligence and good sense, one may overcome the parochialism of one's own understanding. Thus, functionalism and Marxism can disclose previously unknown terrain even to their opponents. One might not care to treat their maps as definitive, but they force one to think about phenomena and processes in a new way. As Burgess said in 1954: 'One value the sociologist as social scientist must defend courageously and vigorously is freedom of thinking, teaching, and research. In defending it he should . . . employ the most powerful weapon at his command . . . research upon the issue in controversy.' [79]

Accordingly, we shall invite our readers to consider a succession of interlocking and competing ideas. By the end of this book, they should be reasonably familiar with the basic theories, preoccupations, debates, and authors in the sociology of deviance, or as we call it, 'deviantology'. Our discussion will be ordered historically, beginning with the Chicago School of the 1920s. This beginning is somewhat arbitrary, in that there certainly was a study of deviance before then, but it is with the Chicago School that a sociology develops on the basis of early principles set out in the nineteenth century. The adoption of a chronological organization seems satisfactory enough: ideas do follow one another in time, and sociologists often respond to the work of their predecessors. And we try to show

how one theory anticipates the next and responds to the former. It should not be assumed that the sociology of deviance has evolved smoothly or logically, nor that later ideas necessarily displace those that went before. That would be to commit the 'chronocentric fallacy', which is the unfounded belief that what is argued today must necessarily be superior to what was argued before.[80] On the contrary, the temporary eclipse of a theory may have little to do with its merit. Just as important are the effects of fashion, the desire to innovate, an impatience with the old, changing political and intellectual environments, and the turnover of generations of sociologists. Older ideas also deserve serious attention, if only because they offer a context and contrast for present concerns.

Chapter Summary

In this chapter we have explained that the diversity within the sociology of deviance is due to a number of factors, including social pressures, individual research interests, institutional development, and academic specialization. By recognizing that, we get a behind-the-scenes appreciation of the development of a discipline. However, the result is not a unified field.

The different theoretical perspectives in the sociology of deviance that have developed and been retained represent different ways of examining the same problem, at different times and in different places, by different people.

The argument is made that the sociological study of deviance means being open to the ambiguity of the topic and the 'confusion' of the field. In the next chapter we look at some of the ways in which knowledge of deviance is gained for study.

Critical-Thinking Questions

1. This chapter proposes that some of the ideas that sociology pursues are influenced by political arguments. How do politicians talk about the need for gun control, for example? On what evidence is it based?
2. The authors suggest that the topic of juvenile delinquency changes over time. How is juvenile delinquency discussed in relation to the *Youth Criminal Justice Act*?
3. What are some of the pressures that influence the development of research? Can we find discussions of this in the methodological literature?
4. A discussion feature suggests that even though 'deviance is relative', we can still evaluate the different perspectives relevant to a discussion of, for example, polygamy. Discuss the difficulty of being ethnically neutral while also being critical.

Explorations in Film

This chapter suggests that it can sometimes be difficult to know what deviance is and that there can be conflicting definitions of deviance. In the film *Hoodwinked*, the detective Flippers seeks to find out the truth in this retelling of the classic story of the Wolf, Grandma, Red Riding Hood, and the Woodsman. In the detective's words, 'when there are four suspects there are four stories,' and his job is to get to the bottom of the matter. This device makes for a lot of surprising twists and turns.

Chapter Two

Sources of Knowledge about Deviance

Chapter Overview

Deviance is a term used to refer to various kinds of behaviour that contravene a social norm, rule, or law. For this reason, finding information on deviance is difficult because people need to be secretive about the deviant acts they commit. Sociologists are interested in studying the social implications of all forms of rule-breaking behaviour in society, and so they have developed techniques for investigating deviant behaviour. In this chapter we discuss observation, interviewing, case studies, institutional research, and other methods of research.

Because different societies define the same behaviour in different ways, sociologists also study how rules are created in any society. For this we use historical and comparative approaches to see deviance in a larger context. This chapter is about how we can know what deviance there is in society and what forms it takes. In subsequent chapters we will look in greater detail at how deviance is caused and how it is learned.

■ Introduction

Sociologists of deviance attempt to explain a world of laws, rules, courts, criminals, rule breakers, police, and prisons. That world is vast and changing, and little of it has been charted. Much of it is unusually difficult to observe, and its very obscurity has complicated the problems of exploration. Venturing into it, the sociologist will continually confront dilemmas about the selection of questions and methods. Every decision to examine one possibility entails some risk and also the neglecting of a different question. The framing of such decisions is central to explanation and theory, and debate can turn endlessly around the wisdom and usefulness of particular choices. Certain facts invite the acceptance of certain theories, just as certain theories propel one to search for certain facts. Any exploration of the sociology of crime and deviance must consider the ways in which deviation may be seen and how those ways affect any argument.

■ The Elusive Quality of Deviance

We have not yet provided a formal definition of deviance. That omission, which is deliberate, stems from our observation that the major theories define deviance differently. However, there is a basic, if unwritten, agreement among sociologists that deviance should be considered as banned or controlled behaviour that is likely to attract punishment or disapproval. It doesn't always matter who issues the ban or how many people support it. Those who deviate tend to make their lives more dangerous and difficult because they are breaking rules. Of course, there is abundant deviation that is never recognized, censored, or sanctioned: for example, adulterers will go undetected, and burglars may never be caught. But deviant pursuits do multiply the perils of ordinary existence. Only occasionally will they be displayed publicly; instead, there is a real effort at concealment. As Matza observed, deviation often becomes devious.

In the following discussion we consider some ways in which deviance is 'elusive'.

•*Sociologists working on visible and undisguised processes have problems enough. Their work becomes vastly complex when subjects and events are deliberately hidden.* Not only is deviance generally covert and secretive, but deviants themselves are unlikely to be co-operative when they are detected: after all, they have little to gain from exposure. Consequently, much rule breaking is represented as something else, denied when it is suspected, and shielded behind walls or locked doors. Sociologists must be exceptionally alert to its presence, recognizing otherwise conventional appearances as façades or deceit. They must be skeptical, assuming that all is not as it seems. Thus Jason Ditton[1] and Stuart Henry[2] uncovered widespread deviance in apparently normal settings. Ditton disclosed the existence of systematic 'fiddles' at most levels of the bread industry. Henry revealed how very ordinary places like pubs and clubs were the widely used as marketplaces in which stolen goods were commissioned and distributed. Farberman, too, has described how the American automobile industry is riddled with organized illicit practices.[3] The distribution of alcohol has been similarly documented as an enterprise that has substantial illegalities.[4] Most occupations, it seems, provide opportunities for forbidden but unrecorded activity.[5]

In complex organizations, deviance may become even more invisible because it may be dispersed and difficult to view in its entirety. The European Commission of the 1990s, for instance, was riddled with fraud and corruption, but middle-ranking officials responsible for auditing accounts found it difficult to form anything like a comprehensive view. They saw small disconnected parts rather than whole, and in the face of substantial opposition, it eventually required great personal persistence and enterprise by 'whistle-blowers' to piece together something of what was afoot.[6] It is in this sense that deviance abounds but is methodically veiled. It is only by taking a more skeptical perspective on the world that disreputable life becomes apparent.

Secrecy makes research complex, and it can fold back on deviance itself, because when rule breaking is guarded and surrounded by devious explanations, deviants themselves may not be fully aware of the extent and nature of their own and other people's activity. Many deviants are segregated from one another and therefore unaware of what the others are doing. Child abusers, for example, need take no part in organized abusive activity. Their principal knowledge of sexual deviance may come from the mass media, the Internet, gossip, and everyday conversation. Their conception of misconduct can embody that knowledge, which moulds their description of deviance and its motivation.[7]

> Deviance is everywhere hidden, and to see it cynicism is needed.

Discussion: Deviance Exploration—The Kinsey Report

Kinsey's studies of sexual behaviour sprang on an unsuspecting, but willing, American public. *Time* magazine reported in 1948 that 'In the 15 weeks since its publication, it has risen nearly to the top of the bestseller list.

Its popularity shows that many a grownup is just as curious about sex as adolescents are.'

Kinsey was a biologist teaching at Indiana University, and his original specialty was studying the characteristics of gall wasps, of which he measured 35,000. His collection of wasps is now in the American Museum of Natural History. Kinsey brought this scientific curiosity for detail to the study of human sexual behaviour in an undergraduate course on marriage. However, while there was a tradition of sex research in Europe, little had been done in America on which to base such a course.

So Kinsey and his assistants gathered 12,214 case histories of men, women, and children. The result of this encyclopedic detailing of ordinary people's sex lives resulted in two books, *Sexual Behavior in the Human Male* (1948) and *Sexual Behavior in the Human Female* (1953). This research was done under the Committee for Research on the Problems of Sex, funded by the Rockefeller Foundation, the successor to the Bureau of Social Hygiene founded in 1911 to study 'social evils'.

An example of his findings were that 85 per cent of the total male population have premarital intercourse; nearly 70 per cent have relations with prostitutes; and between 30 and 45 per cent have extra-marital intercourse. Although for some this confirmed the obvious, for others it was shocking and incendiary.

The *Globe and Mail* opined in an editorial in 1948 that 'for the puritanical, the report packs a wallop, while for those who have charged our sexual mores with hypocrisy, it is a bonanza.' The Postmaster General of Canada told the House of Commons that he would see if the book should be banned from the mails as immoral.

The controversy about Kinsey's research ranged from his findings on homosexuality, premarital intercourse, and pedophilia to the statistical techniques used in sampling and the interpretation of the results. The theologian Reinhold Niebuhr was quoted as saying that he found Kinsey's point of view toward sex even more distressing than the sad state of US morals. The National Council of Catholic Women branded the report an insult to the American people, saying that it could only lead to immorality.

A Harvard sociologist, Pitirim Sorkin said, 'Scientists spend their lives studying lower forms of life. . . . But we are not potato bugs, and you cannot take theories that look good in a zoology lab and apply them unchanged to human beings.'

Then, in 1953 Kinsey made the cover of *Time* magazine with his report on female sexuality, which was based on interviews with 5,940 white women. It was even more controversial than the male volume. Some of its findings were that 50 per cent of women have intercourse before marriage; 26 per cent have extramarital relations; and women enjoy sex and continue to do so into old age.

This controversy found its focus in various ways, from conservative religious discussions on the appropriateness of premarital sexual relations, to how to treat women in therapy for problems in sexual response. Educators seemed to favour the need for sex education, and Kinsey himself promoted reform so that sexual behaviour outside the norm, such as masturbation and lesbianism, could be engaged in without shame or guilt.

In highlighting the prevalence of so-called non-traditional sexuality, Kinsey contributed to a detaching of behaviour from identity. However, it was this view of sexual behaviour detached from romanticism that disturbed some commentators. The revelation that many adults broke the law in having oral and anal sex, that premarital and extramarital sex was prevalent, and that sex was fun and was practised for more than procreation was what angered some but inspired others.

However disagreeable, the Kinsey reports helped bring about a new public discussion of sexuality and to challenge traditional attitudes to heterosexual monogamy and female sexual passivity, and led to greater equality between men and women. As well, this discussion helped bring homosexuality out of the closet and to revise sexual offender laws.

Source: Based on C. McCormick, 'The Kinsey Report: When Deviance Became Normal'(Crime Matters column), *Fredericton Daily Gleaner*, 24 May 2007.

• *Deviants rarely engage in collective efforts to interpret their own behaviour.* Some homosexuals did so at a time when being gay was also held to be markedly deviant,[8] and a number of drug users did so in the 1960s, but many rule breakers themselves possess no more than a fragmented and second-hand knowledge of deviance. In one important sense, that knowledge is quite adequate and authentic. It infuses the world of deviance, affecting deviants' own understanding of their actions and their responses to others. In another sense, it should not be confused with a developed sociological description, because there may well be much more to learn and consider. Having successfully penetrated the defences that surround rule breaking, sociologists cannot be entirely uncritical in their response to what they encounter. As Manning observed, they should not assume 'the "underdog's" narrow, often very simplistic view of large complex social segments which directly affect changes in the underdog's behaviour'.[9] An analysis must look at materials that may be beyond the subject's grasp, and the discovery of those materials is quite onerous.

Most research is limited by the fact that deviant practices are likely to be secret and that little information is available; only a considerable expenditure of time and effort may give the sociologist access to a deviant world. Months or years may have to pass before intimacy develops, a reasonable range of acts are observed, and processes are seen in anything near their completeness. What will emerge is almost inevitably a partial sighting. One might acquire some knowledge about a

Because of its nature, deviance is hidden and is difficult to study.

receiver,[10] a delinquent gang, or a hotel for geriatric hustlers.[11] But it would be quite absurd to expect to become familiar with many instances of such deviance. It would be even more absurd to pretend that one had achieved an understanding of its 'essential' or 'universal' characteristics.

Individual subjects will also resist full surveillance. After all, why should a sociologist be given unfettered access to every intimate moment and thought? Why, indeed, should one trust an outsider at all? There are, Jack Katz once said, 'times and places in the subjects' lives that are beyond the ethnographer's reach.'[12] Those who study delinquent adolescents are very rarely admitted to their homes or schools or more secluded settings. Those who study legislators and administrators will not be privy to every conversation and document. On the contrary, research tends to be confined to public and controlled occasions that permit a careful preparation of appearances. Yet even those occasions can be so densely textured that sociologists are still plagued by problems of what to observe, what questions to ask, what to record, and how to organize and edit their observations.

•*It is not at all remarkable that theories and theorists will tend to describe phenomena quite differently.* Not only do phenomena change from time to time and from place to place, but there are also other sources of divergence that reflect the sheer variety of choices facing an observer. The 'same' process can be reduced to quite conflicting analyses, all of which have been produced in good faith.

For instance, early criminology seemed to neglect policing. It was as if police work was thought to be an inconsequential backdrop to the criminal process or a simple response to crime that had already taken place. Then, in the 1950s came the first wave of research on the police, which stressed the dramatic and the spectacular. The police were represented as a besieged and hostile group involved in ceaseless activity and a long succession of violent incidents.[13] In a second phase of research in the 1960s and 1970s, the police were no longer portrayed as violent or frenetic. Instead, policing was seen as reactive, banal, boring, and commonplace, an occupation like any other.[14] More recently, there has been a move to depict the police as besieged *and* bored. Police officers define themselves as agents of order in the midst of disorder, who perform dull work punctuated by spurts of hedonistic and frenzied activity.[15]

Such shifts in emphasis cannot be explained solely by historical changes in the social structure and behaviour of the police. The police of the 1950s also cared about avoiding unpleasant weather and getting cups of coffee; and the police of the 1960s and early 1970s had their violent moments (indeed, in 1970, Bittner defined the police role as 'a mechanism for the distribution of non-negotiably coercive force'.[16] It was not changes in policing alone but also changes in their perception of what was deemed interesting and reportable that led sociologists to turn their gaze towards different facets of policing. The first sociologists of the police considered the petty, everyday features of policing to be analytically unimportant—there was a more absorbing story to be told. That story having become accepted and having grown familiar, a contrasting description could be given that re-emphasized the typical and mundane. And once the police had become uneventful again, there could be a third phase, with a renewed interest in violence.

The sociology of the police has undergone a series of transformations, but it is not always evident that each has been more truthful than the last.[17]

•*Sociological research is constrained by the very structure of its own field.* It consists of a long train of entangling relationships. Every movement about the social world is both obstructed and eased in a number of ways, and not all groups are equally accessible. Sometimes these obstacles are slight and a little work will overcome them,[18] but most of the time sociologists are not capable of passing effortlessly into the group in question. There are always likely to be certain social groups that resist being researched by certain sociologists. James Carey, for example, found that his work on amphetamine users was dangerous and disturbing because his subjects were prone to erratic violence.[19] Few whites could now undertake research on some sections of black society,[20] and blacks might also find it awkward to study some white groups. Men are not welcomed by radical feminists, and the old may be rebuffed by the young. Many of the barriers that divide people from one another in everyday life also keep the sociologist at bay. In fact the barriers facing sociologists are more formidable than those of everyday life because the sociologist, by asking questions and exploring secrets, seeks an intimacy that is not part of polite, commonplace exchanges between strangers or acquaintances.

Most sociologists do know some deviants outside the formal domain of work and research, and they may well be deviants themselves. As one commented about his early and influential writings, 'after all, we were only talking about ourselves'. But it is inevitable that criminologists are generally familiar with only a few forms of rule breaking, and will be tempted to focus on those ones. Their lives are unlikely to encompass friendships with arsonists, rapists, and murderers. More common is an acquaintance with a restricted group of sexual deviants, soft-drug users, and political radicals, who are to be found in and near the sociologist's own world. Others kinds of deviants have been neglected by most sociologists.[21] Unusual subjects often have to stumble or force themselves into the sociologist's life before they receive attention.

• *The criminologist's own experiences also plays a part.* Thus some criminologists have been prisoners,[22] some have been mental patients, and some have been jazz musicians.[23] Some have even been hobos.[24] But they have not known many other deviants. British *sociologists*, in particular, are a somewhat protected and insulated profession. Unlike their North American colleagues, they have not had to work their way through university by taking part-time and vacation jobs such as driving cabs[25] or working as waiters and waitresses. They have not been exposed to the experiences and milieux that can be subsequently exploited for research purposes.

Another, often unacknowledged problem is the sheer volatility of much deviance. Research frequently entails a careful preparation of finances and time: leave may have to be requested, funds sought, and plans made. In turn, there must be some reasonable guarantee that one's research subjects will still be there when one wants them. It is much easier to study the 'gay world' of homosexuals than the solitary homosexual. The 'gay world' is based on a network of bars, public places, and groups; it does not disappear or move unexpectedly. A lone individual, however, may simply leave the sociologist's orbit or decide not to be studied after all.

Organized and settled congregations of deviants are the most readily and intensively observed. Groups that need to maintain contact with strangers are extremely accessible. The 'gay world', for example, is made up in part by a host of anonymous people—the sociologist is just one more visitor. In contrast, more work is required of one who is curious about professional crime, because the professional criminal is suspicious of the stranger.[26] The most work is demanded of sociologists who seek the isolated and unpredictable—the bomber or the blackmailer.

There are also barriers *within* social worlds so that concentrating on one area may bar access to others. A group may not trust a person who has ingratiated him- or herself with a rival faction. The police may not encourage a sociologist who has been with a delinquent group for some time and vice versa. It is usually impossible to predict the inner politics of a group; only when contact has been established will the limits and hazards of research become apparent. By then it may be too late to undo any damage.

■ Some Methodological Strategies

Some analysis requires the cultivation of intimate relationships. On the other hand, many questions cannot be settled by anthropological methods. Historical research, for instance, obviously demands very different strategies. Even when anthropology might be thought appropriate, many sociologists are quite content with formal interviews or the use of indirect evidence. Yet, whatever strategy is employed, there are inherent uncertainties that all sociology must confront. Sociologists have advanced a number of methods to dispel those uncertainties, and we shall examine some of them in turn.

Since this is not a methods text, the treatment will not be exhaustive, but we will outline some of those strategies here.

Observation—Macro

Many deviants are distinguished by their visibility. Particular styles of rulebreaking rely on public assembly. Indeed, the 'skinhead', 'Goth', or 'hoodie' identity would become meaningless without mass display. Klapp has described expressive deviance that requires an audience as 'ego-screaming'. Street gangs, demonstrations, street people, and street prostitutes are reasonably conspicuous, and sociologists can attach themselves to a suitable gathering. It is often possible to join the fringes of deviant activity, witnessing exchanges and exploiting opportunities. The fringes themselves are generally ill-defined since few groups have a strict and enforceable criteria of membership. Sheer physical proximity can signify that one is either sympathetic or uninterested. The mere decision to stand on the road or on the sidewalk will usually proclaim whether one considers oneself to be part of a demonstration. In the absence of self-policing, then, certain forms of deviance may be bared to scrutiny.

> Some kinds of deviance are hidden, while others demand visibility and public display.

Sociologists have certainly moved in on the more visible and public deviant groups. Some have reported the conduct of demonstrations.[27] Stan Cohen monitored the migrations of the 'Mods' and 'Rockers' in Britain in the 1960s.[28] David Downes frequented a café used by local delinquents. In time, he became accepted as a companion.[29] Cavan, too, simply visited the bars of an American city in order to record their deviant under-life.[30] In a situation that could not neatly discriminate between insiders and outsiders, the presence of outsiders was seldom questioned. When deviance is public, access is eased. Even the partially secluded can be laid open to observation. The more involved participants may tolerate or prepare particular identities that can be donned by observers. Voyeurism is not wholly resented by some sexual deviants. Laud Humphreys, for instance, insinuated himself as a look-out or 'watch queen' in American public lavatories, where he could survey casual sexual encounters between homosexuals.[31]

Despite the wealth of behaviour that is exhibited, it must be remembered that a lot of important activity will still remain concealed. After all, public behaviour is usually only a small and perhaps unimportant part of life and is complemented by other conduct that may be equally significant in the understanding of deviance. And people may have private reservations about the apparent demands of public occasions.[32] Matza has described the 'multiple shared misunderstandings' that mould deviant projects.[33] He argues that 'delinquents' may have personal, unvoiced misgivings about public beliefs; and that it would be misleading to assume that they are all as zealous in their support for criminal enterprises as they appear to be. On the contrary, group activity may be at odds with personal beliefs. For instance, McCorkle and Korn described a delinquent episode in which none of the participants was really willing but each assumed that the others wanted a robbery to take place, and so it did.[34]

The language and conduct of public gatherings are not only coercive; they are too standardized and anonymous to permit the expression of individual interests. It is those interests that often influence how general understandings are translated into practical action. It would be a mistake to imagine that the slogans of a public march distill all its members' political perspectives. Equally, it would be a mistake to imagine that all homosexuals embrace the 'gay world' with enthusiasm, for participation may be an unwelcome penalty inflicted on those who seek a partner.

Observation—Micro

Along with an understanding group dynamics, analysis often requires the additional mapping of private feelings. Without such a map, public language would be an incomplete guide to conduct and belief. The behaviour and cries of soccer crowds can be read as a series of feints and mock battles, not as aggression that will inevitably culminate in physical assault, once we understand how people communicate.[35]

These feelings and motivations can become part of a public language as well. In an early and very influential article, Sykes and Matza discussed the 'techniques of neutralization' that delinquents employ in the explanation of their conduct.[36]

Claiming that would-be delinquents do confront the problem of guilt, they catalogued the public formulas of mitigation and extenuation that delinquents use in reference to their acts. For example, they might say that the victim 'deserved' his fate or that he had suffered no real loss. Orthey might argue that higher loyalties were at stake or that those who condemn the delinquents' acts are in no moral position to judge. Reiss, too, has analyzed the accounts that some adolescent gang members gave of their homosexual prostitution.[37] Not permitting themselves to take an 'active' role and affirming that they were 'really' heterosexual, the prostitutes tried not to acknowledge that they had lost any integrity or masculinity. They said they were not gay but that they cleverly exploited men who were.

The methods a sociologist uses are important because deviation may be furtive or disguised or so uncommon as to be unrecognizable to the naïve eye. Its practitioners may be distrustful and wary and unwilling to have dealings with a strange sociologist. After all, sociologists rarely praise what they see.

Interviewing

Where there are no public groups to observe and no home territories to frequent, the sociologist will be obliged to turn to other strategies. One method is 'snowballing', that is, creating a sample of contacts incrementally. For example, if a sociologist is able to gain the confidence of one informant, he or she may then seek introductions to others in the deviant's world. Those introductions will serve as some reassurance to those who are suspicious. In time, a sizable population may be met. A prime example was provided by Nancy Lee's hunt for women who had had abortions in America[38] at a time when it was newly legal but still morally contested Very commonly, such women did not announce that they had had abortions or court the attention of research sociologists. They may even have hidden the fact of their abortions from their own families. Despite their great reluctance, Lee managed to unearth a considerable number of women by being passed from one to the next in a long chain, women that she would otherwise not have had access to.

> When deviance is hidden, it requires that access to a secret world be obtained through informants.

Similarly, in their study of tattoo artists, Hathaway and Atkinson (of McMaster and Memorial universities, respectively) found a snowball sample quite effective in recruiting people willing to talk about tattooing. Given that their research style was conversational, a more rigorous strategy for selecting a sample was unnecessary.[39]

Chief among the limitations to snowballing are the restrictions imposed by a social network. A sociologist will encounter a sample thrown up by the relationships and knowledge of a particular group, and the boundaries around that group will be the boundaries of a sample. However, that constraint may not be especially important because with the difficulties of research every interview and meeting is an accomplishment.

What remains uncertain is the particular character of the group that has revealed itself. In one sense, all groups are unique and none can claim to be typical. In another sense, distinctiveness *can* become a problem. Initial acquaintance is likely to be with someone in or near the sociologist's circle, and he or she may be meeting a group whose politics are similar to his or her own. The drug users, thieves, or those selling illegal DVDs unearthed by snowballing may then compose a rather special network. Drug users may be unusually articulate, and in fact there used to be disproportionately voluminous research on the self-conscious and middle-class addict. Working-class addicts were once relatively neglected, but more recent research is beginning to focus on them.[40] Similarly, snowballing can give salience to politically active homosexuals, thereby generating a misleading impression of social structure and collective behaviour. This method, which is not designed to reach the isolated person, may suggest in fact that deviance is something of a collective achievement.

The Case Study

Sometimes snowballing does not lead very far because introductions are not forthcoming or prove fruitless. Sometimes, too, the sociologist expresses no great desire to construct a sample. On the contrary, the knowledge available to him or her may be so meagre that it warrants an intensive exploration of just one subject. That exploration might be justified by the search for a biographical analysis of deviance or by the exploitation of an extraordinary opportunity. As a result, criminologists have quite frequently collaborated in the writing of a deviant's life story,[41] attempting to understand the part played by rule breaking in the life of one person. The deviant's co-operation is sometimes obtained when sociologist and deviant become intimate after a period of prison visiting or as a result of intense interviewing. More rarely, volunteers are recruited by advertisement in general or special newspapers.

Although a case history can never be described as a basis for substantial generalization, the deviantologist may not want to produce sociological laws. In the place of generality, the deviant biography offers depth and detail. In one respect, it undoubtedly yields more than brief interviews or short spates of observation. It can be conducted in a leisurely manner: questions can be asked or postponed at will; minute knowledge can be acquired; the evolution of deviant careers can be plotted; and disclosures can be made that might otherwise have been withheld. Sociologists of deviance have accordingly returned repeatedly to criminal biographies in order to tap a source of unusually informed knowledge[42] for they are often appear more complex, intricate, and open to diverse interpretations than sociology imagined.[43]

One exceptional case is the biography of Hitler's architect, Albert Speer, in which themes of guilt, knowledge, and acknowledgement are diffusely intertwined.[44]

> Biographies are a way of studying deviance in the full complexity of life.

Participation

Observation, snowballing, and the case study are 'arms-length' methods, but such distance may simply be impossible to maintain if, for example, the sociologist is a deviant or a friend of deviants and the research will consist merely of observing him- or herself and others.[45] On occasion, too, participation may be foisted on the sociologist as a result of the inescapable relationships and encounters that surround research. After all, research is at bottom a social relation, and it is never easy to remain aloof and disengaged; one's sheer presence may be read as an indication of collusion, interest, or complicity. So it is that, little by little, relations can draw the sociologist in and detachment becomes insupportable.[46] Indeed, a refusal to unbend could be read as a sign of unfriendly stiffness that threatens to undermine the research.

Again, some forms of deviance make no provision for spectators, because the activity is dangerous or demands intimacy or discretion. 'Swinging' couples may consent to be interviewed and may provide autobiographies, but the detail of their everyday affairs cannot be monitored from without. An extra person would be intrusive and would transform a relationship into a qualitatively new mode of life.

Research that entails the active collaboration of the sociologist has been called 'participant observation', and it has been employed with special frequency in the study of deviance. Sometimes circumstances throw a sociologist into such an anthropological role. Sometimes it is a theoretical commitment that social behaviour cannot be understood until it has been experienced personally. Sociologists who lean on external accounts and objective evidence cannot appreciate how people act or cannot understand the subjects' environments and history as their subjects do themselves. They are imposing an alien explanation on a situation when what is represented as causal might well have had no influence at all.

Participant observation, then, is supposed to allow the sociologist to experience causes and effects in a particular social setting. Goffman argued that 'any group of persons . . . develop[s] a life of their own that becomes meaningful, reasonable, and normal once you get close to it, and . . . a good way to learn about any of these worlds is to submit oneself in the company of the members to the daily round of petty contingencies to which they are subject.'[47]

It is with that knowledge that explanations can be built. Those who use participation as a strategy[48] are the bearers of a long tradition that may be linked in part with the University of Chicago in the 1920s. One early student recalled how, in general, academic knowledge was thought to be an unreliable basis for speculation, and one head of the sociology department, Robert Park,

> made a great point of the difference between knowledge about something and acquaintance with the phenomena. That was one of the great thrusts in Chicago, because people had to get out and if they wanted to study opium addicts they went to the opium dens and even smoked a little opium maybe. They went out and lived with the gangs and the . . . hobos and so on.[49]

The subject of deviance provides an attractive solution to those confronting the problems of participant observation, because this method requires being both insider and outsider, a person who sees a social world from within yet who also stands apart and analyzes it as a stranger. As insiders, sociologists will attempt to move as their subjects move, learning responses, ways of thinking, and actions as they go. People's actions will become familiar enough that they can be reproduced and described to a larger audience. As an outsider, the sociologist will treat those actions as problematic and uncertain, requiring close examination and questioning. Ideas and practices must be regarded as simultaneously natural and unnatural. Deviance frequently represents an answer to that dilemma since it is a satisfactory meld of the familiar and the unfamiliar, allowing one to imagine that they are inside and outside the worlds it creates. For instance, drug use or sexual deviance in one's own society combines the strange and the known in a composition that excites curiosity but does not defeat understanding. There is an important affinity between the sociology of deviance and participant observation, and a substantial number of studies have adopted an ethnographic style in consequence.

Nonetheless, there are often good reasons why participant observation should not be used. The method may not necessarily furnish the kind of information demanded by a particular problem. There have been allegations that anthropological techniques (and especially covert techniques) pose intricate ethical problems.[50] Many sociologists, who are not interested in the role of meaning and experience in explanation, look for more objective and solid variables. Others find observation difficult in certain settings. Not everyone would pass uneventfully into the world of punks or Hells Angels.[51] Older sociologists might find it awkward to merge with the young, men with women, whites with blacks, Arabs with Jews. Some have pulled it off, though. Liebow, a white male sociologist, conducted a masterly anthropological study of black street-corner society in Washington, DC, and later of homeless women.[52] But he was exceptional. Safer and less taxing methods *can* be productive, and much of the sociology of deviance has turned to them instead.

Institutional Research

There is one very common strategy for reaching deviants without engaging in participant observation. Sociologists can proceed directly to a prison or mental hospital, the advantage being that one who is confined and controlled is likely to be a little more amenable to being interviewed. A meeting with a sociologist might actually help relieve the boredom of a monotonous regime. And, for the sociologist, it is less work to create a sample. The larger problem is in trying to gain access to the institution itself.[53]

Interviews and studies of captive populations can be put to two major uses, one of which raises rather fewer difficulties of interpretation and application than the other. The first transforms an enclosed community into a sociological subject in its own right. There has been a long history of work on the social structures of prisons and asylums. Thus, Ward and Kassebaum explored a women's prison,[54] Cohen and Taylor discussed the effects of long-term imprisonment,[55] Goffman analyzed the mental hospital as a 'total institution',[56] and Comfort described the web of relations between the inmates of San Quentin prison and their partners.[57] Their intention was to explain the social organization of very special institutions, and there was no pretence at an informed and lengthy discussion about deviance outside the walls. Neither was there a very detailed analysis of what inmates did and thought before their confinement. In this case, the institutions themselves were the focus of study.

In the second use, institutions are not objects of particular curiosity, but instead are repositories for people who are of interest to the sociologist. Prisoners may well be the only available representatives of a certain group that is not easily found in the world at large. They lack the fixed social positions and physical locations that aid discovery. Only the most unusual circumstances would bring about a profitable encounter between a sociologist and a murderer or rapist. Sometimes an offence is rare and haphazard and not easily monitored: an observer might have to spend many unproductive months waiting for something to turn up. Deviants are sometimes too well-guarded, threatening, or secretive to be comfortable subjects. Sociologists could well feel trepidation about spending long periods unprotected in the company of those who are violent or disturbed. If certain people are to be seen at all, it will probably be in a prison or mental hospital. In this way, the business of collecting samples is left to the police and official agencies.

There is some risk that organizations will then become sources of distortion. An institutional setting limits inquiry about past conduct. There can be little appreciation of matters that originally escaped the subject's interest and attention. Events before incarceration cannot be observed as they unfold: they must be pieced together retrospectively. The responses of others cannot be witnessed, and there are few external checks on what is said. Institutions tend to deform communication, inhibiting the delivery of unguarded replies and gestures. And the setting is certainly different from the original milieux that prompted the behaviour that the sociologist would describe. Institutions impose their own mark on its inmates' conduct, making it difficult to detach the effects of treatment, punishment, and control from previous experience.

Problems can also flow from the special recruitment of inmates and patients. For example, clinical reports about homosexuals, prostitutes, or drug addicts deal only with those who presented themselves in need of treatment, or who were institutionalized by the authorities. These patients cannot be used to generalize to the unexplored world of untreated deviants.[58] If they have based their knowledge on a selected population, it is generally impossible for sociologists to claim that typicality. Few deviants at large are apprehended, and only a few apprehended deviants enter custody. Indeed, Mack has suggested that inmates are often simply inept.[59] Research on inmates will be further distorted by a tendency to classify deviants by the offences for which they were incarcerated, such as rape or theft. There is some evidence that such a method of identification is misleading, that deviants are quite likely to be arrested for the acts in which they do not specialize precisely because they are inexpert at them. That is certainly the conclusion of Wright in his study of burglars and of Faupel in his study of drug users. Faupel reflected, for instance:

> Total institutions take over and control everything about the individual—their eating, their sleeping, their very identity.

Criminal addicts are disproportionately arrested for crimes that are marginal to their overall pattern of illegal activities. . . . Stable heroin addicts tend to specialize . . . One of the advantages of such specialization is that valuable technical, social and intuitive skills are developed that facilitate the successful commission of these crimes. More important, these skills provide the stable addict with the ability to avoid detection and arrest.[60]

Finally, there is always the additional possibility that a sociologist will be identified with the staff of an organization. Thus the subjects' responses may be become ingratiating, cautious, or hostile.

Saturation Coverage—Self-Reports

There are less focused and discriminating methods of rendering deviant and other populations visible, methods that might be described as sociological saturation coverage. Pursuing certain problems and assuming that deviance is ubiquitous, sociologists will look at a substantially undifferentiated population of people. There will be little or no attempt to single out groups in advance. On the contrary, those groups will surface as the work progresses. Early instances are the self-report studies conducted by Kinsey, Porterfield,[61] Wallerstein and Wyle,[62] Nye and Short,[63] and Nettler.[64] For example, a schoolchild might be asked questions about deviant incidents, and which acts, if any, they committed. One of the most sophisticated examples was Belson's massive study of London boys, a study that revealed, like many of its predecessors, that every boy interviewed had committed some act of theft.[65]

Julian Tanner (of the University of Toronto) provides an example of a Canadian study that used a survey approach of high school students. That study was concerned with the relationship between 'youth culture' and the school. The main proposition it wanted to test was that a low commitment to school is associated with involvement in delinquency. In other words, do adolescents have a high likelihood of being involved in delinquency if they are uninterested in school? He found, unsurprisingly, that self-reported delinquency is generally associated with low commitment to school, for both working-class girls and boys and for middle-class boys as well. [66]

A specific concern with surveys is that unrecorded delinquencies make it difficult to establish the 'true' rate and distribution of criminality, partly because adolescents are unwilling to admit to graver offences and partly because samples of school students are likely to omit truants, who are the most seriously offending group.[67] A recent exception is the Youth Lifestyles Survey that was based on interviews with just under 5,000 twelve-to-thirty-year-olds living in private households in England and Wales in 1998–99. Fifty-seven per cent of men and 37 per cent of women said they had committed at least one offence in their lives, and 19 per cent said that they had committed one or more offences in the last twelve months. Twelve per cent reported they had been formally cautioned or taken to court at some point.[68]

And lastly, a famous study, Kinsey's research on human sexuality used interviewing and self-reporting. While there was much that was important about this research, including the discovery of how extensive sexual variance was, there were also methodological problems. Kinsey's sample relied heavily on two groups unrepresentative of the population at large: university students, and sexual deviants.

Cohort Studies

Cohort, criminal-careers, or longitudinal studies are a second version of saturation coverage. A sample of a generation may be mapped over time by periodic questioning to examine, not only their patterns of involvement with crime and delinquency, as they unfold during the course of a life, but also how those patterns intersect with other events. Measures of matters as diverse as family structure, discipline, supervision, and abuse; educational attainment and school attendance; poverty, social class, and employment; health, intelligence, drug use, and drinking; and parental criminal convictions and the like are taken to assess their statistical connection with law breaking. The findings can enable the criminologist to learn what the precursors and concomitants of offending behaviour are; when people start to offend and when they desist; what offences are committed by whom, how often, when, and in what company; how specialized offending actually proves to be; and whether there are discernible connections between different offences within the span of a single life. The pioneering research was undertaken by Marvin Wolfgang in the 1960s,[69] and it was to be followed, among other studies, by the work of Wadsworth[70] and West and Farrington[71] in the United Kingdom and of Blumstein and Hsieh[72] and of Petersilia and others[73] in the United States.

Crime Survey

A third form of saturation coverage is the crime survey, pioneered in the United States[74] and applied in Holland, Britain, and elsewhere.[75] Mass surveys have been conducted of households, probing the extent of their members' experience of victimization during a particular period of time, usually a year. The original intention was to discover 'real' crime rates. Thus, the first British Crime Survey of 1981 showed that only 8 per cent of offences of vandalism known to victims were reported to the police. The rates for theft from a motor vehicle were 29 per cent, for burglary 48 per cent, for theft from the person 8 per cent, and for robbery 11 per cent.[76] Imagine how surprising such results must have been.

In Canada, the first victimization survey was the Canadian Urban Victimization Survey, conducted in 1982. It found that only 53 per cent of crime was reported to the police. As we would expect, rates were highest for personal assaults and lowest for property crimes. Since 1993, victimization surveys have been conducted every five years as part of the annual General Social Survey, and generally they report rates of crime higher than those known to the police. These surveys are also important for finding out attitudes toward the criminal justice system and feelings of personal safety.

Crime surveys have introduced quite dramatic changes in thinking about deviance, and because they are rich sources of information they revealed new research possibilities, and affected the very agenda of the sociology of deviance. Such surveys are not just exercises in counting, but have given a new analytic prominence to the victim of crime,[77] raised questions about the distress of victimization and the ways in which it may be relieved,[78] directed research at the problem of the fear of crime and the measures that people take to avoid victimization,[79] and encouraged a re-emergence of the social geography of criminal events.[80] Most recently, they are being employed by governments as measures of 'consumer' satisfaction with services delivered by the criminal justice system. The British Crime Survey, for instance, is now annual, and it is being used to judge the efficacy of the police, the prosecution, and Victim Support, the national voluntary organization for the support of victims in England and Wales. It can be used to gauge whether the justice system has managed to improve 'victim satisfaction'.

Crime surveys have had a revolutionary effect on radical sociology. As we shall see, a revelation of the extent of working-class victimization led some radical sociologists to reappraise their attitude towards the social meanings and consequences of deviance. They no longer discuss everyday deviance committed by and against the working class as if they were a petty and irritating diversion from more substantial political issues.[81] They have instead begun to take very seriously certain issues that were once the exclusive domain of their ideological opponents, issues focusing on the problems of police effectiveness and crime prevention.[82]

> Crime surveys have changed the way sociologists think about crime and also how the police deal with it.

Large victim surveys are not without their defects. Being household surveys, they inevitably fail to cover a number of important, high-risk groups, namely, the imprisoned and institutionalized, those in transit, and the homeless. They do not embrace crimes against institutions, such as the often victimized small shops. As they were often conducted in the presence of other family members, they had particular difficulties in unearthing sexual abuse and domestic violence against women, although that has been remedied in later surveys.[83] They do not often cover children, and they omit the many injuries that children suffer. Those deficiencies can be remedied, although often at some expense. More focused surveys are quite able to illuminate the victimization of particular groups.[84]

Comparative Research

An under-used but recently revived approach is the comparative method of cross-cultural and, less commonly, historical study. Although the sociology of deviance was in a sense, born comparative—in such diverse works as John Howard's *The State of the Prisons* (in 1777) and Durkheim's *Le Suicide* (in 1897)—this approach has been largely neglected. The long ascendancy of positivism may in part account for this neglect. If the cause of deviance is to be found in the pathology of individuals or their families, then the comparative method is logically brought to bear only on such factors as might differentiate deviant from non-deviant within a given society at one point in time. However, part of this neglect was because the interactionist stress on situated accounts, motives, and meanings reinforced a delving into the ways of life of deviant groups and agencies of control at the local level. To generalize beyond the groups was felt to be unjustified.[85]

Yet the past three decades have seen a growth of comparative criminology that shows little sign of slackening. A recent bibliography listed some 500 studies.[86] Much of this work is largely descriptive, but increasingly the tenets of theories purporting to 'fit the facts' are being assessed in terms of trends over time and between societies rather than within single societies or at a given point in history.[87] It is Beirne and Hill's argument that 'the explanatory power of theories can be enhanced considerably if they are systematically tested under as diverse temporal and cultural conditions as possible.'[88]

In their cross-cultural study to develop a theory of aboriginal crime, Russell Smandych (of the University of Manitoba) and his colleagues used a comparative technique to look at the problem of aboriginal overrepresentation in the criminal justice systems of Canada and Australia. Possible reasons for overrepresentation have been found to be racial bias, visibility, over-policing—such reasons are called 'extra-legal', or outside the law. They say that any attempt to develop such a theory has to offer a cross-cultural explanation of the problem of aboriginal overrepresentation; account for aboriginal offending patterns that lie outside the official picture of overrepresentation; and use a society-based, rather than individualist, approach. Thus, in looking at the causes of aboriginal overrepresentation in the criminal-justice systems of Canada and Australia, they synthesize existing cross-cultural theories of crime that have been developed by comparative criminologists.[89]

Feminist Research

Deserving of special mention is also 'feminist methodology' because of the critique it offers of the traditional sociology of deviance. As a field of study, its theory and methods are rooted in feminist critiques of the assumptions and procedures of social science. For example, instead of assuming that for deviance gender doesn't matter, a feminist method tries to ascertain how gender does make a difference. When we place women at the centre of inquiry and make it our goal to understand their experience, we find that rape and the experience of being a rape victim varies cross-culturally with varying patriarchal relations. Or we find that white women receive preferential treatment by the police, or that women are more likely to be prosecuted for deviance that violates traditional gender roles.

Feminist methodology is not limited to any single research method. Research designed to get at questions of gender can use both qualitative and quantitative research tools, such as in-depth interviews and case studies, ethnographies and discourse analysis, and historical or comparative research. The important issue is not to treat men and women's experiences of deviance or of victimization as identical.[90]

An interesting example of research that was undertaken to address issues of how gender is related to deviance is Jenness's study of the reorganization of prostitution as a social problem. Prostitution is an interesting topic because it is stereotypically thought of as a woman's crime (even though there are more men than women involved in prostitution). She looked at the work of the group COYOTE (an acronym for 'Call Off Your Old Tired Ethics'), an organization that has sought to challenge traditional definitions of prostitution as a social problem. The research task has been to study how COYOTE has tried to redefine prostitution by replacing the traditional association with sin, crime, and illicit sex with a debate over discrimination and selective law enforcement and the freedom of women to use their bodies as they wish. [91]

This research then takes women and their experience as the central focus, looks at how they are treated by the justice system, and uses different methods to conduct research.

■ Indirect Sources

Deviance is everywhere and it leaves traces everywhere. It marks those who report it, those who attempt to control it, those who gain from it, those who suffer from it, those who describe it imaginatively, and the situations in which it takes place. Properly read, almost every environment can be interpreted as a record of the effects and responses that deviance produces. Gary Marx once argued that 'traces or residue elements are separate from accidents and mistakes, and perhaps surer sources, in that for certain types of infractions they will always be present.'[92] Locks, doors, walls, graffiti, guards, police, prisons, newspapers, films, insurance companies, ticket collectors, and bank vaults all embody the influence of rule breaking. They are a visible reminder of the reactions to deviance, and in turn they provide new opportunities for the commission of further deviance. Mary McIntosh has described this historical co-evolution as a competitive struggle between preventative and illegal technologies.[93]

Looking at indirect evidence can lead to an appreciation of the settings and processes that manufacture deviance. Policing, surveillance, social representations, common-sense assumptions, and physical structures[94] set practical limits to conduct, and sociologists have worked on them all. Their objectives may not always have been congruent, but the outcome has been the development of overlapping perspectives on similar problems. For example, there has been some interest in examining literary descriptions of crime,[95] building on the idea that literature can be treated as a special history of ideas about crime and control. There has been a particularly intense fascination with the part played by the mass media, although it is actually very difficult to disentangle and inspect the effects of crime reporting on its audiences.[96]

There are sociologists who seek indicators that are even more remote from the sites of deviant activity. Looking to explore 'deep' social structures, they turn to indicators which reflect the changes of an underlying order, such as movements of the business cycle,[97] trends in architecture or in educational practice,[98] or signs of political crisis.[99] The idea is that deviance is only a part of society and that transformations of the whole are felt in many areas. Thus Foucault argued that there was a wholesale revolution in the management of people at the beginning of the nineteenth century: new kinds of discipline, which echoed changing attitudes towards deviants, were introduced into factories, workhouses, prisons, schools, and armies. It might seem curious that new styles of handwriting and child rearing are as instructive to the sociologist as penal practices, but maybe they are more instructive because they are *not* obvious.

•*The most common and orthodox form of indirect evidence is that contained in official statistics.* There has been a long tradition of bureaucratic record keeping in the West. For example, censuses have been conducted in Britain since 1801, and in Canada since 1865. As a result, there has been a heavy reliance upon government-sponsored statistics as a measure of social change, and a new science of 'social physics' arose to respond to the opportunities presented by the new evidence.[100] It was believed that it had become possible to produce laws of social motion akin to those furnished by the natural sciences. Quetelet argued in 1869 that a competent statistician could predict the numbers and characteristics of people who would be murdered and who would murder in the years to come, even though they were still alive and oblivious of what would befall them. Statistical rates were seen as independent facts that revealed truths which were superior to impressionistic and subjective evidence. For instance, Chevalier's history of nineteenth-century Paris contrasted the unreliable and partial accounts of novelists and journalists with the sound checks offered by crime rates.[101]

Official statistics provide an unparalleled foundation for speculation. They are neatly tabulated for immediate analysis and use and are compiled without any effort on the part of the sociologist. In some cases, they have no rivals. Historians are particularly prone to defer to police and court records as indisputably sound and objective, and leans heavily on official published rates.[102]

However, there have been growing reservations about the utility of official records.[103] The argument takes two major tacks. Apart from a brief and probably unproductive debate about whether sociologists should accept classifications that have been devised for unscientific purposes,[104] uncertainties hover around the problem of the 'dark figure' of deviance, and the negotiated character of rates. Official crime statistics represent only those crimes reported to the police and are thus incomplete. But there are other problems as well.

In Canada, for example, statistics are not collected on race, and thus it is difficult to estimate whether race and crime are connected. It is also difficult to determine if crimes are motivated by hate or if the police use profiling in the course of their work. So the objectivity of crime statistics is compromised by information that is not collected. Interestingly, Sellin looked at the issue of crime and race in 1928 and, in a note on the 'Negro criminal', came to the conclusion that the overrepresentation of blacks as criminals came from their differential treatment by the police and the criminal justice system.[105]

Case Study—Problems with Crime Statistics

The phrase 'dark figure of crime' refers to that universe of incidents which are not recorded by the police and the courts. It exists in the world regardless of whether it is reported to the police. However, official statistics are not, and do not pretend to be, a report of all illegal activity whatever that might be.[1] They are simply a record of crimes reported to officials.

Sociologists concerned with the 'real' or 'true' rates may then become preoccupied with the events that escaped police attention and reporting. Only when those events have been enumerated, it is argued, will there be a reliable index of crime in society. Sociologists have accordingly devoted themselves to cataloguing the processes that enhance or undermine the validity of official figures. Listed in that catalogue are the ability and willingness of people to recognize crimes, their willingness to report crimes, and the character of the police response to public reports.

Because deviance is often furtive, hidden, or technically sophisticated, burglaries, frauds, and embezzlement may never even be detected by the victim. Even if a crime is known to have occurred, there may be a reluctance to notify the police: it may be thought that the amounts involved do not warrant intervention; the police may be considered uninterested or ineffective; the victim may be implicated (as a collaborator or as the client of a prostitute, perhaps); the victim may be vulnerable; there may be sympathy for the offender; there may be little sympathy for the victim; there may be hostility towards the police (or a fear of not showing public hostility) and accompanying prohibitions on or informing;[2] the crime may itself be condoned; or there may be little practical utility in reporting because the possessions stolen were uninsured or uninsurable.[3]

The police themselves, applying their own, perhaps idiosyncratic 'counting' or classifying rules,[4] may declare that no wrongdoing has been committed or may take no official action.[5] They may focus on particular kinds of crime and record them in particular ways, in the pursuit of any number of goals, including meeting performance targets to escape censure or acquire extra resources.[6]

According to the 1998 British Crime Survey, some 45 per cent of the crimes committed in England and Wales in 1997 were reported to the police, but only 24 per cent were recorded by the police as having taken place, and only 3 per cent resulted in a caution or conviction. There is a long chain of problematic decisions between the commission of a possible crime and its registration, and official records have come to be treated with some suspicion. We will look at crime surveys conducted in other countries later.

However, certain crimes seem to be reflected accurately in statistics. For example, the first British Crime Survey recorded that victims notified 100 per cent of thefts of motor vehicles to the police,[7] and that may be explained quite readily. There is a real enough incentive to approach the police after the loss of a car because a report must be made if an insurance claim is to be made.

But there are gaps in other records of deviance. Only 8 per cent of 'thefts from the person' were reported. Some amounts will be considered too petty to merit action. Some thefts will be mistakenly thought to be the mere mislaying of property. Some thefts will be of things that were obtained unlawfully. Some possessions may not be missed or may not have been insured. The emergence of crime surveys as competing sources of information has reinforced a trend towards analyzing official criminal statistics as records, not of crimes proper, but of the number and distribution of police decisions. Those figures convey little about the 'actual' volume of rule breaking, but they are an excellent guide to the deployment and behaviour of police forces.[8]

But the matter is not simple. There is evidence that the official statistics may occasionally be more useful than their sociological critics have imagined. For instance, crime surveys of the English city of Sheffield suggest that variations between different areas' officially recorded rates of offending are matched quite closely by variations in their victimization rates.[9] Although Sheffield's police statistics may not capture the city's 'true' number of crimes, they may at least reveal the comparative pattern of dispersal of crimes.[10] If such a finding could be generalized, official statistics would provide helpful information about the geographical and social spread of crime.

A second description of crime records has emerged from phenomenology and ethnomethodology. Instead of portraying official statistics as more or less 'wrong', sociologists have defined them as compressed summaries of complicated interchanges between people.[11] A statistic then ceases to be a poor measure of the worrying 'dark figure', no longer simply a self-evident trace of police action, but a condensed, shorthand expression of all the work that is undertaken when a 'suspect' is named, apprehended, charged, and prosecuted. It is a product of copious activity, and it is argued, it will be meaningless until that activity is first understood. Unless one has a grasp of typical processes of plea bargaining, for example, no significance can be attached to the classification of an offence.[12] Unless one has an understanding of interrogation procedures,[13] police strategies,[14] and courtroom practices, it will remain unclear what the statistics represent.

Crime statistics are not impersonal products of mechanical registration. They incorporate operating assumptions and predictions that are intelligible chiefly to their producers. They are the outcome of the social organization of reporting and recording crime and are only indirectly a reflection of wrongdoing in society. An example of the phenomenological critique of crime statistics is provided by Douglas's[15] (and Atkinson's)[16] criticism of Durkheim's *Le Suicide*. Durkheim depicted suicide rates as objective phenomena, which he thought were displayed in cases of intentional self-murder and explained by different states of social integration. However, it was the independence of such rates that Douglas challenged. Rates are not autonomous, he said, but *constructed* by officials who confront the onerous task of deciding how problematic deaths may have occurred. Officials must operate with lay theories and common-sense reasoning about the nature and meaning of death. 'Suicide' is itself a classification that flows out of such theorizing, a classification that embodies assumptions about the possible meanings of loneliness, loss, grief, and social integration. In doubtful cases, for example, common sense suggests that people who are detached and dislocated are the most eligible candidates for categorization as suicides.

In short, suicide rates are compiled by officials; they encase particular hypotheses about the nature of the world. Durkheim came to the study of those rates with certain hypotheses, whereas Douglas argued that suicide rates must be deconstructed before they can be analyzed.

[1] Jason Ditton has pointed out that, rather as in the light of the Heisenberg principle, the amount of rule breaking unearthed is, to an unmeasurable extent, a product of the diligence with which controllers seek for it. See J. Ditton, *Controlology*.

[2] See R. Hood and K. Joyce, 'Three Generations'.

[3] Thus the inhabitants of areas with very high concentrations of crime may well find that they cannot insure their property or that they are charged prohibitive rates. See the *Times* (London), 1 September 1999.

[4] See the 3 (London), 1 August 2000.

[5] See D. McBarnet, 'Pre-trial Procedures and Construction of Conviction'.

[6] See H. Taylor, 'Forging the Job'.

[7] See M. Hough and P. Mayhew, *The British Crime Survey*.

[8] See K. Bottomley and K. Pease, *Crime and Punishment*, for a useful summary of the official statistics of crime.

[9] See A. Bottoms, R. Mawby, and M. Walker, 'A Localised Crime Survey in Contrasting Areas of a City'.

[10] See R. Mawby, 'Crime and Law'.

[11] See J. Kitsuse and A. Cicourel, 'A Note on the Uses of Official Statistics'.

[12] See J. Baldwin and M. McConville, *Negotiated Justice*.

[13] See A. Cicourel, *The Social Organization of Juvenile Justice*.

[14] See E. Bittner, 'The Police on Skid Row'.

[15] J. Douglas, *The Social Meanings of Suicide*.

[16] M. Atkinson, 'Societal Reactions to Suicide'.

Discussion: Deviance and Culture—Suicide

Not only is suicide a depressing topic, but it is often thought to be brought on by depression itself.

However it is also an interesting example of a form of deviant behaviour that has been studied in different ways by various sociologists since the nineteenth century. In this chapter we reflect on how the methodological approach we use to the study of human behaviour affects what we learn about the topic.

Suicide is an act that is illegal and considered immoral but that is widely practised in many cultures. It is a personal solution to social problems. Sometimes it has a noble cause. Soldiers have thrown themselves on their swords on the battlefield rather than risk capture, and in the Second World War, Japanese fighter pilots deliberately flew their planes, known as *kamikaze*, into Allied ships. Usually, however, suicide is thought to have individualistic reasons, locked in the minds of those who are depressed and unable to carry on living any longer.

Durkheim tried to use a statistical approach to determine if there were any patterns in suicide. Using statistics from coroners he found that suicide varied by religion, by sex, and by marital status. One of his findings is that Protestants were more likely to commit suicide than Catholics. This is interpreted to mean that Protestantism is more individualistic, has fewer of the social supports than Catholicism, and also has fewer sanctions against suicide itself.

Similarly, men are more likely to commit suicide than women, probably because they are less communicative and have fewer outlets for expressing frustration and depression. In Western society, since masculinity is associated with independence, strength, and stoicism, males are raised and socialized to express their emotions less. They also have less social support from others than women do.

A stabilizing factor for men is marriage, a fact that explains why suicide rates for men decrease after marriage. The relationship gives them a partner to talk to and to be supported by—and support is what it all comes down to. Whether it is affected by religion, sex, or marital status, suicide is a personal choice affected by social factors.

Rates of deviance may also be examined as influential phenomena in their own right. Journalists, politicians, the police, and lay people ascribe importance to rates and respond to them as vital moral facts. Control policies will be devised to prevent deviance. The police may define rates as performance targets or indicators of productivity that must be defended or changed. Resources may be solicited, staff recruited, and technologies changed in answer to shifts in rates. Public reaction often precipitates political debate about the impressions of success or failure conveyed by rates.

Sociologists now probably treat victimization surveys as the most substantial and useful sources of government information about the distribution and character of deviance. Not only are the surveys interesting descriptions of patterns of victimization, but they also touch on such ancillary matters as the fear of crime, connections between types of housing and crime, and the relations between styles of life and victimization.

In Canada, many different sources of justice statistics are available through Statistics Canada and also through depository-services programs at major universities. In Britain, the surveys are deposited in the Economic and Social Research Council (ESRC) data archive in Essex University, where they are accessible to research criminologists. In the United States, many sources of crime information, including official statistics, victimization surveys, and other crime surveys are available through government sources.

Although crime surveys are a significant corrective to rates of officially notified crimes, they are not without flaws. Reverse record checks, for instance, have established that some 10 per cent of crimes reported to the police would not be disclosed to an interviewer working on a crime survey. Moreover, crime surveys map crimes against people, not against institutions, although there are many thefts and acts of criminal damage committed against organizations.[106] They also do not count crimes committed *by* institutions. In the past there was a severe undercounting of crimes committed against women,[107] the homeless, and ethnic minorities.[108] In time, to be sure, some of these flaws have been corrected and, indeed, recent work has concentrated quite heavily on underrepresented populations of victims.[109]

•*Some sociologists have turned their attention to the social construction and composition of crime news.*[110] As mentioned above, the news media, as vital disseminators of second-hand knowledge about deviance, furnish a landscape of saints, evildoers, and villains that appears to be as real as anything known to one's limited immediate experience.[111] The consumers of this second-hand knowledge are taken to live in a universe that has been prefabricated by news reports.[112]

Richard Ericson (formerly of the University of Toronto), in his three-volume study of crime reporting, analyzes the subtle and complicated relations between the media, sources, subjects, and events.[113] Ericson has shown how the public image of crime is the product of negotiations between people that are trying to convey their sense of the world to reporters, who are themselves policing the world for 'irregularities' and the 'news hooks' that will organize what they can say.

Crime statistics are significant, though the manner of their reporting may prove more significant than the rates themselves. Katherine Beckett (1997) found that the public's fear of crime proved far more sensitive to political and media representations of crime 'waves' than to changes in actual crime rates.

Ken Dowler (of Wilfrid Laurier) has looked at fear and how it is influenced by the media. The public's knowledge of deviance and justice is derived largely from the media rather than from firsthand information. Because it is not based on first-hand experience, it is subject to manipulation. Dowler examined the influence of media consumption on the fear of crime, punitive attitudes toward criminality, and perceptions of police effectiveness. He found that regular viewing of crime shows is positively related to fear of crime, but not to punitive attitudes or perceived police effectiveness.[114]

Watching crime television is positively related to fear of crime.

Jane Sprott and Anthony Doob (of the Universities of Guelph and Toronto respectively) also looked at why Canadians believe the criminal courts to be too lenient in the sentencing of offenders. Because of the common explanation that most people know little of the courts and of sentencing, they felt that the lack of knowledge, and more important, fear are the major factor in such misconceptions.[115] How much of this is due to the effect of the media is clearly an important issue that requires more theoretical analysis.

Since deviance is shaped in its transactions with events and people around it, sometimes it is difficult to distinguish between deviance and its settings. Sociologists have consequently occupied themselves with the social reaction to deviance because an exploration of courts,[116] prisons,[117] and police forces will produce much information about deviance itself.

Such 'secondary' evidence has a major part to play in explanation, and it tends to be easier to compile than anthropological data because newspapers are more tractable than burglars. Further, media evidence is abundant, it may be studied safely in congenial surroundings, and its producers are often more amenable than deviants themselves. Journalism, the police forces, the prison services, and the civil service are occupations with relatively stable memberships. They are part of the everyday middle-class world of the sociologist. In all these senses, they constitute a more accessible research population.

Case Study—Mean Streets

Mean Streets is a field study in the tradition of 'street criminology' conducted by John Hagan and Bill McCarthy of young people who are living on the streets of Toronto and Vancouver.[1] These youth have left home, and do not see school as a way out. The book illustrates the lives of these youths through personal narratives that are reproduced in their own words.

Sociology often studies deviance through school surveys and self-reported criminal behaviour, but this project involved interviewing more than four hundred young people over the course of a summer. One interesting part of comparing Toronto and Vancouver, the authors argue, is that the two cities have different ways of dealing with homeless youth. In Vancouver, the emphasis on crime control is said to create conditions that increase poverty and danger for homeless youth; whereas in Toronto there is more emphasis on social welfare.

The authors look at factors that cause youth to take to the street, the ways in which they deal with deviance and hardship, and their associations with other street youth, especially within street families. The authors speculate on the factors that amplify street crime andon the youths' contacts with the police; and, lastly, they look at the factors associated with leaving the street and rejoining conventional society.

The story is not easy. As they say, 'some of the most compelling moments in our research came when agency workers recalled youth who seemed to bond with them as anchor points, checking in regularly to report on their problems and prospects, but later vanishing without a trace. More than one worker told us of a youth who was later found dead—in an abandoned building or alleyway—the victim of a sex-crime, a drug overdose or a violent attack.'[2]

Major theories of youth crime are also used by the authors in the context of a new social-capital theory of crime, which brings together the major theoretical frameworks in imaginative ways. Strain theory is linked with control theory and integrated with differential association. What is interesting about the use of theories is best said by the authors:

> We found that it was simply impossible to keep separate and competitively evaluate . . . control theory and . . . strain theory. The place of control theory was reflected in the reduced levels of familial control and erratic parenting common among street youth, whereas the importance of strain theory was evident in the increased levels of coercion that characterize the explosive, violent families that many of these youths had left. Both of these processes limited the social capital available to the children of economically subordinate and socially disrupted families. The children of these families were in turn less likely to be committed to or controlled by school and more likely to be in conflict with teachers. . . . Although strain and control theories are typically seen as incompatible, we believe that they can be united when the latter's restrictive assumptions about the basic nature of individuals, family and other social institutions are relaxed.[3]

[1] J. Hagan and W. McCarthy, *Mean Streets: Youth Crime and Homelessess,*
[2] 'The Meaning of Criminology', *Theoretical Criminology*, 4.2 (2000), 234.
[3] Ibid., 237.

■ Implications

The quest for sociological evidence entails an outlay of money, time, and energy. Except for a few instances of indirect evidence, data are actually misnamed because they are rarely *given*. They would more accurately be called *capta*: 'items that are seized with difficulty'. The defects and biases of particular sources of evidence cannot be easily remedied by accumulating a great range of evidence, because there is too little expertise, time, and money to do so. Rather, a commitment must usually be made to a certain group of data. Each group will preclude certain kinds of knowledge yet deliver certain truths.

For example, official statistics cannot produce textured deviant histories or deviant interpretations or the private handling of social control. Such material can be derived only through more nuanced investigations. By contrast, the participant-observer is not able to estimate the typicality of their group. He or she has only the most limited foundation for inferences about the population of deviants at large. More broad-scale comparisons are needed to estimate typicality.

A decision to adopt particular methods and evidence reflects need, vision, and intention. However, *need* is anything but uniform. The requirements of an official at a ministry or department of justice centre on policy and planning issues, such as the projected size of a prison or criminal population or the success of a crime-prevention project turn on demonstrable connections between official action and officially recorded response. The official statistics lend themselves to the satisfaction of those needs (it was for that very reason that they were compiled—the science of statistics originated in the nineteenth century in the compilation and analysis of data about the *State*). But they are tangential to the purposes of many other sociologists because they do not capture the realities that some sociologists would rather study. Those who dwell on deviance as an evolving process tend to ignore statistics and instead generate their own alternative methodologies.

By extension, it becomes apparent that *need* often intersects with *vision*. Prolonged exposure to the world made visible by statistics will, for example, suggest gaps and projects that are defined and answered by statistical means. Greater statistical competence will be at the expense of other pursuits and will demand the use of time that might have been otherwise employed. The participant-observer will probably become more innumerate as observational aptitude increases. And the statistician will find phenomenological arguments ever more alien and unintelligible.

Different forms of evidence are accompanied by different forms of theory, which will lead one to perceive deviance as a property of groups or of individuals; as rooted in profound causes or lodged in the understandings of people immediately involved; as evolving or static; or as predicted by theory or unknown before active enquiry. There are various sociological schools, all of which stress the collection and inspection of the right kind of knowledge, and which develop certain lines of self-contained reasoning. It is perhaps for that very reason that they have become cut off and treated as discrete theories although they are really involved in the same enterprise, the study of deviance, as the *Mean Streets* case study shows.

In making sense of any theory or method, therefore, it is vital to ask what evidence was collected in what way, what evidence was *not* collected, and how answers might have changed had a methodology or data been different. In the next chapter we turn to the development of criminological theory itself.

Chapter Summary

In this chapter we have summarized some of the methods social science uses to 'display' the world of the deviant. The technique or method which is used depends a lot on the behaviour one wishes to illuminate. But it also depends on the theoretical perspective which is used by the researcher. There is no ready reason why a case-study approach is better than a survey instrument, for example—each relies on solving a particular problem and gives us new information. Understanding the strengths and weaknesses of any particular methodological approach is the key to selecting the one best suited for the topic at hand.

Critical-Thinking Questions

1. This chapter proposes that there are different ways of knowing how much deviance there is in society. Branching out from this, we realize that deviance is a 'topic' exploited by certain groups and discussed in the media. To illustrate this idea, discuss how drunk driving has become a topic.
2. John Hagan suggests there are three main ways to measure the seriousness of deviant behaviour. These are, first the extent of agreement about the wrongfulness of the act; second, the societal evaluation of harm inflicted by the act; and third, the severity of the social response to the act. Pick an example, and look at the factors which affect the 'seriousness' of deviance.
3. There are several research strategies used for studying deviance. What technique would work best for motorcycle gangs, punk musicians, or street kids? Or propose your own topic and the best methodology for studying it.

Explorations in Film

Topic: In *Murder on the Orient Express,* Hercule Poirot joins a pantheon of detectives who have tried to solve crime mysteries through the deductive method made familiar by such luminaries as Sherlock Holmes, who said: 'Once you have eliminated the improbable, whatever is left, however impossible, must be the truth.' What methodology is used in this approach?

Websites

Statistics Canada http://www.statcan.ca/
US Federal Bureau of Investigation http://www.fbi.gov/
British Crime Survey http://www.homeoffice.gov.uk/rds/bcs1.html

Chapter Three

The University of Chicago School

Chapter Overview

The Chicago School laid much of the foundation for the contemporary study of deviance in North American sociology. Even though the intellectual beginnings might be set earlier and there were indigenous traditions elsewhere, such as in Europe and Canada, the work at Chicago set the stage for mainstream sociology of deviance.

Here, the sociology of social problems and deviance was studied scientifically as the product of rapid social change, through techniques suited for the study of deviance in its environment. The city was an ideal laboratory for scientific research because deviance was seen as a consequence of social disorganization in urban areas.

Empirical work on deviance and social problems fell into two general categories. The first was *micro-level case studies* of individual deviants conducted by an ethnographic method; the second was a more *macro-level ecological study* of rates of social problems and deviance in different parts of the city. These two streams have had a significant influence on several developments in the sociology of deviance.

■ Introduction

We have chosen to present the sociology of deviance chronologically, describing a succession of important intellectual episodes. Each episode contributed a distinctive set of ideas to the debate that is the sociology of deviance, and each is independent enough to merit separate examination. But it must be recognized that some difficult decisions underlie such an approach, not the least of which is where to start.

Theoretical developments are not neatly insulated from one another, nor are they arranged in neat phases. On the contrary, there is much borrowing, overlapping, and ambiguity at the boundaries. Thoughts emerge from common sources, and they often flow into one another. Sometimes, indeed, the principal difference between theories is their use of language, similar schemes being expressed in dissimilar words.[1] And then there is the problem that a history of formal thought about rule breaking is offered no obvious beginning.

• *The sociology of deviance did not appear full-grown in the nineteenth century.* Crime, sin, and the sheer difference of opinions and behaviour have always been moral and political problems, and thoughtful people have responded by producing a body of writings that we call a proto-sociology. Thus, the oldest form of scholarship, theology, may be understood as a prolonged attempt to make sense of the existence of moral action. Legal commentaries dwell on deviance. Plays, poems, and sagas have revolved around the conflict between good and evil. There has been an enduring series of literary and intellectual essays devoted to the subject of crime. This 'shadow deviantology' is older than the work of the universities and is composed of accounts of notorious people, sinister happenings, and awful institutions.[2]

In the sixteenth century there was a kind of 'low-life reporting' that offered detailed information about the underworld,[3] with its thieves, thief takers and bounty hunters, prostitutes, and pickpockets. It described their social organization and careers, their techniques, and their relations with their victims.

That writing also contains a great deal of unique material and sensible observation, which is almost an anticipation of the theorizing in the sociology of crime and deviance. Rudimentary conceptions of anomie,[4] labelling theory,[5] functionalism,[6] and ecology[7] can be discovered in writings of the seventeenth, eighteenth, and nineteenth centuries. In this sense, contemporary 'deviantology' is a reinvention

> Theology as proto-criminology is the attempt to understand wickedness.

of past explanations. On occasion, too, those writers produced work that is still unsurpassed. The ethnography of Henry Mayhew and John Binney, for instance, is outstanding as a documentation of crime of Victorian London,[8] and its scale and detail have not been reproduced again in England.

The so-called shadow writers are generally forgotten by academic scholars. Some, like Henry Mayhew, Herbert Asbury, Lucas Pike, and Tony Parker,[9] deserve much fuller incorporation into sociology. They have suffered a neglect that is undeserved but quite understandable. Sometimes their writing is superficially naïve and is developed without the conventional forms of scholarship. They worked outside the universities and were not addressing a university audience. More important, these authors, who came from very a variety of occupations, such as journalist, playwright, prison chaplain, magistrate, novelist, policeman, and lawyer, had little organizational support. They were rarely retained as professional experts on deviance, and so their interest was sporadic and amateur and their skills were not transmitted to students or apprentices who would succeed them. After all, it is only very recently that the university syllabus has expanded to cover the projects they initiated, and acceptance was at first difficult indeed.[10]

• *The University of Chicago sociology department was distinctive because it made a decisive break with the haphazard, solitary, and ill-maintained studies that we have described as proto-criminology.* Academic work seeks to make amateur speculation about deviance into an orderly science. The department's first chairman, Albion Small, transformed sociology into a permanent and co-operative enterprise. He employed people to become professional social investigators who would methodically teach what they had learned to others, in the manner of the research seminar of the German university.[11] The first systematic group-related efforts to apply sociological knowledge were made in Chicago during the second and third decades of the twentieth century.'[12] 'In Europe various philosophically minded persons had written books about something called "sociology"' but 'the Department of Sociology at Chicago . . . was really the first big and lasting one in the country; thus, also the world'.[13] 'In Chicago, sociology was implanted in American academic life and after that nothing was the same'.[14]

Albion Small himself stated that, before the founding of his department, sociology was 'more of a yearning than a substantial body of knowledge, a fixed point of view, or a rigorous method of research.'[15] If these claims are warranted, the creation of the University of Chicago provides an opening for the history of the sociology of crime and deviance. Marxism had flourished in Europe, the *Annales* group had been active in France, the Manchester and London statistical societies had performed important work, and certainly sociology courses were being taught in Canadian universities, but it was in Chicago that sociology was industrialized and a coherent sociology of deviance began.

The Chicago School influenced many traditions that came after it. The promise embodied in the Chicago Area project that society could be improved was used to create ideas on the importance of recreational programs to combat delinquency in Toronto, for example. And, as the accompanying 'Discussion—Deviance and Culture' shows, the idea that urban reform could affect delinquency can be seen

It was in Chicago that sociology was industrialized.

even in the development of libraries. In Canada, at least in the early decades of the twentieth century, sociology was strongly tied to the bettering of social conditions that were thought to lead to deviance.

Discussion: Deviance and Culture—A Library for Boys and girls in 1943

It was 1943 and Montreal was worried about the increase in juvenile delinquency. One segment was determined to use culture to do something about it.

The Notre Dame de Grâce Community Council had come together the year before to discuss how it should deal with juvenile delinquency. News reports had warned of an increase in juvenile delinquency in Britain, the United States, and now in Canada.

In retrospect the problem was more apparent than real, but for newspaper readers of the day there would be no way of knowing. While some youth offences had increased, there was probably no youth crime wave. However, it is the interpretation of that increase which matters, and thanks to news articles the crisis of the 'latchkey child', the youth coming home to an empty house, the youth with time on his hands became topical.

What underlay the media reports was of course a deeper social anxiety about families. Many men were away at war, and women were working outside the home. The suspicion that a lapse in parental discipline might be a problem found its focus in concerns about youth crime. Newspapers ran stories about idle youth, purse snatchings, youth crime, and the influence of detective novels and movie houses.

In the *Globe and Mail*, for example, an editorial published on 7 October 1942 and headed 'An Ominous Condition' refers to an increase in juvenile crime: 'There is rife among a large segment of the younger generation an epidemic of undisciplined lawlessness and disrespect for authority and the rights of others which is responsible for spiritual and material damage on an extreme scale.'

In addition, the *Globe* notes, 'young folk are cutting short their education, and finding employment at wages which give them not only a lot of free spending money but an exalted idea of their own importance in the scale of things.'

A bad combination indeed.

In Montreal, to address this concern the Notre Dame de Grâce Community Council united various causes under the same banner. These included the Home and School Associations, the Boy Scouts and Big Sisters, the Child Welfare Association, and the Parks and Playgrounds Association.

The community council lobbied politicians to rescind a pool hall's licence, to ban gangster radio shows, and to criminalize crime comics.

These actions were not that unusual for such an organization, because by the end of the nineteenth century there were a variety of social services designed to respond to the social problems of youth. These included the Children's Aid Society, and the YMCA/YWCA.

The *Juvenile Delinquents Act* had been passed in 1908; however criminal justice was not always the best solution. Separate pre-trial youth detention facilities were often inadequate, youth court judges had little training, psychologists were seldom used, and there were inadequate reformatory spaces.

So the founding of the Notre Dame de Grâce Library for Boys and Girls was an interesting cultural initiative. Given that juvenile delinquency was thought to be related to reading bad books, making good books available in public libraries would be an ideal solution.

Books were seen as a solution in Toronto too, for example, where schools were encouraged to become centres of social life and recreation. The *Globe* editorial mentioned above said that in many communities there was 'a regrettable lack of organized recreational facilities through which young folk could occupy their leisure pleasantly and profitably. The net result is a deterioration in the morale of the younger generation which bodes ill for the future.'

It is unfortunate that the lack of federal support for day care, or tax breaks for married women who worked probably made the problem worse. This was based on the conservative idea that the 'traditional' nuclear family was the solution for juvenile delinquency. But probably the better solution was to improve recreational, educational, and judicial services for youths.

As the *Globe*'s editors noted in 1942, 'if concerted efforts, well supported by the public, are not made to cope with this deterioration, consequences may well prove calamitous.' Thoughtful words, and a thoughtful solution.

Source: Based on C. McCormick, 'Lack of Services Spurs Youth Crime' (Crime Matters column), *Daily Gleaner* (Fredericton), 31 January 2008. See also C. Lyons, 'Children who read good books usually behave better'; J. Keshen, Wartime jitters over juveniles: Canada's delinquency scare and its consequences, 1939–1945.'

■ The University, the Department, and the City

It is a veritable Babel, in that some thirty or more tongues are spoken. . . . Gunmen haunt its streets, and a murder is committed in them nearly every day in the year.[16]

The University of Chicago was an extraordinary invention.[17] John D. Rockefeller donated 35 million dollars to found a university, it pillaged other institutions by offering their staff higher salaries, and a number of departments were established, such as the sociology department in 1892. Those processes were important for the shaping of sociological work: there was freedom to appoint those who were able, with ample funding for research.

Moreover, innovation was defined as the distinguishing feature of a university that was itself quite new and pioneering. Thus Leonard Cottrell recalled that '[we were] rejecting all the traditional answers and institutions that were allegedly the stabilizers of society.'[18] There was no earlier generation of professional sociologists, and the very respectability of the approach was disputed. Few sociologists had been able to study sociology exclusively, having come from philosophy, biology, religion, journalism, and linguistics. One of the most distinguished Chicago sociologists, Robert Park, claimed never to have heard the word 'sociology' while he was a student at the University of Michigan between 1883 and 1887. Indeed, no university course was offered in sociology anywhere in North America during that period.[19]

The tentative and unformed nature of American sociology revealed itself in the long time that elapsed before the Chicago department came into its own. Some of the early appointments had little interest in the creation of an academic sociology, and it was only later that a distinctive style emerged, especially with the second generation of scholars.[20] In looking at their work in connection with the sociology of deviance, though others might tell a different story, [21] we feel the early achievements of the Chicago department influenced functionalism, epidemiology, attitude research, survey methods, and much else. Our own focus is on the anthropological and ecological study of deviance, whose chief author was Robert Park, a head of the Chicago department and author in 1915 of a classic of urban ethnography, 'The City', published in the *American Journal of Sociology*:

> Anthropology, the science of man, has been mainly concerned up to the present with the study of primitive peoples. But civilized man is quite as interesting an object of investigation, and at the same time his life is more open to observation and study. Urban life and culture are more varied, subtle and complicated, but the fundamental motives are in both instances the same. The same patient methods of observation which anthropologists like Boas and Lowie have expended on the study of the life and manners of the North American Indians might be even more fruitfully employed in the investigation of the customs, beliefs, social practices, and general conceptions of life prevalent in Little Italy on the Lower Side in Chicago, or in recording the more sophisticated folkways of the inhabitants of Greenwich Village and the neighborhood of Washington Square, New York.[22]

Most sociology departments seem to ignore their physical and social environments, and perhaps there is no reason why sociologists should concentrate on their immediately surroundings. But Chicago sociology was to become the sociology of Chicago itself, a detailed anthropological mapping of the social territories that made the city.

The city of Chicago was an exploding mosaic of contrasting social worlds. Its growth from a small log fort in 1833 to a substantial city by 1900 was extraordinary. Spectacular population growth was fed by immigrants from a succession of countries: Ireland, Sweden, Germany, Poland, and Italy. Each group had to make a place for itself in the city. Each had to confront a series of recurring problems. Urban life was a welter of shifting scenes and identities. As Park observed, 'everything is in a state of agitation—everything seems to be undergoing a change. Society is, apparently, not much more than a congeries and constellation of social atoms.'[23]

It is not unusual for burgeoning cities to attract a fascinated gaze. In its time, London was itself thought to be an extraordinary object, a new Babylon revealing a vast kaleidoscope of new social combinations and possibilities. Victorian journalists and novelists devoted themselves to reporting the strange and remarkable events that unfolded in the city. But their fascination lacked the social organization to prepare the foundation of an enduring scholarship, and it passed away. It was the Chicago sociology department that allowed curiosity to become a stable tradition. Itself influenced by the work of journalists like Lincoln Steffens and by the newspaper experience of Park, the department sought to document interesting worlds before they changed and disappeared.[24] The city was a laboratory in which all the nuances and interconnections of social life could be observed.[25]

■ The Roots of Responsiveness

As long as one continues *talking*, intellectualism remains in undisturbed possession of the field. The return to life can't come about by talking. It is an act; to make you return to life, I must set an example for your imitation, I must deafen you to talk, by showing you, as Bergson does, that the concepts we talk with are made for purposes of *practice* and not for purposes of insight.[26]

We do not propose to offer a long commentary on the intellectual development of sociology at Chicago.[27] However, it is essential to stress that it did not arise out of simple curiosity or a journalistic impulse or in reaction to the beguiling qualities of a city undergoing a rapid transformation. It was the fruit of a carefully resolved philosophy of thought and action that emphasized the primacy of practice. Many, although not all, Chicago sociologists were wedded to two principal schools, pragmatism and formalism, and it was the fusing of those schools that led to the use of focused, grounded studies of observable social scenes.

The pragmatism of Charles Peirce, William James, and John Dewey (who himself taught at Chicago) extracted themes from German philosophy and translated them into a radical phrasing of the nature of knowledge. In brief, they maintained that knowledge resided neither in properties of the world alone nor in properties of the observer alone. Facts are not self-evident, but are chosen and interpreted by the mind that surveys them. People with different perspectives and different problems will respond to those aspects of phenomena that answer their particular purposes.[28] For example, the meaning of food will not be identical for the chef, the chemist, the waiter, or the guest at a meal. The meaning of food shifts in response to the peculiar dealings one has with it, not whimsically,[29] but in a transaction between the observer and the environment. Knowledge was not defined as a subjective state or as an objective condition but as a *process*,[30] where useful understanding comes from exploring practical problems, from experiences anchored in the world. Experience becomes the guarantee of valid knowledge: 'It is the personal experience of those best qualified in our circle of knowledge to *have* experience, to tell us *what is*. Now what does *thinking about* the experience of those persons come to, compared to directly and personally feeling it as they feel it? The philosophers are dealing in shades, while those who live and feel know truth.'[31]

Such extolling of experience leads to a distrust of systematic, philosophical reasoning, and as George Herbert Mead remarked, 'our own experience in so far as it is not reflective does not involve knowledge. . . . Experiences simply are'.[32] Any attempt to distance oneself from experience and to describe it is a different form of understanding, different from experience itself and not readily transformed back into it.

Robert Park rescued pragmatism and transformed it into a practicable sociology. He had studied under William James, who had taught him that 'the real world was the experience of actual men and women and not abbreviated and shorthand descriptions of it that we call knowledge'.[33] Park had also studied under Georg Simmel,[34] whose formal sociology provided a limited resolution to the difficulties posed by pragmatism.

Formalism held that it was the task of sociology to explore the structures of social activity and that those structures could be regarded as analytically independent of the settings in which they appeared. In one sense, he argued, every social occasion is unique. It will never return with an identical history, context, and membership. In another sense, it is but part of a wider display of formal processes. For example, a university's administration has a number of offices that are utterly distinct. No office is quite the same as any other: it houses different people with different pasts, problems, and ambitions. Yet it is also an instance of the operation of hierarchy, which is a general feature of bureaucracy, which is also general, and of routine transactions, sometimes conflict-laden, with students and staff, which are general too. Simmel would argue that it is possible to examine hierarchy, bureaucracy, and conflict as autonomous forms that manifest themselves in diverse ways. It is those forms that can be analyzed, not the contents themselves. Grafted onto pragmatism, formalism permitted a restricted description of an otherwise indescribable experience. It became feasible to abstract, discuss, and compare examples of social action.

Together, pragmatism and formalism brought about a special phrasing of sociological work. It was argued that the business of research is to understand the social world and the social world is itself manufactured by the practical experience of those who live in it. Such theory deals with a realm of 'facts' and processes which is less solid than the concrete personal knowledge of those who actually produce the behaviour that is to be explained. Thus Park argued that 'sociology is not interested in facts, not even in social facts as they are commonly understood. . . . Sociology wants to know how people react to so-called facts, to what is happening to them'.[35] And Louis Wirth argued: 'the important features of each cultural situation are not immediately evident to the observer and do not constitute objectively determinable data. They must be seen in terms of the subjective experiences and attitudes of . . . individuals.'[36]

Practical experiences themselves are responses to situations and problems, and they change as those problems change. Indeed, the very task of working on a problem transforms it and changes one's knowledge of it. Thus, sociology is not devoted to the study of states but of *processes*, of things and people in change. It must be so organized that it can observe and report processes over time. The most effective research strategy is one that requires sociologists to participate personally in the world that they would analyze. Without such participation, knowledge is not experience but an uncertain commentary on experience. So Park urged a student embarking on an exploration of a religious sect in Los Angeles[37] to 'think and feel Molokan'.[38]

> The key element of research became participation.

The Chicago sociologists tended to proceed to the small social scenes that lent themselves to anthropological research. In particular, they moved out to the territories that adjoined the university. Organized class visits were made to the ethnic communities that littered Chicago; 'term papers and dissertations naturally followed, and in time, research volumes'.[39] Research training itself consisted of a number of seminars that culminated in an instruction to leave the university for the streets. There were studies of gangs,[40] organized crime,[41] prostitution,[42] taxi dance halls,[43] real estate offices,[44] local newspapers,[45] the rooming house district,[46] hobohemia,[47] the central business district,[48] and the Poles,[49] blacks,[50] and Jews[51] of Chicago. Collectively, 'they seem to have emerged as the most durable and widely used bases for describing the community life of the city'.[52]

Put most simply, these studies are based on the idea of studying the individual in their social context, and Burgess' classic 1923 and 1928 articles set the standard for the case study approach. And some of these writers, for example Thrasher, were also skilled at relating the theory to specific settings, such as the school. [53]

■ Ecology

Any situation could be described in terms of its unique and its general properties. Those general properties were features that cut across particular events, giving them a common history and a common character. Conflict, assimilation, succession, symbiosis, co-operation, and invasion are processes that appear to transform events in predictable ways. For certain purposes, it is practically irrelevant whether conflict is waged between the partners of a marriage, street gangs, or nations. It is still conflict.

City life and urbanization were analyzed by a collection of master forms borrowed from biology and based on the workings of an ecological order. Ecology is an emphasis on the patterns and organized changes that are produced by different species living together in the same physical territory. The development of a

> The idea of ecology, or natural area, was a useful metaphor for sociology.

biological ecology was attractive to sociologists who were searching for analogies and principles with which to advance their own new discipline. It proved especially attractive to those who were seeking to explain the evolution of different human groups in the geographical context of the city. Just as plants, insects, and animals convert a physical terrain into a mosaic of distinct communities, so people become separated into a network of disparate communities that form an intelligible whole. As Wirth remarked, 'whatever else men are, they are also animals, and as such they exhibit the effects of physical aggregation and of their habitat.'[54]

Biological ecology was rarely taken to be more than a convenient working description of an otherwise excessively complex process. It was acknowledged from the first that human communities are constructed on different principles from those of animal and plant communities. People are quite capable of detaching themselves from their 'own' territories; they display rational behaviour; they can organize themselves into institutions that impose a distinct order; their works are modified by an elaborate technology; their activities are shaped by conscious planning; and they are governed by a symbolism that interprets and changes what they do.[55] Moreover, ecology was not regarded as a total explanation. It was but a 'segmental view',[56] which neglected much. Ecology offered a systematic framework for analyzing the flowering of interrelated social worlds:

Ppl diff. from animals and plants

> The city is not merely an artefact, but an organism. Its growth is, fundamentally and as a whole, natural, i.e. uncontrolled and undesigned. . . . What have been called the 'natural areas of the city' are simply those regions whose locations, character, and functions have been determined by the same forces which have determined the character and function of the city as a whole.[57]

Of principal interest to the Chicago sociologists was the manner in which cities expand and become internally differentiated. The emergence of Chicago itself was explained by what came to be known as the *zonal hypothesis*, the idea that cities evolve in a series of concentric zones of activity and life. (See Figure 3.1.) At the very centre is the business district, which is typified by a small residential population and high property values. About it is the zone in transition, whose population is fluid and poor, whose housing is deteriorating, and whose stability is threatened by the encroaching business district. About that zone, in turn, are areas of working-class housing, middle-class housing, and, on the fringes, suburbia. Each zone is itself composed of diverse 'natural areas' that abut on one another. They are natural because they are not entirely intended, because they represent unplanned groups of like people, and because they manifest a rough correspondence to the territorial division of species in nature:

> In the course of time every section and quarter of the city takes on something of the character and qualities of its inhabitants. Each separate part of the city is inevitably stained with the peculiar sentiments of its population. The effect of this is to convert what was at first a mere geographical expression into a neighborhood, that is to say, a locality with sentiments, traditions, and a history of its own.[58]

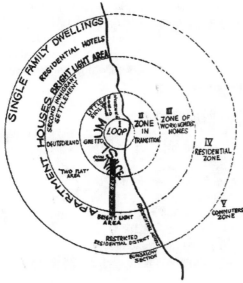

Figure 3:1: The Zonal Model

Source: R. Park, *The City*, there is also a map in Burgess, 'Residential Segregation in American cities', http//www.lib.uchicago.edu/e/su/maps/chisoc/.

Figure 3.2: Map of Chicago showing places of residence of 7,541 alleged male offenders 17–75 years of age placed in the Cook County jail during the year 1920.

Source: Behavior Research Fund, Chicago. Original map held at the University of Chicago Map Collection.

However, it was more than a metaphor for analysis; it was also a model of research, in that sociologists outlined procedures for the study of ecological areas. As Thrasher says, 'No basic understanding of either child or school is possible without a thorough investigation of neighbourhoods, local communities, and metropolitan districts.' Thrasher said the following types of characterization could be used to delimit natural areas:

1. race, nationality, and religion
2. uses of land and buildings: railroads, industrial, residential, etc.
3. types of residential housing: tenements, rentals, etc.
4. density of population, per acre and square mile
5. economic levels based on study of income
6. occupations: labourer, factory, professional, etc.
7. cultural criteria: pathological, bohemian, bright lights, etc.
8. is this an interstitial area (spatial)?
9. is this an area in transition (temporal)?
10. spatial plan of community: radial-axis, gridiron, etc.[59]

The work done at the Chicago School was quite influential, and it appeared in studies of other areas as well. The Burgess zonal model, as it came to be called, was used to study a variety of urban data on crime, dance halls, delinquency, dependency, family disorganization, gangs, mental disorders, suicides, and vice.[60] (See Figure 3.2.)

■ Social Ecology in Montreal

There is an interesting connection between the Chicago School in the United States and what has sometimes been called the Chicago School of the North. In Canada the first formal Department of Sociology was at McGill University. The founder and first chair of the department (from 1922 to 1952) was Carl Dawson. A native of Prince Edward Island, he had studied at Acadia, and done his graduate work at Chicago under two prominent members of the Chicago School, Park and Burgess. Another, later member of the department, Everett Hughes, was at McGill from 1927 until 1938, before he went to the University of Chicago.

As a graduate student in Chicago, Dawson was involved in teaching and in designing social research studies. As a professor in Montreal, he wrote the first Canadian introductory sociology textbook in 1929,[61] wrote and spoke on the concept of regions, and the interaction of individual and community,[62] and conducted several empirical studies of immigrant settlements in western Canada.[63] Dawson headed the Social Research Group, which conducted such research as an exploration of British immigrant experience in Montreal in the first several decades of the century, and supported various notable community studies, such as Hughes's book *French Canada in Transition*, a study of how ethnic relations were changed by industrialization in Quebec.

The 'new science' of sociology wished to understand the forces that led to social fragmentation and social cohesion. However, it was inevitable that human ecology, as it was called, used ideas from the studies of plant and animal ecology, physiology, and cultural anthropology. This became the frame of reference for research projects undertaken by Dawson and his students in the 1920s and 1930s. Particular aspects of research interest were industrial development, transportation, immigration, housing, labour organization, crime, juvenile delinquency, family disorganization, welfare work, and child labour.

Dawson believed that research based on the investigation of urban communities and their institutions would lead to the creation of a better society. As he wrote in 1927: 'A city plan based upon adequate study will not work against the natural forces making for city growth but will direct those forces in the production of more stable, healthy and wholesome neighbourhoods. . . . It can directly and indirectly aid the citizens in meeting some of the most urgent problems of housing, disease and disorder.'[64]

As a 'new direction', Dawson's work represented a combination of the ameliorative interest of social work, the anti-authoritarian tradition of the Baptists, and the rigour of the new social science of sociology. The Baptists of the day promoted prison reform, prohibition, justice for native Canadians, inner-city missions, protection for children, and women's rights. This unique influence made the work of the McGill School different from that of the Chicagoans.[65]

By 1928 Montreal was the fifth-largest city in North America, with thousands of immigrants arriving every year. Electric streetcars enabled thousands of workers to travel daily from the city's inner core into residential neighbourhoods and surrounding suburbs if they could afford to live there. The expansion of the city in all directions from the centre, as in the zonal model, held true for Montreal, but its topographic features distorted the concentric circles into a kidney shape around Mont Royal, as shown in Figure 3.3.

As the city grew, businesses such as machine shops, warehouses, and light manufacturing 'invaded' the Dufferin residential district, a neighbourhood that became a transitional zone when the commercial sector expanded. The more successful among the English, Irish, Scottish, and French families who lived in the district were able to move to the suburbs, and their vacated houses were remodelled into flats and occupied by the less prosperous Asian and European immigrants. In this 'disorganized' physical environment there was constant noise, dirt, stimulation, vice, and despair.

Dawson's graduate students undertook research studies of the area, such as Israel's study of the Negro community, and McCall's study of family disorganization. Margaret Wade conducted a study of the dependent child, and her discussion echoes that of Thrasher:

This is the business area . . . the area of first settlement for the immigrant. Here in any city are found its worst social conditions, and Montreal is no exception. Vice and crime, ignorance and prostitution caused by poverty, and in their turn bringing about poverty, constitute the vicious circle of the

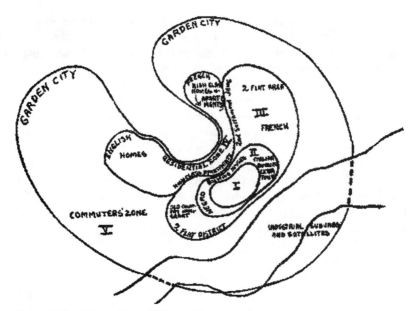

Figure 3.3: Kidney Map of Montreal

Source: *La Revue municipale.*

underprivileged, lower classes of the modern metropolitan city. . . . In these dark, ill ventilated, ill smelling, dirty, unsanitary dwellings are being born and brought up, a large proportion of the future citizens of the city and of the dominion.[66]

In comparison, the 'stable' residential neighbourhoods had more in the way of supporting social institutions such as churches and schools than the Dufferin district. The need for ameliorative institutions is evidenced in the appearance of rescue missions, which first appeared in the Dufferin district in the 1890s.

The work of Carl Dawson and his students, which represents an important period in Canadian deviance studies, was an attempt to apply scientific principles to the study of the natural organization of crime and deviance. For this reason it is sometimes referred to as the Chicago School of the North.

■ Deviance, Crime, and Pathology

It was not the express ambition of the Chicago sociologists to focus solely on deviance, just as it wasn't the sole ambition in Montreal.[67] Deviant populations formed but one segment of the city and were perhaps no more engaging than any other. However there were factors that encouraged the development of 'deviantology'. One was the funding and sponsorship provided by a variety of voluntary and municipal organizations that sought solutions to social problems.

Another was the sociologists' leaning towards practical intervention to improve social conditions. A third was the sheer availability of deviance: graduate students, in particular, were ill-equipped to study any but the relatively undefended public, poor, and exposed neighbourhoods in the zone in transition. Other areas demanded of students an assurance, patronage, and support that were difficult to secure.

What was immediately impressive and obvious to the urban anthropologist was the massive concentration of 'pathological behaviour' in the zone in transition. Partly because of its great visibility, such behaviour appeared to be confined to a narrow territorial belt.[68] Within that belt occurred all those phenomena that are conventionally considered social problems: mental disorder, prostitution, suicide, alcoholism, infant mortality, juvenile delinquency, crime, disease, and poverty.[69] The incidence of pathology could be plotted with data collected from court records, census reports, and special surveys. Burgess wrote: 'In the zone of deterioration encircling the central business section are always to be found the so-called "slums" and "bad lands", with their submerged regions of poverty, degradation and disease, and their underworld of crime and vice. Within a deteriorating area are rooming-house districts, the purgatory of "lost souls"'.[70]

Deviance may have been present elsewhere, but it was hugely conspicuous in the transitional zone.[71]

Analytically, the significance of the zone in transition was that it seemed to possess a distinctive social organization that could not be explained simply by the characteristics of the populations who lived there at any one time.[72] An area with the cheapest rents, an appreciable circulation of inhabitants, and few settled institutions, it tended to be the home of the most recent generation of immigrants. National group after national group lived there. Each in its turn seemed to reproduce very much the same patterns of behaviour. Above all, it produced crime. Part of the Chicago project then turned to the explanation of how deviance arose in a particular quarter of the city.

The zone in transition was unruly, housing people who were unaccustomed to one another, to city life, and to America. Lacking substantial resources and having left much that had been familiar, they were required to establish a way of life in a difficult and shifting environment. One of the prime problems they faced was the sheer array of different worlds around them. When those worlds appeared unstable, the whole invited the description of social disorganization and the lack of a moral consensus: 'The degree to which the members of a society lose their common understandings, i.e. the degree to which consensus is undermined, is the measure of a society's state of disorganization'.[73]

Disorganization also characterized the fragmented, fluid, and anonymous elements of urban life: 'contacts are extended, heterogeneous groups mingle, neighborhoods disappear, and people, deprived of local and family ties, are forced to live under . . . loose, transient and impersonal relations'.[74]

That concept of disorganization is awkward, and it deserves some reflection. Matza, for example, claimed that the Chicago School wrote of disorganization when what they were actually describing was diversity.[75] Whyte asserted that

> The highest concentration of deviance was found in the most disorganized areas.

reference to social disorganization merely signifies that the observer has not understood what has been seen.[76] Quite typical was the remark of another, later Chicago sociologist who stated about his ethnographic research on Jelly's, a bar in Chicago's South Side:

> after being around Jelly's neighborhood for a while and getting to know its people, the outside observer can begin to see that there is order in this social world . . . there is more to social life in and around Jelly's than might be suggested by a cursory inspection, informed by the stereotypes and prejudices of those not involved. Life here cannot be understood as simple 'social disorganization'.[77]

There will always remain the insuperable problem of whether the observer has recognized or imposed the patterns that have been discerned, yet the Chicago sociologists who talked of disorganization themselves went to the jungles of Hobohemia and the streets of the slums and unearthed what they described as very real social structures. Their discovery of structure and order makes their use of the term 'disorganization' appear inaccurate and in need of redefinition. At the very least, it is clear that the word was not actually intended to refer to a collapse of order. On the contrary, the Chicago sociologists displayed an unusual ability to find organization in hitherto uncharted areas. In their work, 'disorganization' actually points to two distinct, but occasionally linked, properties of social life.

•*One such property is the reduction of social relations to a rather rudimentary condition in which mistrust, heterogeneity, and change abound.* In that condition, new opportunities and combinations arise and disappear with some rapidity. Old habits are broken.[78] Life becomes unpredictable. Cohesiveness is threatened. The dependable group shrinks in size. A world so disorganized possesses a palpable order, but it is an uncomfortable order that is sensed as *comparatively* unreliable.[79] Such a world has its own complexities and intricacies that demand a particularly delicate analysis.[80] For its inhabitants, the negotiation of relations in uncertainty is fragile, difficult, and fraught with anxiety.[81] Thus defined, disorganization is mainly a facet of *experience* and, curiously, the experience of disorganization can itself be highly organized.

•*On another plane, disorganization could be described as a property of the wider social structure.* It would then refer to the relations *between* and not within worlds. Social differentiation, a period of excited social change or uneven development can exaggerate the instability of those relations, leading to strain and a breakdown of local order. In turn, particular worlds can become dislocated, thrown up out of their context and exposed. They can achieve a social and moral independence that some sociologists have chosen to emphasize.

In one sense, in keeping with this formulation, the zone in transition was wholly dependent on the city that surrounded it. In another, it could be cast as an isolated and deregulated area, an area uncontrolled by the 'master institutions' of society. Church, law, school, and commonplace morality were thought to have no sway there. A criminal area may be organized and its wider environments may be organized, but there may be little or no articulation between them. Whyte described one instance, the Boston North End of the 1930s: 'Cornerville's problem is not lack of organization but failure of its own social organization to mesh with the structure of the society around it. This accounts for the development of the local political and racket organization and also for the loyalty which people bear toward their race and toward Italy'.[82]

'Disorganization' may be an unfortunate word for such a lack of social integration, but it is evident what was intended. Cornerville and areas like it are akin to the old thieves' quarters of the European cities. They possess a special character, at once attached and detached, and are a part of the city and apart from it. Neatly delimited, they seemed to justify an ethnographic response.

•*Integral to the conception of disorganization was the companion idea of weak social control.* Those who stressed internal disorder could cite numerous obstructions to social control. Moral habits could not be properly implanted.[83] People were not effectively curbed, nor could they curb one another. They did not know each other well, formed few commitments to the area or to its population, were confused by moral diversity, were alienated from the distant authority of the State, and were loath to intervene in the affairs of their fellows.[84] Morality could no longer be taken for granted. It became relativistic and circumstantial, readily adapted for selfish purposes. More particularly, its influence could not extend very far. Those entitled to exercise moral claims were confined to their family and immediate neighbours, all others becoming moral strangers. Such 'amoral familialism' transformed the zone in transition into an unsettled and unsafe region that abounded in potential victims. Fighting gangs may have been represented as a rudimentary effort to defend territory and impose security on the neighbourhood,[85] but they also committed violent acts of law-breaking that increased the insecurity.

Morality was relative in the transition zone.

All these conspicuous moral and structural infirmities could become amplified. The occupants of the zone in transition had often been immigrants from Europe, rural areas, and the southern United States. Their lives had been punctuated by cultural discontinuities that became especially taxing for the second generation.[86] Language, custom, and religion could fall into disuse or change its significance. The children of immigrants sometimes found themselves to be marginal to the new world of the native American and the discarded, old world of their parents. Morally displaced and economically and politically peripheral, they might innovate new modes of social organization. Most often they created a social order that corresponded neither to the old world nor to the new but was a shifting amalgam of both.[87] They also improvised new styles of behaviour and morality that could well embrace deviance as a possible solution to the dilemmas of exclusion and impotence.[88] Those who were successful and, more important, those who could help others to success, were well-regarded, almost becoming local heroes. The racketeer and hustler consequently attain a special importance in the neighbourhood, as Landesco wrote: What needs to be appreciated is the element of genuine popularity of the gangster, home-grown in the neighborhood gang, idealized in the morality of the neighborhood.[89]

•Local politics and local crime were intertwined in the zone in transition; they supported one another and often recruited very much the same people. Police forces were decentralized, under the authority of local politicians, and subject to local control.[90] It was always tempting for the police and local hoodlums and politicians to come to an accommodation in the zone in transition, and there was not much effective resistance from those who tried to oppose them. On the contrary, it was politically and administratively convenient to contain vice and deviance in an area where local resistance was weak and the social standing of the inhabitants was low.[91]

This was not a phenomenon unique to Chicago, of course. Greg Marquis (of the University of New Brunswick), for example, documents the tension between liberals and conservatives in turn-of-the century Vancouver. Although the police were under pressure to crack down on criminal organizations, the practical reality was that crime persisted, especially the 'victimless' crimes of gambling, prostitution, and drinking. The result was a 'negotiation of morality'.[92]

In such transition zones, there was a corresponding growth of prostitution, gambling, and illegal markets. Deviant lifestyles were encouraged commercially and managerially, and that led to the sifting and movement of people: 'Each urban area . . . has its own moral code. A population seeks an area in which its members can be gratified with the least amount of interference.'[93] In turn, said Park:

> What lends special importance to the segregation of the poor, the vicious, the criminal, and exceptional persons generally, which is so characteristic a feature of city life, is the fact that social contagion tends to stimulate in divergent types the common temperamental differences, and to suppress characters which unite them with the normal types about them. Associations with others of their own ilk provides also not merely a stimulus, but a moral support for the traits they have in common which they would not find in a less select society.[94]

> Deviance is tolerated and contained when it can't be controlled.

■ The Normal and the Pathological

Not all sociologists practising at the University of Chicago were unanimous about the methods of their discipline, and moreover, their ideas evolved over time and reflected social changes in the city itself. The crimes that were studied ranged from petty delinquency to organized crime. Different features were emphasized in different studies. The explanation of criminality and deviance proposed by members of the university thus contained a number of apparent contradictions. Such inconsistency would not have worried the Chicago sociologists very much. They were not engaged in a quest for a single theory that covered every contingency. Indeed, Wirth claimed that 'in the face of the imposing series of exploded theories of criminality, prudence dictates that a new theory avoid the persistent error of claiming universal applicability.'[95]

The Chicago sociologists had no binding commitment to the discovery of any single explanation or any single *kind* of explanation. On the contrary, they awarded formal theorizing a lower priority than their own open-ended social anthropology that was capable of leading to unexpected results. They argued that deviance was to be found in a host of confusing and unique settings, that it was difficult to reduce its explanation to a single cause, and that it was even more difficult to explain it by pathological causes alone. The search for the roots of deviance in certain areas—unemployment, the slum, poverty, low intelligence, exploitative capitalism, or family breakdown—is an *ecological* argument associated with the Chicago School that refers to the instability and pathology of the disorganized zone in transition. But there is also the argument that deviance is an unremarkable consequence of normal conditions.

Along this line, in the discussion feature 'Deviance Exploration', we look at events in Toronto in 1942 as commentators discuss the causes of juvenile delinquency in opinion pieces and editorials in the *Globe and Mail*. The time is the Second World War, and the situation is absent parents, but the topic is juvenile delinquency.

Discussion: Deviance Exploration—Juvenile Delinquency in 1942

In October 1942 the *Globe* published an article with the headline 'Big rise in Toronto juvenile crime seen as result of war conditions'. At issue was a 1941 report from the Toronto Family Court. Juvenile delinquency had increased from 1,060 in 1939 to 1,646 in 1941. During the first four months of the war, the article wrote, the rate of juvenile delinquency had risen 28 per cent, and during the next four months it had risen 62 per cent. What's interesting is the explanation offered for the increase.

The executive leader of the Canadian Welfare Council said that the major factors were the absence of the father or mother from the home, employment at an early age, an incomplete education, an unhappy home, emotional upsets caused by the war, and a lack of community recreational facilities. He is quoted as saying that there is 'considerable evidence that the increased number of working mothers is one of the major problems at the present time.'

The president of the Big Sisters Association, and the secretary of the Toronto Big Brothers Movement agreed. The latter said: 'Children grow up quicker during a war. With boys, such conditions result in unusual bravado . . . and a restlessness . . . that results in home and neighbourhood incorrigibility.'

The same attitudes are expressed in articles asking for help supervising children during the day while fathers away at war and women working: 'These children are to be either criminals or of the congregation of those who walk humbly with their God. It is up to us.'

Other articles also stress the failings of parents to teach children the distinction between right and wrong; no less an authority than the Chief Constable said that parents engaged in war work don't have the time to look after their children properly. It was estimated that in the Toronto area alone at least 5,000 children were victims of the situation. This 'serious social and moral problem' could not be neglected without peril to the future of the nation.

Sources: 'Big rise in Toronto juvenile crime seen as result of war conditions', *Globe and Mail*, 6 October 1942, 15; 'Neighbours can help', *Globe and Mail*, 23 April 1942, 6; 'Where lies responsibility?' *Globe and Mail*, 9 March 1942, 6; 'A serious problem', *Globe and Mail*, 18 May 1942, 6; 'Need for day nurseries', *Globe and Mail*, 16 July 1942, 6. See also 'An ominous condition', *Globe and Mail*, 7 October 1942, 6; 'Juvenile delinquency grows', *Globe and Mail*, 7 November 1942, 6.

• *The ethnographic strain in Chicago sociology emphasized moral diversity rather than discord, pathology, or disorganization.* It mirrored John Dewey's 'pluralistic realism', a philosophy of how numerous, equally authentic truths can co-exist.[96] Dewey had defined truth as situated, local and as part of the practical experience of people confronting particular problems. So, too, some sociologists analyzed morality as contingent and parochial. Society was described as a great mosaic of social worlds that housed very different forms of conduct and morality. In this sense, deviance was regarded as simply another form of conduct embedded in social organization, not an absence of order or an assault upon order.

> Deviance was seen as an alternative moral order.

Deviance and delinquency were explained principally by the effects of the isolation of certain natural areas. Deviance became a surrogate social order, an alternative pattern, which replaced the workings of conventional institutions.[97] Their forms were themselves explained as a functional response to deprivation, to the social and moral structures imported by immigrants, and to the experience of growing up in the inner city. Deprived of political control and economic resources, first- and second-generation immigrants produced their own shadow politics and shadow economy. They created rackets, markets, and systems of patronage in which men of influence distributed protection and sponsorship.

Case Study—Is Cornerville a Place?

In 1943, William Foote Whyte published *Street Corner Society*, which became a highly influential study in participant observation. As a community study, Whyte shows that lower-class slums are not pathological or disorganized, but rather are socially organized in such a way as to have an influence on the individual.

In Boston's Cornerville, for instance, an area investigated by Whyte in the Chicago manner, Italian Catholics recognized an affinity between the practical organization of their community and the wider order of the Church and Heaven. The world was held to be hierarchical, divided into big people and little people. Just as saints intercede with God on behalf of sinners, so police captains might intercede on behalf of those given a traffic ticket.

Social conduct hinged on networks of obligation which bound one to local people and substituted personal morality for a more impersonal subordination to law.[1] It was those networks and the reputations which were secured in them that confined the person living in the zone in transition. People did move away, sometimes in groups, but such movement often represented a betrayal:

> To get ahead, the Cornerville man must move either in the world of business and Republican politics or in the world of Democratic politics and the rackets. He cannot move in both worlds at once; they are so far apart that there is hardly any connection between them. If he advances in the first world, he is recognized in Cornerville only as an alien to the district. If he advances in the second world, he achieves recognition in Cornerville, but becomes a social outcast to respectable people elsewhere. The entire course of the corner boy's training in the social life of his district prepares him for a career in the rackets or in Democratic politics.[2]

In recent years there has been some discussion of the theoretical adequacy of Whyte's writings about Cornerville. He has been criticized for focusing too much on the gangs and for imposing a normative interpretation on Italian inner-city life. In turn Whyte insists he had got the story right. And then Norman Denzin weighs in to criticize both sides of the debate for being positivistic.

We won't go further into the debate here, but it poses interesting theoretical issues. References are provided so you can read about it.[3]

[1] Cf. H. Gans, *The Urban Villagers*.
[2] W. Whyte, *Street Corner Society*, 273–4.
[3] See P. Adler et al., 'Street Corner Society Revisited: New Questions About Old Issues'; W. Boelen, 'Street Corner Society: Cornerville Revisited'; W. Whyte, 'In Defense of Street Corner Society'; and N. Denzin, 'Whose Cornerville Is It, Anyway?'

Children raised in the crowded transition zone led a very public life, playing on the street, where they formed small groups that could eventually crystallize into gangs. Thus, the child was under constant surveillance by other people. From an early age, children had a communal identity and reputation. In an insecure social environment, the preservation of reputation acquired strategic importance.

Responsibilities and claims revolved around one's public character. Teasing play repeatedly tested the validity and credibility of character. It became vital to retain face by supporting and initiating joint projects in which reputations could be established or lost. Much of the early delinquency described by Thrasher consisted of a playfulness and daring: stealing fruit from stalls and stores, disrespect for authority, and playing truant.

The gangs Thrasher describes are neighbourhood groups and ethnic associations in schools. He got to know them in fairly informal ways, such as by taking the boys for ice cream in his car or inviting them to his apartment to form a gang. Thrasher advocated that school administrators get to learn who the leaders are in the gangs and use them to assist with 'leadership'.[98] He also tells some interesting anecdotes about getting to know the gangs:

> An incidental question was put as to whether the boys liked school. Yes, the boys liked it, but Tony had recently played truant for two days and the teacher sent a letter home. Tony got the letter and tore it up. He then asked my advice as to what to do. Whereupon some humorist in the gang suggested that I write an excuse as follows: 'Dear Teacher: Please excuse Tony for playing hookey for two days. Signed, The Professor.'[99]

> Labelling was recognized as a problem years before becoming a part of theory.

If ignored, youthful deviance might progress in no discernible direction, although adult criminality was possible. Members of the group could, however, be prosecuted as lawbreakers, and in an anticipation of the labelling theory of the 1960s, it was argued that such public identification could be fateful indeed. Having been categorized as lawbreakers, members of the group could cross a threshold and be publicly regarded as delinquents. But if treated simply as boyishness, the beginnings of delinquency could be channelled into organized sports and neutralized.

What *is* significant is the persistence both of tradition and of structural problems in the zone in transition. Contemporary descriptions of life in the zone in transition seventy years later echo what was written by the first generation of Chicago sociologists.[100] William Julius Wilson describes life in Chicago's inner city as one of 'broken families, anti-social behavior, social networks that do not extend beyond the ghetto environment, and a lack of informal social control over the behavior and activities of children and adults in the neighborhood'.[101] Ideas of conduct are passed on from generation to generation of boys living the public lives of the street: 'to a very great extent . . . traditions of delinquency are preserved and transmitted through the medium of social contact with the unsupervised play group and the more highly organized delinquent and criminal gangs.'[102]

In some measure, it became normal for young people to flirt with delinquency. Those who did not do so were unusually cloistered, marginal, or ostracized.[103] Interestingly, delinquency as portrayed by the Chicago sociologists is obviously not something that only pathological people could contemplate. It became commonplace, petty, and open in its implications for future experience and conduct. More particularly, it became the basis of a career that people might abandon or change unless they were under unusual constraint.

•*Autobiographies and extended interviews were employed to grasp the development of deviance*, emphasis being given to the delinquent's own understanding of his life.[104] That development was placed in the context of peculiar meanings and distinct sub-worlds: 'If we fail to see that a gang has a moral code of its own—however immoral it may appear to the rest of us—we will not be able to understand the solidarity, the courage and the self-sacrifice of which gangsters are capable.'[105]

Thus, the sociology of deviance became an exercise in practical social anthropology, a disinterested analysis of strange peoples and customs. However, the 'naturalizing' of deviance caused it to become a product of its social milieu.

•*The social anthropology of deviance survived to become the core of symbolic interactionism.* In part, survival was made possible in an intellectual dark time by the enthusiasm of Edwin Sutherland. During the 1930s and 1940s Sutherland and his students (Donald Cressey in particular) became the tenacious champions of the argument that deviance is a way of life passed on from generation to generation.

First advanced in 1924, Sutherland's theory of differential association attempted to make systematic the thesis that crime and deviation are culturally transmitted in social groups. The theory was laid out as a series of numbered propositions, which took on the appearance of formal theory and were intended to be a general explanation of crime. Differential-association theory holds that criminal behaviour is learned in interaction with other people and communicated in intimate personal settings. The person learns both the techniques of committing the crime and the necessary motives and attitudes. It is argued that people will become criminal if they are exposed to more definitions favourable to the violation of the law than definitions unfavourable to violation of the law. The process is affected by variations in frequency, duration, priority, and intensity in a manner similar to any learning.

Finally, he claimed that, although criminal behaviour is an expression of general needs and values, it is not explained by those general needs and values, because non-criminal behaviour is also an expression of those same needs and values.[106] Sutherland and his followers plotted the workings of differential association in white-collar crime[107] (a phrase invented by Sutherland himself), professional crime,[108] embezzlement,[109] and even seemingly motiveless crime. An absence of motives, it was claimed, was a powerful spur to deviation and was itself learned. Ironically, perhaps, those studies are probably now valued more for their ethnographic detail than for their development of differential association theory.

The theory of differential association insisted on the ordinariness of the processes by which deviance arose and was transmitted. It located those processes in transactions with others in mundane social settings. It emphasized the central part played by meaning and motive in the formation of deviant projects. And its acceptance by a number of scholars in the 1940s and 1950s ensured that sociology would continue to explore deviance as a shared, symbolic experience that changed over time.

However, the theory promised a kind of mathematical precision which could never be realized. How would it ever be possible, worthwhile, or desirable to add up and evaluate all the competing definitions of law that one is likely to meet in

> Deviance is learned, like any other behaviour.

one's formative years? The theory is riddled with escape clauses and qualifications that diminish its power to predict. Thus, it could always be argued that a great mass of definitions favourable to the breaking of laws can be outweighed by a few definitions of special intensity, priority, or duration. Unless the theory is trivialized to absurdity, one can easily put forward numerous exceptions to the contention that all crime is learned in association with others. Lemert certainly discovered what appeared to be a major anomaly in the example of the naïve cheque forger who had no overt criminal contacts but was still able to commit crimes.[110] Yet differential-association theory stimulated ethnographic work when such work was unfashionable, and it served as a bridge between the early work of the Chicago School and subcultural theory, a significant theory that we shall discuss in a later chapter.

•*Exported to Britain, Chicago sociology affected both the ethnographic work of the 1960s and the sociology of urban social problems.* There seemed to be an affinity between the turbulent and expanding Chicago of the 1920s and the cities of England in the 1960s and 1970s. In particular, the social organization of Birmingham, Liverpool, and Sheffield was analyzed with ideas that bore traces of the zonal hypothesis. Their inner cities seemed to be similar to the zone in transition of an earlier Chicago: they contained a fluid, immigrant population, were characterized by all the conventional signs of social pathology, and were stigmatized symbolically and deteriorating physically. English theory added an important emphasis on the interplay of social classes, denying that natural areas were spontaneous and stressing the political economy of housing. Much was made of the organized struggle for space waged between different 'housing classes' distinguished by their access to and occupation of different styles of housing.[111]

However, not all British sociologists remained at the level of the political economy of the city. Some turned to more focused studies of the politics and history of special areas. Thus it has been argued that housing policy[112] can lead to the concentration of 'problem families' in particular areas[113] and thereby to the stigmatization and criminalization of communities.[114] Not only may there be higher rates of crime and criminals in those places, but areas themselves can acquire reputations that affect the treatment and attitudes of their occupants.[115] Negative definitions, restricted opportunities, and enmity between groups may engender self-fulfilling prophecies that contribute to the perpetuation of deviance.[116]

We shall return to the more recent British work when we discuss some of the new developments in control theory. Now we turn to some criticisms of this approach.

■ Criticism

We have not discussed all the research conducted by Chicago sociologists of the 1920s and 1930s, and thus inevitably some, such as Anderson's *The Hobo*,[117] has been missed. Our intention has been merely to review those arguments that reveal the more important themes of Chicago sociology, in particular, those arguments that have attracted criticism.

Such criticism must be examined rather circumspectly. After all, criticism is usually advanced to promote a particular purpose, and the theories that are attacked often seem to become distorted in the process. Matza praised *The Hobo* as a major innovation that developed 'appreciative' analysis and the sympathetic interpretation of the actor's own stance. Indeed, Matza depicts *The Hobo* as the greatest achievement of the Chicago School. Faris, by contrast, states: '*The Hobo* achieved most of its contribution by way of informal descriptions, using informal research technique and yielding no new sociological principles.'[118]

It appears that criticism is rarely disinterested.

• *The exploratory and unformulated character of fieldwork has attracted criticism.* Those who prefer a natural-scientific model of research find the Chicago ethnographic tradition to be loose, imprecise, and muddled. They argue that there is no clear investigation of hypotheses, no specification of objectives, and no means of finding that a theory is wrong. For instance, Davis remarked, 'In the naturalist's tradition, description for its own sake often superseded theoretical rationales for data analysis.'[119] Similarly, Shils observed that the Chicago School failed to 'set out to demonstrate any explicitly formulated sociological hypotheses'.[120] What these critics demand is a neat theory, a neat and articulate method, and a neat conclusion. They are frequently troubled by the Chicago sociologist's reluctance or inability to provide coherence. Yet as Gusfield remembers: 'What we shared were tacit perspectives without a great deal of concern for rigorous theoretical justifications or deductions. . . . There was, and remained, a certain indifference, even disdain, for the endless efforts of sociologists to develop refined theory or methodological rigor.'[121]

In its defence, it could be argued that the imprecise character of Chicago sociology stems from the pragmatic conception of knowledge as an evolving, grounded and open-ended process. It will be recalled that the pragmatists held that hypotheses should not be too organized or explicit at the very beginning of research. On the contrary, firm expectations would only prevent the sociologist from seeing and responding to phenomena and events as they arose. Theory must not anticipate, deform, or obscure the facts. It must be allowed to emerge as research advances.

In a sense, it may even be argued that the Chicago School's description of research is little more than an unusually honest account of what many sociologists actually experience in the field. Work often seems to develop in a confusing and pragmatic manner.[122] How could it be otherwise? Research almost invariably propels researchers into the unknown, for which one can never be fully prepared.[123] Some dismiss the idealistic recipes of methodologists,[124] but it is quite likely that there are many different worlds of research. There is no good reason to imagine that the cautious survey researcher will experience work in just the same fashion as the ethnographer. But the critics have nonetheless tended to represent Chicago sociology as if it were unnecessarily disorganized and a product of carelessness or oversight rather than a carefully resolved strategy.

> Knowledge was seen as grounded in the experience of research.

•*Criticisms of the substantive work of the Chicago School chiefly turn on the usefulness of the ecological model.* Some have pointed out that the city is *not* an ecological system but is regulated by processes unknown to the biologist.[125] Park and Wirth acknowledged the limitations of the ecological model, and they were aware that the city cannot be completely explained in such fashion; however they sometimes presented ecology as a system of iron laws that contradict the more indeterminate themes of ethnography.[126] Ecology enjoys a fluctuating importance in the works of the Chicago School: in some passages it is a central means of explanation, while in others it is neglected altogether.

Again, it has been alleged that persistent reference to the community and communal group imposed a misleading simplicity and distinctness on phenomena which were actually muddled and ill-defined. Suttles insists that 'natural areas' were very rarely natural. Instead of being unplanned and unanticipated, the early Chicago neighbourhoods *were* planned with great deliberation. Chicago was laid out on the grid pattern and was regulated by many statutes and ordinances, although planned development was confounded by the unpredictabilty of movements in property values.[127] Moreover, the natural areas were not always internally homogeneous, frequently being inhabited by populations who shared no consensus and common identity. When social networks *did* emerge, they could well have been shaped by influences other than the occupation of a shared territory.[128] Indeed, Pahl observes more generally: 'Any attempt to tie particular patterns of social relationships to specific geographical milieux is a singularly fruitless exercise. Some people are of the city but not in it, whereas others are in the city but not of it'.[129]

Such a dissatisfaction with conceptions of the relations between community and territory have stemmed from, or prompted, an alternative phrasing of ideas about urban processes. Some have claimed that the mere fact that events occurred in a physical setting could not justify the deduction that those events must be explained by that setting.[130] Instead, they have proposed that the idea of community be dissolved and replaced or complemented by other variables such as class, race, or political economy. In particular, classes and similar formations have been put forward as more significant actors in urban life.[131] It was class, for example, that dictated the allocation of housing and the uses of space.[132] Certain sociologists have consequently recommended the abandonment of social ecology and the adoption of other theoretical systems. Their arguments are not without merit. The Chicago School did neglect the social history of the business district and the zone in transition, representing their evolution as if it were practically free of human agency:

> Their interpretation stopped abruptly at the point at which the relationship between industrial expansion and high delinquency areas could have gone beyond the depiction of the two as coincidentally adjacent to one another geographically. The interpretation was paralysed at the communal level, a level which implied that either the residents were responsible for the

deteriorated area, or that communities collapsed on their own account. Instead of turning inward to find the causes of delinquency exclusively in local traditions, families, play groups and gangs, their interpretation might have turned outward to show political, economic and historical forces at work, which would have accounted for both social disorganisation and the internal conditions, including the delinquency.[133]

However, while there is some worth in these criticisms, perhaps they imply a different project. *Community* is none the less a useful idea that cannot always be reduced to other elements: 'Unfortunately, this style of research fail[s] to capture what some thought essential to communities, particularly their reputational content and the ethos of local culture'.[134]

Chicago sociologists may have been deficient in their analysis of 'master institutions and contradictory systems of social relations',[135] but the idea of ecology does introduce features of community and territory that have considerable importance for analysis.

• *The Chicago sociologists themselves might well have been more robust in their own defence.* Pragmatists especially would have maintained that 'contradictory systems of social relations', classes, and 'class struggle' are ideas that have no readily observable referents. One cannot see, touch, smell, or hear a contradictory system. Members of the Chicago School tended to suspect such schemes as having no basis in an empirical world that could actually be studied. Class, society, and allied terms were handled circumspectly:

> Society is of course but the relations of individuals to one another in this form and that. And all relations are *interactions*, not fixed moulds. . . . I often wonder what meaning is given to the term 'society' by those who oppose it to the *intimacies of personal intercourse*, such as those of friendship. . . . We should forget 'society' and think of law, industry, religion, medicine, politics, art, education, philosophy—and think of them in the plural. For points of contact are not the same for any two persons and hence the questions that the interests and occupations pose are never twice the same.[136]

Although there are tinges of relativism in this comment, it is important to stress that there was a preference for studying the materials of experience, materials that were lodged in people's attempts to handle specific problems in specific settings.

■ Conclusion

Chicago sociology was a major co-operative enterprise that launched an intellectual interest in the study of the city. Part of that study was occupied with social problems, usually confined to particular districts. The explanation of deviance centred on the peculiar conditions of the zone in transition, a turbulent area that appeared out of joint with the rest of the city. Delinquency was a local effort to restore order and opportunity to disorganization, as well as serving as its cause, and it could become the content of a stable tradition transmitted on the streets. Personal documents, anthropological fieldwork, and the analysis of census and court records were linked together to aid exploration.[137]

The outcome was a detailed contemporary social history of deviance. It prepared the basis for some of the principal sociological developments that were to come. Ethnography endured to become the 'neo-Chicagoan' Symbolic Interactionism of the 1940s, 1950s, and beyond. The investigation of the distribution of social phenomena became sociological epidemiology: research into the connections between events in time and space.

Urban sociology, grounded in the writings of the Chicago School, persisted.

Chapter Summary

This chapter has looked at the development of one of the first university-based attempts at a social scientific study of deviance. Employing an ethnographic, participant-observation style, researchers studied deviance in its natural setting. The researchers produced an array of research into deviance, especially lower-class deviance, such as prostitution.

The Chicago School sociologists argued that deviance arose in a zonal model of the city, a model that found resonance elsewhere. Deviance was said to be related to stages of urban development, and because of the interest in social problems, it was often argued to be a lower-class phenomenon.

Interestingly, elements of the Chicago approach will be found to resonate in other theories that we consider here, such as subcultural theory.

Critical-Thinking Questions

1. The Chicago School developed several different research strategies designed to study deviance. What are they, and how are they unique?
2. How useful would the concentric-zone theory be today for the study of social problems? Perhaps use a city you are familiar with.
3. What are the strengths and weaknesses of differential association?
4. If disorganized neighbourhoods truly do produce crime, how might the police have the greatest impact? Describe several effective strategies that could be incorporated into community policing.
5. One of the discussion features describes events in 1943 that involved taking a 'soft approach' to the problem of youth deviance. How could such an approach be adopted today?

Explorations in Film

Gangs of New York, a film set in nineteenth-century New York, centres on the conflict between immigrant gangs and the native criminal underworld. With the dramatic theme of revenge as its motive, the film relies on the very real economic and social conflicts generated during the waves of immigration in 1860.

Websites

The Sociology Department at the University of Chicago pioneered research on urban studies. For information relevant to their work on poverty, the workplace, immigrants, and maps, see www.encyclopedia.chicagohistory.org/pages/265.html

Chapter Four

Functionalism, Deviance, and Control

Chapter Overview

In this chapter we endeavour to explain some of the reasons why functionalism came to dominate sociology. For several decades it was the mainstream approach in the sociology of deviance. We also summarize how it has influenced some of the other major approaches to the study of deviance, such as labelling theory and critical and post-modern approaches. While it has come to be seen as outmoded and uncritical and has been castigated for being conservative and overly deterministic, functionalism has contributed some essential concepts to the study of deviance, including the ideas that deviance is widespread and normal and that it is necessary for the functioning of society.

■ Introduction

From the late 1930s to the late 1950s, functionalism came as near as any perspective before or since to constituting sociological orthodoxy. Since that time, it has not only fallen from grace, but has been 'ritually executed for introductory teaching purposes. . . . The demolition of functionalism is almost an initiation rite of passage into sociological adulthood or at least adolescence.'[1] In the same vein, Percy Cohen remarked in the 1960s that 'it frequently looks as though anyone in search of theoretical acclaim has only to discover one more defect in functionalism to achieve it.'[2] It seems necessary to point out why, if such is the case, we think it worthwhile to devote a chapter to the subject.

First, functionalism has been vulgarized by its critics. Functionalism is linked with a 'consensus' approach to social problems and a conservative approach to their solution. For example, in Douglas's critique of the structural-functional perspective on deviance,[3] the absurdities of a 'functionalist' approach are contrasted with the 'emerging sociological perspective on deviance'. The latter is supposedly free from errors such as the uncritical acceptance of official statistics, the permeating of a uniform value system throughout society, and a conception of deviance as pathological rather than problematic. However, we see functionalism offering an more sophisticated and subtle model of deviance and control than emerges from such critiques.

Secondly, since Durkheim asserted that crime had to be regarded as not only inevitable but also normal, this has been seen as a 'morally repugnant' argument.[4] Thus, the limited forays into the analysis of deviance by such American functionalists of the inter- and post-war period as Kingsley Davis, Daniel Bell, and Robert Merton, with the exception of Merton's theory of anomie, barely impinged on sociology.[5] A later revival of functionalist arguments, by Erikson and Scott, fared similarly.[6] Despite this neglect, the functionalist approach to crime and deviance continues to survive and to raise questions of an intellectual kind that, as yet, no other perspective deals with at all adequately. At the very least, as Matza argues,[7] the functionalist approach to crime has contributed significantly to the 'emerging sociological perspective on deviance'.

■ The Sociological Background

The main tenets of functionalism seem uncontentious:

  • *First, there is the idea that societies can, for all analytical purposes, be treated as systems.* The parts, such as production, education, government, and belief systems, should be examined in terms of their interrelationships and in terms of their contribution to society in general. For example, it would be pointless to a functionalist to study family and kinship simply in terms of their forms and structures: to do so would be to fail to grasp the significance of family and kinship for other institutions, and vice versa. It follows that changes in any one institution have implications for change in others, though no simple 'functional reciprocity' can be assumed. For example, a change in the distribution of wealth may have immense implications for leisure, but a change in patterns of leisure may have little effect on the distribution of wealth. If this were all that functionalists contended, it would be difficult to dispute Kingsley Davis's assertion that, far from being one school within sociology, sociology and functionalism are virtually one.[8]

> Society is an integrated whole.

Society has needs different from those of individuals.	•*Second, functionalists see the needs of society as different from the needs of individuals.* In general, functionalists pushed the argument further and began to detach the needs of the social system from the needs of the individuals who compose it: this is most obviously the case with Talcott Parsons.[9] The needs of society were also collapsed back onto the needs of individuals, as in Malinowski's cultural functionalism.[10]

•*Third, they postulated an evolutionary trend in the development of society.* There is an evolution from simple agrarian to complex industrial societies, and there is a change in whether institutions are functional or not: this is most marked in the case of Durkheim but was also used by other theorists such as Marx. This idea lends itself to grand and abstract theorizing beyond any possibility of empirical validation; so maybe it deserves the criticism that Douglas, C. Wright Mills, and many others have heaped upon it.[11]

Society evolves, and so do its institutions.

Durkheim's main intellectual purpose, at the beginning of the twentieth century, was to analyze the possibilities of securing social cohesion in the face of rapid social and economic change in France. This problem had been central to social and political theory for much of the nineteenth century. What was novel about Durkheim's formulation was his rejection of purely economic solutions (as Marx had proposed) and of leaving things alone at all costs (as Spencer had advocated) in favour of what we might now define as a 'corporate state' solution.

The division of labour had outstripped the capacity of existing institutions such as the churches to promote moral regulation; yet its result was ultimately to nurture co-operation and lessen conflict by increasing resources and diminishing direct competition between people. The division of labour would therefore ultimately promote moral regulation on the basis of newly emergent 'occupational associations', although this could happen only if the fit between talents and occupations could be brought about 'spontaneously', rather than be 'forced': hence his preference for the abolition of inherited wealth, along with other forms of privilege that intervened between ability and assignment to roles.

The division of labour had outpaced the system of traditional moral regulation.

The task of sociology was to clarify the problems facing industrial society, and to that end, the 'rules of sociological method' were designed to operate on lines of scientific objectivity. No topic was sacred: to emphasize that point Durkheim frequently chose themes designed to shock, such as his analysis of the 'sacred'. In *The Elementary Forms of the Religious Life*, he analyzed the religion of aboriginal ritual as the collective representation of the social: 'Society' was God. The function of religion was the celebration of the social group. How primitive man had accomplished so sophisticated a solution to the problem of social order was left unresolved.[12]

For Durkheim society was God.

Malinowski professed himself at odds with Durkheim's notion of the 'group-mind' and also attacked the method in anthropology of relying on secondary sources of information or what his informants told him about native customs and belief. Proper fieldwork involved a prolonged period of observing what *actually* went on, as distinct from what was *said* to go on. Thus, functionalism enabled one to map social reality as it unfolded. Forms of conduct took on meaning within the context of the patterns of reciprocity and exchange of kinship and tribe. 'It was possible to correlate one aspect of culture with another and show which is the function fulfilled by either within the scheme of culture.'[13] Mali-nowski opposed the 'seamless web' conception of culture so often associated with functionalism, saying, for example, that human culture is neither consistent nor logical, but a mixture of conflicting principles. The functionalist method of rendering culture intelligible *without* resorting to an evolutionist schema did not, however, imply a resistance to acknowledging the reality of change. Fletcher attacked the caricature of functionalism as providing a static portrayal of societies, saying that both 'synchronic' and 'diachronic' accounts are essential and that both are recognized as *processes in time*.[14] This does not solve the logical problem of how, if society 'hangs together' by mutually sustaining functional elements, change is allowed to take place.

The same problem recurs in Parsons' ambitious conceptual attempts to map the 'functional requisites' of social order and the 'structure of social action'. Parsons' work is so little wedded to empiricism and ethnography, by contrast with that of Malinowski and Radcliffe-Brown, that only their underlying shared emphasis on functional relationships makes it at all possible to group them together. Parsons's aim was to combine a 'voluntaristic theory of action' with a model of the social system that would apply to any society. The way this works is through 'value orientations' to action, which match actors' appropriate behaviour and expectations with socially structured role prescriptions. However, such relationships as that of husband and wife, doctor and patient, teacher and pupil are broadly scripted: the individuals improvise the fine detail for themselves. These broad structural constraints are theorized as varying by the type of society and in accordance with the needs that any viable society must meet.[15]

As critics point out, functionalism topples over, especially in its stress on the internalization of common values by the individual, its deterministic profiles of human typecasting, and the circularity of social system reproducing themselves. The first and second reduce the social to the sociable,[16] and nowhere do they convey, or allow for, the active struggle involved in, for example, simply bringing up children, even under relatively favourable conditions. The third hardly allows for the brute facts of conflict, power, and subordination.[17] Deviance is dealt with poorly, either as the product of system malintegration at the margins or as that of inadequate socialization in childhood. What Parsons does achieve, however, is a sense of the magnitude of the accomplishment of social order, even if it is at the expense of an 'over-integrated' view of society and an 'over-socialized' conception of man.[18] It remains the only attempt since the classical theorists to link the processes of interaction on the face-to-face level with the institutional constellations at the macro level worthy of the undertaking itself.

> Parsons creates an oversocialized model of the actor.

It was an attempt, however, that failed. Attempts to supplant it with a superior theory, or indeed to patch it up, have preoccupied sociologists for the past fifty years. It accounts for the revival of Marxism(s), the popularity of French structuralism, the passion for symbolic interactionism, the fascination with Foucault, and currently, with theories of globalization and post-modernity. Marxism and structuralism indeed have great affinities with Parsonian structural-functionalism: compare Hawthorne's summary of Althusser with Parsons's mode of explanation:

'modes of production . . . furnish the limits within which institutions and individuals can act and in that extremely weak sense determine that action. But . . . in any place at any time anything may be more immediately determinant, or "dominant"'.[19]

Functionalist currents also pervade symbolic interactionism. Goffman, for example, in his essay on gambling, falls back ultimately on the notion that 'Character is gambled. . . . We are allowed to think there is something to be won in the moments that we face so that society can face moments and defeat them.'[20] This should not surprise us, for Mead, the founding father of interactionism, wrote a major essay on the functions of punishment for social structure. It looks as though functional analysis persists as an underlying idea, and consider how modern this quotation from Durkheim is: 'We must not say that an action shocks the conscience collective because it is criminal, but rather that it is criminal because it shocks the conscience collective. We do not condemn it because it is a crime, but it is a crime because we condemn it.'[21]

It should be noted that, while there is a functionalist anthropology and a functionalist sociology, there is almost no recognizable functionalist deviantology. Robert Merton, one of the prime functionalists, a man who had a major influence on the sociology of crime and deviance, was reported, for example, to have 'had no interest in criminology and little interest in the nature of crime or its correlates. He explicitly disdained interest in prior research in the field, and he did not bother to summarize the evidence bearing on the empirical relation most important to his theory [of anomie].'[22] At least two general principles explain that indifference and that absence.

•*First, it may be said that functionalism was established to analyze social systems conceived comprehensively*, not the minute parts of any one of the system. It was defined less by an interest in the empirical bits and pieces of society than with the broad formal workings of society as a whole. Like other global theories, then, it does not preoccupy itself much with the detail of substantive problems such as crime and deviance.

•*Secondly, from Durkheim onwards, functionalists maintained that the business of social science is with science* and scientific knowledge, which are themselves held to be quite different from the common-sense knowledge of everyday life. Functionalism was regarded as the scientific study of unintended consequences, hidden processes, deep structures, and 'latent functions'.[23] It was centred on making discoveries that were likely to confound commonplace expectations and mundane reasoning.[24]

The two impulses were contradictory on occasion. Although functionalists did not choose to remain on the level of the small-scale and empirical, they were attracted by the possibility of showing how very surprising the workings of social systems could be. From time to time, as a result, they wrote about deviance precisely because it presented the best opportunity to display the explanatory powers of scientific sociology. Common sense could tell us that deviance is harmful and corrosive of social order and should be eradicated. If functionalism could show that, to the contrary, deviance actually *maintained* social systems, it would have been vindicated indeed. Almost all the major functionalists, with the exception of Talcott Parsons, turned to deviance at least once because it could be used to illustrate the latent functions of what *seemed* incapable of having any such function. Consider the challenge in Durkheim saying: 'Contrary to current ideas, the criminal no longer seems a totally unsociable being, a sort of parasitic element, a strange and unassimiable body, introduced into the midst of society. On the contrary, he plays a definite role in social life. Crime, for its part, must no longer be conceived as an evil that cannot be too much suppressed.'[25]

Being peripheral and *ad hoc*, functionalist studies of deviance may be represented as a piecemeal accumulation of arguments. They are not integrated, organized, or coherent and they have not been the subject of lengthy debate. Others may have criticized what they have done, but those who have been attacked have not usually responded by amending, defending, or clarifying their work. It is as if functionalists had played with problems of deviance without heed to what sociologists of deviance themselves would say. In writing about the functionalist analysis of deviance at all, therefore, we have been obliged to do what the functionalists did not always do themselves, namely, reconstruct (and occasionally construct) arguments in their strongest and most consistent form—sometimes adding to the original to be cogent.

■ The Functions of Deviance and Control
Durkheim and Mead

Durkheim's view of the proper rules of sociological method was based on the idea that the astonishing success of the natural sciences could be matched by the social sciences if similar methods were used. The classification of social phenomena could match the taxonomies of the natural sciences. The social world could be investigated through concepts similar to those of health and disease employed in the study of living organisms. 'Normalcy' and 'pathology' could be established empirically by reference to the generality of phenomena in societies of comparable development and complexity: divergence from the average would indicate degrees of pathology. Two steps were involved in the assessment of normalcy. First, it could be empirically established if a phenomenon existed throughout the range of known societies; if it did, then it could be assumed to be normal, and the sociologist was alerted to its likely functional character. Second, the contribution of the phenomenon to the 'conditions necessary for group life' had to be established. Only if both steps were accomplished could functionality be inferred and a yardstick for the assessment of pathology set up.

The illustration of these methods with reference to deviance led Durkheim to make his most contentious assertion that 'crime is normal. . . . It is a factor in public health, an integral part of all healthy societies.'[26] Or, as in this comment:

> There is no society
> not confronted with
> criminality.

There is no society that is not confronted with the problem of criminality. Its form changes; the acts thus characterized are not the same everywhere;

but, everywhere and always, there have been men who have behaved in such a way as to draw upon themselves penal repression. There is, then, no phenomenon that represents more indisputably all the symptoms of normality, since it appears closely connected with the conditions of all collective life.[27]

The universal character of deviance pointed to its functionality, but Durkheim could only secure his conclusion by stating the manner of the contribution that deviance makes to social stability. This ensues, he argued, from the response that deviance elicits from the group or community, in that the reaction to deviance serves to

- 'heighten collective sentiments';
- sharpen perceptions of moral imperatives; and
- more tightly integrate the community against the transgressor.

Deviance serves to clarify and reinforce the norms and values of the group or, as Durkheim says in *The Division of Labour in Society*: 'We can thus say that, in general, the characteristic of moral rules is that they enunciate the fundamental conditions of social solidarity. Law and morality are the totality of ties which bind each of us to society, which make a unitary, coherent aggregate of the mass of individuals.'[28]

One way in which to think about the utility of deviance is with so-called 'victimless crime'. If a practice has willing participants, is widespread, and seems to have no other effect than to break a moral rule, then what is the purpose of 'deviantizing' it? In a Toronto-based study of the effects of cannabis prohibition, Patricia Erickson (of the University of Toronto) argues that in view of how widely marijuana is used, there is no deterrent effect to the law, and that therefore the criminalization of this drug has more to do with the need to reinforce social norms than to prevent harmful acts. Other deviant acts that are widely tolerated, such as ticket scalping, are studied in research that asserts that deviance is more than a subcultural practice; rather, in many forms it is tolerated or even encouraged and is relatively harmless.[29]

However, while a certain amount of deviance is therefore functional, too little or too much is pathological: 'There is no occasion for self-congratulation when the crime rate drops noticeably below the average level, for we may be certain that this apparent progress is associated with some social disorder.' By the same logic, 'excess [when the crime rate is unusually high] is undoubtedly morbid in nature'. The former implies that the forces of social control have become too strong and that too great a social investment is being made to eliminate deviance the result is social stagnation. The latter implies that deviance is swamping the group's capacity to respond collectively to it and that social cohesion is in grave danger. Commonly accepted beliefs about crime are much more likely to agree with the second than with the first assertion, and Durkheim employed all his customary eloquence to make the argument hold: 'Imagine a society of saints, a perfect cloister of exemplary individuals. Crimes, properly so called, will there be unknown; but faults which appear venial to the layman will create there the same scandal that the ordinary offence does in ordinary consciousness.'[30]

He would no doubt have seen what Stanley Cohen[31] has termed 'moral panics' as forms of communal consciousness-raising that are necessary in order to reactivate social controls:

> We have only to notice what happens, particularly in a small town, when some moral scandal has just occurred. Men stop each other on the street, they visit each other, they seek to come together to talk of the event and to wax indignant in common. From all the similar impressions which are exchanged, and the anger that is expressed, there emerges a unique emotion, more or less determinate according to the circumstances, which emanates from no specific person, but from everyone. This is the public wrath. [32]

Such panics seem fated to recur endlessly. As Pearson has commented: 'The terms and limits within which the problems of lawlessness are understood and acted upon are established within a form of public discourse which has been with us for generations, each succeeding generation remembering the illusive harmony of the past while foreseeing imminent social ruin in the future.'[33] To a functionalist, such continuities are the stuff of which social order is made.

Where Durkheim is deficient is in his analysis of precisely how all those mediations and continuities are accomplished. He failed to describe how authority works. Neither does he consider how it works repressively. As Cotterrell remarks, his more general views about the relations between condemnation, punishment, and social solidarity are not 'merely unproven but dangerous'.[34]

To the functionalist, a 'deviance-free society' is a contradiction in terms, because to bring about the elimination of all deviance would entail such a massive heightening of collective sentiment against it that currently trivial deviations would become magnified to take their place. The attempt to eliminate them would produce a further twist in the spiral, to the point where social life logically seized up. This does not, of course, imply that Durkheim approved of all deviance or all punishment; nor does it stifle debate about the most desirable point at which societies should accept some deviance, but not others, as the norm. What it does insist on as an argument is the impossibility of eliminating deviance from social life altogether, and how deviance is used as a social scapegoat.

Discussion: Deviance and Culture—The Danger in Crime Comics

It was 1929, and the National Council of Education voted to ask Canadian newspapers to curtail the use of American crime comic strips. However the tide would be difficult to turn. Dick Tracy comic strips appeared in newspapers in 1931, Detective Comics published Superman in 1937, and hundreds of comic series appeared in the late thirties. The concern was that adolescents were exposed to murder, cruelty, and sexuality in the crime comics. So in 1949 Canada passed a bill making it a criminal offence to publish or sell comic books depicting crimes, whether it was fictitious or real. However, although the bill passed unanimously in Parliament, it was a different matter when it came under debate before the US Senate Crime Investigation Committee. The conclusion of the Committee was that there was widespread doubt of a connection between crime comics and juvenile delinquency.

In a special article in the *New York Times* on 12 November 1950, the committee was quoted as saying that it had heard that juvenile crime had increased, stimulated by crime comics. However, opinion was divided.

Among the dozens of experts whose opinion was sought before the Committee was J. Edgar Hoover, head of the FBI. He said that he doubted whether banning crime comics would result in a decrease in juvenile delinquency.

On the other hand, the acting director of the Federal Bureau of Prisons said that crime comics 'serve as sources of contamination on impressionable minds, provide explicit instruction by which criminals operate, and contribute to a weakening of the ethical values of the community.'

An outspoken champion of crime comics was a cartoonist, who said, 'In my childhood, it was Tom Mix and William S. Hart movies which were leading us kids to damnation. No doubt Hopalong Cassidy will be blamed for many youthful escapades in the present era.' This raises the question of how different generations demonize different media.

For example, the belief that crime comics caused crime finds its echo in the 1980s in the debate about pornography, and in the 1990s over video games. The underlying idea that the media can shape peoples' perceptions and cause them to act in certain ways is called the 'hypodermic needle' model. The idea is that the media 'injects' people with bad ideas. Crime comics were blamed for adolescent violence because it was believed that juveniles read of lurid violence and criminal behaviour in comics and then acted it out.

Murder, rape, and suicide were portrayed as the effects of reading comic books, and any other causes were omitted from public and political accounts. Juveniles who committed vicious crimes were seen as victims, not of family violence or social breakdown, perhaps, but of looking at bad pictures. Crime comics were vilified for causing what they were, in effect, reporting.

A prominent spokesman against crime comics was Fredric Wertham, a New York psychiatrist, expert in criminal trials and author of *Seduction of the Innocent*. He is credited with single-handedly creating a wave of public indignation against crime comics. Rallies were held, comics were burned, and censorship boards were created. Comic drawings were shown to have subliminal messages, Batman and Robin were accused of homosexuality, and Wonder Woman of encouraging lesbianism.

The claim that crime comics and other salacious literature would lead to prostitution and syphilis, juvenile delinquency, reading disorders, and other educational defects was dubious. It was certainly not supported by trends in juvenile delinquency, which for the most part decreased in the late 1940s. But Parliament decided that it did not need proof in order to decide the issue.

The symbolic crusade against comics had its roots in a deeper less articulate concern about society and the family. And in hindsight, of course, it is easy to condemn those who fabricate moral panics from thin cloth and distract us from real issues. But there is a deeper result as well. Deviance as a topic invites restrictions, which in turn create social solidarity and build cohesiveness.

But for all those boys who were caught looking, the penalty was high, as they were thought to be doing something deviant.

Sources: Augustine Brannigan, 'Mystification of the Innocents: Crime, Comics and Delinquency in Canada, 1931–1949,' 111–44; 'Bill to ban comic books wins in Canadian Senate,' *New York Times*, 8 December 1949, 12; 'Canadians would cut 'crime comic strips,' *New York Times*, 10 April 1929, 38; 'Crime and the comics,' *New York Times*, 14 November 1950, 30; 'Many doubt comics spur crime, Senate survey of experts shows,' *New York Times*, 12 November 1950: 1; 'Comic books and television,' *New York Times*, 5 March 1950, 180.

Unease in the 1970s about the grafting of rehabilitative measures on to the criminal justice system seemed to echo these arguments. It is not, however, that Mead and Durkheim are implicitly at one in their penal theories. Phillipson argues that, to Durkheim, in his *Moral Education*, 'the essential function of punishment is not simply retributive, nor is it to produce individual atonement, nor is it to deter the offender, but rather it is to demonstrate the inviolability of the rule broken by the offender'.[35] If the punishment *is* secondary to the reaffirmation of the rule, then the way remains open for alternative measures to the sheerly punitive.

> The function of punishment is to demonstrate the inviolability of the law.

What those alternatives might be was hinted at elsewhere in Durkheim's work.[36] In his evolutionary perspective, he saw repressive justice as yielding progressively to restitutive justice as society moved from mechanical to organic modes of social solidarity. In the former, uniformity of consciousness could accommodate deviance only by strongly punitive responses. In the latter, restitutive justice, which is the minimum of reparation needed to restore harmony, becomes more appropriate. While Durkheim's chronology may have been partially invalidated by modern anthropology, his ideal types of justice retain their analytical force and can be seen at work in all modern criminal-justice systems.[37] Indeed, the growth of restorative justice in the 1990s and 2000s may prove to be a vindication of Durkheim's thesis, representing, as it does, a strong return to restitutive principles.[38]

> Restorative justice illustrates Durkheim's principles.

Case Study—Punitive Justice

In an article entitled 'The Psychology of Punitive Justice', Mead developed a complementary theme to that of Durkheim.[1] He argued that it is inadequate to account for the social organization of justice by reference to such justifications of punishment as retribution and deterrence. The reason is because these objectives would be as well served by a simpler system, such as lynch law.

Therefore, the ritual solemnities of the criminal law reflect rather the community's need for the deviant to be subjected to a form of punitive justice in which the re-establishment of social order is enacted in dramatic form. At root here is the idea that:

> the common law is an affirmation of citizenship. It is, however, a grave mistake to assume that the law itself and men's attitudes toward it can exist in abstracto. It is a grave mistake, for too often the respect for law as law is what we demand of members of the community, while we are able to regard with comparative indifference defects both in the concrete laws and in their administration. It is not only a mistake, it is also a fundamental error, for all emotional attitudes—and even respect for law and a sense of responsibility are emotional attitudes—arise in response to concrete impulses. We do not respect law in the abstract but the values which the laws of the community conserve. We have no sense of responsibility as such but an emotional recognition of duties which our position in the community entails.[2]

Thus the two major functions fulfilled by the criminal law are the stigmatization of the offender and the reinforcement of inhibitions against law breaking among the community at large. The hostility toward the deviant derives from his or her challenge to the moral boundaries with which the members of the community identify. This hostility cannot be reconciled with the desire to 'reform' or 'treat' the offender: 'It is quite impossible psychologically to hate the sin and love the sinner.'

[1] G. Mead, 'The Psychology of Punitive Justice'.
[2] Ibid., 577–602.

Developments in American Sociology

Despite the radicalism of their tone and style, Durkheim and Mead did not go much beyond asserting the inevitability of deviance and punishment as properties of social order in the societies of their day. Tone and style aside, the American sociologists who took up the functional analysis of deviance came much closer to justifying the pursuit of specific forms of deviance as positively serviceable to the social order, as Matza points out:

The growth of a sociological view of deviant phenomena involved, as major phases, the replacement of a correctional stance by an *appreciation* of the deviant subject, the tacit purging of a conception of pathology by new stress on human *diversity* and the erosion of a simple distinction between deviant and conventional phenomena, resulting from more intimate familiarity with the world as it is, which yielded a more sophisticated view stressing *complexity*.[39]

Appreciation carries the risk of a seeming complicity with the deviance under scrutiny; that is probably the main reason for its relatively late adoption as a method. But there is no reason for appreciation to imply approval: to empathize is not necessarily to agree or approve. Appreciation in this sense is a mere research tool used to enhance the study of any group.[40] However, Matza credits functionalism with several contributions.

•*First, it plays a major role in the growth of 'naturalism' in the sociology of deviance.* By searching for the hidden contributions that deviant phenomena might make to the social order, 'some functional analyses sound suspiciously like the justifications of phenomena rendered by the deviant subjects who exemplify and perpetrate them'.[41] Kingsley Davis's analysis of prostitution for example, which first appeared in 1937, is remarkably similar to the more recent demands by organized groups of prostitutes in the United States and most western European countries. It was claimed that prostitution operates as a social service for those unable to achieve sexual satisfaction in any other way, acting as a safety valve for potential sexual aggression. In Davis's view, this is ultimately the reason why prostitution can never be eliminated, short of abolishing the sanctity of monogamous marriage and requiring 'mutual complementariness' of sexual desire throughout society.[42] In this sense, prostitution complements the institution of the monogamous nuclear family. Both are threatened by the rise of more widespread sexual freedoms, but to push monogamy too far would presumably lead to sexual promiscuity that would chronically affect the social order. Hence, some prostitution is a good thing, an argument taken up and developed with reference to pornography some thirty years later by Polsky.[43] In a fashion analogous to prostitution, pornography makes sexual gratification possible in a commercial transaction that by comparison with adultery, for example, poses no threat to family ties.

> Prostitution serves a social function of sexual release.

Appreciation of deviance is a mixed blessing for sociology. Its appeal is most obvious in the more exotic but victimless forms of deviance, such as smoking marijuana or joining a nudist colony. However, in some cases, it seems to infringe on more widely-held taboos.[44] For example, how do we define the difference between pornography and obscenity, or the age at which being photographed nude is acceptable.

Matza's argument is that it is necessary to apprehend the world 'as it is'; this is exemplified by Daniel Bell's portrayal of the racketeering in New York's dockland. Discussing the problem of why racketeering should flourish there long after it declined elsewhere, Bell characterizes it as a stable organization that actually copes relatively efficiently with the unusually intricate nature of the New York dockside.

That the price is graft, corruption, and exploitation does not detract from the 'beauty' of the racket, which 'provided extraordinary gain on almost no investment other than muscle-men for intimidation'.[45] As Matza comments: 'Such a truth is obviously partial, but it is necessary to begin there. Otherwise, the coherence, form, texture and even utility of deviant phenomena cannot become evident.'[46]

> Functionalism involves understanding the role of deviance in society.

•A second by-product of functionalism is the purging of pathology, which is no small achievement. It is best exemplified in the work of Merton, who distinguished between manifest and latent functions to stress the ways in which social phenomena, however 'immoral' or 'unhealthy' on the surface, may actually contribute to the social order. In fact, there was nothing apart from the terminology employed that was especially new about the idea of latent function. For Durkheim, all functions were latent; he described as 'purposes' those functions that Merton called 'manifest functions'. However, in his analysis of the political machines that were a byword for corruption and graft in American life, Merton sought to establish unintended and unnoticed virtues. These reside largely in the capacity of the political machines, directed by the local Boss, to deliver actual results against the grain of legal constraints and democratic convolutions. 'The functional deficiencies of the official structure generate an alternative (unofficial) structure to fill existing needs somewhat more effectively.'[47]

This analytical model can appear to justify practically anything, a deficiency Merton sought to remedy by introducing the concept of 'dysfunction' to complement that of function. However, Davis, Bell, Merton, and others in the 1930s, 1940s, and 1950s were primarily concerned with the functions of the deviant: the dysfunctions of the conventional were merely the mirror image that supplied a certain analytical symmetry in principle. The most deadly question, which they rarely raised, was 'At whose expense?' and its corollary, 'Functional for whom?' Their intention was not, however, to produce a functionalist theory of deviance, but to use deviance to illustrate functionalist strategies.

• The third achievement of functionalism was to accelerate the movement away from a view of deviance and society as essentially simple to an awareness of its complexity. Deviant phenomena overlap with conventional: the same motives, the same organizational principles, even the same morality, can inspire deviant and conformist alike. In this sense, Al Capone, as Merton stressed, was a model American capitalist. In discussing his 'modes of adaptation' the individual employs skills, Merton said: 'Within this context, Al Capone represents the triumph of amoral intelligence over morally prescribed "failure," when the channels of vertical mobility are closed or narrowed in a society which places a high premium on economic affluence and social ascent for all its members.'

Racketeering was illegal, but it conformed to the canons of good business practice. The irony employed by the functionalists was perhaps less novel than Matza implies. After all, novelists and satirists from Swift and Fielding on, dramatists as celebrated as Shakespeare and Shaw, had employed the device on these very issues to effect. Mandeville, in his *Fable of the Bees* (written in 1714), had argued that the practice of virtue was incompatible with commercial prosperity, which can flourish only in an environment of pride, greed, and emulative luxury. The use of irony in sociology, however, was decidedly novel. 'By the idea of irony, the functionalists revealed social process as *devious* and thus increasingly complex.'[48] Thus Merton said: 'A cardinal American virtue, ambition, promotes a cardinal American vice, deviant behaviour.'[49] And Davis said: 'If we reverse the proposition that increased sexual freedom among women of all classes reduces the role of prostitution (as Kinsey's findings suggest), we find ourselves admitting that increased prostitution may reduce the sexual irregularities of respectable women.'[50]

That deviance could operate as a blessing in disguise was, as Bell put it, nevertheless bought 'at a high price'—a double irony that stemmed from virtue's dependence on evil for the performance of necessary services. In all of this, the American functionalists were prone to neglect the second stage of Durkheim's methodology. Sheer persistence of a phenomenon was not sufficient to establish the functionality of deviance, because the ways in which it necessarily contributes to group life tended to be taken for granted. It is in this sense that Erikson's work represents a return to Durkheimian orthodoxy. But it is an orthodoxy that he takes as a beginning rather than an end of inquiry, as in *Wayward Puritans*:

> This [approach] raises a delicate theoretical issue. If we grant that human groups often derive benefit from deviant behaviour, can we then assume that they are organised in such a way as to promote this resource? Can we assume, in other words, that forces operate in the social structure to recruit offenders and to commit them to long periods of service in the deviant ranks? . . . Deviant forms of conduct often seem to derive nourishment from the very agencies devised to inhibit them. Indeed, the agencies built by society for preventing deviance are often so poorly equipped for the task that we might well ask why this is regarded as their 'real' function in the first place.[51]

If this is so, it may account for the surprising symmetry between the deviant and the conformist—a symmetry far more striking when scrutinized from a distance:

> A twentieth-century American is supposed to understand that larceny and other forms of commercial activity are wholly different, standing on 'opposite sides of the law'. A seventeenth-century American, on the other hand, if he lived in New England, was supposed to understand that Congregationalism and Antinomianism were as far apart as God and the Devil.

His argument culminates in the link between the fear of deviance and the processes by which that very thing is created:

> If deviation and conformity are so alike, it is not surprising that deviant behaviour should seem to appear in a community at exactly those points where it is most feared. Men who fear witches soon find themselves surrounded by them; men who become jealous of private property soon encounter eager thieves. [52]

And the point of this exercise in 'self-fulfilling prophecy' returns us to the most ancient paradox of all: that good can be known only in relation to evil, its

For Erikson, defining deviance defines the limits of the normal.

mirror image. 'In the process of defining the nature of deviation, the settlers were also defining the boundaries of their new universe.' Two subsidiary themes also occur to Erikson.

•*First, he argues that the amount of deviance has more to do with the community's capacity to handle it than with the inclinations towards deviance among its members.* Social control agencies tend to regulate rather than eliminate deviance, whatever they claim rhetorically about the 'war against crime'. Stabilization seems to be preferred to elimination, partly because the control agencies demand some predictability of employment, but also because the very definitions of the problem change.[53]

In a truly Canadian example of this, Kenneth Colburn looks at the issue of violence in hockey. He shows that, rather than being an aberration, violence in hockey is an institutionalized form of 'legitimate' violence that allows players to vent their frustration while at the same time to pursue the goal of winning against an opponent who is frustrating that goal. Referees will even allow some violence as a way to control rogue players and keep violence in line.

This concept of the 'functional indispensability' of deviance can be traced back to Bensman and Gerver's classic article on how deviance maintains the social system within the factory. They document through an observational study how the use of 'taps' to cut screw holes in an aircraft assembly factory, while illegal, is sanctioned by foremen and supervisors as a way to get the job done within acceptable time limits. The penalties for getting caught are severe, but in this setting deviance is part of the negotiated totality of actions.

Similarly, in looking at police work, researchers argue that deviance allows non-deviant members to accomplish their work and satisfy institutional requirements.[54]

•*Second, and as a corollary, societies develop appropriate 'deployment patterns', or strategies, to negotiate the optimum amount of deviance they 'need' for boundary maintenance.* Here Erikson propounds what is virtually a 'conservation of energy' theory of deviance containment. Rag days, charivaris, and festivals, provide outlets for the ventilation of deviance in licensed form. Certain age groups are granted more tolerance: the young are expected to 'sow their wild oats', 'get out of hand', and generally 'raise hell' from time to time, though the tolerance is finely tuned to curb those who go 'too far'. In short, Erikson is probing, so to speak, for a deep structure of deviance and control beneath the myriad forms they have assumed in history and from society to society.

For Christie, too, deviance is in infinite supply and the penal repression applied by any society reveals more about the failure to use other, more sensible ways of managing control than about the relentless politics of demonizing the other and the search to profit from the building of prisons.[55]

In keeping with this idea, some research has focused on the deviance that exists in some workplaces and social settings. Based on the idea used by Robert Stebbins on how deviance involves 'tolerable differences', Stephen Kent analyzes normative strategies in the labelling of religions and cults. He concludes that deviant categories, such as using the word 'cults' are themselves negotiated and are necessary for establishing the legitimacy of own's group.[56]

Discussion: Deviance and Exploration—Bootlegging

Bootlegging is an act made criminal by the passing of a law against it. Unlike murder, for example, which is widely accepted as wrong, bootlegging is a crime because it is prohibited. Murder is *mala in se*, or wrong in itself, while bootlegging is *mala prohibita*, or wrong because it is prohibited.

The profession of bootlegging, if we can call it that, has different forms of organization. If liquor is to be smuggled across a border, it requires those who can organize the boats, cars, planes, or other forms of transportation. It might also require the co-operation of Customs officers, airline cargo handlers, or ports workers.

'Information obtainable tonight was that over the 150 roads leading into Vermont across the Canadian border, high-powered limousines, oftentimes carrying handsomely dressed women, are constantly bringing liquor into the United States. In some cases, it was said, these automobiles are equipped with a special body and tank so designed as to attract no attention from casual observers, yet arranged for carrying a large quantity of liquor. Even the spare tires of the machine, it was said, are often filled with liquor.'[1]

During Prohibition in the United States, denatured alcohol would be purchased for allegedly industrial purposes and then re-distilled for sale to saloons, restaurants, and lunch counters. During Prohibition in Canada, it was legal for doctors to prescribe alcohol for medical purposes, and druggists might also sell alcohol without a prescription. The police were sometimes accused of not enforcing the law, or looking the other way.

'**War on the bootlegger**. While Dominion and provincial authorities are splitting hairs over questions of jurisdiction, the bootleggers are plying their trade with a zeal and industry worthy of a better calling. They have as much regard for the technicalities of the law as the Bolsheviks have for their promises. . . . Attention is called to the fact that the maximum fine of $2,000 imposed sometimes where scores or even hundreds of cases of whiskey is involved are a mere fraction of the profits. Such fines in effect are high license, while the minimum fine of $200 is low license. The latter penalty is indeed a mere travesty of justice. . . . Certain magistrates and officers are not in sympathy with the [Ontario Temperance] Act and are disinclined to take proper steps to enforce it. For these the question of 'discretion' as to the course they ought to pursue should be answered by requests for resignation or by dismissal.'[2]

In 1910 the sale of alcohol was prohibited in Nova Scotia, except for Halifax, which didn't come under a province-wide ban until 1916. Given that it was a densely concentrated military town, blind pigs (illegal bars) and bootleggers continued to frustrate the the police. The tolerance of the general public, the power of organized crime, and drinking establishments with fortified doors resisted the power of the law.

There were criticisms that City Council and the police were not giving enough support to the temperance officers. In addition Customs officers were accused of being corrupted by smugglers and bootleggers. By 1929 opinion was that Prohibition was unenforceable, as evidenced in this comment in the *Halifax Herald*:

> It is my firm conviction that the Nova Scotia Temperance Act has been given a fair trial and has failed in its effect, and while I realize that the Government can enact legislation which would prohibit the legal use of liquor in any form . . . I am not convinced that you can eliminate the bootlegger from distributing his filthy poison, which I believe will become worse if stricter Government regulations are put into effect.[3]

The demise of Prohibition marked the end of an important period, and it shows, perhaps, the difficulty of controlling deviance when it is supported by a majority of the population.[4]

[1] *The Globe*, 8 November 1921, 1.
[2] *The Globe*, 6 August 1920, 6.
[3] *Halifax Herald*, 14 Oct. 1929.
[4] J. Willing, 'The Profession of Bootlegging', 40–4; P. McGahan, 'The Rise and Fall of Prohibition in Halifax'.

Functionalists from Durkheim to Erikson tend to treat social cohesion and the need for boundary maintenance as their ultimate concern, but why the need for boundaries at all—what does it mean to assert that societies must 'cohere'? In what remains the most comprehensive attempt to address those questions, Robert Scott draws, not only on the work of the functionalists, but also on that of the philosopher of science, Thomas Kuhn, on the anthropologically based analyses of rules and meanings of Mary Douglas, and on the social phenomenology of Berger and Luckmann.[57]

From Kuhn, he takes the idea that people explain the world to themselves in terms of a 'paradigm', a self-contained model that is relatively immune to change, except in the form of very rare 'paradigmatic revolutions' that overturn established ways of apprehending reality and replace them by ones that emerge from the new paradigm.

From Mary Douglas he takes the axiom that cultures cannot explain everything, but what cannot be explained is treated as anomalous, as something that 'should not be there': 'Dirt is matter out of place' is her vivid metaphor.

From Berger and Luckmann he takes the notion of 'world-openness', the absence for people of an environmental stability: thus, 'men require a symbolic framework for ordering social reality'. Social order is humanity's creation of 'world-closedness' against the void, a construction to ward off the chaos of nature; it is therefore always precarious and besieged by countless 'alternative' realities. The development of social order is made possible only by humanity's capacity to symbolize actions, which by repetition and reinforcement become reified habits, with the power to exercise constraint over generation after generation. The legitimation of such patterns lends them moral meaning and the patina of 'naturalness'; the integration of such legitimations provides an overarching symbolic framework. Social and cultural cohesion and coherence are achieved when the group as a whole takes a particular system as *the* institutional pattern, in which 'everything makes sense'.

> Social order is created through habit.

In complex societies, many sub-universes of meaning can co-exist, but the dominant order is generally adhered to with a deep conservatism and resistance to change. Gellner assigns the term 'ironic cultures' to those forms of belief that do not ultimately challenge the dominant symbolic order, except on the surface of appearances: people may, for example 'believe' in astrology, but they do not commonly entrust themselves to astrologers for brain surgery or bridge building.[58]

Social order is set in a field of force that has the capacity to overwhelm it. Chaos holds the potential to confront us with things that literally should not exist if the concept of reality that is embodied in our symbolic universe is true. Yet cultures exhibit great resilience in the face of such threats to their integrity. Just as scientific paradigms can explain away, as anomalous, events that science itself postulates ought not to exist or that it has classified and categorized wrongly, so can cultures have mechanisms for smoothing out and resolving threats posed by anomalies. Deviance enters as a property of social order to serve as a category for the anomalous, a catch basin for behaviour outside the usual. Other mechanisms perform similar, complementary functions:

> *Misperception* can quite occur, so that anomalies are simply not noticed;
> *Debunking* can flatten anomalies into everyday events;
> *Normalizing* can redefine deviance as something ordinary;
> If recalcitrant, deviance can be *controlled* coercively;
> If defiant or threatening, *nihilation* can enter deviant's definition of reality;
> Finally, *change* can occur to accommodate the deviance, but is rare.

In sum, deviance is not just what is left over from conformity, nor is it the simple failure to conform; rather, it is inextricably bound up with the preconditions for conformity to exist and is therefore part of how we construct our world.

■ Criticism

In a formidable summary of the strengths and weaknesses of functionalism, Percy Cohen lists three levels of criticism: logical, substantive, and ideological.[59] Of these, the logical criticisms are by far the most severe.

•*First, functionalist theories are viewed as taking a teleological or circular form that is ultimately unacceptable,* despite plausible justifications for this form of argument in the human, as distinct from natural, sciences.[60] Teleology consists in the imputation of cause to beneficial consequence: for example, does religion result from the need for social cohesion, or is social cohesion the benefit of religion? We can see that religion provides cohesion for members of the community, but if we then say that religion comes from a need for social cohesion, that is a teleogical argument.

However, logical problems aside, it can be argued that this presents no real problem, because people have purposes and put them into effect collectively by trial and error. In other words, they have the consequences and benefits of action in mind as an prior condition of their behaviour. The problem here is that functionalism was created in the teeth of the complexities of social life that could not be accounted for solely in terms of intended consequences. As Cohen argues:

> many, if not most, social phenomena are the product of the unintended consequences of social actions; these social actions are themselves purposive; but many of their consequences have no direct connection with these purposes. Thus, men may participate in their religion in order to achieve a state of salvation; if this widespread participation has consequences for the moral order, this may be quite unconnected with the purposes envisaged by the participants. This is not to deny that men sometimes set out to create or destroy social phenomena. . . . But whatever men do in this respect, they always unintentionally produce certain social and cultural items which, though they appear to have been devised for certain purposes, were not.[61]

The problem then becomes how to avoid a purely circular explanation, in which the grounds for the existence of the phenomenon are simply read into the alleged functions it serves. It is one thing to assert that deviance can be made to serve some social end or other *once it has occurred,* for example, to heighten solidarity by uniting society against the offender. It is another step altogether to show that deviance is promoted in advance by society to bring about that end of social unity. There are, to be sure, examples of that process, such as: witch hunting, scapegoating, and the activities of *agents provocateurs.* In such cases the more plausible causal agency is usually particular groups that are seeking specific ends, and not some emanation from the social processes of the group as a whole.

We do have our own misgivings about Cohen's stress on the unanticipated consequences of social action. Indeed, we would argue that there must be quite substantial resort to teleology in a discipline devoted to human activity. People do have purposes, and they are quite perceptive and far-sighted. They often seek what functionalists would wish to describe as unintended ends. Functionalist analyses of deviance actually give us very little evidence about stated intentions; they do not busy themselves with what people *say* they are doing, although it is never very difficult to find someone, somewhere, on the social scene who is capable of putting an identifiable version of the functionalist case. After all, judges

Crime serves to unite the community, but this does not mean that the community creates crime for that purpose.

themselves state that they try to promote solidarity amongst the virtuous, prostitutes that they are performing a vital social service, and organized criminals that
they are exemplary capitalists, mediators, and patrons.[62] No scholar needs to point
them to the latent functions hiding beneath the manifest surface of things. And
once the pointing occurs, functionalism becomes self-falsifying. When a description of the unintended and latent functions of action is published, it can no
longer be safe to assume that the literate are innocent about the consequences of
their behaviour. The result has been an odd, distorting view of social life that
removes much that is purposeful and recognizable about conduct. Mary Douglas
has put the argument well:

> [Functionalism] proposes an unacceptable view of human agency. . . . The
> argument depends on a form of sociological determinism that credits indi-
> viduals with neither initiative nor sense. It was partly for this failing that
> sociological functionalism has been in low repute for the last thirty years. It
> had no place for the subjective experience of individuals willing and choos-
> ing. To suppose that individuals are caught in the toils of a complex machin-
> ery that they do not help to make is to suppose them to be passive objects,
> like sheep or robots.[63]

•*A second vexing problem concerns the testing of the theory.* How could one possibly falsify a functionalist proposition? In the case of crime, for example, it may
be possible to apply the normal/pathological distinction to different societies on
the basis of their crime rates. The United States would undoubtedly emerge at the
pathological end of any such spectrum, a finding that indeed might point to the
myriad defects that socialists have long noted as built into American society,
whereas Canada has sometimes been called the 'peaceful kingdom'.

But functionalism at this point offers an embarrassing number of solutions to
the problem of accounting for those defects.[64] Deviance may be a 'warning light'
or a 'safety valve' or a price to be paid for the maintenance of valued institutions,
such as a commitment to 'free enterprise'. It may be the 'functional equivalent'
of what, in other societies, appear as high rates of political oppression, religious
fanaticism, or mental illness. Similarly, religion has divided communities as well
as united them, but this is viewed as confirming its unifying function, albeit
within each sub-community. Nothing can ever be disproved, nor can the promise
of comparative analysis be fulfilled, as items can only be evaluated in their own
context.

•*Third, functionalism promotes holism,* the tendency to analyze societies as
'wholes' or systems, thereby inhibiting the exploration of just how a phenomenon
affects different groups within it. What is functional for one group may well be
dysfunctional for another. Functionalists recognize this problem but hope to overcome it by a complicated cost-benefit analysis in which the functions and dysfunctions for various groupings are somehow added up to produce a sociological
balance sheet. Functionalism in this sense is, as Gouldner has noted, no more
than sociological utilitarianism,[65] in which it is quite proper for a minority to

suffer, in principle, for the social cohesion of the majority. As a cartoon might put it, the victim of muggers should be gratified that he has played his part in reactivating social solidarity. The main logical defect of such a position is that the vantage point from which such a cost-benefit analysis proceeds is inescapably value-laden.

One reason for opposing functionalism is that little empirical work has been mounted to test its core assumptions.[66] Erikson is the main exception in the sociology of deviance, but his chosen ground—Puritan New England—is reachable only through historical accounts.[67] It is also lacking in the very complexity that functionalists point to as the chief characteristic of modern societies. As Gellner has stressed, structurally simple and small-scale societies allow more scope for 'functionalism as a doctrine' because the problem of feedback of unintended beneficial consequences is minimized.[68]

Moreover, the effect of deviance is often the reverse of that assumed in functional analysis, for far from drawing together 'upright consciences', it all too often triggers a retreat into isolationism. It may not be well-known, but the community in which the *In Cold Blood* murders occurred reportedly withdrew from any semblance of social life in the aftermath of those murders. The Yorkshire Ripper murders allegedly had the same effect on the social life of women. 'Indifference' phenomena are widely reported in the United States in the context of the seemingly intractable deterioration in inner-city victimization.

On the other hand, the Toronto Boxing Day shooting of 2005 or the Los Angeles riots after the trial acquitting the officers who beat Rodney King, did result in a shocked collective reaction that was amplified by politicians, campaigners, and the mass media anxious to use the deaths to impart moral and political lessons about social conditions. Why they should have so shocked the *conscience collective* while other equally appalling crimes did not is not clear. It is a problem begging for theory and research, and it underscores the sad reflection that the main tenets of functionalism have not prompted anything like an adequate mass of empirical work or a viable methodology for undertaking such work in future.

•*Fourth, and finally, functionalists are accused of ignoring conflict*, failing to explain change, and employing conservative ideology as a consequence. However, these criticisms have been discounted. Conflict can be regarded as functional, and indeed, Simmel[69] and Coser[70] have produced long essays arguing that a period of open conflict can resolve otherwise gnawing strains in society; that conflict promotes the social solidarity of those who are bound together to confront a common enemy; that conflict is a clear warning of the presence of social problems; and that conflict is often surprisingly orderly, being a social process locked into other social processes and less disruptive than naïve spectators might suppose. Where conflict is not regarded as functional, it can be described as the outcome of 'malintegration'. Change is no less well accounted for than persistence, and as Merton pointed out, to assert that things 'hang together' in society as an argument against reform tends as much to revolution as to preservation of the status quo.

Merton observed that if social structures are as integrated in functionalist analysis as its critics maintain, all change, however petty, would indeed be revolutionary because no part would remain untouched. Indeed, functionalists are not the defenders of any one form of political or social order. They are interested in very abstract and general principles of structural organization, principles so abstract that they are intended to apply to Utopia as well as to Hell. Robert Merton reflected that 'it is not at all the case that whatever is, is right, or, for that matter, that whatever is, is wrong. Rather, it is only the case that whatever is, is possible.'[71]

Moreover, the allegation that functionalism must be dismissed because it is conservative is itself an ideological rather than a sociological response. It assumes that conservatism is indisputably at fault, and that is not an assumption that can be made on safe philosophical or empirical grounds. The merit of conservatism is a metaphysical matter. If it is found that functionalism is well-argued and solid and if the theory makes conservatism intellectually compelling, then its critics should reconsider their position on conservatism instead of using it as an argument for the rejection of functionalism.

Finally, none of the above applies to functional analysis as a method where the purposes of institutional arrangements and their effectiveness in terms of specific aims are concerned; nor are the unintended side-effects of phenomena any less central a topic if functionalism is abandoned. As a part of sociological enquiry, functional analysis remains in order. 'It is essential to evaluate the functionalist method, in the sense that it suggests to us where to look, in isolation from the functionalist doctrine, that tells us what we will find there.'[72]

As long as it is maintained that certain institutions 'fit' other institutions more than others and that some minimal congruence is suited to human association, functionalism is in principle a better guide than other approaches to many sociological questions. As soon as it is admitted, say, that modern industrial society requires some kinds of family structure, or certain types of education, rather than others, the functionalist method is also admissible. It may be that functionalists have tended to overplay their hand, but at least they appear some times to be playing the right sort of game. And it should be noticed, too, that functionalism still seems to be persuasive and pervasive enough to surface in a variety of disguises throughout sociology. There may be very few sociologists who would now advertise themselves as functionalists, but there are some who are close to being functionalist in style.

Christie Davies, for instance, has written extensively about the functions of humour in upholding social control and social stratification, and about the functions of deviance in enforcing sexual boundaries. His is a straightforward teleology that argues, for example, that 'it is clear that the strong taboos that exist against homosexuality, bestiality and transvestitism in the West are the result of attempts to establish and defend strong ethnic, religious or institutional boundaries. Where such pressures are weak or absent the taboos against these forms of sexual deviance are also weak or absent.'[73] The voice of Christie Davies in 1982 could have been that of Kingsley Davis in 1939.

More recently, David Garland has revived a Durkheimian sociology of punishment that talks about the symbolic work of the penal sanction in constructing social order.[74] Punishment, Garland says, is a:

> serious and symbolic issue in any society because it lies directly at the roots of social order, as well as having a prominent place in the psychic formation and development of individual persons. As regards the political order, punishment operates as a sign of ultimate authority and is the final materialization of that authority's force: as such it is universal and indispensable.[75]

Braithwaite, too, has revived Durkheim in his analysis of the vital part played by shame in the workings of informal social control.[76]

And even if sociologists are not at all overt in their functionalism, there are many calling themselves by other names who resort to functionalist ideas. When a Foucault or a radical criminologist like Steven Box, Stuart Hall, Jeffrey Reiman,[77] or Colin Sumner proclaims that the effect of publicized working-class crime is to support capitalism by deflecting attention from the doings of the powerful, functionalism is being advanced. When a structuralist like Mary Douglas states that the suppression of deviance promotes the integrity of cognitive orders, functionalism is being advanced. When a phenomenologist like Jack Douglas points to the symbolic interdependencies of good and evil, and of deviance and respectability, functionalism is being advanced. In short, there is a tacit but perfectly potent functionalism still lurking in much of the sociology of deviance.

The functionalist message is clear.

Chapter Summary

In this chapter we have explained the central concepts of functionalism and described some of the major figures associated with it. As a theoretical approach, functionalism was the mainstream position for decades. In functionalism, we can see how sociologists see deviance as central to the social order, as necessary for boundary maintenance and social control.

There are of course problems that limit the utility of the approach as well. For example, it has been criticized for its untested hypotheses, its confusion of cause with consequence, and its level of abstraction. Nonetheless, it has remained a core approach in the sociology of deviance on the basis of the simple idea that if something exists, it must exist for a purpose.

Critical-Thinking Questions

1. Discuss how it should be determined how much deviance is beneficial for a society. Is there an optimum level of deviance that could be tolerated?
2. Explain why the functionalist perspective in the 1950s replaced the Chicago School's social-disorganization perspective. Does it deal with different questions in different ways?

3. In your opinion, what are the most valuable contributions made by the functional perspective to an understanding of the origins of crime? And on the other hand, what are its major weaknesses?

Explorations in Film

In the movie *Serpico*, the title character is a New York city police officer, and new to the job, he's keen to do well, but he soon finds that he is expected to take bribes. His desire to maintain his personal integrity and his fight to expose police corruption result in a backlash from officers in the very department he is trying to protect. Done in a documentary style, the 1973 film shows the organizational normality of deviance; it is a real-life story that resulted in the 1971 Knapp Commission into police wrongdoing.

Chapter Five

Anomie

Chapter Overview

This chapter looks at the sociological concept of anomie, originally devised by Durkheim, revised by Merton, and criticized by many. Anomie is a psychological state of confusion and disorientation due to insufficient regulation in society; it is also seen as characteristic of society, particularly under capitalism. In Durkheim's formulation, anomie as a condition of society occurs as society evolves from an agrarian to industrial state. Despite criticisms, anomie remains a strong way to situate deviance as a response of the individual to structural conditions within society. Thus the concept helps explain the dissatisfaction of the individual in modern, Western, capitalist society, and contemporary theorists point to structural changes in the late twentieth century that may be preconditions to anomie.

■ Introduction

Anomie theory has been considered out of fashion, though there are signs of its continued relevance. Like functionalism from which it derives, it has become a routine conceptual folly to be demolished before one moves on to more rewarding ground.

The critical onslaught has been particularly fierce in the case of Robert Merton's version of anomie theory, as in Clinard's collection of critical essays in 1964.[1] By contrast, Durkheim's original statement of anomie as a source of deviant behaviour has received more sympathetic treatment, largely because Durkheim is so central a figure in sociological history and anomie is so central a concept in his thought. That is not the same thing, of course, as continuing to take it seriously. For example, both Lukes and Horton, discern in Durkheim's conception of anomie a philosophical critique of capitalist society in relation to which Merton's theory of anomie is at best confused and at worst 'dehumanized'.[2]

However, Douglas attacked the entire methodology on which Durkheim's sociology rested, Rex views Merton's central idea as 'extraordinarily oversimplified', and Lemert, Gagnon, and others attacked both the theoretical and empirical weaknesses of the theory. By the 1970s, Paul Rock and Mary McIntosh could refer prosaically to the 'exhaustion of the anomie tradition'.[3]

What are we, students of the sociology of deviance, to make of all this arguing? Because of its centrality to the sociological tradition of theorizing about deviance, anomie theory has among its strengths

- the analysis of a key feature of capitalism, namely, material consumption;
- a meta-theory applicable to societies other than capitalist; and,
- the capacity to explain the conditions that may cause social breakdown.[4]

So powerful a theory cannot be disregarded, and its effects have been both diffuse and lingering. Anomie theory was at first so compelling that after Durkheim and Merton, there followed Cloward and Ohlin, Spergel, Downes, and others working in a kind of tacit co-operation that appears only rarely in sociology. Much of the theory was never fully developed, but it has been expanded to become one of the most ambitious attempts to explain deviance.

> Anomie theory is the most ambitious attempt to explain deviance.

Anomie theory was under cultivation at a time of energetic social engineering in the United States, and it was appropriated to give intellectual coherence and legitimacy to the Mobilization for Youth program.[5] It thereby became one of the few well-documented instances of the sociology of deviance achieving a major impact on policy formation.

It may also be remarked that anomie theory has been reincarnated again and again. It has an anonymous presence in Jock Young's essay on labelling theory, *The Drugtakers* and appears under its own name as one of the principal themes in his account of the making of left realism in the 1980s.[6] It is the invisible prop to the radical work of the Birmingham Centre for Contemporary Cultural Studies on class, youth, and deviance in Britain. Indeed, just as Karl Mannheim was called the *bourgeois* Marxist, so Hall, Clarke, and Hebdige of Birmingham could be called the radical anomie theorists. Extensive echoes of the theory will be discerned in any sensitive reading of the contemporary sociology of deviance.

■ Durkheim's Theory of Anomie

There are two distinct usages of anomie in Durkheim, stated as follows:

> In the '*Division of Labour in Society*', [anomie] characterizes the pathological state of the economy, 'this sphere of collective life that is in large part freed from the moderating action of [moral] regulation', where 'latent or active, the state of war is necessarily chronic' and 'each individual finds himself in a state of war with every other'. In '*Suicide*', it is used to characterize the pathological mental state of the individual who is insufficiently regulated by society and suffers from 'the malady of infinite aspiration'. . . . It is accompanied by 'weariness', 'disillusionment', 'disturbance, agitation and discontent', 'anger' and 'an irritated disgust with life'. In extreme cases this condition leads a man to commit suicide and homicide.[7]

Anomie is both a condition of society and a psychological condition.

As this passage makes clear, anomie is conceived of as a constant property of industrial society, and as a variable with social-psychological implications. [8]

Now Durkheim's conception of anomie must be set in the context of his theory of social evolution.

•*In his first use of the concept, it is in the transition of society from mechanical to organic solidarity that the division of labour assumes an anomic form.* In the mechanical state, the division of labour is minimal, and paradoxically, the term 'mechanical' is employed to refer to the uniformity of consciousness, a single normative system, in the simplest societies. In the organic state, it is assumed that the division of labour is highly differentiated and has generated mediating institutions that ensure social cohesion despite marked moral diversity. In the transition, however, anomie results from the rapid growth of the economy without a corresponding growth in the forces that could regulate it. 'Sheerly economic regulation is not enough . . . there should be moral regulation, moral rules that specify the rights and obligations of individuals in a given occupation in relation to those in other occupations'.[9]

Anomie results from rapid social change without a corresponding development of controls.

A prerequisite is that individuals must be able to fill occupational positions that accord with their talents and that they will accept as legitimate. This cannot prevail where the class system inhibits the chances of large numbers of people attaining positions that fit their abilities. Such a forced division of labour can only be abolished if all external inequalities, such as the hereditary transmission of property, are ended. It is in this sense that Taylor, Walton, and Young refer to Durkheim as a 'biological meritocrat', for he assumes that an ideal correspondence is possible between internal qualities and social position.[10] 'Labour is divided spontaneously only if society is constituted in such a way that social inequalities exactly express natural inequalities.'[11]

Anomie, then, is the peculiar disease of modern industrial society, for it is accepted as 'normal, a mark of moral distinction, it being everlastingly repeated that it is man's nature to be eternally dissatisfied, constantly to advance, without relief or rest, towards an indefinite goal'. Religion, governmental power over the economy and occupational groups have lost their moral sway. Thus 'appetites have become freed of any limiting authority' and 'from top to bottom of the ladder, greed is aroused without knowing where to find ultimate foothold. Nothing can calm it, since its goal is far beyond all it can attain'.[12]

In this analysis, class conflict and industrial crises are a symptom, not a cause, of anomie.

•*In his second use of the concept, in* Suicide, *Durkheim elaborates on the sources of variation in the personal experience of anomie.* In this pioneering study, it can hardly be maintained that Durkheim treated anomie simply as a constant and invariable property of industrialism. His argument rests on the crucial nature of the distinction between social *integration* and social *regulation*, which are viewed as causally related to different forms of suicide (see Table 5.1).

With certain exceptions, the excessive strength of integration and regulation are linked with pre-industrial societies. The types of suicide characteristically prevalent in such societies, such as the honorific and the ritualistic, are derived from the excessive subordination of the individual to the group. The reverse obtains in the case of industrial societies. Nevertheless, 'altruistic' suicide may still be found, for example, in the case of soldiers taking their own lives after being found guilty of 'dishonourable conduct'; 'fatalistic' suicide in the acts of self-immolation by Japanese *kamikaze* pilots in the Second World War; and 'suicide terrorism' in the Middle East and by al-Qaeda and allied groups.[13]

The egoistic form of suicide was seen by Durkheim as the product of excessive individuation, which he saw as the moral counterpart of a specialized division of labour. It was exemplified by the fact that the suicide rate was higher among Protestants than Catholics, among the unmarried than the married, and among the childless than parents. The force of the thesis was most strikingly displayed by the explanation Durkheim gave of the lower rates that obtained at times of political crisis compared with periods of political stability, as in France in 1830, 1848, and 1870: 'Great social disturbances and great popular wars, rouse collective sentiments, stimulate partisan spirit and patriotism and, concentrating activity towards a single end, at least temporarily, cause a stronger integration of society.'[14]

Suicide, therefore, varies inversely with the degree of integration of society.[15]

> Poor social integration leads to higher suicide rates.

Table 5.1: Effect of Integration and Regulation on Type of Suicide

Integration	Regulation	
	Too strong	**Too weak**
Too strong	Altruistic suicide	Fatalistic suicide
Too weak	Egoistic suicide	Anomic suicide

Discussion: Deviance Exploration—Suicide

Suicide, the last act over which a person can be said to have control, is a highly individualistic decision. Made perhaps in the depths of despair, the decision nonetheless has social causes, patterns, and consequences related to the individual's place within the social structure.

Males are more likely to commit suicide. In Canada in 2004 there were 2,734 suicides for males of all ages and 879 for females. However, females were hospitalized for attempted suicide at about one and a half times the rate of males in 1998–99. Almost 10 per cent of those who are hospitalized for attempted suicide have been hospitalized more than once before for a suicide attempt in the same year.

The World Health Organization estimates that, around the world, for people between the ages of 15 and 44, suicide is the fourth-leading cause of death.

The overall rate of suicide in Canada is 10.8 per 100,000, compared to a homicide rate of 1.7. However suicide is not even across the population. According to Statistics Canada, immigrants are less likely than native-born Canadians to commit suicide. And immigrants living in Toronto, Montreal, and Vancouver have lower suicide rates than immigrants in other parts of Canada.

The Canadian Mental Health Association also reports that rates are higher among specific groups. For example, the suicide rate for Inuit peoples living in northern Canada is between 60 and 75 per 100,000, significantly higher than the average rate for the general population cited above. Other groups that are at an increased risk of suicide for their age group are the young and the elderly, inmates in correctional facilities, and people with a mental illness.

Contrary to a common belief, studies show that suicide rates are actually lower during the Christmas season. Late July and August have the highest suicide rate, and some research suggests that this is a high-risk time for vulnerable teens because they are going back to school. The rates are so high among aboriginal youth at this time of year that the Centre for Addiction and Mental Health refers to autumn as the 'suicide season'.

Sources: Statistics Canada, 'Suicide in Canada's Immigrant Population, 1995 to 1997' 'Suicides and Suicide Rate, by Sex and by Age Group'; Suicide Deaths and Suicide Attempts'; and Canadian Mental Health Association, www.ontario.cmha.ca/content/about_mental_illness/suicide.asp?cID=3965

Economic crises produced the contrary effect: a sharp increase in the suicide rate. This, argued Durkheim, is *not* due to the sudden loss of livelihood or amenities, for an increase in prosperity produces the same result as a decline. To account

for this, Durkheim invoked the concept of anomic suicide, caused by the disturbance such crises create in the regulatory aspect of social activity. Subject to deregulation in such crises, people's aspirations overshoot socially contrived limits and
fix on the unattainable. Durkheim spent a great deal of time accounting for people's inherent capacity to adopt this course *unless* they are curbed by social regulation. In striving to convey the character of anomie, Durkheim was driven to his
most rabbinical purple passages. Writing in 1897, he says:

> To pursue a goal which is by definition unobtainable is to condemn oneself
> to a state of perpetual unhappiness. . . . Nothing appears in man's organic nor
> in his psychological constitution which sets a limit to such tendencies . . .
> [i.e., the] quantity of well-being, comfort or luxury legitimately to be craved
> by a human being. . . . It is not human nature which can assign the variable
> limits necessary to our needs. They are thus unlimited so far as they depend
> on the individual alone.[16]

So it was that the entertainer, Elton John, could spend £40,000,000 on himself in a mere twenty months, buying, for instance, £50,000 worth of jewellery a
week and a wig costing £3,500, and owning cars worth an estimated £2,000,000,
including four Bentleys.[17]

If human nature does not set limits, people must receive regulation from an
external authority they respect, and that can only be provided by society. Hence,
economic disasters and sudden surges in prosperity alike disrupt the capacity of
society to exercise this influence, and for a time all regulation is lacking. 'Consequently, there is no restraint upon aspirations. . . . At the very moment when traditional rules have lost their authority, the richer prize offered these appetites
stimulates them and makes them more impatient of control. The state of de-reg-
ulation of anomie is further heightened by passions being less disciplined, precisely when they need more discipline.'

The causal flow is from the prior fracturing of social regulation to the adoption
of unattainable goals to suicide.

It is essential, in Durkheim's view, to avoid confusing that type of suicide—
stemming from the 'malady of infinite aspirations'—with that resulting from the
weakening of the social bond, in which the individual is 'detached from life
because, seeing no goal to which he may attach himself, he feels himself useless
and purposeless'. The two types also display distinctive psychological states at the
point of suicide and affect different groups in society. Egoistic suicide is associated with lassitude, weariness, and a lack of goals; it has its principal victims
among those in intellectual careers. Anomie is associated with irritation, self-dis-
gust, and normlessness, and it draws its recruits from the industrial and commercial world in which anomie is endemic and 'chronic'.

In 1938 Louis Wirth penned a classical contribution to the discussion of
anomie in his essay 'Urbanism as a Way of Life'. He characterized urban life as
superficial, anonymous, and transitory. He felt that while the urban individual
gained a sense of freedom from the emotional ties that were present in life in an

integrated society, he or she also lost a spontaneous self-expression, morale, and sense of participation. He called this a social void, or *anomie*. As he said: 'The clock and the traffic signal are symbolic of the basis of our social order in the urban world. Frequent close physical contact, coupled with great social distance, accentuates the reserve of unattached individuals toward one another and, unless compensated by other opportunities for response, gives rise to loneliness.' [18]

Wirth was also concerned that with the transfer of responsibility for the socialization of the individual outside the family to specialized institutions, the family is weakened as a source of control and the traditional basis of solidarity is undermined.

Despite Durkheim's eloquence, his attempts to differentiate egoism from anomie, and integration from regulation strike many observers as overdone.[19] Indeed, the main point is the tendency for industrialism to lead to what Weber termed the 'disenchantment of the world', with its existential doubts and insecurities. However, a separate issue is whether a state of normlessness is conceivable. This is, after all, an extremity beyond anarchy, which is a society without government. A society without norms seems, on the face of it, a contradiction in terms.

•*Illustrative Research.* In general, cases where such extremes are approached empirically are infrequent, appearing mainly in the very young and the very old. Our only approximations to the anomic in everyday terms are the feral child, the senile and demented, and the psychopath. There are, however, a few good descriptions of societies and communities that come close to Durkheim's conception of the anomic.

In one example, Rainwater's *Behind Ghetto Walls*[20] depicted the mistrustful, nasty, alienated, and fragmented world of the Pruitt-Igoe housing development in St Louis, Missouri. So suspicious and isolated had the tenants of the project become that there was no longer anything approaching a viable social life. People were reluctant to leave their homes for fear of break-ins; everyone was a potential predator. In time, the municipal authority concluded that existence in Pruitt-Igoe was so intolerable that the apartment blocks would have to be physically destroyed by dynamite.

Other examples have been given by Kai Erikson, who described the impact of such diverse disasters as the pollution of a river upon a fishing community; fraud and default upon a group of poor Haitians whose savings were stolen; the Hiroshima bomb; and the near-catastrophe of the Three Mile Island nuclear plant.[21] His most extensive study, *Everything in Its Path*,[22] narrates the devastation caused by the collapse of a dam in the mining community of Buffalo Creek, West Virginia. As 132 million gallons of mud rushed down the creek, it carried away houses, people, roads, and possessions. Neat settlements were replaced by a haphazard trailer camp that had no substantial social and spatial organization. There was an accompanying loss of moral regulation, a decline in co-operativeness, a pervading sense of meaninglessness and a lack of purpose. People retreated inwardly, and rates of alcohol abuse and illegitimate births soared.

Other societies could also be described as anomic. One was that of New Guinea, which, in the path of the American attack on the Japanese in the Pacific in the Second World War, had seen the sudden and inexplicable arrival of military airplanes carrying strange, powerful men and vast treasures and had then seen the airplanes just as inexplicably depart again, never to return. The old economic and religious rationalities seemed to make no more sense. It was better to pray and wait for the strangers to return with their wonderful cargoes. In effect, the emergence of the 'cargo cults' signified a major loss of meaning and purpose.[23]

Another anomic society was the Ik of Northern Uganda, as documented by Turnbull.[24] These 'mountain people' were subjected to a sudden deregulation born of economic catastrophe when their traditional hunting grounds were designated a national park. Though Turnbull does not invoke Durkheim, he lists a mixture of Ik characteristics reminiscent of both egoism and anomie: 'acrimony, envy and suspicion' even among hunting parties;[25] 'excessive individualism, coupled with solitude and boredom';[26] 'lassitude and inertia'.[27] Children over the age of three, and the old or disabled, were abandoned or robbed.

Like Durkheim, Turnbull stresses the similarities between the anomic and the lives that we lead. However, in other respects, Durkheim's analysis does not fit the Ik. They did not lack a goal (as in egoism) for their goal was survival; nor did they 'aspire infinitely' (as in anomie), for they aspired very specifically towards such mundane goals as food and water. Yet, in crucial respects, Durkheim offers more of a vocabulary for the understanding and prediction of the Ik than other classical theorists. The Ik come close enough to anomic to show that sudden deregulation may bring social disaster. The irony is that the best-documented example of this 'disease' of modern industrial man should be a pre-industrial people.

As Turnbull stresses, however, there are echoes of the Ik in the crime-ridden neighbourhoods of America, France, and Britain[28] and in public housing projects where attempts to establish Neighbourhood Watch and similar initiatives fail because neighbours simply do not trust one another to watch their homes. One such divided and fearful London project was described graphically by Sampson:

[An] important feature was the multi-dimensional nature of residents' fears. Their lives were blighted by social conflicts and tensions. Some of these conflicts reflected divisions between gender, race, and age while others were about divergent life-styles, divisions between the employed and the unemployed, disparate values and the use of space on the estate. These differences engendered significant resistances to care watches, improved neighbouring and more effective social control between neighbours and their children. The fear of being attacked was found to be widespread, and for women this was a fear of sexual attack. The interviews with burglary victims showed that fears about burglary were also fears of being personally harmed. Living in run-down high density housing contributed to these 'fears'. Isolation seemed to be another source of anxiety.[29]

Indeed, anomic disorder is studied by many sociologists of deviance. Much of the world appears to them to be veering towards a disequilibrium in which the State and formal social control, as well as community and informal social control, can no longer be taken for granted. One of the most graphic examples has been provided by Mike Davis in his description of a Los Angeles similar to the nightmare worlds in the movies *Blade Runner* and *Mad Max*. Davis argues that public, comprehensive regulation has collapsed in Los Angeles. The rich buy private safety in their own defended enclaves. The poor are exposed only to perfunctory policing that keeps them under token control but offers no security. The outcome is that in the poorest areas, beyond the fortified core in which the rich live and work, may be found 'the halo of barrios and ghettos [where there] is now a free-fire zone where crack dealers and street gangs settle their scores with shotguns and Uzis. . . . Both cops and gang members already talk with chilling matter-of-factness about the inevitability of some manner of urban guerilla warfare.'[30]

What Davis claimed for Los Angeles has been extrapolated to states. 'Institutional anomie' is a term applied in the context of human-rights abuses to describe states verging on illegitimacy because judges and police are corrupt and brutal.[31] Some have alleged that disintegrating economies, dysfunctional governments, unenforceable frontiers, uncontrolled population movement, and the globalization of crime have combined to render the State inoperative as the effective maker and enforcer of law. Governments can no longer ensure security or law and order. Corruption will be endemic. In short, there has arisen in many parts of the world an 'appalling expression of . . . the obliteration of any distinction between political dispute and criminal violence'.[32] War itself will cease to be a relatively disciplined process conducted between the armies of States that wield a monopoly of violence. Rather, it will be replaced by a ubiquitous 'low-intensity conflict' that inflicts previously unsurpassed violence on civilians and armed forces alike.[33]

In '*The Coming Anarchy*', Kaplan writes about the increasing lawlessness of several African countries, the emergence of criminal anarchy, the pursuit of war as an end in itself, the 'privatization of violence', and the breakdown of armies and police forces. His future is bleak indeed: there will be a 'rundown, crowded planet of skinhead Cossacks and *juju* warriors, influenced by the worst refuse of Western pop culture and ancient tribal hatreds, and battling over scraps of over-used earth in guerilla conflicts that ripple across countries and intersect in no discernible pattern'.[34] And there is evidence enough to sustain his argument. When the police of several countries are massively corrupt,[35] when the police molest and rape women complainants,[36] when criminal warlords assume control,[37] when an army smuggles contraband,[38] when a president's airplane is found carrying large quantities of cocaine,[39] when a country's president[40] has been accused of cannibalism, and when a state is called a kleptocracy,[41] it is not difficult to acknowledge the disarray to which Stan Cohen pointed when he wondered whether it was possible any longer to distinguish clearly between crime and politics.

Discussion: Deviance and Culture—Toronto's Jane-and-Finch District

The news was shocking. A young student named Jordan Manners had been shot dead in a school in Toronto's Jane-and-Finch area. Two of his friends were then charged with first-degree murder. The national news had headlines like 'Canada's toughest neighbourhood: Where boundary issues turn deadly.'

As a result, a provincial panel was set up to examine youth violence in Ontario. An inquiry was also held into safety at Jordan's school. In a subsequent police raid on the gang in the public housing project where Jordan lived, 100 arrests were made, and dozens of guns and over a million dollars' worth of illegal drugs were seized.

The easy theme of 'Canada's toughest neighbourhood' played well. Youths interviewed said things like: 'You've got to be deadly. You've got to be strong and brave, and you've got to be willing to fight.'

There were two gangs in the district, the Driftwood Crips, who live north of Finch Avenue, and the Bloods, who live in public housing on the south side of Finch. Each has its own turf, and the intersection of Jane Street and Finch has become the buffer zone between the two groups. The Crips have a violent reputation, but their leadership is weak. On the other hand, the Bloods are less violent and have a more stable organization, more like a traditional organized crime group. The senior leaders look out for the younger members, encouraging them to stay in school and avoid guns.

In this neighbourhood many young people come into conflict with the law for theft, assault, and minor property crimes. And if a legitimate job doesn't exist, one option is to sell crack cocaine. Crime is part of the subculture, a way out, a way to make a living.

The Jane-and-Finch area is the result of the need for public housing in Toronto in the 1960s. The idea was to create an urban suburb with access to transit and close to public services. However, the result was huge housing complexes, where many came from households where the fathers were missing, and the parents had poor jobs or were living on social assistance.

The problem is made worse by funding cuts in education and social services, and the lack of recreational programs for young people. It's called causing crime through the lack of social development. Today, a majority of the residents are visible minorities, and twice as many live in public housing as in Toronto as a whole or in the rest of Canada.

Seven months later a report on the problem of school violence was issued. The author is Julian Falconer, a lawyer and chair of the School Community Safety Advisory Panel. The report, called *The Road to Health: A Final Report on School Safety*, contains more than 100 recommendations to help improve the safety and enhance the culture of the Toronto District School Board.

Falconer says that the problem of school violence is not confined to schools just in that area. On the basis of staff and student surveys, the Panel came to the conclusion that there are guns in schools across the city and that sexual assaults in school have increased. Twenty-three per cent of students reported knowing someone who had taken a gun to school, and 7 per cent of female students said they had been the victim of a major sexual assault at school.

Eighty per cent of students said they would not report cases of violence even if they were the victim. For this reason, Falconer has been quoted as saying that not only is there systemic violence in the school system, but there is also a culture of silence.

These are significant findings, and they point to a problem beyond the stereotypical areas. Far from being a Jane-and-Finch issue, the authors conclude, the problem is city-wide. Furthermore, because of inconsistencies in reporting, the panel concluded that they were probably seeing only the tip of the iceberg.

Since the report was issued, however, the reaction has been divided. The *Toronto Star* has declared that the culture of silence must end, while a school board trustee says it is a myth. The teen's mother blames the school board, while the *National Post* say Falconer hoodwinked the *Toronto Star*.

The long-term solution will require hard work, but only after all sides stop fighting.

Source: Adapted from C. McCormick, 'Fighting over Violence in Toronto Schools' (Crime Matters column), *Daily Gleaner* (Fredericton), 17 January 2008.

Merton's Theory of Anomie

Merton took the conception of anomie as a starting point for fresh theorizing.[42] For Merton, the crucial feature of American society in the Depression of the 1930s was the contrast between the American Dream and the enduring reality of harsh economic inequality.

The difference between that society and the France of the 1890s, in which Durkheim had written, lay chiefly in the dream and not the inequality. In Europe, centuries of inequality were institutionalized in a class society, where despite the French Revolution of 1789, hereditary privilege and status still counted. In contrast, America still held out the promise of an open society. In America, there was no hereditary aristocracy, and in the end it was simply money that counted. Hence the American Dream promised that with hard work anyone would have the opportunity to realize their talents.

In this context, Merton argued that anomie is not exceptional but becomes a routine feature of the social world.[43] In this respect, he came closer to Durkheim's first Hobbesian depiction of anomie as endemic in industrial capitalism.[44] But the *source* of anomie for Merton was not the asymmetry between talent and reward; it lay rather in the lack of symmetry between the culture and the social structure. The 'culture' of the United States was taken to be, at bottom, the American Dream; but the social structure could not yield limitless opportunities for all. As a culture, however, North America pivots on the hope that ultimately everyone can attain prosperity. Infinite aspirations are the very seam of the cultural fabric of the American way of life. Only in America were the conditions of advanced industrial society combined with a distinctive ideology of classless egalitarian democracy. However, the basic argument on which it was based, the consequences of the disjunction between goals and the means of goal attainment, could be applied to any social situation where the same type of disparity arose.

> The American Dream doesn't work in the middle of the Depression.

The pursuit of infinite aspirations was seen by Merton, not as an innate human tendency that emerged whenever social regulation was weakened, but as the product of a particular culture. An essential feature of Merton's theory is his recognition of the dramatic growth of advertising. A necessary adjunct to the growth of mass production and mass distribution was mass consumption. In this respect, Merton is at one with Marx.[45] The fostering of consumption, with its creation of wants and dissatisfactions, is basic to economic growth in 'free-market' economies. American ideology supplied the cultural counterpart of economic accumulation: fluid social mobility, the capacity to make it from log cabin to White House, was transmitted as a core value by the churches, the schools, and the mass media. The 'success' goal was sacred, failure profane, but in a society founded on the repudiation of monarchy and aristocracy, success came to be symbolized by sheer material gain. 'Money-success' was coined by Merton as *the* core value of American society, a 'cultural goal' extolled above all others, and one to be analyzed for the sake of simplicity in what would otherwise be an excessively complicated theory.[46]

For Durkheim, deregulation led to infinite aspirations; for Merton, infinite aspirations led to deregulation. However, the result for both was the same: high rates of deviation. The 'strain to anomie' crystallized in Merton's view in four types of deviance, differentiated by their combination of either acceptance or rejection of the goal and the means for realizing the goal (see Table 5.2).

Despite the formidable strain to anomie, the majority of the population adhered, in Merton's view, to *conformity*. The mass of middle America remained small-town Puritans, wedded to cautious advancement but with an eye to the main chance. Their conformity ensured some social stability. For those unable to hold the socio-cultural tensions in balance, however, four 'deviant adaptations' were available.

Table 5.2: Types of Individual Adaptation to Goals and Means

		Institutionally Available Means	
		Acceptance	Rejection
Culturally prescribed goal(s)	acceptance	Conformity	Innovation
	rejection	Ritualism	Retreatism

The first of these, '*innovation*', basically involved the adoption of illegitimate means to the attainment of the cultural goal, 'money-success'. This was not so much a crisis of meaning, as a crisis of means, in that deviance became a different way to the same end, whether that was crime or joining a cult.[47] Racketeering was the deviant response to the small-town Puritans' recipe for conformity, namely, Prohibition, but any chicanery in politics or worldly affairs would exemplify deviant innovation just as well.

> Racketeering is the response to Prohibition.

Its mirror image, '*ritualism*', entailed the elimination of the goal and an obsessive attachment to the institutional means, such as the celebration of sticking to the rules that characterizes much of respectable lower- and middle-class life.

'*Retreatism*' involves the rejection of both goals *and* means, by dropping out of conventional society and yet not consciously striving to construct one afresh; his key examples are the tramp, the hobo, and the drug user.

Finally, '*rebellion*', not in the table, is seen as the rare attempt to resolve the tensions, by rejecting both aspects of the status quo, and by actively seeking to replace them by alternative goals and means. Merton illustrated his thesis with a wealth of symbolic references to cultural myths.

Durkheim had argued that the social pressure exerted by the layers above them limit the aspirations of the lower orders: 'Those who have only empty space above them are almost inevitably lost in it'.[48] And John Hagan later agreed, arguing that those at the summit of business corporations can experience a kind of giddy lack of restraint that permits them to deviate.[49] However, Merton's conclusion is that owing to the more intense and widespread experience of the disparity between the goal and the means at the bottom of the social hierarchy, deviance is inversely related to social status:

> Of those located in the lower reaches of the social structure, the culture makes incompatible demands. . . . In this setting, a cardinal American virtue—'ambition'—promotes a cardinal American vice—'deviant behaviour'. . . . Within this context, Al Capone represents the triumph of amoral intelligence over morally prescribed 'failure' when the channels of vertical mobility are closed or narrowed in a society that places a high premium on economic affluence and social ascent for *all* its members.[50]

Merton's brief statement of anomie theory was first published in 1938 and was revised in the four more editions that his major textbook has gone through in the last seventy years. For almost half that period, it received almost uncritical acceptance; however, since the early 1960s, it has been over-critically rejected. Before going on to the criticisms that have real substance, it is useful to look at those that appear misplaced.

• *The first of these is that Mertonian anomie theory presumes a simple consensus about the primacy of 'money-success' as a cultural goal.* It is necessary to point out that sharing a goal does not imply simple consensus. Anomie theory does not collapse when confronted with the realities of class and value conflict. In his analysis of class conflict, for example, Westergaard documented the division of life chances, in terms of wealth, income, health, educational achievement, mobility, and even access to welfare. An aggravating feature of class conflict is the revolution in rising expectations that surpasses the material possibilities of their fulfilment and promotes what Marshall termed 'mild economic anomie'. The fostering of consumption means that all come to share the aspirations once reasonable only for the élite: 'the luxuries of today become the necessities of tomorrow'.[51] This process is entirely in accord with Merton's theory.

•*A second criticism is that, as Merton himself had recognized, in a diverse and complex society, 'money-success' is not the only goal.* It competes with a myriad of other goals for a claim on energy and time, or it is itself mainly a *means* to quite different goals, such as family support and well-being. It may be successfully resisted by a minority of active 'rebels', but so all-pervasive is the cash nexus that such 'rebellion' is rare and may well be replaced by an equally exclusive 'cultural goal', such as membership in a religious elect or of a party élite. The abolition of private property heightened the attractiveness of the perquisites of high office in State socialist societies. Merton's own defence would be that to consider all the goals pursued by Americans would have unnecessarily complicated the analysis. Nonetheless, it is interesting how successive theorists have discussed deviance as an alternative means to an end, whether the goal being promoted is material success or celebrity status.

•*A third criticism is that Merton's theory is both ahistorical and lacking in critical perspective.* Laurie Taylor compares Merton's image of society to that of a giant slot machine,[52] whose pay-outs are rigged but which most players delude themselves into believing them to be fair. The deviants are those who try to rig the machine to *their* advantage, or play it blindly and obsessively, or ignore its existence, or smash it up and seek a better model. Nowhere, however, says Taylor, does Merton tell us who is taking the profits and who put the machine there in the first place. This criticism applies more to Merton's exposition of his theory than to the validity of the theory itself, for it would strengthen the theory rather than the reverse if it were to be prefaced by a history of American capitalist exploitation and a synopsis of who owns what.

■ Anomie and After

Merton would never have described himself as a sociologist of deviance. His interest lay in formal theorizing and in the sociology of science and knowledge. Although his account of anomie was central to the analysis of deviance, it was also oddly brief. Anomie was discussed in two essays that were never long enough to develop more than a few of its possibilities. There was to be very little reply to many of the criticisms subsequently levelled at his thesis. It would not have been difficult to form a response or adapt his theory, but his ideas on anomie were left in limbo.

•*In a sympathetic but critical reappraisal of Merton's theory by one of his students,*[53] *Albert Cohen noted that its author had laid it out in a way that was surprisingly insulated,* not only from allied work in the sociology of deviance in the 1920s and 1930s, but also from his own contributions to general sociology, that is, reference group theory and role theory.[54]

Reference group theory has alerted us to the limited social worlds in which people invest their energies. We usually compare ourselves, not with the upper echelons or the supremely successful, but with the peer groups of our own age, sex, and approximate social position. For example, manual workers tend to compare themselves with other manual workers, rather than with dukes.[55]

Role theory is concerned with the kinds of people it is possible to be in a society and with how roles are allocated and taken on; we are mostly preoccupied with roles that are accessible to us, and not with those beyond our reach. Had Merton combined these different aspects of his own theorizing, he would have made a more realistic thesis. As it stands, anomie theory is static, individualistic, and mechanistic and is focused on 'initial states and deviant outcomes rather than on processes whereby actions are elaborated and transformed'.[56] People do not jump from conformity to deviance without a prior sounding-out process. Cohen's contribution to meeting this difficulty, while retaining the strengths of the goals-means formulation, was the concept of subcultural process. It is in the development of different versions of subcultures of deviance that anomie theory has remained most influential. Merton was himself later to acknowledge that a neglect of differential association had been a defect in his work. He had, he wrote candidly, 'simply failed to "seize the opportunity" of consolidating the two strands of sociological thought'.[57]

> The idea of subculture explains one way that anomie works as a process.

Otherwise, anomie as an explicit concept has been little more than marginal in the development of post-war theories of social problems and has been almost totally absent from theories of social structure. Empirically, despite many attempts, it did not lend itself to survey work or field methods of observation.[58] Becker parodied the theory in mocking students who failed to find it on visits to car factories.[59] Like phlogiston in eighteenth-century physics, it increasingly appeared to be an artefact of an outmoded view of the social universe. The few serious attempts to measure its incidence have not established support for the theory in any direct sense.

Stinchcombe found the strongest pressures for 'rebellion' lay among middle-class high-school boys, whose commitment to success goals was most marked and whose failure to achieve the most resented.[60] This finding has implications for any theory that invokes anomie and/or subcultural variants as an explanation for middle-class delinquency, but it undermined confidence in Merton's overall theoretical emphasis on high rates of deviance among the lower classes.

Mizruchi complicated the model further by suggesting that middle-class anomie ('boundlessness') differed fundamentally from working-class anomie ('bondlessness').[61] Srole's 'anomie scale' employed questions designed to elicit the extent to which people felt at home in the world, but items such as 'little can be accomplished in a society that is seen as basically unpredictable and lacking order' appeared more as tests of political orthodoxy than existential unease.[62] Such tests were so reliant on ambiguous indicators and subjective measures of 'deviance' that the theory faded from serious consideration.

• *Yet the questions raised most profoundly by anomie theory recur in various guises*, not least as the central strand in left realism, and also as the underlying concern in theories of crime, modernization, and development.[63] The inference is that:

> in the pre-modern age sanctions controlled individual actions by external controls. But with the development of civilization, controls are slowly shifted inwards. . . . If Elias's hypothesis is correct that interpersonal relations change with the civilization of society, then so should the nature of interpersonal violence and crime. Important indicators of this process of civilization would be a decline in violent crime and an increase in self-inflicted harm (i.e., drugs) on individuals.[64]

In Garland's summary:

> . . . typically, the civilizing process in culture involves a tightening and a differentiation of the controls imposed by society upon individuals, a refinement of conduct, and an increased level of psychological inhibition as the standards of proper conduct become ever more demanding. . . . It is the specific and fragile outcome of an evolutionary process which was socially determined though by no means inexorable, and which may at any time be reversed if wars, revolutions, or catastrophes undermine the forms of social organization and interdependence upon which it depends.[65]

These changes of sensibility became widely diffused in the course of the twentieth century and are seen to entail a shift from brutal and degrading to less punitive and more restrained forms of punishment.[66] Yet, as Garland notes, the thesis underplays the force of political, economic, and institutional change.[67] Garland says some support can be found for a long-term and substantial decline in violent crime in English society from the thirteenth to the twentieth centuries'. Gurr[68] attributes this decline to the growing sensitivity to violence and the development of increased internal and external controls on aggressive behaviour, as do others.[69] There seems little doubt that, whatever the reasons, violence and aggression in civil society were massively and progressively reined in over the period from the late medieval to the mid-twentieth century.

> Violence and aggression have decreased since medieval times.

• *The very strength of this evidence, however, serves to magnify the problem of how one might account for trends since the mid-twentieth century* in terms of this theory. For if, as Elias contends, psychic configurations have been restructured and profound cultural transformations have enveloped whole societies, the rise in rates of violent crime since the 1950s becomes truly anomalous. One can only assume that the growing sensitivity to violence widened the net to include minor assaults that would previously have gone unreported and unrecorded;[70] or we must assume a greatly increased propensity to violence among a minority somehow untouched by the civilizing process.

An allied problem with the thesis is its inability to account, not simply for wars, revolutions, and catastrophes, but also for the capacity of the most highly

civilized societies to degenerate into what can only be called genocidal abat-
toirs.[71] These questions remain largely unanswered,[72] but they present particular difficulties for a thesis pivoting on a conception of civilization that does not,
as in Durkheim's idea of anomie, allow for the sudden collapse of hard-won
moral regulation.

'Modernization' theories of crime stress the disruptive impact of industrialization and urbanization on traditional ways of life.[73] For example, Heiland and
Shelley argue:

> Modernization is a continually developing process of structural differentia-
> tion, combined with an increase in the complexity of the norms of social
> organization. . . . Modernization does not always lead to more contentment
> and harmony. Rather, enhanced social tensions, conflicts and social dishar-
> mony are the results of social differentiation, the growing number of life
> choices, and the relative deprivation that accompanies the modernization
> process. . . .With modernization, a shift occurs in the relationship among
> forms of criminal behavior. Violent offenses become less important as prop-
> erty offenses achieve pre-eminence. . . . As modernization proceeds, inequal-
> ity still exists, . . . [and] the crime pattern begins to change from crimes
> typical of poverty to crimes common to the affluent society. Many property
> crimes are not caused by societal or individual crises such as unemployment
> or illness, but by wealth and the abundance of goods.[74]

Empirical support for the theory was found by Schichor,[75] who explored the
relationship between patterns and trends of crime and various socio-economic
factors in forty-five countries: 'Modernization is negatively associated with violent crime (homicide) and positively associated with property crime (larceny).'
Economic development increases the availability of material possessions and their
cultural importance. Property crimes are also more likely to be reported and
recorded in more modern societies so that insurance claims can be made.

Overall, theories of civilization, modernization, and crime cover much the same
ground as anomie theories, but they avoid, presumably deliberately, the emphasis on the damage wrought by the pursuit of 'infinite aspirations' that links
Durkheim and Merton. The analytical need to integrate the 'civilizing process'
with that of 'modernization' leads to loose rule-of-thumb judgments, such as
'Japan appears to be a developed society that has succeeded in both developing
and civilizing' and 'it would be presumptuous to suggest that the tendency
towards civilization is absent in the USA', but high rates of violent crime and
punishment do show 'how difficult it is to maintain the standards of a civilized
society'.[76]

Similar problems arise in the use of evolutionist concepts in the work of
Clinard and Abbott on crime in developing countries.[77] Rapid urbanization and
uneven industrialization in developing countries are seen as the crucial preconditions for soaring rates of crime and delinquency. In what has come to be

regarded as the orthodox perspective on crime in developing countries, they proposed a neo-Durkheimian perspective based on the mismatch between rapid change and social regulation, and hinged on the assumption that once developing countries 'catch up' with the developed, delinquency rates will level off, at least in their violent form. Sumner is scathingly critical of this fundamental misconception of modernization in the developing world as a 'delayed replay of nineteenth-century European development with its extensive urbanization and industrialization . . . held up (mainly) by the deep sleep of 'custom' or the rigid ties of 'tradition'.[78]

It is all too evident that no such exact parallel exists. The global expansion of nineteenth-century Western capitalism was relatively unfettered, unlike the situation in late twentieth-century developing countries. As Sumner says, 'modernization' theory sees crime only as a result of 'development' and the criminal law as the necessary counterpoint to crime. What it does not see is all the criminal law and crime that went into the very making of 'underdevelopment'. Sumner is, however, too sweeping in his condemnation. In Hong Kong, for example, anti-corruption measures and economic development made some impact on rates of violent crime.[79] In short, there are huge variations to be mapped, and while some of the studies we have cited have made an impressive beginning, the dismissal of anomie theories or the stripping down of them to their critical elements in the pursuit of somewhat bland notions of 'modernization' and development, seem premature.

A major exception to the above is Messner and Rosenfeld's 'institutional-anomie theory'.[80] In an important development of Merton's theory, they 'assign a critical role to structural dynamics and the balance among major social institutions such as the economy, the family, and the polity. Accordingly, the form of institutional structure that is particularly conducive to high levels of crime is one in which the economy dominates the institutional balance of power'.[81] The economic institutions weaken the capacity of the family and the school to socialize the young and exert informal controls effectively. The concept of the 'decommodification of labour' can be used to measure the degree to this, in societies that make the political choice to intervene in the market in order to guarantee citizens adequate levels of welfare, militates against high crime rates.

Decommodification exhibits a strong negative effect on homicide rates. This lends credibility to the larger theoretical framework of anomie theory. It also explicitly supports the belief that a mixed economy and generous social security provision offer the best basis for stable prosperity. As Messner and Rosenfeld point out, however, in the aftermath of the Cold War, the 'balance of institutional power' is now threatened as capitalism undermines the welfare and citizenship gains brought into being as a result. The commitment to welfare has now been empirically linked cross-nationally with protections against high rates of homicide and higher levels of imprisonment.[82] Too marked a reduction in welfare spending would, in all likelihood, have unwanted consequences on both fronts.

■ The Crisis of Social Capital

Concerns about social and economic change have increasingly taken the form of anxiety about a decline in social capital, the latest phase in the long-standing preoccupation with the retreat from 'community'. The adoption of the term 'social capital', notably by Bourdieu, Coleman, and Putnam,[83] has reinvigorated and reshaped those concerns.

Community had come to have a folksy connotation and has been devalued by its endless invocation by politicians. It had also been lent a disciplinary dimension in community crime-prevention programs[84] and in the exclusion of deviants who threaten family and group cohesion. However, social capital connotes the importance of social networks as a whole rather than purely neighbourhood-based relations.

Bourdieu notes that social capital involves 'transforming contingent relations, such as those of neighbourhood, the workplace or even kinship, into relationships that are at once necessary and elective, implying durable obligations subjectively felt (feelings of gratitude, respect, friendship, etc.)'. Thus, network ties must also be of a particular type—trusting and positive.[85]

In a society denuded of social capital, people can literally take nothing for granted. Such a society would be scarcely worthy of the name, would, in short, be little more than a state of anomie.

Social capital has, as a concept, strong Durkheimian roots. As Durkheim wrote in *The Division of Labour in Society*:

> But it is not only outside of contractual relations, it is in the play of those relations themselves that social action makes itself felt. For everything in the contract is not contractual. . . . The greater part of our relations with others is of a contractual nature. If, then, it were necessary each time to begin the struggles anew, to again go through the conferences necessary to establish firmly all the conditions of agreement for the present and the future, we would be put to rout. For all these reasons, if we were linked only by the terms of our contracts, as they are agreed upon, only a precarious solidarity would result. . . . In sum, a contract is not sufficient unto itself, but is possible only thanks to a regulation of the contract which is originally social.[86]

Social capital is much the same, therefore, as Durkheim's notion of the noncontractual elements of contract—the active ingredient that makes societies both tick and hang together. Shorn of social capital, people are not only adrift in a state of anomie but are also more liable to fall prey to authoritarian remedies born of desperation. If social capital drops too far democracy is on the line.

Hence the urgency with which the issue is addressed in two major works: Robert Putnam's *Bowling Alone* (2000) and Richard Sennett's *The Corrosion of Character* (1998). Putnam documents the withdrawal of Americans from group and community life at every level since the 1950s—from the family to voting, from bowling to having friends over for dinner, from voluntary work to attending home-and-school meetings, from churchgoing to trade union membership. Four main reasons are explored empirically, more or less in order of importance:

- Television and the computer keep people at home and apart even there;
- Residential sprawl keeps people driving alone as commuters for three hours a day, draining them of time and energy for joint social activities;
- Two-career families experience pressure to put their jobs first and everything else second;
- Each successive generation after the Second World War has increasingly withdrawn from social life.

Putnam says getting ahead has become much more highly valued than getting together. Making good is pursued far more intensively than doing good.

> Getting ahead is valued more than getting together.

There is some debate over Putnam's thesis. For example, Paxton[87] has challenged some empirical aspects of Putnam's thesis, notably the stable rates of group membership over the four decades 1950–90. However, the important issue is that Putnam argues that states with high social capital do better economically, in the human-capital terms of health and education, democratically in terms of tolerance and freedom from persecution, and socially in terms of lower rates of deviance and disorder. Can the decline be reversed and social capital revived? He claims that it happened before—in the 'Progressive' era of 1900–1915 following the extreme inequalities of the Gilded Age of the late nineteenth century—and therefore can happen again. However, his prospects for the revival of community pin their hope on such things as the encouragement of extracurricular activities in high schools, a remedy dwarfed by the scale of the crisis it is meant to resolve.

Putnam does not engage with the post-1970 rise of globalization and the changed political economy. Nowhere does he mention the huge rise in imprisonment in the United States, and yet arguably the greatest perverse side-effect of dwindling social capital is its replacement by *penal* capital. Despite the severe limitations of equating more punishment with less crime, *some* effect is to be expected from imprisonment on so huge a scale as that experienced in the United States over the past three decades, in which two million adults, some 2 per cent of the male labour force, half of them black and one-fifth Hispanic, are locked away, and a further two million are under the disciplinary constraints of probation and parole. Without invoking that harsh reality, Putnam is unable to account for the coincidence of declining social capital and falling rates of crime.

Many democratic societies are now perilously close to re-imposing a segregative regime of penal exclusion combined with punitive surveillance on its most discriminated-against minority groups.[88] 'Governing through crime' entails increasing claims to legitimacy by 'punitive populism',[89] surveillance, and exclusion, a symbolic politics replacing those of inclusion and solidarity. This trend remains most developed in the United States.

However, although 'dual career' families may be thought to contribute to a decline in social capital, they could equally well be seen as enriching social capital.[90] Also, too little regard is paid to policies that have succeeded in tempering

American individualism on the grounds of equality of opportunity. The post-1970 era of globalization and de-industrialization legitimized a more *macho* form of individualism than at any time since the Gilded Age, and not only in the United States.

Current trends in policing can be related to the decline of more indirect sources of social control. There has been a marked decrease in employment in a range of occupations providing natural surveillance, in part as a result of the development and spread of new labour-saving technologies such as ticket machines and automatic barriers in train and transit stations, CCTV, and automated access control to buildings and parts of buildings. The spread and impact of such technologies were encouraged by public policies that sought to maximize profit through reductions in labour costs.[91]

The huge rise in private, commercial security has been at the expense of the public police. The loss of social capital does not, however, figure on the economic capital balance sheet. In the longer term, however, the loss of trust has profoundly adverse economic consequences, as neoconservatives now acknowledge a century after Durkheim spelt them out.[92]

To John Hagan, in contrast to Putnam, the resurgence of inequality is pivotal. The central point is that the concentration of poverty intensifies the links between weak labour force attachment and deviance. As Baron and Hartnagel point out, youths who experience unemployment and who also perceive labour market unfairness are at much higher risk of committing deviance.[93]

The result of inequality, according to Hagan, is a dramatic loss of all kinds of capital, from physical and financial to social and cultural.'[94] Delinquent subcultures are a form of *re*-capitalization in the wake of the huge capital disinvestments in previously prosperous industries and the communities they sustained. The most abundant evidence for that equation can be found in the illicit drug economies that have flourished in the most economically and socially deprived areas. Several studies, both ethnographic[95] and quantitative[96] draw out the links between structural changes and community-level consequences that make for depleted social capital and burgeoning crime. It is not simply that low social capital deprives those it disadvantages (especially young men) of job opportunities and exposes them to heightened risks of crime. It is also that high social capital protects those it advantages from being labelled as criminals for youthful misdeeds, as would happen in lower-class areas. 'Deviance service industries' for drugs, vice, gambling, and 'protection', become yet more central to local economies depleted of social capital, just as changes in the macro-economy entail the shedding of yet more mainstream jobs.[97]

There is in all of these big pictures of social change a tendency to reify and stereotype. Just as Herbert Gans challenged Whyte's picture of conforming suburban man in his detailed study of diversity, *The Levittowners* (1967), so may Sennett be over-generalizing and over-interpreting from a very few sources and accounts. Yet the 'new' order shows the force of his arguments to have even more to them than he allows. Durkheim was right—capitalism and its attendant utilitarian philosophies depend on the 'non-contractual elements in contract' after all.

> Crime is a form of economic activity.

Case Study—Work in the New Capitalism

Richard Sennett explores similar themes to Putnam's in his *The Corrosion of Character: The Personal Consequences of Work in the New Capitalism*. He argues that the 'new capitalism' generates work of a quite different character to that of the 'old'—it is not only more insecure and short-term but more mystifying and fragmented. Power has been reconstituted rather than democratically constrained. Political economy now 'consists of three elements: discontinuous reinvention of institutions; flexible specialization of production; and concentration without centralization of power'.[1] All are lauded as integral to success in the globalized marketplace. All entail a 'loss of narrative' on which to base not only identity but also trust, loyalty, and commitment. Not surprisingly, social capital—the commitment to community and shared ways of resolving conflict—is gravely weakened by these conditions. Freedom is not enhanced by this shift, and older forms of resistance to exploitation are continually eroded.

Sennett's sources are non-traditional, but real. Rico, the son of a caretaker who, unlike his father, had become a 'success', had nevertheless been drained of any sense of a meaningful relationship to work in the process of several job changes. Rose, in middle age, ventured into advertising from her own business of running a bar, yet returned after a year baffled and defeated: 'I lost my nerve.' A group of former IBM employees, victims of seismic downsizing, go through phases of blaming the Jewish Chief Executive and cheap Asian labour before settling on their own lack of entrepreneurship as the cause of their job losses. Sennett uses these sources creatively in his analysis, much as Max Weber used the key figure of Benjamin Franklin to authenticate his thesis on the Protestant ethic and the spirit of capitalism.

The case is immensely persuasive but also problematic. The best of the 'old' capitalist order, its coherent career building for the middle class and its stable and worthy employment for the working class, is compared with the worst of the 'new'—the amoral and blame-free culture of the advertising world, for example. But what became of David Riesman's 'other-directed' conformists of *The Lonely Crowd* (1950) or the bureaucratic time-servers of William H. Whyte's *The Organization Man* (1956)? There wasn't much sense of character or narrative drive there, either; so what has changed? It can be argued that what Sennett has done is take on the task that C. Wright Mills (1959) urged on his fellow sociologists over fifty years ago: to answer the question 'What kinds of character will come to predominate in our social structure?' The answer seems to be a set of super-predators on top (not the delinquents of DeIullio but the CEOs of Enron, World.com, and Arthur Andersen) and a vast array of what Durkheim termed 'disaggregated individuals' for the rest. What has changed is the trained incapacity to resist.

[1] R. Sennett, *The Corrosion of Character: The Personal Consequences of Work in the New Capitalism*, 47.

There is one further point to be factored in. The road to anomie in Western social democracies has been cleared of a significant roadblock—the spectre of communism no longer haunts the world. It was that threat that galvanized capitalism to adopt the mixed economy, the 'welfare state', the right to unionize, and the full panoply of social-democratic alternatives to the extremes of capitalism or communism. With the spectre removed since 1989, there are already signs of significant shifts away from social democracy to neo-liberal models of political economy. The implications for deviance and its control are, from the anomie perspective, clear. It is a race for crime control between a reliance on penal capital[98] and the recovery of social democracy.

Towards an Anomic Culture?

In his most recent book, *The Culture of the New Capitalism* (2006), Richard Sennett takes his analysis a stage further, seeing a new kind of character that is needed in order to flourish in the fragmented society that has ensued from economic growth in an environment of de-industrialization and the dominance of the electronically powered, global institutions of corporate financial 'service' industries. This character is 'a self oriented to the short term, focused on potential ability, willing to abandon past experience . . . an unusual sort of human being. Most people are not like this'.[99] While 'the new economy is still only a small part of the whole economy' and should *not* be regarded as the inevitable future, its influence is becoming all-pervasive—in welfare, education, and health care as well as in its core location in the hi-tech conglomerates.

Culture cannot long be immune to such fundamental changes in social and economic structures. In the realm of production and employment, the rise of what might be termed 'hit-and-run' capitalism in the 1980s devalued long-term growth in favour of short-term gains. The leveraged buyout, which transcended management, became the ideal. Stable, lasting careers became subject to delayering, casualization, and non-linear sequencing. Rampant inequality brought in its wake what Jock Young has termed 'a veritable chaos of reward',[100] consisting of huge gains for those at the pinnacle of the new hierarchies of wealth and power and uncertain earnings for those at the base of the service industries.[101]

The replacement of stable bureaucracies by 'fluid' organizations, staffed by the graduates of the new business schools, jettisons two essential components of social and personal cohesion: deferred gratification and long-term strategic thinking. Other resulting social deficits are a low commitment to the institution, low trust in the top echelons, and poor institutional knowledge, much of which inhered in low-status workers. Talent in the form of experience and expertise that had developed over time is replaced by talent measured by indicators of 'potential', such as flexibility and presentational skills. These are the surface 'knowledge' of the consultancy, not the practical and long-honed skills of the craftsman and the professional.

Three new 'sources of uselessness' now render job holding even more precarious: (1) the export of skilled work to low-wage economies, sometimes called moving production offshore, usually to countries with weaker environmental regulations; (2) 'true' automation, in which microelectronics and computers have pushed mechanization to levels where very large numbers of skilled workers become expendable (though this was long predicted for manual workers, it now affects routine white-collar work as well); and (3) the expansion of ageing, now pervading the culture to such an extent that even thirty-year-olds in certain jobs feel 'over the hill'.

The result for the middle-class and middle-aged is a generation of Willy Lomans (in Arthur Miller's classic *Death of a Salesman,* 1949), whose predicament is now far more prevalent.

Despite a catalogue of economic casualties, environmental and social costs, as long as the system keeps on delivering greater prosperity, the show stays on the road. Momentum is sustained by new forms of what Marx termed commodity fetishism. Rising levels of consumption are no longer driven only by the prime modern phenomena of built-in obsolescence and the 'motor of fashion'.[102] To them can now be added 'branding', based on the increased technological capacity to 'gold-plate' products, Sennett's term for the superficial differentiation of a basic standard object 'so that the surface is what counts': add-ons to any goods or services that inflate price for minimal production cost.[103] An example is business-class travel by train or plane that makes no difference at all to travel time but offers a bit more space. A second innovation is the exploitation of 'potency', or the selling of unrealizable potential. The SUV stuck in traffic is the emblem of unrealizable potency in its starkest form. The innovations of ceaseless 'choice' and unrealizable fulfillment are all too redolent of the pressures towards states of anomie.

Political parties also 'gold-plate' their differences but increasingly share common ground in offering a far narrower range of choices: a neo-liberal economy with a decreasing commitment to public sector welfare, and an increasing reliance on the 'market' for future delivery of health, education, criminal justice, and income-maintenance policies. Unrealizable potency inheres in the vast investment in armaments that dwarfs foreign aid, and penal policies that aim to eliminate not only deviance but much anti-social behaviour. Moreover, an enfeebled culture flows from the new capitalism, a culture that veers towards the anomic and away from sustained relationships. Anomic culture may be a contradiction in terms, but the paradox may become all too real unless countermovements to such trends can be generated.

■ Criticism

Durkheim's demand that 'social facts' should be 'treated as things' is the basis for his particular form of sociological positivism. But even the most sympathetic reader of *Suicide* cannot fail to be struck by Durkheim's boldness in bending 'the facts' to suit his theory. 'Crises' are classified as such on several occasions to suit the suicide rate, rather than being allowed to stand as anomalies. For example, the unification of Italy is treated as an economic, not as a political, event, primarily because it coincided with a rise rather than a decline in the suicide rate. Certain elections that produced, in Durkheim's view, a change in the suicide rate comparable in scale and intensity to the major crises of 1830, 1848, and 1870 lead him to comment, 'Mild as they are, mere election crises sometimes have the same result (as crises of war and revolution)'.[104]

Criticism One

We have already pointed to Douglas's argument that Durkheim's whole approach was based on a methodological fallacy.[105] The flaw can be illustrated by Durkheim's treatment of the different suicide rates of Protestants and Catholics, important to his concept of egoism. Durkheim asserted that *both* groups strongly opposed suicide on theological grounds and therefore the differences between the two groups' rates of suicide could not be accounted for in terms of their belief structures. Rather, it was the Protestant emphasis on free inquiry that weakened the social bond and promoted greater strain towards egoistic suicide among Protestants. Douglas criticizes Durkheim for not going beyond sheer assertion on so crucial a point, since the Catholic doctrine concerning suicide which entails eternal damnation is far more emphatic than Protestant doctrine. The point for Douglas, however, is not simply that Durkheim was wrong on a specific point, however crucial; it is that his method of reliance on official rates eliminated the possibility of eliciting such meanings from individuals.

Criticism Two

Differences in the official rates of suicide were taken by Durkheim to be social facts sui generis. Douglas asserts by contrast that they are prone to all the weaknesses inherent in official statistics and are most prone to distortion in just those respects where differences in the rates are most crucial, as in the case of Protestants and Catholics, or at times of crisis. Durkheim tried to defend himself against the charge that many of the variations he noted were administrative artefacts caused, for example, by the disruption of the administrative machinery for the registration of suicides. He argued on several occasions that if this was the case the rates would be affected only in the areas where disruption was located, whereas in reality the variations were far more widespread.

Douglas, however, is concerned to stress the ways in which officials are themselves influenced by the social meanings of suicide. For example, the view that social situations such as isolation may promote suicide, may cause coroners to return such a verdict in otherwise ambiguous cases. Researchers then proceed to establish isolation as a 'cause' of suicide, and the theory appears confirmed.

Social meanings also pervade the presentation of death in everyday life. Durkheim's confidence in the suicide statistics is summed up in his phrase 'a corpse is a corpse', but if, for example, some groups rather than others, for doctrinal and/or social reasons, have a strong interest in concealing or disguising suicides, the official rates may compound this practice.

Durkheim himself allowed for the passive as well as the active suicide, the person who fails to stop him- or herself from falling as distinct from jumping, but failed to follow this insight through. In his enumeration of suicides classified by manner of death, such processes as drowning, leaping from a high place, and hanging outnumber poisonings and other forms of self-inflicted destruction less amenable to ready classification as suicide.[106]

Douglas's alternative approach, the close scrutiny of suicide notes and allied correspondence, was expressly ruled out by Durkheim, who assumed that official rates were valid because of the regularity and stability of such rates. But the fallacy is to assume that official rates and indices are somehow constructed independently of social meanings.

Criticism Three

This criticism was employed with even greater force against the assumption of Merton that the lower class were pressured into higher rates of deviance than the middle and upper classes. 'Anomie theory stands accused of predicting far too little bourgeois criminality and too much proletarian criminality.'[107] This time it is the acceptance of the official rates of crime and delinquency, rather than that of suicide, which is seen as unwarranted. By accepting a simple inverse relationship between deviance and social status, Merton reduces anomie theory to that of 'relative deprivation'.[108] Once this prop is removed, the theories that base themselves upon it can be seen as mystifications blurring our view of 'deviance, reality, and society'. Such a perspective is reproduced in police practices, which focus far more on public working-class than on private middle- or upper-class criminality. These practices naturally lead to official statistics that lend credence to the theory, and so, in a self-confirmatory circle, a politically innocuous conception of deviance is propagated.

Criticism Four

Lindesmith and Gagnon note the severe limitations of both Merton's theory of anomie and one of its variants, the 'double failure' hypothesis of Cloward and Ohlin, in accounting for the social character of addiction.[109] Merton had typified addicts, along with vagrants, inebriates, and psychotics, as retreatists, that is, 'as non-productive liabilities' and as 'asocialized persons who are *in* society but not *of* it', who have both 'relinquished culturally prescribed goals and abandoned the quest for success'.[110] Even if it is conceded that not all anomie produces deviance and not all deviance flows from anomie, Lindesmith and Gagnon argue that the theory fails to specify clearly *which* forms of addiction may flow from anomie; or to confront the reverse proposition, that addiction may lead to anomie; or to square with the specialized social skills that addicts must develop if they are to survive the control measures against them and finance a highly expensive habit; or to convey the complexity of the social worlds constructed by the diverse groups so readily tagged 'asocial'. The application of anomie theory to a specific form of deviance raises doubts about its capacity either to explain or to enhance our understanding of the origins, consequences, and processes of development of deviance in general.

Criticism Five

Lemert argues that the theory 'strains credulity' for reasons that go beyond the purely logical or empirical.

First, the very terms so confidently used by Merton to sustain his theory are problematic: 'social structure' and 'culture' are abstractions that are exceptionally difficult to substantiate. 'Inescapable circularity lies in the use of "culture" as a summary to describe tendencies in the behaviour of human beings and, at the same time, as a term of designating the causes of those tendencies.'[111] The same term, 'culture', tends to be applied across the board to the small-scale, relatively unified societies, and also to the highly differentiated agglomeration of often diverse sub-societies.

> It is theoretically conceivable that there are or have been societies in which values learned in childhood, taught as a pattern, and reinforced by structured controls, serve to predict the bulk of the everyday behaviour of members and to account for prevailing conformity to norms. However, it is easier to describe the model than to discover societies which make a good fit with the model.[112]

Lemert prefers a model of a pluralistic society, in which different groups and associations negotiate compromises that are close to a consensus over some ultimate values.

> One objection to Merton's view of choice and action by individuals is that it simplifies something enormously complex. Instead of seeing the individual as a relatively free agent making adaptations pointed toward a consistent value order, it is far more realistic to visualize him as 'captured' . . . by the claims of various groups to which he has given his allegiance [familial, occupational, religious, ethnic, and political ties]. It is in the fact that these claims are continually being preemptively asserted through group action at the expense of other claims, frequently in direct conflict, that *we find the main source of 'pressures' on individuals in modern society*, rather than in 'cultural emphasis on goals'.[113]

It is possible to refine Merton's conception to take account of Lemert's quite distinct model of social structure and culture, but only at the cost of reducing the intensity of the 'strain' induced by the discrepancy between goals and means to far milder levels than he proposed.

Secondly, Merton's theory neglects altogether the implications of social control for the shaping of deviant behaviour. Lemert's critique takes two major forms.

One is the need to allow theoretically for the promotion of 'active' as well as 'passive' social control; the second is the need to differentiate between 'primary' and 'secondary' deviation. Active social control refers to the growing organizational tendency in complex industrial societies with a high rate of technologically induced growth to regulate activity in purely instrumental ways. For example, the regulation of pollution, industrial safety, traffic, and commercial and financial transactions is only negligibly concerned with the imputation of stigmas and moral evaluations and is primarily designed to enforce minimum standards of compliance that do not signally interfere with production and profits. Innovation, far from emerging as a 'deviant or non-conforming response of structurally disadvantaged individuals'

> In modern society behaviour is regulated to conform to the needs of capitalism.

> has become organized or institutionalized in our society. . . . Nowhere is the contingent nature of deviation made more apparent than in the action of government regulatory agencies with adjudicative and punitive powers in situations where they are confronted by consequences of technological and organizational change. Large areas of action to do with business, finance, health, labor, housing, utilities, safety and welfare are subject to control through administrative rules discontinuous in origin and form from the culturally derived norms which impressed Merton and others seeming to favor a conception of passive social control.[114]

In other words, an increasing proportion of control measures are active and cannot be seen to flow in any simple or direct fashion from the norms that are assumed to inhere in patterns of childhood socialization.

Passive social control, however, still operates in the sphere of the sacred, and it is in this respect still potent in the operation of the justice system. Moral character and status degradation remain part of the armoury that produces 'secondary deviation'; that is, deviance becomes part of a person's reputation, which then affects his or her future behaviour. In secondary deviation, the original causes of the (primary) deviation give way to the central importance of the disapproving, degrading, and isolating reactions of society. Lemert holds this to be pragmatically a more pertinent' research problem and one to which anomie theory has as yet contributed nothing. To put it crudely, it may be that the majority of people steal, but only a minority are processed as thieves; anomie theory alerts us to possible reasons for the former but precludes analysis of the processes underlying the latter.

In a more structurally inclined critique of Merton, Gouldner makes the point that:

> the allocation of the means to succeed and, with this, of position in the class system, is in appreciable part a function of the institution of private property and its hereditary or testamentary transmission. Thus the distribution of anomic responses is a function of this institution. But it does not follow that those on the top of the class system are less anomic, if by this is meant that they have more of a genuine belief in and devotion to their culture's

moral values. Indeed, there is reason to predict that their genuine commitment to these moral values is undermined by the very institution from which they derive their advantages. For this institution makes it possible for them to sever the connections between gratification and conformity to cultural values. . . . In short, the spoiler of the society's morality is . . . 'vested interest', the right to do something for nothing.[115]

To this critical catalogue, we would wish to add only four more problems.

•*First, although he later attempted to plug the gap,*[116] *Merton ignored the reverse situation to the malintegration of goals and means that occurs when results exceed expectations.* The 'anomie of success' is more prevalent at the top, and it applies whether success is earned or not. The overnight star, the author of an unexpected best-seller, are candidates for anomie just as much as the relative failures.[117] There is, argues Hagan, the problem of too much 'social capital': 'The trust that derives from successfully being embedded in powerful occupations and corporate networks can be a source of freedom and, therefore, power to commit large-scale white-collar crimes.'[118]

•*A second problem is the difficulty of conceptualizing the chronology of anomie and deviance.* Once formulated, deviant adaptations exist in the world as social institutions possessing stability and continuity. They may be encountered before any exposure to the 'strain to anomie' has occurred. However, if the 'solution' is embraced before the 'problem' is encountered, as described, for example, in Whyte's depiction of neighbourhood rackets in an Italian-American slum, then the experience of anomie is pre-empted.[119] It becomes a purely structural property without subjective counterpart. The problem of investigating anomie empirically may therefore elude available methodologies, since the only indicators of anomie that remain are its presenting symptoms, such as high rates of delinquency.[120]

•*Thirdly, anomie seems to be conceived as the outcome of a yawning gap between aspiration and the prospect of final achievement.* It is presumably most grievous in its effects on ambitious but disadvantaged young people who look ahead to judge their life chances. But people actually tend not to project their lives very far ahead; adolescents plan only a little into the future.[121] Expectations and motives are frequently confined to limited periods of time, shifting with each significant turning point in the life cycle. Experiences, perspectives, projects, and acquaintances evolve continuously, and ambition and failure are parts of that phased growth. They are not usually set but emergent, they are often short-term, and anomic disjunction itself may not be as profound as Merton claimed. To be sure, there are groups whose deprivation is so great that their frustration can never be modulated. It is unclear if anomie theory is intended to refer chiefly to them or to others whose lives are rather too complicated to be captured so simply.

•*Lastly, there is the problem posed by the stable institutionalization of deviance in the routine activities of central organizations of state and business.* Bauman, in his

Can people experience anomie if they don't plan far into the future?

analysis of the Holocaust, and Punch, in work on corporate misconduct,[122] have shown how difficult it can be to distinguish deviance from conformity or claim it is a consequence of relative deprivation or deregulation.

In conclusion it may well be that Durkheim's methodology is flawed, but that does not invalidate the general support for his theory that can be drawn from a revised view of the official statistics. Douglas's alternative method for analyzing the communicative actions that can be observed in real-world cases of suicide, such as the examination of suicide notes, simply adds a new layer on the analysis. Even though Durkheim focused on suicide rates alone as providing sufficient evidence for analysis, the two methods are quite compatible. As Atkinson's work testifies, however, there are perhaps intractable problems in a reliance on the rates alone.[123] While support for Durkheim's theory is mixed, it is still a formidable source for theory and research.

Merton's application of the concept draws both its strengths and its weaknesses from his 'westernization' of anomie. The weaknesses stem from too facile an acceptance of the apparent implications of the official rates of deviance, and too standardized a view of the prevalence of the American dream. However, in Western cultures, generations of immigrants from diverse cultures were and are subject to a relatively unbridled ideology of egalitarian consumerism. The content and consequence of these processes have been too little researched and explored: 'In contemporary America children must be trained to *insatiable* consumption of *impulsive* choice and *infinite* variety.'[124] The impact and nature of the collective representations of advertising remain relatively unknown, but such evidence as we have gives point to Merton's thesis.

The effect spreads to all consumer societies, which have experienced rising rates of crime and delinquency in the context of growing affluence; and anomie theory remains one of the most plausible attempts to account for this seeming paradox.[125] In the most systematic review of the evidence to date, Braithwaite concluded that it supported 'a strong *prima facie* case . . . that reducing inequalities of wealth and power will reduce crime'.[126]

> Anomie theory helps explain rising deviance in an affluent society.

Lemert may be right in proposing the general inadequacy of anomie theory in any simple sense to convey the processes involved in deviance and control. His own critique, however, fails to differentiate between social change resulting from innovation that falls *within* the realm of institutional means and social change resulting from innovation that does not. An example of the latter is the extent to which the 'hidden economy' is producing considerable distortions in taxation and consumption.[127]

Even planned social change can disrupt lives for the worse. For example, the unemployment that can result from technological obsolescence falls unevenly on the population, and for those adversely affected, the goals-means equation may be subject to sharp deterioration. It remains an empirical question as to whether that promotes higher rates of deviance of whatever kind. In sum, though substantial revision is in order, there is a great deal of unexplored mileage in anomie theory, whichever version we prefer.

Chapter Summary

This chapter has laid out the theory of anomie as a characteristic of modern society as well as a social psychological condition experienced by individuals as they fail to succeed according to society's goals. As such it is a macro-structural theory of micro-individual strain that continues to be influential today. Perhaps it is within subcultures that anomie is reinforced by others, which is the focus of our next chapter.

Critical-Thinking Questions

1. What are some of the changes that take place as society moves from an agricultural form of production to an industrial one that weakens social controls? How are these changes related to deviance?
2. What are the consequences of increased active control and decreased passive control for increasing the likelihood of deviance in general and among youth?
3. What are some of the major criticisms of anomie theory?
4. In one of the discussion features, the issue of school violence is discussed as only a symptom of much deeper problems in society. In this sense, how could we go about addressing the root, underlying causes of the problem, while also ensuring that students can go to school safely?

Explorations in Film

Children of Men is a combination of science fiction and suspense thriller. The main character is a disillusioned bureaucrat who becomes the unlikely hero in a world that has fallen into anarchy and chaos. The world's youngest citizen has just died at eighteen, and no children are being born because of an infertility defect in the population. Humankind is facing the likelihood of its own extinction, with a struggle between totalitarian state against disaffected individuals.

Websites

At http://www.statcan.ca/english/kits/suicide/sucid1.htm, the table called 'Suicides, and suicide rate, by sex, by age group' can be used to create a bar chart from which a class discussion can be generated about suicide and the differences between the sexes.

See the Emile Durkheim archive at http://durkheim.itgo.com/main.html, and look up quotations on topics such as suicide, anomie, solidarity, and division of labour.

Chapter Six

Deviance, Culture, and Subculture

Chapter Overview

This chapter looks at some of the approaches that have sought to delineate the 'lived (sub)culture' of deviance. Cultural theories in general try to see the sociality of individual's feelings of anomie and alienation.

Originally developed in the 1960s, cultural theories have their roots in older approaches. The traditional subculture perspective has focused on lower-class masculinity and has seen delinquency as a solution to social problems rather than simply a problem in itself.

The subcultural approach has much in common with conflict theories and societal reaction approaches. There are also many different variations, which accord different levels of meaning to actors. In this chapter we look at a variety of these approaches and the contributions they make to the sociology of deviance.

■ Introduction

Attempts to explain and understand social deviance, in particular juvenile delinquency, in terms of adherence to distinctive cultural patterns became commonplace in the 1960s and 1970s. Sociologists, with respectful nods in the direction of anthropology, tried to divide up the population in relation to parents' class cultures, varieties of subcultures, and burgeoning countercultures, each with its distinctive norms, values, and beliefs. And there were real gains, not the least of which was establishing the proposition that the most apparently senseless forms of aggressive delinquency could be made intelligible by taking account of their authors' 'definitions of the situation' and by seeing delinquency as a solution, rather than as a problem, to dilemmas they faced.

There was an excessively schematic quality about the subcultural theories of delinquency of this period, with society categorized into classes, sectors, age groups, and sex roles.[1] However, this was a stage in the evolution of the theory, with these characteristics:

•*First, especially in Cohen's work, there loomed the 'dominant' culture*: white Anglo-Saxon Protestant culture, the ascetic, achievement-oriented, highly competitive, middle-class way of life. Everyone was pulled to this centre of cultural gravity, though in line with Merton's theory of anomie, those most embroiled in the imperfections of the system could rebel in various ways. Deviant subcultures were seen as a reaction against it; once they came into being, they became a form of constraint in themselves. Delinquents acted out delinquent subcultures; the real analytical problem was to theorize why such deviant solutions could be generated in the first place. The sociologist credited that behaviour with rationality, collective problem solving, and group process.

•*Second, the break with these variations on the 'delinquent subculture' theme came with the work of Matza.*[2] It was only a partial break, for Matza retained certain features of these theories in his own work. But with the help of labelling theory, he helped to create a new set of questions, with his emphasis on free will, the argument that all prior theorizing had 'overpredicted' delinquency, and the rejection of the attempt to differentiate deviants from non-deviants. Initially, the focus of labelling theory on such variables as police bias against gang boys complemented subculture theory.[3] However, by the 1970s, work in cultural and subcultural theory shifted to markedly different theories and methods.

•*Third, after 1967, subcultural theory languished.* Little substantive work appeared that was derived from its central tenets or that developed its major propositions. The similarities of subcultural theory to anomie theory became more obvious, and the defects of anomie theory were extended to subcultural theory. Both rested on the assumption that deviant behaviour originated in socially induced 'strain' or 'tension'. Underlying that 'strain' was the image of society as basically stable and consensual, though flawed by remediable inequalities of opportunity. Such an image was unattractive to the labelling theorists, who favoured a more pluralistic model of society as a mosaic of disparate social worlds, and also to the more radical sociologists who based their theories on the central assumption of class struggle.

•*Fourth, it was not until 1972 that a perspective emerged that was capable of accommodating such diverse strands.* Phil Cohen's analysis of working-class youth cultures in East London became the basis for the substantial work on deviance and control by the Birmingham Centre for Cultural Studies.[4] Its work concentrated on the interplay between class conflict, youthful rebellion, and media representations and did not entail first-hand ethnographies. Paul Willis's work at the Centre was the exception, in that he engaged with the complexities of fieldwork in the mode termed 'passionate ethnography'.[5] He attempted to describe and analyze the subjective unfolding of 'contradictions and problems' as they are 'lived through to particular outcomes'.[6] The result was research on the re-creation of cultures, not subculture, but subordinate cultures, which was significant for the development of theory.

In the 1970s a flood of work appeared in Britain that tried to capture cultural meanings and to contextualize them in the larger social structure, usually in terms of their contradictions.[7] Some drew more than others from labelling theory, while others retained the ethnographer's interest in the transmission of beliefs in an urban environment. Overall, the priority accorded formal theory testing receded in the face of an enthusiasm for more extensive explorations of diverse social worlds.[8] The materials gathered in the process enhanced the possibilities for cultural and subcultural theories to develop in a less constricted way than in the past. There is a tendency now for theories to be couched in terms of 'cultural capital' rather than subcultural terms. However, the proliferation of recent cultural ethnographies raises the question whether it is possible in a rapidly changing multicultural society for media-fuelled cultures to crystallize long enough to be studied.[9]

Now let us look at some of the theoretical developments in more detail.

■ Theoretical Perspectives
The Strain Theory of Albert Cohen

Strain theories constitute the first truly systematic use of the concepts of culture and subculture, such as in the work of Albert Cohen. The problem, as he stated it, was that previous theories had made only a limited and circular use of such concepts. To say that delinquency was 'part of' a culture or was 'culturally trans-mitted' did not take one very far. What was needed was a theory of the *origins* of such culture. Previous theories of delinquency had mainly looked at the acquis-itive kind, which is akin to adult forms of theft and robbery. Yet the more puz-zling forms of delinquency were primarily *expressive* in character. Violence, vandalism, joyriding: these kinds of activity were simply not explained by exist-ing theories. Cohen argued that theory should address the character and distrib-ution of both forms of delinquency; and it should employ the concept of culture to specify the functions it performs and the problems it solves for the groups whose behaviour it influences so strongly.

> Fredric Thrasher had looked at expressive deviance, an idea that Cohen now picked up.

This conception of culture is characteristically functionalist. Culture consists of traditional ways of solving problems created by the social structure, which are transmitted through the process of childhood socialization. However, if there is such a strong basis for conformity, how could there be any possibility of innova-tion? Cohen's answer, which echoes Merton's anomie theory, accepts that at some point in the social system normative conflict is possible. Structure and culture make incompatible demands, and at these points of pressure subcultures have evolved to solve the problems that arise. Subcultures usually borrow elements of the larger culture, such as violence and hedonism, and rework them into dis-tinctive forms. 'The crucial condition for the emergence of new cultural forms is the existence, *in interaction with one another, of actors with similar problems of adjustment.*'[10] Cohen conveyed vividly the scope for distinctive subcultures to emerge as solutions to problems posed for different groups: 'Each age, sex, racial and ethnic category, each occupation, economic stratum and social class consists of people who have been equipped by their society with frames of reference and confronted by their society with situations that are not equally characteristic of other roles.'[11]

The task was to theorize 'the role of the social structure and the immediate social milieu in determining the creation and selection of solutions' applicable to gang delinquency. In Cohen's theory, his characterization of gang delin-quency is that it amounted to a way of life in deprived metropolitan and inner urban neighbourhoods, This echoed Wirth's classic essay on urbanism, in that city life is seen to undermine traditional communities, creating individuation and normlessness.[12]

Cohen's pattern of delinquency displays the following six characteristics:

- non-utilitarianism: goods stolen for kicks are given away or destroyed;
- malice: destructiveness such as vandalism that accompanied some break-ins;
- negativism: much delinquent behaviour actually inverted respectable values;
- short-run hedonism: instant gratification existed in delinquent gangs;
- versatility: male gang activities included theft, vandalism, and aggression;
- group autonomy: gang loyalty came first, other allegiances were subordinate.

This profile of the delinquent subculture did not aim to be an exhaustive catalogue, but an inventory of the most serious forms of group delinquency.

Cohen was accentuating tendencies that occasionally became reality, rather than a set of everyday activities. Criticisms of the theory that caricature it for conjuring up an image of incessant warfare between youth and the adult world often ignore its ideal-typical character.

For Cohen, this profile of delinquent subculture helped explain the initial conformity of youth to the established cultural order and then their break from that order. For subordinate groups in a society stratified along lines of social class, adhering to the values of the dominant culture makes for the creation of problems rather than their resolution. The rationale for the motiveless and meaningless behaviour of delinquent gangs is found in the problems faced by lower-class, urban teenage boys. They commonly experience tension and strain in handling the paradoxes of democratic schooling. Schools exist to make children care about social status and academic achievement, but they deny that status and achievement to all but a minority of the working class. Faced with a common problem of adjustment caused by failing at school, the rejected evolve the delinquent-gang solution as a means both to acquire status and to hit back at the system that has branded them as failures. The gang takes the rules of respectable society, turns them upside down, and enjoys the difference, as in the heavy metal fan recorded by Arnett:

> Schools appear meritocratic, but they restrict the success that can be achieved by the lower class, thus creating a push toward delinquency.

> It's all about reality, dying . . . that's reality, you know. I have a hard time with all these people that put down [heavy metal bands] and say they're satanic and they worship the devil and all this, but if you listen to the words in their songs, it's all reality. Dying is reality, nuclear war is reality, going out and killing somebody is reality, living on the streets is reality, and they talk about reality problems. . . . [Opponents of the music] don't want reality facts, don't want to look at what's going on in our world.[13]

Cohen's theory accounts for the much lower rates of delinquency among the middle class (who are more likely to attain success by the conventional route); among girls (who at least in his research were found to value marriage to an successful man far more highly than success in a career of their own); and in non-urban areas (where schools hold less sway as the route to respected crafts and trades). It seemed to fit the facts extremely well, to help explain the group character of most delinquency, and to go beyond previous theories while retaining their more valuable insights.

The Subcultural Theory of Cloward and Ohlin

Cohen's theory stimulated variants of the same model and attempts at empirical testing. The most sympathetic was Cloward and Ohlin's study, dedicated to Robert Merton, the father of the American version of *anomie* theory and to Edwin Sutherland, the Chicagoan father of *differential association* theory.[14] They proposed a similar structurally generated model of delinquency causation to Cohen but argued he had underrated the degree of *specialization* that existed and

Cloward and Ohlin proposed three different juvenile gangs.

overrated the role of the school as the crucible of delinquency. They discerned three types of delinquent subculture arising in different types of neighbourhood: criminal (gangs pursuing quite utilitarian forms of robbery and theft), conflict (fighting gangs), retreatist (drug-using gangs).

The major source of variation was the presence of stable recruitment into adult criminal enterprises: where that existed, the criminal gang would predominate; where it did not, the conflict gang would predominate. Boys who failed to succeed either legally or illegally would slough off this 'double failure' by resorting to using drugs and 'hustling'. The root cause of the original emergence of delinquent subcultures was not so much the school as the pursuit of 'money-success' earlier emphasized by Merton in anomie theory as the prime source of embittered frustration in the metropolitan slums.

Empirical studies based on the testing of these two theories became a major focus of criminology in the late 1950s to mid-1960s. The main conclusions to emerge from the most meticulous of these projects[15] inclined towards Cohen's more generalized characterization of gang delinquency but rejected his emphasis on the oppositional character of the subcultural values in favour of acknowledging situational elements. For example, the precipitating motive for gang fights was threats to the leader's status; while chance dragged large numbers of otherwise only marginally delinquent youth into the fray. Furthermore, gang boys had the ability to accommodate quite contradictory value systems. That is, they could have values favourable to delinquency without significantly disaffiliating themselves from the values of conventional society. A major problem was the difficulty of testing more than a few facets of the theories, but the data pointed to the conclusion that delinquency was far more autonomous and contingent than earlier theories had allowed.

The Neutalization Theory of Matza

The work of David Matza had more influence by making a crucial break with the underlying assumptions of strain theory in proposing an alternative theory of delinquency.[16] He condemns strain theorists for overpredicting delinquency but keeps some of strain theory's central features, notably the stress on group process and the assertion that 'preparation' and a sense of 'desperation' are preludes to delinquency. In this way he conjures up an implication of strain akin to the earlier subcultural theorists.

Matza's builds his theory around the axiom that delinquency is *willed* behaviour and is in general intermittent and mundane and that it also drops off sharply with the onset of adulthood. The earlier idea that delinquency flowed from a deeply held commitment to a set of oppositional values embodied in delinquent subcultures could not account for these patterns. Instead, he proposed that a state of *drift* usually precedes delinquency. Drift entails a loosening of controls, from which delinquency is only *one* possible outcome. 'The delinquent transiently exists in a limbo between convention and crime . . . postponing commitment, evading decision.'[17]

Delinquency, however, does not occur in a vacuum. It is facilitated by a 'subculture of delinquency', which both releases the delinquent from the constraints of law and custom and mocks commonly held values. Techniques of neutralization solve the problem of moral scruples: 'I didn't mean to do it', 'They had it coming to them', 'Everybody does it', 'Nobody got hurt', and 'I only did it for my friends' are common justifications for deviance in general and not just for delinquency. In their analysis of juvenile delinquency, Teevan (of the University of Western Ontario) and Dryburgh, who looked for first-person accounts found that neutralization techniques best described the reasons why boys fought and committed other acts of deviance.[18]

> Techniques of neturalization salve a guilty conscience.

Case Study—Research in the News—'Sports Machismo May Be Cue to Male Teen Violence'

'The sports culture surrounding football and wrestling may be fueling aggressive and violent behavior not only among teen male players but also among their male friends and peers on and off the field.

'Sports such as football, basketball, and baseball provide players with a certain status in society, . . . but football and wrestling are associated with violent behavior because both sports involve some physical domination of the opponent, which is rewarded by the fans, coaches and other players.

'Using a national database of 6397 male students from across 120 schools, [researchers] analyzed the effects of team sports—football, basketball, and baseball—and individual sports—wrestling and tennis—on male interpersonal violence. . . .

'. . . Compared with non-athletes, football players and wrestlers face higher risks of getting into a serious fight by over 40 percent. High-contact sports that are associated with aggression and masculinity increase the risk of violence, . . . however, the violent behavior is not restricted to players alone. . . .

'Males with all-football friends are expected to have a 45 percent probability of getting into a serious fight, more than 8 percentage points higher than similar individuals with no football friends and almost 20 percentage points higher than males with all-tennis friends.

'As for individual sports, wrestlers are 45 percent more likely to get into a fight than non-wrestlers, while tennis players are 35 percent less likely to be involved in fights. The team sports, basketball and baseball, on the other hand, do not lead to fights.

'The findings run contrary to a belief that participation in sports discourages anti-social behavior among boys because of the emphasis on teamwork, discipline and practice, and good sportsmanship and fair play.

'. . . High-contact sports fail to protect males from interpersonal violence, . . . Players might be getting cues from parents, peers, coaches, and the local community, who support violence as a way of attaining "battlefield" victories, becoming more popular, and asserting "warrior" identities.

'Pressure on teams to win games may be contributing to the problem, because it makes coaches want to build a stronger team by selecting aggressive players and encouraging a "win at all costs" attitude both on and off the field. . . .'

Source: Penn State, 'Sports Machismo May Be Cue to Male Teen Violence', *Science Daily*, 24 January 2008. Accessed 25 January 2008 at http://www.sciencedaily.com /releases/2008/01/ 080123150510.htm. See also D. Kreager, 'Unnecessary Roughness? School Sports, Peer Networks, and Male Adolescent Violence', 705–24.

Similarly, delinquency is attractive, not by adherence to a morality unique to young offenders, but by their exaggerated appreciation of widely circulating 'subterranean' values: the pursuit of excitement, the disdain for routine work, and the equating of toughness with masculinity. This combination encourages adolescent males to manufacture excitement by breaking the law. As well, the process of drift helps account for the episodic and mundane character of delinquency. The closeness of the delinquent's values to those of conventional society helps account for the relative ease with which maturation out of delinquency is accomplished with the onset of adulthood and more structured role playing in work and family life.

However, in setting out to remedy theories that overpredicted delinquency, Matza overcorrects to the point at which his own theory *underpredicts* both its scale and its violence. Matza employs the idea of 'desperation' in violence, but the theme is left relatively unexplained. 'The drifter is not less a problem than the compulsive or committed delinquent even though he is far less likely to become an adult criminal. Though his tenure is short, his replacements are legion.'[19] It is as if, in crucial respects, Matza is discussing a different problem than the earlier theorists, who focused on the 'committed' rather than the 'mundane' delinquent.

Similarly, when Quinn discusses the problem of deviance in outlaw motorcycle gangs, he finds a diversity of behaviour to be explained. Rather than being homogeneous, these gangs have radicals who are heavily involved in crime; they suppress the countercultural aspects of the subculture in comparison to the conservatives.[20]

Evidence does not wholly support Matza's image of the drifting and episodic rule breaker. For example, almost all the British youths in West and Farrington's and Belson's self-report studies had engaged in deviance, much of it petty, but there was violence too. By the time they are 28, some 30 per cent of men in England and Wales have appeared before the courts.[21] While most of those who offend are not serious or committed rule breakers (they are like Matza's episodic delinquents), there is a small minority of some 6 per cent who *do* offend repeatedly and, it has been estimated, are responsible for about two-thirds of all offences.[22] The concept of drift is helpful because some delinquents do not always grow out of offending.

'Drift' does not account for a small committed core of chronic offenders.

In another criticism of 'drift', the quantitative analysis of cohorts of recorded offenders suggests that statistically defined groups behave very differently over time.[23] There are marked variations in the ways in which they start and cease to put themselves in danger of arrest and conviction. More important, a very recent and substantial self-report survey of 10,000 people in England and Wales, *The Crime and Justice Survey*, found that 60 per cent of active offenders were younger than 25 and 'many desisters' had relatively short criminal careers,[24] but that 40 per cent of offenders were nevertheless over 25. The qualitative analysis of offences, including unrecorded crime, suggests that the perpetrators may simply change from the more hazardous and exposed forms of offending to ones that are more circumspect. Some research shows that delinquents do not necessarily cease to break rules altogether on achieving maturity but may instead start to break rules more *discreetly*. They come off the streets, where they are the highly visible perpetrators of public-order and status offences, to enter the less visible world of the informal economy. In short, the scale or duration of crime and delinquency in the West should not be underestimated.

Some New Approaches?

More recently, Elijah Anderson has managed to move us further forward. His *Code of the Street* is a masterly ethnographic account of black life in Philadelphia. There is a spectrum, he argues, of adherence to law. At one pole, there are predominantly religious families, often with a father in the home, that are lawfully employed, aspiring towards a secure and law-abiding existence, and struggling to exercise control over their children. At the other pole were those who achieved conspicuous monetary success through crime, principally drug dealing. The streets are dangerous for those growing up in black inner-city Philadelphia, where the threat of violence, robbery, and exploitation is ever present. Security can be only by acquiring a reputation for physical prowess and attachment to a group of other young people who will defend or revenge one. It is dangerous to be unattached, so boys, especially, must work to gain entrance to those territorially based groups, and they do so by proving themselves to be tough and streetwise.

The dilemma for the sons of the conforming and aspiring families is that since they are in danger if they venture out into the streets, they must either be imprisoned at home or acquire the streets' colouring. They become the inhabitants of the remotely linked worlds of the law-abiding family and the law-breaking street group, speaking two languages and subscribing to two cultures, confronting the difficulties of crossing the boundaries, and negotiating the contradictions between them. In this sense, the mother's cry 'he was always a good boy' may have considerable validity, but his goodness had necessarily to be contingent. For girls it was different. One of their chief difficulties was that they were often obliged to try to achieve social and economic success by attaching themselves to sexually predatory men who passed as financially secure but were not, or who professed to be faithful and supportive, but were not.

One virtue of subcultural theories was that they lend themselves well to comparative cross-cultural work. The causes of delinquency exist in all industrial, urban societies with democratic political institutions, and for example, the lower murder rate in Britain than the United States may be partly explained by the fact that hand guns are less readily available in Britain.[25] With the possible exceptions of Glasgow and some groups of football supporters,[26] the violent fighting gang has not emerged as a phenomenon in Britain. Three main structural and cultural differences may help explain this variation, all of which can be related to class allegiances that appear to be stronger in Britain than in the United States: (1) adherence in Britain to individual success or failure has been lower; (2) there has been a relative absence of minority-group loyalties based on ethnicity that cut across class allegiances; and (3)post-war 'affluence' was combined with relatively stable employment.

These points of difference have lost much of their force over the past two decades, and there have been corresponding changes in delinquency as a result. Acquisitive crimes as measured by official statistics rose in the late 1980s,[27] only to start falling again from the mid-1990s.[28] Indeed, research shows a negative correlation between the number of crimes against property and general patterns of consumption: 'When people are increasing their spending very little, or even reducing it, property crime tends to grow relatively quickly, whereas during years when people are rapidly increasing their expenditure, property crime tends to grow less rapidly or even fall.'[29]

The interpretation of official records does require caution, of course, as it is sensitive to the willingness to report crimes.[30]

In a recent study, researchers tried to find a link between crime booms and levels of economic development.[31] Whereas constructionists argue that crime booms are rare, and modernizationalists say that booms are limited to industrializing nations, globalizationalists claim that such booms have existed in all nations since the Second World War. In a rigidly defined test for booms, homicide victimization rates were used for thirty-four nations between 1956 and 1998. Twelve nations satisfied the criteria for crime booms, which was too many to support the constructionist argument, and too few to support the globalizationalists. However, in support of modernizationalists, 70 per cent of industrializing nations qualified as having had booms. The theoretical difficulty posed by such research, of course, is that once we make the link between crime and economic development, we must then find the cultural organization that enables deviance to be sustained or negated.

For example, class identity as a variable that diminished the strain to anomie loomed large in Downes's observations of delinquency among a small number of adolescent boys in East London in the early 1960s; it recurs in similar respects in Wilmott's study in Bethnal Green at much the same time.[32] 'Status frustration', 'alienation', and 'delinquent subculture' were concepts that did not seem to fit descriptions of boys involved intermittently in offences of the fighting, joyriding, theft, and vandalism variety. Most were not members of structured delinquent gangs with a marked sense of territory, leadership, hierarchy, and membership.

Delinquency was a *fact* of life, but not a *way* of life. Educationally, their talk of school implied dissociation from its values rather than embitterment at academic failure. Their occupational goals and expectations were pitched realistically low, consistent with their experience of a succession of 'dead-end' jobs. Early marriage and 'settling down' were already in view.

In a negative sense, though, the necessary conditions held to be essential for the emergence of gang delinquency were largely absent. In a study carried out in a school in a comparable inner-city area, boys in the C and D streams (the lowest streams) engaged in behaviour analogous to that described by Albert Cohen, but of a milder 'delinquescent' character. Copying, cheating, messing around, and rowdyism were the converse of the 'pupil' ideal but fell short of full-blown delinquency.[33]

Such research unites Downes's theme of delinquency as a hedonistic response to the anomic strains of life with Hargreaves's theme of delinquency as oppositional. The delinquents whom they studied were 'outsiders', younger members of a loosely structured and discredited public-housing estate. Their delinquency was rowdiness in cinemas and clubs, sexual misbehaviour, and public drinking. It was argued that the respectability of the village *generated* the deviance of the estate as part of the 'peculiar guerilla warfare waged almost incessantly between established sections . . . and socially produced outsider groups, in this case outsider groups of the younger generation'.[34]

The question that remains in the British context is to account for delinquency at all, given the rough correspondence that obtains between aspirations and expectations. American ethnographic work also points to such a correspondence in certain inner-city areas, with just the consequences that Downes and Hargreaves discerned.[35] It is at this point that Matza's theory seems to have most to offer. The most frequent reason given by the boys for their delinquency was boredom, a word that takes on additional meaning when used with reference to leisure, the one domain in which they have the opportunity to express their character through action. Because their fatalism about school and work is so entrenched, leisure assumes immense significance, not least when the expectation of action is met with the reality of 'nothing going on'. It is out of their response to this impasse that not only much delinquency, but also the successive styles of youth culture, have emerged, particularly since the post-war employment boom for young workers led to the lucrative 'teenage market'. Even so, for working-class adolescents in particular, leisure is too often a counterpart of work: they have nowhere to go and too little money.

In this context, delinquency allows for the display of toughness and daring. The streets, soccer matches, and the law itself provide the setting and raw material for action: delinquency is 'something happening'. The meanings and forms are immensely varied, from 'weird ideas' that emerge from hanging about 'doing nothing', to clashes between groups contriving different expressive styles: 'One has to strip all the hub caps off every car in a parking ground, one has to wait until the last possible moment before dropping an object from a bridge onto the railway line, one has to paint a slogan on the opposite wall of the underground train tunnel.'[36]

There are three ways
that delinquency and
excitement are
related.

There are by now at least three links between delinquency and excitement. Delinquency is the means to buying excitement (alcohol, girls, cars, pot) with the proceeds of the theft;[37] delinquency is the raw material of excitement (in Matza's and Cusson's view[38]); and delinquency is a by-product of the pursuit of actions that are exciting in themselves (vandalism is Corrigan's example).[39]

There seems no particular reason to regard these as mutually exclusive alternatives, because at different times and places, one option may be preferred to another. Indeed, in a study of 100 young English car thieves, their careers in 'taking without consent' started in the hedonism of stealing and fast driving but progressed in time to cars being stolen so that they could be sold whole or in parts.[40] There is similar evidence from American ethnographic work.[41] Many deviants change the way they offend as they become less agile and strong. Eventually perhaps, they will slow down so much that they will be able neither to enjoy the physical exploit of crime nor to keep up so well with their younger, more agile confederates.[42]

An affinity with strain theory is that excitement tends to be the taken-for-granted goal of young male adolescents, on the assumption that this is so in leisure because other goals have been denied them in school and work. With the rise in the 1960s of deviance among relatively privileged youth groups, such as drug use among middle-class hippies and student 'violence' in universities and polytechnics, these theories lost some of their force. Labelling theory assumed greater plausibility.

Discussion: Deviance Exploration—The Culture of Auto Theft?

National statistics show that rates of auto theft in Canada increased from about 300 thefts per 100,000 people in the early 1980s to 541 per 100,000 in 2003. It is a crime that costs about $1 billion per year: $600 million for insurance premiums and $400 million for criminal justice and health care.

In Canada, vehicles are most likely to be stolen from parking lots, followed by streets, home garages, and driveways. Thefts are most frequent in low-income, high-crime communities. Routine activities theory predicts that this is because of the higher number of motivated offenders, less guardianship, and more vulnerable targets.

Rick Linden (of the University of Manitoba) surmises that it is because of the presence of large numbers of motivated offenders, combined with the availability of older cars that are easy to steal and a lack of private or enclosed parking facilities, that the poor are the main victims of vehicle theft.

Aggregate statistics show provincial variations, but at a level that makes it hard to determine if municipal or regional factors are at work. In 2003, for example, when the national rate was 541 per 100,000, provincial rates varied from 126 per 100,000 in Newfoundland and Labrador to 1,111 in Manitoba.

Most stolen vehicles are recovered, but again, the rate of recovery varies provincially. In 2003 in all of Canada, 75 per cent of all stolen vehicles were recovered, and in some communities the recovery rate can be over 90 per cent. However, the patterns differ from one community to another and may also change over time, so crime prevention has to adapt to meet those changes.

In 2002 the recovery rate varied from 56 per cent in Montreal to 62 per cent in Ontario's York Region to 68 per cent in Ottawa-Gatineau. At the other extreme, the recovery rate was 97 per cent in Regina, 95 per cent in both Victoria and Winnipeg, 92 per cent in Edmonton, and 91 per cent in Vancouver. The high recovery rate in the west compared to the low recovery rate in the east, suggests that joyriding is the typical pattern in cities in western Canada, while professional vehicle theft is more prevalent in the east.

Professional vehicle theft is facilitated by a lack of co-operation among provinces. Professional thieves can transport stolen vehicles into another province and sell them by using a Vehicle Identification Number (VIN) taken from a salvaged vehicle and installed in the stolen vehicle.

Joyriding, on the other hand, is made easier because some older cars are easier to steal. For example, in Winnipeg about one in twelve 1990–1994 Dodge Caravans and Plymouth Voyagers are stolen each year because these cars are so easy to open and drive away. In other parts of Canada, older Hondas and Toyotas have high theft rates. These older vehicles are more likely to be owned by poorer people living in low-income neighbourhoods.

Most vehicle thefts are reported, and as a result sociologists know a lot about the victims. However, we know less about the thieves, because the low clearance rate (12 per cent) means we cannot be sure that those who are arrested are representative of all those who steal motor vehicles. However, we can make some inferences:

- Young people make up 42 per cent of those arrested in 2001, a higher proportion than for any other offence.
- Research has found that vehicle theft is a *precursor* offence, meaning that youths who are first arrested for vehicle theft are more likely to continue their criminal behaviour than those whose first involvement is for any other offence.
- Most vehicle thefts are committed by males—91 per cent of adults and 82 per cent of youths (in 2002).
- A large proportion of vehicle thefts are committed by small groups of chronic offenders, whether they are joyriders or professional vehicle thieves.

The high recovery rate for stolen cars in most Canadian communities indicates that cars are being stolen for joyriding rather than for profit. The most frequently stolen vehicles are older vehicles of low value, and there is evidence that stealing cars is part of the youth culture in some inner-city schools. Interviews done by researchers with incarcerated young offenders have shown that their primary motivation for stealing cars is excitement rather than profit.

Research has also found that joyriders are more likely to have an adversarial relationship with the community, to feel excluded by dominant institutions and culture, and to be poorly supervised by their parents. Joyriders also report low rates of participation in sports and other non-criminal recreation and high rates of school truancy. Joyriding is usually committed in the company of peers.

Source: Based on statistics reported in R. Linden and R. Chaturvedi, 'The Need for Comprehensive Crime Prevention Planning: The Case of Motor Vehicle Theft'.

Strain and Labelling Theory

Labelling theorists do not address themselves to the 'causes' of delinquency but focus on the impact of social reactions on deviance. Labelling theory emerged from symbolic interactionism.

Becker, Lemert, Cicourel, and other theorists in the labelling tradition were the first to approach the social reaction to deviant behaviour as a *variable*. They argued that the relationships that developed between deviants and social controllers are in themselves important influences that help to shape and transform deviant phenomena.[43] The process of *becoming* deviant was conceived in terms of the gradual construction of a role and identity that mirrored the conventional career. The early emphasis was on the reaction of others and thus, the amplificatory potential of social control for deviance.

State agencies could create more deviance than would otherwise exist by criminalizing morally disturbing activities (for instance, certain forms of drug use); by mobilizing bias and unduly heavy penalties against groups low in power and status; and by attributing spurious and stigmatizing features to deviant groups. The media in particular could be singled out as promoting stereotypical images of the deviant, which are then contrasted with over-typical picture of 'normality'.[44] The result is to polarize society into a conforming majority and a deviant minority, a dynamic process that helps create a self-fulfilling prophecy, since those to whom deviance is attributed become both objectively and subjectively more at risk: they are subjected to forms of exclusion (from jobs, housing, or recreation)[45] that worsen their situation, and they are under pressure to collude with the majority view that they are 'essentially' deviant.[46]

In Cohen's classic study of the 'moral panic' induced by the Mods and Rockers fights in the mid-1960s, we see the nuances of social control of one moment in British social history.[47] Loose stylistic associations were metaphorically transformed by the media into tightly knit gangs. Ideal-typical 'folk devils' were created: the youth who offered to pay his fine by cheque was parodied as a symbol of youthful affluence, defiance, and indifference to authority. Even non-events were news: towns 'held their breath' for invasions that did not materialize. Cohen argues that the sensationalistic treatment of the initial events sensitized far more adolescents on the fringes to a novel form of action than would have been the case with more modest and realistic reporting.

That emphasis on the impact of the outsider's uncomprehending gaze has been revived to great effect recently by Katz, who claims that 'gangs' are a lazy and misleading description imposed by sociologists who have failed to consider the implications of their arguments. It is easy to invoke the idea of gangs when more complicated and nebulous processes are at work.[48]

Work in this perspective carried out in the 1970s tended to ally it with class conflict and culture conflict theories,[49] or with functional approaches.[50] All stress the inadequacy of labelling theory alone to account for the phenomena concerned, but they see it as addressing an essential dimension missing from previous theorizing. Thus, Gill traces the emergence of 'Luke Street' as a delinquency area from the initial policy that allocated a cluster of larger than average, publicly owned houses in one small neighbourhood to families already classified as 'problems'. These families faced considerable difficulties owing to their large size, low incomes, and high unemployment. Adverse labelling impinged, in various cumulative ways, on the lives of the relatively large number of adolescents who came of age together in this situation. Coming from the 'worst' areas, they found they could not get even 'dead-end' jobs; episodes of street delinquency were given wide press coverage, which reinforced the stereotype; local youth clubs banned them; they felt they were subject to unusually fierce police harassment. Gross exclusion fuelled a sense of local territoriality that escalated into conflicts with the police.

It is improbable that any wider youth culture had very much to do with Luke Street delinquency, but the study conveys a sense of determinism. It is as if the fate of Luke Street was sealed the moment the Housing Authority decided to allocate a critical mass of the housing to large poor families. The press, the police, and the authorities in general closed the trap progressively, Delinquency was the boys' only option.

In another study of interaction among boys who stole car radios,[51] observational work depicts the boys' 'conversation culture' with immense sensitivity and skill. Over three years, changes are observed in the boys' views of themselves and the world. Yet no clear-cut picture of their 'culture' emerges because their 'culture' is not clear-cut. The interactionist technique allows for improvisation, negotiation, and the emergence of new ways of defining the situation and moving on to different ways of handling it. But the boys' autonomy was bounded by the rules of the larger society, and eventually they acceded to that power after a calculated appraisal of the risks. Theoretically, the study shows affinities with strain theory (the 'good times' must be wrung from a penny-pinching society); with labelling theory (the subjective shift from a sense of apartness to a sense of alienation results from first-hand experience of the police and the courts); with control theory (the 'streetwise', who are in trouble from early childhood eventually decide that the costs outweigh the benefits); and conflict theories (the 'iron cage' ultimately clamps down on their horizons and life chances).

Nevertheless, certain themes that recur in different studies of boys engaged in various kinds of trouble seem to reaffirm the reality of subculture. In their study of soccer hooliganism, Marsh argues that such behaviour is basically a ritualized form of aggression that would not escalate into real violence were it not for the disruptive influence of the police. He explains the fans' apparently 'schizoid' accounts of their behaviour in terms of a 'conspiracy':

> In conspiring to construct a reality which seems to be at variance with their tacit knowledge of orderly and rule-governed action, fans are engaged in the active creation of excitement. For fans, regularity and safety are things to be avoided. . . . What the soccer terraces [spectators' area] offer is a chance to escape from the dreariness of the weekday world of work or school to something which is adventurous and stimulating. But in order to achieve the contrast it is necessary to construe, at least on one level, the soccer terraces as radically different from the weekday world.[52]

The media collude with the conspiracy. The police play a more complicated role, since the fans use them to defuse a situation without loss of face to themselves. If the police either over- or under-react, things go awry. This agrees with Matza's notion of delinquency as the 'manufacture of excitement'. In the case of soccer hooliganism, however, the delinquency is mainly a matter of rule-governed symbolization and fantasy. In his anthropological account of 'the Blades', Armstrong agrees: 'hooligan dramas are contextual, negotiated and improvised. . . . For most people in Britain now there is no epic of poverty or war, for life is relatively safe. . . . Modern-day consumer lifestyle increasingly lacks any sense of danger or ordeal and the problem then becomes one of transcending monotony'.[53]

The 'risk society' is no longer *risqué*, and hooliganism redresses the balance, creating a ritualized and therefore *non*-violent context for the display of masculine attributes of daring, prowess, and panache. Interestingly, medieval warfare had many of the same qualities. The last thing many soldiers and mercenaries wanted was to be hurt or killed; the first things were loot and the establishment of character. Much military manoeuvring actually involved armies wheeling about trying to avoid one another.[54]

Similarly, in a close-grained ethnography of youth groups and cultural styles, Blackman shows how violent masculinity is far more contained and symbolic, erupts only rarely in actual combat, and is more significantly related to territorial responses than an expression of social-class resistance:

The mods' promenade of male solidarity was more significantly related to territorial responses as a youth cultural style than an expression of social class resistance. Their 'tough behaviour' did not in any sense become an anti-intellectualism: the mod boys pursued fighting and gaining qualifications with equal rigour. In school it was their potential for violence rather than the reality which formed the basis of their authority.[55]

For those averse to physical combat, adrenalin can be sought in other ways. Wilson studied the experience of engagement with a 1970s music scene. Two decades later, interviews with former followers testify to its long reach into middle age. The heady cocktail of music, dance, drugs, and 'life as party' did not, for the substantial majority, impinge on their life chances. They went on to become wage or salary earners and raised families. But the 'scene' remained their pivotal site of intense experience, group life, and heightened interaction. However, for a small minority it was more fateful: already mired in problematic family backgrounds, the 'scene' was their route to crime, arrest, and in some cases, early death. What emerges is that involvement in youthful subcultures is varied in its character and aftermath, ephemeral for some, and tragic for others.[56]

Culture Conflict Theory

Culture conflict theories are based on the idea that the clash of conduct norms plays a central role in the explanation of crime. Such a view was presented in succinct form by Thorsten Sellin: 'If the conduct norms of a group are, with reference to a given life situation, inconsistent, or if two groups possess inconsistent norms, we may assume that the members of these various groups will individually reflect such group attitudes.'[57]

The most obvious conflicts of conduct norms arose in the process of migration to North America of people from a variety of cultural backgrounds. Sociology then became interested in the cultural conflicts that arose. The model could be adapted to explain aggressive delinquency by invoking the sheer magnitude of the cultural differences between the middle and working classes (without implying any necessary built-in antagonism, as do class conflict theories); and without implying that working-class adolescents are significantly influenced by middle-class culture, as do strain theorists. Culture conflict theory shares with control theorists a definition of the dominant society as unable to gain any effective purchase on the 'hearts and minds' of the working class. They hold that working-class culture is profoundly lodged in a 'generations-old shaking-down process' born of industrialization and urbanization. As yet it is little affected by the changes and reforms, such as affluence, that are so often heralded as the promoters of classlessness.[58]

Miller simply argues that lower-class group delinquency, far from representing a counterculture, is the direct, intensified expression of the dominant culture pattern of the lower-class community. This culture comprises six 'focal concerns' to whose polarities each individual can orient him- or herself:

- trouble (the tension between law-abiding and law-violating behaviour)
- toughness (masculinity—effeminacy)
- smartness (sharp-wittedness—dull-wittedness)
- excitement (activity—passivity)
- fate (luck—being unlucky)
- autonomy (independence—dependency)

For Miller, engagement with these 'concerns' tends to involve lower-class adolescents in a head-on clash with a dominant society whose morality is underwritten by middle-class values. The delinquent gang intensifies such commitment since its members are likely to be socialized in female-dominated households where little reliance is placed on the stability and earning power of the male. The gang helps solve sex-role problems by providing a vehicle for the pursuit of masculine status and reassurance. Miller claims much empirical support for this theory. In particular, the fact that there is a high proportion of intra-group aggressive acts, which are verbally expressive of focal 'concerns' and rarely directed against middle-class or even adult targets, suggest that ambivalence about status in those terms is negligible.

Most delinquency is non-violent, and while thefts are more common than any kind of assault, they are, relatively rare. Violence, when it does occur, is a response to apparent insults or rejection by specific people, not a random outpouring of 'senseless' aggression. It is a source of group cohesion and an affirmation of group values, rather than a springboard for hostility against 'society', the 'adult world', or 'middle-class values'.

A similar type of explanation is afforded by Oscar Lewis's concept of the culture of poverty. Generated by the experience of poverty, this culture takes much the same form whatever the national or structural context.[59] Whether it is studied in Buenos Aires, Glasgow, Calgary, or New York, the same combination of values is observed. It includes an inability to defer gratification, a stress on *machismo* and the sexual prowess of the male, and a profound fatalism about the possibility of influencing events. Violence, particularly as an outcome of the impugning of masculinity and honour, finds fertile soil in such values. Adherence to this culture alone would vitiate any prospect of betterment.

The theme of masculine consciousness as a legitimation of crime and delinquency is a recurrent one from the work of the Chicago School onwards.[60] Similarly Paul Willis discerns, throughout the culture of motorbike boys, a concern with the elaboration of masculine imagery, an imagery that 'owed nothing to the conventional notion of the healthy masculine life. . . . Valued tenets of this code . . . such as impudence before authority, domination of women, humiliation of the weaker, aggression towards the different, would be abhorrent to traditional proponents of honour and labelled criminal by agents of social control.'[61] In early rock and roll, they found a musical form that corresponded perfectly to their self-image.

Bourgois employed the theme to explain domestic violence in New York City, arguing that Latino men, who resented being overshadowed by socially and economically more successful Latina women, resorted to violence to reassert their superiority and keep women in their proper place. And in his analysis of murder in Australia, Polk claimed that insult, respect, and face were crucial concepts in a violent culture of honour among lower-class males. Interestingly, it was Elias's argument that honour has been displaced by shame in the West that allowed him and others, such as Leyton, to explain the decreasing rates of homicide over the last two hundred years. Though relatively small-scale as yet, increases in the homicide rate may signify a reversal of that trend.[62]

Naturally, a host of criticisms have been directed against the conception of working-class culture propounded by Miller and others. Some have held that it is dubious to attribute the toughness and defiance of authority found among the 'roughest' communities to the working class in general. However, part of that criticism may result from a misreading of Miller's concept of 'lower-class culture' because in American sociology the lower class is *not* the same as the working class.

Nevertheless, these approaches do resonate with some aspects of the more serious forms of violence in a way that the more abstract Mertonian theories do not.

Class Conflict Theory

Class conflict theories apply much the same set of ideas to the explanation of crime and delinquency as do other theorists; but they do so within a broad Marxian framework which says that class conflict is inevitable in capitalist societies and that the dynamics of such conflict must be related to issues of deviance and control. This does not necessarily mean that delinquency is a simple symptom of class warfare or that delinquents are seen as fighting the system. But it does mean that connections are sought between the structural contradictions of capitalist societies, deviance, and control.

The concept of subculture, for example, has been applied to innovations in youth culture,[63] which emerge where the contradictions of capitalist political economy work their chief effects—in the working-class inner city. Post-war changes in housing, transport, and technology have, despite some gains in affluence, served to fragment the working-class community. The costs of the faltering of the machinery of prosperity in the 1970s and 1980s fell quite disproportionately on working-class youth and on immigrant minorities. The inability of the parent working-class generation to cope with these problems means that they were refracted onto the young. Their response to the resulting family tensions and economic insecurity was symbolic; it was the creation of subcultural styles that express the contradictions hidden or unresolved in the parents' culture.

Thus, for example, the skinhead style was an attempt to recover and assert the traits associated with hard manual labour under threat from technological change. And if there is a certain uniform pattern to the rise and fall of successive styles, it is because revolts into style[64] cannot resolve the contradictions that give rise to them.

Stuart Hall and his colleagues have applied the same model to the issue of delinquency, in particular to middle-class expressive movements.[65] The rise of the hippy counterculture is attributed to the growing incompatibility between the traditional puritan ethic and the new-found affluence and consumerism of the expanding middle class. The breakdown of traditional middle-class constraints began from *within* the dominant class. It was then transformed and pushed to expressive lengths in both the hippy and student protest movements, where it was perceived as a threat to social order.

Case Study—Learning to Labour

In his study of how working-class young people get working class jobs, Willis tackled a subject that is almost worn out by the sociological repetition of the observation that schooling is perceived by such youths as a massive irrelevancy. His work gained insight by combining interviews and observations of a small group of boys in a typical British comprehensive school during their last year at school and first year in work. What they revealed was their clear sense of their limited life chances in the industrial division of labour and the implications of that sense for their resistance to schooling. Their own hidden curriculum was escape from the tedium of the everyday round. Their culture stressed the perennial themes of 'symbolic and physical violence, and the pressure of a certain kind of masculinity'.[1] 'Sexism' and 'racism' were part of the price to be paid for achieving a form of masculine self-image that rendered the prospect of routine manual work palatable.

Willis uses the terms 'culture' and 'counterculture' in a dialectical sense to convey the 'profane creativity' of subordinate cultures as a route to radical cultural change.[2] By implication, earlier approaches define cultures as 'simply layers of padding between human beings and unpleasantness'.[3] The active appropriation and reworking of cultural items junked by capitalist commodity fetishism can provide the materials for at least temporary challenges to the cultural dominance of the bourgeoisie. Willis's analysis of the cultures of motorbike boys and hippies and Hebdige's of punks share a view of profane culture as a refusal to be silenced by superior cultural forces.[4] In his study of the school counterculture and shop-floor cultures, Willis goes further. He acknowledges that it would be wrong to impute to 'the lads' individually any critique or analytic motive, yet 'their collective culture shows both a responsiveness to the uniqueness of human labour power and in its own way constitutes an attempt to defeat a certain ideological definition of it'.[5]

Though he fights shy of using the term 'alienation', he is in effect applying Marx's original use of that term to the realm of cultural production. Capitalism ultimately determines the conditions by which the limited 'penetrations' that the lads collectively make into the mysteries of bourgeois ideology become a weapon for their own willed subordination. They were in no sense colluding with bourgeois ideology. They fashioned their own independent critique of the system—the higher values placed on manual labour in particular—the logic of which was their eventual entrapment in labouring. The system won, though a certain autonomy at the cultural level was salvaged.

[1] P. Willis, *Learning to Labour*, 36. The colloquialisms roughly translate as avoiding work, catnapping, and fooling around.

[2] P. Willis, *Profane Culture*, 1.

[3] P. Willis, *Learning to Labour*, 52.

[4] R. Hebdige, *Subculture: The Meaning of Style*.

[5] P. Willis, *Learning to Labour*, 132.

Corrigan adds a historical dimension to the paradox that the long struggle to win the right to schooling for working-class children was so largely wasted on them. We should not be too surprised about the result, he argues, in view of the fact that what has been won is the right to a form of schooling originally *imposed on* the working class in a struggle that robbed them of their own emerging educational institutions. Corrigan also proposed a different interpretation of Matza's idea that much street delinquency is the manufacture of excitement. In rule breaking, the 'rules are not broken *specifically because they are rules*; rules are broken for the most part as a by-product of the flow of activity engaged in by the boys.'[66]

His work compares well with Jack Katz's phenomenology of street crime in America and Cusson's later analysis of delinquent motives in Canada. To Katz, violent crime has its own hedonistic and sensual aesthetics centred on excitement. Skinheads, for instance, take violence to have a seductively glorious significance, and not simply to be a matter of using posture and violence to raise terror.[67] With Cusson's subjects, the pursuit of deviance is linked with four broad sets of goals: action, appropriation, aggression, and domination. Action itself 'is the commission of deviance to expend energy and to get the sensation of living intensely'.[68] But in all cases, the class context both limits and subverts autonomy.

The work of the cultural criminologists addresses these themes afresh. Hayward argues that hyperconsumerism is contributing to social problems in ways that are new and qualitatively different from those expressed in classical strain theory,[69] because consumption rather than production provides young people's very sense of identity with expectations of claims to key symbolic goods. The market swamps all competing values with its own credo of force-fed consumerism. This agrees with studies of youths who engage in street robbery, not for survival or even profit, but for the cash to buy the latest fashion accessories. Symbols of deviance are fed into marketing, even mainstream advertising videos, which trade on transgressive images of violence, pillage, and drug use.[70] Moreover, both hemmed in and excluded from public and private space, demonized youth are goaded into manufacturing excitement by conjuring up 'carnivals of crime'.[71] These analyses, whatever their claims, do not logically break with strain theories and allied approaches, but seek to relate them anew to the changed social and economic conditions of late modernity.

A recent, similar approach looks at the punk subculture of British Columbia. In an extensive set of interviews, punks are shown to be a heterogeneous, classless youth culture, reacting to their apparent failure at school, family difficulties, and unemployment.[72]

Other British studies are centred on the subcultural reproduction of crime and deviance, but they are based on a very different foundation of theory, being more redolent of the Chicago School in their emphasis on the embedded and normal character of rule breaking in urban settings. Deviation is not necessarily taken to be a spirited or half-spirited gesture of refusal, frustration, or anger at capitalism and its structured deprivations. It is, instead, part of the fabric of everyday life, transmitted uneventfully as a tradition in certain working-class communities, as in one working-class public-housing estate:

Discussion: Deviance and Culture—The Case of West Coast Punks

A recent sociological study of West Coast punk rock music subculture was done in the field, which means that the researcher, Stephen Baron of Queen's University, went out and interviewed young people where they lived and interacted on the street. Since Canadian adolescent subcultures have been a largely unexplored area, the research was quite informative.

The researcher conducted unstructured interviews with subculture members, where there was a give and take in the conversation. He found that getting access to the youths was relatively easy, especially when he said there was no interest in their criminal activities. He wanted to hear their views on unemployment, school, how they saw themselves fitting into society, and what society could offer them. He hung around with them, talked to them, and then got names of others who might consent to be interviewed.

Surprisingly, about one-third of those interviewed were conformist; that is, they believed it was possible to achieve their goals without compromising their principles by fitting in. However, others were what he calls retreatist, being quite negative about their long-term goals, and giving up on fitting in. These youths had ceased to believe in society's goals and were pessimistic about ever getting there by being conventional.

What is nice about Baron's study is that he includes the voices of those he interviewed, as in: 'I'm downwardly mobile and proud of it. Like I don't know about the way my parents live. Like get a job, work nine to five, do it for thirty odd years, then get shipped off to some lousy pension. I couldn't handle that. Like my dad worked thirty years to get a pension. You might as well live on welfare.'

Commenting on what he did every day, another youth said: 'Panhandling for the dog, scamming a little bit here, scamming a little bit there. It's a living.' Does it sound easy? When he was asked about what the future held for him, he said: 'Generally I don't like to think about it. You walk down the street and you see old men crashed out and you just hope that it's not you in a few years.'

These youths came from different social classes, but they all felt the effect of the lack of employment opportunities. And they didn't seem to think that school was the way out. On this there was open resistance, as in: 'I hated it. Teaching you useless stuff. You really don't learn anything, all you learn is to follow orders. They don't teach you how to think and survive. They just try to mold you into their little working part of society.'

If you think that's a pretty cynical comment, how about this one: 'Basically I think the school system is just to teach the kids how to be good followers. Like you're taught all the stuff you're learning is what other people have to say and repeating it back. You're not supposed to think, you're supposed to say yes ma'am, yes sir. The law has been decreed by their standards.'

The obvious defeatism in these comments and the belief that society has little to offer them by following a conventional route was reinforced by the perception that political resistance was also futile. And even worse, the males were more likely to opt out of conventional dreams than were girls, and they of course are more likely to resort to criminality.

To be fair, there were different responses to their conditions, and the comments presented here are among the more defeatist, but they serve to illustrate how when youths feel that they cannot change conditions of unemployment, poverty, and alienating labour, sometimes they seek to achieve status through participation in alternative deviant subcultures.

Source: Adapted from C. McCormick, 'Punks Have Goals, but Not the Mainstream's (Crime Matters column), *Daily Gleaner* (Fredericton), 2 August 2007.

Criminality was intimately interwoven with the social life of the estate. Dominant features of the social life . . . were the typically long tenancies; the fact that many had grown up on the estate and absorbed its way of life; and the closely interlocking family networks, especially in south-east Gardenia. Where, as in the south-east of the estate, there is a particularly high proportion of 'rough' families, this group of social features produces a distinctive way of life which is obviously related to the mainstream working-class culture, yet which differs somewhat from it: in short a *subculture* . . . [One] feature of the subculture was that criminality was in some circumstances tolerated—so many or most members of the subculture (including women) were occasional offenders; some were career criminals, consistently seeking out opportunities for . . . material gains through criminal activities; and all accepted that some activities (such as dad 'fixing' the electric meter or mum buying a carpet 'very cheaply' off someone in a pub) were part of the normal pattern of life.[73]

Ethnographic studies have illuminated the processes buttressing such a 'normal pattern of life'. For example, in a study of a stable, high-crime area, criminality imposed an organization on social relations, and insiders claimed that they felt protected, and less fearful, because they knew the local offenders and did not suffer from their predations. In another study, of a city neighbourhood not especially notorious for its criminality, the researcher came eventually to focus on '"street-wise" teenagers . . . [who] were not professional criminals but mundane and petty offenders, who graduated from a highly visible and public juvenile street life to the private, institutionalized exploitation of black economy outlets as adults'.[74] One of the chief conclusions was how very mundane, orderly, and conventional those teenagers' delinquency could be. It fitted into the structure of local life. Members of each generation seemed to progress quite smoothly from public, expressive rule breaking to a more secure, inconspicuous and lucrative participation in the informal economy. Members of each generation were ambivalent about the deviance of people younger than themselves, not only condoning their delinquencies, but also subjecting them to mild criticism. Delinquency was confined and regulated informally by a working consensus about the limits of tolerable rule breaking.

Similarly, Dick Hobbs's *Doing the Business*[75] explored the individualistic, entrepreneurial world of the working class. Hobbs's subjects were forever 'duckin' and divin', wheelin' and dealin' around the borders of legality, searching for the good deal, the market opportunity, and the clever score. Theirs was also a shadow criminal tradition, and it was not imbued with a marked spirit of resistance, refusal, or frustration.

Case Study—Crime and the Labour Market

The 1980s in the West proved to be a decade of the New Right, which culminated in the collapse of the socialist regimes and a return to a free-market economy. With the jobless growth born of the new information technologies, unemployment, long-term unemployment, underemployment, and seasonal employment emerged as central trends.

In terms of subcultural theory of delinquency, this was a recipe for anomie, although it occurred unevenly. In the worst-afflicted neighbourhoods, youths with no apparent hope of gaining manhood in the traditional breadwinner role sought fulfilment in the manufacture of excitement.[1] Forms of delinquency evolved that transcended the intermittent and the mundane: 'steaming' brought the force of numbers to bear for robbery and theft in crowds and shops; 'hotting' meant bravura displays of racing stolen cars around local public-housing estates; and 'ram-raiding' entailed smashing stolen vehicles into shops or even houses as a method of gaining forcible entry. Official crime rates increased, only to mirror a fall from the 1990s onwards. It was not surprising that public anxiety mounted and declined.

The most convincing analysis of the link between unemployment and deviance, particularly property offences, has been supplied by Wells and Dickinson. Allowing for a time lag between movements in the business cycle and changes in the crime rate, they demonstrated that there is a decline in property offences during years of economic recovery and a rise during recession.[2]

More surprisingly, successive governments resisted the view that deviance and unemployment was connected. Lack of personal morality, inadequate discipline in the home and school, and increased opportunity were officially cited as the reasons for the growth of crime. Theories about how these attributes derive from a new 'underclass' born of welfare dependency were debated.³ Dennis and Erdos, who argued from within 'ethical socialism', disputed the 'underclass' thesis and contended that the rising lawlessness could be explained only in terms of the decline of the traditional family: the 'anomie of fatherlessness' rather than of unemployment.⁴

In this welter of assertion and counter-assertion, the exclusivity of the focus on employment or on single parenthood is the most striking trait. In an outstanding attempt to rethink the complex issues and evidence involved, Elliott Currie in *Confronting Crime: An American Challenge* argued that, first, economic trends and inequalities not only affect employment opportunities but also destabilize communities and families; and, second, that under-employment may be little better than unemployment as a source of livelihood sufficient to support a family and to provide an active sense of citizenship.

A basic component of anomie theory, namely, the long revolution of rising expectations, interacts with the changing meaning of joblessness in the late twentieth century to produce a new moral calculus. In comparison, in the 1930s, however scarring the experience of unemployment, the shared hope was that jobs were being withheld and would reappear when times and governments changed.⁵

As Lea and Young argued, 'The first Industrial Revolution involved the exploitation of labour by capital. The second Industrial Revolution involves the emancipation of capital from labour.'⁶ Rising aspirations of consumption combined with falling expectations of productive employment lead to a particularly corrosive sense of exclusion.⁷ A striking metaphor for this intensification of cultural inclusion and structural exclusion is 'bulimic culture', a process of force-fed ingestion followed by compulsive expulsion.⁸

Fine shows the scale and complexity of the problems involved:

> The declining economy had its effect on the quality of life in the city. . . . Detroit as of 1987 had the second highest infant mortality rate in the nation, about 65 per cent of its families were single parent households. . . . Violent crime was of special concern to Detroiters, the per capita homicide rate being 3 times higher in 1987 than in 1967 and higher than that of any other city. . . . Were the Detroit of the late 1980s to return to the conditions prevailing in the city of 1967 . . . it would be hailed as a remarkable and happy achievement. And yet it was in 1967, not 1987, that Detroit experienced its great riot. How is one to explain this seeming anomaly?

Fine's answer is that, despite some positive changes (the emergence of a black leadership in city government and an integrated police force), the mood of Detroit was

> one of despair rather than hope. . . . The rioting of 1967 was born of hope, not of despair, the hope that improvement would follow the

disorder in the streets. . . . The 'inescapable reality', wrote Barbara Stanton, was that there was 'far more destruction and violence in Detroit in 1987 than in 1967. . . . It is as if the riot had never ended, but goes on in slow motion. Instead of a single stupendous explosion, there is a steady, relentless corrosion.'[9]

The evidence tends to support Currie's re-analysis of trends in deviance and unemployment. Rising youth unemployment in the early 1980s was followed by the spread of 'hard' drug use in the most deprived areas, and the emergence of new crime groups that were extensively involved in much higher rates of property offences to pay for their drugs.[10] Rates of opioid use correlated strongly with rates of unemployment.[11] The quality of work and under-employment vied with unemployment as causes of deviance. In a rare study using both variables,[12] unemployment was found to be most strongly associated with high juvenile (14–17) arrest rates, but under-employment was associated with high young-adult (18–24) arrest rates.

Against the view that arrest rates reflect police numbers rather than deviant activity,[13] one study based on victim survey data found that the probability of victimization from burglary and theft increased significantly with the rate of local unemployment.[14] In another study, the exigencies of street life increased the involvement of dropout and homeless youth in property offences.[15] Ethnographic work in three contrasting neighbourhoods established the links between access to primary-labour-market jobs and relatively petty and short-lived delinquency, on the one hand, and restriction to secondary labour-market job networks and more serious offending, on the other.[16]

Although it is tempting simply to assume that work is an antidote to youthful delinquency, reductions in deviance could prove all too ephemeral if extremes of inequality persist or increase:

> In the developed world, as much as half the variation in population health, in homicide rates and in social cohesion appear to be due to income inequality alone. . . . Nor is this picture based on an unrealistic contrast between the levels of inequality common in modern societies and some unreachable level of total equality. Rather, the picture reflects the importance of the relatively small differences in inequality . . . between the developed market democracies.[17]

McAuley shows how on a public-housing estate the crime-drugs nexus fills the vacuum created by de-industrialization. And Winlow shows the rise of entrepreneurial crime alongside craft and traditional petty crime, with masculinity expressed in 'bouncing' not ship-building.[18]

In *Bouncers: Violence and Governance in the Night-time Economy*, Hobbs and colleagues present an analysis of how changes in political economy connect with trends in street violence and disorder. In the wake of deindus-trialization, local authorities in the worst-affected cities and towns received little help from central government in making up the loss of industrial rev-enue. As the day-time economy based on production foundered, they exploited the night-time economy based on consumption.

For example, Manchester City Centre now attracts crowds of up to 100,000 people on Friday and Saturday evenings, with thirty to forty police officers are engaged in public-order duties and an estimated 1,000 bounc-ers working each night. This creates social environments in which aggres-sive hedonism and disorder become the norm. In the night-time economy, locations 'bad' for crime and disorder are invariably 'good' for business.[19]

The new 'leisure infrastructure', far from being a panoply of diverse recre-ational services, has seen traditional pubs, cafés, and restaurants driven out. Currently, in the UK, concern about drink-fuelled disorder centres on the legalization of 24-hour opening times. However, the key move towards opening up the night-time frontier to a licensing free-for-all had already taken place. Authority to consider new liquor licensing applications has been transferred to local authorities, themselves complicit in weakening con-straints against whatever expansion the 'market' will bear.[20]

As cities compete for the marketing of corporate conferences and tourism, such rising violence and disorder will be met by tougher policing and more punitive sentencing. Yet the police may be hopelessly swamped at peak times, and the number of bouncers and private security will increase. There are already more private police in Canada than public, and in some areas alliances between the two are crucial to crime control.

While Hobbs et al. are keen to avoid scapegoating bouncers for their often marked associations with illicit drug-dealing, organized crime, and 'protection', and while bouncers are increasingly subject to modes of pro-fessionalized training, and certification, their growth as a form of quasi-but unaccountable policing shows an important aspect of the definition of the rule of law in modern societies: the State's monopolization of legit-imate violence. Although many clubs and bouncers operate to regulate rather than propagate deviance, their ambience is still contrived to stim-ulate a transgressive aura, where displays of 'face', 'respect', and the more *macho* masculine profiles are a recipe for descents into violence. One of the authors of *Bouncers* remained behind in the night-time economy to document how drinking establishments were to be designed and man-aged, not only to maximize the sale of alcohol but also to regulate drink-ing behaviour; how the police and informed outsiders came in time to argue that such concentrations were not conducive to public order and how they began to contest licensing applications. His conclusion is that the police and councils are being out-gunned by those who champion deregulation.

Some new studies have strengthened the 'blocked opportunities' approach associated most distinctively with the subcultural theory of Cloward and Ohlin. These are not theories linking crime to sheer deprivation or working-class culture or, indeed, to an 'underclass'. They view the most serious and pervasive forms of deviance and delinquency as the consequence of a combination of complex experiences born of relative deprivation in a highly competitive, increasingly fragmented social order.

Those most liable to become career delinquents are the politically and economically marginalized youths most disaffected from the core institutions of family, school, work and the standard forms of leisure. As a number of projects have shown, however, they are far from unreachable, and one of the key interventions may have been the growth in further and higher education which has had cultural, economic, and regulatory implications for young people who might once have been deemed at risk. What remains elusive is the political will to fund basic community resources to which they will demonstrably respond. Yet the same tendencies to anomie which strain theorists argue underlie their delinquency also furnish the motives for social polarization, the pursuit of wealth, and the 'crimes of the powerful'.

[1] B. Campbell, Goliath: Britain's Dangerous Places.

[2] See J. Wells, 'Crime and Unemployment' and Dickinson, Crime and Unemployment.

[3] C. Murray, Losing Ground; W. Wilson, The Truly Disadvantaged.

[4] N. Dennis and G. Erdos, Families without Fatherhood, 102.

[5] See H. Mannheim, Crime between the Wars.

[6] J. Lea and J. Young, What Is to be Done about Law and Order?

[7] It is interesting that, in an ethnographic study of American young men, McLeod found that blacks were less delinquent, in part because they perceived themselves to be on a rising curve of prosperity, whereas whites were more delinquent because they thought themselves to be in decline as a group. See J. McLeod, Ain't No Makin' It.

[8] J. Young, 'Merton with Energy, Katz with Structure: The Sociology of Vindictiveness and the Criminology of Transgression'.

[9] S. Fine, Violence in the Modern City, 459, 461, 462–3.

[10] H. Parker et al., Living with Heroin.

[11] G. Pearson, The New Heroin Users.

[12] E. Allan and D. Steffensmeier, 'Youth, Underemployment and Property Crime: Differential Effects of Job Availability and Job Quality on Juvenile and Young Adult Arrest Rates'.

[13] R. Carr-Hill and N. Stern, Crime, the Police and Criminal Statistics.

[14] R. Sampson and J. Woolredge, 'Linking the Micro and Macro Levels of Lifestyle Routine Activity and Opportunity Models of Predatory Victimization'.

[15] J. Hagan and B. McCarthy, 'Streetlife and Delinquency'.

[16] R. McGahey, 'Economic Conditions, Neighborhood Organization and Urban Crime',

[17] R. Wilkinson, Mind the Gap, 64.

[18] R. McAuley, 'The Enemy Within: Economic Marginalization and the Impact of Crime on Young Adults'; S. Winlow, Badfellas: Crime, Tradition and New Masculinities.

[19] D. Hobbs et al., Bouncers: Violence and Governance in the Night-time Economy, 43, 247–8.

[20] D. Hobbs et al., Bouncers, Violence and Governance in the Night-time Economy, 41.

■ Criticism

The promise of subcultural theory was that it would be better than any other at fitting the facts. Those 'facts' clustered around one central assumption: that the most serious forms of delinquency are found in a highly localized form in one sector of the social system, that of the male, lower-class, urban adolescent. However there are some criticisms of this assumption:

•*First, a basic problem from the outset was that the prevalence of delinquency was far from general, even in this sector.* The problems encountered by members of this category led only a minority to serious delinquency and only a minority of a minority to serious *gang* delinquency. Yet the other options open to such boys, the 'college' (upwardly mobile) and the 'corner-boy' (respectable, working-class) adaptations, were never successfully differentiated causally from the delinquent option. The question 'Why should similarly situated youths sometimes choose delinquency and sometimes the alternatives?' was left open, so that subcultural theory became all too vulnerable to David Matza's criticism that it overpredicted delinquency by accounting for far more than actually existed. Matza's own approach, with its characterization of most delinquency as 'mundane' and 'periodic', veers towards the opposite fault of 'underprediction'.

> Subcultural theory over-simplified the problem of delinquency.

•*Second, a related problem in the assessment of the theory revolves around its dependence on official statistics.* Numerous self-report studies threw serious doubt on the subcultural theories' identification of the more serious forms of delinquency with lower-working-class, male, urban adolescents. The more sophisticated studies narrowed the differentials between male-female and lower class–middle class.[76] Moreover, throughout the 1960s, forms of social deviance such as drug use and even instrumental violence became associated with just those groups that were theoretically most immune to delinquency: the middle-class college boys. Were subcultural theories addressing a non-problem, and were they incapable of addressing emergent ones?

•*A third difficulty was that the theories had always relied heavily on analytic imputation.* Subcultures were alleged to arise in situations of socially structured strain, where the 'contradictions of capitalism' were experienced most intensively. This search for correspondences between problems and solutions could lead all too easily to the circularity of explanation already familiar in the social disorganization and functionalist schools. The saving grace of earlier subcultural theories had been an insistence on evidence that adherents to a subculture should be aware of the problems to which it was a response and of the values around which it was held to cohere. In later subcultural theories, this safeguard has been eclipsed all too frequently by the decoding subcultural style into what are assumed to be its immanent properties.

Attempts to solve the problem of analytical imputation—that is, to establish whether or not the distinctive meaning systems of the various subcultures are in reality those imputed to them—have taken successively complicated forms.

> The problem of imputation is central to analysis; however it also needs evidence.

•*In one solution, subculture was inferred from the distinctive linguistic vocabulary used by pickpockets and sneak thieves.*[77] The homology between language and practices was complete. A self-enclosed, relatively unchanging way of life was depicted. Such unity was never established in the more variegated instances of expressive delinquency, though Willis establishes a considerable symmetry in the relations between lifestyles and musical forms in his studies of profane cultures.

•*In another solution, early subcultural theorists such as Cloward and Ohlin tried to link distinctive sets of norms, values, and beliefs to allegedly distinctive types of delinquent subculture.* In such work, the relationship between the parent culture and deviant subcultures was essentially static. The only source of change was the apparently growing instability of the inner city. Hence, it was reasonable to attempt to 'trap' subcultural norms by standard techniques of interview and survey methods.

•*In yet another solution, labelling theory introduced a fresh source of change, the nature of the social reaction.* Dynamism was injected into the static conception of subculture, through the analysis of the societal reaction of others to deviance. Social reaction could be seen to reinforce subcultural cohesion, as in Young's depiction of the impact of police harassment on drug users.[78] Such work complemented earlier approaches, and the preferred method of the labelling theorists, participant observation, enriched available accounts of cultural meanings. Sources of change in delinquency still did not seem to be explained adequately by such methods, however. This failing was most pronounced in the analysis of what Hebdige has termed the spectacular subcultures of adolescence that periodically emerged as apparent symbols of youthful defiance.

•*The introduction of fresh dynamic, developments in class conflict in post-war Britain, promised a means of accounting for the shape such subcultures took.* New methods were employed, in particular semiotics, to capture the nuances of each successive style as a *mélange* of signs, or *bricolage*, as Lévi-Strauss would call it. But the problems of imputation have become, in the process, more rather than less evident.

In a searching critique of the work of the 'new' subcultural theorists, Stan Cohen addresses the problem of imputation at three levels of analysis: structure, culture, and biography.[79]

•*First, at the level of structure, the main innovation has been an appeal to history.* In the work of such theorists as Phil Cohen, Corrigan, and Pearson, working-class delinquency is placed in the context of class struggle. This perspective enables the theorist to analyze both continuity and change afresh. The daily toll of routine delinquency can be related to the reproduction of order by normalized repressive means. The spectacular subcultural innovations can be related to crucial moments in the class struggle. For example, the skinhead style emerged in the attempt to retrieve traditional symbols of working-class cohesion devalued by post-war affluence. The problem, however, is that such an approach easily drifts into historicism, where a single historical trend is picked out—commercialization, destruction of community, erosion of leisure values—and then projected onto a present which is more complicated, contradictory or ambiguous.'[80]

•*Second, at the level of culture, Cohen says these new approaches:*

are massive exercises of decoding, reading, deciphering and interrogating. These phenomena *must* be saying something to us—if only we could know exactly *what*. So the whole assembly of cultural artefacts, down to the punks' last safety pin, have been scrutinised, taken apart, contextualised and re-contextualised. The conceptual tools of Marxism, structuralism and semiotics, a Left Bank pantheon of Genet, Lévi-Strauss, Barthes and Althusser have been wheeled in to aid this hunt for the hidden code.[81]

The dominant themes of resistance to subordination through symbolic displays usually mean that the real enemy (the bosses, the State, or the dominant class) remains unscathed. The essentially subversive nature of the subcultures can be inferred from their styles. As Hebdige put it: 'These "humble objects" (bikes, clothes, make-up) can be magically appropriated: "stolen" by subordinate groups and made to carry "secret" meanings that express, in code, a form of resistance to the order that guarantees their continued subordination.'[82] This may, as Stan Cohen puts it, be 'an imaginative way of reading the style; but how can we be sure that it is also not imaginary?'[83] Ultimately, however, symbols may mean what they appear to mean; or be taken to mean the opposite, as Hebdige claims they should in the case of the punks' wearing of the swastika emblem. However this has been criticized for overemphasizing the political significance of style[84] and for producing a cultural Freudianism.[85]

•*Third, at the level of biography, much the same problems recur, in a fashion akin to earlier subcultural theory.* With delinquency as with other phenomena, many are called but few are chosen or choose themselves. The subcultural deviants are greatly outnumbered by the conforming majority, despite their common exposure to similar pressures. No fresh insights are offered as to which variables might intervene to differentiate the two. In this respect, there is continuity with, but no significant improvement on, earlier cultural approaches: that delinquent and troublesome youth cultures signify a reaction (with degrees of commitment, consciousness and symbolic weight) to growing up in a class society.[86]

A final criticism of subcultural theory in general applies with particular force to the exponents of the various class conflict approaches. It may be termed 'differential magnification', that is, the tuning of the analytical lens to an almost exclusive degree on the subordinate cultures while neglecting the more dominant cultures. In these works, the worlds of teachers, social workers, policemen, prison officers, employers, and even academics are treated with the very disregard for ambiguity, complexity, and resistance to ideology that would be condemned if applied to working-class or delinquent cultures. This massive over-simplification is at times justified in terms of structuralist method: whatever they think they are doing, those in authority are doomed to support the system. The limitations of this position could be overcome by extending to these groups the forms of research reserved as yet for 'subordinate cultures'. The idea that upper- and middle-class cultures comprise merely 'stultification, reification and pretence'[87] deserves a skeptical examination.

Indeed, there has been an unfortunate neglect of the methodological problems involved in exploring, describing, and analyzing entities so complicated and intangible as 'culture' and 'subculture'. It is as if culture were a self-evident body of monochromatic beliefs laid out as propositions that any intelligent observer could read. Little heed has been given to the situated, heterogeneous, and fluid nature of belief; to its ambiguities, anomalies, and contradictions; and to the sheer difficulty of pinning it down and arranging it as a 'system'. On the contrary, subcultural theorists have embarked on their work without any but the most token of nods to the sociology of knowledge, or cultural anthropology, which could aid in discussing such epistemological questions.

Causal explanation and interpretative approaches have both been addressed, though the focus has been almost invariably limited to juvenile delinquency and adolescent trouble making.[88] Criticisms of the factual basis for much theorizing in this vein have in their turn been subjected to substantial attack, not least for their tendency to overstate the impact of selective forms of policing on the construction of delinquency.[89] Certain basic assumptions have resisted invalidation.[90] Above all, perhaps, the logic of subcultural theories predicted with some success such developments as the emergence of a 'hustling' culture among African-Caribbean youth and the appeal of extreme authoritarianism among the most disadvantaged white adolescents.[91] It may well be that such predictions are eminently possible without the aid of subcultural theory. But they at least support the view that such theories have strengths that have barely been explored, as well as glaring weaknesses.

Finally, the Cultural Studies School has reanimated the possibilities of making culture more than a synopsis of the problems it explains. Indeed, culture has been resuscitated in the emergence of what is now called 'cultural criminology', a blend of symbolic interactionism, phenomenology, the work of the Chicago and Birmingham schools, and radical sociology. The sociology of deviance has a habit of forgetting its past and then reinventing itself, and in this, its latest guise, it celebrates as new a culturally framed description of such phenomena as street racing, graffiti, and 'masculine fantasy and the internet'. It is set, as some of its predecessors were, in juxtaposition to a demonized and over-simplified representation of competing work as positivistic, not recognizing that many other diverse strands of 'deviantology' also take an interpretive stance. Ferrell and his colleagues declare, for instance, that cultural criminological writing and research tend to look and feel different from the normal science of positivist criminology because cultural criminologists remain conscious of pluralities of meaning and the possibilities of alternative perception.[92]

Cultural criminology emphasizes, as did its predecessors and contemporaries, the biographical and lived reality of subordinate groups. It rehearses familiar themes of political economic crisis. It traces elements of ideas current elsewhere in theoretical sociology—ontological insecurity, globalization, post-modernism, the commodification of leisure, the ever-growing stress on consumption, the lack of biographical continuity over time, and the fracturing of community. It celebrates deviance as 'transgressive excitement' and, in so doing, it tends rather to forget the victim, who may well *not* celebrate what is done and whose cultural work is not taken to be worth inspection.[93] And it also tends to follow members of the Birmingham School in its portrayal of those who respond negatively to deviants as cardboard figures without depth or complexity. For example, in contrast to the sympathetic interpretation of the graffiti writers' activities and arguments, anti-graffiti campaigners amount to 'one-dimensional ciphers of a one-dimensional culture'.[94] The criticism is that cultural criminology extends the right to create and inhabit webs of meaning to some but not to others.

It may be that what is new about cultural criminology is that it places analysis in a media-saturated world and adds to it the special inflection lent by Jack Katz in his interpretations of the seductive excitement of the criminal exploit. Essays in the *genre* focus on stylized transgression and subversion as a form of cultural resistance to oppression.'[95] Typical of its world view is the following:

As identities and meanings become more fluid and contested, populations become more transient, and citizens become more wary of face-to-face interaction, traditional forms of collectivism, sociality and communality appear to fragment and disintegrate. New media technologies provide a means of achieving a sense of identity, belonging and community in this climate of uncertainty.[96]

Despite perhaps not being quite as novel a departure as some of its proponents pretend, and despite ignoring some of the qualifications that victimology might have introduced, cultural criminology is nevertheless a welcome return to an engagement with the complexities of the lived reality of deviance. It performs a useful service in tracing the many forms of deviance with its attendant motives and accounts, reminding us once more of the importance of will, exploit, and meaning in transgression.

Chapter Summary

Subcultural theory involves the interesting idea that deviance is supported by others in similar circumstances, usually those who are similarly oppressed. In this sense, then, deviant action is not in any simple sense voluntaristic, but results from sharing the similar experiences of others.

Here we have considered the difficulties and contradictions in this approach and also how it is enhanced through adding in alternative perspectives. Those perspectives differ in various ways, one of which is the amount of independence accorded to the actor and also the extent to which the reaction of others is taken into account.

Critical-Thinking Questions

1. Various adaptations to Merton's approach are considered here. What are they, and how do they extend Merton's work?
2. How is strain an element in subcultural theory?
3. What are Cohen's solutions to the problem of imputation?
4. What is the difference between instrumental and expressive deviance, and how is it important for studying subcultures?
5. How can we explain the variations in auto theft as cultural variations?

Explorations in Film

The Outsiders, a film by Francis Ford Coppola, is based on a popular teenage novel by S.E. Hinton. It was originally filmed in 1983, and then remade in 2005. The film is set in Oklahoma of the 1960s, and the plot (and much of the tension) hinges on the conflict between a group of poor youths called the 'greasers' and the more affluent group called the 'soshes'. What is interesting about the development of this film is that Coppola was asked by a high school class to film the novel.

Websites

Department of Sociology, McMaster University:
http://www.socsci.mcmaster.ca/sociology/research/culturemedia.cfm

Culture and the media is a diverse field within the Department of Sociology at McMaster University. It covers ideology, popular culture, subcultures, news media, the political economy of the mass media. Faculty members are studying such topics as the role of popular subculture in sports, bodies, and tattooing; and have published research on youth drug and straightedge subcultures on and off the Internet.

Chapter Seven

Symbolic Interactionism

Chapter Overview

This chapter looks at the symbolic interactionist perspective, which developed in reaction to, but also in accordance with, some of the principles of the Chicago School. In fact, the interactionists are sometimes called the second Chicago School.

Symbolic interactionism is known for its focus on societal reaction and labelling rather than the causes of deviant behaviour itself. It is based on the idea that society's reaction is important for the understanding of deviance, both that of oneself and of others.

Symbolic interactionism also includes research based on the idea of collecting the 'lived culture' of deviance, for which it owes a debt to the ethnographic work developed in Chicago. It is best known for its research on marginal cultures, but it can also be adapted to the work of conflict theories and the micro-social workings of power.

■ Introduction

For two decades the pre-eminent department of sociology in the United States was the University of Chicago Sociology Department. Its students were to set the agenda for the evolution of mainstream sociology, which remained virtually unchallenged until the appearance of structural-functionalism in the late 1930s. As work proceeded and scholars dispersed, the various strains of Chicago sociology tended to undergo separate development. Ethnography became associated with one wing, subsequently described as symbolic interactionist. The connection and continuity have been real enough for some to call interactionists 'neo-Chicagoans'[1] and others to call them a second Chicago School.[2]

> Symbolic interactionism is associated with Chicago School ethnography.

There is some debate about the unity of this 'origin myth', and Louis Wirth said he couldn't understand what people meant by the Chicago School, because of the diversity of ideas and styles of work among his colleagues.[3] However, it is a name associated with a distinct perspective and strong research strategies, especially when compared with Parsons' work at Harvard, and Merton's at Columbia.[4]

Interactionists were to be overshadowed during the 1940s and 1950s by functionalism, which was dominant in that period.[5] However, Sutherland, his colleagues, and his students did continue to explore deviance as an example of differential association, writing about embezzlement,[6] drug addiction,[7] professional crime,[8] the crimes of business corporations,[9] and deviant motivation.[10] Everett Hughes wrote about matters that were of some oblique interest to sociologists of deviance and, in particular, about the moral division of labour into clean and dirty work, with its accompanying stocks of innocent and guilty knowledge about the world.[11] One man, Edwin Lemert, was to be recognized later as a vital forerunner of the interactionist sociology of deviance. He borrowed from symbolic interactionism to construct a general theory of social pathology.[12] But all this work seems to have been considered at the time as rather peripheral to the main body of sociological writing.

It is not at all clear why the Chicago School should have been eclipsed.[13] Nor is it clear why its heir, symbolic interactionism, should have come to prominence in the sociology of the 1960s. Symbolic interactionists were a little puzzled themselves, and Howard Becker, the man held chiefly responsible for the renaissance, expressed considerable surprise at his own influence.[14]

However, it must be remembered that the possibilities of the functionalist and anomie models had not been exhausted; indeed, they had never been fully exploited in sociology. In contrast, it cannot be alleged that the Chicago School had practised a kind of withdrawal and return. There had been no willing retreat; nor had there been any lack of work on deviance.

• *First, the re-adoption of interactionism may be explained by what seems to be the natural life of sociological fashions*: there is an ingrained impatience with the old that condemns every set of ideas to a limited vitality. But there is no reason why this must happen.

• *Second, it may also be explained by the great expansion of higher education that took place in the 1960s*, an expansion that disrupted routine and introduced marginal academics to teaching and research. This would allow for the broader interest in a diversity of approaches.

• *Third, it may have been connected with what were thought to be some of the distinctive qualities of the decade*: the flowering of expressive deviance, an interest in countercultures, and the novel sense of openness and a toying with what Horowitz has called the politics of experience.[15]

There was indeed something of an affinity between a particular social world and a particular kind of writing. Interactionism was held to be an existential sociology that had animation and openness enough to capture new understandings of the social world. Thus Gouldner argued:

> This group of Chicagoans finds itself at home in the world of hip, Norman Mailer, drug addicts, jazz musicians, cab drivers, prostitutes, night people, drifters, grifters and skidders, the cool cats and their kicks. To be fully appreciated this stream of work cannot be seen solely in terms of the categories conventionally employed in sociological analysis. It has also to be seen from the viewpoint of the literary critic as a style or genre and particularly as a species of naturalistic romanticism.[16]

Although interactionism was pursued actively long before the emergence of the special low life of the 1960s, and participation in that life was no prerequisite to becoming an interactionist, a number of interactionists have apparently accepted a history of themselves as crypto-deviants.[17] They have not vociferously rejected the biographies that were constructed for them. Interactionism did suddenly seem to loom large. It became sovereign for a while. Sections of certain works have been described as 'catechisms' for the sociology of deviance.[18] One book in particular, Becker's *Outsiders*, was to become one of the two most frequently cited of all American criminological writings between 1945 and 1972.[19]

Symbolic interactionists take part of their job to be a formal description of the little social worlds that constitute a society. Schools, gangs, families, pubs, and hospitals are not unlike the natural areas studied by the Chicago School. They are bounded social situations, created by people who experience them as sets of changing resources, opportunities, contexts, and constraints. Any social situation will be a blend of activity, history, and material props that achieves its definition and coherence from shared symbols. It is to be expected that some features of those worlds will be familiar and general and that others will not. How they will combine and under what conditions can never be clear until they have been examined. Indeed, interactionists would say that an explorer can never know what he or she is exploring until it has been explored. It requires a particularly patient, cautious, and attentive methodology to chart such a delicate and complicated process as social life. It is all too easy to impose an alien explanatory scheme that obscures vision, ignores problems, and pre-empts solutions. Gusfield remarked: 'What stands out for me is the intensive focus on the empirical world; on seeing and understanding behavior in its particular and situated forms. Data that do not stay close to the events, actions, or texts being studied are always suspect.'[20]

Becker's *Outsiders* is an all-time favourite.

Above all, it is held that an analysis must grasp the meaning that inspires, animates, and shapes social activity. Consequential meaning is that employed by the social actors themselves, not by the sociologist. Interactionism is designed to take the observer and audience as far as is practicable inside the actors' own perspectives on themselves, their acts, and their environments. Howard Becker, the most influential of all the interactionist sociologists of deviance, reflected 'The so-called "labelling theory" revolution should never have been required. It was not an intellectual or scientific revolution. . . . [It merely] directs us to understand how the situation looks to the actors in it, to find out what they think is going on so that we will understand what goes into the making of their activity.'[21]

Interactionists thus tend to practise the anthropology of participant-observation, a technique that marries surveillance to an involvement in the affairs of a social world. The resulting reports cannot but be limited, since they dwell on the particular character of one constellation of events, but first, they should be able to reproduce what is both intricate and subtle; and second, what they report should be generalizable aspects of social behaviour.

> Participant observation is a technique used by symbolic interactionists.

■ Symbolic Interactionism and Deviance

There is a modest compatibility between interactionism and deviance that stems from the propensity of rule breakers to gather in the small, bounded social worlds that interactionist ethnography can map. Stereotypical deviants such as heroin users, thieves, and prostitutes may draw themselves apart, seeking out those who share common problems, experiences, and solutions; but so also do journalists, lawyers, and professors. When they gather together, people create groups whose peculiarities can stimulate the sensitivities that are indispensable to interactionism.

We have already argued that ethnography requires sociologists to reconcile the two contradictory states of participation and observation. They must so distance themselves that they can define commonplace actions and utterances as problematic, and yet their knowledge must be intimate enough to permit a reasonable interpretation of the meanings of those selfsame actions and utterances. Deviant phenomena can take the form of people doing extraordinary things in an ordinary and familiar world, or *vice versa*, and they lend themselves to special study.[22] Theft, drug taking, and prostitution are a useful blend of the common and the uncommon that permits the sociologist to be both provoked and appreciative.

In a 2004 interview Howard Becker topicalizes his technique in reaction to a question about the beginning of his interviewing in 1949:

> I took drugs, I smoked dope, and I used what I learned doing that to understand. I took advantage of what my life gave me. I was a musician, so I was immersed in it before I ever thought of being a sociologist. A lot of the work I did relied on what is called participant observation, that is to say, you get involved in the life of people you are studying. I studied medical students for

three years. I didn't pretend I was a medical student. So, 'Here I am, I'm a sociologist, I'm going to be around here for the next couple of years so get used to me'. I just went everywhere, watched what they did; it was immersion in that sense, being there a lot, being there all the time. When you interview people they tell you about things they think are important, but they don't tell you everything because that would be James Joyce doing Dublin for a day. They don't tell you everything, they tell you what they think you want. I don't mean that they mean to please you, they are just trying to be helpful. But if you are there you can see all the things that happen and it gives you something concrete to attach your questions to. You don't say to a medical student, 'What do you think about patients in general?' You say, 'That guy in the bed there that we just talked about with the teacher, what do you think about him?' So you get something very specific, which is always a more accurate reflection of what those people are doing than a generalised answer.[23]

The Issue of Labelling

In the last chapter, on subcultures, we mentioned the idea that the phenomenon of deviance was both action and reaction. What this means is that deviance is not only action outside the norm, but also action characterized as such by others who are reinforcing the norm.

In that vein, we look here at how deviance is defined as a product of the ideas that people have of one another. It is argued that social action cannot be a response to people as they 'really' are and in every detail. After all, encounters are often brief and much is unknown, concealed, irrelevant, or ambiguous. People are constrained to react to a filtered, adapted, and limited conception of themselves, one other, and the situations in which they meet. Activities are necessarily based on working definitions that are situated and negotiable. Central to such conceptions are the names and symbols upon which definitions are built: as names change, so do actions. For a while, the naming associated with deviance was held to be so important to its interactionist analysis that the entire approach was generally, if misleadingly, termed 'labelling theory'. The remarks of Becker, Kitsuse, and Erikson are frequently cited:

> Labelling theory looks at the reaction to action, and how it names acts as deviant.

> Social groups create deviance by making the rules whose infraction constitutes deviance and by applying those rules to particular people and labeling them as outsiders. From this point of view, deviance is *not* a quality of the act the person commits, but rather a consequence of the application by others of rules and sanctions to an 'offender'. The deviant is one to whom that label has successfully been applied; deviant behavior is behavior that people so label.[24]

I propose to shift the focus of theory and research from the forms of deviant behavior to the processes by which persons come to be defined as deviant by others. Such a shift requires that the sociologist view as problematic what he generally assumes as given—namely, that certain forms of behavior are *per se* deviant and are so defined by the 'conventional or conforming members of a group'.[25]

The critical variable in the study of deviance . . . is the social audience rather than the individual actor, since it is the audience that eventually determines whether or not an episode of behavior or any class of episodes is labeled deviant.[26]

There is a recommendation in all three remarks that the sociologist should concentrate on the work that naming accomplishes. Deviance is held to be a kind of description used in the conversations that order social life. As Kitsuse and Erickson say, they are not interested in the causes or effects of deviance, but rather in the business of making *claims* that acts are deviant.[27]

Conversations have distinct and analyzable qualities, and it is those qualities that organize some of the character of deviance. It should be noted that interactionists do not take conversation to be confined entirely to activities outside the self. Their discussion of deviance hinges on a larger conception of names, selves, and conversations, and it is imperative to turn to that conception before the more focused analysis becomes clear.

The Question of the Self

Chief among the problematic objects confronting an observer is the self. Unlike the phenomenologists, interactionists maintain that people lack a sure knowledge of what they are and what they can accomplish. New problems and settings pose new tasks, and it is not always certain that one is equal to them. It is not even certain that one can always repeat past achievements. Indeed, one experiences oneself as a somewhat erratic and shadowy entity: one can let oneself down or surprise or embarrass oneself. Every situation has the capacity to establish, educate, and redefine the self.

•*Any action requires an appraisal of one's capacities and of the implications of the actions for oneself.* There are certain things one can or cannot do, certain things that might seem inconsistent with past performances, and things that either humiliate or elevate the self. It follows that monitoring and assessment of the self are indispensable to any intelligent social strategy. A mind must scan itself just as it scans other objects in its environment once it has learned to externalize itself as an object in a world of other subjects. Only then will it be able to form conjectures about what it appears to be, what an environment will permit it to do, and how it may work back on the environment to shape it to its will. In all this activity, it is evident that there is a vital division within consciousness. One phase or aspect of reasoning becomes a surveying subject; the other becomes a surveyed object. Bending their minds back on themselves, people become an observing 'I' and an observed 'me'. Activity may then be likened to a kind of intellectual acrobatics in which mind becomes contorted in an effort to view itself.

> Monitoring the self is part of social interaction.

> Mead worked with this idea of the 'I' and the 'me'.

•*The internal gyrations of the self would be virtually impossible without language.* Words have a power to fold back on the speaker with a special force: people cannot see themselves, but they can hear themselves speak (so to speak), and it may well be that their hearing is not too dissimilar to the hearing of others. Speaking, they can become their own stimulus: they are able to act and then react to themselves. In this fashion, speech encourages a sense of self-estrangement, an opening-up of the 'I' and the 'me', which allows one to become one's own audience.

Words have an additional power in that they tend to be relatively anonymous and accessible to anyone. Describing oneself, one has to employ terms that are universal and universalizable. Those terms transform private experience into a public matter, thus making the unique general and social. As one uses words, particular circumstances receive a common classification. Furthermore, that public currency of speech is also used by those about one. It becomes possible to imagine some of the responses that others have to one's action and projected self.

> Discourse makes possible the objectification of the self.

•*An imagination of the replies of others is the vital prerequisite of social action.* It distinguishes mere actions from concerted and co-operative behaviour. Imagination permits the construction of the 'significant gesture', a gesture that is at the very core of all sociability. A person who acts is rarely heedless of the effects of what he or she does. Whether action is benevolent or malevolent, it is normally intended to achieve some response. Thus, the planned action must be tailored to the anticipated reply that others might make. Anticipation requires one to take the role of another, to envisage how he or she views one's display and predicts one's intentions. It forces one to mould one's gestures so that their significance is conveyed properly and efficiently.

•*The work of composing a significant gesture is complicated, and it entails rehearsing one's own reply to the other's reply, conceiving the other's answering response, and so on.* It also entails a running interpretation of the complementary activities that the other does. Imaginations thus become intertwined and mingled in a common social undertaking. The private and subjective are locked into a wider structure. It does not follow that one's interpretation of the other is 'correct'. Indeed, there is no sure method of establishing the inner meaning of one's own and another's acts. But all joint behaviour rests on a series of working conjectures and definitions.

> Being successful requires anticipating how others will react.

In summary, interactionists hold that life is patterned by symbolic indications. People continuously interpret themselves, their settings, and their partners. They must make sense of the past, make plans, and infer intentions. Indications are predominantly linguistic, although gestures, expression, clothing, and context also convey meaning. Language permits the identification and stabilization of social affairs. It allows one to assume persistence and similarity so that responses become available. It is the common medium that integrates public activity.

It is in this sense that the self has been compared to a dialogue within consciousness. The 'I' and the 'me' talk to one another, stimulating one another, interpreting one another, and relying on words for their understanding. The process of recognizing and negotiating deviance is thus merged with the inner moral world of the self. Decisions about future conduct turn on readings of the meaning of deviance, the acceptability of deviant identity, the significance of particular acts, and the possible responses of others. They revolve around the character of potential selves, and they are all made within the self.

An early and important article by Becker, reprinted in *Outsiders*, traced some of the stages of one such private conversation.[28] It discussed the manner in which the marijuana user came to terms with the known and likely definitions of drugs: 'I was with these guys that I knew from school, and one had some, so they went to get high and they just figured that I did too, they never asked me, so I didn't want to be no wallflower or nothin', so I didn't say nothin' and went out in the back of this place with them. They were doing up a couple of cigarettes.'

When the article was written, marijuana was thought to be much more dangerous substance than we think it is today. The prospective user was obliged to consider moral consequences, especially, in terms of what kind of person he or she might become. Plans were moulded by an acceptance, rejection, or redefinition of stigmas. Management of the problem had little to do with the social control emanating from direct confrontations with other people, the police, or the courts. But it did centre on the social control embedded in the meanings of deviation and the self.

Discussion: Deviance and Culture—Emily Murphy

In 1922 Emily Murphy wrote *The Black Candle*, in which she advocated the need to change the Canadian narcotics laws. She wrote that 'when coming from under the influence of [marijuana], the victims present the most horrible condition imaginable. They are dispossessed of their natural and normal willpower, and their mentality is that of idiots. If this drug is indulged to any great extent, it ends in the untimely death of its addict.'

She also quoted from a pamphlet published by the Children's Aid Society of the City of Montreal: 'The cocaine habit must be stamped out in Canada. It is under-mining our boyhood, and cutting away the moral fibre of our girls. It is turning our young people into criminals and imbeciles.'

She also wrote, 'The physical aspect I can but liken to consumption. The deadly work of the drug is done before either the victim or the relatives perceive it. . . . The victim becomes emaciated, extremely irritable, nervous, suspicious, fearful of noise and darkness, depressed, without ambition and bad tempered to the extent of viciousness. Boys and girls lose all sense of moral responsibility, affection and respect for their parents, their one thought being to get the dope and be with their friends.'

Needless to say, Murphy is credited with contributing to the 'deviancy amplification' that resulted in the criminalization of marijuana in 1923. However, what is also interesting in the following quotation is that she was aware of the influence of the media in dramatizing drug problems:

In 1918, the late Chief of Police McLennan, who was brutally murdered by a drug-fiend, called attention to the prevalence of the drug habit in this city which he stated was then becoming alarming. The police authorities claim that although the drug habit has been growing here, it has certainly not been growing any more rapidly than in other cities proportionately to population, but that greater prominence has been given to Vancouver on account of the publicity given to the subject in the daily press, and also on account of the great activity and success of the police department in prosecuting drug traffickers and seizing drugs.

Murphy remains a famous Canadian claimsmaker, for her influence in the public debate over marijuana.

Sources: E. Murphy, *The Black Candle*, 150. Retrieved 31 March 2007. Available at http://www. freeworldnews.com/frontmatter.html.

The experience of oneself as free to deviate depends in part on having access to the right names and explanations, first discussed in a classic article by C. Wright Mills in 1940, taken up by Sykes and Matza in 1957 and then by Scott and Lyman in 1963.[29] It is easier to do something if one has a sympathetic description of the act. When acts and states can be reassessed as worthy or innocuous and when they can be presented as not 'really' deviant, it is a little easier to accept them. We have already described how, arguing that deviation requires a mastery of guilt, Sykes and Matza listed the techniques of neutralization that offer more or less honourable motives for dishonourable acts.[30] An appeal to higher loyalties or the denial of injury can exculpate the deviant and permit a drift into rule breaking.

> Techniques of neutralization are justifications for deviant acts.

Hannah Arendt once recalled how Dostoevsky said in his diaries that 'in Siberia, among scores of murderers, rapists and burglars, he never met a single man who would admit that he had done wrong'.[31] The very absence of an apparent motive can itself become a motive and can liberate the offender from personal responsibility for his or her conduct.[32]

The Role of the Public

Deviance becomes qualitatively transformed when it ceases to be the subject of purely private contemplation. One is then required to rehearse and provide an account to those who may be curious, offended, perturbed, or charged with the enforcement of rules. The account must not only satisfy oneself but also manage the responses of the suspicious outsider. Strategies are used routinely to contend with the problems that deviance brings in its train. Among them are penitence and the acknowledgement of fault.[33] Not all deviation is magnified when it is confronted by accusation or sanction,[34] for it may decline and the rule breaker can feel shame or fear. And there are the alternative strategies of denying blameworthiness, representing deviance as some other phenomenon, or deflecting attention away from treacherous signs.[35] Quite commonly, problems are solved by retreating to the company of those who are similarly beset. When deviance is co-operative and dependent on joint activity or on a division of labour, it is especially likely that errant sub-worlds will emerge.[36]

> Sharing deviance makes it normative, making subcultures desirable.

•*In those sub-worlds, pretences may be partially abandoned, unwelcome relationships avoided,[37] skills learned, and supportive interpretations acquired.*[38] Deviant subcultures represent limited answers to the difficulties of living in a hostile, critical, and discouraging world. Over time they can come to offer a modest refuge, providing new meanings to overcome the opprobrium that deviance attracts. Such subcultures have come to be the special province of the interactionists. Their research is replete with the histories of small deviant circles.

In one such history, Lemert's study of the forger,[39] the naïve forger usually acts alone, but the professional or 'systematic' forger lives in more of a subculture, which has an *argot* that distinguishes members of the group from outsiders. This vocabulary, or language, is studied by the interactionist.[40]

Or in another example, Becker's classic study of the professional dance musician, he records how musicians delineate themselves as different from their clients, whom they define as 'squares'. In many ways, the subculture of musicians is a way of isolation from the demands required for commercial success, as well as a way to assert occupational autonomy. Eventually, even in leaving the subculture, the member asserts the importance of the subculture: 'I'm glad I'm getting out of the business, though. I'm getting sick of being around musicians. There's so much ritual and ceremony junk. They have to talk a special language, dress different, and wear a different kind of glasses. And it just doesn't mean a damn thing except "we're different".'[41]

Thus, membership in a group creates a special sense of inside and outside, of who belongs and who doesn't, part of which is necessary and part of which is contrived.

Becoming an insider itself is an involved process that can be studied. For example, in *The Rebels: A Brotherhood of Outlaw Bikers*, a more recent study of organized motorcycle gangs in Canada, Daniel Wolf (of the University of Prince Edward Island) uses a scene from a chapter called 'Forming Bonds of Brotherhood', to describe the process of accepting new affiliates into a motorcycle gang before they can ever become full members:

After the Sunday dinner the four of use went riding, and I decided to treat everybody to a movie. We were the centre of attention—stares and gawking from the local citizens—while standing in line for the movie. Amidst all this attention Jim pulled out a plastic bag from his leathers. He very nonchalantly proceeded to roll a couple of joints of marijuana: 'Tell you what, Coyote, I'll roll, you get the popcorn!' Feeling somewhat paranoid and at a loss for words, I replied: 'Yeah, but there's no way I'm buying popcorn if we get busted before the movie.' These types of social encounters act as informal screening processes. A friend of the club gets a good idea as to whether or not he is compatible with members in terms of their personal values and social strategies, such as the risk involved in committing an illegal act in public. The commission of such an act simultaneously reinforces a member's self-identification as a biker and differentiates him from the citizens around him. In effect, Jim was teaching me to say, 'Fuck the world.'[42]

•*In the main, it is the public meanings and structures of deviation that interactionists choose to study.* Not only does interactionism deny the sociologist the capacity to reach the inaccessible processes that make up a subjective experience,[43] but it also asserts that recognized deviance is the proper topic for sociology. Deviance enters social life when it receives a response. Accordingly, interactionists may be a little indifferent to finding the first causes of deviance.

In the analysis of mental illness, for example, there are those, like Thomas Scheff, who argue that the origins are diffuse, numerous, and often untraceable. The important sociological problem is not the medical or even social explanation of those origins but the fashion in that mental illness becomes identified and shaped in public interaction.[44]

> To an interactionist, mental illness is a topic of discussion, not a cause.

Similarly, Lemert observed that breaking rules is common in everyday life. However, sociology should not focus on the multiplicity of petty, undistinguished, and unacknowledged breaches. It should analyze the forms that those breaches take when there is some reaction from others. Deviance is then transformed from a private event to public behaviour; it intrudes into the public arena to become a socially consequential event.[45] In a supporting illustration, Becker returned to Malinowski's description of a Trobriand Islander who had committed incest.[46] The incest was tacitly condoned until denunciation made it inescapably public. This advertisement transformed what had been a tolerated private act into an intolerable public act, impelling the Islander to face an untenable situation and kill himself.[47]

> Deviance is the transformation of private problems into public troubles.

Discussion: Deviance Exploration—Thomas Szasz on Ideology

History is full of people clinging to erroneous ideas believed to be religious or scientific truths. As the physicist Max Planck (1858–1947) observed: 'A new scientific truth does not triumph by convincing its opponents and making them see the light, but rather because its opponents eventually die, and a new generation grows up that is familiar with it.'

In the natural sciences, the lifetime of belief in false truths tends to be brief. In contrast, beliefs in false truths about custom, religion, politics, and law can linger for decades, centuries, even millennia.

Coercive world savers have always been blinded by their reforming zeal. . . . Drug prohibitionists deny the importance of the need for mind-altering chemicals, a propensity they perceive as 'drug abuse' and call individuals that cater to that need 'narcoterrorists'. . . . [P]rohibitionists . . . seek to cast the ignoble war on drugs into a noble, therapeutic rhetoric, and the more they fail, the more they insist that they are on the right track.

According to a September 2006 report in *The New York Times*, Afghanistan's opium harvest has increased almost 50 per cent from last year and reached the highest levels ever recorded. . . . People who grow and sell opium, like people who grow and sell olives, are engaged in agriculture and trade. The opium trade is said to constitute one-third or more of Afghanistan's gross domestic product. Cultivating and selling a plant or plant product is not terrorism. Using explosives and herbicides to destroy crops—especially the crops of far-away people with different traditions and religions—is terrorism.

. . . In the United States alone, intoxicated drivers cause an estimated 17,000 traffic deaths per year, one every 30 minutes. Twenty per cent of all traffic fatalities are due to driving while under the influence. . . . [P]eople say, 'I work hard and I'll be damned if I'm not going to have a beer or two on the way home.'. . . There's a church, a school, and 10 bars in every town. . . .

Customs and traditions are more powerful than laws, guns, and herbicides. We have our customs, other people have theirs. 'Why,' asks an unidentified Afghan, 'does the government tell us to stop growing opium when it's doing nothing about alcohol use and prostitution? Opium is not mentioned in the Koran, but alcohol and prostitution are.' A scholar of Iranian culture reminds us that before Qajar period (in the nineteenth century), 'opium was deeply integrated into Iranian social and daily life. People consumed opium each morning in order to be in a good mood to go to work. . . . Opium functioned in Iranian society the way that wine does in French society.'

People who grow and sell opium are engaged in providing people with a much sought-after product. The market is a place to sell and buy goods, not an opportunity for engaging in mayhem and murder. Conversely, people who use explosives and chemicals to destroy other people's agricultural products are engaged in aggression and pillage.

We define certain goods, in particular opium and cocaine (but not alcohol and pornography), as presenting irresistible temptations . . . and persecute the tempters. And we define the persecution of the producers of these goods as the protection and promotion of public health; call the people who justify and promote it 'medical scientists' and 'lawmakers'; and honour the individuals who engage in the mayhem and murder integral to the enterprise as heroes in a noble 'war on drugs'.

Afghans who grow poppy are criminals. Americans who use heroin are patients suffering from a 'diagnosable no-fault disease' we call 'substance abuse'. . . .

Could all this deception, self-deception, effort, and expense be the consequence of a conceptual error and our unwillingness to admit that it is an error?

Source: Abridged from T. Szasz, 'On Not Admitting Error', 21–2. Available at Cybercenter for Liberty and Responsibility, http://www.szasz.com/freeman19.html.

The emphasis here is on the transformation of a private issue into a public problem. It is important to note that a concentration on public response does not entail the claim that there is no deviation without labelling by others. Considerable confusion has arisen from the critic's belief that interactionism treats public labelling as a fundamental prerequisite of deviance. Indeed, some critics have maintained that 'hidden' or 'secret' deviance poses insuperable problems for the interactionist.[48]

We have shown that interactionism does indeed recognize the way in which people answer and adapt to their own private descriptions of self without any intervention from outsiders and that it has demonstrated that the consequences of such self-labelling are real enough. Indeed, a recent and influential study has argued that what affects whether prisoners re-offend or not is the character of the narratives of the self that they can construct and project into the future. One who has reformed through religion, 'self-realization', a new understanding of the consequences of crime, and the like may then base his or her life on a new 'me' as a person now 'straight'.[49]

Interactionists do also attach uncommon significance to the public recognition of deviance. When rule breaking receives a reply from the outside world, it must be defended, ended, or disguised. It must be altered to cope with novel, often painful restraints. The deviant may have to contend with the imputation of sinister intentions, the awarding of an unpleasant identity, and social placement with pariahs. Just as important, such deviation can become a feature of others people's lives. Their conception of the world, its character, and its dangers will be framed by knowledge about publicly ratified transgressions. There is a significant difference between the experience of one who has 'merely' stolen and one who is a certified thief. Stealing might not have been incorporated into core definitions of the self. It might have been construed as a lapse or atypical adventuret that was rather peripheral to the kind of person that one is. Public definition can translate that stealing into a 'master status' or pivotal feature of the offender's personality. It will affect the manner in which he or she is treated by others. The thief may become obliged to reconsider who he or she is and what he or she might do in times to come. There is, Lemert argues, the possibility of a symbolic

A master status is a main feature of one's personality.

reorganization of the self: 'When a person begins to employ his deviant behavior or a role based upon it as a means of defense, attack, or adjustment to the overt and covert problems created by the consequent societal reaction to him, his deviation is secondary.'[50]

•*Secondary deviation can occur in any of the transactions that centre on the overt deviance of a person.* It may arise in informal relations. Indeed, official intervention by the police and other agents being relatively uncommon, it is the informal response by others that is most often encountered. Quite crucial will be the general and local assumptions that people apply to detected deviation. People who are influential in secondary deviation are, foremost, friends and family. In this way, as Hagan suggested,

> the identifying characteristic of the labelling approach is the casting of the 'reactors', rather than the 'actors,' in the casually significant role. . . . Labeling theory would likely benefit empirically from the acknowledgement of a reciprocal relationship between actor and reactor, stimulus and response, and, most importantly, between pre-existing differences and 'reaction effects.[51]

It is evident that much rule breaking is tolerated, as long as certain informal 'secondary rules' are themselves observed. There is theft in the workplace. There is lying in everyday life. Sexual transgressions occur. It is not every instance of such rule breaking that is reported to law-enforcement agencies. Some is condoned, some falls outside the authority of the law, and some is thought not serious enough to merit action. It is equally evident that what is intolerable in one group may be approved in another. For instance, what is proper in a bar is not always proper in a lecture theatre. Deviation is defined by its situation, by its perpetrators, and by its audience. In the course of a day, a person will pass through innumerable settings, and the rules of one will not be the rules of another. The conventional order of a family does not apply to relations between strangers in the street or to the organization of a workplace.

Deviance is defined by the situation.

More dramatically, there may be quite marked discontinuities between worlds, discontinuities that turn the 'normal' order upside down. For instance, Barbara Heyl has described how the madam of an American brothel educated novice prostitutes by attempting to insulate them from the universe of 'squares': there was a systematic inversion of strategic sexual and social conceptions about men, money, and intercourse.[52]

Or in another example, Gresham Sykes describes how men in prison adopt styles of survival that involve 'force, fraud, and chicanery'. These survival styles he characterizes as those of 'men, merchants, and toughs', which are ways in which individuals adapt to prison circumstances. It is the creative adaptation to social circumstances, negotiated through interaction, that is the subject of study.[53]

It is not the simple presence of deviance but its quality, scale, and location that usually shape a reply to it. Very often, deviance can be 'normalized' and accommodated[54] inside the fabric of accepted standards. It is only when it is inexplicable, disordering, harmful, or threatening that a critical reaction can take place.

A crisis occurs when others cannot or will not cope with the behaviour. The precipitation of deviance hinges on prevailing ideas about propriety and harm, the social organization of the audience, and the appreciation of possible remedies.[55]

•*Some groups are tightly organized, others have a loose order, and others little apparent order at all.* In turn, there is a great variation among the schemes that confer coherence on the world and among the abilities of people to monitor one another. The army is regulated by elaborate, interconnecting, and precise rules of conduct. It assigns special personnel to the business of administering order and judging disputes. By contrast, a group of youths who 'hang out' on a street corner inhabit a rather simpler world: it *is* rule-governed, but its rules are often implicit, ad hoc, negotiable, and unenforced. Remedies are also coloured by social ideology. There is an appreciable difference between the punishments inflicted by an army, a street-corner group, and a therapeutic community. Each punishment mirrors something of the symbolic vision of those who impose it. For example, a Quaker body might use discipline to underscore the importance of forgiveness and tolerance.[56] An army might use it to emphasize the need for subordination. Even so, connections are rarely simple and uniform. Quakers *do* expel members and call upon the police. The army *does* exercise clemency, recognize religious objections to certain practices, and make use of psychiatry.

> More than the deviant act itself, what is at stake is the limits of others' acceptance.

Institutionalization

The interplay between social control, social organization, deviance, and identity is neatly illustrated by Scheff's *Being Mentally Ill*. It is Scheff's contention that mental illness is a social role. Initially a disconcerting and anomalous breach of an unnamed, unnameable, 'residual' rule, mental illness is given form by lay and professional stereotypes of madness. There are abundant labels and definitions that describe the character and behaviour of the mad, and they are available to those who witness strange conduct. They are also available to those who have otherwise inexplicable and disturbing experiences. Labels may not be applied immediately. They may not be accepted without qualification when they are applied, and there is often some scope for negotiation.[57] But labels do embody general and seemingly objective ideas.

Labels are a way to make sense of problems by suggesting ways in which one can and should go mad and subsequently seek help. In particular, they inform psychiatric practice by providing a basis for diagnosis and treatment. Scheff would argue that much psychiatry is devoted to the 'apostolic mission' of persuading people to accept one of a limited number of mad roles. Patients are encouraged to comply with therapeutic authority, gain insight, and accept a particular definition of themselves. It is a paradox if a patient rejects a diagnosis, this is taken only to confirm his or her lack of insight and the astuteness of the diagnostician.[58] It little matters whether psychiatric analyses are correct or not, because the social consequences of analysis would remain the same. The sociological import of labelling is that certain versions of mad behaviour are rewarded and reinforced.

> Psychiatry persuades patients to take on the 'mad' role.

People learn to be mad, and others learn to see people as mad, confirming the validity and utility of the original stereotypes.

Partly because of how consequential it is, formal social control has been subjected to considerable analysis by the interactionists. It was interactionism that enlarged the task and complexity of sociology by insisting on the creative role played by outsiders in the production of deviance. So it was that Howard Becker reflected that 'deviance' includes both a possible infraction of a law or rule and a process of acting in some fashion against whoever might be thought to have committed the infraction'.[59]

Scheff and others demonstrated that it was difficult to explain the social organization of deviance by referring to properties of the offender alone. They argue that deviance is identified, answered, and formed by those who deal with rule breakers. The character of the response given by bailiffs,[60] the police,[61] psychiatrists,[62] magistrates,[63] and doctors[64] will provide the materials for the deviant's own significant gestures. At the very least, the deviant will be obliged to construct his or her actions around the probable reaction that they will elicit.

In a twist on the traditional paradigm, Scott Kenney (of Dalhousie University) looks at how people are treated by others when they fall victim to being survivors of homicide, that is, they are related to someone who has been murdered. He considers how victims are subject to labelling and reaction by others in the same way that deviants have been considered to be. They experience negative social consequences, and even though they are innocent bystanders, they can be blamed for their plight, as in this case of a woman whose husband killed her children: 'Some asked me "How could you let him kill the kids?" A few other people I counted as close friends suddenly were distant. The press had picked up that when [the offender] was arrested he shouted that I had done it. Some of these "friends" seem to have doubts about my involvement.'[65]

Imagine her distress at being blamed as, in effect, a co-conspirator in the death of her children. Is the reaction of others justified, and does it reflect perhaps their own emotional confusion rather than any deviance on her part?

The violation and enforcement of rules depend upon place, time, and character. Certain rules are not enforceable because, it seems, they are expressly designed not to *be* enforced.[66] Law officers are not automatons who are insensitive to the need to exercise discretion. They are also responsive to setting and organization, so that they behave rather differently in the inner city, the office, and the suburbs.[67] When offences are comparatively mild (and the definition of mildness is itself contingent), much may hinge on the demeanour and response of the deviant. Whereas compliance and deference on the part of a citizen may bring about a decision not to charge a person, surliness and tardiness can have the opposite effect.[68]

Choongh would argue that in many cases the police make it a practice to use the law simply as a resource for disciplining and confirming the subordination of particular populations, the 'dross' above all, and thereby upholding a moral order on the streets.[69] All this will be negotiated in a moving context of plans and relations. Police officers may be just about to come off their shift, they may be looking for overtime work, or they may be under scrutiny either for poor performance or excessive zeal.[70]

The police use their own discretion when rules are broken.

•*The agencies' intentions and capacities will be central.* Certain enforcement institutions are geared to regulating occupations or industries, and their prime objective is not to punish but to transform behaviour. The Oxford Centre for Socio-Legal Studies has produced a spate of studies of those who employ such 'compliance-based strategies'. Hawkins, for instance, has examined the control of the industrial pollution of rivers and canals,[71] and Hutter has written about environmental health officers.[72] The business of the environmental health officer is not to make moral pronouncements or punish those who produce contaminated food. It is to stop contamination and unhygienic practices. Yet, when people resist reasonable attempts to make them comply, they may well be treated as if they were conventional deviants. In all those studies may be found distinct pariah roles conferred on those who persistently, flagrantly, and disrespectfully ignore compliance strategies by disobeying enforcement officers. A neutral process will then give way to moral outrage at the deviance of those who disobey rules and the enforcers of rules.

That research has also pointed to the manner in which the wealthy, well-informed, and powerful are able to make creative use of the law's provisions in its own avoidance. It is the business of tax lawyers and accountants continually to discover gaps and inconsistencies that permit their clients to escape compliance.[73]

•*Other institutions lack the power or means to manage deviants as outsiders.* After all, enforcement is an expensive and laborious process when it is waged against those who have no wish to comply. Those institutions will then create identities that are expressly designed to ease their work. Being perhaps unable to control hostile and alienated people, they may instead emphasize the normality and conventionality of those whom they may privately define as abnormal. In the case of mass debt collection, for example, enforcement procedures are designed principally to persuade most defaulters that they are fundamentally honest, albeit forgetful people. Were enforcement to antagonize them, the routine collection of small debts would become impossibly expensive and time-consuming.[74]

> Enforcing some rules needs to be done sympathetically.

For rather different reasons, it was the policy of a home for unwed mothers to convince its clients that pregnancy was a misadventure that should not be blamed on them. The mothers were innocents, not sexually experienced women who used contraceptives.[75] In both cases, the regulation of deviance contributed roles that protected the self of the rule breaker. In the latter case, the proffered role confirmed the woman's virtue and her lack of any need to take future precautions, permitting future unintended pregnancies and a further drift into deviance.

•*There is thus a tendency to treat rules as tools rather than as binding instructions.* It is a tendency that creates considerable flexibility in the organization of relations between deviants and agents of control. The rule breakers themselves may be co-opted as allies or informants,[76] they may become part of a game-like and well-regulated exchange,[77] they may be effectively ignored, or they may be pursued with great vigour. For instance, it is so difficult to obtain information about deviant activities that have no willing complainant that the police have to offer incentives to insiders.[78] Drug suppliers may trade information for immunity.[79] And relations may also change: shifts in personnel, policy, or politics can

> Rules are guidelines, not recipes.

introduce pressures to abandon old strategies or adopt new ones. In one celebrated case, the appointment of a new chief constable led to a wholesale transformation in the control of homosexual importuning. What had been neglected became a target for energetic prosecution.[80]

There is also great scope for injecting variety *within* relationships. Willis observed that there was no uniform suppression of drug use in one English town. On the contrary, the users and the members of the local drug squad appeared to enjoy a symbiotic relationship. The police arrested those whose offences were relatively flagrant and substantial, and the users themselves reported 'pushers' whose behaviour was held to be exploitative and bullying. Most consumers were allowed to proceed undisturbed and co-existing quite amiably with the police.[81]

In summary, then, the orderly production of deviance and deviants therefore hinges on a complicated set of interchanges. It cannot be distilled down into a series of mechanical and predictable processes. Interactionism is accordingly somewhat reluctant to rely on schematic descriptions of social control. Instead, it turns sociology towards the detailed analysis of specific events. General themes *do* dominate that analysis, but they are not held to have the character of iron laws. On the contrary, outcomes are treated as uncertain and possibly surprising.

Case Study—The Construction of Blindness

Scott's *The Making of Blind Men* is an important demonstration of the intricate and largely unexpected forms that social control can take. The book, which stresses the interdependence of control and deviation, claims that the blind are manufactured by the special agencies which care for them. Organizations must achieve some success by displaying their capacity to train blind people for work and activity in the world of the sighted. Not every blind person can be educated. Only a few are eligible as candidates for transformation into the acceptably functioning blind. It is those few who are heavily recruited by the voluntary agencies for redemption. They are the: 'blind children who can be educated and the blind adults who can be employed. The system largely screens out the elderly, the unemployable, the uneducable and the multiply-handicapped—in other words, the vast bulk of the blindness population.'[1]

Blindness is rarely a total loss of vision. Many of those in the charge of blindness agencies can see a little. They are methodically encouraged to play the blind *role* by relinquishing any use of their residual sight and adopting the methods of the utterly sightless. They are required to learn incapacity and to conform to embedded institutional definitions of blindness. In this fashion, skills and senses are surrendered, being replaced by an orderly incompetence:

The disability of blindness is a learned social role. The various attitudes and patterns of behavior that characterize people who are blind are not inherent in their condition but, rather, are acquired through ordinary processes of social learning. Thus, there is nothing inherent in the condition of blindness that requires a person to be docile, dependent, melancholy, or helpless; nor is there anything about it that should lead him to become independent or assertive. Blind men are made and by the same processes of socialization that have made us all.[2]

[1] R. Scott, *The Making of Blind Men.*
[2] R. Scott, *The Making of Blind Men,* 14.

The awarding of deviant identity cannot then be portrayed as an elementary reflex action on the part of the State, powerful institutions, or even significant others. To be sure, the State does have considerable power to describe its subjects. It is a power that sometimes allows the subject little scope for negotiation or rebuttal. And in many transactions, the authoritative expert on control or treatment can impose his or her will on the deviant. And family and friends can be significant to personal assessments of deviance. Yet the definitions offered vary, and they may have remarkable differences. Becoming deviant is not always a straightforward process of amplification. The rule breaker may be coaxed into any one of a number of roles, wickedness being ascribed only when an agency or witness holds to ideas of free will, when the offender was thought to know what he or she was doing, and when he or she could have done otherwise.[82] This is what McHugh calls the 'theoretic' orientation.

Equally available are penitent, sick, or probationary roles, as Gusfield describes in his famous article 'Moral Passage'.[83] These roles serve to preserve the symbolic role of the law and to differentiate the deviant designations possible, as in this discussion of the 'sick deviant':

Acts which represent an attack upon a norm are neutralized by repentance. The open admission of repentance confirms the sinner's belief in the sin. His threat to the norm is removed and his violation has left the norm intact. Acts that we can perceive as those of sick and diseased people are irrelevant to the norm; they neither attack nor defend it. The use of morphine by hospital patients in severe pain is not designated as deviant behavior. . . .

Talcott Parsons has pointed out that the designation of a person as ill changes the obligations which others have toward the person and his obligations toward them. . . . He has to become an object of welfare, a person to be held rather than punished. Hostile sentiments toward sick people are not legitimate.

We have used the language of role and role playing, and there is some confusion in the suggestion that the world is neatly scripted and organized for dramatic purposes. As Goffman observed, 'all the world is not a stage—certainly the theater isn't entirely'.[84] Roles are adapted and created in use, breaking down their stereotyped character and replacing it by innovation.[85] Deviant roles themselves resist precise classification.

For example, increasingly interactionists have begun to write of homosexualities instead of homosexuality and to stress the diversity of sexual deviation.[86] It would be misleading to argue that the business of deviating consists merely of stepping into an arranged part. Interactionism casts deviance as a process that may continue over a lifetime, that has no necessary end, that is anything but inexorable, and that may be built around false starts, diversions, and returns. The trajectory of a deviant career cannot always be predicted. However constrained they may seem to be, people can choose not to commit certain actions.

Phillipson has likened this life process to a long corridor with many doors; one is not compelled to travel the entire length but may leave at almost any stage.[87] Indeed, one might go farther, just as deviant careers are likely to become chaotic and *disorderly*,[88] 'careening'[89] rather than organized because of the marked instability of the deviant's world; it is an instability created by cycles of boom and bust in drug dealing,[90] the unexpected arrest or experience of violence, and the lack of firm structures and controls.[91]

Luckenbill and Best argue:

Riding escalators between floors may be an effective metaphor for respectable organizational careers, but it fails to capture the character of deviant careers. A more appropriate image is a walk in the woods. Here, some people take the pathways marked by their predecessors, while others strike out on their own. Some walk slowly, exploring before moving further, but others run, caught up in the action. Some have a destination in mind and proceed purposively; others view the trip and enjoy it for its own sake. Even those intent on reaching a destination may stray from the path; they may try to shortcut or they may lose sight of familiar landmarks, get lost and find it necessary to backtrack. Without a rigid organizational structure, deviant careers can develop in many different ways.[92]

Becoming deviant is itself described dialectically as a series of phases that tend to supersede one another, each phase reworking the significance of what has gone before. In turn, each phase is held to be causally important in its own right. It is not enough to describe the initial conditions of rule breaking (be they social disorganization, conflict, or defective personality); it is also necessary to appreciate the evolving character of the deviant career. Thus Lindesmith and others have been somewhat scathing about psychiatric analyses that presume that traits diagnosed in treatment were somehow invariant dimensions of personality. They insist, instead, that those traits may have arisen in the treatment or control of deviation. Prostitutes or drug addicts may not have been passive or inadequate when they made their first moves towards deviation.

Becker accordingly stressed the need to employ a model of sequential causation that can comprehend the developing, staggered, and changing qualities of deviation. It is a model that requires an expenditure of time, patiently eliciting information in order to monitor or reconstruct events as they unfold. Like its ancestor, the Chicago School, interactionism defines research itself as emergent and exploratory. Knowledge about the social world is built up little by little in an active process of inquiry that continually transforms an original problem and the questions that can be asked about it.

Interactionism and labelling theory were given a new and possibly somewhat awkward emphasis in the British sociology of deviance of the 1960s. Independently of and simultaneously with the emergence of 'labelling' theory in the United States, a social statistician, Leslie Wilkins, had drawn certain inferences about the effects of the distribution of phenomena in social space.[93] He had observed that deviants were statistically uncommon, an odd claim unless it was intended to refer to *assumptions* about the frequency of rule breaking. Wilkins proceeded to argue that there was a tendency for deviants to become structurally isolated from the majority. This was also an argument that *might* be said to hold about popular *assumptions*. He concluded that since information about such an isolated minority was necessarily transmitted over a distance to the majority, it was second-hand or 'mediated', and thus was liable to distortion.

The effect is called 'deviancy amplification'. Amplification occurs when the majority or its agents react to a deforming representation of the deviant minority so as to create a new situation, problems, identity and context for deviation. The answering replies of deviants are again distorted, generating a new response and a new reply. Incorporated by Cohen[94] and Young,[95] amplification theory explained the dialectical progression of deviant processes: action producing reaction in a spiralling chain of ever more alienating gestures. Some slight initial difference in dress, expression, or conduct can lead to a sequence of events that magnifies and exaggerates the difference and creates deviance. Thus the Teddy Boys were given a demonic cast in the England of the 1950s and came to stand for much that was corrupt and evil.[96]

Amplification theory seems to be most telling when it is applied to symbolic or expressive deviation, that is, deviation that is proclaimed publicly and designed to invite a public response. It is not clear how such amplification cycles start and end, nor is it clear why particular cycles amplify visible deviation whereas others serve to reduce it.[97] At stake, it may be supposed, are not only the problems of recruitment confronted by deviant groups that have become ever more estranged from the mundane world, but also the difficulties faced by those who remain, difficulties of increasing censure and isolation. Becoming and staying deviant can become simply too costly.

> Amplification occurs when the media distort events for an unsuspecting public.

■ Criticism

As the interactionist sociology of deviance became more important, criticism developed as well. Predictably, one response was from those whose work had been overshadowed. However, there was also a reaction from those who had exploited developments within interactionism, pursued them beyond the limits of interactionist analysis, and returned to interactionism with their new arguments. As Plummer remarked in 1979, 'In just ten years, labelling theory has moved from being the radical critic of established orthodoxies to being the harbinger of new orthodoxies to be criticized'.[98] The history of interactionism has followed the conventional pattern of much sociology: the extraordinary has become ordinary and then banal.

Attacks have usually been coloured by the parent perspectives of the critic. What one takes to be a conservative stance[99] is thought by another to be radical. Interactionism is defined as overly empiricist by one person[100] and not empiricist enough by another.[101] Interactionist debates are complex because of questions about the positions of the questioners.

•*The first and most obvious objection to interactionism challenges its scientific standing.* The disciplines of the natural sciences are articulate, precise, and reasoned in their methods. Thus, it is held that sociology should proceed by scanning problems logically, formulating hypotheses, and applying them rigorously. However, interactionism is heir to the assumptions and practices of the Chicago School, and it is as resistant to an orderly logico-deductive methodology. It patently fails to conform to the strict scientific procedure.[102] It is hesitant about elaborate planning and exposition because, it argues, such work blinds one to the possibility of learning in the field. Thus, Laud Humphreys observed that 'hypotheses should develop *out* of . . . ethnographic work, rather than provide restrictions and distortions from its inception'.[103] Interactionists would preserve their openness to the social world so that they can be educated as they pursue their research.

Humphreys' *Tearoom Trade* is a classic of observation.

Hostile critics perceive this as a deliberate and unsatisfactory lack of preparation. They portray interactionism as ambiguous, ill-resolved, and evasive. They are particularly distressed by its refusal to offer conjectures that might sustain or refute its fundamental propositions. Adopting a falsificationist philosophy of science,[104] they remark that interactionism is not scientific, because it is a closed system that resists refutation. There is some merit in the observation, for it could be said that symbolic interactionism has woven such a subtle system of indeterminate ideas that the rejection of one can always be explained by invoking another. Its proponents would retort that science should respect the qualities of the materials it explores, and since the social world is distinguished by ambiguity, contradictoriness, and openness, it would be foolish to impose schemes that block out those qualities. To pretend otherwise could lead, in Rorty's words, to the kind of ahistorical scientific method that would be employed by one who 'knows in advance what results he or she desires and has no need to adjust his or her ends'.[105]

However, perhaps interactionism is engaged in a different project. There are many occasions when the perspectives and methods of interactionism are peculiarly suitable, particularly, Katz argues, where new, complex, hitherto unexplored, or especially vivid phenomena are emerging.[106] And it may well be that sociology cannot be otherwise, that efforts to make it conform to a simplified version of the natural sciences do violence to inquiry, and that society cannot be distilled into clear formulas. It may well be that sociology can never be stereotypically scientific. Yet the appeal of interactionism must retreat towards the sheer persuasiveness of its imagery of people, and it is evident that not all *are* persuaded.

•*More telling is the phenomenological assertion that interactionism fails in its core task.* If interactionists resist the codification and formalization of their approach, it is because they would faithfully reflect central properties of social order. It is their ambition to capture the authentic workings of symbolic process. The world and its workings are not reproduced 'naturally' by sociology, because sociology is a distorting activity that answers special purposes and employs a special language. But there is assumed to be correspondence between the structure of social life and the structure of its reports. Some phenomenologists have argued that that correspondence is less than sure. They claim that there is a problematic gulf between the interactionist vocabulary of 'role', 'deviance', and 'process' and the actual procedures by which people organize their affairs.

> Is a 'role' a sociological concept or a thing in the world?

Cicourel, for instance, questioned whether one does, in fact, order one's life by role analysis.[107] If one does not, it is uncertain what status the word 'role' is supposed to occupy. Are roles sociological inventions or features of the social world? People presumably turn to different practices and ideas when they behave, and Cicourel would have the sociologist inspect *them* rather than the concept of role itself.

We have observed that roles are not discussed as if they were binding instructions to people. We have also observed that roles are imprecise, fluid, and negotiated. Nevertheless, roles sometimes appear to be the invention of the sociologist, and not the role player. Similarly, Phillipson and Roche have subjected the very term 'deviance' to an examination which suggests that the rules that are broken are those devised by sociologists, not those of people in everyday life.[108] Deviance is *not* a label that people bestow on one another very freely. A person is more likely to be called a 'cheat', a 'punk', a 'thief', or a 'liar'.

There may be some formal similarity in the consequences of such acts of identification. But the overarching term 'deviance' is more generally a sociological artefact; it is not just a natural phenomenon that the sociologist discovers in an undisturbed state. Interactionists are unprepared to define that term very precisely, because to do so would compound the error that the phenomenologists have already emphasized. Instead, *deviance* is tacitly taken to be a 'sensitizing concept', especially when we are discerning how people use the concept in everyday life: 'Hundreds of our concepts—like culture, institutions, social structure, mores and personality—are not definitive concepts but are sensitizing in nature. They lack precise reference and have no bench marks that allow a clean-cut identification of a specific instance and of its content. Instead, they rest on a general sense of what is relevant.'[109]

Little intellectual capital has been sunk in the interactionist's sensitizing concept of deviance. The concept maps out a vague idea and propels sociologists towards it. It does not inform them about what exactly they will find there. Such information would be misleading, for by definition, it would make research redundant. *Deviance* has become a loose working concept whose details have been supplied progressively by studies of concrete events. The interactionist would not care to amalgamate or sift all those details. Rather, the conception is built up 'crescively'[110] and gradually, including marginal cases, such as those of dwarfs, giants, stutterers, prostitutes, strippers, and thieves. Whether those disparate figures do share a list of common properties that exclude all ambiguous cases is not discussed. Perhaps it is not thought to be analytically important. Interactionists maintain that cross-reference and comparison have been helpful and that prostitutes can be understood by applying analysis derived from studies of drug addicts. More significant is the utility of an approach that uses the term and ideas of deviance.

•*Quite different criticisms have come from radical sociology and its sympathizers.* Radical sociologists try to place the analysis of specific and general events in the context of a particular master vision of society. It is a vision that borrows heavily from Marxism and the sociology of conflict. Every individual phenomenon is thought to acquire its significance from the whole and from its contribution to the whole. Radical criminologists, who dwell on the structures and transformations of capitalism, relate crime and its control to the larger organization of capitalism itself. Deviance is said to be an objective reality caused by the economic structures of capitalism, and thus not a pathological problem caused by anything other than the conditions of society.

Sociological theory is also given meaning by ideas about deviance that are critical in a wider struggle for power and authority. For example, if a theory blames deviance on individual traits, and the society has itself created that deviance, then theory is helping to disguise the true reasons for deviance. Theories are not simply dispassionate commentaries that can be examined for their logicality, coherence, and appropriateness, because sometimes politics defines deviance.

Thus defined, the business of a more radical sociology of deviance is very unlike the interactionist project. It is concerned with a critical mapping of the major systems of power and their interconnections with the State and its enforcement apparatus. Interactionism does touch on power, and it has offered histories of law making and control. But it also refrains from translating such work into a schematic, political theory of society, that is, into what post-modernist critics would call foundational narratives. On the contrary, the interactionists hold that the sociologist is offered only a series of partial glimpses that may lack overall unity. They argue that delinquent groups change from time to time, situation to situation, and place to place and the intensive study of a delinquent group cannot provide the truth about all delinquents. It certainly does, however, not furnish information about the innermost workings of capitalism.

Interactionists and radical criminologists have melded many of their ideas,[111] but there is still an irreconcilable gulf between them. In particular, there is no agreement about the character or very existence of social structure. While radical criminologists hold to a view of structure that supports strong political recommendations, interactionists would doubt that there is a self-evident structure that can be investigated by any actual defensible empirical means.

•*Interactionism has also been subjected to more minute criticisms*, which are a response to the central importance that some have awarded to labelling. Studies of police and judicial reaction have been taken to argue that there would be no deviance without formal intervention. Furthermore, it has been said that the theory portrays deviant careers as a steady progression into ever increasing alienation. Gouldner stated that interactionism has 'the paradoxical consequence of inviting us to view the deviant as a passive nonentity who is responsible neither for his suffering nor its alleviation—who is more "sinned against than sinning"'.[112]

Akers, too, observed: 'One sometimes gets the impression from reading this literature that people go about minding their own business and then—'wham'— bad society comes along and slaps them with a stigmatized label.'[113]

There are certainly strains and vulgarizations in the interactionist sociology of deviance that could encourage such opposition.[114] On occasion, deviants are presented as if they were the innocent, passive targets of signification; but those strains are not necessary or widespread. Deviation can take place without the manifest interference of others. We have also remarked that the effects of labelling are not determinate, but contingent and variable, having no predictable outcome in individual cases. Criticisms of the species offered by Gouldner really reflect a response to only one narrow version of interactionism.

•*A more recent, robust, and sometimes puzzling attack on symbolic interactionism and labelling theory is that of Colin Sumner*, who argued in *The Sociology of Deviance: An Obituary* [115] that the theory has evolved from being a liberal and tolerant response to borderline infractions to an understanding of the necessity of focusing on 'political resistance and revolt'.[116] That new appreciation meant that deviance could no longer be represented as part of a project to enforce coherent values. If capitalism strenuously controls the dissident, the different, and the disadvantaged, there should be a theory appropriate to the theme, a new fusion of the ideas of Durkheim and Marxism in the concept of 'censure', and how deviance is a ban which embodies the ideology and power of the State.

From a distance, it is a little difficult to understand why Sumner should be so adamant that invoking ideas about censure and the State repression of serious deviation must mark the demise of symbolic interactionism and why, indeed, he should have felt obliged to write its 'obituary' at all. Not only has symbolic interactionism succeeded in analyzing serious crime[117] and, indeed, the State in the past, but *there are no principles in interactionist theory to preclude such an analysis of the State*. Of course, that work has had to be done in a compatible manner so as to lead to distinctively interactionist portraits of crime and the State;[118] but why should that have been otherwise? Moreover, interactionism has been found by some to be perfectly complementary to larger theories of the State, and it has entered the writings of Marxists and others who have examined the impact of power on particular social settings.[119]

It is curious that Sumner argues that there must be only one monopolistic model of crime and control. Our own contention would be, first, that the politics of symbolic interactionism is not unambiguous;[120] second, that there is more than enough room for competing theories to co-exist within a division of intellectual labour; third, that the chosen terrain of interactionism is far from exhausted; and, last, that the insight that the State can be oppressive and protective of class interests has no plausible bearing on the validity or appeal of the labelling approach.

Symbolic interactionism held sway over the sociology of deviance in the 1960s and early 1970s. Antipathetic to systematic theorizing and insistent on empirical research, it emphasized the active discovery of knowledge in the research setting, reviving the ethnographic tradition of the Chicago school. Some interactionists have even denied that they have a 'theory' at all. Instead, they insist that theirs is a perspective, a sensitizing approach which enables them to venture out into society to observe people doing things together.[121]

One of the prime contributions made by interactionism is its compilation of detailed information about deviant practices. Its practitioners are not content to speculate about how deviance is transacted; on the contrary, they have been urged on by an active curiosity. Returning with focused and detailed descriptions, they have presented deviance as a series of complicated processes without a fixed structure. Deviants are those who construct activities and assess meanings in the company of others. They are not always constrained. Neither are they always free. They are restricted by circumstances, by the significance that behaviour can attain, and by their ability to negotiate meaning. The interchanges in which they engage have a spatial and temporal dimension, so that rule breaking is not necessarily the same in St Petersburg, Russia, and St Petersburg, Florida; in Hemel Hempstead, Hertfordshire, or Hempstead, Long Island; in 1900 and in 2000. Interactionists do not claim to manufacture grand theory. They do not answer all the pressing social problems that bedevil people. They proceed more modestly and slowly. As Plummer suggests, 'symbolic interactionism is only one theory that need be used within the labelling perspective, but it has an affinity with the study of marginality and deviance and it is a useful corrective to grander, more general theories. It has a useful role to play.'[122]

Chapter Summary

This chapter looks at some of the basic elements in the idea that 'deviance is in the reaction, not (simply) the action.' The key concept is that the deviant actor is but one person among many that define action as deviance, in the sense that we are looking at the reaction of others who see behaviour as deviant.

The process of defining deviance is an interactional one that takes place within the use of language and is described with language. The definition of deviance is illustrated with ethnographic work. Here we consider some of the basic elements in that process and illustrate it through various examples.

The deviant must act, others must react, and the actions of the self must be understood through the reactions of others. Power is at play in this micro-social arena, but there are implications here for wider processes of power at work as well.

Critical-Thinking Questions

1. Blumer coined the term symbolic interactionism in 1937; what concepts are being used here?
2. The *Pygmalion Effect*, a study by Rosenthal, documents how children are labelled by teachers and how this affects their performance. How is power involved in self-fulfilling prophecies, and in what settings?
3. Erving Goffman uses a dramaturgical approach to describe social interaction; how is role a feature of a social situation?
4. In one of the discussion features, the idea of 'claimsmaker' is described; pick a present-day issue and discuss how there are people who are in a position to make certain publicly influential claims about deviance.

Explorations in Film

Being There traces the change in life for Chauncey Gardener, played by Peter Sellers. Through a series of humorous interactions, his fortunes change dramatically, from being a gardener to being seen as a presidential adviser. Part of his success is the ambiguity of the interpretations of others. This is a must-see film for sociologists.

Websites

The Society for the Study of Symbolic Interaction (SSSI) is the association for symbolic interactionists: http://www.soci.niu.edu/~sssi/, which publishes *Symbolic Interaction*.

Chapter Eight

Phenomenology

Chapter Overview

This chapter continues on from symbolic interactionism in its discussion of the more philosophical basis of the 'interpretive project'. To some, phenomenology is the philosophical basis for symbolic interactionism and also for ethnomethodology and conversation analysis.

Phenomenology introduces the idea of doubt, of whether we can know the world as it is. Thus, phenomenology questions the possibility of functionalist descriptions of social systems and turns its attention back to the subjective work of the social actor in real situations. To understand deviance, we must appreciate how it is seen from the subjective viewpoint of the actor and also from the point of view of those around them.

This is a difficult theory, but it is important for understanding the philosophical underpinnings of many concepts in the sociology of deviance, such as labelling, attribution, societal reaction, and social constructionism.

■ Introduction

Phenomenology came out of debates about the character, scope, and certainty of knowledge. Those debates have only a remote bearing on our theme, and we shall not explore them in any detail. It is enough to recall that, although there have always been some misgivings about human ability to make sense of the world, a severe doubt became central to the writings of particular English empiricists and German philosophers at the beginning of the nineteenth century. The claim was made that the methods of science provided no foundation for believing that iron laws of existence could be discovered by social science as they had been for nature. It was even argued that observed objects are not necessarily what they seem. Phenomenology was a challenge to scientific certainty, as in this comment by Schutz: 'The safeguarding of the subjective point of view is the only but sufficient guarantee that the world of social reality will not be replaced by a fictional non-existing world constructed by the scientific observer.'[1]

Let us reconstruct one version of that argument. It was stated that observation is manifestly constrained. It is affected by the physical capacities of the body and brain, by assumptions about the patterning of things, and by memories of past connections. One usually sees, not confusion, but order, and it is difficult to determine how that order arose. At the very least, perspectives are shaped by a rank inability to pay attention to more than a limited range of sensations at any one time and in any one place. Order may inhere in the world, but things cannot be grasped without the active workings of consciousness. Consciousness moulds what may be known, and it is impossible to disentangle features that belong to objects from those that are bestowed by their observers.

In particular, appearances are structured by the present and future purposes of the observer, by experience, and by stocks of knowledge. For example, what is known hinges on practical objectives. A desert is simply not the same thing to oil prospectors, readers of *Dune* and *The Seven Pillars of Wisdom*, ecologists, botanists, painters, Bedouins, and tourists. Each has a different relation with the same thing and each sees and interprets that same thing in different ways. Even to an oil prospector, the desert is not always the same thing. It is a *phenomenon*, a phenomenon being 'that which appears to be the case, that which is given in perception or in consciousness, for the perceiving and conscious subject'.[2]

Phenomena are those organized experiences that are available to us as we explore the world with our senses and imagination. They are utterly distinct from *noumena*—what are assumed to be the undeformed, unchanging, and absolute essences of things. This idea of an 'absolute essence' is an 'imputed unobservable', which is held to anchor our selves in the uncomfortable fact that perhaps the world can never be understood immediately and without interference. Its distorted appearance is related uncertainly to its unobserved, uninterpreted, innocent, and 'real' state. Indeed, it is possible to conclude only that the true nature of a thing is unascertainable. To do otherwise would require, in Rorty's words, 'a God's-eye standpoint—one which has somehow broken out of our language and beliefs and tested them against something known without their aid. But we have no idea what it would be like to be at that standpoint.'³

Phenomenology explicitly addresses the possibilities of phenomena as located in human apperceptions. Phenomenology represents a series of answers to the problems posed by the sheer inaccessibility of sure knowledge about things as they 'really' are. In response to an apparently inescapable uncertainty, some of its authors proposed that philosophy should turn away from the search for an impeccable truth about the external world. They proclaimed their belief that that search was absurd, that one can never know something that is uncontaminated by its own investigation. Support for this came from an unexpected direction, that of physics, which had realized with the 'Heisenberg principle, that uncertainties and imprecision always turned up if one tried to measure the position and the momentum of a particle at the same time.' All that remain are phenomena and the processes that give them birth.

Phenomenology accordingly tended to redefine the proper business of philosophy as a descriptive analysis of how things are grasped by consciousness. It drew attention to a relatively certain area whose limits are the limits of effective knowledge itself. It no longer asked whether knowledge was correct, but how it came into being, a very post-modern idea before the term existed. By extension and with a little irony, a number of phenomenologists could proceed to argue that almost all knowledge becomes correct in context. After all, there is no accessible deeper, higher, or more fundamental truth with which it may be compared and revealed as false. However, this would also lead into relativism without showing how values and opinions are debated and a consensus on truth achieved, in social contexts.

Phenomenology was to become a substantial intellectual enterprise. However, like any such enterprise, it acquired its own peculiar conflicts and ambiguities. Not only does it encompass what might be described as rather marginal and inconsistent themes,⁴ but it is not always clear what unites those who call themselves phenomenologists. There are profound contradictions between the ideas of Hegel, Heidegger, Scheler, and Schutz, who share few ambitions and methods. Indeed, much of the argument we have advanced should actually be qualified to incorporate the dissenting statements of major phenomenologists. There is not one important proposition with which all would agree, something that was not a cause for much concern.

Happily, what passes for phenomenological sociology is a partial interpretation of the opportunities offered by the school. Many complexities have never been imported into the analysis of deviance. The sociology of deviance has yet to be based on the writings of Husserl, Jaspers, and Merleau-Ponty. Disharmony inevitably remains, and it should be stressed that disagreement *has* been taken into 'deviantology'. Moreover, the exponents of different versions have not even been entirely faithful to their own principles. Phenomenological sociology does not offer an integrated logic and methodology. Rather, it forms a loose collection of observations that sometimes fail to support one another. Applied to deviant phenomena, those observations tend to provide irreconcilable perspectives and recommendations. It is important to be alert to results that are both inconclusive and fragmentary. An expectation of coherence would only be confounded, but there are some basic conceptual principles worth exploring.

■ Phenomenology: Some Premises

Outcrops of phenomenology are scattered throughout sociology, but their distribution and character are a little capricious. The very reliance on phenomenology suggests that some sociologists identified social meaning as a subject or problem. Such an identification is more likely to be made when there is a deliberate attempt to understand the social organization of thought that takes place in the sociological study of religion, ideology, knowledge, science, and literature. Phenomenology is manifestly busier in the study of religion than in the study of the State. But the connection between topic and interpretation is not at all straightforward. Not every sociologist of religion would find phenomenology persuasive, although he or she may have to contend with its arguments. Those who do turn to phenomenology can move in quite different directions.

It could be argued that the sociology of the State would be enhanced by an injection of phenomenology[5] (after all, phenomenologists can claim that *every* topic is a problem in the explanation of consciousness). The State, it would be maintained, is not independent of the imagination. As Berger asserted, 'the "stuff" out of which society and all its formations are made is human meanings externalized in human activity. The great societal hypostases (such as "the family", "the economy", "the state", and so forth) [should be] reduced by sociological analysis to the human activity that is their only underlying substance.'[6] Thus conceived, the 'State' is an aspect of consciousness, and it is to consciousness that the phenomenologist should go to study deviance.

The usefulness of phenomenology resides, not in the subject, but in the sociologist's knowledge and sense of what is fitting. Deviance itself is not taken by all sociologists to be so infused with problems of meaning that it must be submitted to phenomenological analysis: it may be thought that meaning is unimportant, or that it is 'objective' enough to forestall the demands of phenomenology.[7] Indeed, the very definition of deviation as a process rooted in symbolism and consciousness appears to stem from a prior commitment to phenomenology or interactionism. Most sociologists lacked that commitment, and 'deviantology' was pursued for decades before it experimented with phenomenology.

The experiment, which was rather short-lived, was confined to a peculiar, slender version of phenomenology that had been exported to America in the 1930s, remained unnoticed for some time, and was rediscovered and put to use in California in the late 1950s and early 1960s.[8] The phenomenological sociology of deviance and crime was principally the work of Cicourel, Douglas, Bittner, Sudnow, and a few others. Later in Europe, it was also developed by Atkinson, Phillipson, Coulter, and Drew. It is that joint work that we shall describe.

Our description of phenomenology is simplified and limited. It is confined to a few arguments that are at the centre of the imported version accepted by sociology. The imported version is an incomplete reflection of the wider span of phenomenology, but its framework is orthodox enough. It is designed to explore the practical knowledge that people have of their social world, knowledge that is accorded a paramount significance.

•*Society is not taken to be something apart from practical consciousness.* Rather, it is represented as an object or process which exists in, wells up from, and *is* the workings of common sense. It cannot be analyzed or considered until it is experienced. Experienced, it becomes a phenomenon. It must be examined as a facet of thought.

The sociological phenomenologist is particularly concerned about the nature and ownership of the experiences that make society available to consciousness. Those experiences are not entirely and always his or her own. Approaching phenomena outside the social domain, the philosopher need reflect only on his own responses and the responses of some imaginary and typical other introduced to generalize his observations. When one approaches social materials, it is apparent that reflection is directed at the responses and reflections of others. Those others may not share the phenomenologist's sensibilities. They are independent of his or her will. In this sense, sociological phenomenology is a reaction to the reactions of others, a consciousness of the consciousness of others, and a knowledge of the knowledge of others.

•*Schutz emphasized the distinction between constructs of the first and second degrees*, arguing that social phenomena are shaped chiefly by constructs of the first degree:

[The social scientist's] observational field, the social world, is not essentially structureless. It has a particular meaning and relevance structure for the human beings living, thinking and acting therein. They have preselected and preinterpreted this world by a series of common-sense constructs of the reality of daily life and it is these thought objects which determine their behaviour, define the goal of their actions, the means available for attaining them. . . . The thought objects constructed by the social scientist refer to and are founded upon the thought objects constructed by the common-sense thoughts of man living his everyday life among his fellow-men. Thus, the constructs used by the social scientist are, so to speak, constructs of the second degree, namely constructs of the constructs made by the actors on the social scene.[9]

Social reality must be real for someone somewhere—its reality must be publicly endorsed and publicly visible. It may be presented as a system of running descriptions that receive life only in the activities of people in the everyday world. It is those activities, not the analysis of the phenomenological observer, that create and animate social phenomena. The description offered by the phenomenologist is secondary and at one remove from that experienced by the actor. Phenomenology is actually a rather pallid facsimile of reality devised for special purposes unrelated to most practical action.

•*Social reality appears when people decipher their environment; put forward proposals and interpretations*; respond to their own constructions and those of others; modify, accept, or reject what is about them; and thereby build a world for themselves. In this manner, the description, the describing, and the described are much the same. What gives them authenticity and solidity and makes them properly social is recognition and acceptance by others. The phenomena of society emerge when they are given a public response; in Berger's words, they are sustained in conversation.

• *The phenomenological project is involved with discussing the manufacture and use of measures for understanding the subjective experience of others.* In practice these measures tend to consist of an amalgam of introspective, functionalist, literary, and observational techniques. Particularly important is introspection, which is defined by the phenomenologist as the phenomenological or eidetic reduction. The mind is turned back on itself to examine its own processes and replies to the world. Read as a practical demonstration of method, much phenomenological writing becomes an examination of how its author imagines he or she understands his or her reactions to his or her surroundings. It stands as a distillation, a stripping away of the inessential and the murky, which reveals the formal rules and procedures of the conscious mind. The only mind that is naked to the phenomenologist is his or her own. Others are opaque, impatient, and fleetingly present. Thus the practices of people in the social world are almost inevitably portrayed for pragmatic purposes as identical to the phenomenologist's own conduct, conduct that is subject to unusual scrutiny.

•*Phenomenological analysis reflects the understanding of the sociologist, and its authority rests on an appeal to plausibility and a community of experience.* It is as if the author had added a rhetorical preface which not only asserted that things could not possibly be otherwise, but also called upon the reader's own memory and sensibility to confirm everything that is to come. Such a preface is supported by the implicit functionalism of much phenomenology. Many of the more general treatises tend to assemble a list of rules and qualities which are indispensable to a viable existence in society. It is not that the phenomenologist can prove or observe the presence of all the phenomena described. But it can quite cogently be announced that these phenomena *must* be so ordered if people are to live with one another.

One instance is Berger's claim that social order is an overarching canopy of objectified beliefs which keep madness at bay.[10] Another is Schutz's observation that one must make certain assumptions before any social conduct emerges. Those assumptions are described by Schutz as 'pragmatically motivated basic constructions', constructions that are brought into being so that action can go forward. This includes the facts that:

> people exchange perspectives when they exchange positions ('the idealization of the interchangeability of standpoints'); people interpret the world in the same way despite their diverse personal histories ('the idealization of the congruence of relevance systems'); and 'the life-world which is accepted as given by me is also accepted by you, indeed, by us, fundamentally by everyone'.[11]

Schutz could never offer an indisputable demonstration of these propositions. He *could*, however, argue that it is difficult to imagine or plan a social world constituted in any other fashion.

Schutz did not often obey his own injunction to move beyond introspection to a properly described and close observation of behaviour, but a number of phenomenologists did become empirical. Variously referring to themselves as ethnomethodologists, existential sociologists, and sociologists of everyday life, they rely less obviously upon a search within. Believing that talk makes a social world, they have undertaken meticulous examinations of the conduct of conversation.[12]

One methodological 'trick' was to stage disconcerting encounters that are designed to make subjects and themselves newly aware of rules that were previously taken for granted.[13] And they have improved new methods for alienating people from themselves, necessitating a self-consciousness and a production of accounts that had hitherto been undemanded.[14]

All this work is directed to the same ends as those of the phenomenologists of the eidetic reduction: there is a quest for knowledge about interpretative practices which are so familiar and understated that they are normally beyond the reach of the conscious mind, practices and understandings that are so taken for granted that they are part of lived-in tacit knowledge, necessary for social life but not necessary to refer to.

The task of inquiry, as Garfinkel says quite succinctly in his description of ethnomethodology, is to make topical, and engage in 'an organizational study of a member's knowledge of his ordinary affairs, of his own organized enterprises, where that knowledge is treated by us as part of the same setting that it also makes orderable.'[15]

■ Phenomenology, Sociology, and Deviance
The Tradition

Phenomenologists tend to be preoccupied with the general and formal properties of rules. The use of rules in any concrete setting may provide an opportunity for empirical work, but whatever the setting, the exploration of rules is unlikely to detain the phenomenologist for very long. Most phenomenologists, reluctant to become sociologists of education, politics, or development, do not attach themselves permanently to one substantive area.

> What is important is not the cause of deviance, but rather the rules that make deviance visible.

Indeed, there is a strain that encourages the recognition of two distinct kinds of rule, variously defined as 'deep' and 'surface' or 'syntactic' and 'semantic'. Deep rules regulate the construction of phenomena by making it possible to constitute, for example, 'teachers', 'students', and 'lessons'. Surface rules are directed at the understanding and manipulation of intact phenomena, thereby enabling a teacher and students to embark on a lesson. Phenomenology is also taken up with an analysis of deep rules, which is the manufacture of deviant phenomena as phenomena rather than with the relations of deviance themselves. That manufacturing process is held to be substantially similar to any other: the peculiar facts of deviance are not so peculiar that they demand specialized attention. It was in this sense that Phillipson argued:

[we should] turn away from constitutive and arbitrary judgments of public rule breaking as deviance towards the concept of rule itself and the dialectical tension that ruling is, a subject surely more central to the fundamental practice of sociology where men and sociological speakers are conceived as rule-makers and followers. What is now the sociology of deviance might then be pushed to the margins of sociological discourse as a museum piece to be preserved perhaps as that antediluvian activity which sought to show oddities, curiosities, peccadilloes and villains as central to sociological reason.[16]

The uninterest in matters of the surface has perhaps prevented the emergence of much of a corpus of empirical phenomenological sociology. Nonetheless, curiosity about the conditions of rules and rule observance has produced a limited affinity between deviance and phenomenological sociology. At some phase in their lives, many phenomenologists flirted with the sociology of deviance. An important generation of American West Coast sociologists passed their apprenticeship in symbolic interactionism before the rediscovery of Alfred Schutz in the 1960s. Interactionist work on symbolism, meaning, and rules fostered a sensitivity to interpretative analysis. A number of those who had become thus sensitive proceeded to phenomenology. But their early research experience was grounded in an interactionist study of deviance.

Empirically and methodologically, the investigation of rules can lead to those marginal and strange situations where the constitution of social life seems particularly stark. Phenomenological sociologists are especially interested in common-sense reasoning. Precisely because it *is* common-sense, it tends to appear natural, familiar, and problem-free. It is liable to be approached with what Schutz called the 'natural attitude', an attitude that does not question or disbelieve and thereby hides the more important and interesting aspects of how people construct actions. The phenomenology of Schutz recommends the suspension of the natural attitude. It proposes that the ordinary should be treated as if it were extraordinary and that mundane phenomena should be regarded with an anthropological naïveté that refuses to take the world for granted.

One difficulty is that any suspension of the natural attitude is difficult. It is almost impossible to cease believing in the objectivity and permanence of the social world around one. Disbelief may have to be created forcibly by jolting one's trust in appearances.

Garfinkel, who had met Schutz and corresponded with him, invited his students to haggle over prices in supermarkets and to behave as if members of their family were complete strangers.[17] Creating 'trouble' in such 'breaching experiments' is a method of disrupting normal appearances and flouting normal expectations. In the shocked and newly questioning reactions of its audience it can lay bare what is usually so silently presupposed that it is unnoticed.[18] It is as if people can sometimes affirm the existence of rules only when the rules are not obeyed; in for example, it is so normal during a conversation to face the person one is speaking to that to turn one's back would lead to a sudden realization of the practical rules of proper behaviour.

Breaching experiments would raise ethical questions now.

Trouble is also a form of mild deviance. The deviant, like the blind, are customarily endowed with a special vision. They are offered unusual perspectives on social phenomena. They are beset by questions that little affect others, questions about the character and presentation of the normal. How, that is, does one identify and apply those often indistinct rules of conduct that can make one appear commonplace?

Garfinkel went to a hermaphrodite to learn about sexual meanings. He maintained that marginality imposes a heightened awareness of conventional social arrangements. Agnes, the hermaphrodite he consulted, had something of a sensitivity to phenomenological issues. She seemed to have suspended her natural attitude. Garfinkel was a sociologist, yet he sought out deviant occasions because they nursed the sensibilities that Schutz and Husserl had praised.

Deviance can be even more intimately implicated in the phenomenological conception of rules. It is held that the social world is constituted by rules of description and classification, that classification is a process whose formal properties can work back on the world, and that an understanding of the power of classification can disclose the forms that society will assume. Mary Douglas has observed that a 'heavy social load . . . is carried by apparently innocent-looking taxonomic systems'.[19] We have already illustrated the character of that load in our discussion of functionalism. But the topic is important enough to warrant some repetition and amplification.

•*Phenomenological sociology argues that society can be analyzed only as a set of experiences*, that experiences are ordered by consciousness, and that order is built on a vital framework of editing, categorization, and sifting. In some of its guises, phenomenology would then proceed to argue that social order is a fragile human accomplishment achieved in the face of meaninglessness. If the universe is not intrinsically significant but has meaning heaped upon it by people, any system or set of phenomena is an area of organization sometimes arbitrarily carved out of disorganization. Society itself can be defined as sense surrounded by things that make no sense. Moreover, there is not merely one society but a number that crowd upon each other and the order of one may be the disorder of another.

Any classification system must recognize its own. The integrity, clarity, and coherence of society must be defended against threats to meaning—indeed, against the very collapse of meaning. Minor instances of such collapse have been documented: societies can seem to lose corporate identity and purpose.[20] But some phenomenologists would claim that death, nightmares, and madness present glimpses of the unreason that lurks at the boundaries of society. As Peter Berger said, in his study of religion:

> Society is the guardian of order and meaning not only objectively in its institutional structures, but subjectively as well, in its structuring of individual consciousness. It is for this reason that radical separation from the social world or anomy, constitutes such a powerful threat to the individual. . . . He becomes anomic in the sense of becoming worldless. . . . The socially established nomos may thus be understood, perhaps in its most important

aspect, as a shield against terror. The ultimate danger of . . . separation is the danger of meaninglessness. This danger is the nightmare *par excellence*, in which the individual is submerged in a world of disorder, senselessness and madness. Reality and identity are malignantly transformed into meaningless figures of horror.[21]

Those who deny or defy important separations and definitions within society may then do more than merely break a rule. They may be thought to challenge the very legitimacy and structure of sense, thus becoming agents or instances of chaos. Sexuality or madness, for example, can thereby become laden with a significance that bears on the entire project of maintaining social order. Describing that project as a 'programme', Berger observed that serious deviance 'provokes, not only moral guilt, but also the terror of madness. . . . The so-called "homosexual panic" may serve as an excellent illustration of the terror unleashed by the denial of the programme'.[22] It makes for an interesting way to think about social panics in the media, for example, as embodying a threat to the underlying assumptions of what should happen and of what normal people should do.

> Social panics are not about deviance, but about the threat to social order.

•*Some forms of deviance are translated into a symbolic refutation of organization, an affirmation of meaninglessness, which demands control and suppression.* Its forms may be interpreted as phenomena that borrow from the particular fears and order of a society, so that when threats to sense are encountered, they usually take the shape imposed by the sense that is under assault. So it was that Erikson described a symbiotic relation between ideas, ideology, and deviance. He asserted that the crime waves of the early Massachusetts Bay colony mirrored central disturbances in the society's classification scheme: Quakers, witches, and Antinomians were the unreason of one small seventeenth-century community.[23] They would not be so now. Again, Shoham claimed that the Nazi stereotype of the Jew was a simple antithesis of the Teutonic Superman.[24] The image of the Jew owed less to the social organization of Jewry than to the structure of Nazi cosmology. *The system of belief manufactures its own deviants.* People 'covenant implicitly to breed a host of imaginary powers, all dangerous, to watch over their morality and to punish defectors'.[25] In another theory we might talk about the interaction between claim makers, scapegoats, and symbolic threats.

> Belief systems manufacture their own deviants.

•*When eruptions from without are considered dangerous, it becomes evident that danger, its forms, and its magnitude will be affected by the character of the frontiers that must be breached.* All societies are defined, but they are not identically marked off from what is about them. Mary Douglas would argue that they can be ranked by the emphasis that they place upon their boundaries. Those that stress their apartness will generate a distinct kind of explanation for deviance. Deviants will then more commonly be presented as outsiders to the virtuous group, evil itself being produced, not by the group, but by a dangerous environment. The threats presented by AIDS, mad-cow disease, terrorism, and organized crime tend characteristically to be located symbolically and geographically outside the system. The weakly bounded, however, tend to lodge the origins of deviance in their own community and look to their fellows as a source of danger.[26]

Discussion: Deviance and Culture—AIDS

During the early 1980s AIDS came on the scene as a new disease. A dominant theme in AIDS coverage was its portrayal as a plague-like disease spread by sexual predators to an innocent public. The first striking thing about the coverage of AIDS in the news is the sheer amount and intensity of the coverage.

In 1983, Canada's major daily papers published ninety-nine news stories on AIDS; they are indexed in the *Canadian News Index* (CNI) under 'diseases'. By 1985, AIDS had its own category, and 643 articles are indexed for that year. This 474 per cent increase in news articles shows that HIV/AIDS had gone from being considered a relatively rare disease to being seen as a major public-health threat.

By 1987 there were 1,423 entries, the highest number during the 1980s. After that, the number of articles published every year dropped until the early 1990s, when 'AIDS and women' and 'AIDS and health care workers' were added as categories to the CNI. The growth of articles on AIDS reveals the prominence of this disease in the news.

In a science column in the *Globe and Mail*, Stephen Strauss commented on the fact that some diseases are reported more than others. Writing in 1993, he said that in the previous two years 600 stories had been published on AIDS, six on arthritis, eleven on prostate cancer, twenty-five on diabetes, and forty-four on heart diseases.

However, although 50,749 Canadians died of cancer in 1988, cancer was written about only 219 times; on the other hand, only 1,097 people died of AIDS in 1991, but the disease received more extensive coverage. The US Center for Disease Control said that fewer than two hundred women died of AIDS between 1990 and 1992, as was reported in twenty-five articles; however, 10,000 women died of breast cancer, which was written about thirty-nine times.

What is also striking about AIDS coverage is how 'being at risk' is portrayed. Having AIDS is not a crime, but by being linked to 'deviant' groups, it was certainly treated that way in the early 1980s. Initially termed GRID (gay-related immuno-deficiency), AIDS was linked to the deviant lifestyle of gay men, to prostitutes, and to the use of intravenous drugs. The disease was seen as a threat to the 'general population' from those (already deviant) groups.

The unfortunate consequence of the early portrayal of AIDS is that it created a view of the disease that lingered long after it became patently untrue. The result was that many people did not realize they could contract AIDS, and the spread of the disease was increased.

Source: Adapted from C. McCormick, *Constructing Danger*.

Deviance is sometimes more than a simple threat of disorganization. It can also take the guise of an orderly and solid enough antithesis to familiar morality. An example of what this means is that part of the fascination of strangers is that they are outsiders who not only confirm our own identity but also offer glimpses of a tantalizing freedom because they are not bound by our rules. Societies are defined by what they are not, and we can only know what we are by identifying things that negate us. Jack Douglas argued that good and evil, God and Satan, morality and immorality are inseparable twins. Meaning and social organization would be impossible without the continuous presence of their contrasts.

Enemies, such as Communists and capitalists, can draw symbolic sustenance from each other.[27] Indeed, the contradictions of politics often seem staged to dramatize rectitude and confirm organization. The far left and the far right *need* one another. Moderates require extremists. The manner in which the adversaries portray one another may depend as much on the dialectics of the political process and the ideology of the definer as on any 'real' or 'independent' properties of the defined. They create one another. And that work of creation is never a fixed or stable activity. As a society changes and its moral frontiers move, so its companion forms of deviance will also shift. For example, Davis maintained that pornography will always be discovered just outside the boundaries of conventional sexuality and that its definition changes with every alteration of convention.[28]

•*Internally, the defence of social order rests upon the preservation of neat distinctions between the classes and phenomena that constitute a society.* Those things and processes that are recognized as detached must retain their separation. Confusion would erode social organization, and the chief instruments of confusion are ambiguity and anomaly. Following Douglas and Berger, Scott states that 'no social order can survive unless it develops mechanisms for protecting the symbolic universe against the threats that chaos and anomaly present to it. . . . The property of deviance is conferred on things that are perceived as being anomalous from the perspective of a symbolic universe.'[29]

The contention is that danger emanates from those who seem responsible for blurring and disrupting the outlines of categories. The hermaphrodite is neither male nor female, but a disturbing exception.[30] So, too, do witches, sexual deviants, and the mad wreak damage on the socially constructed world. They cannot be contained but threaten to expose the fragility of conventional meanings. Significantly, those who straddle categories are sometimes accorded non-human or superhuman qualities. Witches were once thought able to assume the shapes of beasts and to be capable of flight. The mad were thought to be possessed and to be able to communicate with spirits. They were described as the inhabitants, not only of the ruled world of human beings, but also of the chaotic world of unruled nature. It was their unruliness that required discipline: some deviants could be avoided or seen as harmless, while others would have to be destroyed because they were dangerous.[31]

Perhaps the very starkest example of the man who straddled boundaries was Oedipus, who was so abominably unnatural that he killed his father and became the lover of his own mother; he thereby brought a plague on Thebes and had to

> Are strangers more acceptable in strong or weakly-bounded groups?

be banned or killed before the pestilence abated. However there are many examples of 'monsters' that stir revulsion and threaten the symbolic boundaries of social conduct and normative order: today we think of the serial killers, the pedophiles, the juvenile super-predators, and the white-collar corporate criminals.

All classification systems must engender anomalies because none can be exhaustive. It is intrinsic to organization that it produces the unmanageable cases that subvert it.

•*Deviance is sometimes a response by deviants to the apparent disorderliness of everyday life.* Deviants may experience the social world as absurd and morally unstable. There are many situations that seem to be governed by no consistent rules and where any conduct is forced to break some precept or principle of order.[32] Heller's *Catch 22* is a vivid literary example of such a contradictory, 'crazy' system:

> There was only one catch and that was Catch-22, which specified that a concern for one's own safety in the face of dangers that were real and immediate was the process of a rational mind. Orr was crazy and could be grounded. All he had to do was ask; and as soon as he did, he would no longer be crazy and would have to fly more missions. Orr would be crazy to fly more missions and sane if he didn't, but if he was sane he had to fly them. If he flew them he was crazy and didn't have to; but if he didn't want to he was sane and had to. Yossarian was moved very deeply by the absolute simplicity of this clause of Catch-22 and let out a respectful whistle.[33]

In a pluralist society there are many settings that are condemned by those who don the trappings of an absolute morality. Disinclined to subscribe to a single, absolute, and unequivocal truth, and well before the post-modernist turn, the more libertarian phenomenologists of deviance were prone to describe society as a welter of competing and contradictory worlds that constitute no unified whole.[34] Deviance is evidence of a moral diversity that others would repress in the name of an oppressive uniformity. Deviance was the exemplar of disorder that had to be contained.

Much of this phenomenological analysis lodges the roots of deviance in the formal properties of classification. It is not the contents of a scheme, but its structure, which creates deviation. The cleavages, links, and limits of systems are thought to be important in their own right. The very existence of internal differentiation can work characteristic effects upon deviance. Douglas has argued that 'sets of rules are metaphorically connected with one another, allowing meaning to leak from one context to another along the formal similarities that they show'.[35]

This leakage is exemplified by the influence exerted by hierarchy. Social phenomena tend to be ranked, ranking tends to be a moral matter, and matters clustered around the various ranks tend to borrow their moral meanings. For example, in aggregate, stratification by social class can be so dominant that it absorbs other major systems of classification. Classes can become morally meaningful categories that colour the artefacts and conduct of those who are assigned to them.[36]

As an example, Duster has asserted that opiate addiction carried little stigma when it was widely dispersed in the nineteenth century. It was only when middle-class addiction was confined in discreet private clinics and the poor and discreditable user could be seen lining up for supplies that drug use became publicly identified with the disreputable and was held to be disreputable itself.[37]

In Canada, opium was first criminalized in 1909, and involved the labelling of Chinese workers as a source of contamination. The resulting legislation, endorsed by Mackenzie King, was to become the basis for Canada's drug laws, and as we saw in the previous chapter was subject to much claims making by people like Emily Murphy.

> Canada's drug laws are an example of class and race intersecting to produce deviance.

In summary, the work we have reviewed so far is ambitious, devoted as it is to the resolution of grand questions about the fabric of the social universe. It is representative of one tradition of speculative phenomenology associated with the New School for Social Research in New York, the philosopher Alfred Schutz, and the anthropology of Mary Douglas. In the main, it is unfortunate that sociologists have either ignored its arguments or regarded them as tangential to the central problems of their discipline. Sociology and deviantology are probably the poorer for that neglect. If they do still recognize phenomenology, it is a different tradition that receives acknowledgement.

That tradition, based largely in California, preserved an emphasis upon the futility of a quest for absolute and fixed truth. It focuses on the phenomena that have been constituted by consciousness. However, the contexts and phenomena that it describes are rather distinct. The sociologists influenced by phenomenology, however, have concentrated upon small, observable settings. Their work dwells on interchanges between probation officers and delinquents and between prostitutes and their customers, on the physical design of abortion clinics, on the structure of homosexual encounters, and on the social order of nude beaches. It is a more humble, exact, and empirical enterprise.

Yet, in one important sense, its goals and ideas are quite consistent with the more speculative analysis. Both are firmly anchored in phenomenology. Both explore the constitution and operation of rules. Both display some indifference about the specific phenomena that rules produce. A juvenile delinquent and a cosmos are equally the artefacts of interpretative practices.

The Other Tradition

What made the second tradition especially significant to criminology was its commentary upon the way official criminal statistics are created. We have argued that police statistics have always served as an important resource for theorization and inference. However, it had long been understood that they were atypical of the larger 'real' population of criminals and criminal incidents. It was recognized that there *was* a worrying dark figure which had to be ascertained in some fashion. Moreover, analyzing the flow of decisions that make up the processing of deviance in the justice system, shows there is an 'attrition' in the number of cases flowing through the system. This has also been called a crime funnel. Not all crime is reported to the police, but then not all crime is treated equally within the system.

The problem with the previous, literal interpretation of crime statistics was that the statistics were seen as independent of theory. So, while the phenomenological excursion into the social construction of crime rates was unexceptional phenomenology, it was momentous for the sociology of deviance. Rates were newly treated as phenomena that were produced, as all phenomena are, by interpretative work and social organization. Crime rates were no different, say, from the rates of academic success and failure manufactured by schools.[38] However, what was relatively unremarkable in other spheres, say reporting or policing, became the catalyst for considerable debate and revision. The solid facts of crime seemed to melt into a rather fluid and unreliable phenomenon. Kitsuse and Cicourel argued: 'In modern societies where bureaucratically organized agencies are increasingly invested with social control functions, the activities of such agencies are centrally important 'sources and contexts' which generate as well as maintain definitions of deviance and produce populations of deviants.'[39]

Theories and hypotheses employing crime statistics were redefined as constructs of the second degree. Rates were seen, not as the raw, objective, and unprocessed indices that Émile Durkheim and Louis Chevalier had supposed them to be, but on the contrary, as condensed interpretations of the world. They were embedded in background information and contexts of meaning that often remained unanalyzed. They compressed numerous decisions, preoccupations, and practices. As Douglas stated, Once we follow . . . 'disembodied numbers' back to their sources to see how they were arrived at and what, therefore, they actually represent, we find that they are based on the most subjective of all possible forms of activity.[40]

Thus the categories of 'juvenile delinquent' and 'thief' do not emerge spontaneously from the doings of everyday life. Work has to be done before they are animated and applied. Juvenile delinquency rates reflect, not the objective reality of youth crime, but rather practical assumptions about troublesome behaviour, rules of classification, and the assignment of people to different classes. Crime rates turn on assumptions about the meanings of past conduct and predictions about conduct in the future. Clustered together and given a numerical form, those categories are more or less unintelligible unless those who scan the statistics know how they were put together. The language, conceptions, and knowledge of those who encode and tabulate statistics must be available to those who decipher them; however as Cicourel said: 'Sociologists have been slow to recognize the basic empirical issues that problems involving language and meaning pose for all research.'[41]

•*Borrowing from Mannheim,*[42] *ethnomethodologists*[43] *adopted the word 'indexical' to refer to the dependence of meaning on environment.* All utterances and signs are to be understood as indices that point to and stand for the wider and fuller situations in which they arose.[44] Suicide rates, for instance, incorporate the lay and scientific reasoning of those officials who determine the cause and character of death. They reflect shorthand definitions of typical motives, circumstances, and courses of action.[45] For this reason, suicide rates reflect (indexically) the decisions that combine to produce them.

> Crime statistics are products of interpretation.

> A suicide has to be decided, and these procedures are examinable.

Similarly, judicial statistics record the routine practices and conceptions of the courtroom. The staff in busy courts tend to standardize their tasks, establishing patterns of co-operation, a division of labour, and sets of stereotyped operations. Those operations, in turn, can be performed only when the work material is itself stereotyped and standardized. Cases must be predictable, simple, and repetitious, so that the ordinary activity of the court can go on. They will become 'normal cases',[46] those unambiguous and elementary scenes that can be produced efficiently by the existing organization of the court. In those jurisdictions that rely heavily on plea bargaining and 'negotiated justice',[47] there will be a systematic strain towards the discovery and reproduction of such normal cases. Defendants or incidents that are anomalous may be subject to an unusual pressure to undergo redefinition.

In all this, phenomenologists are concerned to investigate 'the processes by which persons come to be defined, classified and recorded in the categories of the agency's statistics'.[48] Their concern is part of a wider interest in the social production of knowledge. Only rarely will it be confined merely to the problems of those who compile and consume statistics. As Troy Duster has said in a retrospective piece:

> As the Sixties dawned, a third set of key players would quickly shift the focus to challenge the epistemological foundations of the whole playing field, and not just of theory and research on deviance. Egon Bittner, Aaron Cicourel, and Joseph Gusfield would ride around in police cars and see just how and when police used discretion in their arrest procedures. . . . If the site of rate construction was the preferred focal point for inquiry and theorizing about these data, then surely it would have bearing and impact on all manners of rate construction, from epidemiological work in public health to coroner's collective accounts of the causes of death. . . . If sociology was a behavioral science, I reasoned, it was the behavior that should be the focal point, not the already-collected statistics where the behavior was assumed to be reflected in the numbers.[49]

Kitsuse and Cicourel are mentioned above as having adapted the philosophy of Schutz to the study of social problems. They published an early article on the analysis of social statistics, after some initial difficulty, because they argued that it was not the social conditions that produced deviance which should be the object of study, but rather the process by which behaviour came to be classed as deviant:

> An individual who is processed as 'convicted,' for example, is sociologically differentiable from one who is 'known to the police' as criminal—the former may legally be incarcerated, incapacitated and socially ostracized, while the latter remains 'free'. The fact that both may have 'objectively' committed the same crime is of theoretical and empirical significance, but it does not alter the sociological difference between them. The *pattern* of such 'errors' is

among the facts that a sociological theory of deviance must explain, for they are indications of the organizationally defined processes by which individuals are differentiated as deviant.[50]

Kitsuse makes this methodological approach more empirical in his examination of the societal reaction to homosexuality. Using a series of questions he elicits the interpretive process by which assessments of 'sexual deviance' are made, sometimes retrospectively, or after the fact. As he says, what is relevant and consequential to the label of deviance is people's interpretations, and not the accuracy or reasonableness of those interpretations in such instances.[51]

> Interpretations are neither correct nor incorrect, but made.

Similarly, Bittner examines the ways that the police use their discretion in deciding what to do about cases of mental illness where there is no crime that requires action but there is also no apparent need to take the person to hospital.[52]

In such work, the concerns of these researchers, some focusing on societal reaction, and some on ethno-methods, is part of a more general campaign against the procedures and claims of 'orthodox' sociology. By challenging the very basis for knowing some things, such as crime rates and deviance statistics, theorists were breaking new ground and challenging old assumptions. Phenomenology and ethnomethodology, in particular, tended to be championed as a rival to sociology and not as a complement or source of correction.[53]

Case Study—Phenomenology and Domestic Violence

In a phenomenological analysis of domestic violence, Norman Denzin[1] looks at husbands' violence toward wives and children. He draws upon the qualitative literature on wife battering for excerpts of experience, and applies phenomenology to examine the inner side of the violent experience in the home more deeply, looking at how emotionality and the self are at the core of domestic violence.

Denzin looks at the phenomenon of domestic violence from within, as lived subjective experience. Specifically, he is interested in negative symbolic interaction and the relationship between emotionality and violent conduct. He draws on his own interviews and observations of violent individuals as part of the Emotions Project.

In looking at how the structures of bad faith are at the core of domestic family violence, Denzin opens up analysis to the validity of subjective experiences. The selves of violent family members are seen to be located in a circuit of progressively differentiated violent and nonviolent conduct that transforms the family into a conflict-riddled, 'painful field of experience that moves, if not checked, into self-destruction'.

Denzin uses the term 'schismogenesis' (from Bateson) to describe the genesis of schisms from conflicts and contradictions within an interactional network. The process of schismogenesis is at said to be 'temporal, historical, dialectical, and self-referencing, while based on emergent, spurious, and fearful spontaneous interactions'. This negative exchange system destroys the values on which interaction is based. The schismogenesis of producing stable structures of negative symbolic interaction locks the family of violence in a circuit of aggressive selfness that connects everyone into the web of violence.

The central theme here is that the violence becomes stabilized in the relationship. When the violence first erupts it is isolated, perhaps even defined as insignificant, and there is a strong tendency to deny that it has occurred. Research has shown that the wife usually takes responsibility for the husband's violence. For example, he quotes research by Dobash from the qualitative literature on wife battering:

> It was just he couldnae [sic] bear anything wrong with his food. . . . I did his breakfast in a hurry and he complained about the grease. . . . He threw the plate at me. . . . I said something like, 'Oh well, we'll have to stop having greasy eggs in the morning.'[2]

The internalization of the abuse by the wife, and the initiation of the violence by the husband stabilizes matters for a short time as he achieves some measure of control over his wife through his use of violence. However, as the violence persists, it escalates because hostility on the wife's part increases and the husband becomes hostile toward her in response to her hostility. Not surprisingly, a loss of affection for the violent spouse begins to appear, as in, again quoting research:

> 'I'd begun not to like him. I began to not like him then, really. I don't mean not love him, but not like him.'[3]

The cycle of violence increases as subjective misunderstandings over the causes of the violence continue. The husband attempts to place the responsibility for his violence on his wife, and though she tries at first to deny what is happening (because that is self-preserving), gradually she comes to realize the dynamic (because that is the role of the powerless). As one wife reported, again from published research:

> He would always make out it was my fault. If I said this or if I hadn't done that it would never have happened. He always claimed that I provoked him. It was always I provoked him.[4]

Denzin says that the dilemma that the wife experiences is a classic double bind. If the husband loves her, why does he abuse her? However, if he doesn't love her, perhaps there's a reason for the abuse. She is the one who has to make sense of it, and the history of the relationship will work against her.

The destructive cycle of abuse will involve the denial of the victimizer, the denial of injury, and the appeal to higher loyalties. To upset the stabilized abuse will require certain other factors to change: 'a change in the level of violence, a change in resources available to the woman, a change in the relationship, despair and surrender by the woman, a change in the visibility of the violence, and the intrusion of external definitions of the relationship.'[5]

A subjective factor that works against the wife is that there is always the hope that the next time there will be no violence. However, in order for her to remain in the relationship she must somehow

> tell herself that the physical violence she received was not intended, was accidental, or was somehow only an episodic outburst on the part of her spouse. She must lie to herself and say that what occurred did not really happen to her, or to the real her. Nor did the real man she loves do this to her. She and he must fall into bad faith in order to sustain this fiction about themselves and their relationship.[6]

The abused and the abuser are trapped within an interactional world that feeds on violence but, more important, on doubt and fear, deceptions and lies. The family of violence destroys itself: either they break up, or the members remain within the structures of bad faith that prevent the open disclosure of what is happening to them.

What is useful about Denzin's analysis is that it looks at the process of how a structure of negative experience that traps its members can be built up. The innovation of locating domestic violence in emotionality and interaction reveals how the feeling self stands at the centre of the violence that permeates so many families. A phenomenological inquiry into this pressing social issue shows how wife battering, which starts as a private problem, hidden behind the closed walls of the family home, becomes a public problem, but only after certain problems of self-awareness are themselves surmounted.

[1] N. Denzin, 'Toward a Phenomenology of Domestic, Family Violence', 483–513.
[2] R.E. Dobash and R. P. Dobash, *Violence against Wives*, 95.
[3] Ibid., 138.
[4] Ibid., 118.
[5] Ibid., 294.
[6] R.E. Dobash and R.P. Dobash, *Violence against Wives*, 299.

The Analysis of Conversation

After some time, ethnomethodology turned from its focused studies on members' practical activities in producing clinical records, and so on, to develop a branch of study using the so-called 'linguistic turn', called conversation analysis. Conversation analysis looked at members' practices in actual situations, as did ethnomethodology, but it looked specifically at how discourse accomplished the work of doing school lessons, 911 calls, police dispatches, coroners' inquests, and so on. While ethnomethodology could easily be seen to be an outgrowth of interactional analysis, by way of Goffman and Becker, conversation analysis turned to the analysis of how language structures social order. Maynard describes the following reasons to look at language:

- Studying vernacular ways of speaking allows a researcher to appreciate the diversity of groups, and how group members conceptually see their worlds, reinforce social boundaries, and resist outside attempts at social control.
- Diversity also potentially means conflict, so being able to see conflict depends upon first documenting the organized system of language in terms of which members of a particular subgroup operate.
- Employing distinctive speech modes may involve enacting social identities, so where relations of power are of concern, sociology requires analysis of turn taking and other organized aspects of interaction.
- If 'labelling' and 'societal reactions' set careers of deviance in motion, this depends upon ordered activities of telling troubles and proposing problems.
- Investigating commonsense reasoning that is embedded in institutional discourse permits access to wider organizational experiences and cognitions that are social structural in origin.
- Perceptions of social problems are filtered through the news, and rhetorical analysis of messages regarding social problems shows they attempt to persuade people of the existence of problems, especially those that are disruptive of a sense of social order.[54]

In summary, there are theorists who have sought to incorporate the analysis of perception, the negotiation of identity, and the role of subjectivity into the analysis of deviance. Jack Douglas, Jack Katz, Peter Manning, and Aaron Cicourel, for example, have been especially active in charting deviant worlds. Douglas's *Observations of Deviance* has chapters on abortion clinics, nudist camps, prostitutes, topless barmaids, homosexuals and lesbians, motorcycle gangs, hustlers and cons, and hippies and drug use.[55] When their writing occasionally dwells upon the manufacture and preservation of unusual styles of behaviour, it is indistinguishable from the ethnography of symbolic interactionism.[56] Indeed, it must be remembered that titles like 'interactionist', 'phenomenologist', and 'qualitative sociologist' are close and easily confused.

Discussion: Deviance Exploration—Discursive Deviance in Class

In an article about deviance in the classroom, Graham and Jardine examine some contemporary sociological conceptions of 'deviance' and 'resistance' in the study of youth culture. They explore how a notion of 'play' or 'playfulness' can contribute to the understanding of disruptive behavior in a classroom. Using a transcript of a lesson sequence in life skills, paying special attention to the 'asides' made by certain class members, they contend that these asides remain linked to the Elicitation-Response-Feedback structure of the official lesson.

They take as their standpoint 'children's culture', which they say was intended to open up the possibility of studying children's activities as phenomena in their own right, rather than as faulty approximations of desired adult conduct. This standpoint allows them to recover the 'good sense' of youth conduct, activities which under a different viewpoint would be treated as incompetence or deviance.

They argue that conventional research takes the normal adult world as the standard against which to measure what children and youths do. The developmental model views children's behaviour as inadequate attempts to mimic fully adequate adult conduct, while the deviance model views youth behaviour as potential deviations from the normal conduct that actors are expected and obligated to perform.

They refer to the idea that play is 'distinct from "ordinary life"', both as to its locality and duration. The 'play space' is characterized by seclusion in that it requires the proximity of the players while keeping out non-players. Play also is said to have its own time, its own internal sense of how long it can last.

Using this idea of play, the authors seek to distinguish some classroom talk as play within the context of the lesson, even though the talk might appear at first glance to be normatively deviant or age-appropriately incompetent.

In looking at the communicative organization of the talk, their concern is with the formal features of some disruption that was noticed during the process of reviewing audiotapes of a classroom lesson on textiles. In particular, their attention was drawn to a form of disruption that appeared to be a prank but seemed to be more than sheer rule breaking (deviance) or more critically, a rejection of schooling as such (resistance).

The disruption can be seen against the background of the routine sequence of interaction that forms the communicative basis of the day's lesson. The ongoing construction of the lesson corpus is seen by the analyst to achieve the status of knowledge through the turn-by-turn structure of interactions between the teacher and the students. This distinguishes classroom discourse from informal conversations, where interaction tends to be structured in terms of paired utterances such as exchanges of greetings, questions and answers, and so on. In comparison, the lessons exhibit a distinctive three-part sequence in which (1) the teacher initiates an exchange by eliciting a student response, (2) a student responds, and (3) the teacher provides feedback.

In the following excerpt, the teacher has asked what tufted fabric could be used for. See what sense you make of the exchange:

24 T: You could. Yup. What else?
25 B: Shoes
26 T: How about, uhm . . .
27 B: Alligator shoes.

28 T: Well with the fluffy slippers, sure.
29 B: Oh, here we go with your em, Porky Pig slippers again, eh?
30 A: D'ya know for every fur coat there's about seven animals killed?
31 B: Great.
32 C?: Who cares?
33 ?: (laughs)
34 B: Beavers do.
35 E: Bedroom slippers.
36 T: Great. Anything else . . .

While it is apparent that the students are having fun, and that their remarks might not appear to be sensible contributions to the knowledge the teacher is trying to develop, they are uttered as asides within the context of the topic. In the researchers' words:

'We view the troublesome form of student talk analyzed here—which we have termed asides—as distinctly playlike in its properties. The playfulness of the aside provides respite from the adult-controlled world in which not any response will do. The serious business of producing an acceptable corpus item positions the respondent precisely at that point where he or she can be held publicly accountable as the kind of speaker required by the lesson organization. Through the aside, the boys continuously work at the production of another possibility, a shadow lesson constructed at the interstices of the official one, concerted with it so that both streams of talk can be preserved simultaneously.'

So discourse does work, and discourse can be play(ful).

Source: Adapted from P. Grahame and D. Jardine, 'Deviance, Resistance, and Play: A Study in the Communicative Organization of Trouble in Class'. *Curriculum Inquiry*, 20, no. 3 (1990), Blackwell Publishing.

■ Criticism

•*Perhaps the most telling criticism of phenomenological work on deviance proceeds explicitly and implicitly from phenomenology itself.* We have related how importance is attached to understanding and describing constructs of the first degree. The phenomenologist would learn how his or her subjects make sense of themselves and their world, reproducing the subjects' own procedures and assumptions. It is apparent that utter fidelity can never be attained: any piece of written analysis must change and distort its object. Indeed, the business of analysis is largely unfamiliar in everyday life. There is seldom time to 'stop and think': thinking requires the interruption of stopping, it usually happens after the event, and it is rarely trained on phenomenological ends. Furthermore, sociological analysis embodies practices, ideas, and objectives that are necessarily different from those of the natural attitude. Phenomenology must disrupt life to analyze it.

What phenomenologists do is to advocate the use of one or more tests of adequacy that might help to undo some of the deformations imposed by their own sociology or philosophy. One such test is the provision of an effective scheme of translation that could eventually permit the subject to recognize him- or herself in any description that has been offered. It is the test that is most seldom applied,[57] and its results are uncertain. Translation transforms meaning: what is recognizable may not be phenomenology, and what is phenomenology may not be recognizable. The subject is unlikely ever to have pondered the constitution of his or her consciousness in the intense manner of the phenomenologist. What he or she would be offered could thus be 'correct' but still almost wholly foreign. The subject could as readily be converted by a description as recognize himself or herself in it. After all, descriptions can work on people and change them.

A prime example is that of the controversy surrounding the idea of 'multiple personalities' and 'recovered memory'.[58] While some maintain that intensive therapy can disclose buried memories of abuse, including satanic abuse, others hold simply that such therapy is part of a collusive enterprise in which patients are guided towards fabricating false pasts and false selves.[59] In all this, the gap between constructs of the first and second degree remains unbridged, but the phenomenological sensitivity remains to trouble those who examine their own and others' accounts by maintaining that what is at issue is, of course, 'accounts'.

Cicourel, for example, turned on the sociology of deviance and asked what was intended by central phrases that had never been properly amplified or explained:

> 'Recent advances recognizing the problem of how members of a group come to be labelled as "deviant", "strange", "odd and the like, have not explicated terms like "societal reaction" and "the point of view of the actor", while also ignoring the practical reasoning integral to how members and researchers know what they claim to know.'[60]

Applied liberally, such observations are likely to lead to the demise of much of what passes for the phenomenology of deviance.

The use of words like 'rules', 'deviance', and 'social order' is also vulnerable to the accusation that they are not defined. After all, the experience of everyday life does not encompass many of the ideas lodged in phenomenology. Any investigation of the basis of that experience is calculated only to move one from deviance to an analysis of quite different phenomena and problems. In practice, that move has taken place. Phillipson, Cicourel, and others deserted deviance for the more fundamental problems of deep rules. It is as if they tended to represent deviation as a clumsy idea that belongs neither to phenomenology nor to lay experience.

•*External criticism of ethnomethodology and the phenomenology of deviance has been somewhat scarce.* The study of deviance tends to remain an eclectic discipline that subordinates an activity called 'theorizing' to practical ends, theory sometimes being taken to be an encumbrance that is independent of policy, methodology, and serious problems. Theory which complicates analysis is a distraction. 'Reflexive' theory that urges the theorists to study themselves as they theorize is difficult. Having noted the mass of phenomenological observations about the significance of data, the conventional sociologist might exhort people to be cautious in their interpretation of official statistics, but that is all.

To some, phenomenology is not particularly salient to the resolution of critical sociological problems. In the division of intellectual labour, the pursuit of phenomenology is dismissed as not much more than an interesting enterprise:

> The 1960s were indeed a revolutionary and romantic period, for well known reasons, at least on the major campuses and in California. If one wanted to project or translate its distinctive mood, the cult of subjectivity, the rejection of external structures, into the language and *problematik* of sociology, then one should quite naturally end up with something just like Ethnomethodology. So this movement would be the manner in which subjective, 'Californian' mood enters the otherwise sober, scientistic, sociological segments of the groves of academe.[61]

Other sociologists describe phenomenology and ethnomethodology as substantial projects, but may not find it pertinent to their work. McDonald asserted in her study of crime rates:

> What the phenomenologists do is change the level of inquiry. It is not just that they do their research in a different way, but they ask different sorts of questions—*how* social control agencies work, *how* officials and the public interact, as opposed to who becomes a client of such an agency in the first place and *why*. . . . Questions as to why certain societies have high crime rates and full prisons and others do not, cannot be addressed with phenomenology and this is the sort of question I wished to entertain.[62]

It is apparent then that this criticism presents phenomenology as marginal to 'real' issues. Radical criminologists used the accusation that phenomenology refused to appreciate the character of the setting in which it is lodged. Quinney attacked 'the epistemological assumption of a social constructionist thought [phenomenology] . . . that observations are based on our mental *constructions*, rather than on the raw apprehension of the physical world'.[63] And Taylor, Walton, and Young would also have wished to restore an absolutist conception of the social order, a conception that deferred only to one essential and true description of society:

> In essence the ethnomethodological critique of sociology . . . is that our shorthand concepts like alienation, class, deviance, etc. are either meaningless or if they do have meaning, they are no more meaningful than the generalization made by members. . . . Our final assessment of ethnomethodology's contribution to the study of deviance is that in 'bracketing' away the question of social reality, it does not allow of any description of *the social totality* we assert to be productive of deviance.[64]

Such a criticism is superficially naïve in that the obvious rebuttal is that the critique is based in the wish to rely uncritically on a static world as a source of knowledge.

Allied to this argument about the absoluteness of reality is a companion criticism of the absurdity of reflexive analysis. It will be recalled that phenomenologists urge sociologists to examine their own practices as they examine the practices of their subjects. They proposed that methodology and theory should bend back on themselves to become their own topics. The radical and absolutist tend to maintain that an interpretative analysis of interpretative analysis raises the spectre of the infinite regress of reflexivity. The observing observer would have to be observed by one who would be observed by others in an endless chain. Some wished to avoid reflexivity and interpretative work altogether.[65]

The phenomenological reply might well ask its own questions about the status of conceptions of 'social reality', 'social totality', 'the real world', and the like. The critics of phenomenology do not seem prepared to trust ordinary people or one another with a reliable sense of the real.[66] Ernest Gellner, Richard Quinney, and others berate ethnomethodology for its subjectivism, but they would themselves have manifestly failed to agree on the objective and the real. Perhaps social reality is not really so objective or self-evident after all. It is contingent, in part, on description, describer, purpose, experience, time and place, as the reality of one is the fantasy of another. It is perhaps barely possible that one definition is correct and all others are false, but it is also clear that the acceptance of any one definition has yet to be unanimous. The phenomenologists may well be right: ideas about social reality are constructed like any other: they are mediated, and positivists have not offered any formulas for grasping the physical world as it 'really' is. Furthermore, those who uphold the dignity of sociology by avoiding the absurd have not refuted arguments for reflexivity. They have merely proclaimed them to be disagreeable. *A priori*, there is no reason why sociology and, indeed, social life itself, should not be a little absurd or disagreeable.

• *Our own reservations about the phenomenology and ethnomethodology of deviance centre on one pivotal problem (but we disagree on this).* Gellner put the matter well when he wrote about the 'scandal of undemonstrated privacy'.[67] The inner subjectivity of the phenomenologist's mind is mined by the phenomenologist for ideas about ideas, and what emerges is plausible to many because it awakes a shock of recognition. Indeed, much of it seems convincing to us, but it is not accepted by all, and perhaps there is no reason to expect that it should.

There are other, lesser problems allied to the first. Some ethnomethodologists and phenomenologists are blandly indifferent to questions about the scope and validity of their work. Their indifference has been compounded by their conception of indexicality that insists on the situationally embedded character of all phenomena. If utterances and processes can attain significance only in context, it is argued, they cannot be examined as if they were ever context-free, general, or abstract. There is an ingrained resistance to the asking of questions about the nature, typicality, distribution, and incidence of processes and phenomena described by phenomenological sociology. It is a resistance that is quite understandable. Perhaps the phenomenologists are justified in their tacit assertion that there is no answer to the problem of generalization. But their resistance seems to be contradicted by other arguments that are offered *as if* they were universal. It has not been alleged, for instance, that examples of phenomenological or ethnomethodological analysis should be treated as temporally, spatially, or socially limited. Sudnow's courtroom seems somehow to be presented as an archetype for all courts anywhere; Agnes appears to have a mandate to proclaim the character of human sexuality, and abortion clinics are implicitly claimed to resemble the one studied by Ball.[68]

The problem, is that if we insist on an objective answer, there are no cautionary words to advise one to the contrary, and there is no road map. The point is that what we are left with is subjective appraisals, much like movie reviews, which feed into social workings.

It may appear that phenomenological analysis has been left in a limbo from which it cannot easily be retrieved, but that is the case only if you begin from an objectivist position. If it really is important to know whether Agnes's perspective is unique (and *how* it is unique) or whether Sudnow's courtroom is typical (and of what) and (heaven forbid) what uniqueness and typicality themselves are, we are given no help in reaching an answer. (This is where we really disagreed.) Neither has the pivotal idea of 'context', the idea that limits generalization, been made very clear. Contexts are not at all self-evident: they are contingent, shifting and biographical, and of indefinite scope and uncertain meaning. How is one to identify those problematic things called contexts and establish their effects? (However, it is done all the time; we're disagreeing again.) In short, it is difficult to know quite how phenomenological analysis should be assessed and what it is intended to accomplish. As a result of that difficulty, perhaps, phenomenological sociology fell on a sword of its own making, as others might say.

The unfortunate outcome of this has been that generations of sociologists writing after the 1970s seem to have no collective memory of the phenomenological period. What is more important, however, is that they have instead re-invented some of its arguments, calling them 'post-modernist' or, borrowing from Berger's *Social Construction of Reality*, 'social constructionist' and have consigned the residue to an unacknowledged oblivion. The phenomenological (and the symbolic interactionist) have been reincarnated as constructionism, and their past, a very important past indeed, has been forgotten.

Chapter Summary

The importation of phenomenology by Schutz to North American sociology went largely unnoticed until it was picked up by interactionists such as Goffman and Cicourel. And later it was turned to a different use by ethnomethodologists such as Garfinkel.

These various adaptations have resulted in different brands of work that challenged theoretical orthodoxy. Phenomenology has also entered into the 'mainstream' of sociological thought and resulted in a transformation in the sociology of deviance.

The phenomenological shift has since been reinterpreted as constructionism or post-modernism and has allowed for the possibility of more critical approaches to develop beyond individualism and functionalism. In particular, ethnomethodology and conversation analysis used philosophical concepts developed from phenomenology.

Critical-Thinking Questions

1. Using the idea that subjective evaluation of an act is necessary for its constitution as deviant, give an example of how people have a difference of opinion on whether something is normal or deviant.
2. How are the actor and deviance considered differently by phenomenology and functionalism?
3. What kind of questions would an ethnomethodologist ask in assessing a suicide?
4. How is conversational style part of what teachers assess in students' competence, over and above the knowledge they may possess?

Explorations in Film

Twelve Angry Men (1957) is said by some say to be one of the greatest legal dramas of all time. The director himself, Sidney Lumet (who also directed *Serpico*), is noteworthy because he made a career out of exploring the workings of the judicial system. In the film, a teenage boy has been accused of killing his father and the jury sees the case as pretty much open and shut. However, while the jury members may think they are anxious to deliver a quick guilty verdict, their personalities get in the way. One of the jurors is Henry Fonda, who tries to convince the others that a boy on trial for his life deserves due consideration. The central question that the film asks and that is pertinent here is whether it is possible for a jury to be impartial. So the movie can be read on two levels: as an endorsement of the legal system or as an illustration of how easily a jury can be swayed by the assumptions and conjectures of its members.

Websites

A list of the Yale University Library's extensive holdings of Schutz's manuscripts and letters is held at Yale University: http://webtext.library.yale.edu/xml2html/beinecke.SCHUTZ.com.html.

A wide-ranging listing of secondary sources related to this philosopher and social scientist can be found in *The Bibliography of Secondary Sources on Alfred Schutz, 1932–2002*, at: http://www.phenomenologycenter.org/asbib32-59.htm.

Chapter Nine

Control Theories

Chapter Overview

This chapter introduces some of the ideas of social control theories. Such theories are based on the idea that deviance is everywhere possible if it is allowed. Instead of inquiring into the causes of deviance, as in the various dispositional theories, it assumes that it will occur, and simply asks how deviance can be controlled.

In this approach we look at factors that weigh in the inhibition against committing crimes, such as parental involvement and a stake in conformity. Also considered are programs that apply the theoretical principles to situational crime prevention.

■ Introduction

Control theories have a formidable pedigree, which can be traced back through Durkheim to Hobbes and to Aristotle: 'It is in the nature of men not to be satisfied. . . . The fact is that the greatest crimes are caused by excess and not by necessity.'[1] The curbing of desires, not the equalization of property, was the right remedy. Hobbes asked: 'Why do men obey the rules of society?' He himself answered: 'Fear. . . It is the only thing, when there is appearance of profit or pleasure by breaking the laws, that makes men keep them.'[2] Similarly, Durkheim wrote in *Suicide*: 'It is not human nature which can assign the variable limits necessary to our needs. They are thus unlimited so far as they depend on the individual alone. Irrespective of any external regulatory force, our capacity for feeling is in itself an insatiable and bottomless abyss'.[3]

Bentham attempted to base social and legal controls on the principle of rational calculation. The 'felicific calculus' assumed that human beings have a capacity to align their actions with whatever course would maximize their pleasure and minimize their pain, a premise which opposed overly severe, as well as too lenient, penalties for infraction.[4] In this vein, householders who lock their doors at night are expressing one aspect of such theories, the belief that *opportunity* in itself is a cause of crime.

How, then, do we account for the fact that, until very recently, control theories have been virtually discounted in sociological theorizing on deviance and control? One of the principal control theorists, Ron Clarke, lamented: 'Despite its improved theory and its growing record of success, [it] still meets with indifference or hostility from criminologists'.[5] Perhaps sociologists think that science should busy itself with the unintended and latent consequences of social action. Perhaps they believe that consequential discoveries are those which lay people cannot make.[6] Perhaps it is thought that control theory has little intellectual interest. Haggerty asserted, for example, that

> rather than attending to questions of social causation or individual pathology, situational criminology [control theory] concentrates on reducing crime through loss prevention, target hardening and enhanced visibility. Many

criminologists have resisted calls to focus on measures like fence height, lock strength or surveillance capacity, perceiving them as belonging to the domain of security consultants more than research criminologists.'[7]

• *The neglect of control theory may also have been due to the unpopularity in liberal sociological circles of work that appears to support discipline, punishment, and regulation.* Far more congenial are ideas which debunk control strategies. For example, the work of the Gluecks,[8] whose attempts to predict delinquency in the 1930s, 1940s, and 1950s, became associated with a stress on the pathological, the individualistic, and the psychological. The three variables that they came to employ in their predictive studies—mother's affection for the child, mother's supervision of the child, and family cohesion—have now resurfaced in modified forms in the work of Hirschi and Harriet Wilson.[9]

The Gluecks' work was neglected in the 1960s, but studying such variables is central to the revived forms of control theory. Interest in this approach remained even in the ascendancy of strain and labelling theories. Reckless, for example, elaborated the notion of 'self-concept' as an 'insulating factor' in delinquency.[10] Such work was ignored, however, in the sociological reaction against the psychoanalytical and family-centred explanations of delinquency, which were viewed as dated products of the 1920s and 1930s. That period also produced the main sociological version of control theory: Shaw and McKay's concept of 'social disorganization'.

The dissatisfaction with the strain theorists' tendency to place the weight of explanation on deviant motivation led to several attempts to give some emphasis to control variables. Sykes and Matza argued that delinquents commonly adhered to the same set of values as everybody else. Deviants differed chiefly in their invocation of 'techniques of neutralization', which freed them from guilt and shame and which temporarily neutralized the social bond to enable them to engage in delinquent activities.

Jackson Toby[11] proposed a more sociological version of control theory by asserting that delinquents were distinguished from non-delinquents by their minimal 'stake in conformity'. In this approach, the common impetus to deviate interacts with varying commitments to conformity stemming from family as well as school and work experiences and opportunities.[12] Briar and Piliavin added the notion of 'situational inducements' as a fresh motivational slant.[13]

• *The combination of variations in the inner commitment to conform and the external opportunities to deviate was already furnishing an alternative* to the by now over-elaborate 'motivation' offered by the strain theorists.

> A lack of conformity and presence of opportunities creates deviance.

Homans and Blau[14] provided a model for the analysis of the individual in society much like the control theorists. In 'social-exchange' theories, a sociological version of *homo economicus* held that human behaviour is explained by individual gratifications provided by 'exchange' and that moral values emerge from ongoing exchanges.

One of Homans's examples is drawn from the famous Westinghouse Electrical Company study, in which informal group norms emerged to restrict production to levels set by the workers, not the management. In other words, deviants (rate-busters) were sanctioned in order to enforce group conformity. The pay-off for the group as a whole was superior to what would result from outright individualism.

This makes sense, because social behaviour is based on tangible forms of exchange which provide the bases for rational choice. In this respect, the theory is close to that of the symbolic interactionists[15] but differs in its relative indifference to meanings and interpretations., Homans's view of people is more attuned to the behaviourism of Skinner than to the interactionism of Mead. To Gouldner, his 'is the most unabashedly individualistic utilitarianism in modern sociology'.[16] People act to maximize the pay-off, whether that takes the form of material well-being, status, or affection.

The approach doesn't say how people choose *between* different pay-offs. But, as Heath points out, 'Skinnerian man is based on the common pigeon . . . a practical creature who learns from experience, avoiding what has proved painful in the past and seeking out what has proved rewarding.'[17] The implications for deviance and its control are not as stark as this might imply, but the scope for applying exchange theory to these phenomena has often suffered, since it is assumed that any truck with Skinner, pigeons, and control must be bad for any sociology. The more recent forms of control theory may have been keen to avoid such imputation,[18] but the affinity between control theory and theories of rational choice remains strong.

Discussion: Deviance and Culture—Crime and the Full Moon

It's a common belief among the public, the police, and hospital workers that there is a connection between phases of the moon and human behaviour. In fact in eighteenth-century England, a murderer could plead 'lunacy' if the crime was committed during the full moon and hope to get a lighter sentence.

Lunacy still appears in the news today. Toledo police claimed in 2002 that crime rises by 5 per cent during the full moon, while Kentucky police also blamed temporary rises in crime on the full moon. In the UK, a 2007 survey found that car accidents rose by up to 50 per cent during full moons, and senior police officers announced they were planning to deploy more officers over the summer to counter trouble linked to the lunar cycle.

However, while it's suspected to be an old wive's tale, when NASA was asked if the phases of the moon affect the crime rate, it said there is no relationship, but suggested that since people are more likely to notice if the moon is full when crimes, births, and strange occurrences happen, they talk about the association.

Whether the link is symbolic or real, it has a name, the 'Transylvanian effect', according to Wikipedia. The research, you will see, is equivocal.

For example, a study in Philadelphia found that with a full moon, 'psychotic' crimes such as murder, arson, dangerous driving, and kleptomania were at their peak. And in another study, psychologist Arnold Lieber decided to test the full-moon 'lunacy' theory by using Miami homicide data over a period of fifteen years. He found that as the moon waxed the murder rate rose, and then declined as the moon waned. He thought that since the human body is composed of almost 80 per cent water, it experiences a 'biological tide' that affects the emotions.

A similar study in the *British Medical Journal* in 1984 looked at crime reported to three police stations to see if it varied with the lunar cycle. They found that the incidence of crime committed on full-moon days was much higher than on all other days but that there was no increase on the 'solar days' of the equinox and solstice. They also thought that the increase of crimes on full-moon days might be due to 'human tidal waves' caused by the gravitational pull of the moon.

On the other hand, another study looked at the effect of the full moon on the number of patients admitted to emergency departments. The authors concluded that the full moon had no effect on the number of patients, ambulance runs, general admissions, or emergency admissions.

However, another study looked at whether animal bites increase at the time of a full moon. Using observational analysis of a general hospital, the researchers compared 1,621 patients who attended an emergency department from 1997 to 1999 after being bitten by an animal with the lunar phase in each month. The study, which found that the incidence of animal bites rose significantly at the time of a full moon, concluded that the full moon is associated with a significant increase in animal bites to humans.

And then there's the study which looked at all of the violent deaths in the US over two years and found that there were clear monthly and daily variations. Suicide peaked in the spring and fall, whereas homicide peaked in July and December. Suicide was more common on Mondays; homicide on Saturdays and Sundays. Homicide was more common on national holidays, while suicide tended to be less common. However, no lunar variation was found.

Similarly, an Australian study looked at whether there was an increase in violent and aggressive behaviour among hospitalized psychiatric clients at the time of the full moon. Using data from five inpatient psychiatric settings, the authors could find no relationship between total violence and aggression or level of violence and aggression and any phase of the moon despite the belief in among health workers of the 'lunar effect'.

Source: Adapted from C. McCormick, 'Crime and the Full Moon' (Crime Matters column), *Daily Gleaner* (Fredericton), 16 August 2007.

■ Sociological Control Theories of Deviance

The Contribution of Travis Hirschi

Hirschi states that the common property of control theories is their assumption that 'delinquent acts result when an individual's bond to society is weak or broken.'[19] He specifies four elements of that social bond: attachment, commitment, involvement, and belief.

'*Attachment*' to others is an antecedent variable. If one cares about the opinions and wishes of others, it is because of one's strong sense of attachment. Theoretically this is seen as a better concept than the 'internalization of norms' since deviation is only possible if a person does not care about the wishes, expectations, and opinions of others.

'*Commitment*' signifies that:

> the person invests time, energy, himself, in a certain line of activity, say, getting an education, building up a business, acquiring a reputation for virtue. When or whenever he considers deviant behaviour, he must consider the costs of this deviant behaviour, the risk he runs of losing the investment he has made in conventional behaviour. . . Most people, simply by the process of living in an organised society, acquire goods, reputations, prospects that they do not want to risk losing. These accumulations are society's insurance that they will abide by the rules.[20]

'*Involvement*' is the behavioural counterpart of commitment. A person who is engaged in conventional activities has little time to engage in deviance, or, as the saying goes, idle hands are the devil's workshop. Involvement in conventional activities is also more likely to associate people with others they are attached to and to increase their commitment to and investment in the community.

Finally, deviants and 'norm-abiding' citizens may share a common value system, but there is variation in the extent to which people's '*belief*' they should obey the rules of society. The 'less a person believes he should obey the rules, the more likely he is to violate them.'[21]

• These four variables interact to produce an ideal-typical portrait of a non-delinquent who is strongly attached to conventional others, strongly committed to conventional activities, heavily involved in them, and imbued with a strong belief in the need to obey the rules. The delinquent is relatively free from such controls and hence more at risk of deviation. Deviance is not automatic; it is simply no longer ruled out as a possibility. The significant fact that those who offend while on bail tend disproportionately to have no fixed address and to be unemployed[22] is an indicator of the controls exerted by commitment and involvement. And, for the same reasons, it is also significant that leaving or not attending school are strongly linked to delinquency.[23]

As Hirschi acknowledged, the most disconcerting question remains: 'Yes, but why do they do it?' Cohen and Short say control theories imply 'that the impulse to delinquency is an inherent characteristic of young people and does not itself

> The conformist is bonded to others; the deviant is not.

need to be explained; it is something that erupts when the lid—i.e. internalised cultural restraints or external authority—is off'.[24] Hirschi's reply is to accept that while certain motivations of a situational character are consistent with control theory, they are 'by no means deducible from it. . . . The question "Why do they do it?" is simply not the question the theory is designed to answer. The question is 'Why don't we do it?'[25] Kornhauser also says that it is not necessary for control theory to explain the motivation of delinquency in order to explain its occurrence.[26]

The strength of Hirschi's work, however, is empirical rather than theoretical. Much of *The Causes of Delinquency* tests a variety of propositions derived from subcultural theory. He finds that control variables correlate with delinquency quite closely and consistently. For example, parental supervision was measured by the extent to which the parent(s) knew where and in what company their boys were when they were away from home. Parents of non-delinquents reported high supervision, while not surprisingly parents of serious delinquents reported low supervision.[27] 'Intimacy of communication' and 'affectional identification' with parents showed similarly strong links with delinquency: the less strong the child's reported bond with his family, the greater his involvement in delinquency. Findings on links with the school and teachers showed the same trend. Hirschi's data were based on a large-scale self-report survey of over four thousand children aged 12 to 17 sampled from a predominantly urban-industrial area designed to be representative of society.

The Contribution of Steven Box

Steven Box[28] tried to redress some of the deficiencies of control theory. He tried to align control theory with labelling theory, and he furnished a theory of delinquency that was sensitive to the issue of motivation. The need for the alignment with labelling theory stems from Box's attempt to explain how and why social class and ethnicity have such weak links with delinquency in self-report studies but such strong links in official statistics. The answer he offers is that the first capture 'primary' and the second 'secondary' deviations. With official intervention, the more powerful members of society are at an advantage, and as a result official deviants are predominantly lower-status. Labelling processes interact with control variables to make matters worse for those defined as deviant, because the bonds they had with conventional society are eroded, and their exposure to the risks of fresh deviations is heightened.

Motivation to commit deviance is also more important for Box than for earlier control theorists. 'Whether or not an individual with the option to deviate decides to, depends to some extent on what he makes of the issue of *secrecy, skills, supply, social* and *symbolic support*.'[29] The first is related to chances of concealment; the second to the knowledge required for deviance; the third to the necessary equipment; the fourth to the support of associates; and the fifth to support from the wider culture. A pot-smoking campus party scores high on all points. These elements, however, do little to suggest why some individuals, and not others, would choose to take up this particular option.

Control theory is interested in why people don't commit deviance.

Parental supervision is inversely related to delinquency.

Box makes more extensive attempts to develop a theory of the will to delinquency in discussing the work of Albert Cohen and Matza. The delinquent is both frustrated by, and resentful of, the experience of failing at school. But *status frustration* is more important than *resentment*, since the former implies a prior internalization of middle-class norms, while the latter implies only that boys are not indifferent to the imputation of failure. The former leads to 'reaction formation', the denial of a (real) attachment by the ostentatious display of rule breaking. The latter leads to behaviour that seeks to assert independent standards. In Box's view this is far more in line with social reality. The weight of the evidence on this point is against Cohen, although the delinquent subculture, as he conceived it, both restores status and provides the social means to hit back at the source of imputed failure. Phenomenologically, however, it seems eminently possible to be frustrated about social status and resentful of even caring about status in the first place.

A similar criticism is made of Matza's attempt to depict the delinquent as both aiming at restoring 'the mood of humanism' and rationalizing his delinquency away as the result of being 'pushed around'. These, says Box, are incompatible: either you are restoring the mood of humanism and mean it, or you genuinely feel pushed around and 'objectified'. Box prefers to treat the second technique as a purely situated account in the context of arrest. Again, the logic of strain theory is pitted against that of control theory. In strain theory, which Matza partially adheres to, delinquents care about breaking the law; hence they invoke 'techniques of neutralization' to justify their deviations ('I was pushed', etc.). To control theorists, no such commitment to the rules exists in the first place; hence 'I was pushed' is an excuse after the fact which the offenders hopes will result in leniency. There is no way of settling this issue here, but Matza's 'techniques' have a double purpose; that is, they both express an existential state of mind and serve as an excuse for the offence.

Case Study—The Contribution of Harriet Wilson

Harriet Wilson's study of socially deprived families in inner Birmingham, *Parents and Children of the Inner City*, has produced findings in line with the tenets of control theory. Using an index of 'chaperonage'[1] she measured the degree of protection parents gave to their children to ensure their safety. Scores were allocated to parents on such items as fetching children from school, allowing them to roam the streets, and whether or not there were rules for coming in at night. The families she studied shared certain characteristics: the were intact families, they had five or more children, and they lived in old housing in a deprived inner-city area. Within this group, the 'chaperonage' variable sharply distinguished delinquents from non-delinquents, whereas other factors, such as the happiness of the home atmosphere, did not. A high chaperonage index was positively related to strict rather than permissive standards of morality:

'Strict' parents insist on a degree of tidiness and cleanliness in the home, they tend to discourage or punish genital play, children looking at each other when undressed, or giggling over the toilet and parents tend to avoid undressing in the children's presence.[2]

> The families who exercised chaperonage and who tend to adhere to traditional standards of strictness are motivated in many different ways, but they share the belief that the deprived neighbourhood and its inhabitants are bad and that their children need protection against this badness. . . These parents were driven into applying child-rearing measures which under more normal conditions in a friendly and known neighbourhood they would not be likely to apply. They kept their children indoors or under close supervision in the back yard; they accompanied them to and from school; they forbade them to play with undesirable youngsters in the streets. If the boys played out, their mothers knew where to find them. These measures are applied at great cost to themselves.[3]

In a further study Wilson extends the support for this conclusion, but she is careful to state that:

> the essential point of our findings is the very close association of lax parenting methods with severe social handicap. Lax parenting methods are often the result of chronic stress, situations arising from frequent or prolonged spells of unemployment, physical or mental disabilities among members of the family and an often permanent condition of poverty. . . . If these factors are ignored and parental laxness is seen instead as an 'attitude' which by education or by punitive measures can be shifted, then our findings are being misinterpreted. It is the position of the most disadvantaged groups in society and not the individual, which needs improvement in the first place.[4]

In such an analysis, a control theory of delinquency is combined with a strong sense of structural context. It has received consistent empirical support[5] in, for example, the attempt by criminologists to provide recipes for the explanation and prevention of criminal violence. Amalgamating ideas flowing from the Chicago School, anomie theory, and control theory, they argue that violence is most likely to occur in communities marked by social heterogeneity, by rapid change (both economic decline and 'gentrification'), by the growth of an illegal market in drugs, and a more general ensuing social disorganization. Those communities can no longer exert informal controls over their younger members. Parents are unable to distinguish local youths from outsiders, 'to question each other's children, to participate in voluntary organizations and friendship networks and to watch neighborhood common areas. Many old heads, community elders who took responsibility for local youth, have left urban communities.'[6]

What offers a limited buffer against delinquency is an intact, two-parent family that continues to exercise discipline over its children:

> Two parents, together with the extended network of cousins, aunts, uncles . . . can form a durable team, a viable supportive group engaged to fight in a committed manner the problems confronting inner-city teenagers, including drugs, crime, pregnancy and lack of social mobility. This unit, when it does endure, tends to be equipped with a survivor's mentality. It has weathered a good many storms. . . . The parents are known in the community as 'strict'; they impose curfews and tight supervision, demanding to know their children's whereabouts at all times. Determined that their offspring will not become casualties . . . they scrutinize their children's associates, rejecting those who seem to be 'no good' and encouraging others who seem on their way to 'amount to something'.[7]

Of course, perhaps we should heed Hagan and McCarthy's warning that the family can itself on occasion be a place of abuse which young people may be only too eager to leave.[8] Far from protecting its own, it may expose them to danger. In the 1980s, the Ministry of the Solicitor General of Canada proposed a campaign to restore missing children to their homes, but it reversed its decision on discovering some of the reasons why the children had left. Even when the family does exercise benign control, its capacity to do so tends to decline quite rapidly when children reach their middle teens and acquire a substantial degree of independence from parental scrutiny and discipline.[9]

[1] First employed by J. and E. Newson, *Seven Years Old in the Home Environment*.

[2] H. Wilson and G. Herbert, *Parents and Children*, 176.

[3] H. Wilson and G. Herbert, *Parents and Children*, 177.

[4] H. Wilson, 'Parental Supervision', 233–4.

[5] See for instance, C. Flood-Page et al., *Youth Crime*, 32–3; and H. Juby and D. Farrington, 'Disentangling the Link between Disrupted Families and Delinquency'.

[6] National Research Council, *Understanding and Preventing Violence*, 15.

[7] E. Anderson, *Streetwise*, 123.

[8] J. Hagan and B. McCarthy, *Mean Streets*, 58.

[9] See D. Riley and M. Shaw, *Parental Supervision and Juvenile Delinquency*.

Control theories have begun to attract a considerable following. For example, Hagan and McCarthy examined how the children of large working-class families 'are more likely to take to the streets and that street life increases serious delinquency'.[30] The erosion of family controls is exacerbated by the structured strains of living on city streets.

Both Sampson and Laub's *Crime in the Making* of 1993 and Laub and Sampson's *Shared Beginnings, Divergent Lives* of 2003[31] examined the onset of, and desistance from, delinquency in the lives of men studied over decades. Both books pay particular attention to the manner in which the social bonds of family, friends, employment, and military service work as controls that moderate the influences emanating from the wider social structure. Marriage, the onset of work, and military service may be turning points in a person's life; they create new sets of social relations, dependencies, and responsibilities; introduce new disciplines into social life; and invite stock-taking and reflection.

Conversely, involvement with the criminal justice system and imprisonment may interrupt or undermine a person's participation in stabilizing social environments, stigmatize the offender and prevent him or her from returning to the 'straight' world, encourage cynicism about criminal justice, and introduce the offender to other lawbreakers who help to amplify deviance through association. Laub and Sampson represent the process, not as an inevitable progression into deviance, but as a sequence of actions that is influenced by how people interpret and respond to their situations. This part played by human agency makes it difficult to predict future deviance from present circumstances.

> The criminal justice system can be criminogenic.

The appeal of control theory has strong links with the political demise of rehabilitation and the call for a return to sentences based on 'harm done'. Morgan[32] argued that delinquency was fostered by permissiveness in family life, education, and crime control. In her view, adolescents had too much freedom to act out their fantasies. Although Morgan was writing in 1978, this sentiment fitted the sentiment of the 1980s that 'nothing works'. In even sterner vein, James Q. Wilson argued that incapacitation alone provides a guarantee against criminality, calling for the incarceration of offenders as a costly but sure means of combating crime.[33] Control theory is not a package deal that commits its adherents to the 'war against crime' and punitive sentencing: Harriet Wilson and James Q. Wilson are not so easily merged. But there is little doubt that control theory lends itself to the technology of crime control and agrees with lay theories that deviance is caused by inadequate preventative measures. This is quite explicit in 'situational' control theories.

■ 'Situational' Control Theories

The Contribution of Clarke

Criminological theories have been little concerned with the situational determinants of crime. Instead, the main object of these theories (whether biological, psychological, or sociological in orientation) has been to show how some people are born with, or come to acquire, a 'disposition' to behave in a consistently criminal manner. This 'dispositional' bias of theory has been identified as a defining characteristic of 'positivist' criminology, but it is also to be found in 'interactionist' or deviancy theories of crime . . . a dispositional bias is presented throughout the social sciences.[34]

The focus of situational control theories, by contrast, is on the technical, cost-benefit-ratio aspects of crime, that is, the opportunities for crime available in the environment and the risks attached to criminal activity. In the short term, reducing the opportunities for deviance produces results more quickly than trying to influence psychological events, social, or economic conditions. The argument is important, because when Clarke, for example, declared that policy-relevant research should focus on containment, deterrent sentencing, police effectiveness, and crime prevention.[35] the outcome was the commissioning of a series of research reports on small practical campaigns to modify crime.[36]

Situational crime prevention theories are consistent with a model of the offender as capable of rational choice. Rational deviants making choices are fairly susceptible to intelligent control strategies. Moreover, the presumption of rationality had a common-sense appeal, because that is how most people, including politicians and officials, would care to explain their own and behaviour and that of others. It lent itself to neat, demonstrable experiments in prevention. Clarke lists some examples: airline hijackings were prevented by the introduction of baggage screening in the 1970s; the robbing of bus drivers was stopped by introducing exact-fare systems; and graffiti on subways was eliminated by the prompt removal of graffiti as soon as they appeared.[37]

The Economist's Angle

Rational choice theory has come to have an increasingly important place in the arguments of control theory itself. This success is due to the authority that economic models of behaviour are beginning to exert over sociology. One particularly important early paper was Gary Becker's 'Crime and Punishment: An Economic Approach',[38] which assessed the balance between expenditure on control and punishment on the one hand, and, on the other hand, the social losses from criminal offences.[39] Becker adopted the economist's assumption that people will offend if the utility of doing so exceeds the utility of not doing so. Offending was not a matter of motivation, he argued, but of costs and benefits weighed by people who choose deviance 'because of the benefits it brings to the offender. This holds in all cases of crime, with the possible exception of some crimes committed as a result of serious mental illness.'[40]

That simple economic calculus was subsequently extended by the inclusion of a larger cast of actors seen to make decisions about the rewards and penalties of committing crime, reporting crime, and enforcing the law. It was never utterly rational but was based on imperfect information, improvisation, and experience. Its use was staggered over time, organized by scripts that chart decisions in sequence, breaking down complex acts into 'aggregations of simpler elements',[41] from preparation, through target selection, entry to the setting, commission of the act, and escape to aftermath. The calculus seemed to have support in 'the evidence of ethnographic studies of delinquency[42] [which] strongly suggest that people are usually aware of consciously choosing to commit offences.'[43] It is most powerfully exemplified by organized crime.[44]

In short, control theory is in line with theories of social learning and rational choice; and it has no difficulty, unlike dispositional theories, in accepting that 'the bulk of crime—vandalism, auto-crime, shoplifting, theft by employees—is committed by people who would not ordinarily be thought of as criminal at all'.[45] Control theory enriches its possibilities because explanation is focused on the criminal event, explanations are developed for separate categories of deviance, and the individual's circumstances and the features of the setting are given more explanatory significance than in dispositional theories.

Furthermore, studies of traffic control, reducing fare evasion, and graffiti show that proponents of situational crime prevention have understated the importance of situations. It is necessary to study how people and the social and physical environment interact. In this way we see that people develop and change in response to their experience in particular situations, and changes in situations can produce more persistent changes in people.[46] What Clarke terms 'standing decisions' can become, in effect and over time, changed norms and values.

•*Measures for crime prevention have two linked emphases: reducing the physical opportunities for offending and increasing the risk of an offender's being caught.* The first includes such measures as the replacement of vulnerable coin-boxes with stronger ones, which can eliminate theft from telephone booths; and the dramatic fall in the suicide rate when supplies of non-toxic gas were installed in people's homes, for example in Birmingham.[47] Several well-researched instances of specific successes in crime prevention can be adduced to bear this approach out. Those include 'target hardening' (that is, making the desired target harder to appropriate), which led to a decline in burglaries at pharmacies[48] and property-marking schemes to reduce residential burglary.

Possibly the most exciting application of this approach has been the attempt to see the environment as potential predators see it. The researchers conducted extensive interviews with burglars, using videotapes of residential districts and going on tours with an accompanying commentary from experienced criminals. It has become clear that signs of occupation, surveillance by neighbours, and ease of access are crucial in the decision to break into a house.[49] In contrast, the activities of the police are relatively inconsequential.

The result has been an increasingly meticulous mapping of the visual controls built into the social spaces through which people move. It is as if the built environment could be transformed by control theory into a bundle of observed possibilities for offending. One clever demonstration of those links between design and crime may be found in a study of burglary in schools. Hope contrasted two different styles of school building in Britain—the large, modern, sprawling schools which were often set in spacious grounds and the small, old, compact schools with only a modest amount of space around them. Unsurprisingly, the average number of burglaries was four times as high for the large and sprawling schools than for the small and compact schools. The conclusion is that the differences in burglary rates could be attributed to features of design: the small schools were less accessible to predators and afforded 'greater opportunities for surveillance by the public and by school caretakers'.[50]

> Control theory relies on a model of rational choice.

> Neighbours are more important than the police in preventing break-ins.

• *The second prong of the preventive approach builds on the assumption that there is 'a good deal of unrealized potential for making use of the surveillance role of employees* who come into regular and frequent contact with the public in a semi-official capacity'.[51] Control theory has translated the physical environment into a terrain patrolled, watched, and guarded by numerous official and unofficial custodians. Doormen, bus conductors, parking lot attendants, caretakers, and the like have a considerable effect on deviance. For example, on double-decker buses without conductors, the areas of least supervision attracted the most damage from vandalism. The drivers could observe the lower deck but not the upper, and there was about twenty times as much damage on the upper as on the lower deck.[52]

A similar example is that of the municipal public-housing developments, where during the 1960s, a drive for economy and rationalization centralized administrative and maintenance work in main offices. Repairs and caretaking tasks were undertaken by mobile teams. However, as a result it was discovered just how much informal social control was exercised by local caretaking staff, who 'play a key role in helping to reduce vandalism, patrolling public areas and supervising the cleaning of them and dealing at first hand with tenants' problems.'[53]

The Contribution of Newman

Passive improvements in environmental design can reduce deviance.

Oscar Newman's study, *Defensible Space*, has been the most discussed theory on the passive controls that can be mobilized by improvements in housing design, demonstrating the link between high-rise public-sector housing and increased rates of delinquency. Jane Jacobs had laid its foundation in her classic lament for the rapidly disappearing intimacy and diversity of city life,[54] which chronicled the progressive extinction of the street as the urban form most in harmony with human scale. The street had evolved as an arena for diverse activities and safe associations, particularly for children at play and was enhanced by passers-by, the presence of merchants and street vendors, and ease of surveillance from houses and shops.[55]

The criticism is that the high-rise housing complex has planned these features of urban concourse away and has created areas of space of an 'indefensible' character—deserted through-ways and underpasses, and unobservable elevators and stairwells. The entrances to buildings are used by so many people that it is no longer certain who has a right to go through them and who has not, who is safe and who is not. In particular, there has been a proliferation of anonymous areas that belong to no one and are cared for by no one. It has become impossible to decide who has a reasonable claim to be present on a piece of land or in a building. In turn, people are unable to establish practical or symbolic boundaries around territory that is their own or to exercise informal social control within them. The result has been a great increase in deviance. Ironically, inner-city building was planned to pack the maximum number of people into the minimum amount of space, for whatever reason, but it then created new problems.

Subsequent criticisms have dented Newman's authority somewhat.[56] First, the argument has been put that Newman neglected the social effects of communal reputation on the behaviour of those who lived in crime-ridden neighbourhoods, that is, that people who are part of a morally stigmatized area experience discrimination, impaired life chances, and unhelpful neighbours. Second, there has been the charge that Newman was insensitive to the effects of different policing strategies and that the high crime rates of the problem housing development reveal police assumptions and policies as much as real variations in behaviour; for example, such housing developments seem to be *under-policed*.[57] Third, a community's characteristics reflect renting decisions. Newman made the assumption that deviants do not belong to an area but are outsiders against whom space can be successfully defended. This is not necessarily the case. And fourth, Newman assumed that a sense of territoriality is a widespread human drive; however, people may not invariably wish to have a symbolic stake in space.[58]

Nonetheless, Newman's work was original, and it did succeed in drawing together a number of strands usually considered in isolation from each other by urban planners, sociologists, and environmentalists. Although it focused on the control aspects of the environment, his theory implicitly raised questions of a more symbolic character. There are many as yet largely unanswered questions to be asked about what features enhance the social sense of 'belonging' to a neighbourhood and make for a feeling of involvement rather than indifference. In this respect, his work combines both situational and sociological control variables.

Perhaps the most direct application of Newman's concept of 'defensible space' has been the study of housing development that lists the design features that seem to be correlated with such measurable signs of disorder as graffiti, litter, vandalism, and the number of children in care.[59] The assumption has been that it is poor physical design that causes social breakdown by estranging members of a community from one another, by letting marauders in, and by preventing an effective response. Crime itself is believed to result from the uncontrolled circulation of strangers along walkways of poorly planned housing developments; the residents' loss of a sense of territoriality; an abundance of escape routes for predators; and inadequate opportunities for surveillance.

Crime and deviance can be reduced by redesigning housing complexes so that the entrances can be controlled, the movement of strangers restricted, spatial ambiguity reduced, and monitoring improved. In newly created small, private, and enclosed residential areas, outsiders may imagine that they are more conspicuous and insiders that they have a greater stake in territory.

Alice Coleman also emphasized the importance of design over social and symbolic variables.[60] However, others have repeated the criticisms that were first directed at Newman, arguing that focusing on design neglects the influence of stigma, social organization, and formal social control; for example 'Crime and violence arise from interactions between the social environment and the physical environment, which cannot be controlled entirely through manipulations of the physical environment.'[61]

Yet in this work,[62] there does remain a provocative line of reasoning whose potential is far from exhausted.

Case Study—Situational Crime Prevention

Situational crime prevention is an evidence-based approach that deters offenders through the use of architecture as a *place-improvement process*. Through the proper planning of space and places, crime can be reduced simply by making that space or place less attractive. This type of crime prevention emphasizes taking the whole situation into account in order to reduce the potential for nuisance behaviour and deviance in public and private spaces. Two important benefits are also the increase in the sense of public ownership, and the decrease in public fear.

This approach is less concerned with the cause of crime than with its prevention. Whereas traditional crime prevention has focused on offenders, this approach looks at geography as a 'filtering process' that channels people to situations in which deviant behaviour can take place. For this reason, to prevent deviance, planners need to consider the characteristics of situations which give them opportunities for deviant actions.

We know from research that it is a small proportion of criminal offenders are involved in very large proportions of all crimes. We also know that many crimes are precipitated by opportunity as much as by motivation. Similarly, some places are more likely than others to be scenes of victimization. In considering crime from this perspective, we should look at what routines bring people into a situation with a potential for crime.

Offences can be prevented at a general level, programs that try to reduce the attractiveness of deviance in vulnerable situations before the specific problem arises. Other programs look at an area's immediate need to reduce an existing crime problem; while a third type of program works to prevent the reoccurrence of offences. These three categories are usually called *primary*, *secondary*, and *tertiary* prevention.

Primary prevention tries to reduce deviance by correcting the underlying factors that have a basic influence on everyone, such as social disorganization, a lack of social cohesion, economic pressures, and the basic physical design of cities.

Secondary prevention focuses more narrowly on individuals who are known to be likely to become involved in crimes. An example cited by Brantingham of Simon Fraser University is the Wise Owl program in British Columbia, which provides education to the elderly concerning various frauds, such as telemarketing fraud and home renovation scams.

Tertiary prevention tries to prevent recidivism, for example, by modifying repeatedly victimized buildings, setting up offender rehabilitation programs, offering hot-spot deterrence programs such as Bullwinkle the Moose, or helping those who are trying to leave the sex trade. In Victoria, BC, the Capital Region Action Team program on the Prevention and Early Intervention of Sexually Exploited Children and Youth helps children and youth who have recently been recruited into prostitution and who have common risk factors, such as having been sexually abused, having poor employment potential, and having difficulties at school.

Through situational crime prevention, sociologists want to develop specific crime-prevention programs and ways of measuring their impact. One such program was intended to prevent auto theft in suburban Vancouver commuter lots. During April 1995, a bicycle-mounted security patrol was introduced into a vehicle-theft 'hot spot', the largest park-and-ride commuter parking lot in British Columbia. In 1994, motor vehicle thefts and thefts from motor vehicles had accounted for 57 per cent of all recorded thefts and almost a quarter of all recorded criminal code offences in the province.

The majority of British Columbia auto thieves appear to be juveniles who steal for joyriding and transport purposes, and who are attracted to malls, large parking lots, and other easily accessible locations that feature large numbers of older vehicle makes and models, which are physically easy to steal. An initial security plan included fencing the lots, allowing access only by a single main entrance, upgrading the lighting, trimming shrubs, introducing a closed camera television surveillance system, and patrolling by a mobile security guard. For several reasons only the security patrol, on bicycles, was introduced.

Before the bike patrol was instituted, the average number of cars stolen per month was twenty-four. After the introduction of the bike patrol, vehicle thefts dropped substantially, to three a month and remained low even after the bike patrol was withdrawn. This pattern of crime reduction can be seen in Figure 9.1.

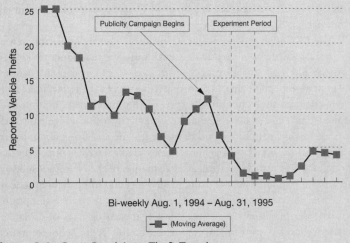

Figure 9.1: Scott Road Auto Theft Trends

Source: Barclay et al., 'Preventing Auto Theft in Surburban Vancouver Commuter Lots'. Reprinted by permission of the publisher.

One factor that is probably decisive was not only the visibility of the bicycle patrol in the parking lot itself, as a situational deterrent, but also the publicizing of the campaign before the experimental period. This would have had the effect of increasing the perceived risk to those planning to commit crimes in parking lot. There didn't appear to be a displacement to adjacent areas, and the overall result was a net reduction in vehicle thefts.

Sources: P.L. Brantingham and P. J. Brantingham, 'Situational Crime Prevention as a Key Component in Embedded Crime Prevention'; idem, 'Environment, Routine and Situation: Toward a Pattern Theory of Crime', 259–4; idem, 'Criminality of Place: Crime Generators and Crime Attractors', 5–26; P. Barclay et al., 'Preventing Auto Theft in Suburban Vancouver Commuter Lots: Effects of a Bike Patrol', 133–1.

The Broken-Windows Hypothesis

Prevention of situational crime, defensible space, and other facets of control theory point to the growing role of informal and formal surveillance in the regulation of everyday life. Especially significant was the concept of 'broken windows', discussed first by Jane Jacobs and then celebrated in an essay published by James Wilson and George Kelling in 1982.[63] Broken windows, graffiti, and malicious damage were held to be the visible and obvious signs of a neighbourhood that was in decay and was open to depredation and about which no one effectively cared. They seemed to be linked in the public mind with disorder, crime, and the fear of crime. By extension, broken windows signified that social control itself had been eroded as families move out and unattached adults move in. In short, broken windows were to be regarded as a phase in a natural history of communal disorganization.

Wilson and Kelling exercised influence over the reform of policing in a number of cities, American and Canadian. 'Incivilities', beggars, 'squeegee kids', graffiti, and the like had formerly been dismissed as 'not real police work' and certainly not as important a part of the police mandate as serious crime. The new argument was that intervening in the cycle of communal deterioration by joining local residents and police together in campaigns to discourage panhandling, littering, and public drinking could reverse a decline and bring about a reinvigoration of informal social control. The successes claimed have included the decline in the rates of crime associated with the reclamation of the New York subway, the practice of zero-tolerance policing, and neighbourhood improvement schemes.[64]

The most rigorous empirical test of the thesis rebuts the core assumption that signs of disorder precipitate a vicious spiral of increasing rates of deviance and social deterioration. Sampson and Raudenbush criticize the whole argument as tautological, mistaking symptoms for causes. Using an ingenious method of videotaping some 23,000 street 'segments' or blocks in Chicago, they constructed scales of physical and social disorder for 196 neighbourhoods. These variables were then analyzed together with other data sets from the census, the police, and interviews with residents to assess the significance of 'broken windows' compared with that of 'collective efficacy' (a version of social capital) and 'structural constraints' (especially concentrated poverty) in explaining lower rates of offences.

> Contrary to the 'broken windows' theory, the relationship between public disorder and crime is spurious, except perhaps for robbery. . . . Put differently, the active ingredients in crime seem to be structural disadvantage and attenuated collective efficacy more so than disorder. Attacking public disorder through tough police tactics may thus be a politically popular but perhaps analytically weak strategy to reduce crime, mainly because such a strategy leaves the common origins of both, but especially the last, untouched.[65]

The new talk about intervention and surveillance alarmed some sociologists, who stressed the darker side of control theory by focusing on the increasing surveillance by the State both indirectly and directly, similar to Foucault's conception of the carceral society.[66]

Discussion: Deviance Exploration—The Broken-Windows Promise?

It was so simple it had to work.

The 'broken-windows' theory developed by Wilson and Kelling in 1982 was based on the idea that controlling *symbolic signs* of public disorder, such as graffiti and vandalism, and *minor misdemeanours*, such as solicitation, jaywalking, and fare jumping, could reduce crime.[1]

The New York City Police adopted the approach in the 1990s, with reputedly remarkable drops in crime. In fact, eventually the three most populous cities in the United States, New York, Chicago, and Los Angeles, all adopted at least some aspect of Wilson and Kelling's theory, primarily more aggressive enforcement of minor misdemeanour laws.

Between 1991 and 2001, the most frequent explanation given in the media for the decline in crime was those innovative policing strategies.[2] And who could argue with it? It was an approach attractive for its no-nonsense conservative simplicity.

However, criminologists have questioned whether the drop in crime is connected to aggressive misdemeanour arrests or is simply due to other factors, such as an aging population, a better economy, a lower proportionate youth population, higher prison populations, increases in policing, or the downgrading of offences in police reports.

Some, such as Harcourt[3] say it doesn't matter and cite a rise in civil liberties and civil rights costs; for example, allegations of overall police misconduct increased by 68 per cent between 1993 and 1996; Amnesty International found racial disparities among persons who complained of police misconduct; claims of police abuse increased by 39 per cent; and settlements paid on claims alleging improper police actions increased by 46 per cent.

And while some might argue that if you can produce a large drop in crime, communities might well be willing to sacrifice their civil rights and civil liberties, there is no reason to ask communities to make that trade because others say that retrospective analysis of evidence provides no support for a simple first-order disorder-crime relationship or for the idea that this policing model is the best use of scarce law-enforcement resources.[4] Moreover, Sampson and Raudenbush[5] say bluntly that any relationship between public disorder and crime is spurious, and they argue for the need to look at measures of collective efficacy.

At best, it seems, a jurisdiction receiving more police attention will inevitably experience a decrease in crime. At worst, any decrease will be due to other factors, such as the under-reporting of crimes to make it seem as if the crime rate is going lower. Because, although it may seem illogical, putting more police on the job is going to drive the crime rate up, so there has to be a way to make the crime rate go down at the same time.

Perhaps the theory is related more to a cultural need for an explanation than to an empirical trend in crime.

[1] George L. Kelling and James Q. Wilson, 'Broken Windows: The Police and Neighborhood Safety.'
[2] S. Levitt, 'Understanding Why Crime Fell in the 1990s', 163–90.
[3] B. Harcourt, 'Broken Theory: Broken Windows'.
[4] B. Harcourt and J. Ludwig, 'Broken Windows: New Evidence from New York City and a Five-City Social Experiment'.
[5] R. Sampson and S. Raudenbush, 'Systematic Social Observation of Public Spaces'.

The Idea of Surveillance

Underlying Foucault's metaphor of surveillance is Bentham's panopticon, a design for a prison conceived in the late eighteenth century.[67] The panopticon was meant to be a vast, circular building with cells housing prisoners about its rim and a dimly lit central tower with inspectors at its centre. The very architecture of the prison gave dominion to authority. From their central tower, only a few inspectors would have been needed to monitor multitudes of inmates. And those inmates could never be sure when they were being monitored or by whom. Their cells would have been illuminated, but the tower would not, and thus the prisoners would have found it difficult to tell whether the observers were actually there, and whether they were watching any particular cell. In the panopticon, the gaze was to be sovereign in that the prisoners were seen but they could not see.[68] Since control would have been efficient and omnipresent, there was no need for violence or coercion because inmates would have become individualized and isolated. Power so perfected, Foucault maintained, rendered its practical use unnecessary.

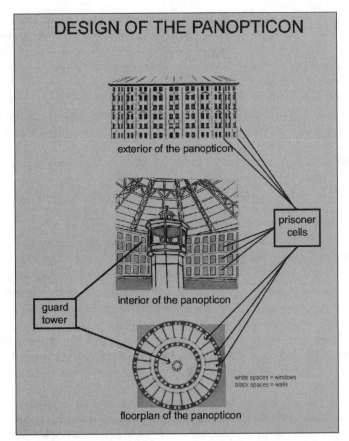

Figure 9.2: Panopticon

Source: From the c-cs.us website. Drawn by James J. Soshoski

Liberally transposed to contemporary society, the panoptic metaphor suggested that social controls were being pushed, dispersed,[69] and extended[70] by technological towards a growing dependence on surveillance, electronically generated information,[71] and calculations of risk. There was, in Stan Cohen's phrase, 'a deeper penetration of social control into the social body'.[72]

Populations and territories, it is held, are now under general, often remote surveillance by closed-circuit television,[73] helicopter, satellite, and the collating of electronic traces generated by banking transactions, credit payments, drivers' licences, and the like. In the 1990s, hundreds of thousands of closed-circuit television (CCTV) cameras were installed in public places[74] to operate with uncertain success, in the widespread public belief that cameras would reduce crime and lead to the apprehension of offenders. But the crime rate is not reduced that easily, and fear of crime was reduced only marginally.[75]

The broad result has been the fashioning of new 'scanscapes'[76] of control and new mechanisms of indirect regulation and self-policing, including the watching of the police by other police for evidence of misbehaviour.[77] Surveillance, argues Graham, has added layer upon layer to the urban terrain: 'Each layer has its own finer and finer mosaic of socio-spatial grids; its own embedded assumptions and criteria for allocating and withdrawing services or access; its own systems for specifying and normalizing boundary enforcement through electronically defining the "acceptable" presence of individuals in different urban 'cellular' space-times.'[78]

Very general, categorical assessments of risk, it has been argued, are beginning to supersede a system of control and justice that had been distinctively individualistic. And those assessments and controls are increasingly been driven by a technology that is less and less centred on moral or indeed social judgement and more on 'operational efficiency'.[79]

•*In summary, two intellectual influences are at work in this new vision of control.*[80] The first is the analysis of the partial retreat of a now 'hollowed-out' State and its formal agencies of control into core activities centred on the maintenance of order over especially troublesome groups and spaces. The State has become less and less able to guarantee the safety of all its citizens. Those who can afford to buy additional safety in the form of walls, gates, alarms, surveillance systems, and private guards will do so. Those who cannot will be left with only the most vestigial of defences against crime.[81] The result is a new urban landscape in which the rich can afford to live in 'security bubbles' set in the midst of insecure space.

In Houston, Texas, for instance, an extensive network of safe underground streets is being developed to protect office workers from the dangers above.[82] The most apocalyptic description of the new topography is Los Angeles, where fortress-homes surrounded by gates, fences, moats, and alarms separate the urban rich from the urban poor; in which the private areas of the wealthy cannot be reached by the public transport used by the poor; and in which the poor, the underclass, and the homeless are confined to dangerous areas and free-fire zones.

In another, more mundane example Shearing and Stenning's describe Disney World as a private domain ingeniously engineered to exercise discreet, diffuse control over its visitors from their very first entrance to their final exit.[83]

The second influence is a growing criminological emphasis on the importance of 'risk'.[84] Ulrich Beck proposed that risks are phenomena mediated by people's dependence on social institutions. Populations are differentially affected by risk: some are relatively exposed, and there are hierarchies of vulnerability. This conception of social groups defined by risk has proved attractive to the sociologist.[85] For example, Feeley and Simon contend that the State's focus is beginning to shift away from the control of individuals to the actuarial identification,[86] classification, and management of social aggregates deemed to be dangerous or problematic. Deviance is no longer discussed professionally in a moralizing discourse but in probabilistic statements. Control becomes risk management. Less is expected of formal sanctions: rearranging the distribution of offenders in the community and incapacitating them in prison are beginning to replace rehabilitation as a goal.[87] And there is also a new privatization of culpability based on a rejection of the social foundations of offending and a devolution of responsibility for prevention onto the potential victim.[88]

Surveillance is becoming more diffuse.

The control of risk is the new control strategy.

■ Miscellaneous Theories of a Control Character

'Control' is a term of such common currency in the sociology of deviance that it is essential to distinguish between three separate usages. First, there are control theories, discussed above, which take control variables of different kinds to be the most significant causes of deviance. Second, there is control as a substantive phenomenon in its own right, that is, the sanctions that are brought to bear against deviancy.

Third, there is that aspect of all theories of deviance that deals with control, either implicitly or explicitly. In strain theories, for example, that aspect is largely unexplored, but a generally neutral set of control responses to deviance tends to be assumed. In labelling theories, controls that are applied differentially are viewed as a major source of 'secondary' deviation. In some culturally framed theories, which cite the causes of deviance in 'culture conflict' (Sellin) or 'cultural diversity' (Miller, Mays, and Lewis), the controls exerted by the dominant culture are seen to be weakened by the offenders' adherence to a lower-class culture, or culture of poverty; in Sutherland's theory of 'differential association', variation in exposure to such alternative cultures is viewed as sufficient to explain different rates of deviance.[89] The concept of 'social disorganization' of Shaw and McKay also rests on the premise that lax controls generate deviance. Durkheim's theory of anomie alone discerns greater attenuation of controls at the top, rather than the bottom, of the social hierarchy.[90] In general, however, it would be incorrect to call the third set of theories 'control theories', since the weakness or absence of controls is caused by adherence to alternative cultures or subcultures, rather than by contingent or random events that serve to deregulate individual families or careers or that exist as a built-in feature of certain milieux.

Psychology and Control

Many approaches rest on the efficacy of psychodynamic controls, although it is not predominant in all psychological theories.[91] Perhaps the archetypal example is Eysenck's theory of crime and personality and its social psychological variant, Trasler's concept of 'inadequate socialization'.[92] The main premise of Eysenck's theory is that extroverts are more resistant to conditioning than introverts and that in all contexts save a criminal sub-society, extroverts will tend to be more amenable to criminality than introverts. It is also argued that neuroticism interacts with extroversion to heighten the likelihood that inhibiting responses will be overwhelmed by excitation. Trasler argued that, in addition, the techniques of child socialization employed by lower-class families were less efficient than those used by the middle class in the reinforcement of inhibition. The typical delinquent on this basis would be the lower-class, neurotic extrovert.

Cochrane[93] listed some twenty tests of Eysenck's theory, which in all cases but one, contradicted rather than verified the central point of his theory concerning extroversion. It remains a classic instance of a control theory, however, not least for Eysenck's proposal that 'conscience is a conditioned reflex'. Nonetheless it may be the case that certain social contexts do indeed produce neuroticism in more extroverted children. Harriet Wilson says some permissive mothers have quiet, withdrawn children who give little cause for friction and if parental demands are minimal, conflicts rarely arise. Others reported much trouble, which they linked with explanations of their temperament: 'He's got a terrible temper, if you cross him he throws things—you've got to get round him.' 'If he can't have his own way, he shouts and kicks the furniture—in the finish I give him his own way—I have to.'[94]

It may well be that, in the circumstances of poverty and overcrowding, the more extroverted children are socialized into neuroticism, not because that is an innate condition, but because faced with intolerable physical constraint they cannot withdraw into protective apathy as do their more introverted siblings. Again, James suggests that mothers living in conditions of hardship may well become clinically depressed, withdrawing and responding punitively to their children. Those children, especially boys, could develop in turn a heightened wariness and sensitivity to the reactions of others, sometimes responding violently to perceived threat.[95]

Psychological control theories of the kind developed first by Eysenck have more recently been resuscitated in a new guise, which is described by some as radical behaviourism sympathetic to rational choice theory.[96]

Consider Wilson and Herrnstein's *Crime and Human Nature*.[97] Any theory of deviance, they contend, is usually no more than an instance of a more general theory of behaviour, and it should be able to explain the forces that control individual behaviour. Crime is held to be a preferred choice determined by its consequences, that is, by the pleasures and pains that flow from particular decisions. More particularly, decisions to offend are defined as the outcome of an interaction between innate drives and secondary reinforcers of behaviour, that is, between the biological and the cultural, and social conditioning supplies the links between the two. While the rewards of crime to the offender may be tangible and immediate, the losses tend not only to be more remote but also more indefinite, and delay and uncertainty in apprehension and punishment enhance criminality.

Or consider Gottfredson and Hirschi's *A General Theory of Crime*, which argues that deviance stems from low self-control: it provides an immediate, easy, and simple gratification of desires that is attractive to those who cannot or will not defer their enjoyment. It requires little skill or planning. It can be intrinsically pleasurable because it involves the exercise of stealth, agility, deception, or power. It demands a lack of sympathy for the victim. But it does not provide medium- or long-term benefits equal to those that may flow from more orthodox careers. In short, it is committed by those who are 'impulsive, insensitive, physical . . . risk-taking, short-sighted and non-verbal.'[98]

Low self-control, in turn, is associated with a lack of discipline, training, or nurturing and those are properties vested in a number of institutions, including schools, friendship groups, and the family and its child-rearing practices. Successful socialization requires that someone care enough for a child to monitor his or her behaviour, recognize deviance, and punishing that deviance consistently and reasonably manner.

> Deviance stems from low self-control, a need for gratification.

Feminism and Control

Another variant of control theory, this time feminist, arises from turning a conventional criminological observation on its head. It used to be argued that women were not of great interest because they committed so little crime.[99] Feminist criminologists and others adopting a control perspective retorted that that was precisely what made women so important analytically, asking how it was that women offended so rarely. It was held that differential controls are applied quite differently in private and public space. The domestic sphere is held[100] to be a feminine preserve in which emotional disciplines are imposed, and the consequences of a young woman transgressesare the more effective and private sanctions of the home. The public sphere is held to be a male preserve, and the less effective formal disciplines exercised there are more likely to propel young men into the justice system and hence towards secondary deviance.

> Are men and women reacted to and controlled in different ways?

■ Routine-Activity Theory

Another, more recent theory of control based on everyday life is the routine-activity theory of Cohen and Felson. They argue that the focus of attention should shift to the ordinary circumstances of offending and to simple models of rational choice rather than more complicated descriptions of human motive and interpretation.[101] Echoing Hirschi, they hold that the big question is, not why people commit deviance, but why everyone does not.[102] Like other control theorists, they offer an imagery of innate human susceptibility to temptation, original sin, and the perils of idleness. Sociology should assume that people will offend if they are sufficiently provoked or enticed, that they will not offend if they are prevented, and that any pattern of offending must be analyzed as a product of the way in which temptations and controls are woven into the fabric of society. Unlike situational crime prevention theorists, they are macro-sociological and they concentrate on 'broad social trends',[103] but the two approaches are perfectly compatible.

The principal contentions of routine-activity theory are, first, that the probability of offending will be affected by the manner in which 'likely offenders', 'suitable targets', and 'capable guardians' converge in space and time[104] and, secondly, that those factors will reflect the commonplace structures of social life.

> Crime requires a motivated offender, an available target, and a lack of guardianship.

For instance, an increase in the number of cars is liable, not only to expand the number of 'suitable targets', but also to make it easier for likely or motivated offenders to travel widely and anonymously, conceal stolen goods, and make a rapid departure. Moreover, such increased car ownership will act to spread housing more thinly in space, reduce population density, and lessen the number of capable guardians who might witness and report suspicious phenomena.

Again, changes in family structure can bring about a growth in the number of single people living alone, a proliferation of households containing property, and a consequent reduction in the population of capable guardians. After all, single people are more likely to leave their homes unattended. Mundane social change can influence opportunities for offending. Cohen and Felson produced a relevant list of propositions: (1) opportunities play a role in causing all crime; (2) crime opportunities are highly specific, differing between bank robbery, mugging, and burglary; (3) all crime opportunities are concentrated in time and space; (4) crime opportunities depend on everyday movements and activity; (5) one crime produces opportunities for another; for example, burglary may lead to the selling of stolen goods; (6) some products offer more tempting crime opportunities; (7) social and technological changes produce new crime opportunities; (8) reducing opportunities can prevent crime; and nine, reducing opportunities does not normally displace crime.

Furthermore, Hagan and McCarthy argue that deviance is amplified when young people leave home, either voluntarily or involuntarily, live a vulnerable existence on the streets, and not only suffer greater victimization but also commit more infractions and are exposed to a considerably higher risk of being processed as deviants. 'Consistently', they claim, 'hunger causes theft of food; problems of hunger and shelter lead to serious theft; and problems of shelter and unemployment produce prostitution.'[105]

It's all about routine activities.

■ Criticism
The Problem with Control Theory

Control theorists are open about criticisms of their approach.[106] However, there is a tendency to overdraw the differences between what are presented as the empirically sound but modest claims of control theory and the empirically unsound but more pretentious alternatives. Leaving aside for the moment the question of whether or not such theories do indeed 'make delinquency necessary', the chief point at issue is how far these theories are addressing the same problem as control theory.

In one respect, there is agreement that all theories attempt to explain the social distribution of delinquency. In other respects, there is substantial divergence, for the equally important aim of sociological theories is to account for the character and motivation of delinquency. It is hardly adequate for control theorists to assert that we would all be deviant if we dared. How deviant, and deviant in what ways? Shorn of any meaning, deviance is presumably pursued for the sheer gratification of appetites—acquisitive, aggressive, and sexual. But it is also difficult to account for the very phenomena that other theorists set out to explain: why delinquency is so often non-utilitarian; why aggression is so frequently ritualized and non-violent in its outcome; why sexual gratification takes such complex forms. In short, control theorists make far too little of both deviance and conformity, so why bother with motivation?

Small wonder, then, that control theorists dismiss as negligible the role that norms and values play in social behaviour. These are viewed as almost entirely dependent on attachments to those whose opinions we value. Weaken or remove those attachments and we feel free to deviate. It may well be that Parsons's assumption that, once adequately internalized, norms and values are with us for life is hopelessly overblown and that it constitutes, in Dennis Wrong's memorable phrase, an 'over-socialized conception of man'. Nor would we wish to dissent from the view that norms and values are fluid, negotiable, and subject to constant revision. But to link adherence to norms and values so strongly to personal attachments, whether to families or to institutions, is to go too far towards a purely 'other-directed' and 'under-socialized' view of man. Norms may be shed and values revalued, but that can take place in the context of strong attachments, as well as in their absence. Rates of deviation may rise after marital break-up, but most divorced people remarry. Children who fail at school may resent the school, but it has not yet been established that they do so without reference to alternative norms and values. In sum, norms and values cannot easily be reduced to attachments as control theorists contend.

The Problem with Situational Control Theory

Situational control theorists are also well aware of the weak link in their arguments. Clarke argues that 'the specificity of the influences upon different kinds of deviant behaviour gives much less credence to the 'displacement' hypothesis; the idea that reducing opportunities merely results in deviance being displaced to some other time or place has been the major argument against situational crime prevention'.[107] He argues that displacement is least likely in cases of opportunistic offences and most likely in cases of professional crime. Even for the bulk of offences that lie in between these extremes, he cites success in specific cases (such as kiosk design and vandalism, or the installation of compulsory steering locks and theft of cars) and refers to a review by the Dutch ministry of justice of fifty-five situational prevention projects. No evidence of displacement was found in twenty-two of the projects, and only partial displacement in the remainder.[108]

The issue of displacement has exercised Mayhew, who remarked that 'advocates of 'situational prevention' . . . encounter particular difficulties in dealing with the criticism that the effectiveness of opportunity-reducing measures is undermined by displacing offenders' activities to other times, places, targets, or types of crime'.[109] It seemed, for instance, that older vehicles began to be stolen when more modern cars were fitted with steering-column locks and that there was an increase in street robberies after the police had acted against muggings in the New York subway.[110] An examination of data on trends in the theft of cars, motorcycles, and bicycles in West Germany, England, and the Netherlands, concluded that the introduction of laws making the wearing of motorcycle helmets compulsory *had* brought about a decline in the theft of motorcycles.[111] It seemed to have become much more difficult for the casual, opportunistic thief to steal a motorcycle. Moreover, the drop in motorcycle theft was not matched by a commensurate increase in car theft, there being no effective displacement. In another article, Mayhew returned to the same data to observe that the increase in bicycle thefts in West Germany was 'much greater than would have been predicted by displacement'.[112] She concluded that displacement was not evident in this case, but, elsewhere, an international survey did suggest that there were puzzling signs of displacement from car thefts to bicycle thefts, a finding which suggested that some thieves will make do with two wheels instead of four. The results run counter to the general finding that displacement is rare.[113]

Much situational theory, having deliberately eschewed ideas of disposition and motivation, can sometimes be at a loss to explain its findings. It tends to be a one-dimensional sociology that is unable to theorize motive and meaning, not only in relation to *expressive* delinquency, but also with regard to deviance in general.

Again there is also some doubt that gun control would do much to reduce violence. As Clinard has pointed out, there are guns in most homes in Switzerland, owing to the system of national defence, and yet crimes of violence are very rare.[114] The vast differences in rates of violence between the United States and Switzerland can hardly be accounted for by the availability of firearms alone; presumably socio-cultural differences play a larger part. Indeed, a recent international survey suggests that, even if the influence of guns is eliminated, the United States would still have higher rates of homicide and serious violence than almost every other country.

Control theorists would doubtless reply that it is easier to control firearms than to change a culture, and it would be absurd to deny that certain control measures demonstrably deter certain offences at what Matza has termed the 'invitational edge'. However, as David Smith points out,

> . . . judgments about what can and cannot be changed are highly contestable . . . [They] may too easily emerge from cultural biases, rather than analysis. For most British people, gun control would 'obviously' be the most effective and efficient method of reducing homicide in the United States, but for most Americans it is equally 'obvious' that such a policy could not be implemented. This example starkly illustrates the limits of [J.Q.] Wilson's robust pragmatism.[115]

Situational prevention theory simply cannot cope with the paradox that, in the United States, gun control is ruled out for 'cultural' reasons while drug prohibition, which is hugely invasive of personal liberty, is deemed perfectly acceptable.

• *There are also dangers that situational crime control may prove self-defeating in unforeseen ways.* First, as Clarke acknowledges, there is the danger that it acts *repressively*, excluding particular groups defined as risks from private or semi-public space and subjecting the population as a whole to surveillance techniques which restrict freedom of movement, privacy, or action. Clearly, however, circumstances change, and few airline passengers now resent screening for firearms or explosives, and most people accept the spread of CCTV. Similar arguments can be advanced for fingerprinting or DNA-banking the entire population. Clarke, however, would dismiss any anxiety, claiming that the benefits of the strategy tend to outweigh its inconveniences and that 'many situational prevention measures are entirely unobtrusive or can even improve the quality of life'.[116]

•*Second, situational prevention may operate regressively* as the bill for semi-offi-cialdom to monitor stores, public buildings, and transport systems is heaped on the consumer regardless of ability to pay.

•*Third, it may deflect attention from attempts to make those difficult social and eco-nomic changes* that control theorists regard as too remote for contemplation, such as the reduction of inequality. And yet, as the race riots in several countries in the past few decades have borne witness, steering locks do not prevent police cars being overturned and fire-bombed. The 'technological fix' is double-edged; it may ease the crime problem in certain specific respects, but it may also blunt our awareness of the need to examine the more fundamental causes of high rates of deviance. Housing built on the cost-benefit principle, without regard to the human factor, cannot be rescued by cost-benefit crime control.

One of the most pressing problems of control theory stems from combining assumptions about the rationality of behaviour with the measurement and com-parison of objective behavioural indicators. It is as if a sensible sociologist sitting at a keyboard in an office or library knows everything about how people conduct their affairs, how they go about stealing, burgling, or on the other hand control-ling deviants. It is assumed that we are quite familiar with the routine practices of residents, caretakers, and others as they go about their tasks. It also seems to be assumed that the simplicities of rational choice theory afford us a good enough comprehension of the way in which predators decipher their environment, for-mulate plans, and are deterred or seduced by signs, obstructions, and opportu-nities. It is the environment that is sovereign in rational choice theory, and those who move about in it are reduced to ciphers.

However, control theorists have done little to observe ordinary behaviour. Sup-position and the easy assumptions of rational choice theory have been allowed to replace observation. People are prone to do untoward and surprising things, and supposition is not enough. Not everyone—and certainly not the delinquent— is risk-aversive. On the contrary, some people can find risk attractive or even seductive,[117] and delinquents are reported to be attracted especially to what Matza called the 'manufacture of excitement', that is, to making things happen in a dull, disenchanted world in order to get an 'adrenalin buzz' or a sense of the important and the thrilling.[118] Others may act in the spirit of what Matza described as a mood of fatalism.

Neal Shover, in his foreword to Richard Wright and Scott Decker's ethnogra-phy of armed robbers, reflected that 'street-level robbers typically make decisions in contexts of hedonism and desperation in which the likely consequences of their acts are neither weighed carefully nor taken seriously'.[119]

His comments were echoed by a later study in England and Wales of street robbers who seemed to be driven by a sense of edgy excitement and of life as play and to be infused by a short-term hedonism and pleasure in fighting. There are cultural dimensions to the assessment of risk, and it may not be obvious to the observer whether people attach what seems to be excessive importance to slight risk, or little importance to great risk.[120]

The 'low self-control' theory of Gottfredson and Hirschi counters all such niceties of motivational analysis with the assumption that deviance is the outcome of the inability to defer gratification. While low self-control is not equated with deviance, it is the universal and necessary, if not sufficient, cause of deviance. The major problem for so all-encompassing a theory is how to account for the decline in rates of deviance with the onset of adulthood. The maturation out of delinquency was seen by Matza in particular as presenting insurmountable problems for strain and subcultural theories. Yet those theories did attempt to deal with the problem by arguing that the sources of strain, such as the search for status, manhood, and 'respect', are at least attenuated by having a job, marriage, and parenthood. Gottfredson and Hirschi are scathingly dismissive of such tenets, on both theoretical and empirical grounds.[121]

Other studies of desistance have weighed the evidence somewhat differently. For example, Maruna[122] states: 'Substantial research confirms that desistance from crime is at least weakly correlated with stable employment. . ., getting married, . . . completing education . . ., and becoming a parent.' Weak correlations are belittled by Gottfredson and Hirschi, but they are the pointers to more effective prevention that in recombination can produce more substantial effects, as the 'what works' literature stresses.

Given their investment in this single, stable variable of low self-respect, Gottfredson and Hirschi acknowledge that the phenomenon of growing out of delinquency needs explaining. A stable factor should produce stable outcomes, that is, continuingly high rates of deviance throughout the life cycle. But it is the onset of adulthood, not just old age, that is associated with declining deviance.

There are two ways of handling this problem. The first is to argue that delinquency does not so much decline with age as change its form, from the predominantly expressive to the largely instrumental. But Gottfredson and Hirschi reject the instrumental-expressive polarity as meaningless. The second is to analyze what it is about 'maturation' that outweighs low self-control; however this is treated as self-explanatory: 'Deviance declines with age. Spontaneous desistance is just that, changes in behavior that cannot be explained and changes that occur regardless of what else happens.'[123] This is particularly lacking as an explanation of how young adult offenders, facing the full force of economic realities, somehow raise their levels of self-control to desist from deviance. At the minimum, consumer capitalism is a sophisticated set of devices for *lowering* self-control with the attainment of the age of majority, and just how every incentive to consume anything from fast food to fast cars via fast credit or fast crime suddenly proves so resistible flies in the face of the logic of low self-control theory.

Sometimes control theorists are quite candid about the problem. Tilley, for instance, noting that the installation of CCTV cameras in parking lots did seem effective, was moved to argue about one scheme that the 'data does not allow us to clarify the mechanism through which car crime has been reduced, beyond saying that usage changes and natural human surveillance does not seem to have played a part. Thus, we do not know what it is about the CCTV set-up which has led to the reduction.'[124]

One of the central tasks of a sociology of deviance is to replace wild or informed guesses about conduct with more reliable charts of the social world. There is interesting research, such as interviews with burglars and robbers,[125] or interviews with offenders on probation or doing community service.[126]

Responses of offenders to CCTV, for example, were so varied that they seemed to display no discernible pattern, although the willingness to commit public-disorder offences did seem to be affected, and some offenders actually welcomed the intensification of surveillance. Norris and Armstrong watched the watchers in the control room at the heart of a network of CCTV surveillance and found, not only that they were not particularly adept at recognizing deviant conduct, but that they were as much interested in following the movements of attractive women or observing couples making love.[127] A similar study described how some watchers spent as much time reading newspapers, dozing, or talking on their cell phones as monitoring the screens. There was also a poor liaison between civilian watchers, security guards, and police dispatchers.[128]

And there were technical shortcomings as well. In the beginning, many opportunities to survey crime electronically were marred by grainy pictures or by video cameras that were not loaded or defective. For example, the IRA bomb that was left outside the Carlton Club in London in June 1990, injuring twenty-one people, was covered by cameras that were not turned on. Matters may be changing: one interesting instance where controls did seem effective was the use of CCTV cameras in police stations where suspects seemed to feel a little safer and the police better protected against charges of improper conduct.[129] They have also been instrumental recently in solving bombing attacks in London.

And Shapland and Vagg have studied the informal social surveillance and control practised by people in everyday life, recounting, for example, how villagers will step outside their front doors and clatter their garbage cans to advertise to suspicious strangers that someone is about and watching them.[130] Again, Dowd has undertaken secondary analysis of the social composition of witnesses and bystanders, discovering, perhaps unremarkably, that they are very similar to victims and offenders in specific cases.[131] Much offending, after all, is the result of similar people milling around together in the same place at the same time. For instance young men are often injured by young men in the presence of other young men. But that work is only a beginning, and quite an edifice has been built on a foundation of unsubstantiated surmise about the invasion and defence of territory, the creation and loss of attachments, and mutual surveillance.

It can be asserted in reply to some of the earlier criticisms that control theorists do not wish to rule out the search for patterns of motivation that help us to understand deviance: they merely argue that no theories so far advanced actually work. Situational controls need not rule out the search for dispositional causes, but they help us cope with problems we face here and now. At the very least, both aspects of control theory point to a dimension that is missing from existing theories and that needs to be included. The approach has the potential for considerable development.

Chapter Summary

This chapter has looked at an array of theories that propose ways in which deviance can be controlled, from the simple iteration of attachment to the futuristic concept of surveillance. Control theories, in all their variety, are based on the assumption that deviance will occur if certain conditions are met. These conditions might include a motivated offender, an opportunity, and a lack of guardianship. Control theories are based on theories of rational choice and deterrence, and are less interested in the dispositional causes of deviance than its control and prevention.

Critical-Thinking Questions

1. What is Hirschi's model of attachment, and how does it explain deviance as an absence of social controls? How do these controls normally inhibit deviance among conforming individuals?
2. Does Hirschi's model account for deviance committed by law-abiding members of the community? Does this model make it possible to examine deviance among apparently conforming individuals?
3. How does the idea of surveillance work to decrease risk and thus move us away from an individualistic explanation of deviance? Why is it such a useful theory today?
4. What was the broken-windows theory of crime control? Who proposed it, how was it implemented, and how was it measured for its effectiveness?

Explorations in Film

The Czech film *Sileni*, or *Lunacy* (2006), is based on two short stories by Edgar Allan Poe and inspired by the works of the Marquis de Sade. Set in nineteenth-century France, a young man is plagued by nightmares in which he is dragged off to a madhouse. It just so happens that on the journey back from his mother's funeral he is invited by a Marquis to spend the night in his castle. After witnessing incredible events, he tries to flee but the Marquis insists he conquer his fears and takes him to a surrealistic lunatic asylum where the patients are free and the staff are locked up.

Websites

The Institute for the Prevention of Crime (IPC) in Ottawa is an educational resource site which collects scientific knowledge from authoritative sources on how to lower rates of crime and victimization. The web site is oriented to policy makers, practitioners, the media, and the public. It contains information on crime trends in crime, evidence from projects on how to reduce crime, and reasons for investing in crime prevention of crime, including its cost effectiveness and support by the public.

http://www.sciencepolitique.uottawa.ca/ipc/eng/ipc.asp

Chapter Ten

Radical Criminology

Chapter Overview

Critical theories have their beginnings in the nineteenth century but did not make a resurgence until the mid-1950s and onward. Since then they have gone through various transformations, from Marxist to radical, to feminist, and left realism. A distinctly Canadian form of political economy lends its analysis well to critical theory.

The interest in critical deviance theory is always in looking at how power is important in the commission of deviance. For example, corporate deviance is committed by the powerful, but often ignored by the State. On the other hand, deviance committed by the powerless often occurs because of their lack of power.

In these theories we are looking at integrating the rationality of the actor within the larger economic structure: that is, deviance is revolution, political act, and sign of desperation; deviance is power, control, and a sign of domination.

■ Introduction

At the time of its emergence in the early 1970s, the very phrase 'radical criminology' seemed a contradiction in terms. There had, after all, been a *concerted* attempt to differentiate criminology, which was associated with political conservatism, from the sociology of deviance, which espoused a more 'radical' definition of the subject and a preference for participant observation.[1] To reintroduce the term criminology seemed to fly in the face of much that had been gained symbolically over the previous decade. To yoke it to the term 'radical' (or 'new', 'critical', or Marxist) seemed both perverse and overambitious. The directive in the phrase, however, was clear: to break with the seeming limitations of the 'sociology of deviance' without returning to conventional criminology.[2]

What had happened in such a short time? The answer lies in the context of the times. In Western countries, the late 1960s produced students 'radicalized' by the Vietnam war, racial conflict, feminist consciousness, and new forms of drug use. Draft dodgers fled to Canada, where a Liberal government under Pierre Trudeau decriminalized abortion and homosexuality, and introduced a panoply of criminal justice reforms. A fierce impatience was expressed with the gradualism of liberal, social-democratic politics. The American 'War on Poverty' and the Labour government in Britain, were seen as failing to correct structural inequalities of class, status, and power. At this point, the longer-standing project of the New Left, to dissociate Marxism from the 'State socialist' regime of the USSR and to regenerate it as a critical force, bore fruit. A variety of neo-Marxist philosophers reinterpreted Marxist theory in an attempt to account for the crises that arose, the inability of capitalism to resolve them, and the inevitability of new and more devastating conflicts.

Compared to the appeal of Gramsci, Habermas, and Althusser,[3] the work of even such gifted interpreters of deviance as Matza and Becker seemed tame and that of Merton and Albert Cohen old-fashioned and conservative. Whereas the latter offered tentative 'processual' models for an enhanced understanding of 'becoming deviant', or theories aimed at explaining lower-class forms of delinquency, the former seemed to provide a basis for grasping the 'total inter-connectedness'[4] of deviance and capitalist society.

The appeal of the application of Marxist theory and method to deviancy studies was also increased by the growing visibility of what came to be termed 'deviance of the powerful'. None of the theories in vogue in the 1950s and 1960s addressed white-collar or corporate deviance at all satisfactorily. To adapt Sutherland's dictum about the limitations of psychoanalytical theories of crime, it seemed absurd to regard a bank as suffering from 'status-frustration', or corporations as victims of 'secondary deviation'.[5] The problem is neatly summarized by

> Marxist theories were ideal for analyzing corporate crime.

Taylor, Walton, and Young's criticism of earlier theories as 'predicting too little bourgeois and too much proletarian criminality'.[6] Such theories could not be readily adapted to resolve their shortcomings;, so a new paradigm was called for. The adequacy of the Marxist criminology that emerged as an alternative to other perspectives, and the ways in which it is applied to the sociology of deviance, are the subject of this chapter.

■ The 'New' Criminology

The most vigorous attempt to supplant existing approaches by a neo-Marxist alternative occurs in the work of Taylor, Walton, and Young (*The New Criminology*, and *Critical Criminology*). Their first book is a comprehensive appraisal of the full range of theoretical approaches in criminology. The main criterion by which such approaches are evaluated and found wanting is their capacity to provide what the authors term, in the book's subtitle, a fully 'social theory of deviance'. Their own model for a fully social theory is Marxism, but it is the Marx of the *Economic and Philosophical Manuscripts of 1844*, as well as of *Capital*, that they commend— Marx the dialectician rather than the determinist, Marx the action theorist as much as the analyst of political economy who was concerned with alienation and consciousness as much as modes of production.[7] To establish the new criminology as superior to the old involved a ground-clearing critique, which forms the bulk of the 1973 book and which is concerned to salvage certain elements from prior theorizing for integration into an improved Marxist criminology.

Taking issue with eight major approaches and their variants, the authors attempt a synthesis of their most useful insights. First, the philosophical bases for liberal criminology are located in the work of Hobbes, Locke, Bentham, and the utilitarian tradition. This 'classical criminology' and its neo-classical variants are viewed as incapable of reconciling forms of inequality rooted in property relations and the extension of rationality to those who offend against the law.[8]

Second, the 'appeal' of positivism is viewed as residing in its claim to be capable of accounting for criminality in neutral, scientific terms that situate pathology in the individual offender and deflect attention from the social context of unequal social relations which basically frame the offence. Third, they challenge the conventional image of Durkheim as a functionalist who argued that deviance is both inevitable and necessary if *any* society is to survive. They argue instead that Durkheim restricted his view of the functionality of deviance to societies that fell short of true 'organic' solidarity. On this reading of Durkheim, the proposition that 'crime is normal' need not inhibit the pursuit of a 'crime-free' society.

They also deal critically with ecological and anomie theories, labelling theory, American naturalism and phenomenology, Marx and Engels's own view of crime, and Bonger's attempt to apply formal materialism to its study, and to the conflict theories of Turk and Quinney.[9] All are found wanting in terms of their potential as a basis for a 'fully social' theory of deviance, because they dehumanize the deviant or fail to furnish an adequate context of political economy, or both.

> Critical criminology constituted a wide-ranging critique of traditional approaches to deviance.

Ecological theory is valued for its move away from individualistic accounts, but it placed far too great an emphasis on purely urban processes, such as the emergence of 'natural' delinquency areas, which it divorced from the play of economic forces. What economic forces, for example, resulted in the formation of disorganized areas?

Anomie and its subcultural variants related deviance to the social structure but reduced the deviants themselves to people who were purely reactive or adaptive and therefore not creative.

Labelling theory made a crucial break with positivism by treating deviance and control dialectically, as variable and dynamic processes implicated one with the other, but ultimately it merely substituted one over-simple model—in which control leads to deviance—for another, in which the opposite happens. Images of deviance remained flawed as a result, since deviant motivation was reduced to passive resistance to or acquiescence in the superordinates' definitions of reality. In Gouldner's phrase, the deviant is regarded as 'man-on-his-back' rather than 'man-fighting-back'.[10]

Naturalism attempted to restore a more humanistic model of deviance, but 'appreciation' as a method merely gave unwarranted primacy to the deviants' own view, thus abdicating the sociological task of mediating the relations between that view and those from other vantage points.

Phenomenology moved even further away from a concern with the social context to a preoccupation with individual perceptions of deviance and control. Even Marx and Engels, in the occasional passages where they discussed crime, were prone to a determinism at odds with the role accorded creativity and consciousness elsewhere in Marx's work, a mechanistic lapse mistaken for a truly Marxist approach to crime by Bonger and other formal Marxists.

Finally, non-Marxist radicals, in particular Turk and Quinney, while attempting to relate deviance to the structural sources of conflict in advanced societies, confused authority relations with power relations, and thus obscured the actual foundation of deviance in class conflict.

In all these approaches, partial gains are offset by significant flaws. They attempt to synthesize the gains and eliminate the flaws by recovering them for a fully Marxist model of deviance and control. It is axiomatic that capitalism is criminogenic, as are all societies based on exploitation and oppression. The only form of society that in principle holds out any possibility of being crime-free is one embodying the principles of 'socialist diversity'. 'Socialism' entails an absence of material differences and a willed commitment to equality. It removes the rationale for offences against property, which make up the bulk of offences in any capitalist society.

'Diversity' entails a commitment to the toleration of minority beliefs and activities which many formally socialist states proscribe, such as drug use, sexual deviance, and gambling. To do otherwise than to work for the demise of capitalism and the transformation of society to one of socialist diversity is to implicate oneself in correctionalism, that is, the coercive use of the criminal sanction to 'correct' behaviour on a personal basis when its roots lie, on one level, in social structural inequalities of wealth and power and, on another, in the ideological mystifications that mask those inequalities.

In Taylor, Walton, and Young's introduction to their later work, *Critical Criminology*, these themes are recapitulated, but not greatly elaborated, save for the argument by Young that working-class control over policing should be greatly extended.

■ The Birmingham School

In the 1970s the Centre for Contemporary Cultural Studies at Birmingham University became, under the aegis of its Director, Stuart Hall, of some consequence in the sociology of deviance and control. While its members' interests were diverse and embraced the fields of industrial relations, the media, and race relations, the unifying feature of their work was the reproduction of order in capitalist Britain, a theme they came increasingly to theorize in the context of youthful deviance and adult control.

> The Birmingham School added the important dimension of culture to the study of deviance.

This theme had been dealt with by the media and by some sociologists as a product of 'intergenerational conflict', a mode of explanation that the Birmingham School rejected at the outset as misleading. The Birmingham School held that, in a class society, youthful deviance is most profoundly lodged in the refusal to accept, and the struggle against, relations with authorities that administer, on the State's behalf, institutions based on a rule-bound set of interests that are ultimately those of a capitalist ruling class. Youth is a crucial point of vulnerability for the reproduction of order, for if capitalism allows the members of its subordinate working class a moment of truth, it is at the point of entry into the occupational order. Willis is especially preoccupied with the manner by which that structural problem is culturally resolved by 'the boys' themselves.[11] Phil Cohen supplied the School with a method for bringing class struggle far more centrally into focus in the analysis of youthful subcultures than earlier, non-Marxist theorists had envisaged.[12]

However, these studies took no more than marginal note of societal reactions to deviance and of the details of the manifestations, both social and economic, of the 'contradictions of capitalism' to which subcultures were allegedly a symbolic response. In *Policing the Crisis*, Stuart Hall and his colleagues make a most ambitious attempt to integrate these various levels and aspects of analysis around the phenomenon of 'mugging'.

Policing the Crisis is by no means the complete expression of the kind of 'critical' criminology urged by Taylor, Walton, and Young, for it deals only fleetingly with the third and the sixth 'formal requirement' of their 'fully social theory': the 'actual act' and the 'outcome of the social reaction on deviants' further actions'. On the remaining five such requirements, however, it attempts an exhaustive analysis and still provides the most sophisticated basis so far[13] by which we might assess the claim that critical criminology is superior to alternative approaches.[14]

> *Policing the Crisis* is a classic of critical criminology.

The book is divided into four parts, each dealing with a major aspect of 'mugging, the State and law and order', as the subtitle puts it. Part I deals with the rise of a generalized concern about 'mugging' in England in the early 1970s. Part II follows the particular case in which three youths from Handsworth, Birmingham, received sentences of ten and twenty years for one such offence. Part III sets both the pattern of offences and the official and societal reactions within the context of the crisis of hegemony afflicting the British State in that period; and Part IV links these aspects together in the depiction of a 'politics of mugging'. It connects street crime, among black youth in particular, to fundamental contradictions of political economy in Britain. It is these which promote the real crisis; street crime is both a product of, and a palliative for, an intensifying class conflict, rather than the source.

• *The study opens with a painstaking examination of the 'facts'* that were held to justify the importation from the United States of a term, 'mugging', to describe crimes of robbery with violence long extant in England. It signified a trend that came to justify the creation of 'anti-mugging' squads and in turn to justify far longer sentences than were normal, even in a period when the length of sentences had been rising anyway. It was widely alleged, by press, police, and judiciary alike, that the ever-rising crime rate was, one, a product of the 'permissive' society coupled with, two, too lenient a pattern of sentencing; three, that certain aspects of street crime *were* novel; and, four that these features had been the subject of rising public anxiety.

Hall and his colleagues argued that only the label, not the crime, was new. Different crimes were conflated or put together to give the impression of a sharp and unprecedented rise in street crimes of violence. In some instances, even pickpocketing, by definition a crime of stealthy non-violence, was added to the 'mugging' total. They are able to show that the link between the rise in crime and lenient sentencing had no basis even in official facts, since the 1965–72 period saw a *lower* rise in the crime rate than the 1955–65 period, though sentencing in the 1960s was far tougher than in the 1950s There was no change in the rate of acquittals, and even in the specific case of robberies with violence, there was no uniform or steeper trend in either London or the provinces in 1972–5 than in 1955–65. The much-quoted rise of 129 per cent in 'muggings' in London over the 1968–72 period was derived from figures clouded in ambiguity. Most surprising of all, 'we have never had any figures at all concerning the scale and rate of increase, of provincial muggings'.[15]

This unpacking of the 'mugging' scare is the foundation for all that follows, for it enables the authors to ask: 'If the reaction to mugging cannot be explained by a straightforward reference to the (official) statistics, how *can* it be explained?'[16] Their answer is:

> When the official reaction to a person, group of persons or series of events is *out of all proportion* to the actual threat offered, when 'experts', in the form of police chiefs, the judiciary, politicians and editors *perceive* the threat in all but identical terms. . ., when the media . . . stress 'sudden and dramatic'

increases . . . and 'novelty', above and beyond that which a sober, realistic appraisal could sustain, then we believe it is appropriate to speak of the beginnings of a *moral panic*.[17]

A 'referential context' is built up in which the 'meaning of mugging' is taken to be the growing social malaise of the inner city, a symbol of urban violence long associated with America (to which frequent allusions are made) but now increasingly evident in Britain. The crucial novelty is not the rise in crimes of violence, but the involvement of black youths and white victims. The orchestration of consensus by police, media, and judiciary now assumes a *vox populi* role, in which the media represent the judiciary as speaking *for* the public and the judiciary can quote the media as evidence of the strength of public opinion. They interact to produce an ideological and control certainty around the issue. At this point the media, without any recourse to conspiracy or dragooning, operate as an 'ideological State apparatus' (a tip of the hat to Althusser).

> The construction of mugging is a social problem.

• *The second stage of the analysis concerns the particular response elicited by the case of Paul Storey* and two accomplices, who 'mugged' an elderly man in Handsworth and whose sentences were for twenty and ten years' imprisonment respectively. The case made for saturation media coverage, in part because the boys returned to inflict further injuries on the victim two hours after the original attack. The age and defencelessness of the victim, the small sum of money stolen, and the second assault, were pointed to as features of the menace of mugging. In addition, Storey was half West Indian and one of his accomplices was of Cypriot background: the link with 'race' and danger was reinforced.

The local press treatment of the case is analyzed in detail, and while much was made of the associations between deviance and urban decay, the loss of neighbourhood and family cohesion, and poor recreational facilities, the structural background remained absent from even feature articles. The national press probed no deeper, and 'liberal' papers, such as the *Guardian*, were largely silent on the issues involved. Letters to the press were analyzed, as were anonymous and abusive letters to the Storey family. Certain root concepts, which can be read as English ideologies of deviance, emerge from all sources. 'Englishness' equals a belief in the necessity for work to be undertaken as a source of livelihood. By contrast, deviance is parasitic.

> The English ideology of crime undergirds the reaction to mugging.

Certain key symbols recur: the family, the need for discipline, respectability and decency; and the police and the law as guarantors of these core values, to which the working class adhere as fiercely as others. Detestation of crime transcends and ultimately unites classes. The black mugger is thus the perfect 'folk devil' and a scapegoat for all the social anxieties produced by the change to an affluent but destabilized society. Unable to generate a political solution to these problems, the working-class response is that of corporate, defensive class consciousness, a regressing to the *exclusion* and *stereotyping* of a surrogate enemy; the lower middle class react with moral indignation. Against the full force of English common sense and traditionalism, liberalism wilts and runs for cover.

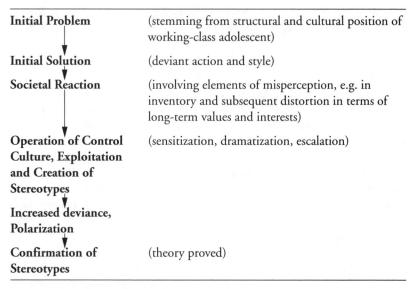

Figure 10.1: Deviancy Amplification Model

Source: *Folk Devils and Moral Panics: The Creation of the Mods and Rockers*, Stanley Cohen, 2002, Routledge.

•*If crime is one of the few symbolic sources of unity in an increasingly divided and embittered class society*—if, moreover, the traditional armoury of consensus (power, deference, fatalism, and external enemies) is exhausted, diminishing, or absent— then it follows that the State, faced with a 'crisis of hegemony', will need little incentive to use the 'war against crime' as a source of re-legitimation. The management of consensus had, in this view, only recently become of truly critical significance for the British ruling class. While Britain's economic decline can be traced back to 1870, it was only in the 1960s–1980s that the international situation had been so transformed that the decline was beyond dispute. The breakdown of the machinery of prosperity coincided with the loss of empire, a conjuncture that left the working class as the only serious candidate for bearing the costs. Yet the working class had been incorporated into political society and 'pragmatically accept[ed]' the status quo only as long as certain conditions hold. As the economic crisis deepened, hegemony became increasingly difficult to sustain.

> Crime is functional for the State.

The 1960s and 1970s revealed the bankruptcy of democratic reform in the face of stubborn working-class resistance to a change in the rules of the game that had evolved over the previous century. Important concessions had been wrung from the ruling class, such as making the rule of law applicable to all groups, the guarantee of certain union immunities and rights, and universal suffrage. A host of others, such as universal education, the welfare State, and an increasingly mixed economy, were administered by a massive increase in the numbers of bureaucratic State employees, who stood in a 'subaltern' relation to the hegemonic class.

By the late 1960s it was evident that the inter-class truce based on full employment, free collective bargaining, and rising wages could not be sustained. Working-class resistance to the erosion of first one and then the other led most dramatically to the three-day week, the miners' flying pickets, and the fall of the government, a sequence that coincided with a fresh wave of immigration and alarm about the numbers of immigrants still flooding into the country as dependents of those already here.

As *Policing the Crisis* pointed out, these themes—political and economic crisis, ideological struggle and race—came together within an organic conjuncture that was aggravated by the rapid deterioration in Britain's economic condition. There was an increasing readiness to arm the police in the light of terrorist attacks connected with Ulster, an upsurge in armed robbery and hijackings, and the erosion of civil liberties in the process of criminal justice.

• *The State's main concern was to define the crisis away, and remove the focus on class relations.* Instead the crisis was framed as a crisis of legitimate authority which was prevented from doing its job by deviants: criminals, industrial dissidents, scroungers, or political malcontents. Images of deviance became commonplace in the realm of industrial relations. Enough confusion was created to lead the working class to 'misrecognize' their enemy; thus the crisis was deflected on to youth, crime, and race and away from class relations onto authority relations.

> A crisis makes good news, but it also has to be explained away.

Finally, the 'politics of mugging' emerged so that policing the blacks (the poor and the unemployed) amounted to policing the crisis. There was a reality to young black crime, especially in the wake of unemployment that affected the black labour force most severely. To meet sheer material needs, there emerged a semi-criminal mixture of informal dealing, rackets, semi-legal practices, and small-time crime. But it also serviced the black community's leisure in a context where they could less feasibly aspire to a common class identity with whites. The young, second-generation blacks experienced both exploitation and expendability, but increasingly they refused to accept the reserve-army-of-labour role assigned to them under capitalism. Yet the refusal to carry out so-called 'white man's shit-work' entailed a wagelessness that was a forcing ground for hustling. Crime became a predictable and quite comprehensible consequence of this process.

Discussion: Deviance and Culture—Jamaican Danger

The headline on the *Toronto Star* screamed 'Urban Terrorism', and reflected a comment by the police after a twenty-three-year-old woman named Georgina Leimonis was shot and killed in a café known as Just Desserts. The date was Tuesday, 5 April 1994, and the place, downtown Toronto.

As details about the incident were revealed, people asked how it could have happened 'here'. Videotape showed several men surveying the store from the door before leaving and then returning, only to rob the patrons and kill Leimonis. Newspapers announced that the police were seeking several men, including a suspect who had immigrated to Canada from Jamaica during his early childhood. This helped create a fear bound up with concerns about a category of person—the 'Jamaican criminal'. That suspect was later convicted and imprisoned for the crime.

One of those charged with manslaughter and robbery in the case was Oneil Grant, a permanent resident who had come to Canada from Jamaica in 1983. He had been ordered deported by the Immigration Department in 1992 but appealed the order and won a stay of the deportation order for five years. The Immigration Minister refused to say why Grant had been ordered deported.

As Stephen D'Arcy notes in his news article 'The Jamaican Criminal in Toronto', this depiction of the Jamaican criminal was not new to Toronto in April of 1994. Two years earlier the *Globe and Mail* had published a series of articles entitled 'Crime Story: The Jamaica Connection'. Its author, a police reporter, Timothy Appleby (and sources such as Toronto police officers), spoke about 'Jamaican criminals' and claimed that a criminal subculture in Jamaica had been exported to the streets of Metro Toronto and to Montreal.

Allegedly, one of the sources Appleby cites claimed that Jamaicans are more aggressive and violent than other people in the West Indies. Furthermore, these traits are due to the ancestors of present-day Jamaicans having been unloaded in Jamaica from slave ships because they had been rebellious on the trip.

In 1994 the Canadian Association of Chiefs of Police warned Canadians of the 'immense dangers' they faced from an increase in violent crime. Three shootings were grouped together to make the point: a Constable Todd Baylis, killed in the line of duty; Georgina Leimonis, murdered in a Toronto restaurant; and Nicholas Battersby, slain in an Ottawa driveby shooting.

The picture that is created of Jamaican crime, first in the 1992 articles and then in 1994, confirms the link to violent crime. The result is creating a link in the media between criminality and racial minorities that results in discriminatory treatment at the personal level and also in tighter immigration controls.

Source: S. D'Arcy, 'The "Jamaican Criminal" in Toronto, 1994: A Critical Ontology'; 'Island crime wave spills over', *Globe and Mail*, 10 July 1992, A1; 'The twisted arm of the law', *Globe and Mail*, 11 July 1992, A1; 'Identifying the problem', *Globe and Mail*, 13 July 1992, A1.

■ Radical Criminology in America

In America, as in Britain, radical criminology moved from a 'radical liberal' stance in the late 1960s to a more thorough commitment to a Marxist position in the 1970s. The American Marxist criminologists were more concerned with a relatively uncomplicated application of Marx's most central concepts to the analysis of deviance and control. By comparison the British theorists' attempted to draw more fully on critical neo-Marxists such as Habermas and Gramsci. This difference may reflect a more obvious and uncomplicated set of relations between crime and capitalism. The shift is well drawn out by Klockars, who juxtaposes passages written by Chambliss and Platt, in 'The Contemporary Crisis', which had been revised in a Marxist direction: for example, by the substitution of terms like 'ruling class' for the apparently vaguer and more pluralist 'the social order'.[18] There is also, especially in the work of Chambliss and Quinney, a desire to expose the threat to the integrity of community by the graft and corruption of business, government, unions, and crime. The last theme was not included in the work of C. Wright Mills, its most celebrated exponent.[19]

Case Study—The Contribution of Chambliss

In *On the Take*, Chambliss found the perfect topic for expressing the concern over corruption and power in the character of racketeering in Seattle. The book's subtitle, 'From Petty Crooks to Presidents', summarizes its major finding, namely, that the 'hidden hand' in organized crime in America is not the Mafia, but leading representatives of the city's ruling class. A diagram which at first glance resembles a high school chart of civic worthies, with its list of financiers, businessmen, politicians, and law-enforcement officers, is headed 'Seattle's Crime Network'.

The evidence for this profile is gathered from several years' participant observation in Seattle. Chambliss began by frequenting bars that were known for gambling and drugs and where vice connections might be made. After several months' involvement Chambliss found several contacts that had inside knowledge and were willing to talk. It was from these informants, who were motivated in part by grievance or substantial experience of victimization, that he pieced together the links between the front-line operators and the more shadowy entrepreneurs who ultimately controlled the crime networks—powerful members of the police force, the legal profession, business, local government, and the public prosecutor's office. Both Nixon and Johnson as presidents had dealings with men whose business profits were derived at least in part from illegal business.

Thus, to Chambliss deviance is not a by-product of an otherwise effectively working political economy, but a main product of that political economy. The conclusion, for Chambliss, is that the logic of capitalism makes the emergence of crime networks inevitable. Such networks are also pervasive in Europe and Scandinavia. Does the existence of crime networks in other countries weaken the argument that it is the structural characteristics of capitalist democracies that create and sustain crime networks? Not at all, because if socialism includes a rigid class system, the use of money for exchange, and the alienation of workers from the product of their labour, to mention only a few, crime networks can occur. Interestingly, Chambliss concluded with the idea that one solution to organized crime would be to decriminalize gambling and the drug trade; this would lessen the hold of the rackets on these illicit goods and the provision of deviant services.

The Contribution of Platt

Tony Platt also was interested in the relationship between deviance and capitalism in almost identical terms, except he dealt with the phenomenon of 'street crime': 'They [crime studies sponsored by the US government] supported the conclusion that "street" crime is not simply a *by-product* of the capitalist mode of production. . . . Rather, it is shown to be a phenomenon *endemic* to capitalism at its highest stage of development'.[20]

The victim surveys tapped an incidence of street crimes (theft, car theft, burglary, rape, assault, and armed robbery) almost four times as great as the rate reported to the police. Police brutality, corruption, and incompetence were seen to account for much of the difference, particularly as far as working-class and black minorities are concerned. Moreover, such crimes are primarily an *intra-class* and *intra-racial* phenomenon. Platt pointed out that the highest incidence of violent and property crime is among poor and unemployed working-class young men, and single or separated women. The death rate for black males by homicide was over eight times that for white males. This was the starkest illustration of the extent to which the costs of crime are regressive in their effects.

The conditions under which crime and deviance was political in the past were destroyed by capitalism. 'Social banditry' was purged as a form of 'expressive deviance' by the new technologies of control and superseded as a means of rebellion by the rise of the political organization of the working-class movement. What remained was predatory 'street' crime that offers no hope of a political solution for the

> super-exploited sectors of the working class. Monopoly capitalism emiserates increasingly larger portions of the working class and 'proletarianizes' the lower strata of the bourgeoisie, degrades workers' skills and competency in the quest for higher productivity and organizes family and community life on the basis of its most effective exploitability. It consequently makes antagonism rather than reciprocity the norm of social relationships.[21]

The Contribution of Reiman

A latter-day 'new criminologist' is Jeffrey Reiman, who is able to blend the ideas of Taylor, Walton, and Young, Marxist functionalism, and the Birmingham School together. Consider the abstract from his 1981 publication on Marxism and justice policy:

> Conventional analysis takes changes in criminal justice policy to be a response to shifts in the public's mood or to new developments in knowledge. Marxism views such policy changes as reflecting the shifting needs of the capitalist system of production. In this essay, we shall try to show how the so-called justice model in correction, the rejection of the goal of rehabilitating offenders, and the resurgence of the death penalty are characteristic responses of capitalist states to economic crisis.[22]

In his famous *The Rich Get Richer and the Poor Get Prison*, Reiman claims that the American justice system methodically created a misleading image of the deviant as young, black, working-class, and male, an image that filters out the middle-class and the white-collar offender by differential treatment.[23] The American criminal justice system, argues Reiman, *generates* and reproduces crime by criminalizing drug use, maintaining recidivist-producing prisons,[24] neglecting to address issues of social and economic inequality, and stigmatizing offenders so that re-entry to the conventional world is blocked. The conclusion to be drawn was that:

> The goal of our criminal justice system is not to reduce crime or to achieve justice but to project to the American public a visible image of the threat of crime. To do this, it must maintain the existence of a sizeable or growing population of criminals. To do this, it must fail in the struggle to reduce crime. . . . The practices of the criminal justice system keep before the public the *real* threat of crime and the *distorted image* that crime is primarily the work of the poor. The value of this *to those in positions of power* is that it deflects the discontent and potential hostility of middle America away from the classes above them and toward the class below them.[25]

■ Allied Approaches

A continuing source of inspiration for Marxist criminologists has undoubtedly been the longer-standing project of socialist historians to recover what has come to be termed 'history from below'. From the work of Hobsbawm, Thompson, and Rudé on social banditry, machine breaking, and the London mob to the detailed documentation of working-class history by the Ruskin History Workshop, the attempt has been made to rescue the lives of people consigned by orthodox scholarship to the margins of history from what Thompson has aptly termed 'the enormous condescension of posterity'.[26] The focus of such work has been almost entirely on deviance and political resistance to ruling-class or State power, rather than more predatory victimization.[27] However there are relatively few attempts to apply this approach to equivalent contemporary forms of deviance. Pearson has sought to explain violence against ethnic minorities in part by using much the same framework: 'Paki-bashing' in an economically blighted town in northern England is related to the resentment felt against immigrants taking jobs and apparently making good in a time of rising unemployment.[28] As we have seen, the work of Phil Cohen, Stuart Hall, and his colleagues is informed by a similar approach.

A historical approach has also been employed in the analysis of relations between social control and the political economy of the capitalism that emerged from the Industrial Revolution. Scull has viewed the nineteenth-century asylum- and prison-building programs as promoting the iron discipline that employers enforced in the period of maximum capitalist growth. By comparison, the stagnant capitalist economies of the 1970s and 1980s tried to unload their institutional charges for cut-rate 'community care'.[29] Ignatieff has explored the religious connection between some forms of prison discipline and the symbolic order of capitalist political economy.[30] In a series of works, Foucault used a 'structuralist' method along similar lines: capitalist industrialism employed a logic which its agencies applied to ruthless effect in one institutional sphere after another—the asylum, the prison, the clinic, the school, and the factory.[31] Charles Dickens had conveyed the same insight with more poetic force, but he believed in the power of the human heart to reform such organized cruelty.

Mathiesen and Fitzgerald saw the prison as a functional and continuing necessity for capitalist society.[32] Evidence for the use of the prison as an instrument of class oppression was inferred from the relative over-use of the prison for proletarian populations and its under-use in connection with offences of the powerful. Even in the courts, allegedly the most neutral and disinterested forum for the promulgation of the rule of law, class bias was seen to persist. Carlen,[33] who analyzed modes of courtroom interaction, concluded that they functioned so as to bestow a sense of impotence and inferiority on the largely working-class defendants and to buttress the superiority of the overwhelmingly middle- or upper-class lawyers and judiciary. The very language of the courtroom polarizes defendants and prosecution along class lines; and Griffith has documented the unified class character of the judiciary, both in its social composition and its ideology.[34]

The offences of the powerful and their relative immunity from prosecution and penal sanction were a central theme for Marxist analysis, though it is by no means the case that they pioneered its study—that honour must go to Edwin Sutherland.[35] This important topic remains slightly explored, but his argument is a simple one based on these propositions:

1. White-collar crime is real, being in violation of the criminal law.
2. White-collar crime differs from lower-class crime principally in an application of the criminal law that segregates white-collar criminals administratively from other criminals.

3. The theories of the criminologists that crime is due to poverty or to psychopathic and sociopathic conditions statistically associated with poverty are invalid because, first, they are derived from samples that are grossly biased with respect to socio-economic status; second, they do not apply to the white-collar criminals; and third, they do not even explain the criminality of the lower class, since the factors are not related to a general process that is characteristic of all criminality.
4. A theory is needed that will explain both white-collar criminality and lower-class criminality.
5. A hypothesis is suggested in terms of differential association and social disorganization.[36]

Following in this tradition is Frank Pearce's *Crimes of the Powerful*, a largely historical study of violations of the anti-trust laws in the United States and a critique of the Mafia myth. Before Chambliss, but drawing on the work of Albini,[37] he argued that organized crime in America is far more subservient to the imperatives of Big Business, to which it stands in a 'servant-class' relationship (for example, in strike breaking), than contemporary analyses allow. In a different vein, Colin Sumner tried to integrate the interactionists' emphasis on labelling with the Marxists' emphasis on class conflict s by means of a focus on criminal sanctions or 'censure' as the ultimate means by which class rule is secured and symbolically expressed through ideology.[38]

Thus, in a relatively short time, Marxist analysis attempted to redefine and extend the purposes and boundaries of the field.

■ The Emergence of Left Realism

In the 1980s, some radical theorists found their older position untenable. In response to external critics and to a series of changing circumstances, there was a revolution within radical 'deviantology'. Built on the structure created by Taylor, Walton, and Young and members of the Birmingham School, but also in reaction against it, there emerged a new form of pragmatism which is not very different from the older, conventional sociology of deviance that was deserted in the early 1970s. Jock Young (and Richard Kinsey, John Lea, Roger Matthews, and Geoffrey Pearson) were to be the architects of what Young called 'left realism', which inserted itself between what was defined as the hysterical overreaction of 'law and order politics' and the gross insensitivity to deviance by the left in Britain. It is an approach that has had analytic and political promise; it lies between the astructural lay and professional criminologies of the right and the wilfully myopic and 'impossibilist'[39] political analysis of the left.

Jock Young reflected:

Those of the right frequently attempt to suggest that levels of crime have no relationship to . . . changes in work and leisure but are rooted in the supposedly autonomous area of child rearing, drug use or a world of free-floating moral values. On the other hand, those on the left repeatedly attempt to suggest that changes in imprisonment, patterns of social control, the emerging actuarialism, etc. are political or managerial decisions unrelated to the problem of crime.[40]

So Young looked for a way to mediate these polar positions. Left realism has diverse social and intellectual roots. The arguments about the class-bound nature of deviance, the forgotten importance of political economy, and the neglect of Marx had become well-worn. The academic and commercial appeal of radical studies was appreciated by publishers; the Academic Press established its radical *Law, State and Society* series, and Macmillan its *Critical Criminology* series; Penguin published books sponsored by the Socialist Society, and Martin Robertson its largely radical *Law in Society* series. Thus it became less and less plausible to contend that critical themes were ignored and that the bourgeois sociology of deviance exercised intellectual hegemony.

• *On the contrary, sociology was awash with critical argument.* To some of its advocates radical analysis began to seem increasingly scholastic, established, and ritualistic. There were diminishing marginal returns in calling for a socialist analysis of deviance. The 'new criminology', Matthews and Young concluded, 'was never able to offer a competing alternative. Its critique was essentially negative and reactive.' Moreover, it was a critique that had its affiliations with a position rapidly being discredited by revelations of the terror exercised in the name of Marxism in Europe.[41]

• *Second, a number of radical theorists discovered that there were new contexts and opportunities for practical engagement.* In some jurisdictions, city councils had begun to espouse a politics with a marked affinity to the politics of critical work. Many of those councils were composed of people who had had some confrontation with radical thought at university and polytechnic, who were often radical intellectual activists, and who looked for intellectual support from a wider network of the left. A new 'shadow' sociology monitored the police, lesbian and gay rights, and the treatment of minorities. The radicals' words and ideas acquired a new political influence.

For example, in 1981 the Toronto police raided several bathhouses and arrested more than 300 men. This proved to be a turning point in gay rights in Canada, with social protests eventually turning into the first gay pride day march. Police relations with the gay and lesbian community have not been the same since.

• *Third, the left realists who taught probation officers, social workers, and others became bowed down under the repeated retort of 'it's all right for you to talk'.*[42] Nellis observed that, for those students, the issue of '"what is to be done?" was a question they had to ask themselves every day of their working lives'.[43] A faith in the redemption of socialist diversity after the revolution was no guide to action now. 'Deviantology' was obliged to become a little more practical.[44]

• *Fourth, the rise of feminism in the 1970s generated an attack on critical analysis.* In 1977 a student of Ian Taylor's at Sheffield University, Carol Smart, published her *Women, Crime and Criminology*. She reproached radical criminology for ignoring the politics of gender, for forgetting the extensive victimization of women, and for celebrating what seemed to be patriarchal oppression. Feminists began to analyze rape, sexual abuse, and battering. They were to be radical champions of the *victim*. Previous descriptions had dwelt on mental illness, prostitution, homosexuality, and drug use—all forms of deviance without immediate and visible victims. Some had refrained from discussing victimization altogether, as if deviance occurred in a void. Some had rather grandly assumed that victims were impersonal organizations or members of the property-owning classes and therefore politically peripheral or, indeed, blameworthy. There had been little attention paid to the ordinary, abundant suffering which crime inflicts on the working class. The criminal had been romanticized and the victim ignored. The rediscovery of the female victim had momentous consequences:

> Studies of domestic violence, rape and sexual harassment have been central to the feminist case since the mid-sixties. Feminist victimology was to create enormous theoretical problems for the radical paradigm in criminology. . . . [which] had tended to focus on crimes of the powerful and on the way in which vulnerable groups in society are criminalized. All very worthy stuff, but the traditional concern of criminology—crimes occurring within and between the working class—was a conceptual no-go area. This was part of a general tendency in radical thought to idealize their historical subject (in this case the working class) and to play down intra-group conflict, blemishes and social disorganization. But the power of the feminist case resulted in a sort of cognitive schizophrenia amongst radicals.[45]

Left realism, then, had one beginning in an emphasis on the female victim and the acknowledgement that radicals had neglected to say anything about her condition or her assailant. It had another beginning in the American, Canadian, and British national and local victimization surveys of the 1970s and 1980s. Survey after survey deconstructed the radical demystification of crime. It became increasingly evident that it was not the bourgeoisie but the proletariat who were the chief victims of crime, that they were less capable of coping with crime when they *were* victimized,[46] and that deviance was a major problem in their lives—a problem that threatened to subvert community and destroy happiness.

Gottfredson and Hirschi had criticized radical work in saying that 'crime is an ill-conceived mechanism for the redistribution of wealth or for the extraction of revenge on one's oppressors. . . . It is implausible to argue or believe that the pain of inequality may be alleviated by assaulting, robbing or stealing from similarly situated people'.[47] John Lea and Jock Young conceded:

> There was a schizophrenia about crime on the left where crimes against women and immigrant groups were quite rightly an object of concern, but other types of crime were regarded as being of little interest or somehow excusable. Part of this mistake stems . . . from the belief that property offences are

Feminist criminology identified new topics for analysis.

directed solely against the bourgeoisie and that violence against the person is carried out by amateur Robin Hoods in the course of their righteous attempts to redistribute wealth. All of this is, alas, untrue.[48]

Radical criminology was confronted with the facts of victimization.

•*Left realism set itself a number of tasks.* The first and most important was a program of empirical inquiry. Earlier crime surveys were held not to have paid enough attention to the victimization of women and ethnic minorities. The Islington Crime Survey disclosed the suffering that crime inflicts on people. Thus, deviance and control became identified as pressing problems that were no longer to be dismissed as insubstantial distractions or ideological mystifications. Deviance was redefined as painful, and the police and crime prevention as necessary.

The second task was to rewrite radical scholarship on deviance. For example, *What Is to Be Done about Law and Order?* discusses the manner in which crime takes place *within* the working class. Following an earlier book, *Policing the Riots,*[49] it also recognizes the heavy participation of young British blacks in crime, a recognition that encouraged other radicals to accuse its authors of racism.[50] Having identified the significance of black crime, they could proceed to an analysis of the interplay between police, victims, and young, marginalized blacks in areas of high unemployment.

The argument runs that effective policing is reactive, not proactive, and is dependent on the willing co-operation of witnesses and victims. Yet there are particular forms of crime in the inner city that inhibit a reactive stance. Street crime, for instance, is not easy to detect, being anonymous, committed by strangers and often unreported. As unemployment and political marginality increased the alienation of certain groups in the inner city, so their co-operation receded and the police received less and less voluntary information. The police response was aggressive patrol, saturation policing, and the harassment of young minority males. These strategies only increased the marginalization and triggered a spiral of confrontation. Deviance was thereby amplified, and co-operation declined further.

•*Crime surveys, particularly the local crime surveys conducted by left realists, encouraged the next turn in radical analysis.* These surveys were taken to be the foundation of new policies and prevention strategies. John Lea remarked in 1986 that 'the research techniques at our disposal in the development of crime prevention policy have progressed in leaps and bounds during the last decade. The importation of the victim survey gave us a qualitatively new type of data on which to base policy formation.'[51] Surveys had thereby not only illuminated new areas of the world and justified a new political attitude towards the nature of social problems under capitalism; they had also become a guide to practical action.[52] Where once radical sociologists would have disparaged surveys as positivist and action as correctionalist, they now embarked on a program of policy-making as vigorous as that of any government department. The dominant model they worked with was that of a parallelogram of forces composed of the State, society, and the offender, but which is fuller still because it now makes provision for the victim.

Crime surveys became a crime-fighting tool for the left.

In the 'square of crime', there are four minimal elements necessary for the definition of a crime (see Figure 10.2). In this square, the four corners are the offender, the victim, police agencies, and the public. When an offence is committed, there is a victim who is hurt or harmed by the offender's action; the offence then elicits a formal response by agencies of government enforcing the law; and the 'public' or community sees the act as an offence. To produce crime, each of these elements must be present and must interact socially to produce crime.

Effective analysis and intervention flowed from a new synthesis of twin intellectual antecedents: anomie theory, which supplies a vision of the relations between crime, motive, and structured inequality (as labelling theory had not), and labelling theory, which focuses on the existential consequences of control (in a way that anomie theory had not.) In incorporating the interactions between the State, victim, offender, and society, the analysis gives special emphasis to the community and its informal social controls. Much of what is recommended is little different from the ideas of secondary crime prevention[53] developed by the British Home Office Crime Prevention Unit or the Canadian Ministry of the Solicitor General. Left realists have advocated improved street lighting to reduce crime and the fear of crime,[54] better street design to foil prostitutes and curb crawlers,[55] improvements in public housing, and better-co-ordinated policing. They would use crime surveys to establish more effective police priorities. They would found hostels, youth clubs, drop-in centres, and clinics in areas with high crime rates.[56] From time to time, however, their radicalism takes them beyond the conventional reformism of government. They felt able to argue that, where necessary, crimes could be displaced from the most vulnerable and poorest sections of society to areas occupied by the more well-to-do. That is certainly not what the officials of any existing department of state would propose, and in such remaining differences, we see the 'leftness' of the new left realist theorists.

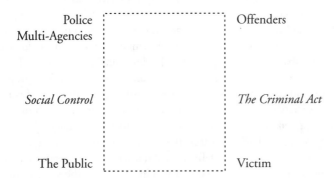

Figure 10.2: Young's Square of Crime Model

Source: Young, J. 1992. 'Realist Research as a Basis for Local Criminal Justice Policy.' Pp. 33–72 in *Realist Criminology: Crime Control and Policing in the 1990s*, edited by J. Lowman and B. MacLean. Toronto: University of Toronto Press. Reprinted by permission of the author.

Within radical politics, left realism was a new beginning. It has a political agenda, but in its evolution it has become more and more a practical administrative sociology of the left[57] that takes the problems of victimization seriously but gives a modestly radical inflection to their solution, awards prominence to politically preferred victims, and seeks to influence the police response to the needs of those victims.[58]

Within the mainstream sociology of deviance, the *applied* version of left realism is starting to look very much like any other digest of orthodox theory, and not an intellectual revolution at all but a return to convention, 'the criminology that has come in from the cold.'[59] Empirically, it has the local crime surveys to its credit, but it is now difficult to discern quite what distinguishes it from a combination of anomie, interactionist, and subcultural theories with a covert addition of social and situational control theories.

• *Theoretically, however, left realism took on a new direction* and a vitality with the publication of two books, Ian Taylor's *Crime in Context* and Jock Young's *The Exclusive Society*. Just as *The New Criminology* reflected the big sociological ideas of the early 1970s, so these two books reflect theoretical themes current in sociology at large at the end of the twentieth century. They talk about the common problem of crime in late modernity and come close to the 'fully social theory of deviance' which they had promised in 1973.

Crime in Context lists a series of social transitions in the political economy of society and the fashion in which they press down on poverty, class, gender, race, and the family to affect the national and transnational contexts of deviance. Socialism as a utopian alternative to capitalism, pronounced Taylor, 'is dead, not least because of the collapse of the only existing experiment with that form of societal organization, the Soviet Union.'[60] However, capitalism is continually beset by a series of crises: unemployment; poverty; social uncertainty; problems of social inclusion and the racialization of crime; crises of masculinity caused by a loss of power by newly insecure, largely proletarian men; ensuing crises in authority, power and relations within the family; and related crises of poverty in childhood and in the transition to adulthood. This amounts to a formula for delinquency among the poor and, with the emergence of a transnational capitalism, for a globalization of organized and institutional crime among the rich.

The Exclusive Society also plays on the theme of social transitions, in particular the causes and consequences of vast increases of crime in the West. Late modern capitalist society has become mapped into an inner core that is flourishing economically; a '*cordon sanitaire*' that serves as a buffer about that core; and a rim of outer regions, populated by a threatening, marginalized, and regulated underclass. Deviance is no longer defined as abnormal and the property of a pathological minority who can be restored therapeutically to the security of a moral community at one with itself, but *normal*, the actions of a significant, obdurate group who are stigmatized and ostracized from protected spaces in a world newly insecure, fractured, and preoccupied with problems of risk and danger. The whole is blanketed by the blandishments of a consumer society that motivates members of the underclass to crave the goods and services that large groups take to be properly their own. Such an order is inherently fragile and is punctuated by out-breaks of implosive rioting, on the one hand and, on the other, the 'slow rioting of crime' that combine to rebound on the people and property of the nether regions, making miserable conditions worse.

Both descriptions are graphic. They synthesize masses of ideas into a coherent analytic model. But it is moot whether they should be taken to refer to a state of affairs that is itself transitional or one that will endure and become ever graver over time. Unemployment rates decline as well as rise—and they have been *falling* at the end of the twentieth and beginning of the twenty-first century—although the nature of work itself has been changing and insecurity has undoubtedly appeared to mount.

Case Study—The Media and Corporate Crime

John McMullan (of Saint Mary's University) has studied how the press covered the Westray mine disaster of 1992. His interest is in looking at the relationship between news sources, knowledge claims, and the social construction of crime. Using Foucault's concept of the 'politics of truth' and Cohen's concept of 'states of denial', he demonstrates how the formal media create various 'regimes of truth' which dominate how we think about the event.

In this situation, what truth gets told is important because both corporate and state institutions were accused of wrongdoing. The mining company, Curragh, was accused of failing to maintain proper safety conditions in the mine, and the province was accused of failing to inspect the mine properly. The ultimate conclusion was that a methane explosion was what killed the twenty-six miners. Given that the explosion was both predicted and preventable, the potential for a legitimation crisis was inevitable.

So whether what happened at Westray is seen as a natural accident, a legal tragedy, or a political scandal is important. And the way in which the story played out in the media became the truth for the public. The examination of thousands of news stories shows that the media presented divergent and changing versions of what had happened.

What is especially important in this truth telling is the absence of a social vocabulary of corporate crime. This absence of a discourse of corporate crime marks the inability of the media to tell the truth about corporate and state interests, and this means that the media's stories tend to perpetuate those interests. In the process, workplace crime is made invisible in popular culture.

And Westray is a significant event in popular culture. There is a National Film Board film about it, as well as plays, radio shows, and documentaries. To date there are at least three books, and numerous websites on the subject. A public inquiry mapped the causes of the tragedy, the likes of which had not been seen in decades. For the public, the truth of Westray was still being debated many years later. In the months after the explosion, charges of safety violations were filed by regulatory agencies under the *Occupational Health and Safety Act* against Curragh Resources, only to be dropped in favour of criminal charges of manslaughter and criminal negligence.

The eventual criminal trial cost an estimated $4.5 million and ended in a mistrial and a staying of all charges against the accused. The public inquiry, which cost $4.8 million, and concluded that the disaster 'was a complex mosaic of actions, omissions, mistakes, incompetence, apathy, cynicism, stupidity, and neglect,' And it called it a 'predictable path to disaster.'

At the inquiry, corporate officials and politicians tried to exonerate themselves by attacking the credibility of victims ('the mine blew up because of what happened that morning'), accusing the inquiry of being biased against them ('they just want to blame someone'), or excusing their actions through appeals to other loyalties ('we had to cut corners in order to meet production quotas'). In this way the accused were able to condemn the condemners in a 'language of necessity and trivialization'.

At each stage the media coverage of the charges, the trial, and the public inquiry is framed differently from news coverage in the immediate aftermath of the explosion.

In the first period of coverage, the legal and human-interest elements of the disaster each received about the same amount of coverage. During the second period, coverage of the legal elements of the case more than doubled, whereas during the third period, the discussion of the legal elements declined, and the human-tragedy coverage resurfaced.

Moreover, in the process of representing the event as news, the crime is 'imagined' out. Or as McMullan says,

> This was the limit of the press's ability to tell the truth to powerful corporate and state interests, the place where media truth telling was made coincident with the exercise of power. The media produced their own version of 'interpretive denial': 'What happened at Westray' was really 'something else'! . . . They convey the novelty of the disaster rather than the mundane character of the criminal actions leading up to the event. The press did not demarcate the corporation as capable of 'killing' or its agents as capable of 'homicide,' and the news coverage, while registering a 'view from below,' does not constitute the truth of Westray as state-corporate criminality.

In the process of coverage, corporate crime disappears as a topic, and the conditions that allowed the crime to happen in the first place continue: the lack of criminal sanctions, economic development in an unevenly developed region, high unemployment, government regulations favourable to industry, and a lack of media preparation for covering such disasters.

As Laureen Snider of Queen's University says, the lack of punishment for corporate crime is accompanied by the increasing punitiveness of the justice system when it came to lower-class crime. Furthermore, the 'disappearance' of corporate crime was 'argued into obsolescence because new truth claims were developed which were more compatible with concerns of dominant groups. . . . The reception of these claims, then, can only be understood by relating it to the hegemonic dominance of those interests who stood to benefit from their acceptance as "truth".'

Sources: J. McMullan, 'News, Truth, and the Recognition of Corporate Crime'. See also idem, 'The Media, the Politics of Truth, and the Coverage of Corporate Violence: The Westray Disaster and the Public Inquiry', 67–86; idem, *News, Truth and Crime: The Westray Disaster and Its Aftermath*; L. Snider, 'The Sociology of Corporate Crime: An Obituary', 169–206.

■ 'New Directions' in Canadian Criminology

In the 1980s, social scientists became interested in what might constitute a uniquely Canadian study of deviance. This was fuelled by a reawakening of interest in Canadian political economy, a reaction against American functionalism, and of course, developments in critical analysis in Britain. As one commentator said, " 'there was much to be critical about, since the narrowly "applied" character of much of what then passed for criminology research represented little more than specious control-oriented projects that obscured connections to market and power structures—falling abjectly short of a "fully social theory" of crime.'[61]

As Thomas Fleming stated in the preface to *The New Criminologies in Canada*, editor of the first critical collection on the subject to emerge in Canada, it was a revolutionary approach and one that provided an alternative to those mainstream approaches that viewed deviance as simply that which violated laws and regulations. Instead, the writers who were brought together in that work sought to ask such questions as: who makes the law, how it is applied, and whether some people get preferential treatment while others are punished severely.[62]

The challenge of this 'new direction' was based on the idea that the traditional sociology of deviance allied itself with the ruling apparatus of the State in the administration of the justice system. In the process of adopting a correctionalist posture, social science helps to perpetuate social control in that the causes of problem behaviour are looked for in the individual so that they can be corrected.

Through various essays, the contributors tried to engage critical issues, such as the need to develop working-class research, a criticism of the romanticism of radical analysis, and the reasons why some kinds of behaviour are punished while others are not. This was an important period in the history of Canadian studies.

An analysis of the historical development of drug legislation, for example, looks at the role of the State in mediating class conflict. Compared to previous approaches that have used a labelling approach to connect opium to the Chinese, Elizabeth Comack looks at the role of the State in using the criminal law to solve the problem of surplus labour in turn-of-the-century British Columbia.

She comes to the conclusion that it is not simply a matter of labelling, but a matter of class conflict, a conflict over the 'problem' of surplus labour that is at the heart of the criminalization of opium.[63]

Other analyses included in *New Criminologies* are Russell Smandych's analysis of anti-combines legislation, John Casey's analysis of how corporations attempt to alter the law through political pressure and to avoid sanctions for crimes against workers, John Hagan's discussion of how corporations use the courts to their own advantage, and Laureen Snider's urging of sociologists to use historical inspection, interdisciplinary links, and political economy to conduct empirical analyses of crime and criminal justice.

New Directions also includes analyses of crooked lawyers; the economy of penal reform; male hegemony in the development of penal law; youth, unemployment, and moral panics; the rise of the State; law, conflict, and order; and the punishment industry.

Other notable contributions in the development of a critical, Canadian deviantology are *Realist Criminology*,[64] and *Post-Critical Criminology*.[65] The former includes analyses of the regulation of prostitution, feminism and realism, woman abuse in Canada, women's fear of crime, critical victimology, and local crime research. *Post-Critical Criminology* includes analyses of zero-tolerance policies on family violence, lawlessness and disorder in historical perspective, youth and school violence, masculinity and crime, and panopticism.

In one, retrospective article, Ratner is not very optimistic about the future:

> The siren calls of faith, family, and orderly community may prove too seductive amidst the frenzied ideological space of 'anti-terrorism,' inducing even self-professed critical criminologists to rally behind such dubious panaceas as 'restorative justice' and crime prevention,' which tend to individualize culpability, on the one hand, and territoriality displace criminality, on the other.[66]

In another, Chunn and Menzies say:

> Academic criminology had followed the . . . trend for social sciences to reconfigure themselves as applied sciences. . . . In these hyper-modern times of all-pervasive risk . . . academic criminology . . . represents an enticing paradigm. . . . For Canadian criminologists immersed in crime-prevention research, administrative criminology, clinical criminology, biological criminology, computational criminology, crime-mapping, police science, forensic psychology, forensic science, penal science, risk assessment, and other 'insider' pursuits, times have never been so good.[67]

However, what is *important* about these developments is the application of a Marxist approach to issues that affect workers, women, and youth and a critique of power relations that distort crimes of the powerful and pathologize deviance in individualistic theories. What is *unique* about these collections is their development in Canada and their use of local issues and historical analysis.

Discussion: **Deviance Exploration**—Canada's Drug Laws

It is a mystery why certain substances were criminalized as dangerous narcotics in the early twentieth century. Before 1908 there were no restrictions on the sale or consumption of opiates, for example, and tonics, elixirs, and cough syrups containing opium were widely available.

Much credit for the opium legislation of 1908 is given to then deputy minister of Labour, Mackenzie King, who travelled to Vancouver to investigate the anti-Asiatic riots of early September, 1907. The result of his seeing the 'drug' situation was the *Opium Act* of 1908, which was revised in 1911, 1919, and 1929.

Carstairs argues that the Vancouver anti-drug campaign was pivotal to the extension of Canada's drug laws in the early 1920s and that the highly racialized drug panic resulted in legislation which provided for severe penalties, including six-month sentences for possession. Like the labelling theorists, she argues that this had a disproportionate effect on Chinese-Canadians, who were targeted by enforcement officials and who could be deported. However, the drug panic also affected all drug users, who were faced with long sentences for possession as well as (to us) violations of civil liberties in the course of searches and restrictions on the right to an appeal.

Malleck, who takes a different tack, examines the arguments about drug addiction made by medical and non-medical reformers in Victorian Canada to explain the emergence of anti-narcotic legislation in the early twentieth century. Rather than see the motive for the 1908 *Opium Act* and its unanimous acceptance by Parliament as simply anti-Chinese sentiment, he suggests it is necessary to explore wider discussions of drug addiction available in physicians' self-prescribed role as protectors of national health.

Furthermore, in an excellent analysis, E. Comack who takes the research into an even more divergent direction, looks at opium legislation in relation to the State's need to deal with an increasingly difficult labour situation. Chinese labour was both a real and a symbolic threat to the British Columbia working class, which was itself being deskilled and unionized. Relations between management and labour were approaching a crisis by the turn of the century, and drug laws were part of a strategy to manage class conflict by removing the threat posed by Chinese labour.

The genius of having King deal with the 1907 Anti-Asiatic Exclusion League riot was that it pinned responsibility on foreign agitators, translated the problem into a 'race problem', and made the issue one of immorality.

The result of the opium laws was to transform a private issue of drug use into a public problem, which was blamed on the 'Mongolians', in King's term, and to turn people away from socialism, which saw the labour crisis as a class issue rather than an ethnic issue, and thus preserve the legitimacy of the State.

Did the State intend the crisis to further its legitimation? Probably not. Did it benefit? Certainly.

Sources: A. Comack, 'The Origins of Canadian Drug Legislation: Labelling versus Class Analysis'; C. Carstairs, 'Deporting "Ah Sin" to Save the White Race: Moral Panic, Racialization, and the Extension of Canadian Drug Laws in the 1920s', 65–88; D. Malleck, '"Its Baneful Influences Are Too Well Known": Debates over Drug Use in Canada, 1867–1908', 263–88. See also S Cook, 'Canadian Narcotics Legislation, 1908–1923: A Conflict Model Interpretation', 36–46.

■ Criticism

If all that was being asserted by Marxist 'deviantology' were series of propositions to the effect that capitalism and deviance were interconnected, that deviance and control assumes a distinctive form under capitalism and so on, then there could be little to object to in adopting such premises as a basis for further analysis and research.

The problems that plagued the earlier structural approaches would still need to be surmounted—that of reification of 'structure', for example, and the adoption of deterministic models of deviance—but all approaches linking deviance to the social structure share these pitfalls. Indeed, it was only with the advent of an interactionist approach that such problems were teased out and elucidated. But the advocates of a Marxian perspective tend to assert far more than this.

The 'new' criminologists, for example, assert the 'total interconnectedness' between deviance and capitalism. Class conflict is viewed as *the* form of group conflict in advanced industrial societies.

• *The first criticism is that the search for a 'total interconnectedness' leads to a revival of functionalism, in which deviance is viewed as an expression of, or resistance to, capitalist exploitation.* Correspondingly, ban, censure,[68] and control are viewed as necessary for the maintenance of bourgeois hegemony.[69] For example, Young argued that State prosecutions for marijuana offences is an example of ruling-class irrationality that contributes to the maintenance of bourgeois institutions.[70]

However, it is not clear how such 'irrationality' does in practice contribute to bourgeois hegemony, since the processes by which this aim is accomplished are not examined. If certain offences are decriminalized, it can equally plausibly be argued that the purpose is to secure bourgeois domination by 'repressive tolerance'.[71] This form of circular argument is endemic in the search for 'total interconnectedness'.

Underlying this mode of analysis is a 'new' form of determinism and essentialism. Determinism is shifted from the socio-cultural context to the realm of political economy. Essentialism is in that

> other-worldly realm of real processes which must not be confused with mundane appearance, everyday belief and social phenomena. It cannot be understood by entering the lifeworld of those who actually experience those processes. The consciousness of essential truth is distinct from the false consciousness of ordinary people. . . . Radical criminology . . . rejects a dependence on empiricism and *Verstehen*. . . . After all, empiricism merely investigates the sensory world, a world which is not metaphysically authentic. Verstehen, too, simply reproduces false consciousness and is incapable of explaining what is real.[72]

It would be idle to pretend that 'false consciousness' does not, in some form or other, constitute both a major problem for sociology and its chief justification. If perfect social knowledge could be assumed to exist, sociology would be superfluous. However, there is a marked difference between the assumption that knowledge is inadequate or partial and that it is 'false'. The one assumes at least a relative openness to fresh information and insights; the other a pre-structured falsity which can be corrected only by a total transformation of consciousness itself. Sociology is, in general, wedded to the former, with its corresponding hard-core commitment to the principle of falsification. Marxism, in general, eludes or rejects that criterion.

• *This point is germane to a consideration of the second issue, the Marxian theory of class conflict as a necessary outcome of capitalist structure.* If Marx was correct in identifying the central properties of capitalism, then class conflict will inevitably grow as the crises of capitalism intensify. It might be thought that Marx's clear specification of a particular evolutionary sequence *could* be tested, particularly as societies based upon a socialist alternative were constructed. However, the defence is that the proletariat have not been progressively 'emiserated' under capitalism because their affluence has been secured at the expense of the Third World. If proletariat and bourgeoisie have not as yet been polarized, that is because, as Marx predicted, the bourgeoisie has exploited to the full the capacities of their technologies to buy time and buy off opposition. Yet prosperity remains precarious, as the proletariat presses home its strategic advantages, prosperity can be sustained only at the cost of successive crises and hidden forms of exploitation, for example of migrant labour.

Even when those societies, one by one, collapsed quite spectacularly after 1989, there are still some radical theorists who do not seem to act fully on what they see:

> Despite current rhetorics and feelings against a certain kind of communism and indeed against the very mention of the word socialism in some countries, this is not a time for socialistic capitulation on questions of theory. The theoretical work done by socialists within sociology of crime and law, however much it may be dubbed 'neo-Marxist' or 'marxisant', remains the most vibrant and explanatory available.[73]

This limitation does not extend to alternative theories of conflict, including class conflict, that stem from the sociology of Max Weber.[74] The major difference between Marx and Weber lies in their fundamental assumptions about the development of capitalism. For Marx, capitalism rests upon a particular mode of exploitation; for Weber, it rests upon a particular form of rationality. These are not mutually exclusive ideas in principle, but in their philosophical development they become so. For Marx, class domination culminates in the revolutionary transcendence of capitalism and the opportunity to construct a classless, free, and equal communism. For Weber, rationality generates bureaucratic authority, which can be harnessed, with immense difficulty, only by the retention of charismatic authority in the framework of constitutional democracy.

In a sense, both have been invalidated by history. Marx failed to predict the logic of the Russian Revolution, and Weber, the rise of Hitler and Fascism, which was the yoking together of charisma and bureaucratic authority.[75] Ultimately, however, if a choice between the two must be made, Weber at least provides the conceptual vocabulary with which to make sense of such developments, whereas to some, Marx does not. The sociology of Weber can handle the growth of State powers, the rise of bureaucracy, the routinization of charisma, and the myriad forms assumed by conflict between classes, racial groups, the sexes, and religions; Marxian sociology collapses these into endless variations of the class struggle.

• *The strengths and weaknesses of Marxian sociology are well exemplified in Policing the Crisis.* Theoretically, the advance made by this book was the attempt to integrate the interactionist insight concerning 'moral panics' with the Marxian insight into the nature of the 'crisis' wrought by capitalism in Britain in the early 1970s. Empirically, however, this integration is not accomplished. The reality of the 'moral panic' is skillfully analyzed and conveyed,[76] but the grounds for asserting that the official reaction tried to promote such a panic for larger ideological and political ends are not established. This is not to say that they could not be established, for even if they are unlikely to issue forth from the mouths of the 'master institutions' themselves, they might be inferred from the demonstration that 'crises' and 'panics' are correlated. But this kind of evidence is not advanced, and indeed, it perhaps could not be advanced, without firmer criteria for the identification of 'crises'.

• *There is also a central inconsistency in the analysis.* Young black second-generation immigrant men are exonerated from any undue contribution to the rise in crime but are simultaneously described as a 'super-exploited sub-proletariat' whose increasing contribution to crime is 'inevitable'. On inspection, that inconsistency *can* be resolved, but the main grounds for its resolution in *Policing the Crisis* seem far less defensible in the light of critical analyses of its statistical basis. Ironically, the attempt by Hall *et al.* to be more precise in their definition of a 'moral panic' than was usually the case opened up that terrain for reappraisal.

Pratt has shown that the London police kept records of events called 'muggings' in their area, and those events did both increase at the end of the 1960s and also shift in location from the classic sites of such crime—towpaths, tunnels, and commons—to far less avoidable main streets.[77] More significantly, Wadding-ton has shown that there was a real and continuous national rise in muggings before the 'moral panic' allegedly arose. There may have been a slight decline in the *rate* of increase, but there was no decline in the propensity of street crime to grow steadily and uninterruptedly: 'the only valid conclusion to be drawn from the figures presented by Hall *et al.* . . . is the opposite one to that drawn by the authors themselves. It is that crime during the period immediately preceding the onset of concern about "mugging" was indeed increasing and doing so by increas-ing increments.'

Moreover, 'the lack of any criteria of proportionality allows no distinction to be drawn in general between a "sober, realistic appraisal" of a problem and a "moral panic"'.[78]

Reviewing evidence about the experience of crime in the inner city some years later, radical theorists observed that fears about mugging are not panicky but sober and sensible: 'people's perceptions of crime are not based on moral panic'.[79] Suggestive as the work of Hall and his colleagues remains, one may con-clude that, both statistically and conceptually, their interpretation of the social his-tory of mugging is flawed.

Even if one does accept the statistical argument of *Policing the Crisis*, the offi-cial reaction can be indicted for a premature rather than a faulty analysis of the situation. Similarly, the media and judiciary are assailed for their frequent invo-cation of the American comparison as a prefiguration of the inner-city future. Yet the authors themselves make much the same comparison, though in more sociologically acceptable terms. This seems to extend to sociology a benefit denied to those engaged in formal social control. In short, the prior commitment to a particular version of class struggle over-determines the analytical outcome.

In the work of Platt and Chambliss there is above all a conviction that Amer-ican capitalism is capitalism, that American crime is crime, and that elsewhere may be found less of much the same thing. Platt sees American capitalism as the highest form of capitalism, though he gives no reason for this assumption. Gid-dens could equally plausibly make quite the opposite assumption in his study of the advanced societies.[80] In general, however, the main limitation of their work is that no intermediate or distinctive forms of political economy other than cap-italism and socialism are considered worthy of analysis.

• *The symmetry between deviance, control, and capitalism is questioned by com-parative work.* For example, Hagan and Leon, in a study of juvenile justice in Canada, could find no basis for the links implied by Platt to exist between the reform of the juvenile justice system and capitalist interests in the child labour market in the United States.[81] Clinard, in his study in Switzerland, *Cities with Lit-tle Crime*, found a surprisingly low rate of working-class criminality in a supremely capitalist society. The variations in deviance that obtain in widely differing cap-italist societies seem scarcely to be addressed by this approach. And if the net is broadened to include the history of the former State socialist societies, the yield drops even lower. In short, it is difficult to make the connections between deviance and capitalism fit.

• *Finally, we might return to an inspirational source for the 'new' studies in deviance:* Gouldner's insistence that theory should encompass 'man-fighting-back' rather than 'man-on his-back'. This theme has been embroidered into a rich symbolic tapestry of deviant resistance. It has been argued that the crime rate can be interpreted as an index of 'the credibility of a propertied society at particular stages of its development—the extent to which the distribution of property is latently accepted or rejected amongst certain sections of the working population'.[82] It is difficult to reconcile this political reading of deviance with actual patterns of criminal victimization, which takes place overwhelmingly within rather than between groups. Such a reading also obscures the extent to which deviance is only at several removes a problem for the State. It primarily affects local communities, whatever their class composition. Much evidence suggests that working-class communities desire more, rather than less, policing and are less critical of police work than middle-class groups.[83] To sustain the case for deviance as a 'misrecognition' of the 'real mechanisms'[84] of subordination involves the risk of reducing crime to a 'very bad case indeed of false consciousness'.[85]

On the other hand, some Marxist scholarship, such as Thompson's social historical studies and Willis's ethnographic work, provides outstanding examples of rigorous research. Thompson describes his method in *Whigs and Hunters* as resembling 'a parachutist coming down in unknown territory: at first knowing only a few yards of land around me and gradually extending my explorations in each direction.' In his already classic defence of the rule of law, he remarks that the Whig oligarchy employed the law

> very much as a modern structural Marxist should expect it to do. But this is not the same thing as to say that the rulers had need of law, in order to oppress the ruled, while those who were ruled had need of none. . . . Most men have a strong sense of justice, at least with regard to their own interests. If the law is evidently partial and unjust, then it will mask nothing, legitimate nothing, contribute nothing to any class's hegemony. . . . We reach then not a simple conclusion (law [equals] class power) but a complex and contradictory one. On the one hand, it is true that the law did mediate existent class relations to the advantage of the rulers. . . . On the other hand, the law mediated these class relations through legal forms, which imposed, again and again, inhibitions upon the actions of the rulers.[86]

His own conclusion is that to dispense with the restrictions of bourgeois legalism in favour of Utopian projections is to throw away a whole inheritance of struggle *about* law and within the forms of law.

• *Crime rates have been falling, not rising, in the West*, although they are falling from high levels. When and how unemployment and crime will rise again is not clear. In some respects late modern societies are markedly less exclusionary than those of high modernity. The mentally ill and handicapped may be adversely affected by deinstitutionalization, but very large numbers are no longer consigned to highly regimented mental hospitals and are treated in the community. In Britain and Canada mainstream secondary schooling is now comprehensive, however flawed that may be. Higher education is no longer the preserve of the top 5 per cent, and so on. Moreover, however strident they may be, the more overt forms of racism have not really become politically influential in most places.

Again, the current fashion for restorative justice in Canada, Australia, and the United Kingdom underscores contradictory trends towards *inclusionary* models of control. In France and Germany, too, there is a strong emphasis on 'solidarity' as well as on exclusion in criminal justice practice. It remains uncertain how crime, deviance, and control, and with them, the radical or critical criminology that tries to capture them, will evolve. What is sure is that the greater part of radical deviancy project has now been absorbed into the theoretical mainstream.[87]

Not all radical theorists have taken the 'realist' route. Some remain unreconstructed, disavowing any connection with the mainstream sociology of deviance and lamenting the passing of the radical moment.[88] Pearce talked about the need for a commitment '*not* to take the claims of the powerful at face value' and about how 'notable and depressing' and 'how unusual is this commitment' in academic sociology. 'There is now', he said, 'a whole generation of academics . . . many of whom lack any basic training in Marxist concepts or modes of analysis.'[89] Theirs is a radical sociology which looks back to Poulantzas[90] to portray the academy as a medium for the construction of bourgeois ideology, intellectuals as the servants of capitalism, and the sociology of deviance itself as a lackey of the State. They would return to the Schwendingers[91] and others to reject bourgeois definitions of crime and insert in their place the evils of racism, imperialism, and capitalism as proper subjects of study.

Chapter Summary

This chapter has looked at the lineage of radical, or critical theory as it applies to the sociology of deviance. There is a rich theoretical heritage to this tradition. Although the original authors failed to address much of their work to this topic, it has been taken up by their contemporaries in Britain, Europe, and North America.

Of particular importance is the work of the Birmingham Cultural School, the new realists, and the diverse work of the Canadian political economists. These branches of radical thought, while quite different, all illustrate the need to examine the interconnections between power, deviance and control.

In a fairly short time, because of the influence of the critical tradition, deviance has gone from being seen as a threat to the social order to being treated as a symptom of social inequality.

Discussion Questions

1. What overall contribution is made by the 'new criminology' to an understanding of deviance?
2. How is the work of the Birmingham School important? Can it be applied, for example, in an analysis of the factors used to justify a crackdown on mugging?
3. How can we use labelling theory in a critical theory of deviance? Are the two compatible?
4. In the analysis of media coverage of the Westray disaster, how does the lack of a critical discourse of 'crime' affect both the possibility of such a crime occurring again?

Exploration in Film

In 1989, Michael Moore released his satirical documentary *Roger and Me* about the closing of the General Motors plants in Flint, Michigan. The resulting layoffs cost 33,000 people their jobs and left the one-industry town destitute. In the film, Moore tries to interview Roger Smith, the head of GM and the man responsible for the layoffs.

Websites

Simon Fraser University Media Analysis Lab
http://www.sfu.ca/media-lab/risk/index.html

Chapter Eleven

Feminist Criminology

Chapter Overview

In this chapter we look at the feminist critiques of the sociological study of deviance. These critiques are important because they undermine some of the basic assumptions of mainstream sociology and of how the study of deviance has developed. What comes in for particular criticism is not only the academic neglect of women as a topic but also the stereotyping of women as deviants.

Then we look at several examples where a feminist contribution has made a difference in analysis: that female emancipation leads to deviance, and that male chivalry explains the low deviancy rate of women, as well as the neglected area of victimology. The Discussion features are meant to highlight some key issues where gender and deviance intersect.

■ Introduction

Since the late 1970s, one of the most notable developments in theorizing about deviance has been the emergence of what has been termed 'feminist criminology'. This is a diverse body of work united by the critical view that the understanding of female offending and the role of gender in theories of deviance in general have both been ill-served by traditional sociology. So successful has that development been that, by the early 1990s, it was possible for Mariana Valverde of the University of Toronto to claim that 'it is now no longer true that women's issues are being ignored, for there are whole shelves of work on women as victims of male violence, women offenders and women police officers. The more extreme examples of sexism found in criminological theory have been discredited—at least in the eyes of those who read feminist works.'[1]

Despite earlier statements, in both Britain and the United States, that anticipated much of the force of the feminist critique,[2] the emergence of feminist scholarship on deviance is generally assigned to the publication of Carol Smart's *Women, Crime and Criminology* in 1977.[3] Though it was not without its critics among female criminologists[4] and was received skeptically by some male sociologists,[5] the work of those in the forefront has tended to reaffirm Smart's fundamental analysis. It is worth looking in some detail at her critique of the field as a template for feminist criminology in the past three decades.

The basis for Smart's critique is that, not only is there a lack of material on female criminality, but also what does exist

> shares an entirely uncritical attitude towards sexual stereotypes of women and girls. From Lombroso and Ferrero (1895) to Cowie, Cowie and Slater (1968) and from W. I. Thomas (1923) to Konopka (1966) the same attitudes and presuppositions reappeared, confirming the biologically determined inferior status of women not only in conventional society but also in the 'world' of crime and delinquency. [Despite rare exceptions], the majority of these studies refer to women in terms of their biological impulses and hormonal balance or in terms of their domesticity, maternal instinct and passivity.[6]

The neglect of female criminality by the predominantly male criminological profession had several undesirable consequences.

•*First, the 'arrested development' of the subject as regards female offenders left it ossified at the positivist stage of development.* Women offenders alone are subject to a form of intellectual atavism aping the Lombrosian theory of crime: the theorizing about female deviance is a throwback to the earliest stage of criminological evolution. This sort of perspective elides discussions of context and process in that there is no discussion of what produces such delinquency. It is neither a situational theory nor a dispositional one.

•*Second, policies and attitudes towards female deviance mirrored such determinisms.* In advanced industrial societies, there is a cultural assumption that women are irrational, compulsive, and neurotic. Unfortunately, sociological theories of deviance have reflected this predominant stereotype.

As well, adolescent girls face much higher risks of institutionalization than boys for non-criminal forms of sexual deviance, a fact adeptly proved by Joan Sangster of Trent University in her work on the regulation of female delinquency in Canada. In her analysis of women incarcerated under the *Female Refugees Act* (*FRA*), she says that:

> A short list of the qualities most condemned in the FRA women tells us much about the dominant ideals of femininity and its polar opposite, the bad woman in the 1930s and early 1940s. The FRA women most rebuked were those who were described as willful, stubborn, disobedient to elders and family, overly sexual or easily led to engage in sex, lacking in sexual guilt, having no sense of appropriate sex partners, and disrespectful of marital boundaries with regards to sex.[7]

In Britain, such regimes as the 'new' Holloway prison confirmed the biological determinist view, with therapy but no vocational training for women prisoners.[8] The 'sick' role model 'is a consequence of the failure of theorists to explicate or treat as topics for analysis the understandings which they share with those engaged in formulating penal policy'.[9]

Third, unreconstructed notions about women's 'nature' have lent undue prominence to 'sexual deviance' as the focus of inquiry best suited to the study of female deviance. 'Double standards' become institutionalized across the board in theory, research, law, treatment, and control. Prostitution is studied more than rape, as an example of female pathology—despite the male clientele—while the study of rape, when it takes place at all, leans heavily towards the imputation of victim precipitation[10] or the need to protect the accused against false conviction. Though Smart overlooks his work, Heidensohn has pointed out[11] that even so relatively sophisticated a theorist as Albert Cohen assumed that 'female delinquency is relatively specialized. It consists overwhelmingly of sexual delinquency or of involvement in situations that are likely to spill over into overt sexuality.'[12] To paraphrase Gouldner, patriarchally inclined criminologists have portrayed the female deviant as 'woman-on-her-back, rather than woman-fighting-back'.

> Double standards for gender roles are institutionalized in deviance topics.

The Critique of Lombroso

In their wish to expose the defects of both classical and contemporary studies of female criminality, feminist sociologists have been energized as much by the belief that the task has been unduly neglected by their male colleagues and predecessors as by the view that such work has exerted a malign effect on public policy and

Discussion: Deviance and Culture—Moral Panics and the 'Nasty Girl'

In a recent article, two researchers at Simon Fraser University examine how female crimes have been interpreted as a sign that today's girls are increasingly violent. They argue that the 'nasty girl' phenomenon is actually the product of a moral panic and part of the backlash against feminism.

They begin with the murder of Reena Virk by a group of mostly female teens in Victoria in 1997, which led Canadians to believe that something had gone terribly wrong with teenage girls. When that belief was given prominence in the media with the release of the CBC documentary *Nasty Girls* in the same year, the stage was set for the belief that girl violence was rampant.

The idea is that moral panics are an exaggeration of a condition that is already generating widespread public concern. In the subsequent media storm, the public becomes sensitized to the threat, and its perception of danger and risk solidifies.

The first component of a moral panic is said to be the misuse of statistics. In this case, the statistics show that the number of young women charged with assault between 1980 and 1995 increased by 525 per cent; however the researchers assert that the increase reflects changes in charging practices more than changes in behaviour. If true, that's quite a distortion in police charge rates.

The second component of the moral panic is an exaggeration of isolated acts and a connection between them and an imputed larger trend in girl violence. This is a good technique for creating a crime wave about anything, whether it's youth crime, satanic cults, or illegal aliens.

A third component of a moral panic is that experts identify some characteristic of the 'nasty girl' as a concern for panic. This tradition, of describing female deviants as masculinized, insensitive, lacking moral values, envious of men, psychologically maladjusted, and promiscuous goes back a long way.

Morality is central to the identification of dangerous females, because women are supposed to be guardians of the moral sphere. In the past, social-purity movements criminalized (working-class) women who used their sexuality to survive, seeking to rescue 'fallen women' and delinquent girls.

The researchers' point, then, is that through distortion, exaggeration, and statistical manipulation of data, the media have constructed a new breed of female, the 'nasty girl'. The significance of this folk devil is that danger is repackaged into mainstream advice to parents and educators, thereby causing undue anxiety for the public.

However, the real anxiety which underlies the reaction to the violent girl is said to be rooted in the larger social structure. In other words, changes in modern society have fractured our common values, leaving us with a heightened sense of risk and uncertainty. In such a precarious climate, crime acquires a powerful symbolic value. Deviants are really scapegoats who are made responsible for our feelings of insecurity.

If, then, there isn't really an epidemic of violent female offenders, what are the deepest social anxieties that are projected on to the 'nasty girl' today and what threat to social values does she represent? The authors argue that our culture associates young female offenders with feminism and that thus the moral panic over the 'nasty girl' is part of a backlash against feminism. Girl power is seen as the source of social anxieties, and 'the moral panic over the statistically insignificant nasty girl is a projection of a desire to retrieve a patriarchal social order characterized by gender conformity.'

The evidence for their analysis of the characterization of female deviance is provocative, especially the idea that the identification of deviance betrays deeper anxieties in society. However it should also be pointed out that this particular analysis of moral panic is weak. There is no sample for the media analysis, the statistical analysis of changes in crime trends is dismissed on dubious grounds, and there are no experts cited to criticize.

And as for whether the alarm about 'nasty girls' represents a backlash against feminism, well this article will convince those who accept its premises, but not those who require convincing evidence.

Source: Based on C. McCormick, 'Moral Panics and the "Nasty Girl" Syndrome' (Crime Matters column, *Daily Gleaner* (Fredericton), 27 September 2007.

State control. In this way, in feminism, as in much of the sociology of deviance since the work of Matza,[13] the sociological critique of positivism has generated much debate.[14]

In contrast, the apparent resilience of Lombrosian influences in the realm of female deviance and control has shown that feminist criminologists such as Smart and Heidensohn have read the main sources closely and attentively. Tedious as it may be to the jaded palate, the defects of criminological positivism have to be exposed once again, though this time with a female rather than a male subject as the target for concern. The work of Lombroso and Ferrero is not,[15] in the view of feminist criminologists, an antique intellectual curiosity, but a living body of thought which set an agenda that is still operative—the subordination of women to the view that female deviance is biological destiny, a view long since dispelled in the case of men.

The durability of the Lombrosian legacy in relation to female deviance is not simply due to its neglect as a topic; rather, it inheres in the long-standing prescriptions about the female role and the 'essence' of the nature of women in society. Lombroso and Ferrero accounted for their discovery of fewer signs of degeneration among female, by comparison with male, offenders by resorting to the view that 'as all women are relatively "primitive", the criminals amongst them would not be highly visible and would be less degenerate than their male counterparts.[16]

Citing their belief that the greater conservatism of women must be sought in the immobility of the ovule compared with the zoosperm, Smart criticizes their view that the female deviant was seen to have all the criminal qualities of the male plus all the worst characteristics of women, that is, cunning, spite, and deceitfulness. It could be that such scholars, when confronted with female deviance, confused sex and gender, and simply attributed masculine traits to female offenders, as was done later in the work of Pollak and others. The work of Cyril Burt[17] escapes Smart's net, but he tended to this view, referring to posing as 'masculine hobbledehoys' (awkward, bad-mannered adolescent boy) as typical of female delinquents. The early theorists, indeed, gave more coverage to female delinquency than those writing after the Second World War.

The combination of the 'worst of both sexes' led to attributions of a third abnormality in this conception of the born female criminal: the lack of a maternal instinct. In this respect, Lombroso and Ferrero reproduced in scientistic form the set of common-sense beliefs about female deviance that is exemplified in the popular detestation of Myra Hindley, the accomplice of Ian Brady in the notorious 'Moors Murders' of several children, or of Karla Homolka, the accomplice to Paul Bernardo in his serial sex murders. The majority of female offenders are not, however, so depicted; in fact, Lombroso and Ferrero viewed them as inferior criminals compared to the male, inadequate, and more easily caught. In this respect, Pollak[18] was later to take the opposite view while sharing the belief that female nature is the source of female deviance.

The Critique of Pollak

The work of Pollak so perfectly embodies what feminists critique that it might be said that, if it did not exist, it would have been necessary to invent it. Pollak's main empirical contention is that rates of female deviance are much the same as those of male deviance but appear far lower because of under-reporting, lower detection, and greater leniency in prosecution and sentencing: 'Men hate to accuse women and thus indirectly to send them to their punishment, police officers dislike to arrest them, district attorneys to prosecute them, judges and juries to find them guilty and so on.'[19]

None of these assertions is particularly outrageous (to men), and some self-report studies can be found to lend some credence to at least the basis of the first assertion, that the disparity between 'real' and official rates of crime is quite marked for first offences[20] and reduces the sex differential in general to two to one rather than several to one in respect of boys and girls. However, it was the manner of exposition and the nature of the theories he advanced that strained the credulity of successive generations of sociologists.

•*First, Pollak sought evidence of greater female criminality, mainly in domestic and employment spheres, using highly problematic sources* and ignoring the potential for 'masked' male criminality in these self-same contexts.

•*Second, he imputed to women the time-worn catalogue of vices,* such as cunning, deviousness, and deceit, as a way of accounting for the putative 'concealment' of their crimes.

•*Third, he located the ultimate source of legendary female deceitfulness in the woman's capacity to simulate sexual arousal.* Although he did give cultural factors some weight, Smart says: 'rather than considering the implications of the sexual politics which produce a situation in which many women endure intercourse when they are neither aroused nor acquiescent, Pollak takes the existence of a passive engagement in sexual activity as a basis of assumptions about women's ambiguous attitude towards honesty and deceit.'[21]

•*Fourth, he claimed in the 'chivalry' hypothesis that the police and courts deal leniently with women offenders.* This is seen as an acceptance of the deceptive view that women's nature is essentially passive, a myth used to justify women's inferior social status. Even though Pollak apparently recognized the darker side of chivalry and the possibility of scapegoating the 'fallen' woman, he neglects to incorporate these elements into his study. While Lombroso and Ferrero were at least working in sympathy with the grain of their time—a period that also saw the rise of eugenics and the widespread acceptance of social Darwinism[22]—Pollak's study bore no resemblance to the then burgeoning sociological theories of crime and delinquency.

Sutherland and Cressey pointed out in a dismissive reference to Pollak's work that he had made an earlier foray into the realm of hidden criminality among the aged.[23] However, a more pointed criticism is from Meda Chesney-Lind:

> It is clear that few women commit serious crimes and that those who violate the law do so largely out of desperation and in relatively minor ways. Women's general conformity to social norms is not mysterious not does it appear to be a product of 'femininity'; research indicates that women are closely monitored. The few women who escape domestic discipline find themselves confronting powerful correctional forces.
>
> The response of the criminal justice system to women's deviance falls far short of chivalrous despite rhetoric to the contrary. It is increasingly evident that both the construction of women's defiance and society's response to it are coloured by women's status as male sexual property. Once a female offender is apprehended, her behaviour is scrutinized for evidence that she is beyond the control of patriarchy and if this can be found she is harshly punished. For this reason, continued study of the role of women's punishment as criminals in the enforcement of female subservience seems vital. It is possible, for example, that definitions of and responses to women's deviance are informed by a concern that any success women have in challenging the bounds of domesticity might ultimately jeopardize the entire structure of women's oppression.[24]

Empirical work on the 'chivalrous' treatment of the female offender by the justice system has been done to ascertain whether such differential treatment occurs and what its nature is. Anderson investigated three characterizations of the female offender which have influenced the perpetuation and survival of the 'chivalry' proposition: the instigative female offender, the sexualized female offender, and the protected female offender. She came to the conclusion that researchers must view women as motivated by human needs in the same way as any deviant offender, rather than by sex-based needs. For example, in studying the economic motivations behind women's involvement in deviance, researchers have looked for ways in which women are different from her male counterpart, rather than look for similarities. She concludes that the notion of a 'chivalrous' justice system is largely a myth.[25]

The Critique of Thomas

A more formidable figure in the pantheon of sociologists critiqued by feminism is that of W.I. Thomas, author of such key interactionist insights as 'What men define as real is real in its consequences'. Applying that dictum to his study of female delinquency, *The Unadjusted Girl*,[26] feminist criminologists have found it to be depressingly accurate. For what Thomas defined as real was that the

> source of female criminality, which he believed to be mainly sexual, was the breakdown of the traditional restraints on women who formerly would not have thought of working outside the home or marrying outside the ethnic or community group. . . . Because they have been most repressed, therefore, Thomas argued that women are more likely to become 'maladjusted' when social sanctions are removed.[27]

On this basis, Thomas favoured the earliest possible intervention by welfare agencies into the lives of 'pre-delinquent' girls and resistance to further moves away from existing social relations. The more enduring legacy of his work is to be found in the impetus it gave to the focus on treating individual maladjustment so characteristic of social-work agencies and the shying away from any analysis of the structurally wrought constraints on improvements in women's social and economic situation. More damningly, Thomas is seen as the most authoritative link in the chain of sociologists who lend their voices to the resistance to female emancipation on the grounds that it would inevitably entail an increase in female deviance. This issue was later to become explicit in the work of Adler.[28]

The Break from Tradition

Contemporary studies of female criminality are divided into those that carry on the classical tradition of Lombroso and Ferrero, Thomas, and Pollak, with no fundamental change to the terms of reference they set; and those in the field of role theory, which takes the social differentiation of gender roles as the point of departure for analysis, thus breaking with the biological and psychological determinism of the classical tradition. Smart sees a marked continuity between the Lombrosian tradition and the study by Cowie, Cowie, and Slater,[29] which takes an institutionalized sample of girls as representative of delinquents; takes sex roles to be constitutionally predetermined; and reduces social and cultural factors to 'channels' for abnormal biological states. Chromosomes, rather than culture, are seen as the root of the problem. The work of Thomas is influential in the study by Konopka,[30] with its emphasis on liberal treatment strategies as the best response to female delinquency. Although sympathetic to the problems posed by poverty and unequal opportunities for women, it views those difficulties as secondary to personal maladjustment. Both fail to distinguish the biological variable of sex from the socially constructed and culturally fluid character of gender.

> Chromosomes, not culture, are the problem.

It was this crucial distinction between sex and gender that opened fresh possibilities within sociology. From the late 1960s, presaged by such pioneering works as Hannah Gavron's *The Captive Wife*,[31] a veritable flood of sociological work challenged taken-for-granted axioms about the nature, status, and role of women in contemporary society and tried with varying success to mount a feminist critique and alternative mode of study to covertly male chauvinist orthodoxy. Early work in this vein in sociology mapped out an agenda for the analysis of female deviance in terms of such factors as differential socialization, differential illegitimate opportunity structures, and differential reactions of society.[32]

Although focusing on such neglected topics as the extent to which the greater conformity of women may be attributable to quite different methods of socialization and supervision during childhood, and the generally subordinate character of their participation in deviance as reflecting their role and status in the social structure in general, Smart argues that work until the mid-1970s still lacked the capacity to 'situate the discussion of sex roles within a structural explanation of the social origins of those roles'.[33] Nor did it address the motivation of those women who did engage in deviance. She concluded by arguing that the time for a feminist analysis of deviance was ripe, but no precise shape could be given to its character. There was the clear risk of ghettoization on the one hand and tokenism on the other. Recognizing that a critique alone cannot constitute a new theoretical approach, she believed that further research was needed before the goal of a 'women's perspective' could be achieved on such questions as typical patterns of offending, the 'leniency' hypothesis, the treatment of female deviants, and the role of gender in the framing and execution of laws.

And if one thought it was unimportant how sociological theories conceptualize deviance, in a notable essay she says:

> The implications of theorizing have frequently been overlooked by those sociologists or criminologists who perceive themselves merely to be observers or recorders of everyday life. Yet social theories do have indirect social implications either by confirming common-sense and culturally located beliefs or by altering the consciousness of people in their everyday lives through a criticism and demystification of accepted values and beliefs.[34]

In a paper on feminism and the sociology of deviance in Britain, Gelsthorpe and Morris[35] took stock of what had been achieved in the decade following the publication of Smart's critique. Though much had been accomplished to redress the balance and undo the neglect of gender in the study of deviance and control, they assert that a single feminist criminology cannot exist. Just as we had to talk of 'feminisms' in sociology, it was important to delineate feminist perspectives within criminology. The shared concerns are the opposition to positivism, stereotypical images of women, the use of sympathetic methodologies, and the analytical centrality of gender and the subordination of women. The active pursuit of such concerns is far from transforming the subject; and the study of female criminality and its control, as well as the issue of gender in more general theories, faces constant problems of marginalization, incorporation, and tokenism.

Gelsthorpe and Morris, following Heidensohn,[36] regard existing theories as deformed by the almost unrelieved focus on the deviance of males and the invisibility or, at best, marginality of women and girls to the field. Nor can the situation be remedied by 'inserting' women into theories already formed on so patriarchal a basis: 'These critiques demonstrated that theories of criminality developed from and validated on men had limited relevance for explaining women's crime.'[37]

Heidensohn criticizes the sociology of deviance in general for neglecting gender in an assessment of the validity of the various theories.[38] However, Gelsthorpe and Morris answer that deviance theories have also neglected other variables, such as crimes of the powerful, and ethnicity. Such blind spots reflect themes which can be developed. Second, emptying such theories of their sexism does not render them valid since they can still be classist, or racist, or empirically unproved. Third, masculinity has also been subject to stereotyping, owing to the failure to consider that there might be varieties of masculinity and that males might be subject to discrimination as well. Fourth, variables mediating the significance of gender, such as class and race, tend to be ignored by feminist criminologists; the result is an exclusive focus on gender to the neglect of their interaction with those other factors. Fifth, sources of sexism tend to be analyzed as if they were one-dimensional and emanating from some global notion of men as hegemonic or from the capitalist mode of production as a patriarchal system. To some, the study of victimization is the sole area in which gender has transformed research,[39] though even here the emphasis is on the oppression of women and women's fear of crime, rather than their subordination to male domination as the source of that fear.[40]

Real achievements may, however, be more impressive than this self-appraisal from a feminist perspective might allow. Significant work has been done in four substantive areas: the 'female emancipation leads to crime' debate; the invalidation of the 'leniency' hypothesis; the emergence-from-within control theory of a gender-based theory of both male and female delinquency; and the raising to greater prominence of the female victim in political and academic analysis, a matter perhaps more properly reserved for victimology than sociology, which we shall touch on only lightly.

■ Female Emancipation and Crime

That females commit markedly fewer crimes than males, that their crimes are less serious, and that they are less likely to offend after the first conviction has been acknowledged by criminologists for most of the past century. In 1999, for example, only 15 per cent of those arrested and only 17 per cent of 'known offenders' in England and Wales were women.[41] Statistics Canada reported in 2008 that in Canada only one in five persons charged with a Criminal Code offence in 2005 were female. Furthermore, the rate of crime among females is about one-quarter the rate among males. For every 100,000 females aged 12 and older in 2005, about 1,100 were arrested for Criminal Code offences, compared to a rate of about 4,200 for males.[42]

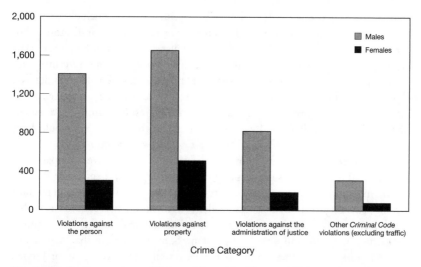

Figure 11.1: Comparison of Rates of Arrest for Men and Women, Canada, 2005

Source: Adapted from Statistics Canada publication *JURISTAT—Female Offenders in Canada,* Catalogue 85–002, Vol. 28, No. 1, Released 24 January 2008, page 3; http://www.statcan.ca/bsolc/ english/bsolc?catnop=85-002-x.

Recent work has suggested that women have a lower threshold of shame and guilt than men and are less prone to 'deviance disavowal' as a result.[43] Barbara Wootton wrote, in short, that 'if men behaved like women, the courts would be idle and the prisons empty'.[44]

Two sets of theories have addressed this difference quite explicitly. Subcultural theories have assumed that females pursue less deviant and more attainable goals than men, namely marriage and family life, and are therefore insulated from the social sources of delinquency, the main exception being the strain to sexual deviance. Control theories specify with some precision the far more intensive and extensive informal social controls that are brought to bear on girls compared to boys, controls that constitute powerful inhibitors against deviance. Insofar as female emancipation weakens or alters either or both sets of conditions, to that extent, it can be argued, females will converge with males in their exposure to criminogenic influences. The assertion that that has already happened as a result of the liberation movement, or that it will necessarily occur in the future if emancipation becomes greater than it is now, is strongly disputed by feminists. In view of the crude ideological battles that have been fought over the 'maternal deprivation' of delinquent children by working mothers,[45] it is not surprising that such a proposition should be fiercely challenged. For the 'female emancipation leads to more female crime' thesis offers a new guise for the same old double standard: the Angel in the House must not—for the sake of the social order—be allowed to 'fall'.

The thesis that the fall from grace has already begun and that both the extent and character of female crime have converged quite significantly with those of males has been argued by Adler[46] and Simon.[47]

In the most rigorous review of the available evidence, Box concludes that when trends in offending are properly related to social and economic indicators of liberation on the one hand and economic marginalization on the other, it is the latter which best accounts for the modest convergence in property-crime rates between the sexes. He concludes that the 'new violent' female offender is a myth.[48] Even the convergence in convictions for property crime can be seen as the effect of changes in arrest and prosecution practices resulting from the apparent changes in the criminality of women, though, on that basis, one would have expected as great, or greater, a rise in female rates of violent crime.

If it is indeed the economic marginalization of women over the past four decades that best accounts for property-crime convergence, then female emancipation in its most basic form has not occurred at all—a view that is held by most feminist sociologists. In that respect the debate remains open. It should be emphasized, however, that the 'emancipation causes more female crime' view assumes that structured inequalities are held constant. Some support for that view can be gleaned from one of the few studies of female as well as male youth cultural styles:

> The only real challenge to the mod boys' patriarchal power came from the new wave girls. Most importantly, the girls showed that they could see through the mod boys' public face rituals of exaggeration. . . . They were the only group of pupils who successfully opposed and countered the ritualistic patriarchal behaviour of the mods. . . . The new wave girls, through their spoken interactions and written communications, reverse the symbolic order of language; they demonstrate the denial of speech and then set about reclaiming the right to speak, define and know.[49]

When women are deviant, they pose the typical difficulty for feminist theorizing. Feminists have as much difficulty perhaps in addressing the issue of women's violence as male theorists have. The so-called Violence against Women movement in the 1970s focused feminist research on the widespread and pervasive nature of male violence against women. Male violence, which was a neglected topic in traditional 'deviantology' was seen as part of patriarchy, the structure and ideology that privileges men over women. To focus on that violence was to name the gendered nature of the victimization of women.

However, as a result, when the issue of violence by women began to be discussed in the 1990s, the difficulty was how to theorize it. Was women's use of violence a consequence of their own victimization experiences, such as in self-defence against an abusive partner (Lavallee), or perhaps a result of mental illness as in the case of Karla Homolka.

Comack and Brickey of the University of Manitoba conducted in-depth interviews with eighteen women who had committed acts of violence in order to discover these women's own understanding of their crimes. What they found was that the women had the greatest ability to articulate their experiences from the point of view of the victim, rather than that of the offender. However, they also rejected the role of the victim. On the other hand, they denied that their behaviour was due to mental illness. In some cases, as in this case:

> When a man made it obvious to her that he was going to force her to perform fellatio and that he had no intention of paying for it, Jennifer brandished the knife. In talking about the incident, Jennifer remarked how good it felt to finally be the one in control: 'He was really scared. And that's something that I wasn't used to, I was always the one being the victim, I was always the one that was in control of, and this time I was being in control.' After this incident, Jennifer regularly 'jacked up johns.'[50]

One lesson Comack and Brickey got from this research is that identity is not 'static or [single] but changing, multiple, and fractured.' The women have experienced a diversity of roles, as wives, mothers, daughters, friends, workers, and even robbers and prisoners, and their accounts are none the less complicated.[51]

■ Leniency and Control

The view that women and girls are treated more leniently for reasons of 'chivalry' or self-deception, proposed by Pollak but shared by others, has been refuted and in significant respects even reversed by a number of studies over the past twenty years.[52] In the most authoritative study of sentencing, Farrington and Morris[53] found that the lighter sentences passed on women offenders in a Cambridge court were accounted for by the nature of their offences and their previous convictions. Similar findings explained the greater proportion of females cautioned by the police.[54]

In a review of the evidence, Heidensohn[55] finds much support for the view that women are doubly punished when their rule breaking is compounded by perceived role breaking. Carlen's interviews with Scottish sheriffs[56] elicited views consonant with a dual morality that justifies imprisonment more readily for women offenders who have 'failed' as mothers. The Cambridge study found that divorced or separated women or those from 'deviant' family backgrounds were more likely to receive severe sentences. This holds open the possibility that women who conform to the conventional female role do benefit from judicial discretion, for which some support can be found.[57] Eaton[58] has found, however, that family and employment factors of mitigation are used in a similar way for males and females. But it is in the realms of 'protective' custody for non-criminal behaviour that dual morality looms largest: girls are far more likely than boys to be 'taken into care' for various kinds of misconduct, which may include truancy as well as sexual waywardness.[59]

More important, 'reverse sexism' shows that leniency is even more apparent in cases of domestic violence for men who victimize their female partners, where non-prosecution is the norm.[60] and in cases of corporate or white-collar crime, which women are rarely given the occupational opportunities to commit, but where non-prosecution of cases tends to be the norm. In these major respects, women—by comparison with men—are 'under-protected and over-controlled', a significant critique of the justice system.[61]

In the case of domestic violence, presumptive protocols for arrest in situations where there was assumed to have been an assault were not adopted in most Canadian provinces until about 1990. This followed the feminist criticism that police did not take domestic violence against women seriously.

Prostitution is perhaps the most notorious instance of 'double standards', with a long history of vilification by statute and stereotype. 'Common prostitutes' are seen as 'fallen' women, whereas men, whether they are prostitutes or clients, escape both forms of censure.[62] Despite the fact that there are more men involved in the buying and selling of sex than women, women are more likely to be thought of as prostitutes, and more likely to be prosecuted for prostitution related offences. Moreover, despite the strong economic incentives, in view of job discrimination, for women to become prostitutes, their motivation is usually considered to be psychogenic.

Discussion: Deviance and Culture—The Media and Prostitution

In 2006, the *Canadian Review of Sociology and Anthropology* went beyond standard depictions of prostitution as deviant by publishing a series of articles that presented a different view of the trade. One article, 'Fallen Women and Rescued Girls', examines media portrayals of people who work in the sex industry. The authors' aim was to understand how the media contribute to constructing and reproducing social stigmas associated with working in prostitution.

The analysis draws upon media discussion of the sex industry in Victoria, British Columbia, between 1980 and 2004 as represented in the regional daily newspaper, the *Victoria Times Colonist*. The newspaper's subject index was used to find 425 articles concerning the sex industry. The researchers developed seven narrative categories: 'vectors of contagion, population at risk or endangered, sexual slavery, moral culpability, predatory pimps, criminal culpability, community failure, and other.'

For most people, who are unlikely ever to encounter sex-trade workers, the media are their main source of information about sex work. Unfortunately, the media are also also a source of misinformation, for it is here that stigmas of sex work are produced and consumed.

However, it is important to underscore the fact that the mainstream media are 'structurally embedded within hegemonic moral, economic and political orders.' The news is told from a particular social point of view, which corresponds with positions of moral, economic, and political power. For this reason, using a cultural-studies approach allows us to pay attention to the role of power in the media and how it is pivotal in the transmission of knowledge and values.

With prostitution, there is a social stigma that is part of the normative knowledge about the sex trade. This stigma reduces the sex-trade worker from a whole person to a tainted one. This stigma becomes the reality for the public, and also it can become internalized by the person. The identity of the self incorporates the interpretation of the self available within the media.

In the study, it was found that sex-industry workers are portrayed as vectors of contagion, that is, as moral pollutants or as sources of disease. The dominant media motif was gendered, with virtually all the media coverage focusing on women (as adults, teenagers, and children) and that men appeared infrequently and only as clients, pimps, or law enforcers.

There were thematic shifts over the study period. After the late 1980s, the assigning of criminal culpability to sex-industry workers disappeared and responsibility moved toward clients, pimps, and the 'global sex trade'. However, between 1980 and 1990, media discussion centres frequently on the risk of physical contagion posed by prostitutes and on the need for 'spatial containment solutions'.

Table 11.2: Discussions of the Sex Industry in the *Times Colonist* (Victoria), 1980–2004

Theme	1980–1990 N=115	1990–2000 N=182	2001–2004 N=128
Vectors of contagion	43 (37%)	51 (28%)	25 (20%)
Risk	0	33 (18%)	45 (35%)
Sexual slavery	0	27 (15%)	31 (24%)
Moral culpability	17 (15%)	18 (10%)	0
Community failure	19 (17%)	11 (6%)	0
Predatory pimps	0	42 (23%)	6 (5%)
Criminal culpability	30 (26%)	0	0
Other	6 (5%)	0	21 (16%)

Source: H. Hallgrimsdottir et al., 'Fallen Women and Rescued Girls', 270.

The authors make the point that these (mediated) rhetorical practices about risk tell us how the (media's) narrative conventions sustain social stigmas. For example, it is argued that the consequence of the coverage of the Vancouver police department's investigation of the 'women missing from Vancouver's East Side who were struggling with drug addiction and involved in the sex trade' was (unintentionally) to reassure the readers that the risk was far removed from them.

It is argued that the public relies on culturally available scripts about gender, sexuality, and morality in part (obviously it seems) because it lacks the experience with which to know the experience of others and then (as second-order knowledge) to judge the credibility and truthfulness of media narratives.

Cultural scripts (already present within the society) organize media narratives by directing what is considered newsworthy, so that 'media attention is paid to the titillating and illicit aspects of trading sex for money, while its less glamorous, ordinary reality is ignored'. At the same time, these narratives 'thus place the worker at the margins of society, as the stigmatized other, and direct the moral obligations of the audience in particular ways: abandoning fallen women and rescuing lost girls.'

Source: Adapted from H. Hallgrimsdottir et al., 'Fallen Women and Rescued Girls: Social Stigma and Media Narratives of the Sex Industry in Victoria, BC, from 1980 to 2005', llgrimsdottir 265–80.

■ Gender, Crime, and Social Control

The study of gender and control in two notable studies by Hagan, Simpson, and Gillis[63] addresses the relations between gender, crime, and social control through a synthesis of control and conflict theories of deviance. This is not a feminist theory per se, but a control theory that address notions of gender; that is why it is included here.

Case Study—Power-Control Theory

The first study by Hagan, Simpson, and Gillis, which was based on data gathered from a mixed-sex sample of several hundred Toronto high school adolescents, tested and explored the theory that the self-reported rates of delinquency both within and between males and females would be linked to differentials in socialization and informal social control: 'There is a sexually stratified inverse relationship between structurally differentiated processes of social control such that women are more frequently the instruments and objects of informal social controls.'[1]

Segregative formal control is seen as emerging with industrialization, with the site for informal social control increasingly confined to the private realm of the home,[2] from which men are increasingly absent and in which women are more and more frequently sequestered. Men became subject to formal social control, while women did not. The larger exclusion of women from the economic sphere and their lower crime rate are thus jointly rooted in family-based patterns of informal social control. It was stressed that informal social control in the home is not synonymous with less control, but probably with more. And since even career women tend to inherit the responsibility for the care and control of children, intergenerationally transmitted gender roles flow from the earliest experiences.

The data bore out the hypotheses that subjecting girls to a dense array of informal social controls, primarily mediated by their mothers, would ensure greater compliance; while young males are freed to pursue more active forms of risk taking, with the consequence that they are more likely to encounter the world of formal control. Males more than females defined risk-taking positively, defined delinquency more positively, and engaged in delinquency more often and more seriously. On this basis, Hagan, Simpson and Gillis conclude that, accurate as Dennis Wrong's critique of functionalist sociology may be with regard to men, women are, in effect, over-socialized.

A crucial omission in the study was the interaction between sexual and social stratification, an omission that is rectified in their second study,[3] which was carried out on a similar sample in Toronto. Drawing more fully on a neo-Marxian class analysis than is usually the case, they differentiate four groups in the stratification order: employers, managers, employed workers, and unemployed workers. The power variable was therefore entered into the frame as well as control variables. Class was found to be unrelated to the common forms of delinquency measured, with the predicted exception that the children of employers were reportedly the most delinquent, being highest on power and least fettered by both formal and informal controls. Introducing gender revealed a decrease in the relationship between gender and common forms of delinquency with each step down the class structure.

In sum, as Bonger asserted in 1916, differences in the way of life between the sexes are at their height in the upper reaches of society[4] and at their minimum in the lower working class. Among children of parents excluded from the labour market, delinquency approached unity by gender once parental controls are taken into account. The most serious forms of delinquency are not adequately covered by the early research design, but they are so uncommon that adequate sampling across all social groups would scarcely be feasible.

Reiss and Rhodes established over forty years ago that type of community was a key variable in delinquency rates:[5] working-class delinquency rates tended to increase with the class homogeneity. What such work should stimulate is a redressing of the balance in respects other than gender alone and by methods other than self-reported delinquency alone, in particular, the filling of the gap in ethnographies of 'employer class' crime and delinquency.

[1] 'The Sexual Stratification of Social Control', 25.

[2] Strong historical support for that argument has subsequently been provided by Malcolm Feeley, 'The Decline of Women in the Criminal Process: A Comparative History' and 'The Vanishing Female: The Decline of Women in the Criminal Process, 1687–1912'.

[3] J. Hagan et al., 'The Class Structure of Gender and Delinquency'.

[4] Well caught in Flaubert's parody: '*Young gentleman*: Always sowing wild oats; he is expected to do so. Astonishment when he doesn't. *Young lady*: Utter these words with diffidence. All young ladies are pale, frail and always pure. Prohibit, for their good, every kind of reading, all visits to museums, theatres and especially to the monkey house at the zoo.' (J. Barzun, tr., *Flaubert's Dictionary of Accepted Ideas*, 84.)

[5] A. Reiss and A. Rhodes, 'The Distribution of Juvenile Delinquency in the Social and Class Structure'.

In a number of studies, Pat Carlen advanced the analysis of the links between forms of female deviance and social regulation by pointing to the ways in which the lives of female offenders in Britain seem to have been associated with early ruptures in domestic social control.[64] Women deviants, she claims, come from among the poorest and the least powerful of all social groups. They are disproportionately black or working-class, and many were abandoned by their families in childhood. Such women are disproportionately likely to have been placed in institutional care, where they were free from family bonds and the customary restraints of gender. They have shrugged off what she calls the 'gender deal', the array of quasi-contractual understandings that routinely control the boundaries and character of femininity in a patriarchal society. As women with radically impaired life chances, they have also shrugged off the 'class deal', the understandings about effort and reward that bind men and women to the conventional labour market. Doubly free, they can deviate in ways denied to the traditionally fettered woman.

Of late, work is beginning to suggest that the trend towards the erosion of gender difference has advanced in ways that are particularly significant for delinquency, control, and gender relations. In particular, Hagan and his colleagues conjecture that the decline of male work and the rise of female work have brought about a transformation in patterns and models of domestic control. There has been, they argue, a move away from patriarchal dominance:

Women . . . have become agents of change in the gender schemas that surround work and the family. As these gender schemas are diminished or discarded in families where mothers have gained occupational power . . . adolescent males may benefit less from this [process of] capitalization and still remain at greater risk of involvement in delinquency. The implication is that the male subculture of delinquency is a residue of the former hegemony of a patriarchal power structure. In this sense, male subcultural delinquency may be a vestigial social trait, making male subcultural delinquents the social dinosaurs of a passing, more patriarchal era.[65]

■ Feminism and the Female Victim

Victims of crime were almost wholly neglected by sociologists of deviance until the mid-1970s, when the women's movement began to focus on the victim of rape and domestic violence,[66] women's refuges,[67] and rape crisis centres.[68]

Scholarly work followed; it was at first set largely within the frame established by the politics and ideology of the activists. That is, violence against women was represented as a problem hidden in the private recesses of the domestic sphere; it was a mirror of patriarchal oppression; it was a gendered phenomenon centred on male power and female subordination that could not be compared with the victimization of men; and attempts to introduce it into the public domain were met by parallel patriarchal and oppressive responses that brought about the 'secondary victimization' of the woman complainant by the criminal justice system.[69] At its loosest, the word 'victim' was stretched to embrace the female offender, who was taken in effect to be a casualty of domination acting protectively against repeated male abuse.[70] The outcome has been that there is now a copious body of writing about the experiences of women victims as they confront crime and its aftermath.[71]

Case Study—Theorizing Public Housing and Woman Abuse

In their study of woman abuse in public housing, DeKeseredy and Schwarz argue that while physical, sexual, and psychological abuse of women in intimate relationships occurs in all sociodemographic groups, women who are socially and economically marginal report higher rates of such victimization.

They also argue that there is an absence of in-depth theoretical work on how woman abuse is related to class. On this basis, they develop an economic exclusion/male peer support model of woman abuse in public housing.

In the last several decades, the rate of urban poverty has increased significantly in both Canada and the United States, exacerbating social pathologies such as drug dealing and interpersonal violence. There has been a decline of manufacturing jobs and a shift to a service economy, the proportion working full-time has decreased, inner-city poverty has increased, and rates of those living in public housing who cannot afford alternatives has increased.

Despite an increase in research on social problems in North American urban communities, not much social scientific attention has been devoted to studying and theorizing male physical, sexual, and psychological assaults on women who live in impoverished neighbourhoods. Male-to-female victimization is more common among those who live in these marginalized locations, and thus it is important to recognize class differences in woman abuse.

The Quality of Neighborhood Life Survey, administered to residents of six public housing developments in the west end of a metropolitan centre in Canada, used a modified version of the Conflict Tactics Scale to elicit data on female victimization in intimate relationships. About 19 per cent stated that in the year before the study they were harmed in a way which could be measured by the scale. Significantly, this figure is higher than that found by standard large-scale US and Canadian woman abuse surveys.

DeKeseredy (of the University of Ontario's Institute of Technology) and Schwarz use a theoretical model as a 'heuristic' to explain the role of economic exclusion and patriarchal male peer support (see Figure 11.2). This model incorporates the macro-social: recent major economic transformations in North America, such as the shift from a manufacturing to a service-based economy, which displaces working class men and women who often end up in urban public housing.

The model also incorporates the micro-social: these men are unable to support their families and live up to their culturally defined role as breadwinner. As a result, these now marginalized men experience high levels of stress because their normal paths to personal power and prestige have been cut off. The stress in turn prompts them to seek social support from male peers with similar problems, which while helping them manage their stress, may also have negative consequences because for men with high levels of stress, social ties with abusive peers have been found to be strongly related to woman abuse in some situations.

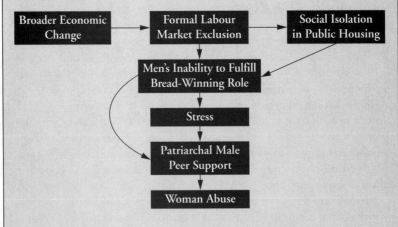

Figure 11.2: Economic Exclusion/Male Peer Support Model

Their research offers a theoretical model that combines both the macro and micro-level factors. And unlike most other woman-abuse theories developed so far, it attempts to explain how broader economic changes in recent decades contribute to woman abuse and to theorize how all-male social networks can perpetuate woman abuse.

Source: Abridged from W. DeKeseredy and M. Schwartz, 'Theorizing Public Housing Woman Abuse as a Function of Economic Exclusion and Male Peer Support'.

Such an introduction of female victims to sociology was to have important repercussions for policy and analysis. As we have shown, it galvanized radical sociology and laid part of the foundations for the emergence of left realism. But there was always a strain between sociology and the feminism that had sponsored the rediscovery of the female victim. It was a strain born not only of the more general tension between the practical engagement of the activist who talked of 'survivors' and the more distant stance of the academic who tended to talk of 'victims', but also of the moralization of the subject, which made it difficult to examine the role played by female victims in criminal transactions.[72]

For example, victim precipitation, a term used to describe how victims could unintentionally initiate an unwelcome encounter, was called 'victim blaming' by Clarke and Lewis, who charged that 'victim blaming has become institutionalized within the academic world under the guise of victimology.'[73] The theory of victim precipitation was meant to identify passive characteristics of victims that set them up for assault, or more active behaviour that could instigate an encounter. However, when women deviants were themselves identified as the casualties and victims of patriarchy, it could become even more difficult to analyze the processes and phenomena of female offending with any scholarly disinterest.[74]

More generally, work in feminist sociology has now started to evolve in two principal directions, reflecting the fundamental division in all social science between the 'empirical' and the 'theoretical'.

•*One wing has increasingly moved from declaratory manifestos and 'immanent critiques' towards empirical studies* of the history and sociology of women, deviance, and control. To be sure, there have been such studies before (many having been inexplicably neglected in the formal feminist history of the discipline), but exegesis and criticism are now being supplemented by a wave of original studies that reflect, in part, the growing number of women who have entered the field.[75]

•*Another wing, as much sociology as feminism perhaps, has added descriptively to what is known about women, deviance, and control.* Campbell, for instance, has explored the extent and character of female delinquency and found no support for Albert Cohen's view that it is predominantly sexual. Rather, it is manifest across the range of offences, though with much lower prevalence than is the case for males in all but a few offences, such as shoplifting.[76] Nor are girls so resistant to becoming gang members as has often been assumed; but within the gang, they can be seen to play roles reflective of the subordinate and supportive female role in the wider society.[77]

Miller's *Street Woman*[78] is a sensitive piece of ethnographic research on the orderly careers of prostitutes in a North American city. Miller recounts how, as a matter of course, young women in segments of the black community take to the streets for a time while their children are tended by grandmothers who were prostitutes themselves in their day. In due course, Miller remarks, the women will move from the streets back to domesticity to look after their prostitute daughters' children in their turn. The pattern is repeated from generation to generation, only interrupted if the women become so addicted to drugs that they cannot return to the more or less conventional world.

Heidensohn's *Women in Control*[79] examines how women in Britain and North America manage the daunting project of 'breaking into' the solitary male world of police officers.[80] Women, she says, are subject to unusual and severe tests before they can prove themselves. Acceptance may depend on passing strategic tests of character and ability. The successful woman, like Cinderella, undergoes a 'transformation scene' that confirms her as a deserving insider.

Zedner's *Women, Crime and Custody in Victorian England*[81] narrates how moral definitions of female deviance gave way to scientific explanations invoking biology and psychology under the spell of Darwin and the medicalization of social problems. Zedner argues that women were less often considered to have a capacity for reason and rational choice, their deviance viewed as pathology, their character being described as mad rather than bad.

And Taylor examined the lives of women drug addicts in Glasgow that were organized, in part, around the distinctively feminine problems of managing pregnancy and raising children.[82]

•*Feminists have also begun to move beyond an insistent focus on women alone to ask larger questions about gender*, about the deviance and control of *men*, and about the different treatment of men and women in the justice system.[83] As Tim Newburn and Betsy Stanko observe, 'the most significant fact about crime is that it is almost always committed by men'.[84] Because men offend often and women do not, the links between crime and gender have engaged the sociologist's attention.

The differential exercise of control has been the target of one kind of analysis, the social construction of gender another. Of particular influence in some of the newer work has been Robert Connell's conceptions of 'hegemonic' (or accredited) and 'subordinated' (or discredited) masculinities, a conception based loosely on the writings of Gramsci, which stresses how certain models of maleness can attain ideological and cultural ascendancy. Power, wealth, and personal strength are some of the components of the hegemonic pattern. Without very much empirical evidence, but nevertheless with some plausibility, Connell points to Sylvester Stallone, Muhammed Ali, and John Wayne as examples of a version of tough masculinity which leads to 'practices that institutionalize men's dominance over women'.[85] They are authoritative prototypes, or embodied scripts, that delineate appropriate actions and relations.

Why hasn't criminology studied why crime is committed by men?

Connell did not write extensively about crime and criminals in *Gender and Power*, but it is evident that an ideal of rough, muscular maleness has a strong affinity with the patterns of behaviour that are associated with assaults, domestic violence, street crime, and the like. That idea is reproduced in schools,[86] on the streets, and on and around the sports field;[87] it legitimates the use of violence; and it explains some of the transactions that unfold between men and women. As Kersten argues in an article in a special issue of the *British Journal of Criminology* devoted to 'Masculinities, Social Relations and Crime', 'such constructs of 'good' or 'real' masculinities are subject to both the self-definition of deviant 'outlaw' masculinities and the construction of the criminal offender and (even more pronouncedly) to the image of the 'gang' as the collective 'other'.[88]

In the same issue of the journal, Bourgois explains the extremes of violence directed by Puerto Rican crack dealers against women in New York City as part of an effort to protect threatened claims to masculine supremacy in an economic environment marked by the rise of female employment and the decline of male employment.[89] It is a matter of defending traditional conceptions of male face, identity, or pride against new attacks, and that is a theme much rehearsed in the work centred on crime and gender. Polk, for example, has argued that many instances of working-class men killing other working-class men in Australia must be referred to attempts to uphold a precarious but highly valued masculine honour.[90]

The other wing would deflect attention away from the deviant woman to urge the ending of what has just begun. Just as an earlier generation did not wish to endanger the politics of race by looking too closely at the links between blacks and deviance (other than in connection with the unjust criminalization of blacks and the racism of the justice system),[91] so have some feminists argued that no good purpose can be served by exploring the deviance of women or reducing rule breaking by women and the stigmatization and punishment of the woman rule breaker. A feminist sociology of deviance, it has been argued, is prone to 'correctionalism' and collusion with patriarchy,[92] being used as an instrument *against* women.

The grand theorists, in some measure like their Marxist[93] or phenomenological[94] forebears, would claim that a preoccupation with the empirical detail of female deviance belittles and circumscribes what should be a larger project altogether, the study of women under patriarchy. The deviant woman is an ideologically generated category that restricts its subject. Feminists, they say, should move beyond such limited entities to their own distinctive terrain[95] to becoming, as Young put it, 'producers of their own discourse, instead of being the mere receivers of a masculinist master discourse'.[96] Like others before them, it would seem, the feminist grand theorists are quitting the empirical and substantive field of sociology for a more elevated plane of systematic reasoning about the social world.[97] Carol Smart, for instance, wrote about how, 'as feminist theory is increasingly engaging with and generating postmodern ideas, the relevance of criminology to feminist thought diminishes. . . . It should be stressed, of course, that this is not exactly a novel exercise. Criminology seems to be *the* enterprise that many scholars desert or reject.'[98]

■ Criticism

Many feminist sociologists have gone much further than deploring the neglect of female deviance and have moved toward theorizing and defining priorities to remedy past omissions. Some have made the issue a criterion for the validity or invalidity of sociological theory; as Box and Harris say, 'any causal explanation of crime which does not include gender-related factors cannot be valid.'[99] Gelsthorpe and Morris[100] argue that 'Theories are weak if they do not apply to half of the potential criminal population; women, after all, experience the same depriva- tions, family structures and so on, that men do. Theories of crime should be able to take account of the behaviour of both men and women and to highlight those factors which operate differently on men and women.' And Heidensohn stated, 'Criminology is poorer in all its forms [because it has] not yet fully accepted and integrated the importance of gender, or its interaction with such factors as race and class.'[101]

Central as its role should be in the sociology of deviance, the impulses behind theorizing are diverse, and they are ultimately irrelevant to the criteria that gov- ern the evaluation of its validity. Deviancy theory has tended to focus on subjects who are predominantly white, urban, lower-class, and usually adolescent males in advanced industrial capitalist societies. The focus was chosen primarily because of who the main offenders were.

It seemed to successive generations of sociologists, particularly in the post-war context of increasing affluence, that common-sense and psychogenic explana- tions were most deficient in explaining the extent and character of delinquency among this sector of the population. In the process, the criminality and/or greater conformity of every other group became marginalized or explained away; not only females, but also ethnic minorities, the middle-aged and elderly, rural com- munities, the middle and upper classes, corporations, and both State socialist and developing countries were neglected as subjects. It is a massive catalogue of neglected topics.

It may well be that the crime-led character of 'deviantology' was profoundly mistaken, being based on a misconception of what constituted deviance (a reval- uation began systematically only with the emergence of labelling theory in the early 1960s. And the questions posed may have been too inattentive to the under- lying problem of order. That was the task consigned to mainstream sociological theory, though the Gluecks and control theorists took it as their point of entry into the field. The possibilities opened up by these approaches have already enlarged the scope of the study of female deviance in particular and the signifi- cance of gender for deviance and control more generally.

The theories whose character we have tried to convey in preceding chapters have, in our view, something to offer in the pursuit of the concerns of feminist criminologists.[102] Matza's concept of 'drift' is *a priori* as applicable to female as to male subjects. The concepts of 'labelling', 'career', 'stigma', and the like should be as fruitful for the understanding of female deviance as that of males. In terms of substantive theories, Albert Cohen did not preclude girls from subcultural formations, though he may have assumed too readily that his formulations of cause and effect did not apply at all to females and that sexual deviancy exhausted their repertoire. The 'manufacture of excitement' is as germane to an understanding of female as of male delinquency.[103] The differences in crime rates by age and sex remain central to theorizing delinquency. However, the existing theories as to why that should be so have not been supplanted by our greater awareness of the oppression of women, on the contrary, that has tended to reinforce their premises.

Much theory is a movable feast. A number of the older, apparently male-centred theories have a good deal of utility in explaining female deviance. Elaine Player, for example, found anomie theory the most satisfactory framework for explaining female burglary and robbery.[104] And, some research has pointed to how young women use violence for the same reasons young men attack young men, citing the need to elicit 'respect'.[105]

Robert Agnew has found that female delinquency may be influenced more by interpersonal strain; and Berger has discussed the role strain inherent in females' attempts to negotiate ambiguous or contradictory gender roles.[106] These are only two examples of the variety of research that has attempted to modify and extend traditional deviance theorizing to account for gender.

It may well be that male-centred theories work for women or that they need to be modified. Matza uses the masculine pronoun throughout his work, but his archetypal deviants in *Becoming Deviant* were all women. Consider, too, the difficulties confessed to by Lyn Lofland, herself a woman, who was writing in 1973 at just about the time when those literary conventions were under challenge:

As to sex, I have attempted to avoid as much as possible the use of the term 'man' to stand for all human beings. I have also attempted to avoid excessive use of the pronouns 'he,' 'his,' and 'him' when referring to both men and women. Neither attempt has been particularly successful. Stylistic convention makes 'man,' 'he,' 'him,' and 'his' difficult words to avoid. At one point, I considered substituting 'woman,' 'she,' 'her,' and 'hers' in all the appropriate places, but finally decided that female chauvinism is no improvement over the male variety. In addition, in reading over a sentence or paragraph where I had made such a substitution, I found that, because of the strangeness of the phrasing, the words drew attention to themselves and even I lost track of what was being said.[107]

Lofland and Matza clearly did not intend the masculine pronoun to refer solely and exclusively to men. Women were included in their analysis, but language may have masked what was said. And they were not alone. Theirs was a common difficulty at the time.[108] This raises the question of whether feminists are right in asserting that sociology has so markedly ignored women.

Perversely, it also raises the question of whether the growing literary convention of using only feminine pronouns in the third person singular should be interpreted as excluding all *males* from analysis. One distinguished exemplar of this practice is Richard Ericson, who insists on the feminine pronoun throughout his more recent writing, even referring to an ideal-typical Hells Angel as a 'she'.[109] Are we, one wonders, to take it that all Hells Angels are women or that 'masculine' theories of crime and control do not apply to them? Nor is the overt neglect of female criminality and the significance of gender quite as marked as the critiques insist. Heidensohn[110] and Morris[111] in Britain and Mann[112] in the United States, have written texts that omit to mention Paul Cressy's *The Taxi-Dance Hall* and Reckless's *Vice in Chicago*. Pauline Morris's *Prisoners and Their Families* somehow escapes attention in what is defined as uncharted territory. Willis's alleged attachment to the glamour of machismo, which is a general shortcoming of male sociologists according to Heidensohn, was accompanied by an unrivalled ability to situate the sexism and racism of his subjects.[113] Such persistent defects mar an otherwise powerful case.

Take two arguments about the impact of certain theories of female crime. It is claimed that the neglect of the positivist remainder in the field of female deviance has had untoward consequences in the treatment of female offenders. This may be so, but the proposition is as yet almost wholly unsupported by evidence; and male offenders are not totally exempt from positivist measures. The jump has been made, for example, from turn-of-the-century Lombrosianism to the 'new' therapeutic Holloway prison for women, or improvements to Canada's prisons for women, but the mediating links are not supplied.[114] On the contrary, the significance of gender and the particular plight of women prisoners is more complex than any straightforward, unilinear history of ideas might suggest. Policy questions are mediated by the political problems of how arguments could be used to best advantage in a bureaucratic environment. The pragmatism of policy-making does not require officials and politicians to make a decision about the real character of female offenders. Neither did they demand unanimity. And it is certainly the case that the name Lombroso does not appear at all in any of the papers or arguments underpinning the development of women's prisons in Britain or Canada. Beverley Brown argued:

> [The] theme in feminist criminology has been, crudely, that traditional criminology is the theory, Holloway [Prison]—especially its psychiatric wing—the practice. An additionally cohesive force is added by feminist criminology's emphasis on the monotonous repetition of criminology's view of the female offender, a few basic themes reiterated from the opening shots fired in 1895 by Lombroso and Ferrero's *The Female Offender*. . . . To invoke this rhetoric is to invoke that powerful and epiphanous moment in which feminist criminology was announced, a moment of foundation and denunciation, indeed foundation-by-denunciation, when feminist criminology could simply constitute itself as *Critique*.[115]

> Conditions changed for women inmates in Canadian prisons after the Arbour Commission report.

Despite these criticisms, the feminist analysis of deviance, broadly defined as women's perspectives within sociology,[116] has significantly reoriented the field. All paradigms are anomalies transformed into novel focus. For feminist studies, the absence of gender, long acknowledged as regrettable, but easily lived with, has inspired the fresh insight that theories of male deviance do not readily fit the facts of female deviance. The sociology of deviance can only benefit from addressing more creatively the question of why the oppression of women has not led to rates of deviance as high as those of males.

All new paradigms transform the banal into fresh focus. Radical sociology retrieved, but then threw away, the failure to study the crimes of the powerful; labelling theorists built on the truism that 'deviant behaviour is that which is so labelled'; control theorists asked if the real question may be 'Why don't we all deviate?'; subcultural theorists looked for motives and meaning in that which was considered 'mindless'; functionalists perceived the sources of conformity in deviance; and the Chicagoans saw that deviant traditions were inescapably social and not products of individual pathology.

Feminist criminology may or may not be a new paradigm in this sense, but it has undeniably revitalized the exploration of existing perspectives.

Chapter Summary

This chapter has looked at some of the feminist critiques of the traditional sociology of deviance and some of the subsequent feminist contributions to the field. We have gone from a discipline where gender did not matter and women were slighted to one where now both genders are studied and masculinity can be a subject of study.

Critical-Thinking Questions

1. Three notables in the history of deviance—Lombroso, Pollack, and Thomas—are selected for criticism by feminist scholars. Pick one, and explain what the criticism is.
2. The feminist critique centres on several questionable claims about female deviance. Pick one, and explain what the criticism is.
3. How has it been suggested that the connection between masculinity and deviance needs to be looked at more closely? Can we extend feminist theorizing to studying male criminality?
4. In a discussion feature, it is suggested that morality is often central to the identification of female deviants because women are supposed to be guardians of the moral sphere. Discuss the significance of how social-purity movements treated (working-class) women who used their sexuality to survive and tried to rescue 'fallen women' and delinquent girls.

Explorations in Film

Though *Thelma and Louise* is an overrated film, it's worth a quick look. The movie features Susan Sarandon as a waitress who persuades her friend, Geena Davis, to hit the road with her for a weekend of freedom. They are fed up with their partners and want to have some fun. One of their first stops is a bar, where the women dance and flirt with some of the locals. When one man tries to rape Thelma in the parking lot, Louise shoots him. They are convinced that the police will never believe their version, and so they take off, fugitives from the law. It's overdone and is by no means a declaration of the emancipation of women, but it's a good victims-take-justice-into-their-own-hands movie.

Websites

http://www.orcc.net/
The Ottawa Rape Crisis Centre (ORCC), which first opened in 1974, was the third such centre in Canada; others had been established in Toronto and Vancouver

Chapter Twelve

Deviance Theories and Social Policy

- ■ Chapter Overview
- ■ Introduction
- ■ The Relationship between Theory and Policy
  - • *Case Study: Canadian Victim Survey*
- ■ Pulling It All Together: Cases
  - • The Case of the Chicago School
  - • *Case Study: An Applied Study of Social Disorganization Theory*
  - • The Case of the Functionalist Theories
  - • The Case of Anomie Theory
  - • The Case of Marxist Theory
  - • The Case of Interactionist Theory
  - • *Case Study: Juvenile Justice Legislation*
  - • The Case of Control Theory
  - • *Case Study: The Priorities Estates Project*
  - • The Case of Feminism
  - • The Case of Phenomenology
- ■ Conclusions
- ■ Chapter Summary
- ■ Critical-Thinking Questions
- ■ Websites

Chapter Overview

In this chapter we look at the various theories of deviance that have been examined in this book and consider how they have contributed to discussions of social policy. Priority is given to tested demonstrations of policy development over statements of policy directives. We attempt to assess the relations between theories of deviance and their implications for politics and policy-making with this considerations in mind. Examples are cited from Britain, the United States, Canada, Australia, and other Western countries.

■ Introduction

In general, sociologists spend most of their time and energy on teaching and research, where the objectives are a greater understanding of the social world. Some work in politics or in the making of social policy, but their attention to this aspect of their work is usually cursory because of several factors: role definition, translatability, and salience.

• *First, role definition, implies a division of labour in which sociological teaching and research take priority.* The rigorously academic may simply reject the pursuit of competing priorities such as politics and policy-making. These activities have their own practitioners in other departments or in other institutions who can make use of sociological research. The simple distinction is between 'pure' and 'applied' science. However, in a more complicated way sociologists may actively resist the agenda setting that a concern for 'social problems' implies. 'Sociological problems' do not necessarily coincide with 'social problems'. What sociology likes to study and what society defines as a problem are two different things. To force the former into a mould formed by the latter would be as absurd as to yoke astronomy to the tasks of space exploration.

> Social problems are not always sociological problems.

• *Translatability refers to the differences between the 'systems of relevance'[1] of sociology and social policy.* Sociological discourse, which uses what Schutz termed 'second-order constructs', is quite distinct from the discourse of policy-makers, who use first-order constructs embedded in the natural attitude of everyday life. Sociological theories differ greatly in their receptivity to the constructs of everyday life. In the case of theories that address the social functions of deviance or the phenomenological analysis of the meaning of anomie, the implications for social policy may be non-existent. However, it is easier to see the relevance of suggestions for how to tackle vandalism through situational crime prevention.

All theories of deviance have implications for policy. However, the extent to which theories are taken up in practice depends only in part on the energy and commitment of the theorist, the degree of empirical support for the theory, or the ease with which the theory can be translated into policy terms.

• *The salience of a theory for policy-makers may have as much to do with the extent and forms of knowledge which officials and politicians have of theory*, the consonance between theory and the practical work of government, the scope of the proposals for action, the resources needed, the extent to which significant interests are engaged as parties or adversaries, and the likely ratio of costs to benefits. Even these factors are likely to be secondary to the correspondence between the theory and the policy-makers' timetables and political platform.

■ The Relationship between Theory and Policy

What is evident, however, is the contingent nature of the relationship between theory, research, and policy.

•*First, and very often, what concerns the politician and policy official is not the academic solidity of a theory but its political relevance.* For instance, the Canadian government's Justice for Victims of Crime Initiative was addressed quite explicitly to the needs of elderly and female victims of crime.[2] Those victims were established by government priorities, not by research, but in view of the Canadian political scene in the early 1980s, a victims' initiative could not have neglected them. It would have been naïve to imagine that an initiative could have been based simply on the findings of victimological research.

The language and emphasis of policy documents and political arguments are not constructed as parts of an academic discourse that is shaped by questions of methodology, evidence, and intellectual pedigree. On the contrary, their nuances flow from concerns about constituencies and the practicalities of implementation. There will sometimes be consultation with experts, and sometimes theory and research will have the effect of discouraging officials from supporting recommendations that experts consider to be naive, discredited, or impracticable.

•*Second, and more generally, theory and research will tend to be a rhetorical resource to cite when needed.* It is always useful to show that proposals are well anchored, even if the demonstration is retroactive. In that process of formulating proposals, the theorist is often transformed into a competent authority who may be relied upon because people and their ideas are judged for their apparent soundness and trustworthiness. Questions of demonstration and method are usually considered to be the business of the expert, and policy-makers accept the academic qualifications of their experts or the logic of their arguments on trust. In turn, theory may well creep anonymously into politics, not because it is a rational extension of phenomenology or control theory, but because it represents the accredited good sense of criminologists and researchers whose job it is to brief officials and politicians. Accordingly, it is often difficult to discover the precise intellectual source of proposals and it is even more difficult to keep track of them as they assume the clothing of political argument.

•*A third feature of the connection between theory and social policy is that it is pervasive, piecemeal, and incremental.* New theories are rarely accepted or rejected in their entirety, but trickle in from many sources. Literate policy-makers and researchers may have encountered Durkheim or Marx at university when they were young. They meet criminologists at social events. They read research reports and newspapers. They gossip at conferences. In all this continuous talk, questions are asked, ideas synthesized, and opinions formed. Quite often, policy-makers will forget the origin of a particular idea. It is never easy to fix when it was that a theory began to influence action or action a theory. Indeed, it would be naïve to attempt to do so.

> Political relevance is as important for a theory as academic validity.

•*Fourth, another property of that contingent relationship is the changing influence of ideas.* As political and practical circumstances fluctuate, so there will be a responsive shift in the direction of theory and research. Circumstances will condition theory, and theory will colour circumstances. Let us illustrate this, again turning to the development of the Canadian Justice for Victims of Crime Initiative.

Case Study—Canadian Victim Survey

A critical turning point in the evolution of policies for victims in Canada was the decision, made in the mid-1970s, to study the possibility of a national survey of victimization. A principal purpose of that decision was to improve the criminal justice database and to learn more about the 'dark figure of crime', that is, crime not reported to the police. The decision was made at a time of concern about the prospective abolition of capital punishment, and there were good political reasons to present it as one of a package of measures intended to evaluate the effectiveness of programs for preventing violent crime.

The fact that victims do not always report violence such as sexual assault to the police means that there are inevitable problems in doing victim surveys as well. Such surveys are usually large and expensive and require thorough planning. As proposals were drafted to survey victimization in Canada, it became apparent that there were major methodological problems which had first to be solved. Canadian research staff consequently undertook extensive consultations about the conduct of victim surveys, such as the US National Crime Surveys. Inevitably, of course, the preoccupation with measuring the suffering caused by victimization became a factor in encouraging the growth of a domestic Canadian interest in the provision of services to victims.

The planning of the Canadian survey was oriented towards an assessment of the impact of victimization, and extensive consultation was undertaken with women's groups across Canada. The use of focus groups, which was a technique that had not been used in other places that developed surveys, allowed the development of a measurement technique especially sensitive to women's issues and their experiences, itself a dialectical exercise. When it was finally carried out, the survey was presented as an exercise designed to support the relief of victims. The survey was thus defined by a succession of practical and political issues, which it also helped to shape. Since there was a dialectical and evolving interchange between research and politics, it is impossible to point to simple, unilateral effects.

Statistics Canada found that 51 per cent of women had experienced violence at some point in their lifetimes, 10 per cent in the previous year (Statistics Canada 1993). This finding must have been shocking, because even though crime surveys had been fairly well developed, specialized surveys to measure the extent of victimization against women lagged behind.

The Statistics Canada survey was considered to be the most comprehensive survey yet conducted, and it has since repeated in a variety of countries.

Sources: Statistics Canada, *Violence against Women*; S. Walby and A. Myhill, 'New Survey Methodologies in Researching Violence against Women', 502–22; R. Dobash and E. Dobash, 'Reflections on Findings from the Violence gainst Women Survey', 457–84; H. Johnson and V. Sacco, 'Researching Violence against Women: Statistics Canada's National Survey'; R. Gartner and R. Macmillan, 'The Effect of Victim-Offender Relationship on Reporting Crimes of Violence against Women'.

•*Fifth, many sociologists of deviance are quite aware of the problematic character of the association between academic ideas and political action* and there have been a number of accounts of how it can change.

Scull, for example, argued that the case for 'decarceration' (or the emptying of prisons and asylums) changed little between its first exposition in the mid-nineteenth century and its reappearance in the mid-twentieth century.[3] He argued that the reasons for its initial rejection and its later acceptance have to be explained in terms of its relevance to changes in the political economy of capitalism. Economies undergoing a 'fiscal crisis' could no longer afford an ever-growing control apparatus. There is argument about this,[4] but it does point to the importance of the political and economic frameworks of penological debate.[5]

Other sociologists have stressed the manner in which long-established theories can come into their own when the times are propitious; for instance, anomie theory had been formulated for twenty years before it was transposed by Cloward and Ohlin into 'opportunity structure theory' and the rapid development of the Mobilization for Youth project. Short has commented that this example

> illustrates a principle of great importance for the relation of sociological theory to social policy: that sociological theory is typically crescive, developing by slow and often uncertain increments suggested by either an empirical discovery or a conceptual modification. One implication is that those who would leap to specific concrete social engineering proposals on the basis of new developments in sociological theory are likely to find themselves on shaky ground. There is a scarcity of both social policy-oriented theory and replicated studies demonstrating valid and reliable knowledge.[6]

The issues of role definition, translatability, and salience combine to make it rare for a theory of deviance to inspire action programs or changes in social policy. It is more common to find competing social policies being justified by their adherents by the support they may derive from theory and research. The theories we have discussed offer distinctive explanations for deviance, and it is logical that they offer distinctive recipes for responses to deviance in political, policy, and practical terms. The search for such correspondences reveals the strengths and weaknesses of the theories anew. For they are subject to the constraint that they specify with some precision just what should (or should not) be changed before there can be a significant improvement in the social response to deviance.

■ Pulling It All Together: Cases

In certain respects, the implementation of social projects or policies based upon a theory can provide exacting opportunities to test that theory more searchingly. Do its propositions hold up? Are there unanticipated difficulties? The difficulties of such evaluations and the results that have been obtained will be alluded to as we deal with each perspective in turn.

The Case of the Chicago School

The Chicago School of Sociology produced one major project based on the characteristic theoretical assumptions of several of its leading members. The Chicago Area Project was inaugurated by Clifford Shaw and Henry McKay in 1934 and has survived in modified form to the present. The Chicagoans' definition of the role of the sociologist was quite compatible with so direct an involvement in practical intervention. Burgess and Thrasher developed responses that embodied their insights into the group nature of delinquency. Thrasher, for example, wrote:

> We need a new penology which shall be penetrating in its insights into the subjective aspect of the boy's life and which shall be much broader in scope than institutional care and the present system of probation and parole. . . . He must not be treated as if he existed in a social vacuum, but . . . as a member of all the various groups to which he belongs—not merely to the gang alone, but the family, the neighborhood, the school, the church, the occupational group and so on.[7]

The theory of social disorganization seemed readily translatable into terms of social practice. If delinquency was caused by the erosion of social controls due to social disorganization, then the most effective response would be to foster the potential for social organization in affected areas. Since the approach stressed the inherent capacity of communities to mobilize their own social control resources, the main burden of the projects should be to enhance the capacity of local residents to take the initiative in promoting links with disaffiliated youth and in seeking indigenous sources for the promotion of their welfare. However, Shaw and McKay argued that problems had arisen from the recruitment of outside professionals who lacked substantial interests in the areas in which they worked. They wished to promote links between local leaders and local youths in terms that were personal and social rather than clinical and individualistic.

They improvised a broad range of community-based programs, the most imaginative of which was the use of ex-offenders to act as youth workers with gangs. Their aim was to redirect rather than repress or break up the gang. At times, their enthusiasm for such redirection seemed naïve. For example, Thrasher said the

Scout movement and the YMCA were suitable outlets for the ganging process. However, their reformist zeal received support and lent a salience to strategies that still clings to their modern counterparts. The strategies of redirection, detached youth work with 'disaffiliated' or 'unattached' youth, and the co-opting of indigenous workers remained basic to the work of the New York City Youth Board in the post-war period,[8] as well as influencing the programs of Mobilization for Youth and other youth-related programs in the American 'War on Poverty' in the 1960s. Such strategies tended to be regarded in Britain as 'experimental' well into the post-war period.[9]

The problems of assessing the work of the Chicago Area Project have been shared by all delinquency prevention programs.

> At the bottom the difficulty rests on the fact that such programs . . . cannot by their very nature constitute more than a subsidiary element in changing the fundamental and sweeping forces which create the problems of groups and of persons or which shape human personality. Declines in rates of delinquency—the only conclusive way to evaluate delinquency prevention—may reflect influences unconnected with those of organized programs and are difficult to define and measure.[10]

The fact that this assessment rested on 'logical and analytic grounds' weakens the conclusion that 'in all probability these achievements have reduced delinquency in the program areas, as any substantial improvement in the social climate of an area must'.[11] The circularity of this conclusion reflects the circularity of the parent theory: namely, if delinquency is both symptom and consequence of 'social disorganization', then social programs to reduce such disorganization must have reduced delinquency.

Finestone challenges Kobrin's view by taking as a basis for evaluation the sheer variety of the projects generated by the Chicago Area Project. He addresses the problem of assessing the variable strength or weakness of the projects as organizations by adopting certain indicators of their performance. Their success in fundraising and their autonomy from state-appointed staff workers are taken as indicators of project success. On these purely organizational terms, the most successful projects correlated conversely with the seriousness of the delinquency problem in the areas: 'The Chicago Area Project has not provided a method of coping with the problem of delinquency in its most serious form in the areas of the city with the highest rates.'[12]

Finestone's assessment is limited by the absence of time-series data; however, it confirms the severe limitations of so exclusive an emphasis on community controls and activities. Such an emphasis precludes any attempt to deal with social and economic processes, such as the expansion of industrial and commercial land use in the inner city which erodes and disorganizes the community, and which can only be tackled by more comprehensive social and economic policies.[13] Such criticisms are important to consider , but we have yet to establish that more fundamental changes would actually promote the reduction of crime and delinquency, or that we have the understanding to implement such changes intelligently.

Case Study—An Applied Study of Social Disorganization Theory

The noted Canadian researcher Carol LaPrairie tried to discover whether certain large Canadian cities contribute to the over-representation of aboriginal people in the criminal justice system. The nine cities she studied are large urban areas that are known as Census Metropolitan Areas; they are located in eight provinces representing four major regions: Atlantic, Quebec and Ontario, the Prairies, and British Columbia. For the study, data on aboriginal offenders were analyzed in order to explore theoretical concepts such as social disorganization and to understand the extent of aboriginal over-representation in the justice system.

Previous research shows that the Prairies have the highest levels of over-representation and that urban areas contribute the majority of incarcerated aboriginal offenders. What LaPrairie shows in her city-by-city analysis is that disadvantage factors, such as low income, low employment, low education, high mobility, and lone parenting, are proportionally higher for aboriginal people and that they parallel the over-representation of natives in the justice system. LaPrairie suggests the need to

> explore possible interventions for the most disadvantaged urban groups and sub-groups, particularly in the 'high contributor' cities, and the resulting policy implications for local, provincial and federal governments. What kinds of reserve and urban models might be developed and tested for addressing disadvantage? Social capital theory, for example, posits that people acquire at birth and accumulate through their lives unequal shares of capital that incrementally alter and determine their life chances. Social capital accumulates not only among individuals but also within communities.[1]

By joining the idea of an ecological-systems model with the social-capital theory, LaPrairie proposes an exploration of how various individual, family, institutional, and community systems create not only risk but also protective factors in child development. The approach is based on the idea that community and family capital can be enhanced through services, increased options and opportunities, and for the individual, longer periods of employment.

She acknowledges that the justice system is not in a position to affect these structural factors, but it is in a position to implement effective crime-prevention strategies.

LaPrairie also cites recent research on collective efficacy that is based on a long-term study in 196 Chicago neighbourhoods (R. Sampson and S. Raudenbush, 'Disorder in Urban Neighbourhoods—Does It Lead to Crime?'). That study found that 'the absence of collective efficacy, which is defined as cohesion among neighbourhood residents combined with shared expectations for informal control of public space, was a significant factor in explaining levels of crime and disorder.'

In those neighbourhoods where the measured rate of collective efficacy was strong, rates of violence were low regardless of the socio-demographic composition of the population. The conclusion here, coupled with the concepts of social disorganization and social capital, is interesting. Increasing collective efficacy will reduce crime, and reducing disorder will reduce crime indirectly by stabilizing communities and promoting collective efficacy.

The challenge will be to establish social development programs and justice policies to facilitate this.

[1] C. LaPrairie, unpaginated.
Sources: Based on C. La Prairie, 'Aboriginal Over-Representation in the Criminal Justice System; R. Sampson and S. Raudenbush, 'Disorder in Urban Neighbourhoods—Does It Lead to Crime?'

The Case of Functionalist Theory

Functionalist theories seem to offer the basis for policies that are comprehensive in scope. After all, the analytical aim of functionalism is nothing short of the total interconnectedness of social institutions. However, as Gouldner notes:

One of functionalism's basic methodological precepts is that there are no 'causes'. Functionalism thinks of systems as mutually interacting variables rather than in terms of cause and effect. Functionalism's elementary domain assumption has always come down to this: everything influences everything else. But functionalism has had no theory about the weighting to be assigned to different variables in the system. It has had no theory about which variables are more and which are less important in determining the state of the system as a whole.[14]

Above all, the functionalists tried to discern a hidden order in apparent disharmony, to suggest that 'when problems arise in a group, there spontaneously emerge *natural* defence mechanisms that restore order and equilibrium'.[15] As a result, translating functionalism into policy options was a contradiction in terms. If what appear to be problems are—at the level of second-order constructs—retranscribed as solutions, then government intervention is likely only to make matters worse. From Spencer through Durkheim to Parsons's early and middle phases, functionalists argued that the power of the State was to be kept at a minimum to allow deep (social) evolutionary processes to hold sway. Since the State could acquire power only from interventionist policies, such policies were best avoided. Their consequences would be likely to proliferate in ways that would be difficult to foresee and control. 'Hands off' would be the major functionalist recommendation.

In Gouldner's view, the seeming irrelevance of functionalism to social policy began to change as the welfare State in America began to assume growing importance, both as an instrument of conflict resolution and resource allocation in the American economy and as a major source of finance for social science research. In this changing context, Gouldner argues, functionalists could not maintain their attitude of detachment from political and policy issues. Even Parsons began to adjust his scheme to take account of 'input deficits' suffered by certain socially deprived groups.[16] And in the cases of Smelser and Moore, leading functionalists undertook an attempted convergence with Marxism in the rush to accommodate social change and policy relevance to their theoretical work. In the process, however, the tensions between the parent theory and its new-found applications in the policy realm became all too apparent. Functionalism lost credibility, and the 1960s witnessed the pursuit of other sociologies, in particular symbolic interactionism, phenomenology, and Marxism.

The Case of Anomie Theory

Ironically, Gouldner ignored the one major respect in which functionalism indirectly led to the development of a theoretical model of great relevance to the realm of policy. Anomie theory, in Merton's version, shared with functionalism the problem of translating its 'second-order constructs'—culture and deviant 'adaptations'—into the achieving of social organization and meaning in everyday life. But its central tenet, that the disjunction between goals and means caused high rates of deviance, was grave, and a causal statement of considerable scope.

The strain towards deviance induced by the gap between goals and means should be reducible by narrowing that gap. Despite his own leanings towards the political left, Merton did not spell out this clear directive towards more egalitarian policies. However, Cloward and Ohlin redefined anomie theory as opportunity structure theory. The crucial modification was their linking of the emergence of delinquent subcultures to the experience of the closing of both legitimate and illegitimate opportunities in adolescence.[17] This change provided a rationale for the Mobilization for Youth project (MFY), whose purpose was to expand opportunities. In its turn, MFY became a major influence on the War on Poverty that dominated US domestic policy in the 1960s.

The immediate origins of MFY lay in the theoretical synthesis offered by Cloward and Ohlin in *Delinquency and Opportunity*. But its salience was partly due to their original responsibility for that task at a settlement house in the Lower East Side, the Henry Street Settlement. They embarked on the process of theorizing with the requirements of policy initiatives in mind, and their formulation accounts for the ready translatability of the theory into the language of social intervention. Because it coincided with the demand for initiatives from the new, reforming administration of the Kennedys, it acquired a prominence that few projects have possessed before or since in either Britain or the United States. As Cloward and Ohlin remark, 'It is our belief that most delinquent behaviour is engendered because opportunities for conformity are limited. Delinquency therefore represents *not* a lack of motivation to conform but quite the opposite: the desire to meet social expectations itself becomes the source of delinquency if the possibility of doing so is limited or non-existent.'[18]

Aware that translating these tenets into practice would be far from easy, they also stated that an appropriate program of action is not self-evident from a theory of causation: 'it cannot be assumed that once we know what the trouble is, we will have little difficulty remedying it'.[19] The difficulties that MFY encountered were not foreseen because the theory dealt only indirectly with power and vested interests. The core of these problems lay in the inconsistency of tackling at the local, community level inequalities that were rooted in the wider social structure. 'In both their employment and their education programmes, the projects were cramped by their inability to supersede the limits of local action and tackle the national problems that underlay their frustrations.'[20]

It was a major irony that theory based on a comprehensive analysis of the links between delinquency and social structure should have been translated into a project which intervened at the community level. Yet the realities of American politics ruled out more sweeping reforms, and community-action programs could be justified in terms of their efficiency as 'demonstration projects'. Demonstration, however, hinged on the effectiveness of the research that monitored the results of the projects, and on this count the project evidently could not cope with the sheer complexity of the evaluation involved. MFY launched enriched educational programs, job training schemes, vocational guidance, and even, on occasion, actual jobs from the resources of the project itself; and it embraced diverse forms of community protest. However, the monitoring of the results, already flawed by the absence of a comparative basis, became routinized into administrative book-keeping. Moreover, the politics of the project proved contentious: 'The Great Society programs were promulgated by federal leaders in order to deal with the problems created by a new and unstable electoral constituency—namely, blacks— and to deal with this new constituency not simply by responding to its expressed interests, but by shaping and directing its political future.'[21]

This view of Great Society politics corresponds with Gouldner's assertion that some sociological backing is actively sought by governments to help legitimize their commitment to limited social reforms. The State must actively promote some reforms, but the reforms must not be too radical, or the State risks conflict with dominant (capitalist) interests. 'The upper apparatus of the Welfare State, then, needs social research that will 'unmask' its competitors; it needs a kind of limitedly 'critical' research.'[22] However, it is difficult to keep 'critical' research within bounds.

The potential for more radical action was explored early and, as a result, drew the fire of local authorities and media. 'Community protest', which was no more than a minor aspect of MFY, took the form of embracing causes, while 'expanding opportunities' came to be defined as entailing 'decreasing the sense of powerlessness' among poor people.[23] Organizing a voter registration drive, aiding a local contingent of the March on Washington, encouraging rent strikes, and supporting a local group of Puerto Rican mothers in their campaign to oust a local school principal led to the pillorying of MFY by the New York *Daily News*. The project was accused of employing Communist sympathizers, of financial irregularities, and of inspiring riots! The charges are evidence of the severe limits within which such projects are politically constrained.

The ultimate limitation on allied projects in Britain was the impossibility of meeting the commitment to expand opportunities with the means available. Even for generously funded projects, it was extremely difficult to creating any but the most temporary jobs. Hence, the project came to focus increasingly on elaborate job-training schemes and placement programs in relation to existing jobs. Some of these schemes, such as simulated work-situation training, were genuinely imaginative attempts to align job preparation with the kinds of jobs available and the lack of sophistication of the recruits, but there was little to offer the trainees at the end of the process, Moynihan concluded that more would have been gained if government had concentrated directly and simply on the stimulation of employment.[24] Marris and Rein note the difficulties of establishing with any precision just what impact the projects made, but they conclude: 'While the projects could claim many individual successes and may well have increased somewhat the range of opportunities, they did so at great cost and without benefit to perhaps two-thirds of those who sought their help.'[25]

Did these activities make any impact on delinquency? One study reports that most lower East-Side gangs 'ignored MFY and at times were openly hostile to 'the organization through vandalism'.[26]In one central respect, however, the project's principal assumption does seem borne out by experience.

> As soon as the projects offered an opportunity that seemed genuine, they encouraged more response than they could handle. . . . The children of the slums responded to the projects, because they recognized the sincerity of the intentions; they became discouraged only as it became clear that the promise could not be fulfilled. Disillusionment is not apathy and to confuse them only complacently displaces the responsibility for failure.[27]

In the end, the aims of the project could be achieved only within 'a framework of national redistribution of resources, which deliberately redressed the balance of opportunities between rich and poor communities'.[28] If we have learned anything about the large-scale social and economic correlates of criminality, it is that countries with the greatest internal inequalities are also marked by the highest rates of crime.[29]

In Britain, similar projects were created by the Community Development Projects program.[30] Despite occasional successes, the projects foundered on much the same rock as the US programs: a chronic shortage of resources to meet well-documented needs utterly beyond the reach of the community itself. In some cases, project members reached the same conclusion as Marris and Rein, namely that national policy needed to reallocate resources from rich to poor. Perhaps the major appeal of such projects for governments is that by their adoption, the thorny political issues involved in such reallocation can be, for a time, minimized.

The price to be paid is that, with each successive failure, the limits of social-democratic reformism are cruelly exposed.

It was in the wake of such failures that *radical theorists* argued that capitalism was so crisis-ridden that reformism had become untenable and revolutionary methods offered the only hope of attaining egalitarian ends.

The Case of Marxist Theory

Marxist theorists have never, in principle, had to face problems of role definition that have so naggingly permeated sociology. 'Philosophers have long sought to understand the world: the point, however, is to change it.' That epitaph on Marx's tomb shows the need for theory and practice to be related, with theoretically informed practice feeding back into practically informed theory in a dynamic and self-critical process. The usefulness of research depends heavily, however, on the interpretations that are drawn from praxis. Until recently, however, the sheer force of the underlying theory had a dampening effect on revolutionary practice in Western academic Marxism. The more orthodox interpretations seemed to offer every reason *not* to act until the right conjuncture of revolutionary possibilities had materialized.

Least relevant of all were the realms of deviance and control. Deviance was defined as the inevitable by-product of capitalism; therefore little could be done until capitalism had been eliminated. Only with the redefinition of the potential of deviant groups for revolutionary struggle could sociologists engage at all in more relevant activity. It was the achievement of the 'new' criminologists to discern in the upsurge of political consciousness among certain deviant and minority groups the basis for a different strategy from traditional class action. Claimants' unions, 'gay liberation', 'women's liberation', prisoners' rights, and welfare rights movements, among others, suggested possibilities for politicizing deviance. Participation in protest movements promoted alliances and more understanding of class conflict.

However, the guidelines for action are thin. Suggestions for the control of policing and the administration of justice to be taken over by working-class communities made little progress.[31] The problems of translating radical theory into practice was formidable, not simply because the obstacles are strong, but also because the theories do not offer criteria for discriminating between the myriad possibilities for action.

• *Two major exceptions are instructive for the contradictory answers they give to a radical dilemma.* There is the accommodation proposed by radicals who are impressed by the need to take working-class problems and reluctant to remove themselves from political engagement. The beginnings of a program of pragmatic reform were drafted by radical sociologists, who launched a revolution from within. In 'left realism', sociologists of deviance are concerned with working-class experience, and, in some respects, their solutions are not so very different from the more liberal proposals of Home Office officials in Britain or their counterparts in Canada, Australia, and New Zealand. There is an interest in propounding remedies for the suffering experienced by poor, vulnerable, and ill-serviced working-class communities in urban areas. There is a demand for more responsive and efficient policing and, in particular, for policing that is directed at priorities that the working class themselves would choose, for policing that eschews aggressive patrol tactics and is directed by a more intelligent system of targeting. There is a cautious welcome for neighbourhood watch programs. 'Left realists' are wary about the displacement of crime from middle-class to working-class areas, and there is an apprehension that working-class communities are too disorganized to support such programs themselves. There is support for a 'multi-agency' approach to crime that would co-ordinate the activities of shelters for battered women, social services, crime-prevention programs, and the police.[32] There is a recommendation that prison should be used much more sparingly and should be replaced by schemes that integrate rather than further 'marginalize' the alienated. All these proposals display a marked affinity with those of experts from other theoretical positions, and there are the makings of a new professional consensus.

One direction which 'left realists' and others may take has been prepared by John Braithwaite. Recall Jock Young's parallelogram of forces that pointed to the importance of the community as a source of informal social control. It was Braithwaite's contention that informal social control is powerful when it uses techniques of shaming directed by those who are respected members of the offender's immediate environment, against offences that flout 'core consensus values'.[33] Shaming, which includes requiring the offender to make apologies, is powerful when it is conducted in public and encourages the eventual moral and social return of the one who has been shamed, thus 'avoiding stigmatization'.[34] The conventional justice system fails because judges, magistrates, and police officers lack authority for the offender, particularly the young, working-class offender. Their moral pronouncements have only a limited effect, and punishments do not bring about reintegration. Braithwaite's argument echoes earlier work in anthropology[35] and that of Durkheim, Hirschi, and labelling theorists. Some see shaming as an erosion of due process and the importance of the wider public interest.[36] Yet it is a successful instance of an academic argument leading to material change, drawing on labelling theory, social anthropology, and the empirical findings of criminology.[37]

• *The other major exception remains the work of Thomas Mathiesen* in the field of penal reform, and it embraces none of the pragmatism of the left realists.[38] Instead, Mathiesen's work addresses the radical's dilemma of whether to pursue short-term reforms or long-term revolutionary aims. Reformism runs the risk of strengthening the system and thereby undermining more radical change; and its advocates tend to become incorporated into the system by endless compromise. To opt for revolutionary ends, however, means being isolated from the system, being considered an 'irresponsible revolutionary', and losing one's credibility in relations with the subordinate groups most affected, in this case, prisoners.

Mathiesen resolves this dilemma by differentiating reforms that are 'system-strengthening' from those that are 'system-weakening'. The latter can be supported and the former resisted, as a means to long-term aims. An example of the former is the 'medicalization' of deviance. Superficially this is a progressive measure (rehabilitation), but fundamentally it individualizes the causes of deviance and therefore defuses its political aspects. It also dehumanizes deviant subjects by reducing their problems to those of a sickness from which, with suitable treatment, the State will enable them to recover.

Examples of 'system-weakening' reforms are concessions which would give greater autonomy to deviants in their relations with the system. Prisoners' rights to certain standards of work, education, and freedom from censorship and to legal procedures in a prison, are in this sense system-weakening. However, the main strategy is the abolition of repressive laws and of coercive institutions. The Norwegian prison-reform movement was partly responsible for the abolition of the vagrancy laws and the cancellation of detention centres that were planned for young offenders.

Mathiesen's strategy has great appeal, particularly in the field of penal reform, and has counterparts in other areas of social work. 'Client refusal' has evolved as a strategy by which radical social workers try not to be co-opted by State power. They refuse:

> to condone the labels which are officially attached to deviants. . . . Client refusal consists simply of blocking the unjust suction of individuals into so-called therapeutic situations where they lose control and responsibility. Thus in the early 1970s, many groups of social workers refused to receive children into care simply because their parents were homeless. . . . Taylor rightly goes further by arguing that client refusal, which in isolation could be seen as another form of rationing, should include an attempt to enlist the client as a political ally.[39]

Similarly, many reformist groups collaborated to mount campaigns for the abolition of capital punishment.[40] In principle, Mathiesen's model can be extended to cover social action in general, not only in the penal field. Its adequacy must therefore be assessed in relation, first, to its capacity to resolve the 'reform'-versus-'revolution' dilemma; and second, to its potential for the achievement of a society based on 'socialist diversity'.

Even within the penal field, an examination of particular cases shows the immense complexity of interpretation involved in assessing the potential of reforms. The view that the 'medicalization' of deviance is automatically system-strengthening seems questionable in the case of drug dependence, where the right to treatment within the health service is one which many States are reluctant to concede.[41] Moreover, the concern with system strengthening hardly seems the main point, which is whether or not 'medicalization' works for the deviant. The main grounds for opposing it ought to be its appropriateness, rather than its implications for the 'system'.

Similarly, research on one therapeutic community-based prison suggests that it's an institution that works rather well.[42] There *does* seem to be a general tendency to neglect what might work. Indeed, McMahon has written about the manner in which critical penological arguments have directed 'attention away from any moderation of penal control that might have taken place'.[43] It may be that the granting of certain rights to prisoners lessens the hold of the State in a repressive sense over certain aspects of their lives.

Yet such a policy is system-strengthening. The State gains in legitimacy from such enlightened procedures. Indeed, the burden of much Marxist 'critical' theory is to 'unmask' the reality of State power behind the façade of 'repressive tolerance' created by the progressive extension of citizenship rights to formerly dispossessed groups in capitalist societies over the past two centuries. In periods of quite significant reductions in the relative use of prison and mental hospitals,[44] system-weakening effects have not resulted, though the impact on certain families and communities may have been burdensome. In short, most reforms have both positive and negative aspects in relation to State power. In the great majority of cases the dilemma is not so much resolved as reconstituted in different and ultimately ambiguous terms by the abolitionist strategy.

Moreover, this complication of the issue is bought at the price of an oversimplified view of the 'State', capitalism, and class society. The problem of whether one might not actually *wish* to strengthen the system in certain respects, on the grounds that the 'not-too-bad' society is better than any revolutionary alternatives, is not even considered. Mathiesen's analysis, much like the work of more structuralist Marxists, provides only one role for the State under the capitalist mode of production: it is basically repressive. Everything is part of the State's repressive apparatus.[45]

Prisons are seen as the quintessential mode of repression under capitalism and, as the crisis in capitalism deepens, so will its reliance on the penalization of working-class offenders. Indeed, Christie argues that the growth of the crime-control industry was one of the major marketing successes of capitalism at the end of the twentieth century.)[46]

Mathiesen's analysis makes little sense of the immense variations in imprisonment between different capitalist societies; nor does it consider the problem of the persistence and even extension of penal powers in the State socialist societies before their collapse. The point at issue is the insistence that all attempts at reform are doomed to 'correctionalism' except those that align themselves with strategies to eliminate capitalism. This entails a drastic foreshortening of perspectives on deviance and control to 'a single-cause theory of conflict (class antagonism)'.[47]

The Case of Interactionist Theory

Symbolic interactionism as a source of policy remained largely untapped until the 1960s. Interactionists had never much preoccupied themselves with the policy implications of their work. It is possible to read the work of Goffman, for example, without finding any systematic policy inferences. What came to be termed *labelling theory* was more precisely foreshadowed in the work of Tannenbaum's *Crime and the Community* and Lemert's *Social Pathology*, neither of which was typical of interactionism.[48] Only with the publication of Becker's *Outsiders* in

1963 were these separate strands fused and implications for policy quickly spelled out. Becker's own definition of the sociologists' role made it clear that their sympathies should lie with the underdogs. Translating labelling theory into practice consisted of variations on the theme of 'delabelling': decriminalization, destigmatization, and decarceration.[49] The importance of such themes grew as the costs of institutional care and custody rose sharply in the 1960s, though the trend towards the reduction of inmate populations had begun in the 1950s with the mentally ill. The importance of labelling theory was enhanced in that attacks on institutionalization came from other quarters.[50]

• *The fact that these proposals found a ready audience did not mean that they were easy to formulate in practice.* 'Decriminalization' has been linked by Schur in particular to 'deviance without victims', such as drug use, prostitution, gambling, homosexuality, and abortion. The criminal sanction was applied to such forms of deviance more extensively in the United States than in Canada or Britain, but since in all those countries the great majority of offences are crimes *with* victims, the scope for applying this principle much further soon runs into difficulties. There is agreement among some[51] that such 'criminogenic interventions'[52] by the State only strengthen the propensity to offend.

Schur advocated a policy of 'radical nonintervention' towards delinquency, with his slogan 'leave the kids alone'. 'Status offenders', those whose offences would not be illegal if committed by an adult, are the primary candidates for this policy.[53] Such offenders should be dealt with within the community rather than in institutions, although Schur is vague about how to respond to runaways, truants, under-age drinkers, and 'ungovernables'.[54] Delabelling does not dispense with the problems to which those labels were applied;[55] however it is an attempt to deal with the issue of stigma, which is of course the emphasis in Canada's youth delinquency legislation.

As J. Osborne noted in 'Juvenile Justice Policy in Canada', the development of diversion programs from the formal court system was associated with the popularity of labelling theory. She also goes on to note that it is unusual for a theory to have been translated so wholeheartedly into policy; and she suggests why that may have happened:

> This may be due to the lack of distinctively Canadian theorizing. . . . Virtually nothing in the way of significant research has been undertaken into the causes or characteristic features of delinquency that have application in the specific context of Canadian conditions. . . . [Furthermore] there is a general reluctance on the part of policy makers to apply the results of criminological research . . . [because] although criminologists use increasingly sophisticated methodology . . . there is a considerable degree of indeterminacy in their findings. They tend to be speculative rather than definitive and are always subject to redefinition and reinterpretation.[56]

However, as Osborne goes on to note in developing a diversion policy based on labelling theory, Canadian legislators actually subverted the liberal premise of the theory. Diversion was only for those that deserved it, being reserved for those juvenile offenders least likely to reoffend, while increasing the criminalization of other offenders, a point drawn from Ericson's 'From Social Theory to Penal Practice.'[57]

•*'Destigmatization' is also fraught with similar problems.* Schemes to 'divert' the young offender from the stigmatizing processes of the juvenile court have resulted in non-serious offenders diverted to hundreds of agencies in lieu of being sent to court.[58] Does diversion lower the number being sent to court, lessen the stigma, or reduce the exposure of children to bureaucratic processing?[59] Does it create a supplementary rather than an alternative means of disposal for juvenile offenders, the younger, less serious offenders whom the police used to caution and release?

One study discerns the tendency to redefine its target population from the relatively serious to the less serious offenders and to those 'at risk' of delinquency.[60] 'Restigmatization' and its extension to hitherto unaffected groups are predictable consequences of rerouting strategies. The new vision of the carceral society in which the State pretends to withdraw from formal social control, actually intrudes more invasively into the lives of its subject population. New classifications and remedies are propounded for the control of deviant groups, but the exceptions and the failures then present problems of management, and new institutions are formed to regulate them. In a series of 'iatrogenic feedback loops', social control is pushed ever further outwards.[61]

In Australia, for example, 'youth at risk' is the currently favoured label for youth with low educational performance who are not expected to complete secondary education. Although some research has identified relevant factors such as individual and family circumstances, as well as characteristics of schools and society,

> policy identification of youth 'at risk' has tended to simplistically focus on personal attributes of young people. Moreover, this identification has set up a false distinction between a supposed problematic minority versus a 'normal' majority. Thus, the dominant conceptualization of youth 'at risk' draws attention to what is wrong with these youth, rather than to what may be wrong with schooling. [We] propose use of the concept of 'marginalized students' instead, which identifies individuals not through their personal characteristics but through their relationship with schooling. This approach allows recognition that marginalization is at least in part a product of schools and society, and requires action in those arenas.[62]

Cohen felt that the State control apparatus had never receded but had merely thrown out webs of new diversionary programs and projects, called 'community corrections', that had the practical consequence of enlarging its sphere of carceral control. Each time offenders broke the terms of their probation or community service, each time they disobeyed a reparation order or failed to pay a fine, they could be penalized by confinement. They might be imprisoned for offences that would never originally have warranted prison. The penal estate grows inexorably, Cohen argued.

Bottoms, in his turn, challenged Cohen by demonstrating how the proportion of prison sentences steadily declined in the same period. McMahon has also pointed to a number of fundamental confusions and misconceptions in the 'net-widening argument'. There are, she argued, many reasons other than net widening why the absolute numbers of prisoners should have increased.[63]

Perhaps Braithwaite's strategy of making offenders ashamed without shaming them, of allowing ritual reintegration into society, and of healing the rift with their victims is the first major theoretically informed and practically effective resolution of the dilemma. It may prove on balance to be inclusionary rather than exclusionary, and not prone to significant net widening at all.

• *'Decarceration' was perhaps the strongest and best attested policy that labelling theorists stressed in past decades.* Supportive theory, empirical evidence on high recidivism rates, and the soaring costs of institutional control swayed governments in a sympathetic direction. However, the dangers of offending the judiciary and alarming public opinion meant that indirect means were usually chosen to reduce the prison population. Such methods tended to backfire or make only negligible impact; parole, suspended sentences, and diversion tended either to encourage 'compensatory' sentencing or to widen the population at risk. A confusion of aims led to policy compromises that in some respects proved counter-productive. Only in the Netherlands did the trend towards shorter sentences prove sustainable, for two decades at least, in the face of rising crime rates.[64]

In one case, however, a more radical decarceration was accomplished. In 1972, all juvenile reformatories in Massachusetts were closed down overnight. A number of community-care alternatives were then been adopted with varying success. The authors of the change in policy claimed that there was no indication of an increase in crime by juveniles.[65] It was claimed that recidivism rates were roughly the same in the community-based programs as in the State training schools.

Less optimism is evident in Scull's evaluation of decarceration and community-care policies.[66] Scull managed to offend both liberals and radicals with his argument that capitalist societies are actively encouraging decarceration but for narrow budgetary reasons and with generally distressing results. He was particularly scathing about the data on Massachusetts, which he lambastes as so sloppy as to be useless for policy evaluation purposes. Not even crime and recidivism figures are presented in such a way as to make before and after comparison possible; costs are given only for the period after the change, and no attempt is made to assess how well families coped with the responsibility for young offenders when alternatives were not available. Scull's main argument is that the rhetoric of community care and decarceration masked a trend in which the State sloughs off responsibility for deviants on to cut-rate private agencies, whose standards of provision were not monitored adequately. Moreover, in many cases, the real costs were heaped regressively on to the deviants' own families and on to those communities least able to mobilize to screen the deviants out. Hence, they gravitate downwards to form 'deviant ghettoes' in the already deprived inner-city slums. It is all too clear that community care can slide into no care at all.[67] The major alternative, which is to improve institutions, is conveniently buried, largely on the grounds of cost.

It should not be assumed that major savings are made by such policies.[68] It is essential to have access to fiscal, behavioural, and research data to make such appraisals. And all too often, the period of time allotted to evaluation is very brief. Programs can change direction in mid-stream. Political demands may well conflict with research requirements.[69] And there has also been an irrational tendency to dismiss a whole line of theoretical reasoning after the purported failure of a single demonstration project or experiment. In most other areas of inquiry, the consequence of negative or inconclusive findings would be to modify the original program in order to change the outcome. Unusually hard criteria are applied quite precipitately in social-reform experiments. It is not surprising that there have been difficulties in demonstrating any 'payoff' from liberal reforms. Apparent failure, coupled with the longer-standing disillusionment with rehabilitative policies,[70] helped to encourage a revival of more conservative penal policies. Governments on both sides of the Atlantic have become 'tough on crime'. They have partly abandoned the arguments for cautioning delinquents, instead adopting deterrence, punishment, and incapacitation instead, with resulting increases in incarceration.[71]

Case Study—Juvenile Justice Legislation

Juvenile justice legislation in Canada is based on particular philosophical assumptions about how young people should be treated when they commit deviant offences. Although these assumptions reflect a certain lay understanding of motivation and responsibility, it is difficult to find theoretical explanations in them beyond simplistic ideas of deterrence or rehabilitation.

The first federal piece of juvenile justice legislation was the *Juvenile Delinquents Act*, which was in effect between 1908 and 1984. It was the result of extensive lobbying by social reform groups interested in the betterment of society. Those groups were successful in achieving separate courts for juveniles, incarceration separate from adults, and *in camera* hearings. This Act signalled a new way of thinking about young people that differentiated them from both children and adults. This identification of adolescence as an intermediate period requiring intervention not coincidentally occurred with the industrialization of Canadian society.

The social leaders of the day were alarmed at the apparent upsurge in the number of truant and vagrant children roaming the streets, and there was doubt about the reformative ability of the industrial schools. W.L. Scott, who was instrumental in the adoption of the *Juvenile Delinquents Act*, referred to such institutions as 'schools for crime'. By the turn of the century, reform-minded élites were rejecting custodial institutions because they were dissatisfied with the way such institutions were governed, and with a new enthusiasm for community-based strategies such as probation were promoting the creation of new forms of laws for young people.[1]

The *Juvenile Delinquents Act*, which applied to young people aged seven to sixteen and was based on principles of 'social welfare legislation', provided for guidance and proper supervision, the State acting as *parens patriae*, or as a parent of the people. One problem with the Act was that it was not applied consistently in every province, because even though it was a piece of federal legislation, the *British North America Act* made its administration a matter of provincial responsibility. Another problem after 1982 was the neglect of the new Charter rights, such as due process.

In 1984 the *Juvenile Delinquents Act* was replaced with the *Young Offenders Act*, which introduced a more 'legalistic', less compassionate model for youth justice, moving away from the social-welfare approach that had received much criticism. Young people were now to be held more accountable for their crimes even though it was recognized that they were not adults and should not suffer the same consequences as adults would for their actions.

There were a number of amendments to the *Young Offenders Act* in the 1990s, and by the late 1990s it was evident that change was in the air. The Liberal political agenda for young offenders was informed more by the public's concerns[2] than by problems in the way in which adolescents are processed by the youth justice system.[3] The 1993 election was the first in Canadian history that juvenile justice was an issue for all four political parties.[4]

In 2003 the YCJA, or *Youth Criminal Justice Act* came into effect. It places an emphasis on keeping young people out of court and out of custody. Youth sentences are often controversial because of the impression that they are too lenient. However, there is the possibility of adult sentences for young persons.

The *Youth Criminal Justice Act* makes provisions for non-court options: extrajudicial measures and extrajudicial sanctions (formerly called alternative measures). The first includes taking no further action, giving a warning, and administering a caution. The second is based on the restorative-justice principle of diverting cases from the formal court process because of the stigmatizing effect.

In these various pieces of legislation we can see ideas of deterrence, rehabilitation, and concern over the effects of labelling. It is more difficult to see a concern with subcultures, social bond, or disorganization. The difficulty perhaps is that justice policy is more often designed to be corrective than to correct the root causes of deviance through social development.

[1] B. Hogeveen,, 'If we are tough on crime, if we punish crime, then people get the message'.

[2] J. Sprott, 'Understanding Public Views of Youth Crime and the Youth Justice System'.

[3] R. Corrado and A. Markwart, 'The need to reform the YOA in response to violent youth offenders: Confusion, reality or myth?': 342–78;P. Carrington and S. Moyer, 'Trends in youth crime and police response', 1–28.

[4] N. Bala, 'What's Wrong with YOA Bashing? What's Wrong with the YOA?—Recognizing the Limits of the Law', 247–70; B. Hogeveen, 'Discontinuity and/in the Early Twentieth Century Ontario Juvenile Court'; idem, 'If we are tough on crime, if we punish crime, then people get the message'.

The Case of Control Theory

The 'incapacitation' argument of James Q. Wilson's is only the most extreme of a wide range of demands for a new traditionalism. The demand for a return to retributivism of the 'just deserts' model[72] and the desire to return to the strict legality of due process in the juvenile justice field are generally in tune with the tenets of control theories. Yet control theories are not necessarily reducible to the demand for control of a more traditional kind. For example, the extraordinary success with which girls and women are socialized into conformity logically suggests the feminization of male role playing and a greater emphasis on informal rather than formal social controls. Instead, we sentence young male offenders to regimes that are in effect designed to promote 'macho' hardness. Nor are the theories necessarily opposed to redistributive policies.

'Stake-in-conformity' and 'culture of poverty' theories essentially imply much the same set of policies as strain theories, namely better jobs, housing, and education for those relatively deprived of such bonds with the social order. The major differences between the two kinds of theories concern the causal priorities of the means to this end. Strain theories stress the need to expand opportunities, and they take motivation for granted. Control theories see motivation as weak or absent and argue that tackling the cultural deprivation of the poor and most discriminated-against minority groups is a precondition for betterment.

A key example has been Operation Head Start, an American project for children in their preschool year who were considered to be in need of an intensive preparation for education. Early results were encouraging, but after the children had been in school for a few years, the 'head start' gained seemed to have been lost. The brief exposure to an enriched educational experience was assumed to have evaporated as more persistent inequalities reasserted their hold. 'Head Start did not seem to promote any lasting improvement in children's school performance despite its popularity'.[73] Much the same assumptions and conclusions applied to the British experiments in the designation of Educational Priority Areas that were allocated extra funding for a variety of teaching aids and strategies. However, an analysis of the *long-term* effects of the more rigorously designed Head Start programs is more encouraging.[74] School 'failure' (as defined by indicators such as placement in remedial classes, failing a grade, and dropping out of school) was markedly higher for control-group children (44 per cent) than for project children (25 per cent).

> To use avoidance of remedial classes and 'grade failures' as measures of effectiveness is to focus on the minimal aspirations of a school's work. On the other hand . . . they are measures of actual educational experience, rather than abstractions like measured intelligence. . . . For a government determined to relieve the handicaps of those who come from poor families, a pre-school program discriminating in their favour seems to be one of the crucial weapons.[75]

The worthiness of the project was reaffirmed,[76] though it has yet to be shown that making a discernible impact on the 'culture' of poverty leads to a reduction in poverty itself. As Currie argued, that would require the provision of worth-while jobs.

The 'situational' type of control theory has the most obvious relevance for policy, but it does not necessarily coincide with traditionalist calls for more policing and harsher sentencing, measures that produce no more success in controlling crime than community policing and milder sentencing.[77] The controls that are successful tend to be preventive rather than punitive. There is obvious scope for a wide array of controls to be experimented with along carefully monitored and relatively economical lines. In a few cases, such as the reduction in motorcycle thefts after the wearing of crash helmets became mandatory, whole classes of crime can be dramatically diminished.[78] In others, initially promising causal links now seem more modest or largely spurious.[79]

Overall, the main criticism remains that excessive reliance on such policies may lead to a 'double displacement' effect: crime takes a more regressive form in relation to the more vulnerable groups in the population and attention is deflected from more complicated variables of a social and economic character.

What does remain are important initiatives in the rehabilitation of disorganized or vulnerable communities, which may do something towards the restoration of informal social control. The mere presence of concerned people, visible consultation with affected agencies, the expenditure of money, and a new responsiveness to residents' problems may be enough to bring about some change. At the very least, local leaders may arise and acquire influence in the process of consultation, and their new influence may inject organization into what had once been disordered. The Priorities Estates Project case study looks at one family of initiatives in a little detail.

Case Study—The Priorities Estates Project

The Priorities Estates Project, which was developed by the British Department of the Environment, was not intended explicitly to reduce deviance. It was supposed to reverse the decline of problem housing developments and to ensure that empty, unwanted property was once again occupied. Nonetheless, it seems to have had quite real consequences for deviance. Consultants claimed evidence of burglary rates decreased. On one estate in north London, the burglary rate dropped by 62 per cent.[1] On another, described as a 'nightmare estate', 'burglaries have virtually been eliminated . . . and the crime rate generally has plummeted'.[2]

The Priority Estates Project explains such changes as an indirect consequence of delegating services, management, and leasings. An elaborate process of negotiation with tenants, local authority departments, the police, and local agencies result in a great deal of practical control returned to people living and working on a housing estate. One major example is the introduction of a devolved system of leasing that allows local people to obtain tenancies on hard-to-let estates. It allows networks of friends, acquaintances, and families to enter once-fragmented communities. Moreover, these new tenants often *want* to live on the estates. Their coming reduces the numbers of vacant and squatted-on properties that damage 'local morale' and are 'a public announcement of trouble'. It helps to construct and restore community and it serves to 'strengthen local ties'.[3] It installs tenants who are prepared to act as the unofficial custodians of space that was formerly unprotected: 'housing would be guarded free of charge by the new occupants'.[4] It imports those who no longer resent living on a 'problem' estate, reversing processes that alienate residents from municipal councils. It increases the homogeneity of a community. It removes squatters and others who have been defined as a source of mischief. Similarly, the decentralization of maintenance work seems to improve the quality and rate of repairs, transforming the physical appearance and symbolic character of an estate. Such a decrease in visible public damage can eventually become self-propelling by reducing the number of cues that invite vandalism. Residents can act as guardians of property and channels of information about deviance.

What complicates any discussion of such policy initiatives is the difficulty of establishing their precise effects. In practice, the impact of the work undertaken by the Priority Estates Projects and similar organizations can easily become lost and muddled, confused with all the other social, economic, and political changes that may simultaneously be affecting a community.

The devolution of practical control may be accompanied by a remodelling of the physical environment. When boundaries are installed, there may be a decline in the amount of confused, impersonal public space and an increase in the area of private, defended space.[5] Consultation with the police and other agencies can enable groups to reassess one another and then collaborate. 'A commonly reported situation is one where, as a result of beat policing allied to better management of the estate, the tenants are more willing to report damage or challenge hooliganism.'[6] Above all, the very business of implicating tenants in plans and programs can soften relations between suspicious neighbours and imbue them with a novel sense of organization, purpose, and effectiveness. It gives an opportunity to reassert control.

[1] T. Zipfel, 'Broadwater Farm Estate, Haringey: Background and Information Relating to the Riot on Sunday, 6th October 1985', unpublished.

[2] T. Zipfel, 'Hard Work Transforms a Nightmare Estate'.

[3] Department of the Environment, *Local Housing Management*.

[4] A. Power, 'How to Rescue Council Housing'.

[5] Department of the Environment, *Reducing Vandalism on Public Housing Estates*.

[6] M. Burbidge, 'British Public Housing and Crime: A Review'.

Although there is some anxiety about the displacement effect of such policies, the decline in the amount of victimization does seem to be absolute. As our discussion of Mayhew's analysis of displacement effects may have shown, crime does not always travel when initiatives are introduced. And since 1995 crime rates have fallen back to 1987 levels, at least as measured by victim surveys,[80] a trend apparent across most of Europe and North America.

Situational crime prevention is a prime variable in explaining such trends, though it is far from being the whole story, for in Canada and Scotland crime rates were relatively stable throughout the post-1980 period.[81]

One of the most widely celebrated of such experiments to restore informal control in high-crime estates was the Kirkholt project.[82] Kirkholt was a housing development that suffered double the rate of burglaries, reported and unreported, characteristic of 'high risk' areas, but its residents *did* declare themselves ready to co-operate in crime prevention. Pease and his associates did not propose to introduce a blanket neighbourhood watch scheme.[83] Instead, they targeted a specific offence, burglary its victims, it 'being their observation that one of the best predictors of future victimization was victimization in the recent past.[84] Neighbours were to be especially protective of those vulnerable victims, a practice which was called 'cocooning neighbourhood watch'. The outcome was a 'large absolute and proportionate reduction in domestic burglary', which was not apparently displaced.

Some areas, of course, are too anomic, too heterogeneous, and too fragmented to be called communities. In Newman's language, they have 'tipped' and have slid into a state of disorder from which there cannot always be a return.[85] Like Rainwater's Pruitt–Igoe project, the only recourse may be to destroy the estate physically and begin again. It was certainly the case that an attempt to introduce 'cocooning neighbourhood watch' on a London housing estate collapsed because, like the anomic residents of Pruitt–Igoe, neighbours did not trust one another enough to erect a defensive shield. Neighbours knew one another too little (or perhaps too well) to co-operate; it was feared that the cocooning neighbours might actually be the very people who had burgled the apartment in the past; and there were anxieties that formal reports to the police and informal personal intervention might lead to retaliation.[86]

There may be other difficulties. Housing estates, projects, and inner-city areas are never neat instances of the uncontaminated laboratory experiment. There is so much and such continual intervention from so many bodies, from the police, probation, social services, and local and central government, that the impact of any single crime-prevention initiative is almost always impossible to establish. In the Kirkholt project, the estate was subject also to experiments in probation practice and an estate rehabilitation program.[87] Efforts to discern the specific impact on crime of a Priority Estates Programme project in London's Tower Hamlets were confounded by the simultaneous workings of changes in local government housing policy.[88]

•*Such studies also show the difficulties of distinguishing the effect of the social from the situational aspects of crime prevention programs.* In principle, the two approaches are very different. Social crime prevention, in so far as it tackles the root causes of deviance successfully, harbours no risk of its displacement. For example, if the search for excitement is met by car repair and racing projects, the displacement effect is nil. Situational measures, however, such as steering locks, car alarms, and CCTV monitors, may raise the excitement stakes and/or deflect crime elsewhere.

In practice, situational measures may carry socially exclusionary effects, as in the barring of shopping centres to known troublemakers, with the result that more crime may be generated elsewhere. But situational measures may enhance feelings of security to the point where community life is revived. The removal of an experienced community police officer can lead to an increase in crime and the fear of crime, upsetting the balance between containing deviance and encouraging it.[89]

Even well-conceived social measures can backfire by inadvertently drawing in a far wider population starved of adequate housing and leisure resources: this is a kind of reverse displacement.[90] It is not easy to strike the right balance between social and situational measures, especially when scarce resources encourage practitioners to opt for the short-term, tangible, purely situational response, such as target hardening

In Britain, policy-making was also heavily shaped by Tony Blair's assertion in 1993 that New Labour would be 'tough on crime, tough on the causes of crime'. Policies were ushered in designed to break with the old government's "soft on crime" image'[91] while retaining a social reformist agenda. What is important in this example is that the latter was rooted in priorities relevant to strain and social control theories and to those of left realism: tackling poverty, social exclusion, unemployment and inequalities of educational opportunity and health care, and regenerating deprived communities.

However, the government underemphasized the growing economic inequality and overemphasized the need to satisfy populist punitiveness.[92] A panoply of liberal measures on youth unemployment and training, on community regeneration and on restorative justice, was accompanied and over-shadowed by a string of punitive measures heavily influenced by the American examples of 'zero tolerance' policing and penal incapacitation. 'Final warnings'; anti-social behaviour orders (popularly known as ASBOs); minimum mandatory sentencing for burglary, drug dealing, and violence; tighter penalties for breaking community sanctions; a lowering of the age of criminal responsibility to ten, parenting orders; and other measures tilted the social service and criminal justice systems towards the disciplinary end of the welfare spectrum.

This new agenda thus rests on a reversal of the meaning of the term 'respect',[93] in which allowing the poor and the dependent a voice in their own situation, and a measure of real autonomy, is essential for effective welfare services and crime-prevention measures. The prison population has increased and a new 'culture of control'[94] has evolved, partly in response to rising crime rates over the long period from 1955 to 1993 but also in response to changing conceptions of responsibility. The fallacy of conflating explanations of crime with excuses for its commission is part of this process.

> Explanations should never be confused with excuses.

The 'new' politics of law and order are now entrenched, not only in Britain and the United States, but also in countries like the Netherlands, a country long associated with minimal reliance on penal measures.[95] The defining criterion for the new politics is the acceptance by all major political parties of what might be called[96] 'governing through crime', that is, the exploitation for electoral ends of public concern about crime as the over-riding condition for governmental legitimacy. This entails a ceaseless raising of consciousness about deviance and control as the issue that above all else constitutes grounds for political credibility. It has greatly extended the trend towards the 'criminalisation of social policy',[97] the danger that

> fundamental public issues may become marginalized, except in so far as they are defined in terms of their criminogenic consequences . . . As a consequence, we may come to view poor housing, unemployment, racism, failed educational facilities, the lack of youth leisure opportunities, and so on, as no longer important public issues in themselves. Rather, their importance may be seen to derive from the belief that they lead to crime and disorder.

A related trend is towards the criminalization of criminal justice policy. Skolnick, in *Justice without Trial*, and Packer, in *Limits of the Criminal Sanction*, distinguished the tension between law and order and between crime control and due process, as fundamental antinomies in the criminal justice framework.

In contemporary Britain, and in other Western countries, the tension is steadily becoming weighted in favour of order and crime control rather than law and due process. For example, anti-social behaviour orders introduced the less exacting canons of civil rather than criminal law in the determination of guilt, despite the fact that criminal penalties of up to five years' imprisonment could be activated for any breach of the order. Justified as needed to ensure rapid case settlement for 'nuisance value' misconduct, they are increasingly used to complement sentencing in criminal cases, logically negating their original purpose.[99] Parenting orders are invoked to coerce parents of young offenders to learn better parenting skills, despite the fact that young offenders are now deemed fully responsible for their own offending behaviour. The concept of individual responsibility for the offence is thereby eroded. The welfare principle in youth justice has been progressively marginalized, not least by the abolition of the *doli incapax* rule by the 1998 *Crime and Disorder Act*. As a result of that Act, children under fourteen are unable to claim lack of awareness of criminal responsibility due to immaturity. This has lessons for other jurisdictions.

The ascendancy of the 'governing through crime' principle has not easily proved reversible in any society that has adopted it as the key electoral strategy, but there are societies that have resisted its allure, not least the Scandinavian countries, Canada, and Germany.[100]

The constant harping on deviance and control in its many rhetorical guises constantly undermines citizens' sense of security, and leaves the fear of crime unchanged. It can be argued that, although the governing-through-crime strategy has proved irreversible in any society that has adopted it, it is actually unsustainable, for good Durkheimian reasons. A crime-free society is a contradiction in terms, since the very processes that lead to an ever-heightened consciousness of crime prevention lead inevitably to the demonization of normal deviance. An infinite aspiration to the elimination of crime logically leads, in Durkheimian terms, to the paradox of anomie.

The Case of Feminism

To paraphrase Lowman,[101] the critical assault against radical sociology was rooted in rape crisis centres and transition houses, as much as it was in women's studies programs. This new feminism championed the woman as victim of violence, legitimated women's perspective, and showed that women's fear of crime was not irrational. Coupled with information from the new crime victimization surveys, a two-pronged assault against traditional theories, buoyed up by experience, was launched against 'deviantology' from within.

The coming together of women to reflect and speak on their experiences informed their experiences dialectically through the collective transformation of private experience into public (shared) reality. That reality was a fear of male violence, a concern about danger in public places, and of course the belief that police and the courts were unable or unwilling to act in their interests.

Feminist work involved setting up shelters for battered women, crisis centres for victims of sexual abuse, and sexual harassment programs in universities and industry. Government work involved setting up crime-prevention programs, often stressing situational crime prevention, such as carrying a cell phone, locking car doors, having a full tank of gas, and so on. However, the stage was set for a clash in perspectives.

The dominant narrative of danger in public places at the hands of strangers clashed with many of women's own experiences of danger. Women already knew the risks of public places, but they also knew of the threat posed to them by their ex-boyfriends, sons, and other male relatives. Because, as Stanko concludes:

> if we are to take women's fear of crime seriously, and if we agree that it is more a reflection of women's social location within intersections of gender, class, race, and ability structures, then we must reconsider what we mean by crime prevention and fear reduction. The fact is that many still place what endangers women the most—familial and familiar violence—on an agenda often separate from that of crime reduction. Others may suggest that better lighting, repairing broken windows, or cleaning graffiti is sufficient for creating an environment that is woman friendly and thus less fear producing. The social context of women's fear of crime is such that unless women's autonomy is promoted—which, I advocate, must address women's freedom from sexual danger—it is unlikely that women's fear will be reduced. Good lighting, good transport, adequate child care, decent education, safe houses, and safe relationships—one without the others is inadequate to address women's needs and, by extension, women's fear of crime.[102]

Examples of feminist responses to crime include safety audits of public places and the demand that spending priorities reflect a concern with women's safety;

public relations campaigns about zero tolerance for violence; and educational campaigns about spousal abuse, women as victims of sexual violence, and violence against women in the sex trade.

The Case of Phenomenology

Finally, *phenomenological* approaches favour a more austere set of relations between sociology and social policy than those that are sought by most sociologists. In some respects they adhere to the methodological principles of Weber, who had argued that while sociologists' own values are implicated in their choice of subject matter and definition of a problem, once they proceed with their investigations their methods and analytical procedures should be as objective as possible. Moreover, the claims of scientific integrity preclude the use of sociological or scientific work for partisan or political ends in which, as citizens, they are quite properly engaged.

Schutz's phenomenology proposed a more radical version of the separation of scientific and natural roles, in which the choice of problem for sociologists should properly be derived from sociological, and not lay or political, definitions of the problems at hand:

> Sociological typifications of action and meaning, Schutz's 'second order con-
> structs', by definition are removed from the common-sense, practical activities
> of members of society; these typifications are a product of certain kinds of
> reflection by sociologists on the common-sense world. This would suggest that
> the main relationship between sociological reflection about the world and
> practical activity in the world lies. . . . in sociology's ability to clarify these prac-
> tical activities. . . . The contribution of sociology, then, . . . is that it can help
> the members of a society pose their own dilemmas more acutely and clearly.[103]

Sociological work, for whatever reason, can enter into public and political dis-course as a resource and stock of knowledge in its own right. It becomes extremely difficult, if not impossible, under such circumstances for sociologists to claim that they are disseminating knowledge simply as citizens and not in any way as scientists. The distinction between the two roles is, however, an important one and clearly holds implications for scientists in general, not sociologists alone.

■ Conclusions

If one theme has emerged, it is that, like facts, theories do not speak for themselves. Sociologists have not, on the whole, taken very seriously Kant's assertion that 'nothing is so practical as a good theory'. There is usually no simple or automatic set of policy prescriptions to be drawn from theories. A variety of interpretations are possible, and ideally the theorist should attempt to clarify their character. Translating theories into practice entails further complex and difficult stages in which the implications for action may be specified, proposals for monitoring and evaluation made, and likely side-effects anticipated. A theory of social problems should be complemented by a theory of policy process. Otherwise, the casting of a theory into the world is naïve. The obstacles to these aspirations are great, both intellectually and practically, so that no great mystery surrounds the relative infrequency with which they are even attempted.

Two obvious recommendations seem appropriate: one, that the monitoring and evaluation aspects of policy implementation be given far more emphasis than is currently the norm; and two, that the timescales on which most projects operate, which seem in general disproportionately short, should be lengthened.

The costs of such recommendations mean that the situation is unlikely to change, though such costs may be minimal compared with the losses from the premature abandonment or non-monitoring of expensive projects. Monitoring is a consequential process in its own right, and it is too often crude and over-simple, dominated by the search for limited effects in a short time period.[104]

Chapter Summary

This chapter has taken on the difficult task of looking at some of the ways in which social deviancy theory has been adapted to the purposes of social policy. There are various projects and policies which can be studied; however the difficulty is that the purpose of theory is not the articulation of policy, and policy is not indebted to theory.

The fit has not always been easy, and as we have seen, politics often puts theory to its own uses.

Critical-Thinking Questions

1. How was a victimization survey in Canada motivated by sociological theory research?
2. How successful was policy motivated by the Chicago School?
3. How relevant was the concept of anomie to an understanding of real-life deviance?
4. One of the case studies was based on the development of juvenile justice policy. How has that been influenced by ideas about the responsibility of juveniles, and society's obligation to them?

Websites

http://www.icclr.law.ubc.ca/ The International Centre for Criminal Law Reform and Criminal Justice Policy (ICCLR) was established in 1991 as an independent, non-profit institute affiliated with the United Nations. Its objectives are to contribute to international criminal justice policy through analysis, research, and consultation.

Chapter Thirteen

The Metamorphosis of Deviance?

- ■ Chapter Overview
- ■ Introduction
- ■ How Theories Illuminate the Millennium—Prediction and Control
  - • The Case of Strain Theory
  - • The Case of Labelling Theory
  - • The Case of Control Theory
  - • The Case of Critical Theory
- ■ Conclusion
- ■ Chapter Summary
- ■ Critical-Thinking Questions

Chapter Overview

In this chapter we evaluate some, but not all, of the social theories of deviance we have looked at in this text. We evaluate them, not for how well they explain deviance and not for their adaptability to social policy, but rather for their capacity to predict and control deviance in changing times. This is clearly much more of a speculative chapter than the rest, but some trends are discussed.

■ Introduction

Four decades since its decisive re-emergence in the mid-1960s, the sociology of deviance has, not surprisingly, encountered a fresh wave of critical analysis. In fact, an entire issue of the journal *Sociological Spectrum* is devoted to discussing 'a sociology of deviance in the new millennium', with articles on conceptual fashions in the sociology of deviance and relativism and on whether the concept of deviance is even still relevant. As Best says in his 'Whatever Happened to Social Pathology?' 'A variety of critics have pronounced deviance "dead," although they cannot agree on whether its demise was due to (a) the failure of sociologists of deviance to embrace a radical sociological agenda . . ., or (b) those sociologists of deviance having fallen into the grip of a radical sociological agenda'.[1]

As Best goes on to say, conflict theorists have criticized deviance studies for focusing too much on street crime and political protest while ignoring social arrangements, such as inadequate housing, that disadvantage the poor. Feminists have criticized the inclusion of abortion and prostitution in deviance, yet the lack of attention to domestic violence, rape, and pornography. Activists have charged that including homosexuality or disability as deviant ignores discrimination as a larger issue.

For the cynical, these objections to the viability of the sociology of deviance are not new. In 1994 Sumner offered the view that deviance studies are exhausted and had in fact died twenty years earlier.[2] Morrison said, more charitably, that the sociology of deviance is unable to cope with new trends in crime and society;[3] and Nelken, that it cannot cope with new perspectives in social theory.[4] As early as 1972 Liazos offered the opinion that the sociology of deviance was impoverished because of its neglect of power.[5]

Erich Goode, however, takes issue with Sumner, or at least with that interpretation of an early death.[6] He says that when Sumner argued that the sociology of deviance had 'died' in 1975, it meant a decline in the 'ideological function of the field for the ruling elite and not its declining intellectual vitality.' Goode says optimistically that although the sociology of deviance has declined perhaps in theoretical vitality since the 1960s, it is still influential:

> What I am proposing—and this is an empirical question—is that an immense number of fields have adopted the deviance concept, transformed it, renamed it, and used it in ways that are parallel to the way it was intended to be used by Edwin Lemert [in *Social Pathology*], or Howard Becker [in *The Outsiders*], and the other social constructionists. As Best says about sociology generally, and as I say elsewhere, deviance specialists are guilty of 'giving it away' for free.[7]

Joel Best, however, is not so optimistic.[8] He notes a decline in the use of the term deviance, just as there was a decline in the use of 'social pathology' decades earlier. He characterizes the sociology of deviance as inherently divisive, and that it is a field where critiques have called into question the very definition of deviance. He is vague about what the future holds, but he suggests that because sociologists disagree on even what should be considered deviant, theorists should be devising fresh questions and new orientations in order to move forward.

And it is obvious that there is no lack of interest in new topics, whether it is old forms of deviance in the workplace or school or new forms of deviance such as pathological Internet communities;[9] or even new directions, such as disorganization theory.[10] John Muncie has predicted that not only will globalization gradually apply to the control of obvious international policing issues such as transnational organized crime and international terrorism, but it will also have its effect in criminal justice reform itself. In his words,

a combination of neo-liberal assaults on the social logics of the welfare state
and public provision, widespread experimentation with restorative justice and
the prospect of rehabilitation through mediation and widely ratified international directives, epitomized by the United Nations Convention on the
Rights of the Child, have now made it possible to talk of a global juvenile/
youth justice.[11]

With such a suggestion, however, we move from the more traditional sociology of deviance to questions more properly dealt with in criminology, two fields
that overlap but are quite separate. Young, for example, sees the complex history
of deviance studies culminating in a fight between two forms of realism, that of
the left and of the right, but what he is talking about is criminology.[12] On the
other hand, Swaaningen says 'critical' criminology is the way forward,[13] whereas
Henry and Milovanovic propose that the future lies in ambitious system of 'constitutive' criminology, a re-working of the phenomenological and critical traditions and the sociology of law.[14]

There are other lines of argument which have only just begun to materialize,
and research on new topics is always developing, such as the current debate over
social capital, already referred to in this book. Raymond R. Corrado of Simon
Fraser University, Irwin M. Cohen of University College of the Fraser Valley, and
Garth Davies of Simon Fraser University argue that the relationship between
social capital and community crime-prevention programs is a direct one.[15] They
recommend that research on social-capital programs shows that they should continue to be established for vulnerable groups living in urban areas, such as marginalized families of recent immigrants, aboriginal families, homeless people,
marginalized youth, and youth living in the street:

> Informal networks developed in programs, such as the National Association
> of Aboriginal Friendship Centres, along with linkages to formal government
> and non-government resource networks are vitally important in allowing at-
> risk youth and adults to make the transition into pro-social relationships and
> employment, thus increasing the communities or neighbourhoods' potential
> to reduce crime and social disorder.

Let us sum up several of these forecasts about the sociology of deviance, and
examine the questions they pose about the state of research.

• *The first critique, that the sociology of deviance is exhausted, tends to devalue
social theories of deviance as lacking purchase on the complexities of the post-
modernist world*, seeing them as 'master narratives' that fitted modernist but
not post-modernist conditions. There is no more reason to accept post-modernist
eschatology as a foundational narrative than any of the other narratives which
post-modernism rejects. As Eagleton[16] has argued in the case of literary theory, such a dismissal is itself a narrative, albeit one that leads nowhere and
that fails to acknowledge the extent to which the condition was well theorized

in the first place by the traditions thus consigned to history. In his view, this 'illusion of post-modernism' reflects the displacement of radical energies in the wake of political defeat. The problem—the difficulties of accounting for the triumph of market capitalism and of reconciling the clash of different world views—is taken to be the solution: that is, all cultures, tastes, and beliefs are equally valid.

There is a sense in which the sociology of deviance was prematurely post-modernist, that is, in its emphasis on the importance of accounts, hierarchies of credibility, and vocabularies of motive. In the highly unequal division of labour that goes into the social construction of reality, sociologists of deviance have long aimed to redress the balance between those in and those outside power. The attempt, however, is to mediate between different accounts rather than to grant them equal validity. In this way perhaps there is still a role for a sociology of deviance.

• *The second critique, that we are witnessing a fight between the left and the right, is more in line with earlier attempts to synthesize diverse theories into just such a super 'master narrative'*, with 'left realism' combining key elements from strain, labelling, control, and radical theories into one. While this synthesis has done much to reinvigorate such theories as anomie and subculture, it skates too readily over fundamental problems of analysis and root causes. Left realism encounters exactly the same problems as the earlier parent theories on which it depends, for example, overprediction. Its core cause, relative deprivation, tries to account for far more deviance than exists, even now, especially among women. Such problems are compounded for left realists by the synthesis of competing causes, which entails a multiplier effect, that is, overprediction cubed.

In contrast, right realists have taken the opposite approach, that of anti-synthesis. Having stripped away all theoretical positions bar one, that human nature causes crime and, as a consequence, only punitive means against it can work at all,[17] they face the difficult problem of accounting for immense differences in comparative social problems without convincing reference to social, economic, or cultural variables. Of the two, left realism offers the more plausible perspective, though perhaps because right realism lends itself so readily to populist beliefs and sound-bite criminology, the latter has been by far the most influential policy prescription. We offer the observation that the political debate over crime is instructive about what has happened to the sociology of deviance—we have moved to a more legalistic definition of deviance.

• *Two other suggestions for change have similar problems to left realism.* 'Critical' criminology[18] embraces the best both of liberalism (universal human rights) and democratic socialism (whose goal is a just society). However, there is only one major respect in which the continental forms of critical criminology differ from much mainstream and 'left realist' criminology in pursuit of these same goals: that is the abolitionist tradition of theorizing alternatives to penal measures. The abolitionist perspective, which aims at the virtual elimination of imprisonment, has proved a fertile source for a host of community responses to crime in several European countries, especially The Netherlands.[19] Despite lacking a popular base and being at odds with 'realist' criminologies of both left and right, it has made an impact, at times, on criminal justice policy.

The tension between the abolitionist strain of critical criminology and left realism is most marked in relation to policing. Through its proponents have so far resisted the implications of its appeal, there is a marked affinity between the reliance of left realism on social control through localized policing and working-class authoritarianism,[20] enhanced by legislation such as juvenile curfews, electronic tagging, coercive parental counselling, and the blurring of the line between civil and criminal proceedings.

'Constitutive' criminology seeks to achieve a new synthesis of phenomenological and critical approaches to crime, law, and society. But it does not resolve the problems pointed to in earlier chapters related to these approaches. In one respect, they propose a novel concept, 'transpraxis', to counter the dangers of (post-revolutionary) authoritarian alternatives—but without adequate analysis of what alternative futures are offered. 'Transpraxis' consists basically of thinking ahead to avoid making things worse, a worthy aim not greatly helped by coining so ambiguous a term.

The questions that arise from these developments are, naturally enough, how far they indicate a fundamental change of direction in the field and whether or not that spells the effective end of the sociology of deviance as a recognizable subject. Would it now, in line with recent texts and a new journal, be better termed 'theoretical criminology' or some other variant on that theme? The important battles were won in the 1960s, with the shift to the sociology of deviance from a field largely framed by medico-legal precepts, and with the acceptance of the premise that crime and deviance were problematic, not immanent, properties of social conduct. Since then, criminology and sociology have become increasingly meshed together, with frequent interchange and borrowings of concepts, methods, and theories. However the two fields are distinctly different.

> Compared to criminology, the sociology of deviance is inherently radical.

In considering these suggestions, we are not so wedded to theories of 'deviance' that we would resist the abandonment of the concept in the face of superior alternatives. To make that shift, however, we would need to be persuaded that such theories had been seriously outpaced by events, fresh theories, or new ideas—and that does not seem to be the case.

One further example justifies that conclusion. Cain, in her *Orientalism, Occidentalism and the Sociology of Crime*, develops her case for a 'transgressive' criminology by reference to the difficulties of applying mainstream Western theories of deviance, and control to non-Western and developing societies. Criminology is entrapped either by *orientalism*—the assumption that non-Western societies are unavoidably different—or by *occidentalism*—the assumption that the Western template can be applied to *all* societies.[21] She is undoubtedly right to criticize superficial and ethnocentric comparative work and to challenge such notions as the assumption that the age-crime relationship which appears to prevail in North America and western Europe holds for Jamaica and Senegal. But to take these shortcomings and those that have occurred in the history of crime and gender studies as grounds for rejecting all previous theorizing, is far too dismissive of its strengths.

In contrast, Stan Cohen, no stranger to the most stringent criticism of the field (especially in his *Against Criminology* and *States of Denial*), finds in Sykes and Matza's theory of 'techniques of neutralization' a cornerstone for the understanding, not only of juvenile delinquency, but also of the worst political atrocities. He is able to take an old idea in the sociology of deviance and apply it to an understanding of a new topic as he does here: 'Yet political accounts most often follow the same internal logic and assume the same social function as ordinary deviant accounts. The narrative acknowledges that something happened, but refuses to accept the category of acts to which it is assigned. The equivalent of "you can't call this stealing" is "you can't call this torture".'[22]

In any field where knowledge is far from perfect, the need to start afresh recurs and does, at times, amount to the semblance of a paradigmatic revolution—a seismic shift in theorizing from a new set of first principles. Such a shift arguably did occur in this field in the 1960s, a shift that drew on sociological work from Durkheim onwards but reassembled it in fundamentally new analytical directions. As yet there do not seem to be the grounds for establishing a comparable shift in perspective. As Keynes remarked, regarding economics, 'No theory is ever dead.' Theories are reworked, and different theories are reassembled in a novel vein; some that were prematurely abandoned are rediscovered and revived in changed times and cultures. Such seems to have been the case of late with the sociology of deviance. Far from being overthrown or eclipsed, it is in the process of metamorphosis. But what exactly is it changing into?

> No theory is ever dead.

Key questions are not only how the theories might compare in the ways they account for deviance and control (both as metatheories and as sources for applied theories relevant to different types and cases), but also how usefully they predicted and handled the changing trends in deviance and its context. For the context has undeniably changed. Whether we term it 'high-', 'late-',or 'post'-modernity, the transformation of economics and of labour markets in the wake of automation and the globalization of the political economy of capitalism have led to profound changes in family structures, problems of urbanization, and formal social control. At best, such changes—in birth control, information technology, and mobility—have created the conditions for new forms of emancipation—of gender, ethnicity, and sexuality.[23] At least, on the cost side, they have engendered new forms and scales of inequality and exclusion—of single parenthood, expendable long-term unemployment, homelessness—once thought incompatible with comprehensive welfare provision. At worst, they presage global havoc, schism, and mass self-extinction by pollution, deforestation, global warming, and other assorted unwanted side-effects of high population and high-consumption rates of growth.[24]

Whatever might be said about such portents, and they may turn out to be the ultimate moral panic, they put deviance in its place. The global trends involved are fundamental properties of modern life rather than aspects of deviant misconduct. They flow from economic virtue under both capitalist and state-socialist versions of political economy, rather than from marginal forms of deviant entrepreneurship. The corrective action needed to halt such trends, not to mention reverse them, will logically create new fields for deviance and control. On this score Marx may have the last laugh. Despite capitalist triumphalism after the collapse of State socialist regimes and the breakup of the Soviet Union, the ultimate opposition to the logic of capitalism, at least of its consumerist heyday, may well be the limits to growth spelt out ecologically—a contradiction even Marx did not foresee.

The condition of post-modernity may be readily imaginable (science-fiction writers have been doing little else for a century); but it is far from being the actual state of affairs, despite tangible signs of its emergence. For that reason, Giddens' use of the term 'late modernity' seems preferable, though even that raises the questions 'How late is late?' or 'Late in relation to what?' or 'Is it too late to have supper before the show?' The condition of late modernity has seemed to incubate trends that have created changes for deviance, and control against which to assess the validity and relevance of theory. No knock-out punch actually seems to have been delivered, given what is currently in view, any more than from past developments.

■ How Theories Illuminate the Millennium— Prediction and Control

All the theories dealt with in earlier chapters have had things to say that illuminate the millennium in ways which show their likely continuing potential for novel synthesis and applications. In a field where continuities and changes are often difficult to differentiate, the following trends seem to have been usefully presaged by some of the major theories.

The Case of Strain Theory

Continuities and change in *strain theory* offer one of the clearest instances of prescience in the sociology of deviance. The fundamental propositions of the anomie and subcultural traditions of theory from the 1930s on were that inequality, whether persistent or growing, combined with rising expectations fuelled by consumer capitalism, would lead to increasing problems and the emergence or growth of more serious forms of deviance. Early subcultural theory was replete with warnings that automation would lead to mass working-class unemployment unless radical changes in training, education, and job creation were made.[25] Little was done and, in the wake of widespread deindustrialization and 'marketization', massive job losses coincided with rampant consumerism to produce a much-analyzed and well-documented widening of inequalities and increase in poverty.[26]

Left realism is the main current vehicle for these concerns. In a recent article, Webber reassesses the concept of relative deprivation and its current relevance. Rather than search for causes of problems in either individuals or social structures, the concept of relative deprivation can sensitize us to the process and emotion of deviance.[27]

In many respects the predicted increase in social problems and changes in the character of deviance took place on cue. In Europe, especially Britain, and in North America, property crime and rates of drug-related crime rose sharply. New forms of inequality and social exclusion generated a series of riots unprecedented in modern Britain, riots which in the 1980s were associated with policing issues and in the 1990s with florid forms of delinquency such as 'hotting'.[28] Crime rates then fell. They fell in England and Wales, to exceptionally low rates. They fell in Canada, probably as the percentage of youths in the population decreased. They also fell in the United States, but one likely reason was the effect of an extraordinarily high prison population, which removed some 6 per cent of the most 'at risk' of crime-age groups—young males—and reduced male unemployment by 2 per cent by the simple process of removing some two million people from the labour market.[29] Even so, according to calculations by Richard Freeman,[30] once allowances are made for this effect, the crime rate of the unincarcerated has still risen—a damning finding for proponents of deterrence, if not of incapacitation.

•*Against this view, several critical remarks have been made.* One is that falling inequality and full employment in the 1960s did not lead to falling crime (quite the reverse) and that mass unemployment and huge inequality in the 1930s did not lead to steep rises in crime.[31] A second is that 'deficit' theories of crime do not account for its growth among the affluent.[32] While both objections are powerful reminders that no simple relationship obtains between deviance and inequality, the essential accompaniment to such links is the context of market-driven rising expectations.

Some of the complexities of this relationship were captured by Simon Field's authoritative study[33] demonstrating short-term cyclical fluctuations in property crime and social wealth. This pattern amounts to anomie in action: when times are bad, people are more likely to buy from the black market, or from the back of a truck;[34] when times are good, people buy from established stores.[35] What remains unclear is how such short-term resolutions to the strain to anomie exhibit a long-term 'ratchet effect',[36] so that net rises in crime acquire some permanence. The most likely result is that an instrumental moral expediency becomes steadily more acceptable, a process which is challengeable only by punitive means or the closer attainment of that Durkheimian ideal of a just society based on a moral framework acceptable by all.

•*The limits to prescience are well exemplified by theorists* who correctly predicted a huge increase in the amount and seriousness of deviance, but failed to deduce where that could lead in the realm of punishment and control. Even the most extreme radical theorists seemed bound by the liberal paradigm that no democratic government would countenance so dramatic a change in the character and scale of the prison population as that which has occurred in the United States since the mid-1970s. Nor did the proponents of penal incapacitation, such as James Q. Wilson and John DeIulio, predict so marked a move to mass imprisonment, much as they may have welcomed it. Penal policy has never before had so profound an impact on American and, given the international situation, world politics. The links between politics, deviance, and control have not, since the rise of Fascism, had so potent an effect on the shaping of Western democracies.[37]

Two interlocking problems that remain unresolved are, first, why official crime rates have fallen rather than risen over the past decade in spite of increased inequality in Britain and the United States; and, secondly, why the fear of crime has remained relatively unchanged despite that fall. On the first question, it is not enough to point to rising imprisonment in Britain and mass imprisonment in the US as the answer. Canada, for example, has experienced much the same rise and fall in homicide rates over the past forty years as the US but at one-third of the American level and without resorting to mass incarceration.[38] Indeed, Canada has seen a notable stability in both crime and punishment rates over the past two decades. In the cases of Britain and the US, it may well be that, even though *some* causes of crime, such as inequality and a rampant winner-loser culture have not been lessened and have even worsened, it is possible to lower the crime rate by punitive and purely situational prevention measures, such as target hardening, CCTV, the proliferation of 'gated' communities, and the denial of access to designated sites to all but holders of ID cards. Such a 'culture of control', as discussed by Garland in *Mass Imprisonment* helps account for both falling crime rates and the persistently high rates of fear of crime. A state of constant red alert and a permanent sense of crisis are not conducive to peace of mind, especially when they are given daily reinforcement by the governments and certain segments of the media.

The Case of Labelling Theory

These trends also raise problems for labelling theory, which, broadly conceived, offered the first step towards dealing with societal reaction and formal control processes as variables rather than constants in the creation and transformation of deviant behaviour. The initial excitement of applying the concepts of Becker, Goffman, and Lemert—moral career, moral entrepreneurship, moral passage, and secondary deviance—to deviance and control tended to give way to premature disillusionment when the most obvious means of delabelling and decarceration failed to lead to crime reduction. Such reactions, however understandable, have tended to obscure the real and continuing impact of labelling theory on social theory and social movements.

•*First of all, two generations of students in the social sciences and their applied fields, such as social work and probation work, have now been exposed to the approach* and have used its insights for the reappraisal of deviant naming. The new-found significance of the politics of naming has derived at least in part from the vocabulary and theories of labelling and has had some appreciable effect in the partial emancipation of women, ethnic minorities, the disabled, and gays. In Canada, marijuana has been effectively decriminalized, abortion is widely accepted, and same-sex couples have won the right to marry and divorce. Even the concept of 'moral panic'[39] has worked its way into the English language, a sign of acceptance that the over-interpretation of extreme instances of deviance can be self-defeating.

The abuses often attributed to this development—political correctness and the 'culture of complaint',[40] has undoubtedly led to excesses in its turn; but it can be argued that the re-defining of *some* forms of deviance as diversity has resulted in net gains in tolerance and heightened understanding.

•*Secondly, labelling theory was given a second wind by the work of Michel Foucault* and its critical development by Stan Cohen, David Garland, and others.[41] The work of Cohen[42] provides a rich vein of concepts—net-widening, mesh thinning, blurring, penetration, and the proliferation of community controls—that presaged such invasive developments as CCTV, electronic tagging, urine testing, and new 'vocabularies of motive' for States violating human rights and restricting civil liberties. Such invasive, pervasive, and exclusionary devices have the powerful legitimation, often shared by communities as well as 'the State', that they are essential to the 'war against crime', a discourse which brooks no alternatives to punitive measures unless they are of a rarely achieved, demonstrable effectiveness, which is a very strict criterion of effectiveness.[43]

•*Thirdly, trends strikingly in line with labelling theorists' predictions about the future of social control in late modernity have taken place in the realm of social exclusion.* This is a field far wider than crime and one that necessitates the use of 'deviance' to capture its reach. For example, school suspensions and expulsions in Britain have risen even more rapidly than crime rates or sentences and have combined their long-term effects with the lack of substantive rights to process. Perhaps the most formidable example has been the use to which the term 'underclass' has been put in the work of Charles Murray.[44]

As MacNicol predicted,[45] the term 'underclass' has been appropriated by the 'New Right' to blame the poor themselves for the resurgence of poverty and for the 'culture of dependency' that allegedly stems from social assistance. There are three important strands to the underclass story.

The first is the social construction of the concept, which, especially in the work of Murray, hinges heavily on the conflation of illegitimate single parenthood, self-induced unemployment, and deviance. 'Underclass', even more than its progenitor, the 'culture of poverty', is a set of attributes that are ascribed to social groups and entrap them into dependence on the State. In contrast, 'social exclusion' implies a set of tendencies, the 'downsizing' of the workforce, the destabilization of work, and the consequent erosion of family and community structures, that exclude certain groups from secure, well-paid jobs, and viable social networks.

Second, the evidence for the 'welfare causes underclass' thesis is comparatively weak. Both in the United States[46] and in Europe,[47] comparisons between levels of social assistance, single parenthood, and crime rates fail to match the theory—quite strikingly so in the European case. The converse theory, that joblessness and poor job quality are the root causes of both the need for welfare and the increased reliance on crime, is strongly supported by a detailed study.[48]

Thirdly, the adverse definition and effective abandonment of the excluded as authors of their own misfortune have helped to justify their ghettoization[49] and has greatly increased incarceration[50] and technologically driven surveillance.[51] The potency of labelling process is well exemplified in these seemingly disparate trends.

It should not be forgotten that labelling theory was always more than a theory of labelling. It centred on the self and the negotiation of social action, and it has proved robust as a way of looking at very diverse settings in which deviance takes place. It provides a crucial component in Giddens' theory of structuration,[52] which is the most ambitious recent attempt to resolve the 'problem of sociology': namely, how society, which is a human creation, may be experienced as beyond human control. Giddens' resolution of the structure-agency problem by viewing human agency as essential to the production and reproduction of social order and of the self does not, however, yield immediate gains for the understanding of deviance. A knowledge of deviance cannot be directly inferred from concepts such as globalization, high modernity, and the sequestration of experience[53] any more than from notions of class and conflict. Partly formed by interactionism, such concepts lend themselves more readily to empirical observation and—as in the work of Bottoms and Wiles[54]—they are beginning to inform theory and research into the most recent developments in policing and risk control.

It is all too easy to forget the most obvious and lasting example of the relevance of labelling theory that lies within the sphere in which its rise to prominence began—with the modest-seeming propositions of Howard Becker about marijuana use. Since then, the reach of drugs control has expanded vastly in significance, not least because of high-profile campaigners, its impact on the American prison population with its grotesquely disproportionate ethnic composition,[55] and the enormous growth of illicit drug use globally.

The 'Great Prohibition'[56] differs from that of the 1920s in several ways. It has spread virtually all around the world; it is being applied to a wide array of drugs rather than just alcohol; it has already lasted far longer than the 'old' Prohibition, which served, lest we forget, to fuel the take-off of organized crime in the United States; and it generates profits that constitute perverse incentives for drug-related crime, the corruption of officialdom, the exploitation of the miseries of a criminalized underclass, the 'drug mules' of the addictive economy, and the economic deformations of money laundering and drug production. These unwanted side-effects of prohibition, rather than the drugs themselves, have been exhaustively chronicled and analyzed.[57] The case has been made endlessly for alternative and, on the balance of the evidence, more effective and harm-reducing regulation.

The main counter-argument, that our inability to prevent every burglary, theft, and robbery hardly makes the case for their decriminalization, ignores the primacy of the key difference between crimes of victimization and those termed 'deviance without victims'—perhaps too readily since crack-cocaine and heroin obviously take a heavy toll. But the fact remains that householders do not welcome burglars onto their property, car owners do not hand their keys to car thieves, and those who are robbed do not willingly part with their wallets or purses.

Drug users in their millions, however, do collude with their sources of supply, and only the sociological labelling perspective can illuminate the refusal of governments, with notable exceptions, to take account of so elementary a fact in their making of criminal justice policy and of the consequent mass production of secondary deviance and secondary controls.

The Case of Control Theory

Control theories are based on concerns which overlap markedly with those of strain and labelling theories, but they differ profoundly from strain and labelling theories in that they explain deviance primarily by the weakening or absence of effective links between individuals and such social institutions as the family, the school, the workplace, the community, and so on. Over the past two decades the condition of late modernity has increasingly been defined as systematically damaging to such bonds. The increased scope for mobility, both social and physical, is believed to fuel an increasingly hedonistic individualism that holds collective well-being in scant regard. The change from full, stable employment to insecure, part-time work is believed to fragment communities and families. Advanced capitalism affords the many what was once the preserve of the few—unprecedented scope for travel, choice, the search for individual self-gratification from the fruits of economic growth. To strain theories, the emphasis lies in the gap between expectations and reality as a motor of endless dissatisfaction which may promote deviance. To control theorists, it is the progressive erosion of social cohesion which is the primary cause of deviance.

Against this background, social cohesion needs resuscitation if it is to survive. The 'communitarianism' of Amitai Etzioni[58] is one model for its recovery. The commitment to being a good parent is becoming more difficult in market societies, he argues. Thanks to an ever more demanding work environment, parents in 1985 spent only seventeen hours a week with their children compared to thirty in 1965, although there is now evidence that this trend may be reversing.[59] But even so civic-minded a reformer as Etzioni accepts 'gated' communities as the price to be paid for the enhancement of social cohesion. Shaming punishments, including electronic tagging, are needed to provide reassurance about security and risk. This drift to a revival of neo-medieval sanctions in the electronic age is seen as the only possible antidote to the centrifugal tendencies of late modernity. It is ironic that, after a twenty-year period of rampant market individualism, even neoconservatives such as Francis Fukayama are acknowledging the need to reassess the claims of the social against the economic. He prefaces his book *Trust* (1995)—a celebration of that precept as a factor in business success—with a quotation from Durkheim (1895):

> A Society composed of an infinite number of unorganized individuals, that a hypertrophied State is formed to oppress and contain, constitutes a veritable sociological monstrosity. . . . A nation can be maintained only if, between the State and the individual, there is interlaced a whole series of secondary groups real enough to the individual to attract them strongly in their sphere of action and drag them, in this way, into the general torrent of social life. . . . Occupational groups are suited to fill this role and this is their destiny.[60]

Paul Ormerod[61] reminds us, also, that Adam Smith, the proclaimed saint of free enterprise, accepted that society rested on a 'moral economy' that should set limits to economic exploitation.

It is perhaps necessary to disentangle the properties of modernity from those of the political economy of capitalism that has fashioned their development in particular ways. John Braithwaite proposes a reading of modernity, and its impact on community, somewhat different from that of Etzioni. First, he argues that, even in a fairly literal sense, the storm centres of modernity are tightly knit communities: 'One of the mythologies of late modernity is that capitalism runs on formal controls to the exclusion of the informal. The fact is that at the very centre of capitalism what you have on Wall Street, in Toyko, and in the City of London is a surprisingly communitarian culture of capitalism'.[62]

Capitalism does not necessarily fragment communities; however, it has wreaked havoc in Hispanic and black minority communities and in traditional white working-class communities in Britain.[63]

Braithwaite's second point is that shaming, in its reintegrative form, largely arose *with* modernity, especially in the family, and is associated historically with reductions in crime, domestic violence, and stigmatizing punishments. Third, although stigmatizing, exclusionary punishment has staged a comeback, the potential for reintegrative shaming is in some ways greater in modern urban societies than in close rural communities. The process of growing interdependencies and role segregation increase scope for shaming in communities of interest; perhaps opening up possibilities of 'global shaming'?:

> The segmented self is a double-edged sword. It affords us day-to-day protection from shame as we move around groups with different values; but it leaves us very vulnerable when an act of wrongdoing becomes so public as to become known to all these groups. The latter vulnerability has maximum force with the shaming of crime, because this is the most public institutionalisation of shaming that we have.[64]

However, stigmatizing shaming can drive the deviant into protective subcultures that are hardened against shame and replete with symbolic defences against it. Inclusionary shaming holds out the prospect of genuine reintegration. Again, however, Braithwaite relies heavily on examples of groups with a strong 'stake in conformity'—the argument is less easily sustained where the only segmented roles people inhabit are those of the dole queue and the soup kitchen, a point of course he would concede.

Situational control theories, more than any other approach, have helped to fashion the character of late modernity. While lacking any explicit concern with theorizing root causes, its principal focus is very much to analyze the temporal, spatial, and technical aspects of crime prevention in a rapidly changing world in order to deter the offender by reducing opportunities and enhancing detection and capture. Every target hardened, every space rendered defensible is a gain in control. Motivation is stripped down to its operative core. The rational deviant, is, as Stan Cohen put it,[65] 'nothing *but* choice'—he is devoid of biographical or symbolic substance, social background, or culture. He is a hedonistic predator, motivated only by gain and defeated only by fear. Guilt, shame, frustration, desperation, and boredom do not figure in the equation. It is a particularly post-modernist conception for a world whose economy is increasingly driven by the impersonal and unfettered money market on a global scale. It harks back to the most modernist theory of all, the utilitarian *felicity calculus* of Jeremy Bentham. And in Bentham's *panopticon* can be found its ideal, a system of total surveillance and control.

In some respects, however, situational control theorists have moved beyond the purely preventative and controlling objectives to a wider concern with citizenship rights. For example, Ken Pease has argued that situational measures are vindicated even if, because of displacement the amount of deviance does not fall. If it is spread more evenly among victims, that is a beneficial result because the overburdening of multiple victims by repeat offending is at least reduced. As well, Hope and Foster have argued for the optimum combination of social and situational policies, which could be a recipe for the transformation of deviance from a blight that falls like a plague of locusts on some communities and groups rather than others, into a manageable set of risks that can be insured against in policy as well as security terms. However, the immediate pain of victimization—and the impact that makes on the politics of law and order[66]—gives the purely situational and punitive a built-in edge over longer-term and more diffuse, but arguably more effective, policies of deviancy reduction.

In an unjust, highly unequal society, the claims of 'restorative' justice are always secondary to those of retribution.

The Case of Critical Theory

Critical studies of deviance have had their own role in the elaboration of just that basic point. Having suffered a number of damaging rebuffs in the late 1970s (at least in Britain and in the United States, but not so much in Canada where it found a receptive audience), it metamorphosed into 'left realism' and a continuing but much reduced neo-Marxist remainder. On the Continent it continued to develop in a less sectarian, more pragmatic way.[67] The debates in the US and Britain, if they can be called that, either did not happen in European criminology or were far more muted. The feminist critique,[68] the social democratic critique,[69] and the internal schism[70] did not appear in Dutch, Scandinavian, Italian, or German criminology. The debates rolled on, though the tenor of the 'law-and-order' politics was far more hostile to radical reform and, in particular, abolitionist ideas in penal policy. The result was a sociology of deviance more 'critical' than left realism, but more pragmatic than 'left idealism'.[71]

There is an obvious reason why a neo-Marxist sociology of deviance will become far more vigorous in the twenty-first century. That is, Marxism, at least of a libertarian kind, is back on track after about a century of 'guilt by association' with Stalinist State socialism; that was a brand of political economy that it never upheld but which it found exceptionally difficult to criticize during the Cold War and to theorize in terms of central canons of Marxism. As Parkin pointed out,[72] Marxism was at a loss to explain Fascism, because the State was meant to be the committee for the management of the affairs of the bourgeoisie, not the means for its domination. With Fascism, Stalinism, and Maoism largely consigned to the past, it is said, the true course of history has been resumed. The very fact of capitalist triumphalism is in line with Marxist tenets, for it was only on the basis of the contradictions of a mature capitalism that socialism was to be truly born. Far from being over, the argument with Marxism is only just about to begin all over again, this time in the context of a capitalism careering out of control and without the communism exerting a counter-pressure for egalitarian policies in welfare, income and wealth distribution, and the international equivalent in the form of the controls that were exercised by nation-states over business and finance before the 'big bang' of global capitalism in the 1980s.

In sociological terms, capitalists have also, for the past two decades, been behaving extraordinarily badly. A host of highly criminogenic trends have been set in motion, at times almost perversely in view of their impact on deviance—financial deregulation, deindustrialization, massive job losses, homelessness, rising poverty and inequality, and the force feeding of the 'new individualism' by consumerist pressures.

The 'new individualism' is said by Giddens to be a mixture of positives and negatives, of emancipation and anxiety, fuelled by new sorts of uncertainty. A basic mistake was to equate the new individualism with the self-seeking of the marketplace and to opt for a theory according to which, through the market, multiple egoisms came to mean the public good.[73]

The resulting rise in crime, especially its drug-related forms, with the side-effects of corruption, money laundering, and racketeering, have been met by increasingly punitive methods of policing and punishment. In Nils Christie's nightmare[74] the whole cycle resembles a scenario of left functionalism: capitalist contradictions produce rising crime, which is used to justify vastly increased reliance on privatized prisons, probation, and policing, which create fresh profits to plow back into yet more of the same; it is a self-justifying vicious circle of instrumental criminalization. Similarly in his study of arms trading, money laundering, and corporate crime, Vincenzo Ruggiero[75] discerns a growing accommodation between corporate crime and so-called 'organized crime'—the 'mafiaization' of business on a global scale.

> Capitalism causes crime, which requires investments in control.

There is enough truth in their accounts to ensure a great deal of mileage for critical analysis in the post-millennial era. It is more difficult than in the past, however, to see where Marxism begins and ends in these approaches. Marxism, as the theorists of social democracy have long pointed out,[76] presented a diagnosis of capitalism that many non-Marxist socialists share. The difference lies in the prescription for what is to be done about its defects. Democratic socialists remain wedded to reformism, Marxists to some version or other of revolutionary change.

■ Conclusion

Images of future deviance and its control, which are implicit in the various approaches discussed in this book, provide one way of assessing their application in the future. Their fundamentally distinct character and the tentative nature of any prediction of how society will evolve make any such overall assessment highly problematic.

Strain theory from the early 1960s predicted the increasing rates in both the seriousness and amount of deviance in the wake of de-industrialization. What it failed to predict was the concomitant rise of offences among the powerful, a problem of imperfect application rather than a theoretical defect. Anomie theory in its Durkheimian form was well-equipped to do so, however. As relative inequality increases on a global scale, strain theory is still relevant to a sociology of deviance.

Radical theories explicitly attacked the 'under-prediction of bourgeois criminality'[77] in the sociology of deviance, but on grounds which practically ruled out any possibility of being an honest capitalist or a dishonest non-capitalist. The overly romantic theories of traditional critical sociology have been replaced with an analysis of the effects of modernization, deskilling, and a global environmental crisis.

For its part, labelling theory was pregnant with forebodings about the future shape of systems of control. Though those were not explicitly cast as predictions of the revival of fear of an 'underclass', the electronic tagging of offenders, or the explosion of imprisonment in the United States, their concerns presaged such developments. In its focus on societal reaction, the punitive reaction to deviance that occurred in the 1990s belies any suggestion of the early demise of labelling theory, as long as it is attuned to a macro-analysis of power and control.

Control theories likewise heralded the shift from informal to formal controls as the predictable response of governments to a rise in deviance in the wake of changes in family structure and the erosion of communities at a time of rapid economic change and deindustrialization. However, how to reorganize society so as to increase social capital and social cohesion without the stigmatizing of deviants will be the challenge for control theory.

It is possible, though in our view premature, to synthesize all these diverse approaches into one master theory that situates the growing strain to deviance and the consequent over-control of some groups rather than others, in the context of the destructive aspects of global capitalism. When taken all together, rather than separately, the weakness of the theories—the tendency to gross over-prediction or under-prediction, the vulnerability to reification, and the risks of over-interpretation—tend to be multiplied rather than reduced.

The opposite tendency—to argue that because no theory works, no theory can ever work—is equally unwise, and it reduces the sociology of deviance unfairly. It is best to advance but with a more sophisticated use of tried and tested methods: comparative study, field study, and a constant openness to fresh developments in other disciplines. The transformative properties of deviance remain a vital, yet neglected resource for the understanding of social order and social change.

Chapter Summary

This chapter has looked at how well some of the social theories of deviance discussed in this book have predicted the relationship between deviance and social context. While anticipating what a sociology of deviance for the 'new millennium' will look like, we assess some of the major perspectives, and comment on some recent trends. One concern we note is that there is a continuing tendency to replace a sociology of deviance discourse with one borrowed from criminology, but in our view that is part of the modern tendency to deviantize difference and professionalize control. Both of these trends are worth watching, but we feel that sociology is still up to the task.

Critical-Thinking Questions

1. How relevant was strain theory in explaining deviance in capitalism?
2. How is situational control theory not about disposition, but about motivation?
3. Why is Nils Christie having nightmares?

Glossary

alienation: In Marxist theory, the feeling in workers of being separated from control over the process of production; the feeling of being out of control of one's life and self. Has parallels to normlessness and also to lack of attachment. See also *class conflict, anomie.*

altruistic suicide: A type of suicide by which a person, such as a kamikaze pilot sacrifices his or her life for the good of the group; associated with the work of Durkheim.

amplification: A process of interaction between deviants and authorities where the police respond to action and define it as deviance, thereby generating further deviance, which requires a more punitive response, and so on in a spiral.

androgen: The male hormone that causes deviance; the concept is used in gender studies and feminist analysis.

anomic suicide: A type of suicide resulting from an absence of norms in society. associated with the work of Durkheim. See also *anomie.*

anomie: A situation, according to Durkheim, where the norms that govern conduct break down, leading to personal uncertainty because of the lack of social restraint. See also *strain.*

argot: A specialized language of any group of people, such as prisoners or cheque forgers. See also *subculture.*

atavism: In the theory of criminal anthropology characteristics that represent an earlier stage of evolution; associated with Lombroso.

attachment: In Hirschi's theory, the strength of the bond one has to others which is an element of control preventing deviance.

breaching: An experimental technique which involves pretending not to understand basic rules, and then observing how people act, associated with Garfinkel.

broken windows: A theory that physical deterioration in a neighbourhood is an element of social disorganization, which leads to increased fears for personal safety and higher crime rates overall.

Chicago School: An approach that emphasizes the study of the ecological distribution of deviance and social disorganization, and the use of ethnography; associated with Parks, Thrasher. See also *ethnography.*

claims maker: A person in a position of authority to make claims about deviance and have them accepted by others. See also *labelling*.

class conflict: Inequalities in wealth and power that cause deviance directly and also indirectly in interaction between authorities and deviants; associated with Marx. See also *labelling*.

cohort: A group of people of the same age who are studied to see how deviance develops over time. See also *longitudinal study*.

commitment: The degree of participation in conventional activities that insulates the person from deviance; associated with Hirschi. See also *attachment*.

conformity: Behaviour that is in accordance with social norms, because of either agreement with social values or fear of sanctions.

consensus: Agreement with basic social values, which is indispensable for social stability; conditions that threaten consensus, such as class conflict, lead to instability and deviance.

conversation analysis: An approach developed from interactionism, and meant to illustrate what people accomplish through discourse, e.g., naming deviance.

corporate deviance: Actions that are committed by individuals in organizations and that benefit those organizations. See also *professional deviance*.

counterculture: A culture created in opposition to the dominant culture, as in the work of Willis. See also *subculture*.

crime: An intentional act that contravenes a law, and that is censured and labelled illegal by authorities; usually seen as more serious than deviance.

crime rate: The number of crimes reported to the police in a year, divided by the population, multiplied by 100,000, to give the likelihood that a crime will occur. See also *dark figure of crime*.

criminal anthropology: The study of anatomy associated with Lombroso and physiology in the late 1800s. See also *atavism*.

criminology: The study of the causes of crime, its basis in law, and techniques for its control; developed as an interdisciplinary study to include sociology, biology, psychology, history, geography, and economics.

culture of poverty: The lower-class values, such as fatalism, that are developed by people who live in poverty and dependency and that lead to failure.

dark figure of crime: Crime that is not reported to the police and that is not evident from official statistics. See also *victimization survey*.

definition of the situation: In symbolic interactionism, the way in which the actor views or interprets the situation and his or her actions.

delinquent: A young offender who commits deviance.

dependent variable: In experimental research, the variable, e.g., deviance, which is affected by the manipulation of the independent variable, e.g., poverty.

deviance: A general term to describe actions that do not conform to group values; actions defined as deviance by the reaction of others; varies across cultures and historical periods. See also *crime*.

deviantology: The sociological study of deviance, which comprises a range of behaviours different from those studied by criminology.

differential association: The idea that deviance is learned like any other kind of behaviour, in association with significant others in a reference group. See also *subculture*.

diffusion of benefits: In situational crime prevention, an unexpected benefit of crime control, where the benefits spill over to other locations. See also *displacement*.

discourse: A specialized term for the use of talk in interaction and in institutions.

displacement: In situational crime prevention, what happens when actions taken to control deviance in one location cause it to occur in other locations. See also *diffusion*.

drift: The tendency of deviants, who are seldom hard-core committed careerists, to drift in and out of conventional activities, committing deviance usually as the opportunity arises.

egoistic suicide: A type of suicide in which a person takes his or her own life because of the lack of ties to a group or community; the idea was developed by Durkheim. See also *attachment*.

ethnography: A research technique made famous by the Chicago School sociologists, where direct observation records the life of the participants.

ethnomethodology: A term associated with Harold Garfinkel that refers to the methods used by individuals both to make sense of social life and to organize their activities.

expressive deviance: Actions, such as social protests, that are motivated by emotions. See also *instrumental deviance* .

feedback loop: A process by which the reaction to deviant behaviour feeds back to escalate the deviance. See also *amplification, secondary deviance*.

feminist approach: A sociology of deviance that emphasizes the study of gender issues, and how gender affects the cause and control of deviance.

focal concerns: Lower-class values, such as toughness, trouble, smartness, excitement, fatalism, and autonomy, which according to Miller, are conducive to the formation of delinquency. See also *subculture*.

functionalism: A theoretical perspective associated with Durkheim and Parsons, where the institutions of society interact to create social order; the challenge of deviance is to account for its 'necessity' in social life.

gender: An identity, distinct from sex or sexuality, that is acquired through socialization; related to deviance in feminist theory and power-control theory.

guardian: In situational crime prevention, a person, such as a security guard, who is in a position to prevent deviant actions.

ideology: A shared system of beliefs about society and the role of individuals in society that cements social relations; also a false consciousness that prevents people from understanding the reality of social inequality.

independent variable: In experimental research, a variable, such as poverty, that is manipulated to study its affect on another (dependent) variable, such as deviance.

institutionalization: The process of transforming social beliefs into more formal laws, e.g., making expressive deviance a crime.

instrumental deviance: Actions that are usually taken for monetary gain, such as robbery. See also *expressive deviance* .

involvement: A person's participation in conventional activities, the degree of which, in Hirschi's theory, influences the degree of control of deviance.

labelling: In symbolic interactionism, the naming by others of an action as deviant, thereby defining the action as deviance and resulting in further rule breaking; labelling is associated with the hidden consequences of an action.

left realism: A branch of Marxist theory that sets itself apart from what it perceives to be the romanticism of critical criminology instead working to develop ways to control working-class deviance.

linguistic turn: A development in symbolic interaction, as in conversational analysis, which looks at the accomplishment of social life through discourse. See also *labelling*.

longitudinal study: A methodological approach that looks at changes in a group over a period of time, used in studying development of chronic delinquency. See also *cohort*.

macro-level research: Investigation of large-scale social interactions, such as the effect of social inequality on deviance; the cross-cultural study of a phenomenon such as deviance or of how it changes historically. See also *micro-level*.

manifest consequences: The intended consequence of an action; used by Merton. See also *latent consequences*.

Marxism: An approach to the sociology of deviance which stresses the underlying role of inequality in causing deviance and the reaction to it. See also *class conflict*.

master status: The dominant label a person acquires, such as ex-convict or mentally ill, which overrides any other aspects of the person.

mechanical solidarity: A term used by Durkheim to describe the state in more traditional societies where social cohesion is achieved through adherence to social norms and through institutions such as the church. See also *organic solidarity*.

medicalization: In modern society, the designating and defining of certain kinds of behaviour as illnesses, in a way not done in more traditional societies.

micro-level research: Investigation of small-scale social interactions, such as classroom interaction, where deviance is defined in that local context. See also *macro-level*.

moral entrepreneur: A person in a position of authority who uses an opportunity to capitalize on defining deviance. See also *claimsmaker*.

moral panic: Response to an exaggerated concern in society about deviance, often promoted through the media in modern society. See also *amplification*.

norms: Non-legal rules that guide the behaviour of the individual in the group.

normlessness: A state similar to anomie and associated with functionalist theory, where the individual is not guided by the norms of the group.

opportunity: The chance to commit deviance. In situational crime prevention, controlling the opportunity works to deter the offender. See also *drift*, *guardian*.

organic solidarity: A state in modern society where social cohesion is achieved through the specialized interdependence of members' roles; developed by Durkheim.

panopticon: A specialized prison designed to maximize the observation of prisoners; more important as a metaphor for surveillance in modern society.

participant observation: A methodological approach in which the researcher acts as a member of the group which is being observed; usually done for sensitive topics. See also *ethnography*.

phenomenology: A philosophical perspective, used by Schutz, to describe the study of consciousness and meaning and the role of interpretation in social life; developed in symbolic interactionism.

positivism: The philosophical view that social phenomena should be studied as objective structures independent of interpretation and meaning; associated with Comte.

power-control theory: A focus on how delinquency is formed as a consequence of power relationships in society that affect the family; associated with Hagan.

primary deviance: An initial action, such as shoplifting, where the negative reaction of others defines the action as deviant, and leads to further, secondary acts of deviance; associated with Lemert.

professional deviance: Action, such as tax fraud, committed by individuals because of their power or institutional position.

Pygmalion effect: The tendency for deviance to result when the self orients to the interpretations and expectations of others. See also *self-fulfilling prophecy*.

recidivism: The repetition of deviant behaviour after the individual has been punished by others.

reference group: The group to which the individual orients him- or herself for membership; used as a way of defining the appropriateness of one's own actions. See also *differential association, subculture*.

residual deviance: The categorization of behaviour as deviant when other ways of understanding an action fail or are unavailable; associated with Cicourel.

retreatists: Persons who reject society's goals, and the socially accepted means of achieving them. The term is part of Merton typology. See also *ritualists, conformity*.

ritualists: According to Merton, those who follow the norms of society even if there is no hope that they will achieve their goals. See also *retreatists*.

routine-activities theory: A form of rational-choice theory that focuses on how the lifestyles of victim and offender contribute to deviance.

secondary deviance: Deviance that results when the social reaction of others to an initial action is so strong that the initial deviance becomes internalized as identity. See also *feedback, amplification*.

self-fulfilling prophecy: Deviant behavior caused by the orienting of the self to the interpretations and expectations of others. See also *Pygmalion effect*.

self-report: A methodological technique for determining the prevalence of deviance in a group where the behaviour is not likely to be reported to the police; often used in studies of student drug use.

signification: A term used in looking at the language used in defining deviance. See also *amplification*.

situational choice theory: Part of rational choice theory that sees deviance as the result of the individual weighing the likelihood of exploiting an opportunity.

situational crime prevention: An approach that tries to prevent deviance by reducing opportunities, increasing guardianship, and making targets less desirable.

social bond: A set of relations that reinforce convention and counter the urge to deviance, especially related to Hirschi. See also *attachment, involvement*.

social pathology: An older term for deviance that fell out of favour, especially after the societal-reaction approach was developed.

somatype: A way of categorizing the shape of a person's body to predict behaviour; associated with Sheldon.

stigma: An internalized negative description that is caused by the reaction of others to primary deviance, and that results in a long-lasting change in deviant identity and becomes a basis for social exclusion. See also *secondary deviance*.

strain: The feeling that is induced in an individual or a group by the failure of one's achievements to match expectations, and that can result in deviance. See also *anomie*.

subculture: A group which shares a set of common values that set it apart from the dominant society and in which deviance may be normal.

symbolic interactionism: A theoretical perspective that focuses on the symbolic interactions through which people accomplish social situations, associated with Becker and Goffman.

techniques of neutralization: Ways in which people can disavow responsibility for deviant actions, e.g., by saying 'he had it coming'; developed by Sykes and Matza.

victimization survey: A technique developed in the 1980s to determine how much crime is not reported to the police. See also *dark figure of crime*.

Notes

Chapter One: Confusion and Diversity

[1] See I. Taylor et al., *The New Criminology*; I. Taylor et al. (eds), *Critical Criminology*.

[2] See T. Hirschi, *Causes of Delinquency*; G. Nettler, *Explaining Crime*.

[3] See K. Davis, 'Prostitution'.

[4] See R. Merton, *Social Theory and Social Structure*.

[5] See K. Erikson, *Wayward Puritans*.

[6] See J. Ditton, *Part-Time Crime*.

[7] See C. Sundholm, 'The Pornographic Arcade'.

[8] See S. Cavan, *Liquor License*.

[9] See M. Yarrow et al., 'The Psychological Meaning of Mental Illness in the Family'.

[10] C. Warren, 'Mental Illness in the Family: A Comparison of Husbands' and Wives' Definitions'.

[11] D. Matza, *Becoming Deviant*, 12.

[12] See J. Douglas, 'The Experience of the Absurd and the Problem of Social Order'.

[13] E. Bittner, 'Radicalism and the Organization of Radical Movements', 934.

[14] T. Swann Harding, 'The Alleged Ignorance of Social Scientists', 850–4.

[15] See A. von Hirsch, *Doing Justice*.

[16] See V. Ruggiero, *Crime and Markets*.

[17] K. Burke, *A Grammar of Motives*, pt. 1, chap. 2, 'Antinomies of Definition'.

[18] For a fuller discussion of the links between the State and different groups in the domain of political crime, see F. Hagan, *Political Crime*.

[19] For a particularly effective demonstration of that assertion, see the analysis of the politicization of crime control in the regulation of Israeli Arabs in A. Korn, 'Crime and Legal Control'.

[20] J. Wilson, *Thinking About Crime*.

[21] See P. Mayhew et al., *Crime as Opportunity*.

[22] See O. Newman, *Defensible Space*.

[23] See P. Morgan, *Delinquent Fantasies*.

[24] E. Schur, *Radical Non-Intervention*.

[25] See J. Braithwaite, *Crime, Shame and Reintegration*.

[26] H. Becker and I. Horowitz, 'The Culture of Civility'.

[27] T. Szasz, *The Manufacture of Madness*.

[28] See F. Pearce, *Crimes of the Powerful*; P. Hillyard et al., 'Leaving a "Stain upon the Silence"'.

[29] See D. Matza, *Becoming Deviant*.

[30] M. Foucault, *Discipline and Punish*.

[31] T. Mathiesen, *The Politics of Abolition*.

[32] R. Quinney, 'Crime Control in Capitalist Society'.

[33] A. Platt, review of *The New Criminology*.

[34] See D. Hay et al., *Albion's Fatal Tree*.

[35] See E. Thompson, *Whigs and Hunters*.

[36] See E. Thompson, 'The Moral Economy of the English Crowd in the Eighteenth Century'.

[37] See G. Rudé, *The Crowd in History*.

[38] See E. Hobsbawm, *Primitive Rebels*.

[39] See L. Humphreys, *Out of the Closets*.

[40] See M. FitzGerald, *Prisoners in Revolt*.

[41] See J. Becker, *Hitler's Children*.

[42] See E. Cleaver, *Soul on Ice*.

[43] See T. Wolfe, *Radical Chic and Mau-Mauing the Flak-Catchers*.

[44] See M. Foucault, *I, Pierre Rivière*.

[45] See A. Scull, 'Mad-Doctors and Magistrates'.

[46] See E. Lemert, *Social Action and Legal Change*.

[47] A. Cicourel, *The Social Organization of Juvenile Justice*.

[48] É. Durkheim, *The Division of Labor in Society*.

[49] R. Merton, *Social Theory and Social Structure*.

[50] See M. Davis, 'That's Interesting!'

[51] J. Douglas et al., *The Nude Beach*, 51.

[52] See A. Lindesmith and Y. Levin, 'English Ecology and Criminology of the Past Century'.

[53] See M. Baumgartner, *The Moral Order of a Suburb*.

[54] I. Karpets, Director of the Moscow Institute of Criminology, quoted in W. Connor, *Deviance in Soviet Society*, 168.

[55] P. Solomon, *Soviet Criminologists and Criminal Policy*.

[56] R. Clarke and B. Cornish, 'Rational Choice', 2.

[57] T. Rawsthorne, 'The Objectives and Content of Policy-Oriented Research', 5.

[58] Kevin D. Haggerty, *Making Crime Count*, 198.

[59] N. Davis, *Sociological Constructions of Deviance*, xi–xii.

[60] In a survey of 106 British criminologists conducted by one of us in 1992, it was discovered that 36 per cent (and 32 per cent of the non-respondents) were in departments of law; 19 per cent (and 18 per cent of the non-respondents) in departments of sociology; 2 per cent (and 15 per cent) in designated research centres; and 9 per cent (and 15 per cent) in the Home Office Research and Planning Unit: P. Rock, 'The Social Organization of British Criminology'.

[61] F. Ianni, *A Family Business*.

[62] F. Thrasher, *The Gang*.

[63] W. Whyte, *Street Corner Society*.

[64] D. Matza, *Delinquency and Drift*.

[65] H. Parker, *The View from the Boys*.

[66] J. Foster, *Villains*.

[67] E. Anderson, *Code of the Street*.

[68] C. Alexander, *The Asian Gang*.

[69] J. Sangster, *Girl Trouble*; 'Girls in Conflict with the Law: Exploring the Construction of Female "Delinquency" in Ontario, 1940–60'.

[70] There were, to be sure, exceptions to this tendency to reduce all delinquents to a single mould. We shall show in chapters 5 and 6 how, following Merton (*Social Theory and Social Structure*), Cloward and Ohlin (*Delinquency and Opportunity*) developed a typology of different forms of delinquency based on systematic variations in their response to structural opportunities and restraints. In its turn, Cloward and Ohlin's work was to

be the basis of Spergel's *Racketville, Slumtown, Haulburg*, a book that pursued that theme of variation yet further by linking forms of delinquency to forms of community organization or disorganization.

71 See H. Finestone, *Victims of Change*.

72 See N. Polsky, *Hustlers, Beats and Others*.

73 See A. Lindesmith, *Opiate Addiction*.

74 See K. Plummer, *Sexual Stigma*.

75 See C. Klockars, *The Professional Fence*.

76 See W. Einstadter, 'The Social Organization of Armed Robbery'.

77 See C. McCaghy, 'Drinking and Deviance Disavowal'.

78 In A. Heath et al. (eds), *Understanding Social Change*, 2.

79 E. Burgess, 'Values and Sociological Research'.

80 G. Morson, *Narrative and Freedom: The Shadows of Time*, 235, 278–82.

Chapter Two: Sources of Knowledge about Deviance

1 J. Ditton, *Part-Time Crime*.

2 S. Henry, *The Hidden Economy*.

3 H. Farberman, 'A Criminogenic Market Structure'.

4 See N. Denzin, 'Crime and the American Liquor Industry'.

5 See S. Henry and G. Mars, 'Crime at Work'.

6 See Van Buitenen 2000.

7 See L. Taylor, 'The Significance and Interpretation of Replies to Motivational Questions'.

8 See L. Humphreys, *Out of the Closets*.

9 P. Manning, 'Deviance and Dogma', unpublished paper, 1975.

10 See C. Klockars, *The Professional Fence*.

11 See J. Stephens, *Loners, Losers and Lovers*.

12 J. Katz, 'Ethnography's Warrants', 399.

13 See W. Westley, 'Violence and the Police', and J. Skolnick, *Justice without Trial*.

14 See M. Cain, *Society and the Policeman's Role*; P. Manning, *Police Work*; and J. Rubinstein, *City Police*.

15 See M. Punch, *Policing the Inner City*; S. Holdaway, *Inside the British Police*; and D. Smith and J. Gray, *Police and People in London*.

16 E. Bittner, *The Functions of the Police in Modern Society*, 46.

17 Punch would argue that the transformation is anything but complete; studies 'have neglected boredom and routine. However hard ethnographers try to tell us what it is really like out there, they invariably end up with rich, gripping material. . . . Researchers concentrate ineluctably on the dramatic (either in terms of hectic action or interpersonal relations) and even conspire to make tedium of interest because they describe the "easing" practices which make inactivity tolerable.' M. Punch, 'Officers and Men', 9.

18 See N. Polsky, *Hustlers, Beats and Others*.

19 J. Carey, 'Problems of Access and Risk in Observing Drug Scenes'.

20 See J. Spiegel, 'Problems of Access to Target Populations'. But see M. Duneier, *Sidewalk* and E. Liebow, *Tally's Corner*.

21 There *are* exceptions. For instance, see W. Einstadter, 'The Social Organization of Armed Robbery'.

22 See J. Irwin, *The Felon*.

23 See H. Becker, 'The Culture of a Deviant Group'.

24 See N. Anderson, *The Hobo*.

[25] See F. Davis, 'The Cab-Driver and His Fare'.

[26] See T. Parker and R. Allerton, *The Courage of His Convictions*.

[27] See J. Halloran et al., *Demonstrations and Communications*.

[28] S. Cohen, *Folk Devils and Moral Panics*.

[29] D. Downes, *The Delinquent Solution*.

[30] S. Cavan, *Liquor License*.

[31] L. Humphreys, *Tearoom Trade*.

[32] See J. Dollard, *Caste and Class in a Southern Town*.

[33] D. Matza, *Delinquency and Drift*.

[34] R. Korn and L. McCorkle, 'Social Roles'.

[35] See P. Marsh et al., *The Rules of Disorder*.

[36] G. Sykes and D. Matza, 'Techniques of Neutralization', and, for a later elaboration, S. Cohen, *States of Denial*.

[37] A. Reiss, 'The Social Integration of Queers and Peers'.

[38] N. Lee, *The Search for an Abortionist*.

[39] A. Hathaway and F. Atkinson 'Active Interview Tactics in Research on Public Deviants: Exploring the Two-Cop Personas', 161.

[40] See P. Rock, Preface to *Drugs and Politics*.

[41] See E. Sutherland, *The Professional Thief*; C. Shaw, *The Jackroller*; W. Probyn, *Angel Face*; and W. Chambliss, *Box Man*.

[42] See H. Becker, 'The Life History and the Scientific Mosaic'.

[43] For an analysis of the new directions research can lead, Plummer was working on the life histories of a number of sexual deviants. He argued that no conventional sexual categorization adequately describes their conduct or self-definition. Instead of 'homosexuality', for example, he preferred to talk of 'homosexualities'. See K. Plummer, *Documents of Life*.

[44] G. Sereny, *Albert Speer*.

[45] See T. Shibutani, *The Derelicts of Company K*.

[46] For a fictional description of such a process, see A. Lurie, *Imaginary Friends*.

[47] E. Goffman, *Asylums*, ix–x.

[48] See P. Rock, *The Making of Symbolic Interactionism*, chap. 6.

[49] Interview with Leonard Cottrell, quoted in J. Carey, *Sociology and Public Affairs*, 156.

[50] See K. Erikson, 'Disguised Observation in Sociology'.

[51] See H. Thompson, *Hell's Angels*.

[52] E. Liebow, *Tell Them Who I Am: The Lives of Homeless Women*.

[53] See S. Cohen and L. Taylor, *Prison Secrets*.

[54] D. Ward and G. Kassebaum, *Women's Prison*.

[55] S. Cohen and L. Taylor, *Psychological Survival*.

[56] E. Goffman, *Asylums*.

[57] M. Comfort, *Home Sweep*.

[58] See A. Lindesmith, *Opiate Addiction*; E. Hooker, 'Male Homosexuality'.

[59] J. Mack, ' "Professional Crime" and Criminal Organization'.

[60] C. Faupel, *Shooting Dope*, 140.

[61] A. Porterfield, *Youth in Trouble*.

[62] J. Wallerstein and C. Wyle, 'Our Law-Abiding Law-Breakers'.

[63] F. Nye and J. Short, 'Scaling Delinquent Behavior'.

[64] G. Nettler, 'Antisocial Sentiment and Criminality'.

[65] W. Belson, *Juvenile Theft*.

[66] Julian Tanner, 'Youth Culture and the Canadian High School: An Empirical Analysis', 89–102.

[67] See M. Sullivan, *Getting Paid: Youth Crime and Work in the Inner City*, 6.

[68] C. Flood-Page et al., *Youth Crime*.

[69] M. Wolfgang et al., *Delinquency in a Birth Cohort*.

[70] M. Wadsworth, *Roots of Delinquency: Infancy, Adolescence and Crime*.

[71] D. West and D. Farrington, *Delinquency: Its Roots, Careers and Prospects*; D. West and D. Farrington, *Who Becomes Delinquent?*; D. West and D. Farrington, *The Delinquent Way of Life*.

[72] A. Blumstein and P. Hsieh, *The Duration of Adult Criminal Careers*.

[73] J. Petersilia et al., *Criminal Careers of Habitual Felons*.

[74] President's Commission on Law Enforcement and the Administration of Justice, *Crime and its Impact: An Assessment*.

[75] See R. Sparks et al., *Surveying Victims*.

[76] See M. Hough and P. Mayhew, *The British Crime Survey*.

[77] See P. Rock, *A View from the Shadows*.

[78] See M. Hough and P. Mayhew, *Taking Account of Crime*.

[79] See M. Maxfield, *Fear of Crime in England and Wales*.

[80] See S. Smith, *Crime, Space and Society*.

[81] See S. Box, *Crime, Power and Mystification*.

[82] See J. Lea and J. Young, *What Is to be Done about Law and Order?*

[83] See P. Mayhew and C. Mirrlees-Black, *The 1992 British Crime Survey*.

[84] For crimes against one population of small shopkeepers, see P. Ekblom and F. Simon, *Crime Prevention and Racial Harassment in Asian-run Small Shops*; and for the victimization of young people, see K. Yousaf et al., *Young Teenagers and Crime*.

[85] See R. Robertson and L. Taylor, *Deviance, Crime and Socio-Legal Control*.

[86] P. Beirne and J. Hill, *Comparative Criminology: An Annotated Bibliography*.

[87] See e.g. J. Braithwaite, *Inequality, Crime and Public Policy*, and *Crime, Shame and Reintegration*.

[88] P. Beirne and J. Hill, *Comparative Criminology*, vii.

[89] R. Smandych et al., , 'Toward a Cross-Cultural Theory of Aboriginal Crime', 1–24.

[90] M. DeVault, 'Talking Back to Sociology: Distinctive Contributions of Feminist Methodology'", 29–50; S. Simpson, 'Feminist Theory, Crime and Justice', 605–32.

[91] V. Jenness, 'From Sex as Sin to Sex as Work: COYOTE and the Reorganization of Prostitution as a Social Problem'", 403—20.

[92] G. Marx, 'Notes on the Discovery, Collection, and Assessment of Hidden and Dirty Data', 86.

[93] M. McIntosh, *The Organization of Crime*.

[94] Cf. J. Jacobs, *The Death and Life of Great American Cities*.

[95] See D. Davis, *Homicide in American Fiction*, and J. Palmer, 'Thrillers: The Deviant Behind the Consensus'.

[96] See S. Livingstone, 'On the Continuing Problem of Media Effects'.

[97] See H. Mannheim, *Social Aspects of Crime Between the Wars*; G. Rusche and O. Kirchheimer, *Punishment and Social Structure*, and J. Wells, 'Crime and Unemployment'.

[98] See M. Foucault, *Discipline and Punish*.

[99] See S. Hall et al., *Policing the Crisis*.

[100] See A. Quetelet, *Essai de physique sociale*.

[101] L. Chevalier, *Labouring Classes and Dangerous Classes*.

[102] See T. Gurr et al., *The Politics of Crime and Conflict*.

[103] See S. Box, *Deviance, Reality and Society*, and R. Hood and R. Sparks, *Key Issues in Criminology*.

[104] See T. Sellin, 'The Significance of Records of Crime'.

[105] T. Sellin, 'The Negro Criminal: A Statistical Note', 52–64; see also R. Park, 'The Bases of Race Prejudice', 11–20.

[106] See E. Smigel and H. Ross, *Crimes against Bureaucracy*.

[107] See the 'Review Symposium' in the *British Journal of Criminology*, Apr. 1984.

[108] See T. Jones et al., *The Islington Crime Survey*.

[109] The 1988 and 1992 *British Crime Survey* rectified some of these deficiencies.

[110] See M. Fishman, *Manufacturing the News*.

[111] See J. Tunstall, *Media Sociology*; S. Cohen and J. Young (eds), *The Manufacture of News*.

[112] See L. Wilkins, *Social Deviance*.

[113] R. Ericson, *Visualizing Deviance* and *Negotiating Control*.

[114] K. Dowler, 'Media Consumption and Public Attitudes toward Crime and Justice', 109–26; K. Dowler et al., 'Constructing Crime: Media, Crime and Popular Culture', 837–50.

[115] J. Sprott and A. Doob, 'Fear, Victimization, and Attitudes to Sentencing, the Courts, and the Police,', 297–1.

[116] See P. Carlen, *Magistrates' Justice*; M. Atkinson and P. Drew, *Order in Court*; and W. Bennett and M. Feldman, *Reconstructing Reality in the Courtroom*.

[117] See M. Foucault, *Discipline and Punish*; T. and P. Morris, *Pentonville*; D. Clemmer, *The Prison Community*; and G. Sykes, *The Society of Captives*.

Chapter Three: The University of Chicago School

[1] See S. Cohen, Preface to *Folk Devils*, 2nd edn.

[2] For general examples, see A. Hayward (ed.), *Lives of the Most Remarkable Criminals*; A. Griffiths, *The Chronicles of Newgate*; C. Gordon, *The Old Bailey and Newgate*; and D. Defoe, *The True and Genuine Account of the Life and Actions of the Late Jonathan Wild*.

[3] See A. Judges, *The Elizabethan Underworld*; and J. McMullan, 'Aspects of Professional Crime'.

[4] See T. Nourse, *Campania Foelix*.

[5] See P. Colquhoun, *A Treatise on the Police of the Metropolis*.

[6] See B. Mandeville, *The Fable of the Bees*.

[7] See T. Beames, *The Rookeries of London*.

[8] H. Mayhew, *London Labour and the London Poor*, vol. 4.

[9] See L. Pike, *A History of Crime in England*; and H. Asbury, *The Gangs of New York* (although an eponymous film, starring Daniel Day-Lewis, revived interest in that latter work).

[10] For a discussion of the difficulty of establishing criminology as an academic discipline in the United Kingdom, see R. Hood, 'Hermann Mannheim and Max Grünhut'.

[11] See E. Shils, 'Tradition, Ecology and Institution in the History of Sociology'.

[12] J. Carey, *Sociology and Public Affairs*, 9.

[13] E. Hughes, Preface to W. Raushenbush, *Robert Park*, vii.

[14] L. Broom, Preface to R. Faris, *Chicago Sociology, 1920–1932*, xi.

[15] A. Small, 'Fifty Years of Sociology in the United States', 802.

[16] Chatfield-Taylor, quoted in H. Zorbaugh, *The Gold Coast and the Slum*, 1.

[17] See R. Faris, *Chicago Sociology*, 22.

[18] Quoted in J. Carey, *Sociology and Public Affairs*, 154.

[19] See W. Raushenbush, *Robert Park*, 78.

[20] See J. Short (ed.), *The Social Fabric of the Metropolis*, xiv.

[21] See M. Bulmer, *The Chicago School*; R. Faris, *Chicago Sociology*.

[22] R. Park and E. Burgess (eds), *The City*, 3.

[23] R. Park, 'Community Organization and Juvenile Delinquency', 107.

[24] See E. Hughes, 'Robert E. Park'.

[25] See R. Park, 'The City as a Social Laboratory'.

[26] W. James, *A Pluralistic Universe*, 290.

[27] For a fuller account of that development see P. Rock, *The Making of Symbolic Interactionism*.

[28] See J. Dewey, 'The Reflex Arc Concept in Social Psychology'.

[29] See C. Peirce quoted in C. Mills, *Sociology and Pragmatism*, 158.

[30] J. Dewey, 'Perception and Organic Action', 648.

[31] W. James, *Pragmatism*, 30.

[32] G. Mead, 'The Philosophy of John Dewey', 74.

[33] R. Park, quoted in W. Raushenbush, *Robert Park*, 29.

[34] See P. Baker, 'The Life Histories of W.I. Thomas and Robert E. Park'; L. Braude, '"Park and Burgess": An Appreciation' and the Preface to R. Park, *The Crowd and the Public*.

[35] Quoted in W. Raushenbush, *Robert Park*, 112.

[36] L. Wirth, 'Culture Conflict and Misconduct', 240.

[37] P. Young, *The Pilgrims of Russian Town*.

[38] Quoted in R. Faris, *Chicago Sociology*, 71.

[39] Quoted in R. Faris, *Chicago Sociology*, 71.

[40] See F. Thrasher, *The Gang*.

[41] See J. Landesco, *Organized Crime in Chicago*.

[42] See W. Reckless, 'The Distribution of Commercialized Vice in the City'.

[43] See P. Cressey, *The Taxi-Dance Hall*.

[44] See E. Hughes, *The Growth of an Institution: The Chicago Real Estate Board*.

[45] See R. Park, *The Immigrant Press and Its Control*.

[46] See H. Zorbaugh, *The Gold Coast*.

[47] See N. Anderson, *The Hobo*.

[48] See E. Johnson, 'The Function of the Central Business District in the Metropolitan Community'.

[49] See W. Thomas and F. Znaniecki, *The Polish Peasant in Europe and America*.

[50] See S. Drake and H. Cayton, *Black Metropolis*.

[51] See L. Wirth, *The Ghetto*.

[52] G. Suttles, *The Social Construction of Communities*, 5.

[53] 54a See E. Burgess, 'The Study of the Delinquent as a Person', 657–80; Ernest Burgess, 'Residential Segregation in American Cities', 105–15; F. Thrasher, 'Social Backgrounds and Education', 69–76; see also F. Thrasher, 'A Study of the Total Situation', 477–90.

[54] L. Wirth, 'Human Ecology', 178.

[55] See R. Park, 'The City', 4; and L. Wirth, 'Human Ecology', 180.

[56] L. Wirth, 'Human Ecology', 188.

[57] R. Park, foreword to L. Wirth, *The Ghetto*, viii–ix.

[58] R. Park, 'The City', 6; see also P. Cressey, 'Population Succession in Chicago: 1898–1930', 59–69.

[59] F. Thrasher, 'The Study of the Total Situation', 477–90.

[60] James Quinn, 'The Burgess Zonal Hypothesis and Its Critics,' 210–18; see also, for example, E. Schneider and E. Young, 'Ecological Interrelationships of Juvenile Delinquency, Dependency, and Population Mobility', 598–610.

61 C. Dawson and W. Gettys, *An Introduction to Sociology*; R. Helmes-Hayes, 'Canadian Sociology's First Textbook: C.A. Dawson and W.E. Gettys's "An Introduction to Sociology (1929)"', 461–97.

62 C. Dawson, 'Population Areas and Physiographic Regions in Canada', 43–56, and 'A Useful Approach', 335–8.

63 K. Raitz, 'Ethnic Maps of North America', 335–50; C. Wittke, 'Review', 369–70; see also C. Dawson, *The Settlement of the Peace River Country*; *Group Settlement: Ethnic Communities in Western Canada*; *Canadian Frontiers of Settlement*; and *The New North West*.

64 C. Dawson, 'The Church and Social Service.

65 M. Shore, 'Carl Dawson and the Research Ideal: The Evolution of a Canadian Sociologist,'.

66 M. Wade, 'A Sociological Study of the Dependent Child'; W. Israel, 'The Montreal Negro Community'; M. McCall, 'A Study of Family Disorganization in Canada'.

67 See J. Galliher, 'Chicago's Two Worlds of Deviance Research', 166.

68 H. Wilson and E. Smith, 'Chicago Housing Conditions, VIII: Among the Slovacs in the Twentieth Ward', 145–169; for a later study in the same vein but a different city, see F. Chapin, 'The Effects of Slum Clearance and Rehousing on Family and Community Relationships in Minneapolis', 744–63.

69 See R. Faris and H. Dunham, *Mental Disorders in Urban Areas*.

70 E. Burgess, 'The Growth of the City', 54–6.

71 E. Lemert, *Social Pathology*.

72 See C. Shaw and H. McKay, *Juvenile Delinquency and Urban Areas*.

73 L. Wirth, 'Ideological Aspects of Social Disorganization', 46.

74 L. Wirth, 'Culture Conflict', 236.

75 See D. Matza, *Becoming Deviant*.

76 W. Whyte, *Street Corner Society*.

77 E. Anderson, *A Place on the Corner*, 2, 4.

78 See R. Park, 'Community Organization', 107.

79 See K. Erikson, *In the Wake of the Flood*.

80 See G. Suttles, *The Social Order of the Slum*.

81 See L. Rainwater, *Behind Ghetto Walls*; G. Suttles, 'The Defended Neighborhood', in his *Social Construction of Communities*.

82 W. Whyte, *Street Corner Society*, 273.

83 See R. Park, 'Community Organization'.

84 See L. Wirth, 'Culture Conflict'.

85 See G. Suttles, *The Social Construction of Communities*.

86 See W. Thomas and F. Znaniecki, *The Polish Peasant*.

87 See H. Lopota, 'The Function of Voluntary Associations'.

88 See C. Shaw, *The Natural History of a Delinquent Career*.

89 J. Landesco, *Organized Crime in Chicago*, 169.

90 See W. Miller, *Cops and Bobbies*.

91 See W. Reckless, 'The Distribution of Commercialized Vice'

92 G. Marquis, 'Vancouver Vice: The Police and the Negotiation of Morality, 1904–1935', 242–73.

93 L. Wirth, *The Ghetto*, 285–6.

94 R. Park, 'The City', 45.

95 L. Wirth, 'Culture Conflict', 229.

96 See J. Dewey, 'Realism without Monism or Dualism—II'.

97 See F. Thrasher, *The Gang*.

[98] See F. Thrasher, 'Social Backgrounds and Social Problems', 121–30

[99] F. Thrasher, 'How to Study the Boys' Gang in the Open', 244–54.

[100] See, for example, M. Dear and J. Wolch, *Landscapes of Despair*.

[101] W. Wilson, *When Work Disappears: The World of the New Urban Poor*, xvi.

[102] C. Shaw and H. McKay, 'Male Juvenile Delinquency and Group Behavior', 260.

[103] Cf. W. Reckless et al., 'The Good Boy in a High Delinquency Area'.

[104] See C. Shaw, *The Jack-Roller*; E. Sutherland, *The Professional Thief*. See also some of the smaller studies, such as W. Reckless, 'A Sociological Case Study of a Foster Child', 567–84; idem, 'Juvenile Delinquency and Behavior Patterning', 493–505; and idem, 'Suggestions for the Sociological Study of Problem Children', 156–71.

[105] L. Wirth, 'Culture Conflict', 237–8.

[106] E. Sutherland and D. Cressey, *Principles of Criminology*.

[107] E. Sutherland, *White Collar Crime*.

[108] E. Sutherland, *The Professional Thief*.

[109] D. Cressey, *Other People's Money*.

[110] E. Lemert, 'An Isolation and Closure Theory of Naive Check Forgery'.

[111] See J. Rex and R. Moore, *Race, Community and Conflict*.

[112] One particular consequence of British housing policy has been that planning can lead to the removal of criminal areas from the inner city. Estates later to be identified as 'problem estates' may, for instance, be placed on the borders of cities. See B. Campbell, *Goliath*; D. Herbert, 'Urban Crime'; and A. Power, *Estates on the Edge*.

[113] See F. Reynolds, *The Problem Housing Estate*.

[114] See A. Bottoms, R. Mawby, and P. Xanthos, 'A Tale of Two Estates'.

[115] See S. Damer, 'Wine Alley'.

[116] See O. Gill, *Luke Street*.

[117] Nels Anderson, *The Hobo: The Sociology of the Homeless Man*.

[118] R. Faris, *Chicago Sociology*, 66.

[119] N. Davis, *Sociological Constructions of Deviance*, 53.

[120] E. Shils, *The Present State of American Sociology*, 9.

[121] J. Gusfield, preface to G. Fine (ed.), *A Second Chicago School?* xi.

[122] See P. Hammond (ed.), *Sociologists at Work*.

[123] See also his *Documents of Life*.

[124] See S. Cohen and L. Taylor, *Psychological Survival*.

[125] See T. Morris, *The Criminal Area*. For an unusually full account of post-war British criminology, from the ecological approach roughly to date, see J. Tierney, *Criminology: Theory and Context*.

[126] Cf. N. Davis, *Sociological Constructions of Deviance*, 46.

[127] See H. Hoyt, *One Hundred Years of Land Values in Chicago*.

[128] G. Suttles, *The Social Construction of Communities*.

[129] R. Pahl, *Whose City?* 101.

[130] See M. Alihan, *Social Ecology*.

[131] See M. Davie, 'The Pattern of Urban Growth'.

[132] See J. Rex and R. Moore, *Race, Community and Conflict*.

[133] J. Snodgrass, 'Clifford R. Shaw and Henry D. McKay', 10.

[134] G. Suttles, *The Social Construction of Communities*, 14.

[135] N. Davis, *Sociological Constructions of Deviance*, 49.

[136] J. Dewey, quoted in C. Mills, *Sociology and Pragmatism*, 426, 430.

[137] Some kinds of evidence were inexplicably ignored. Newspapers and literary reports, for instance, were almost never used.

Chapter Four: Functionalism, Deviance, and Control

[1] H. Martins, 'Time and Theory in Sociology', 246.

[2] P. Cohen, *Modern Social Theory*, 47.

[3] J. Douglas, 'Deviance and Order in a Pluralistic Society', chap. 14.

[4] J. Mays, *Crime and the Social Structure*, 67 ff.

[5] K. Davis, 'The Sociology of Prostitution', 444–55 and 'Illegitimacy and the Social Structure', 221–33; D. Bell, *The End of Ideology*, chaps 7–9; R. Merton, *Social Theory and Social Structure*; and R. Merton and R. Nisbet (eds), *Contemporary Social Problems*.

[6] K. Erikson, *Wayward Puritans, A New Species of Trouble* and (with R. Dentler) 'The Functions of Deviance in Groups', 98–107; R. Scott, 'A Proposed Framework for Analyzing Deviance as a Property of Social Order'.

[7] D. Matza, *Becoming Deviant*, 31–7, 53–62, 73–80.

[8] K. Davis, 'The Myth of Functional Analysis as a Special Method in Sociology and Anthropology'.

[9] See in particular T. Parsons, *The Social System*.

[10] See in particular B. Malinowski, *A Scientific Theory of Culture*.

[11] J. Douglas, 'Deviance and Order'; C. Mills, *The Sociological Imagination*, chap. 2.

[12] S. Lukes, *Émile Durkheim: His Life and Work*, is the fullest account of Durkheim's work, and A. Giddens's Introduction to *Émile Durkheim: Selected Writings* is the most succinct.

[13] B. Malinowski, *Crime and Custom in Savage Society*, 128.

[14] R. Fletcher, 'Evolutionary and Developmental Sociology', 42.

[15] For an analysis of the problems associated with this theme, see L. Sklair, 'The Fate of the "Functional Requisites" in Parsonian Sociology', 30–42.

[16] A. Gouldner, *The Coming Crisis in Western Sociology*, 425–8.

[17] See in particular D. Lockwood, 'Some Remarks on 'The Social System", 134–46; J. Rex, *Key Problems of Sociological Theory*; and Gouldner, *The Coming Crisis in Western Sociology*, part II.

[18] D. Wrong, 'The Oversocialized Conception of Man', 183–91.

[19] G. Hawthorne, *Enlightenment and Despair*, 229.

[20] E. Goffman, 'Where the Action Is', 237–9.

[21] É Durkheim, *The Division of Labor in Society*, 123–4.

[22] M. Gottfredson and T. Hirschi, *A General Theory of Crime*, 78.

[23] See P. Blau, *The Dynamics of Bureaucracy*, 8–9.

[24] See M. Davis, 'That's Interesting!'

[25] E. Durkheim, *The Rules of the Sociological Method*, 63.

[26] É. Durkheim, *The Rules of Sociological Method*, 67.

[27] É. Durkheim, *The Rules of the Sociological Method*, 62.

[28] (1933, p. 398) É. Durkheim, *The Division of Labor in Society*.

[29] P. Erickson, 'Deterrence and Deviance: The Example of Cannabis Prohibition', 222–32; A. Hathaway and M. Atkinson, 'Tolerable Differences Revisited: Crossroads in Theory on the Social Construction of Deviance', 353–77.

[30] É. Durkheim, *The Rules of Sociological Method*, 66–72 and *passim*. For excellent discussions, see M. Phillipson, *Sociological Aspects of Crime*, chap. 3; and A. Cohen, *The Elasticity of Evil*.

[31] S. Cohen, *Folk Devils and Moral Panics* and chaps. 6 and 7 below.

[32] É. Durkheim, *The Division of Labor in Society*, 127.

[33] G. Pearson, *Hooligan: A History of Respectable Fears*, 229.

[34] R. Cotterrell, *Émile Durkheim: Law in a Moral Domain*, 76.

[35] See M. Phillipson, *Sociological Aspects of Crime*, 70.

[36] Lukes and Scull, *Durkheim and the Law*.

[37] E. Lemert, *Human Deviance, Social Problems and Social Control*.

[38] See J. Braithwaite, *Crime, Shame and Reintegration*.

[39] D. Matza, *Becoming Deviant*, 10; see also 31–7, 53–62, 73–80.

[40] See N. Fielding, *The National Front*.

[41] D. Matza, *Becoming Deviant*, 32.

[42] K. Davis, 'Prostitution', 286.

[43] N. Polsky, *Hustlers, Beats and Others*.

[44] See N. Fielding, *The National Front*, which remains an appreciative but disinterested analysis of a fascist group.

[45] D. Bell, 'The Racket-Ridden Longshoremen', *The End of Ideology*, 187.

[46] D. Matza, *Becoming Deviant*, 37.

[47] R. Merton, *Social Theory and Social Structure*, 73.

[48] D. Matza, *Becoming Deviant*, 77.

[49] R. Merton, *Social Theory and Social Structure*,. 137.

[50] K. Davis, 'Prostitution', 283–4.

[51] K. Erikson, *Wayward Puritans*, 283–4.

[52] Ibid., 21, 22.

[53] Ibid., 23.

[54] K. Colburn, Jr., 'Deviance and Legitimacy in Ice-hockey, 63–74; see also K. Colburn, Jr., 'Honor, Ritual and Violence in Ice Hockey', 153–170; J. Bensman and I. Gerver, 'Crime and Punishment in the Factory: The Function of Deviancy in Maintaining the Social System', 588–98; M. Reed et al., 'Wayward Cops: The Functions of Deviance in Groups Reconsidered', 565–75.

[55] N. Christie, *A Suitable Amount of Crime*.

[56] R. Stebbins, *Deviance: Tolerable Differences*; S., 'Deviance Labeling and Normative Strategies in the Canadian 'New Religions/Countercult' Debate', 393–416.

[57] R. Scott, 'A Proposed Framework for Analyzing Deviance'; T. Kuhn, *The Structure of Scientific Revolutions*; M. Douglas, *Purity and Danger*; P. Berger and T. Luckmann, *The Social Construction of Reality*.

[58] E. Gellner, *Legitimation of Belief*, 191–5.

[59] P. Cohen, *Modern Social Theory*, chap. 3.

[60] See e.g. A. Stinchcombe, *Constructing Social Theories*, chap. 3.

[61] P. Cohen, *Modern Social Theory*, 49.

[62] See D. Gambetta, *The Sicilian Mafia*.

[63] M. Douglas, *How Institutions Think*, 32.

[64] For an enumeration of such functions, see A. Cohen, *Deviance and Control*, 6–11.

[65] A. Gouldner, *The Coming Crisis*.

[66] See P. Rock, 'Rules, Boundaries and the Courts'.

[67] See J. Goldthorpe, 'The Uses of History'.

[68] E. Gellner, 'Concepts and Society'.

[69] G. Simmel, *Conflict and the Web of Group Affiliations*.

[70] See e.g. L. Coser, *The Functions of Social Conflict*.

[71] R. Merton, *On the Shoulders of Giants*, xxv.

[72] L. Sklair, 'The Fate of the "Functional Requisites"', 40.

[73] C. Davies, 'Sexual Taboos and Social Boundaries', 1060. See also his 'From the Sacred Hierarchies to Flatland'.

[74] See, in particular, the concluding arguments that David Garland offers in his important *Punishment and Modern Society*, 282–3. On 283, for example, he says, 'to understand penality—we need to think in terms of complexity, of multiple objectives and of over-determination. We need to think of it as a historical emergent which is also a functioning system; as a distinctive form of life which is also dependent upon other forms and other social relations.'

[75] D. Garland, 'Frameworks of Inquiry in the Sociology of Punishment', 11. See, too, his *Punishment and Society*.

[76] See J. Braithwaite, *Crime, Shame and Reintegration*.

[77] See J. Reiman, *The Rich Get Richer and the Poor Get Prison*, esp. 34 f.

Chapter Five: Anomie

[1] M. Clinard (ed.), *Anomie and Deviant Behavior*.

[2] S. Lukes, 'Alienation and Anomie'; J. Horton, 'The Dehumanisation of Alienation and Anomie'.

[3] J. Douglas, *The Social Meanings of Suicide*; J. Rex, *Discovering Sociology*, 234ff; M. Clinard, *Anomie and Deviant Behavior*; and P. Rock and M. McIntosh (eds), *Deviance and Social Control*, xi.

[4] Though see, in particular, P. Berger and T. Luckmann, *The Social Construction of Reality*, and K. Erikson, *In The Wake of the Flood*.

[5] See Mobilization for Youth, *A Proposal for the Prevention and Control of Delinquency by Expanding Opportunities*. It is interesting that an even earlier head-start experiment has recently been claimed to have had a marked impact on the future lives of its participants. The High/Scope Perry Preschool Study was launched in Ypsilanti, Michigan, in 1962 with 123 3- and 4-year-old children from poor families. Data were collected annually for the first eight years and then as the children attained the ages of 14, 15, 19, 27, and, finally, 40. There appears to have been a lasting effect: more of the participants had jobs than their controls (76 per cent compared with 62 per cent); they earned more; and they committed less violent, drug-related, and property crime. Fewer went to prison, although the figures for both groups were high (28 per cent versus 52 per cent). See the *New York Times*, 21 November 2004.

[6] See J. Young, 'Left Realist Criminology'. He was to say later that 'the Mertonian notion of contradiction between culture and structure . . . has run throughout all my work, from *The Drugtakers* onwards' ('Crime and the Dialectics of Inclusion/Exclusion', 553).

[7] S. Lukes, 'Alienation and Anomie', 138–9.

[8] Some say that this process originated with Merton's later adaptation of the concept; see N. Davis, *Sociological Constructions of Deviance*, 109.

[9] A. Giddens, *Émile Durkheim: Selected Writings*, Introduction, 11.

[10] I. Taylor et al., *The New Criminology*, 81ff.

[11] É. Durkheim, *The Division of Labor in Society*, 377.

[12] É. Durkheim, *Suicide*, 256.

[13] Laqueur, 2002

[14] É. Durkheim, *Suicide*, 208.

[15] A striking confirmation of this aspect of Durkheim's theory is provided by P. O'Malley, 'War and Suicide'. O'Malley argued that, if Durkheim was right, then the rate of suicide among Australian women should have fallen significantly at three points in Australia's involvement in the Second World War: her entry into the War, her defeats with other Allies in North Africa, and the fall of Singapore—a real threat to the

Australian mainland. The theory was sustained by the available evidence. The only alternative explanation might lie in the processes by which the definitions of suicide were contrived, and it is conceivable that coroners in wartime are swayed from such definitions for patriotic reasons, since suicides suggest demoralization, etc. But no data exist to substantiate or refute this alternative.

[16] É. Durkheim, *Suicide*, 248 ff for this and subsequent quotations.

[17] *The Times* (London), 16 Nov. 2000.

[18] Louis Wirth, 'Urbanism as a Way of Life', 1–24.

[19] See S. Lukes, 'Alienation and Anomie', 139, n. 14.

[20] L. Rainwater, *Behind Ghetto Walls*.

[21] K. Erikson, *A New Species of Trouble*.

[22] K. Erikson, published in Britain as *In the Wake of the Flood*.

[23] See P. Worsley, *The Trumpet Shall Sound*.

[24] C. Turnbull, *The Mountain People*.

[25] Ibid., 239.

[26] Ibid., 238.

[27] Ibid., 253.

[28] See N. Davies, *Dark Heart*.

[29] A. Sampson, *Lessons from a Victim Support Crime Prevention Project*, 32–3.

[30] M. Davis, 'Beyond Blade Runner', 6, 721.

[31] R. Aldana-Pindell, 'In Vindication of Justiciable Victims' Rights to Truth and Justice for State-Sponsored Crimes', 1466–7.

[32] S. Cohen, 'Crime and Politics', 19.

[33] M. van Creveld, *The Transformation of War*, 58, 192.

[34] R. Kaplan, 'The Coming Anarchy', 62–3.

[35] See *The Times* (London), 24 August 1998.

[36] See R. Kumar, *The History of Doing*, esp. 128.

[37] See *The New York Times*, 19 August 1999; *Evening Standard*, 10 August 1999.

[38] The *Sunday Times* (London), 2 August 1998.

[39] The *New York Times*, 22 September 1996.

[40] The *Times* (London), 2 November 1999; *The Independent*, 25 January 2001.

[41] J-F. Bayart et al., *The Criminalization of the State in Africa*, 20.

[42] R. Merton, 'Social Structure and Anomie'.

[43] R. Merton, 'The Emergence of a Sociological Concept', 10.

[44] Durkheim also regarded the state of anomie as 'chronic' in the 'sphere of trade and industry' in his analysis in *Suicide*; see especially 254–8.

[45] See Gouldner's Foreword to I. Taylor et al., *The New Criminology*, x–xi.

[46] R. Merton, 'The Emergence of a Sociological Concept', 30.

[47] S. Kent, 'Slogan Chanters to Mantra Chanters', 104–18.

[48] É. Durkheim, *Suicide*, 257.

[49] J. Hagan, *The Disreputable Pleasures*.

[50] R. Merton, *Social Theory and Social Structure*, 145–6.

[51] T. Marshall, *Sociology at the Crossroads*; J. Westergaard, 'The Withering Away of Class'.

[52] L. Taylor, *Deviance and Society*, 148.

[53] Merton said, 'Cohen went on to extend and deepen the paradigm by showing how social interaction among those subjected to structurally induced pressures leads to patterned collective responses and the emergence of a delinquent subculture' ('The Emergence of a Sociological Concept', 9).

[54] A. Cohen, 'The Sociology of the Deviant Act', 5–14.

[55] W. Runciman, *Relative Deprivation and Social Justice*.

[56] A. Cohen, 'The Sociology of the Deviant Act', 9.

[57] R. Merton, 'The Emergence of a Sociological Concept', 39.

[58] See the formidable inventory compiled by S. Cole and H. Zuckermann in Clinard, *Anomie and Deviant Behavior*, 243–83.

[59] H. Becker, 'Labelling Theory Reconsidered', 50.

[60] A. Stinchcombe, *Rebellion in a High School*.

[61] F. Mizruchi, *Success and Opportunity*.

[62] See the comments by Merton in Clinard, *Anomie and Deviant Behavior*, 227–8.

[63] H.-G. Heiland and L. Shelly, 'Civilization, Modernization and the Development of Crime and Control', 7.

[64] H.-G. Heiland and L. Shelley, 'Civilization, Modernization and the Development of Crime and Control', 3–4; see also N. Elias, *The Civilising Process* (Vol. 2): *State Formation and Civilization*, and 'Violence and Civilization: The State Monopoly of Physical Violence and its Infringement'.

[65] D. Garland, *Punishment and Society*, 217–18.

[66] P. Spierenburg, *The Spectacle of Suffering: Executions and the Evolution of Repression*, 217–18.

[67] D. Garland, *Punishment and Society*, 229–30.

[68] T. Gurr, 'Historical Trends in Violent Crime'; and Gurr et al., *The Politics of Crime and Conflict*.

[69] L. Stone, *The Family, Sex and Marriage in England*; K. Thomas, *Man and the Natural World*; J. Beattie, 'Violence and Society in Early Modern England'; V. Gatrell, 'The Decline of Theft and Violence in Victorian and Edwardian England'.

[70] F. McClintock, *Crimes of Violence*. Certainly the rise of feminism in the late 1960s and early 1970s was accompanied by an increasing awareness of the problems posed by violence against women and children, particularly in the domestic sphere. What had previously been treated by many as a private matter, not to be brought into the open or managed as a problem for criminal justice, came to be redefined as a crime.

[71] G. Steiner, *Language and Silence: Essays and Notes 1958–1966*, 175.

[72] Z. Bauman, *Modernity and the Holocaust*, esp. 212–13.

[73] L. Shelley, *Crime and Modernization*; M. Clinard and D. Abbott, *Crime in Developing Countries: A Comparative Perspective*.

[74] H.-G. Heiland and L. Shelley, 'Civilization, Modernization and the Development of Crime and Control', 5–6.

[75] D. Schichor, 'Crime Patterns and Socio-economic Development: A Cross-National Analysis'.

[76] H.-G. Heiland and L. Shelley, 'Civilization, Modernization and the Development of Crime and Control', 10.

[77] M. Clinard and D. Abbott, *Crime in Developing Countries: A Comparative Perspective*.

[78] C. Sumner (ed.), *Crime, Justice and Underdevelopment*, chap. 1.

[79] H. Traver, 'Crime Trends', 22.

[80] S. Messner and R. Rosenfeld, *Crime and the American Dream*.

[81] S. Messner and R. Rosenfeld,' Political Restraint of the Market and Levels of Criminal Homicide', 1396.

[82] D. Downes and K. Hansen, 'Welfare and Imprisonment in Comparative Perspective'.

[83] P. Bourdieu, 'Forms of Capital'; J. Coleman, 'Social Capital in the Creation of Human Capital; R. Putnam, '*Bowling Alone: The Collapse and Revival of American Community*.

[84] S. Cohen, *Visions of Social Control*.

[85] Bourdieu, 'Forms of Capital', 249–50; P. Paxton, 'Is Social Capital Declining in the United States?, 92.

[86] E. Durkheim, *The Division of Labour in Society*, 211–15.

[87] P. Paxton, 'Is Social Capital Declining in the United States?'

[88] L. Wacquant. 'Deadly Symbiosis: When Ghetto and Prison Meet and Mesh'.

[89] Simon, 1977; A. Bottoms, 'The Philosophy and Politics of Punishment and Sentencing'.

[90] H. Gavron, *The Captive Wife*.

[91] T. Jones and T. Newburn, 'The Transformation of Policing?' 140–1.

[92] F. Fukuyama, *Trust*.

[93] S. Baron and T. Hartnagel, 'Street Youth and Labour Market strain', 519–533; see also S. Baron, 'Street Youth Labour Market Experiences and Crime'.

[94] J. Hagan, *Crime and Disrepute*, 76.

[95] See M. Sullivan, *'Getting Paid': Youth Crime and Work in the Inner City*; E. Anderson, *Streetwise*; and J. Moore, *Going Down the Barrio*.

[96] R. Sampson, 'Race and Criminal Violence:' 'Effects of inequality, heterogeneity, and urbanization on intergroup victimization' (1986); S. Messner and R. Rosenfeld, *Crime and the American Dream*.

[97] R. McAuley, 'The Enemy Within: Economic Marginalisation and the Impact of Crime on Young Adults'.

[98] N. Christie, *Crime Control as Industry: Towards Gulags Western Style*; D. Garland, *Mass Imprisonment: Social Causes and Consequences*.

[99] R. Sennett, *The Culture of New Capitalism*, 5.

[100] J. Yound, *The Exclusive Society*, 152.

[101] B. Ehrenreich et al., *Undercover in Low-wage USA*; P. Toynbee, *Hard Work: Life in Low-Pay Britain*.

[102] V. Packard, *The Hidden Persuaders*.

[103] R. Sennett, *The Culture of New Capitalism*, 144.

[104] É. Durkheim, *Suicide*, 208, 204

[105] J. Douglas, *The Social Meanings of Suicide*; and also in A. Giddens (ed.), *The Sociology of Suicide*.

[106] É. Durkheim, *Suicide*, 291.

[107] I. Taylor et al., *The New Criminology*, 107.

[108] S. Box, *Deviance, Reality and Society*, 105–6. Box bases his case on the much more random distribution of criminality to be inferred from 'self-report' studies. For a critique of such studies, see A. Reiss, 'Inappropriate Theories and Inadequate Methods as Policy Plagues: Self-Reported Delinquency and the Law', 21–2. Reiss argues *inter alia* that police practices are largely *reactive* and therefore have little probable impact on crime rates.

[109] A. Lindesmith and J. Gagnon, 'Anomie and Drug Addiction'.

[110] R. Merton, *Social Theory and Social Structure*, 142–4.

[111] E. Lemert, 'Social Structure, Social Control and Deviation', 60.

[112] Ibid., 63.

[113] Ibid., 68.

[114] E. Lemert, 'Social Structure, Social Control and Deviation', 89–91.

[115] A. Gouldner, *The Coming Crisis*, 325.

[116] R. Merton, 'Anomie, Anomia, and Social Interaction: Contexts of Deviant Behavior', 219–22.

[117] S. Smith and P. Razzell, *The Pools Winners*.

[118] J. Hagan, *Crime and Disrepute*.

[119] W. Whyte, *Street Corner Society*.

[120] Merton and Srole distinguished *anomie* as a systemic property from *anomia* as a psychological state. This differentiation does not resolve the problem as we see it here.

[121] A. Stinchcombe, *Rebellion in a High School*.

[122] M. Punch, *Dirty Business: Exploring Corporate Misconduct*.

[123] M. Atkinson, *Discovering Suicide*.

[124] J. Henry, *Culture against Man*, 70.

[125] Experience in England and Wales may offer a test of sorts between these versions of anomie theory. Ten years after the end of the Second World War, crime rates were actually lower than in 1945. After their single sharp rise, of 15 per cent in 1950–1, they fell back below their 1945 level. After 1955, they began their almost uninterrupted climb of 5 per cent–6 per cent annually. Durkheim's theory (of suicide rather than crime) does not fit very well with so sharp a rise in crime rates in the middle of the Korean war—in which Britain was fully engaged—and while rationing, which was a tough regulatory framework, was still largely in effect. Merton's theory fits the trends far better: people put up with post-war austerity in the glow of victory and post-war reconstruction. But by 1950, when their patience was wearing thin, the austerity was prolonged by a far-distant war. Aspirations shot ahead of reality. With the election of the Conservatives in 1951 and the Korean armistice, rationing finally ended, and for a few years at least, reality outpaced aspirations. By the mid-1950s, the 'never-had-it-so-good' society was born, and aspirations began to soar, if not infinitely, then at least indefinitely.

[126] J. Braithwaite, *Inequality, Crime and Public Policy*.

[127] See e.g. S. Henry, *The Hidden Economy*.

Chapter Six: Deviance, Culture, and Subculture

[1] A. Cohen, *Delinquent Boys*; R. Cloward and L. Ohlin, *Delinquency and Opportunity*; W. Miller, 'Lower Class Culture as a Generating Milieu of Gang Delinquency', 5–19; J. Mays, *Growing Up in the City*; D. Downes, *The Delinquent Solution*; D. Hargreaves, *Social Relations in a Secondary School*.

[2] D. Matza, *Delinquency and Drift*.

[3] See e.g. I. Piliavin and S. Briar, 'Police Encounters with Juveniles', 206–14; also C. Werthman and I. Piliavin, 'Gang Members and the Police'.

[4] P. Cohen, 'Working Class Youth Cultures in East London'.

[5] J. Henry, *Culture against Man*, 3.

[6] P. Willis, *Profane Culture*, 1. See also his *Learning to Labour*.

[7] G. Murdock and R. McCron, 'Youth and Class; The Career of a Confusion'; G. Pearson, '"Paki-Bashing" in a North East Lancashire Cotton Town'; P. Corrigan, *Schooling the Smash Street Kids*; P. Cohen and D. Robins, *Knuckle Sandwich: Growing up in the Working Class City*; R. Hebdige, *Subculture: The Meaning of Style*; M. Brake, *The Sociology of Youth Culture and Youth Subcultures*; K. Pryce, *Endless Pressure: A Study of West Indian Lifestyles in Bristol*; H. Parker, *The View from the Boys*; O. Gill, *Luke Street*; P. Marsh et al., *The Rules of Disorder*.

[8] This has not been so in the case of traditional criminology, or in the US. See e.g. D. West, *Present Conduct and Future Delinquency*; D. West and D. Farrington, *Who Becomes Delinquent?* and *The Delinquent Way of Life*; see also M. Hindelang, 'The Social versus Solitary Nature of Delinquent Involvements', 167–75; and D. Elliott and H. Voss, *Delinquency and Dropouts*.

[9] See J. Muncie, *Youth and Crime*.

[10] A. Cohen, *Delinquent Boys*, 59.

[11] Ibid., 54.

[12] Ibid., 55; L. Wirth, 'Urbanism as a Way of Life', 3–24; see also C. Fischer, 'The Subcultural Theory of Urbanism: A Twentieth-year Assessment', 543–77.

[13] J. Arnett, 'Three Profiles of Heavy Metal Fans', 423–33.

[14] R. Cloward and L. Ohlin, *Delinquency and Opportunity*.

[15] J. Short and F. Strodtbeck, *Group Process and Gang Delinquency*.

[16] David Matza's work on delinquency and deviance emerged chronologically as follows: with G. Sykes, 'Techniques of Neutralization', 1957; 'Subterranean Traditions of Youth', 1961; with G. Sykes, 'Delinquency and Subterreanean Values', 1961; *Delinquency and Drift*, 1964; *Becoming Deviant*, 1969.

[17] D. Matza, *Delinquency and Drift*, 28.

[18] J. and H. Dryburgh, 'First Person Accounts and Sociological Explanations of Delinquency', 777–93.

[19] D. Matza, *Delinquency and Drift*, 30.

[20] J. Quinn, 'Angels, Bandidos, Outlaws, and Pagans: The Evolution of Organized Crime among the Big Four 1% Motorcycle Clubs, 379–99; see also D. Wolf, *The Rebels: A Brotherhood of Outlaw Bikers*.

[21] See Home Office Statistical Bulletin, 7/85.

[22] See M. Wolfgang et al., *Delinquency in a Birth Cohort* and D. West and D. Farrington, *Who Becomes Delinquent?*

[23] See, for example, M. Ezell and L. Cohen, *Desisting from Crime: Continuity and Change in Long-term Crime Patterns of Serious Chronic Offenders*. The work is a statistically sophisticated secondary review and original analysis of patterns of youth offending. What it does fail to examine, however, is the utility of conviction data as a measure of criminality. After all, only 3 per cent of crimes in England and Wales result in conviction, and the vast bulk of offending passes without any record.

[24] T. Budd and C. Sharp, *Offending in England and Wales*, 8.

[25] See M. Clinard, *Cities with Little Crime*.

[26] See D. Robins, *We Hate Humans*; J. Patrick, *A Glasgow Gang Observed*.

[27] P. Mayhew and N. Maung, *Surveying Crime*, 4.

[28] The fall in officially recorded crime began in 1992 in England and Wales and continued thereafter. The fall in crime registered by the British Crime Survey began later, in 1995 and also continued thereafter, suggesting that the discrepancy was due in some measure to changes in police recording practices.

[29] S. Field, *Trends in Crime and Their Interpretation*, 5.

[30] See P. Mayhew, *Residential Burglary: A Comparison of the United States, Canada and England and Wales*.

[31] G. La Free and K. Drass, 'Counting Crime Booms Among Nations', 769–800.

[32] D. Downes, *The Delinquent Solution*; P. Wilmott, *Adolescent Boys in East London*.

[33] D. Hargreaves, *Social Relations in a Secondary School*.

[34] N. Elias and J. Scotson, *The Established and the Outsiders*, 112.

[35] See M. Sullivan, *'Getting Paid': Youth Crime and Work in the Inner City*, 116.

[36] S. Cohen, 'Directions for Research on Adolescent Group Violence and Vandalism', 337.

[37] H. Parker, *The View from the Boys*.

[38] M. Cusson, *Why Delinquency?*

[39] P. Corrigan, *Schooling the Smash Street Kids*.

[40] R. Light et al., *Car Theft: The Offender's Perspective*.

[41] See M. Sullivan, *'Getting Paid': Youth Crime and Work in the Inner City*, 117.

[42] See N. Shover, *Aging Criminals*.

[43] For a comprehensive analysis of their work, see R. Ericson, *Criminal Reactions*.

[44] J. Young, 'Mass Media, Drugs and Deviance', 241.

[45] See G. Marx, *Under Cover*, 126–7.

[46] D. Matza, *Becoming Deviant*, 179.

[47] S. Cohen, *Folk Devils and Moral Panics*.

[48] J. Katz and C. Jackson-Jacobs, 'The Criminologists' Gang'.

[49] S. Hall et al., *Policing the Crisis*; O. Gill, *Luke Street*.

[50] P. Marsh et al., *The Rules of Disorder*.

[51] H. Parker, *The View from the Boys*.

[52] P. Marsh et al., *The Rules of Disorder*, 82, 97.

[53] G. Armstrong, *Football Hooligans*, 233, 296.

[54] B. Tuchman, *A Distant Mirror*.

[55] S. Blackman, *Youth: Positions and Oppositions*, 254.

[56] A. Wilson, *Urban Songlines*.

[57] T. Sellin, 'Culture Conflict and Crime', 228.

[58] W. Miller, 'Lower Class Culture' and in M. Wolfgang et al. (eds), *The Sociology of Crime and Delinquency*, 267–76 and (with others) 'Aggression in a Boys' Street-corner Group'.

[59] O. Lewis, *Five Families: Mexican Case Studies in the Culture of Poverty*; also *The Children of Sanchez* and *La Vida: A Puerto Rican Family in the Culture of Poverty*. In his introduction to *La Vida*, he made it plain that poverty and the 'culture of poverty' are not mutually inclusive terms. For example, the Jews of Eastern Europe were very poor, but their literacy and religion insulated them from the culture of poverty. However, despite some disclaimers on both parts, the culture of poverty corresponds closely with Liebow's observations of one group of the urban poor in the USA (E. Liebow, *Tally's Corner: Negro Street-corner Men in Washington, D.C.*). For a discussion, see C. Valentine, *Culture and Poverty*. For a criminological statement of much the same position, see M. Wolfgang and F. Ferracutti, *The Subculture of Violence*.

[60] J. Mays, *Growing Up in the City*; J. McVicar, *McVicar by Himself*.

[61] P. Willis, *Profane Culture*, 29–30.

[62] P. Bourgois, 'In Search of Masculinity'; K. Polk, *When Men Kill*; N. Elias, *The Civilizing Process*; F. Leyton, *Men of Blood*.

[63] P. Cohen, 'Working Class Youth Cultures in East London', 23–4

[64] G. Melly, *Revolt into Style*.

[65] S. Hall et al. (eds), *Resistance through Ritual*.

[66] P. Corrigan, *Schooling the Smash Street Kids*, 140.

[67] J. Katz, *Seductions of Crime*, 128, 139.

[68] M. Cusson, *Why Delinquency?* 32.

[69] K. Hayward, *City Limits*, 86

[70] S. Blackman, *Chilling Out*.

[71] M. Presdee, *Cultural Criminology and the Carnival of Crime*.

[72] S. Baron, 'The Canadian West Coast Punk Subculture', 289–316.

[73] A. Bottoms, 'A Tale of Two Estates', 57.

[74] S. Walklate and Z. Evans, *Zero Tolerance or Community Tolerance*; J. Foster, *Villains: Crime and Community in the Inner City*, 2.

[75] D. Hobbs, *Doing the Business: Entrepreneurship, the Working Class and Detectives in East London*.

[76] For a comprehensive review of such studies, see S. Box, *Deviance, Reality and Society*; and M. Gold, *Delinquent Behavior in an American City*.

[77] D. Maurer, *Whiz Mob: A Correlation of the Technical Argot of Pick-pockets with their Behavior Pattern.*

[78] J. Young, 'The Role of the Police as Amplifiers of Deviancy'.

[79] S. Cohen, *Folk Devils and Moral Panics*, introduction.

[80] Ibid., viii–ix.

[81] Ibid., ix.

[82] R. Hebdige, *Subculture: The Meaning of Style*, 18.

[83] S. Cohen, *Folk Devils*, xv.

[84] S. Blackman, *Youth: Positions and Oppositions*, 4–5.

[85] As, for example, in Hebdige's assertion that 'Every time the boot went in, a contradiction was concealed, glossed over or made to "disappear"' (*Subculture*, 60). The drift to a facile idealism recalls Zilboorg's Freudian explanation of why pickpockets plied their trade at public hangings. 'This was their revenge for their own vicarious execution.' As Maurer notes, Barrington, the famous eighteenth-century thief, gave a sounder explanation: 'Everybody's eyes were on one person and all were looking up' (D. Maurer, *Whiz Mob*, 14–16). In this case, however, a clear-cut purpose was involved: thieving as a trade. Expressive 'spectacular subcultures' do not lend themselves so readily to instrumental accounts, so that Hebdige's approach is correspondingly more defensible and in general his methods lend themselves to a more rigorous use of evidence than the above might imply.

[86] S. Cohen, *Folk Devils*, xxv.

[87] P. Willis, *Profane Culture*, 5.

[88] An exception is K. Plummer, *Sexual Stigma: An Interactionist Account.*

[89] A. Reiss, Jun., 'Inappropriate Theories and Inadequate Methods as Policy Plagues'; and R. Mawby (ed.), *Policing the City.*

[90] M. Brake, *The Sociology of Youth.* Brake demonstrates that there is greater agreement over views of the self, other groups, and society within as compared to between the youthful subcultures of Skinheads and Hippies.

[91] See e.g. D. Downes, *The Delinquent Solution*; and S. Cohen, 'Directions for Research'.

[92] J. Ferrell et al., 'Fragments of a Manifesto', 6.

[93] D. Downes, Review of K. Hayward, *City Limits: Crime, Consumer Culture and the Urban Experience.*

[94] M. O'Brien, 'What is *Cultural* about Cultural Criminology?' 603.

[95] D. Brotherton, 'Subversive Subcultures', unpaginated.

[96] C. Geer, 'Crime, Media and Community', 117.

Chapter Seven: Symbolic Interactionism

[1] See D. Matza, *Becoming Deviant.*

[2] G. Fine, 'The Development of a Postwar American Sociology'.

[3] H. Becker, 'The Chicago School, So-called', 3–12.

[4] J. Gusfield, 'The Second Chicago School?'

[5] Cf. K. Davis, 'The Myth of Functional Analysis'.

[6] See D. Cressey, *Other People's Money.*

[7] A. Lindesmith, *Opiate Addiction.*

[6] See E. Sutherland, *The Professional Thief.*

[9] See E. Sutherland, *White Collar Crime.*

[10] See D. Cressey, 'Role Theory, Differential Association and Compulsive Crimes'.

[11] E. Hughes, 'Good People and Dirty Work'.

[12] See E. Lemert, *Social Pathology.*

[13] See A. Reiss and M. Tonry, Preface to *Communities and Crime*.

[14] See J. Debro, 'Dialogue with Howard S. Becker'.

[15] See I. Horowitz, 'The Politics of Drugs', 165.

[16] A. Gouldner, 'Anti-Minotaur: The Myth of a Value-Free Sociology', 209.

[17] S. Cohen, 'Criminology and the Sociology of Deviance in Britain'; I. Taylor and L. Taylor (eds), *Politics and Deviance*; N. Polsky, *Hustlers, Beats and Others*; J. Weis, 'Dialogue with Matza'.

[18] G. Pearson, *The Deviant Imagination*, 52.

[19] See M. Wolfgang et al., *Evaluating Criminology*.

[20] J. Gusfield, preface to G. Fine (ed.), *A Second Chicago School?*

[21] H. Becker, *Tricks of the Trade*, 53.

[22] For an extended discussion of the historical development of different rationales for ethnography, see J. Katz, 'Ethnography's Warrants', 391–423.

[23] Hans Ulrich Obrist interview with Howard Becker,' accessed 23 April 2008 from http://home.earthlink.net/~hsbecker.

[24] H. Becker, *Outsiders*, 9.

[25] J. Kitsuse, 'Societal Reaction to Deviant Behavior', 19–20.

[26] K. Erikson, 'Notes on the Sociology of Deviance', 11.

[27] J. Kitsuse and M. Spector, 'Toward a Sociology of Social Problems', 407–19.

[28] H. Becker, 'Marihuana Use and Social Control', 35–44.

[29] Cf. C. Mills, 'Situated Actions and Vocabularies of Motive'; M. Scott and S. Lyman, 'Accounts, Deviance and Social Order'.

[30] G. Sykes and D. Matza, 'Techniques of Neutralization'.

[31] H. Arendt, *Eichmann in Jerusalem*, 52.

[32] Cf. D. Cressey, 'Role Theory'; L. Taylor, 'The Significance and Interpretation of Replies to Motivational Questions'.

[33] See M. Cameron, *The Booster and the Snitch*.

[34] See H. Parker, *The View from the Boys*.

[35] See F. Davis, 'Deviance Disavowal'; E. Goffman, *Stigma*.

[36] See M. Leznoff and W. Westley, 'The Homosexual Community'.

[37] See D. Tanner, *The Lesbian Couple*.

[38] See A. Lindesmith, *Opiate Addiction*; E. Schur, *Narcotic Addiction in Britain and America*; K. Plummer, *Sexual Stigma*.

[39] E. Lemert, 'An Isolation and Closure Theory of Naïve Check Forgery', 296–307; and E. Lemert, 'The Behavior of the Systematic Check Forger', 141–9.

[40] D. Maurer, 'Prostitutes and Criminal Argots', 546–50.

[41] H. Becker, 'The Professional Dance Musician and his Audience', 136–44.

[42] D. Wolf. *The Rebels: A Brotherhood of Outlaw Bikers*. For a fuller history of the Hells Angels in Canada, see P. Cherry, *The Biker Trials: Bringing Down the Hells Angels*.

[43] Cf. H. Becker, 'The Self and Adult Socialization'.

[44] T. Scheff, *Being Mentally Ill*.

[45] E. Lemert, *Social Pathology*.

[46] H. Becker, *Outsiders*.

[47] B. Malinowski, *Crime and Custom*.

[48] See J. Gibbs, 'Conceptions of Deviant Behaviour'.

[49] See S. Maruna, *Making Good*.

[50] E. Lemert, *Social Pathology*, 76.

[51] J. Hagan, 'Labelling and Deviance: A Case Study in the "Sociology of the Interesting"', 447–58.

[52] B. Heyl, *The Madam as Entrepreneur*.

[53] G. Sykes, 'Men, Merchants, and Toughs: A Study of Reactions to Imprisonment', 130–8.

[54] See S. Cavan, *Liquor License*.

[55] See e.g. R. Akers, 'Problems in the Sociology of Deviance: Social Definitions and Behaviour', 455–65.

[56] See R. Dentler and K. Erikson, 'The Functions of Deviance in Groups'.

[57] T. Scheff, 'Negotiating Reality: Notes on Power in the Assessment of Responsibility'.

[58] See E. Goffman, 'The Moral Career of the Mental Patient'; D. Rosenhan, 'On Being Sane in Insane Places'.

[59] H. Becker, *Tricks of the Trade*, 119.

[60] See P. Rock, *Making People Pay*.

[61] See D. Bordua (ed.), *The Police*.

[62] See E. Goffman, *Asylums*.

[63] See R. Emerson, *Judging Delinquents*; P. Carlen, *Magistrates' Justice*.

[64] See E. Freidson, *Profession of Medicine*.

[65] J. Kenney, 'Victims of Crime and Labelling Theory: A Parallel Process?' 235–65.

[66] R. Baldwin, 'Why Rules Don't Work'.

[67] See E. Bittner, 'The Police on Skid Row'; A. Stinchcombe, 'Institutions of Privacy in the Determination of Police Administrative Practice'.

[68] See C. Werthman and I. Piliavin, 'Gang Members and the Police'; J. Wilson, *Varieties of Police Behavior*.

[69] S. Choongh, *Policing as Social Discipline*.

[70] See J. Rubinstein, *City Police*.

[71] K. Hawkins, *Environment and Enforcement*.

[72] B. Hutter, *The Reasonable Arm of the Law?*

[73] See D. McBarnet, 'Whiter than White Collar Crime'.

[74] See P. Rock, *Making People Pay*.

[75] See P. Rains, *Becoming an Unwed Mother*.

[76] See G. Marx, 'The New Police Undercover Work'.

[77] See H. Sacks, 'Notes on Police Assessment of Moral Character'.

[78] See J. Skolnick, *Justice without Trial*.

[79] See B. Cox et al., *The Fall of Scotland Yard*.

[80] See *Police Review*, 3 August 1963.

[81] P. Willis, *Profane Culture*.

[82] See P. McHugh, 'A Common-Sense Conception of Deviance'.

[83] See J. Gusfield, 'Moral Passage'.

[84] E. Goffman, *Frame Analysis*, 1.

[85] See R. Turner, 'Role-Taking: Process versus Conformity'.

[86] See K. Plummer (ed.), *Modern Homosexualities: Fragments of Lesbian and Gay Experience*, esp. chap. 1.

[87] M. Phillipson, *Sociological Aspects of Crime and Delinquency*.

[88] See J. Katz, *Seductions of Crime*. For a contrary argument, see J. Stander et al., 'Markov Chain Analysis and Specialization in Criminal Careers'.

[89] This is Dave Robins' nice term. See his *Tarnished Vision*.

[90] See C. Faupel, *Shooting Dope: Career Patterns of Hard-Core Heroin Users*.

[91] See P. Reuter, *Disorganized Crime*.

[92] D. Luckenbill and J. Best, 'Careers in Deviance and Respectability: The Analogy's Limitation', 201.

[93] L. Wilkins, *Social Deviance*.

[94] S. Cohen, *Folk Devils*.

[95] J. Young, *The Drugtakers*.

[96] See P. Rock and S. Cohen, 'The Teddy Boy'.

[97] Cf. J. Ditton, *Controlology*.

[98] K. Plummer, 'Misunderstanding Labelling Perspectives', 85.

[99] Cf. A. Platt, review of *The New Criminology*.

[100] See I. Taylor et al., *The New Criminology*.

[101] See W. Gove (ed.), *The Labelling of Deviance*.

[102] See J. Huber, 'Symbolic Interaction as a Pragmatic Perspective'.

[103] L. Humphries, *Tearoom Trade*, 22.

[104] See K. Popper, *Conjectures and Refutations*.

[105] R. Rorty, *Objectivity and Truth*, 68.

[106] J. Katz, 'Ethnography's Warrants'.

[107] A. Cicourel, 'Interpretative Procedures and Normative Rules in the Negotiation of Status and Role'.

[108] M. Phillipson and M. Roche, 'Phenomenology, Sociology and the Study of Deviance'.

[109] H. Blumer, *What Is Wrong with Social Theory?*, 148.

[110] Cf. A. Rose, Preface to *Human Behavior and Social Processes*.

[111] Cf. R. Scott, *Why Sociology Does Not Apply*.

[112] A. Gouldner, 'The Sociologist as Partisan', 38.

[113] R. Akers, 'Problems in the Sociology of Deviance', 463.

[114] Cf. T. Scheff (ed.), *Mental Illness and Social Processes*.

[115] See the introduction to C. Sumner (ed.), *The Blackwell Companion to Criminology*.

[116] C. Sumner, *The Sociology of Deviance: An Obituary*, 246.

[117] See, for instance, L. Athens, *Violent Criminal Acts and Acktors*; and J. Katz, *Seductions of Crime*.

[118] See P. Rock, *A View from the Shadows* and *Helping Victims of Crime*.

[119] Prime examples are S. Hall et al., *Policing the Crisis*, and J. Ferrell, *Crimes of Style*.

[120] They are libertarian interactionists like Schur; conservative interactionists like Klapp; and socialist interactionists like Smith. Most have no clear political markings at all.

[121] H. Becker, 'Labelling Theory Reconsidered'.

[122] K. Plummer, 'Misunderstanding Labelling Perspectives', 119.

Chapter Eight: Phenomenology

[1] Schutz, A., "The social world and the theory of social action," in *Collected Papers*, 2, The Hague, 1964

[2] M. Phillipson and M. Roche, 'Phenomenology, Sociology and the Study of Deviance', 126.

[3] R. Rorty, *Objectivity, Relativism and Truth*, 6.

[4] An instance is the debate about whether significant differences exist between phenomenology and symbolic interactionism. See G. Mead, *The Philosophy of the Act*, esp. 360; D. Miller, *George Herbert Mead*; B. Meltzer et al., *Symbolic Interactionism*; and J. Douglas (ed.), *Understanding Everyday Life*, chaps 1, 11, and 12.

[5] Works which point to the kind of analysis that might ensue include M. Edelman, *Politics as Symbolic Action*; W. Lippmann, *Public Opinion*; J. Douglas, *American Social Order*; and P. Manning, *The Narc's Game*.

[6] P. Berger, *The Social Reality of Religion*, 18.

7 Cf. L. McDonald, *The Sociology of Law and Order*, 18.

8 One of the very first references to phenomenology made by those who later affected the sociology of deviance is found in A. Cicourel and J. Kitsuse, *The Educational Decision Makers*, 11. An earlier one is a reference to Schutz's 1953 piece 'Common Sense and Scientific Interpretations of Human Action' by H. Garfinkel in 'Conditions of Successful Degradation Ceremonies', 1. The question of how these scholars came to be familiar with Schutz's work is less certain, although bridging articles such as the following may have been instrumental: K. Bode and A. Stonier, 'A New Approach to the Methodology of the Social Sciences', 406–23. In addition, Garfinkel referred to Schutz in *The Perception of the Other: A Study in Social Order*, as did T. Parsons in *The Social System*, in 1951, and F. Kaufmann, in *Methodology of the Social Science*. This is a question for the scholars of intellectual history.

9 A. Schutz, 'Common-sense and Scientific Interpretation of Human Action', 5–6.

10 P. Berger and T. Luckmann, *The Social Construction of Reality*.

11 A. Schutz, *The Structures of the Life-World*, 61.

12 See M. Atkinson and P. Drew, *Order in Court*.

13 See H. Garfinkel, *Studies in Ethnomethodology*.

14 See R. Hill and K. Crittenden, *Proceedings of the Purdue Symposium on Ethnomethodology*.

15 R. Turner, *Ethnomethodology*.

16 M. Phillipson, 'Thinking Out of Deviance', 5–6.

17 It is said that Garfinkel himself was not amused when his own students tried breaching experiments on him.

18 H. Garfinkel, *Studies in Ethnomethodology*, chap. 2.

19 M. Douglas, *Rules and Meanings*, 11.

20 See K. Erikson, *In the Wake of the Flood*; T. Shibutani, *The Derelicts of Company K*.

21 P. Berger, *The Social Reality of Religion*, 30, 31, 32.

22 Ibid., 33–34.

23 K. Erikson, *Wayward Puritans*, 7–8.

24 S. Shoham, *The Mark of Cain*, 7–8.

25 M. Douglas, *Implicit Meanings*, xiv.

26 See M. Douglas, *Natural Symbols*.

27 See I. Buruma, 'The Joys and Perils of Victimhood'.

28 M. Davis, *Smut*.

29 R. Scott, 'A Proposed Framework for Analyzing Deviance', 22.

30 See R. Edgerton, 'Pokot Intersexuality', and Y. Teh, *The Mak Nyahs*. Yik Koon Teh analyzes in some detail the conceptual, civil, and religious problems posed for transsexuals and for civic and religious authorities in Malaysia, a predominantly Muslim society.

31 See M. Douglas, *Purity and Danger*.

32 See J. Douglas, 'The Experience of the Absurd and the Problem of Social Order', and D. Hargreaves, *Deviance in the Classroom*.

33 J. Heller, *Catch-22*, 55.

34 See J. Douglas, *American Social Order: Social Rules in a Pluralistic Society*.

35 M. Douglas, *Rules and Meanings*, 13.

36 See J. Douglas, 'Deviance and Respectability', 6–7.

37 T. Duster, *The Legislation of Morality*.

38 See A. Cicourel and J. Kitsuse, *The Educational Decision-Makers*.

39 J. Kitsuse and A. Cicourel, 'A Note on the Uses of Official Statistics', 139.

40 J. Douglas, 'Understanding Everyday Life'.

41 A. Cicourel, *The Social Organization of Juvenile Justice*, 331.

[42] See K. Mannheim, 'On the Interpretation of 'Weltanschauung'.

[43] 'Ethnomethodology' is the study of the common-sense practices or methodologies which ordinary people employ to make sense of the everyday world.

[44] See A. Cicourel, *Method and Measurement in Sociology.*

[45] See J. Douglas, *The Social Meanings of Suicide* and M. Atkinson, *Discovering Suicide.*

[46] See D. Sudnow, 'Normal Crimes: Sociological Features of the Penal Code'.

[47] See J. Baldwin and M. McConville, *Negotiated Justice.*

[48] A. Cicourel and J. Kitsuse, *The Educational Decision-Makers*, 9.

[49] T. Duster, 'The Epistemological Challenge of the Early Attack on "Rate Construction"', 134–6.

[50] J. Kitsuse and A. Cicourel, 'A Note on the Uses of Official Statistics'.

[51] J. Kitsuse, 'Societal Reaction to Deviant Behavior', 247–56.

[52] E. Bittner, 'Police Discretion in Emergency Apprehensions of Mentally Ill Persons', 278–92.

[53] Cf. W. Sharrock, 'Ethnomethodology and British Sociology'.

[54] D. Maynard, 'Language, Interaction, and Social Problems', 311–34.

[55] J. Douglas (ed.), *Observations of Deviance.*

[56] Cf. J. Douglas (ed.), *Research on Deviance.*

[57] The major example was conducted, not by a phenomenologist, but by a Marxist anthropologist, Paul Willis, in *Learning to Labour.* Willis presented his subjects with the somewhat abstract and abstruse commentary which he had constructed to explain their conduct. They flatly refused to accept it as a proper or appropriate analysis.

[58] See, for example, I. Hacking, *Rewriting the Soul.*

[59] See M. Pendergast, *Victims of Memory,* and R. Ofshe and E. Watters, *Making Monsters.*

[60] A. Cicourel, *The Social Organization of Juvenile Justice*, 331.

[61] E. Gellner, 'Ethnomethodology', 435.

[62] L. McDonald, *The Sociology of Law and Order*, 18.

[63] R. Quinney, 'Crime Control in Capitalist Society', 184.

[64] I. Taylor et al., *The New Criminology*, 199, 208.

[65] See B. Hindess, *The Use of Official Statistics in Sociology.*

[66] For an example, see E. Gellner, *Postmodernism, Reason and Religion.*

[67] E. Gellner, 'Ethnomethodology', 431.

[68] See D. Ball, 'An Abortion Clinic Ethnography'.

Chapter Nine: Control Theories

[1] Aristotle, *Politics*, quoted in L. McDonald, *The Sociology of Law and Order*, chap. 2.

[2] T. Hobbes, *Leviathan*, 195; see also the discussion in T. Hirschi, *Causes of Delinquency*, 4–6.

[3] É. Durkheim, *Suicide*, 247.

[4] For a useful discussion, see L. McDonald, *The Sociology of Law and Order*, chap. 2.

[5] R. Clarke, 'Situational Crime Prevention, Criminology and Social Values', 109.

[6] See M. Davis, 'That's Interesting!'.

[7] K. Haggerty, 'Displaced Expertise', 218.

[8] Chiefly in S. and E. Glueck, *Unravelling Juvenile Delinquency.*

[9] T. Hirschi, *Causes of Delinquency*; and H. Wilson and G. Herbert, *Parents and Children in the Inner City.*

[10] See W. Reckless et al., 'Self-Concept as an Insulator against Delinquency', and W. Reckless, *The Crime Problem.*

[11] J. Toby, 'An Evaluation of Early Identification and Intensive Treatment Programs for Pre-Delinquents'.

[12] J. Toby, 'Social Disorganization and Stake in Conformity'.

[13] S. Briar and I. Piliavin, 'Delinquency, Situational Inducements and Commitment to Conformity', 35–45.

[14] G. Homans, 'Social Behavior as Exchange', 597–606; P. Blau, *Exchange and Power in Social Life*.

[15] G. Homans, *The Human Group*, and 'Bringing Men Back In', 809–18.

[16] A. Gouldner, *The Coming Crisis*, 140.

[17] A. Heath, *Rational Choice and Social Exchanges*, 171.

[18] See the opening section of H. Wilson, 'Parental Supervision: A Neglected Aspect of Delinquency'.

[19] T. Hirschi, *Causes of Delinquency*, 16.

[20] Ibid., 20–1.

[21] Ibid., 26.

[22] See P. Morgan and P. Henderson, *Remand Decisions and Offending on Bail*, 48.

[23] See K. Hansen, 'Time to Educate the Criminals?'

[24] A. Cohen and J. Short, 'Juvenile Delinquency', 106.

[25] T. Hirschi, *Causes of Delinquency*, 34.

[26] R. Kornhauser, *Social Sources of Delinquency: An Appraisal of Analytic Models*, 154.

[27] T. Hirschi, *Causes of Delinquency*, 89, Table 18; corroborated by H. Wilson, 'Parental Supervision'.

[28] S. Box, *Deviance, Reality and Society*.

[29] Ibid., 150.

[30] Ibid., 106–9 and 122–33.

[30] J. Hagan and B. McCarthy, 'Streetlife and Delinquency', 555.

[31] A. Sampson and J. Laub's *Crime in the Making*; Laub and Sampson's *Shared Beginnings, Divergent Lives*.

[32] P. Morgan, *Delinquent Fantasies*.

[33] J. Wilson, *Thinking about Crime*. A Home Office study questions the feasibility of this approach: S. Brody and R. Tarling, *Taking Offenders Out of Circulation*.

[34] R. Clarke, 'Situational Crime Prevention', 136.

[35] See R. Clarke and D. Cornish, *Crime Control in Britain*, 41.

[36] D. Cornish and R. Clarke, *The Reasoning Criminal*, 1.

[37] R. Clarke (ed.), *Situational Crime Prevention: Successful Case Studies*.

[38] G. Becker, 'Crime and Punishment: An Economic Approach'.

[39] For a more general and critical discussion of that trend, see F. Fukuyuma, *State Building*, 61 ff.

[40] R. Clarke and D. Cornish, 'Rational Choice', 2.

[41] D. Cornish and R. Clarke, 'Analyzing Organized Crimes', 20.

[42] The reference is to H. Parker, *The View from the Boys*.

[43] R. Clarke, 'Situational Crime Prevention', 138.

[44] Cornish and Clarke observe, 'Whatever the merits of . . . criticisms for other offenses . . . they carry little weight in respect of organized crime. This is rational crime par excellence.' D. Cornish and R. Clarke, 'Analyzing Organized Crimes', 1.

[45] R. Clarke, 'Situational Crime Prevention', 137.

[46] D. Smith, 'Changing Situations and Changing People', 171–2.

[47] P. Sainsbury, in 'The Epidemiology of Suicide', has questioned the inference that trends in the detoxification of gas supplies to domestic consumers in England account for the

sharp decline in the suicide rate between 1963 and 1975. He notes the similarity between rates of suicide in a number of towns in England and Wales and provinces in Holland, despite dissimilar phasing in of the detoxification process. R. Clarke and P. Mayhew, in *Designing Out Crime*, 130, and 'The British Gas Story', rebut this criticism by reference to the inadequacy of the data for Holland and their inconclusive nature for England and Wales, owing to the small number of towns sampled. The balance of evidence now seems to favour control theory on this issue, whose significance as a test of displacement makes it a priority for further research.

[48] G. Laycock, *Reducing Burglary*.

[49] T. Bennett and R. Wright, *Burglars on Burglary*.

[50] T. Hope, *Burglary in Schools*.

[51] R. Clarke, 'Situational Crime Prevention', 142.

[52] P. Mayhew et al., *Crime as Opportunity*, 26.

[53] UK Department of the Environment, *Reducing Vandalism on Public Housing Estates*.

[54] J. Jacobs, *The Death and Life of Great American Cities*.

[55] See the work of M. Duneier in *Sidewalk*, a study that leans heavily on the arguments of Jane Jacobs and which unearths complex webs of informal control practised by homeless entrepreneurs on the streets of New York.

[56] See e.g. the review by A. Bottoms.

[57] See e.g. F. Reynolds, *The Problem Housing Estate*.

[58] See B. Hillier, 'In Defence of Space'.

[59] A. Coleman, *Utopia on Trial*.

[60] B. Hillier, 'City of Alice's Dreams'.

[61] National Research Council, *Understanding and Preventing Violence*, 148.

[62] See B. Poyner, *Design against Crime*, and B. Poyner et al., *Layout of Residential Areas and its Influence on Crime*.

[63] J. Wilson and G. Kelling, 'The Police and Neighbourhood Safety'.

[64] See G. Kelling and C. Coles, *Fixing Broken Windows*.

[65] R. Sampson and S. Raudenbush, 'Systematic Social Observation of Public Spaces', 603, 638.

[66] M. Foucault, *Discipline and Punish*.

[67] See J. Semple, *Bentham's Prison*.

[68] See C. Gordon (ed.), *Power/Knowledge*, 154–5.

[69] See S. Cohen, 'The Punitive City'.

[70] See N. Fraser, 'Foucault on Power'.

[71] See D. Lyon, *The Electronic Eye*.

[72] S. Cohen, 'The Punitive City', 356.

[73] Quite major claims have been made for the capacity of closed circuit television to reduce crime. See S. Graham et al., 'Towns on the Television', 4.

[74] *The Sunday Times*, 14 February 1999.

[75] See Scottish Office Central Research Unit, *The Effect of Closed Circuit Television on Recorded Crime Rates and Public Concern about Crime in Glasgow*. See also J. Ditton, 'Crime and the City'.

[76] The phrase is that of M. Davis in 'Beyond Blade Runner'.

[77] See the *Times* (London), 4 November 1999.

[78] S. Graham, 'Surveillant Simulation and the City', 26–7.

[79] M. Lianos and M. Douglas, 'Dangerization and the End of Deviance', 270.

[80] See P. O'Malley, 'Risk, Power and Crime Prevention'.

[81] See A. Bottoms and P. Wiles, 'Crime and Insecurity in the City'.

[82] S. Graham and S. Marvin, *Telecommunications and the City*, 223.

[83] C. Shearing and P. Stenning, 'From the Panopticon to Disney World'.

[84] U. Beck, *Risk Society*.

[85] See J. Simon, 'The Emergence of a Risk Society'.

[86] See J. Simon, 'The Ideological Effects of Actuarial Practices'.

[87] See M. Feeley and J. Simon, 'The New Penology'.

[88] P. O'Malley, 'Risk, Power and Crime Prevention', 264, 266.

[89] T. Sellin, *Culture Conflict and Crime*; W. Miller, 'Lower Class Culture'; J. Mays, *Growing Up in the City*; O. Lewis, *The Children of Sanchez*, xi–xxxi; E. Sutherland, *Principles of Criminology*, first published in 1924 and since 1955 extensively revised by D. Cressey.

[90] And see J. Hagan, *The Disreputable Pleasures*, and M. Punch, *Dirty Business*.

[91] As A. Cohen implies in his trenchant critique 'Seven Limitations of Psychodynamic Control Theories', in his *Deviance and Control*, 59–62.

[92] H. Eysenck, *Crime and Personality*; G. Trasler, *The Explanation of Criminality*.

[93] R. Cochrane,'*Crime and Personality*: Theory and Evidence', 19–22, and H. Eysenck, '*Crime and Personality Reconsidered*', 23–4.

[94] H. Wilson and G. Herbert, *Parents and Children*, 177.

[95] O. James, *Juvenile Violence in a Winner-Loser Culture*.

[96] See R. Clarke and D. Cornish,'Modeling Offenders' Decisions: A Framework for Research and Policy', 155.

[97] J. Wilson and R. Herrnstein, *Crime and Human Nature*.

[98] M. Gottfredson and T. Hirschi, *A General Theory of Crime*, 90.

[99] See M. Innes, *Understanding Social Control*, 54.

[100] See J. Hagan and A. Gillis, 'The Sexual Stratification of Social Control'; P. Carlen, *Women, Crime and Poverty*.

[101] See R. Clarke and M. Felson (eds), *Routine Activity and Rational Choice*.

[102] M. Felson, *Crime and Everyday Life*, 15.

[103] R. Clarke, 'Situational Prevention, Criminology and Social Values', 1.

[104] L. Cohen and M. Felson, 'Social Change and Crime Rate Trends'; Felson and Clarke (1998)

[105] J. Hagan and B. McCarthy, *Mean Streets*, 184.

[106] T. Hirschi, *Causes of Delinquency*, 29

[107] R. Clarke, 'Situational Crime Prevention', 138.

[108] R. Clarke, 'Situational Prevention, Criminology and Social Values'.

[109] P. Mayhew et al., 'Motorcycle Theft, Helmet Legislation and Displacement', 1.

[110] J. Chaiken et al., *Impact of Police Activity on Crime: Robberies on the New York City Subway System*.

[111] P. Mayhew et al., 'Motorcycle Theft, Helmet Legislation and Displacement'.

[112] P. Mayhew, 'Displacement and Vehicle Theft', 235.

[113] See P. Goldblatt and C. Lewis (eds), *Reducing Offending*, 28.

[114] M. Clinard, *Cities with Little Crime: The Case of Switzerland*, 114–15.

[115] D. Smith, 'Changing Situations and Changing People', 155.

[116] R. Clarke, 'Situational Prevention, Criminology and Social Values', 106.

[117] See A. Giddens, *Modernity and Self-Identity*, 132.

[118] See R. Ericson and A. Doyle, *Uncertain Business*, esp. 10.

[119] R. Wright and S. Decker, *Armed Robbers in Action*, x.; Richard Wright et al., 'The Foreground Dynamics of Street Robbery'.

[120] See M. Douglas, *Risk Acceptability According to the Social Sciences*.

121 M. Gottfredson and T. Hirschi, *A General Theory of Crime*, 138–9.

122 S. Maruna, *Making Good: How Ex-Convicts Reform and Rebuild their Lives*, 30, n. 6.

123 Ibid. 136.

124 N. Tilley, *Understanding Car Parks, Crime and CCTV*, 13.A more recent evaluation of the impact of CCTV reported substantial and largely unexplainable variations in rates of offending. See M. Gill et al., *The Impact of CCTV*.

125 See D. Walsh, *Break-Ins* and *Heavy Business*.

126 E. Short and J. Ditton, 'Seen and Now Heard'.

127 See C. Norris and G. Armstrong, *The Maximum Surveillance Society*.

128 C. Norris and M. McCahill, 'CCTV: Beyond Penal Modernism?'; see also B. Goold, *CCTV and Policing*.

129 See T. Newburn and S. Hayman, *Policing, Surveillance and Social Control*.

130 J. Shapland and J. Vagg, *Policing by the Public*.

131 L. Dowd, 'Witnessing of Incidents and Intervention: Informal Social Control in Action'.

Chapter Ten: Radical Criminology

1 See e.g. S. Cohen's Introduction to *Images of Deviance*; and M. Phillipson, *Sociological Aspects of Crime and Delinquency*, chaps 1 and 2. For a more detailed account of developments from this perspective, see S. Cohen, 'Criminology and the Sociology of Deviance in Britain'.

2 The operative image of conventional criminology was of activity almost exclusively geared to the more precise measurement, prediction, and control of criminality without regard to wider social and economic contexts and by quantitative methods. The reality was naturally more diverse.

3 The work of Antonio Gramsci and Jurgen Habermas has no direct connection with criminological issues, but by the late 1960s it had an immense significance for the New Left. See in particular *Selections from the Prison Notebooks of Antonio Gramsci* (ed. and trans. by Q. Hoare and G. Nowell Smith); and, from Habermas's work, *Legitimation Crisis*. Major themes from their work are closely integrated in S. Hall et al., *Policing the Crisis*, which also deploys some conceptions from Althusser. The structuralist Marxism of Althusser had elsewhere been viewed as incompatible with the study of crime, deviance, and allied concerns. See P. Hirst, 'Marx and Engels on Law, Crime and Morality'.

4 I. Taylor et al., *The New Criminology*, 278.

5 For documentation of these cases, see C. Raw et al., *Do You Sincerely Want to Be Rich: Bernard Cornfeld and IOS: An International Swindle*; and G. Tyler, 'The Great Electrical Conspiracy'.

6 I. Taylor et al., *The New Criminology*, 107.

7 This brought them quickly into dispute with Hirst, whose Althusserian Marxism stressed the latter and largely excluded the former concerns. See P. Hirst, 'Marx and Engels' and the reply by Taylor and Walton in I. Taylor et al., *Critical Criminology*, chaps 8 and 9.

8 'The "solution" in social contract to the problem of inequality . . . is an evasion and is best seen in Locke. He makes a distinction between those numbers of the poor who have chosen depravity and those who, because of their unfortunate circumstances, were unable to live a "rational" life. Thus, crime is *either* an irrational choice (a product of the passions) *or* it may be the result of factors militating against the free exercise of rational choice. In neither respect can it be fully rational action in the sense that conforming action is invariably seen to be. These two alternative views of criminal

motivation have dominated criminology (surviving the attack of positivism) ever since.'
I. Taylor et al., *The New Criminology*, 6–7.

[9] References here are primarily to W. Bonger, *Criminality and Economic Conditions*;
A. Turk, *Criminality and the Legal Order*; and R. Quinney, *The Social Reality of Crime*.

[10] A. Gouldner, 'The Sociologist as Partisan' in *For Sociology: Renewal and Critique in Sociology Today*, 39; first published in *The American Sociologist*, May 1968, this article formed the basis for much of the critique by the 'new' criminologists of what Gouldner termed the 'zookeepers of deviance', that is, the work of Howard Becker and the symbolic interactionists. See chap. 7.

[11] In his *Learning to Labour*; see chap. 6.

[12] P. Cohen, 'Working Class Youth Cultures'; see chap. 6.

[13] Another interesting and unusual example of analysis that comes close to being a 'fully social theory', an example that was to be warmly endorsed by Ian Taylor, is M. Davis, *City of Quartz*. *City of Quartz* is not an explicit piece of radical criminology. Rather it might be called a historically based political economy of the city of Los Angeles that narrates how that city emerged within the labour and industrial markets of the United States, how its social ecology reflected a geographical separation between the physically defended rich and the undefended poor, how policing was devised to protect the one from the other, and how crime, deviance, and gang activity emerged among the blacks and Hispanics as a defensive response.

[14] The formal scope of a fully social theory was held to require coverage of (1) the wider origins of the deviant act; (2) immediate origins of the deviant act; (3) the actual act; (4) the immediate origins of social reaction; (5) the wider origins of social reaction; (6) the outcome of the social reaction on the deviant's further action; and (7) the nature of the deviant process as a whole. See Taylor et al., *The New Criminology*, 270–8.

[15] S. Hall et al., *Policing the Crisis*, 16. See also M. Pratt, *Mugging as a Social Problem*.

[16] S. Hall et al. *Policing the Crisis*, 16.

[17] Ibid. The term was originated earlier by Stan Cohen in *Folk Devils and Moral Panics*.

[18] C. Klockars, 'The Contemporary Crises of Marxist Criminology', *Criminology*, 487 ff.

[19] C. Mills, *The Power Élite*.

[20] A. Platt, '"Street Crime"—A View from the Left', 29.

[21] Ibid., 31.

[22] J. Reiman and S. Headlee, 'Marxism and Criminal Justice Policy', 24–47.

[23] Exactly the same point was made by Chapman in his *Sociology and the Stereotype of the Criminal*.

[24] Exactly the same point was made by Foucault in *Discipline and Punish*.

[25] J. Reiman, *The Rich Get Richer and the Poor Get Prison*, 2, 4.

[26] E. Hobsbawm, *Bandits*; E. Thompson, *Whigs and Hunters: The Origin of the Black Act*; G. Rudé, *The Crowd in History*; R. Samuel (ed.), *Ruskin College, History Workshop Pamphlets*.

[27] D. Hay et al. (eds), *Albion's Fatal Tree: Crime and Society in Eighteenth Century England*, 14.

[28] G. Pearson, '"Paki-Bashing" in a North East Lancashire Cotton Town'.

[29] A. Scull, *Decarceration*.

[30] M. Ignatieff, *A Just Measure of Pain*.

[31] M. Foucault, *Discipline and Punish*; see also his *Madness and Civilization* and *The Birth of the Clinic*.

[32] T. Mathiesen, *The Politics of Abolition*; M. Fitzgerald, *Prisoners in Revolt* and (with J. Sim) *British Prisons*.

[33] P. Carlen, *Magistrates' Justice*.

34 J. Griffith, *The Politics of the Judiciary.*

35 E. Sutherland, *White Collar Crime.*

36 E. Sutherland, 'White Collar Criminality', 1–12.

37 J. Albini, *The American Mafia: Genesis of a Legend.*

38 C. Sumner, 'Marxism and Deviancy Theory' and *Reading Ideologies: An Investigation into the Marxist Theory of Ideology and Law.*

39 See J. Young, foreword to R. Swaaningen, *Critical Criminology: Visions from Europe.*

40 J. Young, 'From Inclusive to Exclusive Society', 64–5.

41 See R. Swaaningen, *Critical Criminology: Visions from Europe*, 6.

42 See S. Cohen, 'It's All Right for You to Talk'.

43 M. Nellis, review of R. Reiner and M. Cross (eds), *Beyond Law and Order*, 348.

44 See R. Matthews and J. Young, 'Reflections on Realism', 7.

45 T. Jones et al., *The Islington Crime Survey*, 2–3.

46 See Mawby, who on the basis of a re-analysis of the 1988 British Crime Survey, was to conclude that 'the evidence . . . points unequivocally to crime having most impact on the most vulnerable members of the community: the poor, council tenants, blacks, women, the divorced and those living alone or in one-parent families'. Quoted in T. Newburn, 'The Long-Term Impact of Criminal Victimization', 33.

47 M. Gottfredson and T. Hirschi, *A General Theory of Crime*, 152.

48 J. Lea and J. Young, *What Is to Be Done about Law and Order?*, 262.

49 D. Cowell et al. (eds), *Policing the Riots.*

50 See J. Lowman and B. MacLean, *Realist Criminology: Crime Control and Policing in the 1990s*, 6.

51 J. Lea, 'Towards Social Prevention', 4.

52 See I. Taylor, 'Left Realist Criminology and the Free Market Experiment in Britain', 97.

53 See P. Brantingham and F. Faust, 'A Conceptual Model of Crime Prevention'.

54 See K. Painter, *Crime Prevention and Public Lighting.*

55 See R. Matthews, *Policing Prostitution: A Multi-Agency Approach.*

56 See R. Matthews, 'Replacing "Broken Windows".

57 See G. Pavlich, 'Critical Genres and Radical Criminology in Britain', esp. 151.

58 See e.g. D. Downes and T. Ward, *Democratic Policing.*

59 P. Rock, foreword to J. Lowman and B. MacLean (eds.), *Realist Criminology: Crime Control and Policing in the 1990s.*

60 I. Taylor, *Crime in Context*, 3.

61 R. Ratner, 'Pioneering Critical Criminologies in Canada', 5.

62 T. Fleming (ed.), *The New Criminologies in Canada.*

63 E. Comack, '"We Will Get Some Good Out of This Riot Yet": The Canadian State, Drug Legislation and Class Conflict'. 48–70.

64 J. Lowman and B. MacLean, *Realist Criminology.*

65 T. O'Reilly-Fleming, *Post-Critical Criminology.*

66 R. Ratner, 'Pioneering Critical Criminologies in Canada', 5.

67 D. Chunn and R.t Menzies, '"So What Does This Have to Do with Criminology?": Surviving the Restructuring of the Discipline in the Twenty-First Century'.

68 A prime example of the radical functionalism of 'censure' is provided by one of Colin Sumner's students, who, in his analysis of corruption, argues, 'The logic is that if the dominant class decides to censure corruption, at the expense of jeopardizing its entrenched interests, then it must have a specific target to achieve, a pressing problem to solve, a hegemonic function to perform. . . . Its aim may be to combat corruption to dispel public discontent, to reclaim its declining legitimacy, to discipline its black

sheep, to isolate political rivals or to eliminate class enemies.' T. Wing Lo, *Corruption and Politics in Hong Kong and China*, 4.

[69] D. Downes and P. Rock (eds), *Deviant Interpretations: Problems in Criminological Theory*, 12–13.

[70] J. Young, Foreword to F. Pearce, *Crimes of the Powerful*, 18.

[71] H. Marcuse, *One-Dimensional Man*.

[72] P. Rock, *Deviant Interpretations*, 75–6.

[73] C. Sumner, introduction to T. Wing Lo, *Corruption and Politics in Hong Kong and China*, x.

[74] For elaboration on Weber's theories of class and social stratification, see F. Parkin, *Marxism and Class Theory: A Bourgeois Critique*.

[75] There is some considerable scope for uncertainty about Weber's capacity to account for German Fascism. Aron states: 'He did not understand the implications of the Bolshevik revolution nor foresee the totalitarian despotism of single party rule. Anxious to spare democracy the reign of politicians without vocation he emphasised the plebiscitary legitimacy of the charismatic leader, unaware of the dangers which the following generation was to experience and suffer' [i.e. Nazism]. R. Aron, 'Max Weber and Power Politics', 99. Yet Weber's sociology is replete with insights into those very dangers, in a way which Marx's is not. As a sociologist, Weber was acutely conscious of problems for which, as a politician, he could not prescribe remedies.

[76] For a dissenting view, see e.g. C. Sumner, 'Race, Crime and Hegemony'. One strand in the analysis of Hall et al., the adoption of tougher forms of policing that are more resistant to democratic controls, is forcefully developed by Hall in *Drifting into a Law and Order Society*.

[77] M. Pratt, *Mugging as a Social Problem*.

[78] P. Waddington, 'Mugging as a Moral Panic', 252.

[79] T. Jones et al., *The Islington Crime Survey*, 35.

[80] A. Giddens, *The Class Structure of the Advanced Societies*, Preface.

[81] A. Platt, *The Child Savers: The Invention of Delinquency*; J. Hagan and J. Leon, 'Rediscovering Delinquency', 922–8.

[82] I. Taylor et al., *Critical Criminology*, 42.

[83] R. Sparks et al., *Surveying Victims*, 187–8.

[84] P. Cohen and D. Robins, *Knuckle Sandwich*, 113.

[85] S. Cohen, *Folk Devils*, xi.

[86] E. Thompson, *Whigs and Hunters*, 16; see chap. 6 for references to Paul Willis.

[87] See K. Stenson and N. Brearley, 'Left Realism in Criminology and the Return to Consensus Theory'.

[88] P. Hillyard et al., 'Leaving a "Stain Upon the Silence"', 383.

[89] F. Pearce, foreword to S. Tombs and D. Whyte (eds), *Unmasking the Crimes of the Powerful*, xi, xii.

[90] See N. Poulantzas, *Classes in Contemporary Capitalism*.

[91] See H. and J. Schwendinger, 'Defenders of Order or Guardians of Human Rights'.

Chapter Eleven: Feminist Criminology

[1] M. Valverde, 'Feminist Perspectives in Criminology', 241.

[2] F. Heidensohn, 'The Deviance of Women: A Critique and an Enquiry'; M. Chesney-Lind, 'The Judicial Enforcement of the Female Sex Role'; D. Klein, 'The Etiology of Female Crime: A Review of the Literature'.

[3] L. Gelsthorpe and A. Morris, 'Feminism and Criminology in Britain', 221.

[4] See e.g. A. Campbell, *Girl Delinquents*, chap. 7.

[5] P. Rock, review of C. Smart, '*Women, Crime and Criminology*'.

[6] C. Smart, *Women, Crime and Criminology*, xiii–xiv.

[7] J., 'Incarcerating "Bad Girls": The Regulation of Sexuality through the Female Refuges Act in Ontario, 1920–1945', 239–75; see also Sangster's 'Criminalizing the Colonized: Ontario Native Women Confront the Criminal Justice System, 1920–60', 32–60, and T. Myers and J. Sangster, 'Retorts, Runaways and Riots: Patterns of Resistance in Canadian Reform Schools for Girls, 1930–60', 669–97.

[8] See P. Rock, *Reconstructing a Women's Prison*, and 'Holloway'.

[9] C. Smart, *Women, Crime and Criminology*, xiii–xiv.

[10] M. Amir, *Patterns in Forcible Rape*.

[11] See F. Heidensohn, *Women and Crime*.

[12] A. K. Cohen, *Delinquent Boys*, 144.

[13] D. Matza, *Delinquency and Drift*.

[14] N. Walker, *Behaviour and Misbehaviour*; P. Cohen, 'Is Positivism Dead?'.

[15] C. Lombroso and W. Ferrero, *The Female Offender*.

[16] C. Smart, *Women, Crime and Criminology*, 32. See also C. Smart, 'The New Female Criminal: Reality or Myth' and, 'Criminological Theory: Its Ideology and Implications Concerning Women'

[17] C. Burt, *The Young Delinquent*.

[18] O. Pollak, *The Criminality of Women*.

[19] Ibid.

[20] M. Gold, *Delinquent Behaviour in an American City*.

[21] C. Smart, *Women, Crime and Criminology*, 84.

[22] R. Hofstadter, *Social Darwinism in American Thought*; D. Kevles, *In the Name of Eugenics: Genetics and the Uses of Human Heredity*.

[23] E. Sutherland and D. Cressey, *Principles of Criminology*, 110, 112.

[24] M. Chesney-Lind, 'Women and Crime': The Female Offender', 78–96; see also J. Belknap, 'MedaChesney-Lind: The Mother of Feminist Criminology', 1–23.

[25] E. Anderson, 'The "Chivalrous" Treatment of the Female Offender in the Arms of the Criminal Justice System', 350–7.

[26] W. I. Thomas, *The Unadjusted Girl*.

[27] C. Smart, *Women, Crime and Criminology*, 41–2.

[28] F. Adler, *Sisters in Crime*.

[29] J. Cowie et al., *Delinquency in Girls*.

[30] G. Konopka, *The Adolescent Girl in Conflict*.

[31] H. Gavron, *The Captive Wife*.

[32] F. Heidensohn, *Women and Crime*; D. Hoffman-Bustamente, 'The Nature of Female Criminality'; K. Rosenhan, 'Female Deviance and the Female Sex Role'.

[33] C. Smart, *Women, Crime and Criminology*, 89.

[34] C. Smart, 'Criminological Theory: Its Ideology and Implications Concerning Women'.

[35] L. Gelsthorpe and A. Morris, 'Feminism and Criminology in Britain'.

[36] F. Heidensohn, *Women and Crime*.

[37] L. Gelsthorpe and A. Morris, 'Feminism and Criminology in Britain', 226.

[38] F. Heidensohn, 'Women and Crime: Questions for Criminology'.

[39] R. Matthews and J. Young (eds), *Confronting Crime*; T. Jones et al., *The Islington Crime Survey*.

[40] E. Stanko, 'Typical Violence, Normal Precaution: Men, Women and Interpersonal Violence in England, Wales, Scotland and the USA'.

[41] Home Office, *Statistics on Women and the Criminal Justice System 2000*.

[42] R. Kong and K. AuCoin, *Female Offenders in Canada*.[43]   R. Morris, 'Female Delinquency and Relational Problems' and 'Attitudes towards Delinquency by Delinquents, Non-Delinquents and their Friends'.

[44] B. Wootton, *Social Science and Social Pathology*.

[45] P. Morgan, *Child Care: Sense and Fable*; M. Rutter, *Maternal Deprivation Reassessed*.

[46] F. Adler, *Sisters in Crime*.

[47] R. Simon, *Women and Crime*; F. Adler and R. Simon (eds), *The Criminology of Deviant Women*.

[48] S. Box, *Power, Crime and Mystification*, chap. 5; F. Heidensohn, *Women and Crime*.

[49] S. Blackman, *Youth: Positions and Oppositions*, 254–5.

[50] E. Comack and S. Brickey, 'Constituting the Violence of Criminalized Women', 23.

[51] E. Comack and S. Brickey, 'Constituting the Violence of Criminalized Women'.

[52] See S. Westervelt, *Shifting the Blame*.

[53] D. Farrington and A. Morris, 'Sex, Sentencing and Reconvictions'.

[54] C. Fisher and R. Mawby, 'Juvenile Delinquency and Police Discretion in an Inner City Area'; S. Landau and G. Nathan, 'Juveniles and the Police'.

[55] F. Heidensohn, *Women and Crime*, chaps 4 and 5.

[56] P. Carlen, *Women's Imprisonment*.

[57] I. Nagel, 'Sex Differences in the Processing of Criminal Defendants'.

[58] M. Eaton, 'Mitigating Circumstances: Familiar Rhetoric'; 'Documenting the Defendant: Placing Women in Social Inquiry Report'; *Justice for Women?*

[59] M. Casburn, *Girls Will Be Girls*.

[60] R. Dobash and R. Dobash, *Violence against Wives: A Case against Patriarchy*; 'The Nature and Antecedents of Violent Events'; S. Edwards, *Female Sexuality and the Law*; 'Police Attitudes and Dispositions in Domestic Disputes: The London Study'. This trend has been reversing, with many jurisdictions adopting a policy of presumptive arrest, or 'automatic charging', a policy originated in part by L. Sherman and R. Berk, *The Minneapolis Domestic Violence Experiment*.

[61] D. Downes and T. Ward, *Democratic Policing*, 17.

[62] M. Sumner, *Prostitution and Images of Women*.

[63] J. Hagan et al., 'The Sexual Stratification of Social Control'; 'The Class Structure of Gender and Delinquency: Toward a Power-Control Theory of Common Delinquent Behaviour'.

[64] See e.g. P. Carlen and A. Worrall, *Gender, Crime and Justice*, and P. Carlen, *Women, Crime and Poverty*.

[65] J. Hagan et al., 'Gender Difference in Capitalization Processes and the Delinquency of Siblings in Toronto and Berlin', 663.

[66] See J. Freeman; 'The Origins of the Women's Liberation Movement'.

[67] There were, for instance, refuges for battered women run by nuns in Quebec in the 1930s, and no doubt other examples could be given, but they have not been given a place in the orthodox histories of the movement. See E. Pizzey, *Scream Quietly or the Neighbours will Hear*.

[68] See M. Wasserman, 'Rape: Breaking the Silence'; and V. Jaycox, *Creating a Senior Victim/Witness Volunteer Corps*.

[69] See Z. Adler, *Rape on Trial*.

70 See J. Nadel, *Sara Thornton: The Story of a Woman Who Killed.*

71 See, for example, S. Edwards, *Policing 'Domestic' Violence: Women, the Law and the State*; J. Gregory and S. Lees, *Policing Sexual Assault*; and J. Temkin, *Rape and the Criminal Justice System.*

72 See S. Westervelt, *Shifting the Blame: How Victimization Became a Criminal Defense.*

73 L. Clark and D. Lewis, *Rape: The Price of Coercive Sexuality*, 147–8.

74 See A. Mattravers, *Justifying the Unjustifiable*; and S. Hayman, *The Evolution of the New Federal Women's Prisons in Canada.*

75 See P. Rock, 'The Social Organization of British Criminology'.

76 A. Campbell, *Girl Delinquents.*

77 A. Campbell, *The Girls in the Gang.*

78 E. Miller, *Street Woman.*

79 F. Heidensohn, *Women in Control: The Role of Women in Law Enforcement.*

80 There have been other studies on such a theme. See e.g. S. Martin, *Breaking and Entering.*

81 L. Zedner, *Women, Crime and Criminal Justice in Victorian England.*

82 A. Taylor, *Women Drug Users*; and L. Maher, *Sexed Work: Gender, Race, and Resistance in Brooklyn Drug Market.*

83 See K. Daly and M. Chesney-Lind 'Feminism and Criminology'.

84 T. Newburn and E. Stanko (eds), *Just Boys Doing Business?* 1.

85 R. Connell, *Gender and Power*, 185.

86 P. Willis, *Learning to Labour.*

87 See J. Williams et al., *Hooligans Abroad.*

88 J. Kersten, 'Culture, Masculinities and Violence against Women', 383.

89 P. Bourgois, 'In Search of Masculinity'.

90 K. Polk, *When Men Kill.*

91 See P. Gordon, *White Law.*

92 See J. Allen, 'The Masculinity" of Criminality and Criminology: Interrogating Some Impasses', and C. Smart, 'Feminist Approaches to Criminality, or Postmodern Woman Meets Atavistic Man'.

93 See P. Hirst, 'Marx and Engels on Law, Crime and Morality'.

94 M. Phillipson, 'Thinking Out of Deviance'.

95 See B. Brown, 'Women and Crime: the Dark Figures of Criminology', and C. Smart, *Feminism and the Power of Law.*

96 A. Young, 'Feminism and the Body of Criminology', 21.

97 See P. Rock, 'Has Deviance a Future?'.

98 C. Smart, 'Feminist Approaches to Criminology, or Postmodern Woman Meets Atavistic Man', 70.

99 F. Heidensohn, *Women and Crime*, 3.

100 L. Gelsthorpe and A. Morris, 'Feminism and Criminology in Britain', 231.

101 F. Heidensohn, 'Women and Crime: Questions for Criminology', 27.

102 Cf. E. Leonard, *Women, Crime and Society.*

103 S. Welsh, 'The Manufacture of Excitement in Police-Juvenile Encounters'.

104 E. Player, 'Women and Crime in the City'.

105 The proceedings were subsequently published as the *Annals of the American Academy of Political and Social Science*, September 2004.

106 R. Agnew and T. Brezina, 84–111, 'Relational Problems with Peers, Gender, and Delinquency,' 84–111; and R. Berger, 'Female Delinquency in the Emancipation Era: A Review of the Literature', 375–99.

[107] L. Lofland, *A World of Strangers*, xii–xiii.

[108] See, for instance, Dawkins, who wrote in his preface to *The Blind Watchmaker*, published in the mid-1980s: 'I am distressed to find that some women friends . . . treat the use of the impersonal masculine pronoun as if it showed intention to exclude them. If there were any excluding to be done . . . I think I would sooner exclude men, but when I once tentatively tried referring to my abstract reader as 'she', a feminist denounced me for patronizing condescension: I ought to say 'he-or-she' and 'his-or-her'. That is easy to do if you don't care about language, but then if you don't care about language you don't deserve readers of either sex. Here, I have returned to the normal conventions of English pronouns. I may refer to the 'reader' as 'he', but I no more think of my readers as specifically male than a French speaker thinks of a table as female', xvi–xvii.

[109] See, for instance, R. Ericson and K. Haggerty, *Policing the Risk Society*.

[110] F. Heidensohn, *Women and Crime*.

[111] A. Morris, *Women, Crime and Criminal Justice*.

[112] C. Mann, *Female Crime and Delinquency*.

[113] P. Willis, *Learning to Labour*.

[114] See e.g. G. Pailthorpe, *Studies in the Psychology of Delinquency*.

[115] B. Brown, 'Women and Crime: The Dark Figures of Criminology', 359–60.

[116] L. Gelsthorpe and A. Morris, 'Feminism and Criminology in Britain', 225.

Chapter Twelve: Deviance Theories and Social Policy

[1] See M. Phillipson, *Sociological Aspects*, chap. 6

[2] See P. Rock, *A View from the Shadows*. Most of the following argument is based on the implications of that case study of Canadian policy-making.

[3] A. Scull, *Decarceration: Community Treatment and the Deviant*.

[4] S. Cohen, *Visions of Social Control*; but see M. McMahon, ' 'Net Widening': Vagaries in the Use of a Concept'.

[5] Cf. Banting's use of the term 'salience' in his *Poverty, Politics and Policy: Britain in the 1960s*, 10ff. For the broader social policy field, see Bulmer (ed.), *Social Policy Research* and his *Social Science and Social Policy* and *The Uses of Social Research*.

[6] J. Short, 'The Natural History of an Applied Theory: Differential Opportunity and Mobilization for Youth'.

[7] F. Thrasher, *The Gang*, 499–500.

[8] See e.g. New York City Youth Board, *Reaching the Fighting Gang*.

[9] See e.g. M. Morse, *The Unattached*; and G. Goetschius and M. Tash, *Working with Unattached Youth*. The use of ex-offenders as social workers resurfaced as 'new careers': see D. Briggs, *Dealing with Deviants*; and C. Covington, 'The Hammersmith Teenage Project'.

[10] S. Kobrin, 'The Chicago Area Project', 323.

[11] Ibid., 330.

[12] H. Finestone, *Victims of Change: Juvenile Delinquents in American Society*, 144. A similar conclusion was reached by J. Mays in his analysis of an allied, smaller-scale Liverpool project in *On the Threshold of Delinquency*.

[13] See J. Snodgrass, 'Clifford R. Shaw and Henry D. McKay', and also P. Townsend, 'Area Deprivation Policies'.

[14] A. Gouldner, *The Coming Crisis*, 346–7.

[15] Ibid., 346.

[16] A. Gouldner, *The Coming Crisis*, 346–7, 358.

[17] J. Short, 'The Natural History of an Applied Theory', 199–200, discusses this issue.

[18] Mobilization for Youth, *A Proposal for the Prevention and Control of Delinquency by the Expansion of Opportunities*, 44–5.

[19] Ibid., ix–x.

[20] P. Marris and M. Rein, *Dilemmas of Social Reform: Poverty and Community Action in the United States*, 124.

[21] F. Piven and R. Cloward, *Regulating the Poor*, 279.

[22] A. Gouldner, *The Coming Crisis*, 350.

[23] G. Brager, 1964, quoted in P. Marris and M. Rein, *Dilemmas of Social Reform*, 77.

[24] See D. Moynihan, *Maximum Feasible Misunderstanding*, 26.

[25] P. Marris and M. Rein, *Dilemmas of Social Reform*, 77.

[26] J. Short, 'The Natural History of an Applied Theory', 199 n.

[27] P. Marris and M. Rein, *Dilemmas of Social Reform*, 124–5.

[28] Ibid. 126. Those strictures about 'genuine' opportunities should be noted. A number of criminologists and Currie in particular, have argued that employment will act as an alternative to crime only if it is not work that is badly paid and devalued. See E. Currie, *Confronting Crime: An American Challenge*.

[29] See J. Braithwaite, *Inequality, Crime and Public Policy*.

[30] The policy background is well analyzed in Marris and Rein's preface to *Dilemmas of Social Reform*.

[31] See J. Young, 'Working Class Criminology' and 'Left Idealism, Reformism and Beyond' and, for a discussion of the issues raised, S. Cohen, 'Guilt, Justice and Tolerance: Some Old Concepts for a New Criminology'.

[32] However, it is becoming increasingly clear that multi-agency approaches have their problems, that the police tend to be the agency that dominates agendas and decisions, and that different agencies often disagree about the nature of the problems they are confronting and the methods that should be used to tackle them. See A. Sampson et al., 'Crime, Localities and the Multi-Agency Approach'.

[33] J. Braithwaite, *Crime, Shame and Reintegration*, 185.

[34] J. Braithwaite, 'Shame and Modernity', 1.

[35] See K. Llewellyn and E. Hoebel, *The Cheyenne Way: Conflict and Case Law in Primitive Jurisprudence*.

[36] See A. Ashworth, 'Victims' Rights, Defendants' Rights and Criminal Procedure'.

[37] See e.g. J. Dignan, *Understanding Victims and Restorative Justice*; and H. Strang, *Repair or Revenge: Victims and Restorative Justice*.

[38] T. Mathiesen, *The Politics of Abolition*.

[39] M. Simpkin, *Trapped within Welfare: Surviving Social Work*, 155. The reference is to I. Taylor, 'Client Refusal'. See also P. Corrigan and P. Leonard, *Social Work Practice under Capitalism*.

[40] 'Control Units' were established in two English prisons in the 1970s to control troublesome prisoners by techniques that amounted to sensory deprivation. They were closed after adverse publicity stemming from the family of one of the prisoners subjected to this form of punishment led to a widespread campaign for their abolition. For a discussion, see M. Fitzgerald and J. Sim, *British Prisons*.

[41] See E. Schur, *Narcotic Addiction in Britain and America*.

[42] E. Genders and E. Player, *Grendon: A Study of a Therapeutic Prison*. See too B. Mason, 'Imprisoned Freedom: A Study of the New Women's Prison in Dublin'.

[43] M. McMahon, 'Net-Widening', 144. See, too, idem, *The Persistent Prison?*

[44] A. Scull, *Decarceration*.

[45] R. Pahl, 'Stratification: The Relation between States and Urban and Regional Development', 9. The reference is to N. Poulantzas, *Classes in Contemporary Capitalism*.

[46] N. Christie, *Crime Control as Industry: Towards Gulags Western Style*.

[47] E. Gellner, 'A Social Contract in Search of an Idiom', 141; See also R. Pahl, '"Collective Consumption" and the State in Capitalist and State Socialist Societies'; F. Parkin, *Marxism*; and D. Downes, 'Praxis Makes Perfect' and 'Abolition: Possibilities and Pitfalls'.

[48] F. Tannenbaum, *Crime and the Community*; E. Lemert, *Social Pathology*.

[49] See in particular *Crimes without Victims* and *Radical Non-Intervention*.

[50] See e.g. P. Townsend, *The Last Refuge*; and T. and P. Morris, *Pentonville*.

[51] See, for instance, J. Hagan and A. Palloni, 'The Social Reproduction of a Criminal Class in Working-Class London circa 1950–1980'.

[52] J. Miller, *Search and Destroy*.

[53] S. Kobrin et al., 'Offense Patterns of Status Offenders', 233 n. 1.

[54] S. Cohen, review of E. Schur, *Crimes without Victims*.

[55] K. Teilmann and M. Klein, 'Juvenile Justice Legislation: A Framework for Evaluation', 423.

[56] J. Osborne, 'Juvenile Justice Policy in Canada', 25.

[57] R. Ericson, 'From Social Theory to Penal Practice'.

[58] L. Empey, 'Revolution and Counter-revolution: Current Trends in Juvenile Justice'.

[59] Ibid., 172.

[60] C. Covington, 'The Hammersmith Teenage Project'.

[61] S. Cohen, *Visions of Social Control*.

[62] K. Riele, 'Youth at Risk: Further Marginalizing the Marginalized?', 129–45

[63] M. McMahon, '"Net-Widening": Vagaries in the Use of a Concept'.

[64] D. Downes, *Contrasts in Tolerance*.

[65] J. Miller, 'Systems of Control and the Serious Youth Offender', 144.

[66] A. Scull, *Decarceration*.

[67] R. Titmuss, *Commitment to Welfare*, chap. 9: 'Community Care: Fact or Fiction?'

[68] P. Lerman, *Community Treatment and Social Control: A Critical Analysis of Juvenile Correctional Policy*, esp. 58–69 and chap. 8.

[69] For an invaluable collection of papers assessing the interplay between research, practice, and policy in the British government's 'evidence-led' crime reduction initiative of the late 1990s, see the special issue of *Criminal Justice*, August 2004, and especially M. Hough, 'Modernization, Scientific Rationalism and the Crime Reduction Programme'.

[70] R. Martinson, 'What Works? Questions and Answers about Penal Reform', 22–54.

[71] Home Office (UK), *Information on the Criminal Justice System in England and Wales: Digest 4*.

[72] American Friends Service Committee, *Struggle for Justice*; A. von Hirsch, *Doing Justice*. However, although the huge increase in imprisonment in the USA since the mid-1970s has stemmed partly from mandatory minimum sentencing with a so-called progressive emphasis, i.e., set penalties for certain offences which increase according to prior convictions, Von Hirsch's concept of 'just deserts', by contrast, rejects any such steepening of sanctions. It was this conception which animated the 1991 *Criminal Justice Act* in Britain and which was reversed two years later by subsequent Home Secretaries.

[73] P. Marris and M. Rein, *Dilemmas of Social Reform*, 330.

[74] A. Halsey, 'Education Can Compensate', 172–3.

[75] Ibid., 173.

[76] Interestingly, work conducted by West and Farrington on their Cambridge cohort research has led to the reiterated assertion that delinquency can be prevented by the

introduction of pre-school programs for poorer children. See D. Farrington and D. West, 'The Cambridge Study in Delinquent Development: A Long-Term Follow-Up of 411 London Males'.

[77] M. Zander, 'What is the Evidence on Law and Order?' 591–4.

[78] R. Clarke, 'Situational Crime Prevention', 141.

[79] See e.g. R. Mawby, 'Kiosk Vandalism', 30–46; R. Clarke and P. Mayhew (eds), *Designing Out Crime*; and P. Sainsbury, *Suicide Trends in Europe*.

[80] Home Office (UK), *The 2001 British Crime Survey: First Results, England and Wales*, iv.

[81] See e.g. D. Smith, 'Less Crime without More Punishment'.

[82] See D. Forrester et al., *The Kirkholt Burglary Prevention Project, Rochdale*; and D. Forrester et al., *The Kirkholt Burglary Prevention Project, Phase II*.

[83] See D. Rosenbaum, 'A Critical Eye on Neighbourhood Watch: Does it Reduce Crime and Fear?' and T. Bennett, *An Evaluation of Two Neighbourhood Watch Schemes in London*.

[84] See N. Polvi et al., 'The Time Course of Repeat Burglary Victimization'.

[85] See O. Newman, *Community of Interest*.

[86] See A. Sampson, *Lessons from a Victim Support Crime Prevention Project*.

[87] See D. Gilling, 'The Evolution and Implementation of the Multi-Agency approach to Crime Prevention'.

[88] See J. Foster and T. Hope, *Housing, Community and Crime*.

[89] J. Foster, 'Informal Social Control and Community Crime Prevention'.

[90] J. Foster and T. Hope, *Housing, Community and Crime*.

[91] D. Downes and R. Morgan, 'Dumping the Hostages to Fortune: The Politics of Law and Order in Postwar Britain'.

[92] Bottoms, 1995, "The Philosophy and Politics of Punishment and Sentencing," in The Politics of Sentencing Reform, C. Clarkson and R. Morgan, eds. Oxford 1995.

[93] R. Sennett, *Respect in a World of Inequality*.

[94] D. Garland, *The Culture o f Control*.

[95] D. Downes and R. van Swaaningen, 'The Road to Dystopia? Changes in the Penal Climate of the Netherlands'.

[96] J. Simon, 'Governing through Crime'.

[97] A. Crawford, *The Local Governance of Crime: Appeals to Community and Partnerships*, 228.

[98] Ibid., 229–30.

[99] E. Burney, *Making People Behave: Anti-social Behaviour, Politics and Policy.*

[100] Zedner, 'Dangers and Dystopias in Penal Theories'.

[101] J. Lowman, *Realist Criminology: Crime Control and Policing in the 1990s*.

[102] E. Stanko 'Women, Crime, and Fear'.

[103] M. Phillipson, *Sociological Aspects*, 16–89 and chap. 6, 'Criminology, Sociology, Crime and Social Policy'.

[104] Models to follow are Lerman's study of the Californian diversion projects (*Community Treatment and Social Control)* and Scott's exploratory work (*The Making of Blind Men*) on the agencies for the blind in the United States.

Chapter Thirteen: The metamorphosis of deviance?

[1] J. Best, 'Whatever Happened to Social Pathology?'

[2] C. Sumner, *The Sociology of Deviance: An Obituary*.

[3] W. Morrison, *Theoretical Criminology: From Modernity to Postmodernism*.

⁴ D. Nelken (ed.), *The Futures of Criminology*.

⁵ A. Lizos, 'The Poverty of the Sociology of Deviance: Nuts, Sluts, and Perverts', 103–20.

⁶ E. Goode, 'Does the Death of the Sociology of Deviance Claim Make Sense?', 107–18; see also idem, 'Is the Sociology of Deviance Still Relevant?', 46–57; and idem, 'Is the Deviance Concept Still Relevant to Sociology?', 547–58.

⁷ E. Goode, 'Is the Deviance Concept Still Relevant to Sociology?'

⁸ J. Best, 'Deviance May Be Alive, But Is It Intellectually Lively? A Reaction to Goode', 483–92; idem, 'Whatever Happened to Social Pathology? Conceptual Fashions and the Sociology of Deviance', 533–46.

⁹ K. Durkin et al. 'Pathological Internet Communities: A New Direction for Sexual Deviance Research in a Post Modern Era', 595–606.

¹⁰ C. Kubrin, 'New Directions in Social Disorganization Theory', 374–402; F. Markowitz et al., 'Extending Social Disorganization Theory: Modeling the Relationships between Cohesion, Disorder, and Fear', 293–319.

¹¹ 'J. Muncie, The Globalization of Crime Control—The Case of Youth and Juvenile Justice: Neo-Liberalism, Policy Convergence and International Conventions'.

¹² J. Young, 'Incessant Chatter: Recent Paradigms in Criminology'.

¹³ See R. van Swaaningen, *Critical Criminologies: Visions from Europe*.

¹⁴ S. Henry and D. Milovanovic, *Constitutive Criminology: Beyond Postmodernism*.

¹⁵ R. Corrado et al., 'Social Capital and Community Crime Prevention Programs'.

¹⁶ See T. Eagleton, *The Illusions of Postmodernism*.

¹⁷ J. Wilson and R. Herrnstein, *Crime and Human Nature*.

¹⁸ See R. van Swaaningen, *Critical Criminologies*.

¹⁹ See H. Bianchi and R. van Swaaningen (eds), Abolitionism: Towards a Non-Repressive Approach to Crime.

²⁰ S. Lipset, *Political Man*.

²¹ See also D. Nelken, 'Comparing Criminal Justice'.

²² M. Cain, *Orientalism, Occidentalism and the Sociology of Crime*; S. Cohen, *States of Denial: Knowing about Atrocities and Suffering*, 77.

²³ A. Giddens, *The Consequences of Modernity*, and D. Harvey, *The Condition of Postmodernity*.

²⁴ P. Kennedy, *Preparing for the Twenty-First Century*.

²⁵ D. Downes, *Back to the Future: The Predictive Value of Social Theories of Delinquency*.

²⁶ W. Hutton, *The State We're In*; O. James, *Juvenile Violence in a Winner–Loser Culture*.

²⁷ C. Webber, 'Revaluating Relative Deprivation Theory', 97–120.

²⁸ A. Power and R. Turnstall, *Dangerous Disorder: Riots and Violent Disturbances in Thirteen Areas of Britain, 1991–92*.

²⁹ B. Western and K. Beckett, *How Unregulated is the USA Labor Market? The Penal System as a Labor Market Institution*.

³⁰ R. Freeman, 'Who Becomes a Criminal?'

³¹ D. Smith, 'Youth Crime and Conduct Disorders', in D. Smith and M. Rutter (eds), *Psychosocial Disorders in Young People: Time Trends and Their Causes*.

³² V. Ruggiero, *Organized and Corporate Crime in Europe*.

³³ S. Field, *Trends in Crime and Their Interpretation*.

³⁴ see also Dick Hobbs's *Doing the Business* and *Bad Business*.

³⁵ M. Sutton, 'Supply by Theft: Does the Market for Second-Hand Goods Play a Role in Keeping Crime Figures High?'

³⁶ J. Pitts and T. Hope, 'The Local Politics of Inclusion—The State and Community Safety'.

[37] See D. Garland (ed.), *Mass Imprisonment: Social Causes and Consequences*; and C. Ugger and J. Manza, 'Democratic Contraction? The Political, Consequences of Felon Disenfranchisement in the United States'.

[38] A. Doob and C. Webster, 'Countering Punitiveness: Understanding Stability in Canada's Imprisonment Rate'.

[39] S. Cohen, *Folk Devils and Moral Panics*.

[40] R. Hughes, *The Culture of Complaint*.

[41] S. Cohen, *Visions of Social Control*; and D. Garland, 'Frameworks of Inquiry in the Sociology of Punishment'.

[42] From S. Cohen, *The 'Punitive City'* to *Visions of Social Control*.

[43] F. Lösel, 'The Efficacy of Correctional Treatment: A Review and Synthesis of Meta-Evaluations'.

[44] C. Murray, *Losing Ground, The Emerging British Underclass* and *Underclass: The Crisis Deepens*.

[45] J. MacNicol, 'In Pursuit of the Underclass'.

[46] C. Jencks and R. Peterson (eds), *The Urban Underclass*.

[47] NACRO, *Crime and Social Policy*.

[48] See W. Wilson, *The Truly Disadvantaged*; R. Freeman, 'Employment and Earnings of Disadvantaged Young Men in a Labor Shortage Economy'; and M. Sullivan, *'Getting Paid': Youth Crime and Work in the Inner City*.

[49] A. Bottoms and P. Wiles, 'Crime and Insecurity in the City'.

[50] See R. King, 'Prisons'; and F. Zimring and G. Hawkins, 'The Growth of Imprisonment in California'.

[51] M. Davis, 'Beyond Blade Runner'.

[52] A. Giddens, *The Constitution of Society*.

[53] A. Giddens, *Modernity and Self-Identity*.

[54] A. Bottoms and P. Wiles, 'Crime and Insecurity in the City'.

[55] Tonry, 1995, 'Malign neglect, race, crime, and punishment in America'.

[56] D. Matza and P. Morgan, *Controlling Drug Use: The Great Prohibition*.

[57] See e.g.V. Ruggiero, *Organized and Corporate Crime in Europe;* and N. South, 'Drugs, Alcohol and Crime'.

[58] A. Etzioni, *The Moral Dimension* and *The Parenting Deficit*.

[59] Quoted in W. Hutton, *The State We're In*, 225. See also 'Kids spend more time with parents than 20 years ago,' *USA Today*, 9 May 2001; and Canadian Research Institute for Social Policy, 'Are Parents Investing More or Less Time in Children? Trends in Selected Industrialized Countries'.

[60] The quotation is from É. Durkheim, *The Division of Labor in Society.*

[61] in P. Ormerod, *The Death of Economics.*

[62] J. Braithwaite, 'Shame and Modernity', 13.

[63] B. Campbell, *Goliath: Britain's Dangerous Places*; and W. Wilson, *The Truly Disadvantaged* and *When Work Disappears*.

[64] J. Braithwaite, 'Shame and Modernity', 15.

[65] S. Cohen, 'Crime and Politics: Spot the Difference'.

[66] D. Downes and R. Morgan, 'Dumping the Hostages to Fortune? The Politics of Law and Order in Postwar Britain'.

[67] R. van Swaaningen, *Critical Criminologies: Visions from Europe.*

[68] C. Smart, *Women, Crime and Criminology.*

[69] D. Downes and P. Rock (eds), *Deviant Interpretations: Problems in Criminological Theory.*

[70] J. Lea and J. Young, *What Is to Be Done about Law and Order?*

[71] R. van Swaaningen, *Critical Criminologies: Visions from Europe.*

[72] F. Parkin, *Marxism and Class Theory: A Bourgeois Critique.*

[73] A. Giddens, *In Defence of Sociology*, 243–5.

[74] N. Christie, *Crime Control as Industry: Towards Gulags Western Style.*

[75] V. Ruggiero, *Organised and Corporate Crime in Europe.*

[76] F. Durbin, *The Politics of Democratic Socialism.*

[77] I. Taylor, P. Walton, and J. Young (eds), *The New Criminology.*

References

Adler, F., *Sisters in Crime*, New York, 1975.
—— and Simon, R. (eds), *The Criminology of Deviant Women*, Boston, 1979.
Adler, P., Johnson, J., 'Street Corner Society Revisited: New Questions about Old Issues',
 Journal of Contemporary Ethnography, 21, 1 (1992).
Adler, Z., *Rape on Trial*. London, 1987.
Agnew, R. and Brezina, T., 'Relational Problems with Peers, Gender, and Delinquency',
 Youth and Society, 29, no. 1 (1997): 84–111.
Akerlof, G. and Yellen, J., 'Gang Behavior, Enforcement, and Community Values', in
 H. Aaron, et al. (eds), *Values and Public Policy*, Washington, 1994.
Akers, D., 'Problems in the Sociology of Deviance: Social Definitions and Behaviour',
 Social Forces, 46, no. 4 (1968), 455–65.
Akers, R., 'Problems in the Sociology of Deviance', *Social Forces*, 46(4) (1968).
Albini, J., *The American Mafia: Genesis of a Legend*, New York, 1971.
Alihan, M., *Social Ecology*, New York, 1938.
Allan, E. and Steffensmeier, D., 'Youth, Underemployment and Property Crime: Differ-
 ential Effects of Job Availability and Job Quality on Juvenile and Young Adult Arrest
 Rates', *American Sociological Review*, 54 (1989).
Allen, J., 'The "Masculinity" of Criminality and Criminology: Interrogating Some
 Impasses', in M. Findlay and R. Hogg (eds), *Understanding Crime and Criminal Justice*,
 Sydney, 1988.
American Friends Service Committee, *Struggle for Justice: A Report on Crime and Punish-
 ment in America*, New York, 1971.
Amir, M., *Patterns in Forcible Rape*, Chicago, 1971.
Anderson, E., 'The "Chivalrous" Treatment of the Female Offender in the Arms of
 the Criminal Justice System: A Review of the Literature', *Social Problems*, 23, no. 3
 (1976).
—— *A Place on the Corner*, Chicago, 1976.
—— *Streetwise*, Chicago, 1990.
Anderson, N., *The Hobo: The Sociology of the Homeless Man*, Chicago, 1923.
Anon., 'The Life Histories of W. I. Thomas and Robert E. Park', *American Journal of
 Sociology*, 79 (1973).
Armstrong, G., *Football Hooligans: Knowing the Score*, London, 1998
—— and Wilson, M., 'City Politics and Deviancy Amplification', in I. Taylor and L. Taylor
 (eds), *Politics and Deviance*, Harmondsworth, 1973.
Arnett, J., 'Three Profiles of Heavy Metal Fans: A Taste for Sensation and Subculture of
 Alienation,' *Qualitative Sociology*, 16, no. 4 (1993): 423–33.
Aron, R., 'Max Weber and Power Politics', in O. Stammer (ed.), *Max Weber and Sociology
 Today*, Oxford, 1971.
Asbury, H., *The Gangs of New York*, New York, 1928.

Ashworth, A., 'Victims' Rights, Defendants' Rights and Criminal Procedure', in A. Crawford and J. Goodey (eds), *Integrating a Victim Perspective within Criminal Justice*, Aldershot, 2000.

Athens, L., *Violent Criminal Acts and Actors*, Boston, 1980.

Atkinson, M., 'Societal Reactions to Suicide', in S. Cohen (ed.), *Images of Deviance*, Harmondsworth, 1971.

—— *Discovering Suicide*, London, 1979.

—— and Drew, P., *Order in Court*, London, 1979.

Bakal, Y. and Polsky, H. (eds), *Reforming Corrections for Juvenile Offenders*, Lexington, Mass., 1979.

Baker, P., 'The Life Histories of W. I. Thomas and Robert E. Park', *American Journal of Sociology*, 79, no. 2 (1973).

Bala, N., 'What's Wrong with YOA Bashing? What's Wrong with the YOA?—Recognizing the Limits of the Law', *Canadian Journal of Criminology*, July, 1994.

Baldwin, J. and Bottoms, A., *The Urban Criminal*, London, 1976.

—— and McConville, M., *Negotiated Justice*, London, 1977.

Baldwin, R., 'Why Rules Don't Work', *Modern Law Review*, 53 (1990).

Ball, D., 'An Abortion Clinic Ethnography', *Social Problems*, 14 (1967).

Bankowski, Z., Mungham, G. and Young, P., 'Radical Criminology or Radical Criminologist?' *Contemporary Crises*, 1, no. 1 (1977).

Banting, K., *Poverty, Politics and Policy*, London, 1979.

Barclay, P. et al., 'Preventing Auto Theft in Suburban Vancouver Commuter Lots: Effects of a Bike Patrol', *Crime Prevention Studies*, 6 (1996).

Baron, S., 'The Canadian West Coast Punk Subculture: A Field Study', *Canadian Journal of Sociology*, 14, no 3 (1989): 289–316.

Barzun, J. (trans.), *Flaubert's Dictionary of Accepted Ideas*, London, 1954.

Bauman, Z., *Modernity and the Holocaust*, Cambridge, UK, 1989.

Baumgartner, M., *The Moral Order of a Suburb*, New York, 1988.

Bayart, J-F., Ellis, S. and Hibou, B., *The Criminalization of the State in Africa*, Bloomington, Ind., 1999.

Beames, T., *The Rookeries of London*, London, 1850.

Beattie, J., 'Violence and Society in Early Modern England', in A. Doob and E. Greenspan (eds), *Perspectives in Criminal Law*, Aurora, Ont., 1984.

Beck, U., *Risk Society*, London, 1992.

Becker, G., 'Crime and Punishment: An Economic Approach', *Journal of Political Economy*, 76, no. 2 (1968).

Becker, H., 'The Culture of a Deviant Group', *American Journal of Sociology*, 51 (1961). Reprinted by permission of Howard Becker.

—— *Outsiders*, New York, 1963.

—— 'Marihuana Use and Social Control', in idem, *Outsiders*, New York, 1963; reprinted from *Social Problems*, 3, no. 1 (1955): 35–44.

—— 'The Self and Adult Socialization', in E. Norbeck et al. (eds), *The Study of Personality*, New York, 1968.

—— (ed.), *Culture and Civility in San Francisco*, Chicago, 1971.

—— 'The Life History and the Scientific Mosaic', in *Sociological Work*, London, 1971.

—— Labelling Theory Reconsidered', in P. Rock and M. McIntosh (eds), *Deviance and Social Control*, London, 1974.

—— *Tricks of the Trade: How to Think about Your Research While You're Doing It*, Chicago, 1998.

—— and Horowitz, I., 'The Culture of Civility', in H. Becker (ed.), *Culture and Civility in San Francisco*, Chicago, 1971.

—— 'The Chicago School, So-called', *Qualitative Sociology* 22, no. 1 (1999): 3–12.

—— 'The Professional Dance Musician and his Audience', *American Journal of Sociology*, 57, 2 (1951).

Becker, J., *Hitler's Children*, London, 1978.

Beirne, P. and Hill, J., *Comparative Criminology: An Annotated Bibliography*, Westport, 1991.

Belknap, J., 'Meda-Chesney-Lind, The Mother of Feminist Criminology', *Women and Criminal Justice*, 15, no. 2 (2004).

Bell, D., *The End of Ideology*, New York, 1960.

Belson, W., *Juvenile Theft*, London, 1975.

Bennett, T., *An Evaluation of Two Neighbourhood Watch Schemes in London*, Cambridge, 1987.

—— and Wright, R., *Burglars on Burglary*, Aldershot, 1984.

Bennett, W. and Feldman, M., *Reconstructing Reality in the Courtroom*, New Brunswick, NJ, 1981.

Bensman, J. and Gerver, I., 'Crime and Punishment in the Factory: The Function of Deviancy in Maintaining the Social System', *American Sociological Review*, 28, no. 4 (1963): 588–98

Berger, P., *The Social Reality of Religion*, Harmondsworth, 1973.

—— and Luckmann, T., *The Social Construction of Reality*, London, 1967.

Berger, R., 'Female Delinquency in the Emancipation Era: A Review of the Literature', *Sex Roles*, 21, no. 5/6 (1989): 375–99.

Bersani, C. (ed.), *Crime and Delinquency*, New York, 1970.

Best, J., 'Deviance May Be Alive, But Is It Intellectually Lively? A Reaction to Goode', *Deviant Behavior*, 25, no. 5 (2004): 483–92.

—— 'Whatever Happened to Social Pathology? Conceptual Fashions and the Sociology of Deviance', *Sociological Spectrum*, 26, no. 6 (2006): 533–46.

Bianchi, H. and Swaaningen, R. van (eds), *Abolitionism: Towards a Non-Repressive Approach to Crime*, Amsterdam, 1986.

Bittner, E., 'Radicalism and the Organization of Radical Movements', *American Sociological Review*, 28 (1963).

—— 'The Police on Skid Row', *American Sociological Review*, 32, no. 5 (1967).

—— 'Police Discretion in Emergency Apprehensions of Mentally Ill Persons', *Social Problems*, 14, no. 3 (1967).

—— *The Functions of the Police in Modern Society*, Rockville, 1970.

Blau, P., *The Dynamics of Bureaucracy*, Chicago, 1955.

——*Exchange and Power in Social Life*, New York, 1964.

Blumer, H., 'Suggestions for the Study of Mass Media Effects', in *Symbolic Interactionism*, Englewood Cliffs, NJ, 1969.

—— 'What is Wrong with Social Theory?', in *Symbolic Interactionism*, Englewood Cliffs, NJ, 1969.

Blumstein, A. and Hsieh, P. *The Duration of Adult Criminal Careers*, Washington DC, 1982.

Bode, K., Stonier, A., 'A New Approach to the Methodology of the Social Sciences', *Economica* 4, (1937): 406–23.

Boelen, W., 'Street Corner Society: Cornerville Revisited', *Journal of Contemporary Ethnography*, 21, no. 1 (1992).

Bonger, W., *Criminality and Economic Conditions*, Boston, 1916.

Bordua, D. (ed.), *The Police: Six Sociological Essays*, New York, 1967.

Bottomley, K. and Pease, K., *Crime and Punishment*, London, 1986.

Bottoms, A., review of *Defensible Space*, *British Journal of Criminology*, 14 (1974).

—— 'The Philosophy and Politics of Punishment and Sentencing', in *The Politics of Sentencing Reform*, C. Clarkson and R. Morgan (eds), Oxford, 1995.

—— Mawby, R. and Walker, M., 'A Localised Crime Survey in Contrasting Areas of a City', *British Journal of Criminology*, 27 (1987).

—— and Wiles, P., 'Crime and Insecurity in the City', in C. Fijnaut (ed.), *Changes in Society, Crime and Criminal Justice in Europe*, The Hague, 1996.

—— et al., 'A Tale of Two Estates', in D. Downes (ed.), *Crime and the City*, Basingstoke, 1989.

Bourdieu, P., 'Forms of Capital' in J. Richardson (ed.), *Handbook of Theory and Research for the Sociology of Education*, New York, 1983.

Bourgois, P., *In Search of Respect: Selling Crack in El Barrio*, Cambridge, 1995.

—— 'In Search of Masculinity', *British Journal of Criminology*, 36 (1996).

Box, S., *Deviance, Reality and Society*, London, 1971.

—— *Crime, Power and Mystification*, London, 1983.

Boyle, J., *A Sense of Freedom*, London, 1977.

—— *The Pains of Confinement: Prison Diaries*, Edinburgh, 1984.

Braithwaite, J., *Inequality, Crime and Public Policy*, London, 1979.

—— *Crime, Shame and Reintegration*, Cambridge, 1989.

—— 'Shame and Modernity', *British Journal of Criminology*, 33 (1993).

Brake, M., *The Sociology of Youth Culture and Youth Subcultures*, London, 1980.

Brannigan, A., 'Mystification of the Innocents: Crime, Comics and Delinquency in Canada, 1931–1949', *Criminal Justice History*, 1, (1986).

Brantingham, P. and Brantingham, P., 'Situational Crime Prevention as a Key Component in Embedded Crime Prevention', *Canadian Journal of Criminology and Criminal Justice*, April (2005).

—— 'Environment, Routine and Situation: Toward a Pattern Theory of Crime', *Advances in Criminological Theory*, 5 (1993).

—— 'Criminality of Place: Crime Generators and Crime Attractors', *European Journal on Criminal Policy and Research*, 3 (1995).

—— and Faust, F., 'A Conceptual Model of Crime Prevention', *Crime and Delinquency*, 22 (1976).

Braude, L., '"Park and Burgess": An Appreciation', *American Journal of Sociology*, 77 (1970).

Briar, S. and Piliavin, I., 'Delinquency, Situational Inducements, and Commitment to Conformity', *Social Problems*, 13 (1965).

Briggs, D., *Dealing with Deviants*, London, 1975.

Brody, S. and Tarling, R., *Taking Offenders out of Circulation*, Home Office Research Study No. 64, London, 1980.

Brown, B., 'Women and Crime: The Dark Figures of Criminology', *Economy and Society*, 16 (1986).

Bulmer, M. (ed.), *Social Policy Research*, London, 1978.

—— *The Uses of Social Research*, London, 1982.

—— *The Chicago School*, Chicago, 1985.

—— *Social Science and Social Policy*, London, 1986.

Burbidge, M., 'British Public Housing and Crime: A Review', in R. Clarke and T. Hope (eds), *Coping with Crime*, Boston, 1984.

Burgess, E., 'The Study of the Delinquent as a Person', *The American Journal of Sociology*, 28, 6, (1923): 657—80.

—— 'Residential Segregation in American Cities', *Annals of the American Academy of Political and Social Science*, 140, (1928): 105—15.

—— 'Values in Sociological Research', *Social Problems*, 2, no. 1 (1954).

—— 'The Growth of the City', in R. Park and E. Burgess, *The City*, Chicago, 1967.

Burke, K., *A Grammar of Motives*, New York, 1945.

Burney, E., *Making People Behave: Anti-social Behaviour, Politics and Policy*, Cullompton, Devon, 2005.

Burt, C., *The Young Delinquent*, London, 1924 (1944, 4th rev. edn).

Buruma, I., 'The Joys and Perils of Victimhood', in Lightman, A. and Atwan, R., *The Best American Essays 2000*, Boston, 2000.

Cain, M., *Society and the Policeman's Role*, London, 1974.

—— 'Orientalism, Occidentalism and the Sociology of Crime', *British Journal of Criminology*, Special Issue, 40 (2000).

Cameron, M., *The Booster and the Snitch*, New York, 1964.

Campbell, A., *Girl Delinquents*, Oxford, 1981.

—— *The Girls in the Gang: A Report from New York City*, Oxford, 1984.

—— 'Self-report of Fighting by Females', *British Journal of Criminology*, 26 (1986).

Campbell, B., *Goliath: Britain's Dangerous Places*, London, 1993.

Carey, J., 'Problems of Access and Risk in Observing Drug Scenes', in J. Douglas (ed.), *Research on Deviance*, New York, 1972.

—— *Sociology and Public Affairs: The Chicago School*, Beverly Hills, 1975.

Carlen, P., *Magistrates' Justice*, London, 1976.

—— review of D. Downes and P. Rock, *Deviant Interpretations*, *Sociological Review*, 27, 4 (1979).

—— *Women's Imprisonment*, London, 1983.

—— (ed.), *Criminal Women*, Cambridge, 1985.

—— *Women, Crime and Poverty*, Milton Keynes, 1988.

—— and Worrall, A., *Gender, Crime and Justice*, Milton Keynes, 1987.

Carr-Hill, R. and Stern, N., *Crime, the Police and Criminal Statistics*, London, 1979.

Carrington, P. and Moyer, S., 'Trends in Youth Crime and Police Response', *Canadian Journal of Criminology*, January 1994.

Carstairs, C., 'Deporting "Ah Sin" to Save the White Race: Moral Panic, Racialization, and the Extension of Canadian Drug Laws in the 1920s', *Canadian Bulletin of Medical History*, 16 (1999).

Casburn, M., *Girls Will Be Girls*, London, 1979.

Cavan, S., *Liquor License*, Chicago, 1966.

Centre of Criminology, University of Toronto, *Handbook and Annual Report 1976*, Toronto, 1976.

Chaiken, J., Lawless, M., and Stevenson, K., *Impact of Police Activity on Crime: Robberies on the New York City Subway System*, Santa Monica, 1974.

Chambliss, W., *Box Man*, New York, 1972.

—— 'The State and Criminal Law', in W. Chambliss and M. Mankoff (eds), *Whose Law, What Order?*, New York, 1976.

—— *On the Take: From Petty Crooks to Presidents*, Bloomington, Ind., 1978.

Chapin, F., 'The Effects of Slum Clearance and Rehousing on Family and Community Relationships in Minneapolis', *American Journal of Sociology*, 43, no. 5 (1938): 744–63.

Chapman, D., *Sociology and the Stereotype of the Criminal*, London, 1967.

Cherry, P., *The Biker Trials: Bringing Down the Hells Angels*, Toronto, 2005.

Chesney-Lind, M., 'The Judicial Enforcement of the Female Sex Role', *Issues in Criminology*, 8 (1973), University of Chicago Press Journals.

—— '"Women and Crime": The Female Offender', *Signs*, 12, 1 (1986): 78–96.

Chevalier, L., *Labouring Classes and Dangerous Classes*, London, 1973.

Christie, N., *Crime Control as Industry: Towards Gulags Western Style*, London, 1993.

Chunn, D. and Menzies, R., '"So What Does This Have to Do with Criminology?": Surviving the Restructuring of the Discipline in the Twenty-First Century', *Canadian Journal of Criminology and Criminal Justice*, 48, no. 5 (2006).

Cicourel, S., *Method and Measurement in Sociology*, New York, 1964.

—— *The Social Organization of Juvenile Justice*, New York, 1968.

—— 'Interpretative Procedures and Normative Rules in the Negotiation of Status and Role', in *Cognitive Sociology*, Harmondsworth, 1973.

—— and Kitsuse, J., *The Educational Decision Makers*, Indianapolis, 1963.

Clarke, L. and Lewis, D., *Rape: The Price of Coercive Sexuality*, Toronto, 1977.

Clarke, R., 'Situational Crime Prevention: Theory and Practice', *British Journal of Criminology*, 20 (1980). Copyright © 2006 by the Centre for Crime and Justice Studies. By permission of Oxford University Press.

—— (ed.), *Situational Crime Prevention: Successful Case Studies*, Albany, 1997.

—— 'Situational Prevention, Criminology, and Social Values', in A. von Hirsch, D. Garland and A. Wakefield (eds), *Ethical and Social Perspectives on Situational Crime Prevention*, Oxford, 2000.

—— and Cornish, D., *Crime Control in Britain*, Albany, 1983.

—— 'Modeling Offenders' Decisions: A Framework for Research and Policy', in M. Tonry and N. Morris (eds), *Crime and Justice*, 6 (Chicago, 1985).

——, 'Rational Choice', unpublished paper, n.d.

—— and Felson, M. (eds), *Routine Activity and Rational Choice*, New Brunswick, NJ, 1993.

—— and Hope, T. (eds), *Coping with Crime*, Boston, 1984.

—— and Mayhew, P. (eds), *Designing Out Crime*, London, 1980.

—— —— 'The British Gas Story and its Criminological Implications', in *Crime and Justice*, M. Tonry and N. Morris (eds), *Crime and Justice*, Chicago, 1988.

Clausen, J., 'Biological Bias and Methodological Limitations in the Kinsey Studies', *Social Problems*, 1, no. 4 (1954): 126–33.

Cleaver, E., *Soul on Ice*, New York, 1968.

Clemmer, D., *The Prison Community*, New York, 1940.

Clinard, M. (ed.), *Anomie and Deviant Behavior: A Discussion and Critique*, New York, 1964.

—— *Cities with Little Crime: The Case of Switzerland*, Cambridge, UK, 1978.

—— and Abbott, D., *Crime in Developing Countries: A Comparative Perspective*, New York, 1973.

Cloward, R. and Ohlin, L., *Delinquency and Opportunity*, New York, 1960.

Cochrane, R., 'Crime and Personality: Theory and Evidence', *Bulletin of the British Psychological Society*, 27 (1974).

Cohen, A., *Delinquent Boys: The Culture of the Gang*, Glencoe, Ill., 1955.

—— 'The Sociology of the Deviant Act: Anomie Theory and Beyond', *American Sociological Review*, 30 (1965).

—— *Deviance and Control*, Englewood Cliffs, NJ, 1966.

—— *The Elasticity of Evil*, Oxford, 1974.

—— and Short, J., 'Juvenile Delinquency', in R. Merton and R. Nisbet (eds), *Contemporary Social Problems*, New York, 1961.

Cohen, L. and Felson, M., 'Social Change and Crime Rate Trends: A Routine Activity Approach', *American Sociological Review*, 44 (1979).

Cohen, P., 'Working Class Youth Cultures in East London', *Working Papers in Cultural Studies* (Birmingham University), 2 (1972); in J. Clarke et al. (eds), *Resistance through Ritual*, London, 1976; and in his *Rethinking the Youth Question*, London, 1997.

—— and Robins, D., *Knuckle Sandwich: Growing up in the Working Class City*, Harmondsworth, 1978.

Cohen, P.S., 'Is Positivism Dead?', *Sociological Review*, 28 (New Series) (1980).

—— *Modern Social Theory*, London, 1968.

Cohen, S., 'Directions for Research on Adolescent Group Violence and Vandalism', *British Journal of Criminology*, 11 (1971).

—— (ed.), *Images of Deviance*, Harmondsworth, 1971.

—— 'Criminology and the Sociology of Deviance in Britain', in P. Rock and M. McIntosh (eds), *Deviance and Social Control*, London, 1974.

—— Review of Schur, E., *Crimes without Victims*, *New Society*, 21 Nov. 1974.

—— 'It's All Right for You to Talk: Political and Sociological Manifestoes for Social Work Action', in R. Bailey and M. Brake (eds), *Radical Social Work*, London, 1975.

—— 'The Punitive City: Notes on the Dispersal of Social Control', *Contemporary Crises*, 3, no. 8 (1979).

—— 'Guilt, Justice and Tolerance: Some Old Concepts for a New Criminology', in D. Downes and P. Rock (eds), *Deviant Interpretations*, Oxford, 1979.

—— *Folk Devils and Moral Panics: The Creation of the Mods and Rockers* (2nd edn., rev.), Oxford, 1980.

—— *Visions of Social Control*, Cambridge, 1985.

—— *Against Criminology*, New Brunswick, NJ, 1988.

—— 'Crime and Politics: Spot the Difference', *The British Journal of Sociology*, 47 (1996).

—— *States of Denial: Knowing about Atrocities and Suffering*, Cambridge, 2001.

—— and Taylor, L., *Psychological Survival*, Harmondsworth, 1972.

——, *Prison Secrets*, London, 1976.

—— and Young, J. (eds), *The Manufacture of News*, London, 1973.

Colburn, K., Jr., 'Deviance and Legitimacy in Ice-Hockey: A Microstructural Theory of Violence', *Sociological Quarterly*, 27, no. 1 (1986): 63–74.

—— 'Honor, Ritual and Violence in Ice Hockey', *Canadian Journal of Sociology*, 10, no. 2 (1985): 153–70.

Coleman, A., *Utopia on Trial*, London, 1985.

Coleman, J., 'Social Capital in the Creation of Human Capital', *American Journal of Sociology*, 94, (1988): 95–120.

Colquhoun, P., *A Treatise on the Police of the Metropolis*, London, 1806.

Comack, E., 'The Origins of Canadian Drug Legislation: Labelling versus Class Analysis', in T. Fleming (ed.), *The New Criminologies in Canada*, Toronto, 1985.

—— '"We will get some good out of this riot yet": The Canadian State, Drug Legislation and Class Conflict'. In Elizabeth Comack and S. Brickey (eds), *The Social Basis of Law*, Halifax, 1991.

—— and Brickey, S., 'Constituting the Violence of Criminalized Women', *Canadian Journal of Criminology and Criminal Justice*, 49, no. 1 (2007).

Conant, R. and Levin, M. (eds), *Problems in Research on Community Violence*, New York, 1969.

Connell, R., *Gender and Power*, Stanford, Calif., 1987.

Connor, W., *Deviance in Soviet Society*, New York, 1972.

Cook, S., 'Canadian Narcotics Legislation, 1908–1923: A Conflict Model Interpretation', *Canadian Review of Sociology and Anthropology*, 6, no. 1 (1969).

Cooke, D., 'Containing Violent Prisoners: An Analysis of the Barlinnie Special Unit', *British Journal of Criminology*, 29 (1989).

Cornish, D. and Clarke, R., *The Reasoning Criminal*, New York, 1986.

—— 'Analyzing Organized Crimes', unpublished typescript, 2000.

Corrado, R., and Markwart, A., 'The Need to Reform the YOA in Response to Violent Youth Offenders: Confusion, Reality or Myth?', *Canadian Journal of Criminology*, July 1994.

—— et al., 'Social Capital and Community Crime Prevention Programs', PRI Project: Social Capital as a Public Policy Tool, *Social Capital in Action Thematic Policy Studies*, September 2005.

Corrigan, P., *Schooling the Smash Street Kids*, London, 1979.

—— and Leonard, P., *Social Work Practice under Capitalism*, London, 1978.

Coser, L., *The Functions of Social Conflict*, London, 1956.

Cotterrell, R., *Émile Durkheim: Law in a Moral Domain*, Stanford, 1999.

Covington, C., 'The Hammersmith Teenage Project: Social Policy and Practice in an Experimental Community-Based Delinquency Project 1975–78', Ph.D. thesis, University of London (LSE), 1980.

Cowell, D., Jones, T. and Young, J. (eds), *Policing the Riots*, London (1982).

Cowie, J., Cowie, V. and Slater, E., *Delinquency in Girls*, London, 1968.

Cox, B. et al., *The Fall of Scotland Yard*, Harmondsworth, 1977.

Crane, D., *Invisible Colleges: Diffusion of Knowledge in Scientific Communities*, Chicago, 1972.

Cressey, D., *Other People's Money*, Glencoe, Ill., 1953.

—— 'Role Theory, Differential Association and Compulsive Crimes', in A. Rose (ed.), *Human Behavior and Social Processes*, New York, 1962.

Cressey, P., *The Taxi-Dance Hall*, Chicago, 1932.

—— 'Population Succession in Chicago: 1898–1930', *American Journal of Sociology*, 44, no. 1 (1938): 59–69.

Currie, E., *Confronting Crime: An American Challenge*, New York, 1985.

Cusson, M., *Why Delinquency?*, Toronto, 1983.

DeVault, M., 'Talking Back to Sociology: Distinctive Contributions of Feminist Methodology', *Annual Review of Sociology*, 22 (1996).

Daly, K. and Chesney-Lind, M., 'Feminism and Criminology', *Justice Quarterly*, 5 (1988).

Damer, S., 'Wine Alley: The Sociology of a Dreadful Enclosure', *Sociological Review*, 22 (1974).

Davie, M., 'The Pattern of Urban Growth', in G. Murdock (ed.), *Studies in the Science of Society*, New Haven, 1937.

Davies, C., 'From the Sacred Hierarchies to Flatland', Reading, UK, 1990.

Davies, N., 'Sexual Taboos and Social Boundaries', *American Journal of Sociology*, 87 (1982).

—— *Dark Heart: The Shocking Truth about Hidden Britain*, London, 1998.

Davis, D., *Homicide in American Fiction*, Ithaca, NY, 1968.

Davis, F., 'The Cab-Driver and his Fare', *American Journal of Sociology*, 64 (1959).

—— 'Deviance Disavowal', in H. Becker (ed.), *The Other Side*, New York, 1964.

Davis, K., 'The Sociology of Prostitution', *American Sociological Review*, 2 (1937).

—— 'Illegitimacy and the Social Structure', *American Journal of Sociology*, 44 (1939).

—— 'Prostitution', in R. Merton and R. Nisbet (eds), *Contemporary Social Problems*, New York, 1961.

—— 'The Myth of Functional Analysis as a Special Method in Sociology and Anthropology', *American Sociological Review*, 24 (1959). Reprinted in N. Demerath and R. Peterson (eds), *System, Change and Conflict*, New York (1967).

Davis, M., 'That's Interesting! Towards a Phenomenology of Sociology and a Sociology of Phenomenology', *Philosophy of the Social Sciences*, 1 (1971).

Davis, M.S., *Smut: Erotic Reality/Obscene Ideology*, Chicago,1983.

Davis, Mike, *City of Quartz: Excavating the Future in Los Angeles*, London, 1990.

—— 'Beyond Blade Runner', *Open Magazine Pamphlet*, 23, Westfield, New Jersey, 1992.

Davis, N., *Sociological Constructions of Deviance*, Dubuque, Iowa., 1975.

Dawkins, R., *The Blind Watchmaker*, London, 1986.

Dawson C., 'The Church and Social Service', *Presbyterian Witness*, 26 October 1922.

—— 'The City as an Organism', *La Revue Municipale*, 1927.

—— 'Population Areas and Physiographic Regions in Canada', *American Journal of Sociology*, 33, no. 1 (1927): 43–56.

—— 'A Useful Approach', *Social Forces*, 9, no. 3 (1931): 335–338.

—— *The Settlement of the Peace River Country: A Study of a Pioneer Area,* Toronto, 1934).

—— *Group Settlement: Ethnic Communities in Western Canada*, Toronto, 1936

—— *Canadian Frontiers of Settlement,* Toronto, 1937.

—— *The New North West,* Toronto, 1947.

—— and W. Gettys, *An Introduction to Sociology*, New York, 1929.

Dear, M. and Wolch, J., *Landscapes of Despair: From Deinstitutionalization to Homelessness*, Princeton, 1987.

Debro, J., 'Dialogue with Howard S. Becker', *Issues in Criminology*, 5, no. 2 (1970).

Defoe, D., *The True and Genuine Account of the Life and Actions of the Late Jonathan Wild*, London, 1725.

DeKeseredy, W. and Schwartz, M., 'Theorizing Public Housing Woman Abuse as a Function of Economic Exclusion and Male Peer Support', *Women's Health and Urban Life*, 1, no.2 (2002). *Women's Health and Urban Life: An interdisciplinary Journal*, is funded by SSHRC and is an open-access journal. Previous issues can be viewed at http://www.utsc.utoronto.ca/~sosci/sever/index.

Dennis, N. and Erdos, G., *Families without Fatherhood*, 2nd edn, London, 1993.

Dentler, R. and Erikson, K., 'The Functions of Deviance in Groups', *Social Problems*, 7 (1959).

Denzin, N., 'Crime and the American Liquor Industry', in N. Denzin (ed.), *Studies in Symbolic Interaction*, I, Greenwich, Conn., 1978.

——. 'Whose Cornerville is it, Anyway?', *Journal of Contemporary Ethnography*, 21, no. 1 (1992).

Department of the Environment, *Local Housing Management: A Priority Estates Project Survey*, London, 1980.

—— *Reducing Vandalism on Public Housing Estates*, London, 1981.

Dewey, J., 'The Reflex Arc Concept in Social Psychology', *American Journal of Sociology*, 2 (1896).

—— 'Perception and Organic Action', *Journal of Philosophy, Psychology and Scientific Methods*, 11, no. 24 (1912).

—— 'Realism without Monism or Dualism—II', *Journal of Philosophy*, 19, no. 13 (1922).

Dickinson, D., 'Crime and Unemployment' (mimeo), Cambridge, 1994.

Ditton, J., *Part-Time Crime*, London, 1977.

—— *Controlology*, London, 1979.

—— 'Crime and the City: Public Attitudes towards Open-Street CCTV in Glasgow', *British Journal of Criminology*, 40 (2000).

Dobash, R. and Dobash, R., *Violence against Wives: A Case against Patriarchy*, London, 1979.

—— 'The Nature and Antecedents of Violent Events', *British Journal of Criminology*, 24 (1984).

—— and E. Dobash, 'Reflections on Findings from the Violence gainst Women Survey', *Canadian Journal of Criminology*, July, 1995.

Dollard, J., *Caste and Class in a Southern Town*, New Haven, 1937.

Douglas, J., *The Social Meanings of Suicide*, Princeton, 1967.

—— 'Deviance and Order in a Pluralistic Society', in J. McKinney and E. Tiryakian (eds), *Theoretical Sociology*, New York, 1970.

—— (ed.), *Deviance and Respectability*, New York, 1970.

—— *Observations of Deviance*, New York, 1970.

—— *American Social Order: Social Rules in a Pluralistic Society*, New York, 1971.

—— 'The Sociological Analysis of Social Meanings of Suicide', in Giddens, A. (ed.), *The Sociology of Suicide*, London, 1971.

—— (ed.), *Understanding Everyday Life*, London, 1971.

—— (ed.), *Research on Deviance*, New York, 1972.

—— 'The Experience of the Absurd and the Problem of Social Order', in R. Scott and J. Douglas (eds), *Theoretical Perspectives on Deviance*, New York, 1972.

—— et al., *The Nude Beach*, Beverly Hills, 1977.

Douglas, M., *Purity and Danger*, London, 1966.

—— *Natural Symbols*, London, 1970.

—— (ed.), *Rules and Meanings*, Harmondsworth, 1973.

—— *Implicit Meanings*, London, 1975.

—— *How Institutions Think*, Syracuse, 1986.

Dowd, L., 'Witnessing of Incidents and Intervention: Informal Social Control in Action'. Paper presented to the American Society of Criminology, Chicago, 8–12 November 1988.

Dowler, K., 'Media Consumption and Public Attitudes toward Crime and Justice: The Relationship between Fear of Crime, Punitive Attitudes, and Perceived Police Effectiveness', *Journal of Criminal Justice and Popular Culture*, 10, no. 2 (2003): 109–26.

Dowler, K., Fleming, T., and Muzzatti, S. (2006). 'Constructing Crime: Media, Crime and Popular Culture', *Canadian Journal of Criminology and Criminal Justice*, 48, no 6 (2006): 837–50.

Downes, D., *The Delinquent Solution: A Study in Subcultural Theory*, London, 1966.

—— 'Praxis Makes Perfect', in D. Downes and P. Rock (eds), *Deviant Interpretations*, Oxford, 1979.

—— 'Abolition: Possibilities and Pitfalls', in A. Bottoms (ed.), *The Crisis in the British Penal System*, Edinburgh, 1980.

—— *Contrasts in Tolerance: Postwar Penal Policy in the Netherlands and England and Wales*, Oxford, 1988.

—— *Back to the Future: The Predictive Value of Social Theories of Delinquency* in S. Holdaway and P. Rock (eds), *The Social Theory of Modern Criminology*, London, 1998.

—— and Morgan, R., 'Dumping the Hostages to Fortune? The Politics of Law and Order in Postwar Britain', in M. Maguire, R. Morgan and R. Reiner (eds), *The Oxford Handbook of Criminology*, 2nd edn., 1997.

—— and Rock, P. (eds), *Deviant Interpretations: Problems in Criminological Theory*, Oxford, 1979.

——and van Swaaningen, R., 'The Road to Dystopia? Changes in the Penal Climate of the Netherlands', in Tonry (ed.), *Crime and Justice in the Netherlands*, 35 (2006).

—— and Ward, T., *Democratic Policing*, London, 1986.

Drake, S. and Cayton, H., *Black Metropolis*, New York, 1945.

Durkin, K., Forsyth, K., Craig J., and Quinn, J., 'Pathological Internet Communities: A New Direction for Sexual Deviance Research in a Post Modern Era', *Sociological Spectrum*, 26, no. 6 (2006).

Dunkel, F., 'Legal Differences in Juvenile Criminology in Europe', in T. Booth (ed.), *Juvenile Justice in the New Europe*, Social Services Monographs, 1992.

Durkheim, É., *Suicide*, London, 1952 (orig. published 1897). Published by Routledge and Kegan Paul Ltd.

—— *The Division of Labor in Society*, New York, 1964 (orig. published 1893).

—— *The Rules of Sociological Method*, New York, 1964 (orig. published 1895).

Durbin, F., *The Politics of Democratic Socialism*, London, 1940.

Duster, T., *The Legislation of Morality*, New York, 1970.

—— 'The Epistemological Challenge of the Early Attack on "Rate Construction"', *Social Problems*, 48, no. 1 (2001): 134–6.

Eagleton, T., *The Illusions of Postmodernism*, Oxford, 1996.

Eaton, M., 'Mitigating Circumstances: Familiar Rhetoric', *International Journal of Sociological Law*, 11 (1983).

—— 'Documenting the Defendant: Placing Women in Social Inquiry Report', in J. Brophy and C. Smart (eds), *Women in Law*, London, 1985.

—— *Justice for Women?*, Milton Keynes, 1986.

Edelman, M., *Politics as Symbolic Action*, Chicago, 1971.

Edgerton, R., 'Pokot Intersexuality: An East African Example of the Resolution of Sexual Incongruity', *American Anthropologist*, 66 (1964).

Edwards, S., *Female Sexuality and the Law*, Oxford, 1981.

—— 'Police Attitudes and Dispositions in Domestic Disputes: The London Study', *Police Journal* (1986).

—— *Policing 'Domestic' Violence: Women, the Law and the State*, London, 1989.

Einstadter, W., 'The Social Organization of Armed Robbery', *Social Problems*, 17, no. 1 (1969).

Ekblom, P. and Simon, F., *Crime Prevention and Racial Harassment in Asian-run Small Shops: The Scope for Prevention*, London, 1988.

Elias, N., *The Civilizing Process*: Vol. 2, *State Formation and Civilization*, Oxford, 1982.

—— 'Violence and Civilization: The State Monopoly of Physical Violence and its Infringement', in J. Keane (ed.), *Civil Society and the State*, London, 1988.

—— and Scotson, J., *The Established and the Outsiders*, London, 1965.

Elliott, D. and Voss, H., *Delinquency and Dropouts*, Lexington, Mass., 1974.

Ellis, A., 'Female Sexual Response and Marital Relations', *Social Problems*, 1, no. 4, 1954): 152–5.

Emerson, R., *Judging Delinquents*, Chicago, 1969.

Empey, L., 'Revolution and Counter-Revolution: Current Trends in Juvenile Justice', in D. Shichor and D. Kelly (eds), *Critical Issues in Juvenile Delinquency*, Lexington, Mass., 1980.

Ericson, R., *Criminal Reactions*, Farnborough, UK, 1975.

—— et al., *Visualizing Deviance*, Toronto, 1987.

—— et al., *Negotiating Control*, Toronto, 1989.

—— et al., *Representing Order*, Toronto, 1991.

—— 'From Social Theory to Penal Practice', *Canadian Journal of Corrections*, 19 (1977).

Erikson, K., 'Notes on the Sociology of Deviance', in H. Becker (ed.), *The Other Side*, New York, 1964.

—— *Wayward Puritans*, New York, 1966.

—— 'Disguised Observation in Sociology', *Social Problems*, 1967.

—— *In the Wake of the Flood*, London, 1979.

—— *A New Species of Trouble*, New York, 1994.

Erickson, P., 'Deterrence and Deviance: The Example of Cannabis Prohibition', *The Journal of Criminal Law and Criminology*, 67, 2 (1976).

Etzioni, A., *The Moral Dimension*, New York, 1990.

—— *The Parenting Deficit*, London, 1993.

Eysenck, H., *Crime and Personality*, London, 1961 (3rd edn., rev., London, 1977).

—— 'Crime and Personality Reconsidered', *Bulletin of the British Psychological Society*, 27 (1974).

Farberman, H., 'A Criminogenic Market Structure: The Automobile Industry', *The Sociological Quarterly*, 16 (1975).

—— 'Symposium on Symbolic Interaction: An Introduction', *Sociological Quarterly*, 16 (1975).

Farberow, N. (ed.), *Taboo Topics*, New York, 1963.

Faris, R., *Chicago Sociology, 1920–1932*, San Francisco, 1967.

—— and Dunham, H., *Mental Disorders in Urban Areas: An Ecological Study of Schizophrenia and Other Psychoses*, Chicago, 1939.

Farrington, D. and Morris, A., 'Sex, Sentencing and Reconvictions', *British Journal of Criminology*, 23 (1983).

—— and West, D., 'The Cambridge Study in Delinquent Development: A Long-Term Follow-Up of 411 London Males', in G. Kaiser et al. (eds), *Kriminalität*, Berlin, 1990.

Faupel, C., *Shooting Dope: Career Patterns of Hard-Core Heroin Users*, Gainesville, Fla., 1991.

Feeley, M., 'The Vanishing Female: The Decline of Women in the Criminal Process, 1687–1912', *Law and Society Review*, 25 (1991).

—— and Simon, J., 'The New Penology: Notes on the Emerging Strategy of Corrections and its Implications', *Criminology*, 30 (1992).

—— 'The Decline of Women in the Criminal Process: A Comparative History', in *Criminal Justice History: An International Annual*, Westport, Conn., 1994.

Felson, M., *Crime and Everyday Life*, Thousand Oaks, Calif., 1994.

—— and Clarke, R., *Opportunity Makes the Thief*. Policing and Reducing Crime Briefing Note, London, 1998.

Ferrell, J., *Crimes of Style: Urban Graffiti and the Politics of Criminality*, New York, 1993.

—— and Saunders, C. (eds), *Cultural Criminology*, Boston, 1995.

Field, S., *Trends in Crime and their Interpretation*, London, 1990.

Fielding, N., *The National Front*, London, 1980.

Fine, G. (ed.), *A Second Chicago School?* Chicago, 1995.

Fine, S., *Violence in the Modern City: The Cavanagh Administration, Race Relations and the Detroit Riot of 1967*, Ann Arbor, 1989.

Finestone, H., *Victims of Change: Juvenile Delinquents in American Society*, Westport, Conn., 1976.

Fischer, C., 'The Subcultural Theory of Urbanism: A Twentieth-year Assessment', *The American Journal of Sociology*, 101, no. 3 (1995): 543–77.

Fisher, C. and Mawby, R., 'Juvenile Delinquency and Police Discretion in an Inner-City Area', *British Journal of Criminology*, 22 (1982).

Fishman, M., *Manufacturing the News*, New York, 1980.

Fitzgerald, M., *Prisoners in Revolt*, London, 1977.

—— and Sim, J., *British Prisons*, Oxford, 1979.

Fleming, T., (ed.), *The New Criminologies in Canada*, Toronto, 1985.

Fletcher, R., 'Evolutionary and Developmental Sociology', in J. Rex (ed.), *Approaches to Sociology*, London, 1974.

Flood-Page, C. et al., *Youth Crime: Findings from the 1998/1999 Youth Lifestyles Survey*, London, 2000.

Foote, N., 'Sex as Play', *Social Problems*, 1, no. 4 (1954): 159–63.

Forrester, D. et al., *The Kirkholt Burglary Prevention Project, Rochdale*, London, 1988.

—— et al., *The Kirkholt Burglary Prevention Project, Rochdale, Phase II*, London, 1990.

Foster, J., *Villains: Crime and Community in the Inner City*, London, 1990.

—— 'Informal Social Control and Community Crime Prevention', *British Journal of Criminology*, 35, no. 4 (1995): 563–83.

—— and Hope, T., *Housing, Community and Crime*, London, 1993.

Foucault, M., *Madness and Civilization*, London, 1967.

—— *I, Pierre Rivière*, New York, 1975.

—— *The Birth of the Clinic*, New York, 1975.

—— *Discipline and Punish: The Birth of the Prison*, London, 1977.

Fraser, N., 'Foucault on Modern Power: Empirical Insights and Normative Confusions', in his *Unruly Practices*, Minnesota, 1989.

Freeman, J., 'The Origins of the Women's Liberation Movement', *American Journal of Sociology*, 78, no. 4, (1973).

Freeman, R., 'Employment and Earnings of Disadvantaged Young Men in a Labor Shortage Economy', in C. Jencks and R. Peterson (eds), *The Urban Underclass*, 1991.

—— 'Who Becomes A Criminal?' Talk to Mannheim Centre of Criminology, London School of Economics, 1996.

Freidson, E., *Profession of Medicine*, New York, 1970.

Fuchs, V., *Who Shall Live? Health Economics and Social Choice*, New York, 1974.

Fukayama, F., *Trust: The Social Virtues and the Creation of Prosperity*, New York, 1995.

Galliher, J., 'Chicago's Two Worlds of Deviance Research', in G. Fine (ed.) *A Second Chicago School?* Chicago, 1995.

Gambetta, D., *The Sicilian Mafia*, Cambridge, Mass., 1993.

Gans, H., *The Urban Villagers*, New York, 1962.

—— *The Levittowners: Ways of Life and Politics in a New Suburban Community*, New York, 1967.

Garfinkel, H., 'The Perception of the Other: A Study in Social Order', Ph.D. Dissertation, Harvard University, 1952.

—— *Studies in Ethnomethodology*, Englewood Cliffs, NJ, 1967.

Garland, D., *Punishment and Welfare*, Aldershot, UK, 1985.

—— 'Frameworks of Inquiry in the Sociology of Punishment', *British Journal of Sociology*, 41 (1990).

—— *Punishment and Modern Society*, Oxford, 1990.

—— *The Culture of Control: Crime and Social Order in Contemporary Society*, Cambridge, 2001.

—— (ed.), *Mass Imprisonment: Social Causes and Consequences*, London, 2001.

—— and Young, P. (eds), *The Power to Punish*, London, 1983.

Gartner, R., and Macmillan, R., 'The Effect of Victim-Offender Relationship on Reporting Crimes of Violence against Women, *Canadian Journal of Criminology*, 37 (1995).

Gatrell, V., 'The Decline of Theft and Violence in Victorian and Edwardian England', in V. Gatrell, et al. (eds), *Crime and the Law: The Social History of Crime Since 1500*, London, 1980.

Gavron, H., *The Captive Wife*, London, 1966.

Gellner, E., 'Concepts and Society', in B. Wilson (ed.), *Rationality*, Oxford, 1968.

—— *Legitimation of Belief*, Cambridge, 1974.

—— 'A Social Contract in Search of an Idiom: The Demise of the Danegeld State?', *Political Quarterly*, 46 (1975).

—— 'Ethnomethodology: The Re-Enchantment Industry or The Californian Way of Subjectivity', *Philosophy of the Social Sciences*, 5 (1975).

—— *Postmodernism, Reason and Religion*, New York, 1992.

Gelsthorpe, L. and Morris, A., 'Feminism and Criminology in Britain', *British Journal of Criminology*, 28 (1988).

Genders, E. and Player, E., 'Women's Imprisonment: The Effects of Youth Custody', *British Journal of Criminology*, 26 (1986).

——, *Grendon: A Study of a Therapeutic Prison*, Oxford, 1995.

Gibbs, J., 'Conceptions of Deviant Behavior: The Old and the New', *Pacific Sociological Review*, 8, no. 1 (1966).

Giddens, A. (ed.), *The Sociology of Suicide*, London, 1971.

—— *Émile Durkheim: Selected Writings*, Cambridge, 1972.

—— *The Class Structure of the Advanced Societies*, London, 1973.

—— *The Constitution of Society*, Cambridge, 1984.

—— *The Consequences of Modernity*, Cambridge, 1990.

—— *Modernity and Self-Identity*, Cambridge, 1991.

—— *In Defence of Sociology*, Cambridge, 1996.

—— *The Third Way*, Cambridge, 1999

Gill, O., *Luke Street: Housing Policy, Conflict and the Creation of the Delinquent Area*, London, 1977.

Gilling, D., 'The Evolution and Implementation of the Multi-Agency Approach to Crime Prevention'. Ph.D. dissertation, University of Manchester, 1992.

Glueck, S. and Glueck, E., *Five Hundred Delinquent Women*, New York, 1934.

—— *Unravelling Juvenile Delinquency*, Cambridge, Mass., 1950.

Goetschius, G. and Tash, M., *Working with Unattached Youth*, London, 1967.

Goffman, E., 'The Moral Career of the Mental Patient', *Psychiatry*, 22, no. 2 (1959).

—— *Stigma*, Englewood Cliffs, NJ, 1963.

—— *Asylums*, Harmondsworth, 1968.

—— 'Where the Action Is', in his *Interaction Ritual*, London, 1972.

—— *Frame Analysis*, Cambridge, Mass., 1974.

Gold, M., *Delinquent Behavior in an American City*, Belmont, Calif., 1970.

Goldblatt, P. and Lewis, C. (eds), *Reducing Offending: An Assessment of Research Evidence on Ways of Dealing with Offending Behaviour*, London, 1998.

Goldthorpe, J. 'The Uses of History', *British Journal of Sociology*, 42, no. 2 (1991).

Goode, E., 'Does the Death of the Sociology of Deviance Claim Make Sense?', *American Sociologist*, 33, no. 3 (2002): 107–18.

—— 'Is the Deviance Concept Still Relevant to Sociology?', *American Sociologist*, 33, no. 3 (2002).

—— 'Is the Sociology of Deviance Still Relevant?', *American Sociologist*, 35, no. 4 (2004): 46–57.

Gordon, C., *The Old Bailey and Newgate*, London, 1902.

Gordon, P., *White Law*, London, 1983.

Goring, C., *The English Convict: A Statistical Study*, London, 1913.

Gottfredson, M. and Hirschi, T., *A General Theory of Crime*, Stanford, Calif., 1990.

Gouldner, A., 'Anti-Minotaur: The Myth of a Value-Free Sociology', *Social Problems*, 10 (1962).

—— *The Coming Crisis in Western Sociology*, New York and London, 1970. Reprinted by permission of Basic Books, a member of Perseus Books Group.

—— 'The Sociologist as Partisan', *American Sociologist* (1968). Reprinted in Gouldner, A., *For Sociology: Renewal and Critique in Sociology Today*, London, 1973.

Gove, W. (ed.), *The Labelling of Deviance*, London, 1975.

Graham, S., 'Surveillant Simulation and the City', paper delivered at the NCGIA annual conference, Baltimore, 1996.

P. Grahame and D. Jardine, 'Deviance, Resistance, and Play: A Study in the Communicative Organization of Trouble in Class', *Curriculum Inquiry*, 20, no. 3 (1990) Blackwell Publishing.

Gregory, J. and Lees, S., *Policing Sexual Assault*, New York, 1998.

Griffith, J., *The Politics of the Judiciary*, London, 1977.

Griffiths, A., *The Chronicles of Newgate*, London, 1884.

Gurr, T., 'Historical Trends in Violent Crime: A Critical Review of the Evidence', in M. Tonry, and N. Morris (eds), *Crime and Justice: An Annual Review of Research: 3*, Chicago, 1981.

—— Grabosky, P., and Hula, R., *The Politics of Crime and Conflict: A Comparative History of Four Cities*, Beverly Hills, 1977.

Gusfield, J., 'Moral Passage', *Social Problems*, 15 no.2 (1968).

—— 'The Second Chicago School?', in Fine, G. (ed.), *A Second Chicago School?* Chicago, 1995.

Habermas, J., *Legitimation Crisis*, London, 1975.

Hacking, I., *Rewriting the Soul: Multiple Personality and the Sciences of Memory*, Princeton, 1995.

Hagan, F., *Political Crime: Ideology and Criminality*, Boston, 1997.

Hagan, J., 'Labelling and Deviance: A Case Study in the "Sociology of the Interesting"', *Social Problems*, 20, no. 4 (1973): 447–58.

—— *The Disreputable Pleasures*, Toronto, 1977.

—— and Leon, J., 'Rediscovering Delinquency: Social History, Political Ideology and the Rule of Law', *American Sociological Review*, 42 (1977).

—— and McCarthy, B., 'Street-life and Delinquency', *British Journal of Sociology*, 43 (1992).

—— and McCarthy, B., 'The Meaning of Criminology', *Theoretical Criminology*, Sage (2000).

—— *Crime and Disrepute*, Thousand Oaks, Calif., 1994

—— *Mean Streets: Youth Crime and Homelessness*, Cambridge, 1998.

—— and Palloni, A., 'The Social Reproduction of a Criminal Class in Working-Class London circa 1950–1980', *American Journal of Sociology*, 96 (1990).

—— Gillis, A., and Simpson, J., 'The Class Structure of Gender and Delinquency: Toward a Power-Control Theory of Common Delinquent Behaviour', *American Journal of Sociology*, 90 (1985).

—— et al., *Structural Criminology*, Cambridge, 1988.

—— Simpson, J., and Gillis, A., 'The Sexual Stratification of Social Control', *British Journal of Sociology*, 30 (1979).

Haggerty, Kevin D., *Making Crime Count*, Toronto, 2001.

Hall, S., et al. (eds), *Resistance through Ritual*, London, 1976.

—— et al., *Policing the Crisis*, London, 1978.

—— *Drifting into a Law and Order Society*, London, 1980.

Hallgrimsdottir, H., Phillips, R, and Benoit C., 'Fallen Women and Rescued Girls: Social Stigma and Media Narratives of the Sex Industry in Victoria, B.C., from 1980 to 2005' *Canadian Review of Sociology and Anthropology*, 43, no. 3 (2006).

Halloran, J. et al., *Demonstrations and Communications*, Harmondsworth, UK, 1970.

Halsey, A., 'Education Can Compensate', *New Society*, 24 January 1980.

Hammond, P. (ed.), *Sociologists at Work*, New York, 1964.

Hansen, K., 'Time to Educate the Criminals?', *Centre Piece*, 5 no. 3 (2000).

Harcourt, B., 'Broken Theory: 'Broken Windows' Policing Carries Potentially High Costs at No Clear Benefit', ACLU of Southern California, 2003, accessed at http://www.aclu-sc.org/News/OpenForum/100424/100434/;

—— and Ludwig, J., 'Broken Windows: New Evidence from New York City and a Five-City Social Experiment', *University of Chicago Law Review*, 73 (2006).

Harding, S., 'The Alleged Ignorance of Social Scientists', *American Sociological Review*, 3, no. 6 (1938): 850–4.

Hargreaves, D., *Social Relations in a Secondary School*, London, 1967.

—— et al., *Deviance in Classrooms*, London, 1975.

Harris, A., 'Sex and Theories of Deviance', *American Sociological Review*, 42 (1977).

Harvey, D., *The Condition of Postmodernity*, London, 1993.

Hathaway, A.,and Atkinson, M.', 'Tolerable Differences Revisited: Crossroads in Theory on the Social Construction of Deviance', *Deviant Behavior*, 11 (2001): 353–77.

—— 'Active Interview Tactics in Research on Public Deviants: Exploring the Two-Cop Personas', *Field Methods*, 15, no 2 (2003).

Hawkins, K., *Environment and Enforcement*, Oxford, 1984.

Hawthorne, G., *Enlightenment and Despair*, Cambridge, 1977.

Hay, D. et al. (eds), *Albion's Fatal Tree: Crime and Society in Eighteenth-century England*, London, 1975.

Hayward, A. (ed.), *Lives of the Most Remarkable Criminals*, London, 1927.

Heath, A., *Rational Choice and Social Exchange*, Cambridge, 1976.

Hebdige, R., *Subculture: The Meaning of Style*, London, 1979.

Heery, D. and Brooks, J., 'Towns on the Television', *Local Government Studies*, 22, no. 3 (1996).

—— and Marvin, S., *Telecommunications and the City: Electronic Spaces, Urban Places*, London, 1996.

Heidensohn, F., 'The Deviance of Women: A Critique and an Enquiry', *British Journal of Sociology*, 19 (1968).

—— *Women and Crime*, London, 1985.

—— 'Women and Crime: Questions for Criminology', in P. Carlen and A. Worrall (eds), *Gender, Crime and Justice*, Milton Keynes, UK, 1987.

—— *Women in Control: The Role of Women in Law Enforcement*, Oxford, 1992.

Heiland, H. G. and Shelley, L., 'Civilization, Modernization and the Development of Crime and Control', in H.G. Heiland, L. Shelley and H. Katch (eds), *Crime and Control in Comparative Perspective*, Berlin, 1992. Reprinted with permission from Walter De Gruyter Inc. Copyright © Walter de Gruyter.

Heller, Joseph, *Catch-22*, New York, 1961

Helmes-Hayes, R., 'Canadian Sociology's First Textbook: C. A. Dawson and W. E. Gettys's "An Introduction to Sociology (1929)", *Canadian Journal of Sociology*, 19, no. 4 (1994): 461–97.

Henry, J., *Culture against Man*, London, 1963.

Henry, S., *The Hidden Economy*, London, 1978.

—— and Mars, G., 'Crime at Work', *Sociology*, 12, no. 2 (1978).

—— and Milovanovic, D., *Constitutive Criminology: Beyond Postmodernism*, London, 1996.

Herbert, D., 'Urban Crime: A Geographical Perspective', in D. Herbert and D. Smith (eds), *Social Problems and the City*, Oxford, 1979.

Heyl, B., *The Madam as Entrepreneur*, New Brunswick, NJ, 1979.

Hill, R. and Crittenden, K., *Proceedings of the Purdue Symposium on Ethnomethodology*, West Lafayette, Ind., 1968.

Hillier, B., 'In Defence of Space', *RIBA Journal*, November 1973.

—— 'City of Alice's Dreams', *Architecture Journal*, 39 (9 July 1986).

Hills, J., *The Future of Welfare: A Guide to the Debate*, York, UK, 1993.

Hillyard, P. et al., 'Leaving a 'Stain upon the Silence', *British Journal of Criminology*, 44, no. 3 (2004).

Hindelang, M., 'The Social versus Solitary Nature of Delinquent Involvements', *British Journal of Criminology*, 11 (1971).

Hindess, B., *The Use of Official Statistics in Sociology: A Critique of Positivism and Ethnomethodology*, London, 1973.

Hirschi, T., *Causes of Delinquency*, Berkeley, Calif., 1969.

—— 'Procedural Rules and the Study of Deviant Behavior', *Social Problems*, 21, no. 2 (1973).

Hirst, P., 'Marx and Engels on Law, Crime and Morality', in I. Taylor, et al. (eds), *Critical Criminology*, London, 1975.

Hoare, Q. and Nowell Smith, G. (eds), *Selections from the Prison Notebooks of Antonio Gramsci*, London, 1971.

Hobbes, T., *Leviathan*, 1651; Oxford, 1957.

Hobbs, D., *Doing the Business: Entrepreneurship, the Working Class and Detectives in East London*, Oxford, 1988.

—— *Bad Business*, Oxford, 1995.

Hobsbawm, E., *Primitive Rebels*, Manchester, 1959.

—— *Bandits*, Harmondsworth, 1969.

Hoffman-Bustamente, D., 'The Nature of Female Criminality', *Issues in Criminology*, 8 (1973).

Hofstadter, R., *Social Darwinism in American Thought*, New York, 1959.

Hogeveen, B., '"If We Are Tough on Crime, If We Punish Crime, Then People Get the Message": Constructing and Governing the Punishable Young Offender in Canada during the Late 1990s', *Punishment and Society*, 7, no. 1 (2005), 73–89.

—— 'Discontinuity and/in the Early Twentieth Century Ontario Juvenile Court', *Journal of Historical Sociology*, 20, no. 4 (2007).

Holdaway, S., *Inside the British Police*, London, 1983.

Homans, G., *The Human Group*, London, 1951.

—— 'Social Behaviour as Exchange', *American Journal of Sociology*, 64 (1958).

—— 'Bringing Men Back In', *American Sociological Review*, 29 (1964).

Home Office Statistical Bulletin 7/85, 'Criminal Careers of those Born in 1953, 1958 and 1963', London, 1985.

Home Office, *Experiments in Social Policy and their Explanation* (Report of an Anglo–American Conference held at Ditchley Park, Oxfordshire, 29–31 Oct. 1969), Community Development Project, 1970, mimeograph.

—— Research Findings No. 2, London, 1992.

—— *Information on the Criminal Justice System in England and Wales: Digest 4*, London, 1999.

—— *Statistics on Women and the Criminal Justice System 2000*, London, 2000.

—— *The 2001 British Crime Survey: First Results, England and Wales*, London (2001)

Hood, R., *Sentencing in Magistrates' Courts*, London, 1962.

—— and Joyce, K., 'Three Generations: Oral Testimonies on Crime and Social Change in London's East End', *British Journal of Criminology*, 39 (1999).

—— and Sparks, R., *Key Issues in Criminology*, London, 1970.

Hooker, E., 'Male Homosexuality', in N. Farberow (ed.), *Taboo Topics*, New York, 1963.

Hope, T., *Burglary in Schools*, London, 1982.

Horowitz, I., 'The Politics of Drugs', in Rock, P. (ed.), *Drugs and Politics*, New Brunswick, NJ, 1977.

—— and Liebowitz, M., 'Social Deviance and Political Marginality', *Social Problems*, 15, no. 3 (1968).

Horton, J., 'The Dehumanisation of Alienation and Anomie', *British Journal of Sociology*, 15 (1964).

Hough, M. and Mayhew, P., *The British Crime Survey*, London, 1983.

—— *Taking Account of Crime*, London, 1985.

Howard, J., *The State of the Prisons*, London, 1777.

Hoyt, H., *One Hundred Years of Land Values in Chicago: The Relationship of the Growth of Chicago to the Rise in its land Values, 1830–1933*, Chicago, 1933.

Huber, J., 'Symbolic Interaction as a Pragmatic Perspective: The Bias of Emergent Theory', *American Sociological Review*, 38, no. 2 (1973).

Hughes, E., *The Growth of an Institution: The Chicago Real Estate Board*, Chicago, 1931.

—— 'Robert E. Park', in *The Sociological Eye*, Chicago, 1971.

—— 'Good People and Dirty Work', in *The Sociological Eye*, Chicago, 1971.

Hughes, R., *The Culture of Complaint*, New York, 1993.

Humphreys, L., *Tearoom Trade*, Chicago, 1970.

—— *Out of the Closets*, Englewood Cliffs, NJ, 1972.

Hutter, B., *The Reasonable Arm of the Law?* Oxford, 1988.

Hutton, W., *The State We're In*, London, 1995.

Ianni, F., *A Family Business*, London, 1972.

Ignatieff, M., *A Just Measure of Pain*, London, 1979.

Irwin, J., *The Felon*, Englewood Cliffs, NJ, 1970.

Israel, Wilfred, 'The Montreal Negro Community', MA thesis, McGill University, 1928.

Jacobs, J., *The Death and Life of Great American Cities*, Harmondsworth, 1965.

James, O., *Juvenile Violence in a Winner–Loser Culture*, London, 1995.

—— *Britain on the Couch: Why We Are Less Happy Than in 1950, Though Richer*, London, 1997.

James, W., *A Pluralistic Universe*, New York, 1920.

—— *Pragmatism*, New York, 1949.

Jaycox, V., *Creating a Senior Victim/Witness Volunteer Corps*, Washington, 1981.

Jencks, C. and Peterson, R. (eds), *The Urban Underclass*, Washington, 1991.

Johnson, E., 'The Function of the Central Business District in the Metropolitan Community', in *Third Year Course in the Study of Contemporary Society*, Chicago, 1942.

Johnson, H., and Sacco, V., 'Researching Violence against Women: Statistics Canada's National Survey', *Canadian Journal of Criminology*, 37 (1995).

Jones, T., Maclean, B., and Young, J., *The Islington Crime Survey*, Aldershot, UK, 1986.

Jones, T. and Newburn, T., 'The Transformation of Policing? Understanding Current Trends in Policing Systems', *British Journal of Criminology*, 42 (2002): 129–46.

Juby, H. and Farrington, D., 'Disentangling the Link between Disrupted Families and Delinquency', *British Journal of Criminology*, 41, no. 1 (2001).

Judges, A., *The Elizabethan Underworld*, London, 1930.

Kaplan, R., 'The Coming Anarchy', *Atlantic Monthly*, February 1994.

Katz, J., *Seductions of Crime*, New York, 1988.

——— 'Ethnography's Warrants', *Sociological Methods and Research*, 25, no. 4 (1997).

——— , and Jackson-Jacobs, C., 'The Criminologist's Gang', in C. Sumner, ed., *Blackwell Companion to Criminology*, London, 2004.

Kaufmann, F., *Methodology of the Social Science,* Oxford University Press, 1944.

Kelling, G. and Coles, C., *Fixing Broken Windows*, New York, 1996.

——— and Wilson, J., 'Broken Windows: The Police and Neighborhood Safety', *The Atlantic Monthly*, March 1982.

Kennedy, P., *Preparing for the Twenty-First Century*, New York, 1993.

Kenney, Scott, 'Victims of Crime and Labelling Theory: A Parallel Process?', *Deviant Behaviour*, 23, 2 (2002): 235–65.

Kent, Stephen A., 'Slogan Chanters to Mantra Chanters: A Mertonian Deviance Analysis of Conversion to Religiously Ideological Organizations in the Early 1970s', *Sociological Analysis*, 49, no. 2 (1988): 104–18.

———'Deviance Labelling and Normative Strategies in the Canadian 'New Religions/ Countercult' Debate', *Canadian Journal of Sociology*, 15, no. 4 (1990): 393–416.

Kersten, J., 'Culture, Masculinities and Violence Against Women', *British Journal of Criminology*, 36 (1996).

Keshen, J. 'Wartime Jitters over Juveniles: Canada's Delinquency Scare and its Consequences, 1939–1945', In J. Keshen (ed.), *Age of Contention: Readings in Canadian Social History, 1900–1945*. Toronto, 1997.

Kevles, D., *In the Name of Eugenics: Genetics and the Uses of Human Heredity*, New York, 1985.

Kincheloe, S., 'The Behavior Sequence of a Dying Church', *Religious Education,* 1929.

King, R., 'Prisons', in M. Tonry (ed.), *The Crime and Justice Handbook*, New York, 1998.

Kirkendall, L., 'Premarital Sex Relations: The Problem and Its Implications', *Pastoral Psychology* 7, no. 3 (1956): 46–53.

Kitsuse, J., 'Societal Reaction to Deviant Behavior: Problems of Theory and Method', *Social Problems*, 9, no. 3 (1962): 247–56.

——— 'Societal Reaction to Deviant Behavior', in E. Rubington and M. Weinberg (eds), *Deviance: The Interactionist Perspective*, New York, 1968.

——— and Cicourel, A., 'A Note on the Uses of Official Statistics', *Social Problems*, 11, no. 2 (1963).

——— and Spector, M., 'Toward a Sociology of Social Problems: Social Conditions, Value-Judgments, and Social Problems', *Social Problems*, 20, no. 4 (1973): 407–19.

Klapp, O., *Collective Search for Identity*, New York, 1969.

Klein, D., 'The Etiology of Female Crime: A Review of the Literature', *Issues in Criminology*, 8 (1973).

Klockars, C., *The Professional Fence*, London, 1975.

———'The Contemporary Crises of Marxist Criminology', *Criminology: An Interdisciplinary Journal*, 16, no. 4 (1979).

Kobrin, S., 'The Chicago Area Project', in N. Johnston, et al. (eds), *The Sociology of Punishment and Correction*, New York, 1962.

—— et al., 'Offense Patterns of Status Offenders', in D. Shichor and D. Kelly (eds), *Critical Issues in Juvenile Delinquency*, Lexington, Mass., 1980.

Kong, R. and Aucoin, K., *Female Offenders in Canada*, Juristat, 28, no. 1 (2008), Statistics Canada catalogue no. 85-002-XIE, 28, 1 (2008).

Konopka, G., *The Adolescent Girl in Conflict*, Englewood Cliffs, 1966.

Korber, R., 'Rethinking Sex: Alfred Kinsey Now', *American Quarterly*, 57, no. 2, (2005): 463–74.

Korn, A., 'Crime and Legal Control: The Israeli Arab Population during the Military Government Period (1948–66)', *British Journal of Criminology*, 40 (2000).

Korn, R. and McCorkle, L., 'Social Roles', in C. Bersani (ed.), *Crime and Delinquency*, New York, 1970.

Kornhauser, R., *Social Sources of Delinquency: An Appraisal of Analytic Models*, Chicago, 1978.

Kraeger, S., 'Unnecessary Roughness? School Sports, Peer Networks, and Male Adolescent Violence', *American Sociological Review*, 72, no. 5 (2007).

Kubrin, C., 'New Directions in Social Disorganization Theory', *Journal of Research in Crime and Delinquency*, 40, no. 4, (2003).

Kuhn, T., *The Structure of Scientific Revolutions*, Chicago, 1961.

Kumar, R., *The History of Doing: An Illustrated History of Movements for Women's Rights and Feminism in India 1800–1990*, New Delhi, 1993.

LaFree, G. and Drass, K., 'Counting Crime Booms among Nations: Evidence for Homicide Victimization Rates, 1956 to 1998', *Criminology* 40, no. 4 (2002): 769–800.

Lambert, J., *Crime, Police and Race Relations*, London, 1970.

Landau, S. and Nathan, G., 'Juveniles and the Police', *British Journal of Criminology*, 23 (1983).

Lander, B., *Towards an Understanding of Juvenile Delinquency*, New York, 1954.

Landesco, J., *Organized Crime in Chicago*, Chicago, 1968.

La Prairie, C., 'Aboriginal Over-Representation in the Criminal Justice System: A Tale of Nine Cities', *Canadian Journal of Criminology*, 44, no. 2 (2002).

Laqueur, W., ' Life as a Weapon', *Times Literary Supplement*, 6 Sept. 2002, 3–4.

Laycock, G., *Reducing Burglary*, London, 1984.

Lea, J., 'Towards Social Prevention', Enfield, Middlesex, 1986.

—— and Young, J., *What Is to Be Done about Law and Order?* London, 1984.

Lee, N., *The Search for an Abortionist*, Chicago, 1969.

Lemert, E., *Social Pathology*, New York, 1951.

—— 'An Isolation and Closure Theory of Naïve Check Forgery', *Journal of Criminal Law, Criminology, and Police Science*, 44, no. 3 (1953): 296–307.

—— 'Social Structure, Social Control and Deviation', in M. Clinard (ed.), *Anomie and Deviant Behavior*, New York, 1964.

—— 'An Isolation and Closure Theory of Naive Check Forgery', in *Human Deviance, Social Problems, and Social Control*, Englewood Cliffs, 1967.

—— *Social Action and Legal Change*, Chicago, 1970.

Lenin, V., *Materialism and Empirio-Criticism*, London, 1908.

Leonard, E., *Women, Crime and Society*, London, 1982.

Lerman, P., *Community Treatment and Social Control: A Critical Analysis of Juvenile Correctional Policy*, Chicago, 1975.

Levitt, S., 'Understanding Why Crime Fell in the 1990s: Four Factors That Explain the Decline and Six That Do Not', *Journal of Economic Perspectives*, 18, no. 1 (2004).

Lewis, O., *Five Families: Mexican Case Studies in the Culture of Poverty*, New York, 1959.

—— *The Children of Sanchez*, New York, 1961.

—— *La Vida: A Puerto Rican Family in the Culture of Poverty*, London, 1967.

Leznoff, M. and Westley, W., 'The Homosexual Community', *Social Problems*, 3, no. 4 (1956).

Lianos, M. and Douglas, M., 'Dangerization and the End of Deviance: The Institutional Environment', *British Journal of Criminology*, 40, no. 2 (2000).

Liebow, E., *Tally's Corner: Negro Streetcorner Men in Washington*, London, 1967.

—— *Tell Them Who I Am: The Lives of Homeless Women*, New York, 1993.

Light, R., Nee, C., and Ingham, H., *Car Theft: The Offender's Perspective*, London, 1993.

Linden, R., and Chaturvedi, R., 'The Need for Comprehensive Crime Prevention Planning: The Case of Motor Vehicle Theft', *Canadian Journal of Criminology and Criminal Justice*, 47, no. 2, (2005). © University of Toronto Press. Reprinted by permission of UTP Inc.

Lindesmith, A., *Opiate Addiction*, Bloomington, Ind., 1947.

—— and Gagnon, J., 'Anomie and Drug Addiction', in M. Clinard (ed.), *Anomie and Deviant Behavior*, New York, 1964.

—— and Levin, Y., 'English Economy and Criminology of the Past Century', *Journal of Criminal Law, Criminology and Police Science*, 27, no. 6 (1937).

Lippmann, W., *Public Opinion*, New York, 1965.

Lipset, S. *Political Man*, London, 1960.

Livingstone, S. 'On the Continuing Problem of Media Effects', in J. Curran and M. Gurevitch (eds), *Mass Media and Society*, London, 1996.

Lizos, A., 'The Poverty of the Sociology of Deviance: Nuts, Sluts, and Perverts', *Social Problems*, 20, no. 1 (1972).

Llewellyn, K. and Hoebel, A., *The Cheyenne Way: Conflict and Case Law in Primitive Jurisprudence*, Norman, 1941.

Lockwood, D., 'Some Remarks on 'The Social System'', *British Journal of Sociology*, 7 (1956).

Lofland, L., *A World of Strangers*, New York, 1973.

Lombroso, C. and Ferrero, W., *The Female Offender*, London, 1895.

Loney, M., *Community against Government: The British Community Development Project, 1968–1978*, London, 1983.

Lopota, H., 'The Function of Voluntary Associations', in E. Burgess and D. Bogue D. (eds), *Contributions to Urban Sociology*, Chicago, 1964.

Losel, F., 'The Efficacy of Correctional Treatment: A Review and Synthesis of Meta-Evaluations', in J. McGuire (ed.), *What Works: Reducing Reoffending*, Chichester, 1995.

Lowman, J. and Maclean, B (eds), *Realist Criminology: Crime Control and Policing in the 1990s*, Toronto, 1992.

Luckenbill, D. and Best, J., 'Careers in Deviance and Respectability: The Analogy's Limitation', *Social Problems*, 29 (1981).

Lukes, S., 'Alienation and Anomie', in P. Laslett and W. Runciman (eds), *Philosophy, Politics and Society*, Oxford, 1967.

—— *Émile Durkheim: His Life and Work*, London, 1973.

—— and Scull, A., *Durkheim and the Law*, Oxford, 1983.

Lurie, A., *Imaginary Friends*, London, 1967.

Lyon, D., *The Electronic Eye: The Rise of Surveillance Society*, Cambridge, UK, 1994.

Lyons, C., "Children who read good books usually behave better, and have good manners": the Founding of the Notre Dame de Grace Library for Boys and Girls, Montreal, 1943', *Library Trends*, 55, no. 3, 2007: 597–608.

Mack, J., "Professional Crime' and Criminal Organization', *International Journal of Criminology and Penology*, 6 no. 4 (1978).

Macleod, J., *Ain't No Makin' It*, Boulder, Colo., 1995.

MacNicol J., 'In Pursuit of the Underclass', *Journal of Social Policy* (1987).

McCauley, R., 'The Enemy Within: Economic Marginalisation and the Impact of Crime on Young Adults', University of Cambridge, Ph.D. thesis, 1999.

McBarnet, D., 'Pre-trial Procedures and Construction of Conviction', in P. Carlen (ed.), The Sociology of Law, *Sociological Review Monographs*, Keele, 1976.

—— 'Whiter Than White-Collar Crime', *British Journal of Sociology*, 42 (1991).

McCaghy, C., 'Drinking and Deviance Disavowal', *Social Problems*, 16 no.1 (1968).

McCall, M., 'A Study of Family Disorganization in Canada', MA, McGill University, 1928.

McCormick, C., *Constructing Danger: The Misrepresentation of Crime in the News*, Fernwood Publishing Co., 1995. Reprinted by permission of the publisher.

McClintock, F., *Crimes of Violence*, London, 1963.

McDonald, L., *The Sociology of Law and Order*, London, 1976.

McGahan, P., 'The Rise and Fall of Prohibition in Halifax', in *Crime and Policing in Maritime Canada*, Fredericton, 1988

McGahey, R., 'Economic Conditions, Neighborhood Organization and Urban Crime', in A. Reiss and M. Tonry (eds), *Communities and Crime*, Chicago, 1986.

McHugh, P., 'A Common-Sense Perception of Deviance', in H. Dreitzel (ed.), *Recent Sociology: No. 2*, New York, 1970.

McIntosh, M., *The Organization of Crime*, London, 1974.

McMahon, M., "Net-Widening': Vagaries in the Use of a Concept', *The British Journal of Criminology*, 30 (1990).

—— *The Persistent Prison? Rethinking Decarceration and Penal Reform*, Toronto, 1992.

McMullan, J., 'Aspects of Professional Crime and Criminal Organization in Sixteenth and Seventeenth Century London: A Sociological Analysis', Ph.D. thesis, University of London (LSE), 1980.

—— 'News, Truth, and the Recognition of Corporate Crime', *Canadian Journal of Criminology and Criminal Justice*, 48, no. 6 (2006).

—— *News, Truth and Crime: The Westray Disaster and Its Aftermath*. Halifax, 2005.

—— 'The Media, the Politics of Truth, and the Coverage of Corporate Violence: The Westray Disaster and the Public Inquiry', *Critical Criminology*, 14, no. 1 (2006).

McRobbie, A., *Postmodernism and Popular Culture*, London, 1994.

—— and Garber, J., 'Girls and Subcultures', in Hall and Jefferson (eds), 1976.

McVicar, J., *McVicar by Himself*, London, 1974.

Maher, L., *Sexed Work: Gender, Race, and Resistance in Brooklyn Drug Market*, Oxford, 1997.

Malinowski, B., *Crime and Custom in Savage Society*, London, 1926.

—— *A Scientific Theory of Culture*, London, 1944.

Malleck, D., "'Its Baneful Influences Are Too Well Known": Debates over Drug Use in Canada, 1867–1908', *Canadian Bulletin of Medical History*, 14 (1997)

Mandeville, B., *The Fable of the Bees*, London, 1714.

Mann, C., *Female Crime and Delinquency*, Alabama, 1984.

Mannheim, H., *Social Aspects of Crime between the Wars*, London, 1940.

Mannheim, K., 'On the Interpretation of "Weltanschauung"', in *Essays on the Sociology of Knowledge*, London, 1952.

Manning, P., 'Deviance and Dogma', *British Journal of Criminology*, 15 (1975).

—— *Police Work*, Cambridge, Mass., 1977.

—— *The Narc's Game*, Cambridge, Mass., 1980.

Marcuse, H., *One-Dimensional Man*, London, 1964.

Markowitz, F., Bellair, P., Liska, A., and Liu, J., 'Extending Social Disorganization Theory: Modeling The Relationships between Cohesion, Disorder, and Fear', *Criminology*, 39, no. 2 (2001).

Marquis, G., 'Vancouver Vice: The Police and the Negotiation of Morality, 1904–1935', in H. Foster and J. McLaren (eds), *Essays in the History of Canadian Law*, volume 6, Toronto, 1995.Marris, P. and Rein, M., *Dilemmas of Social Reform: Poverty and Community Action in the United States*, Harmondsworth, 1974.

Marsh, P., Rosser, E., and Harré, R., *The Rules of Disorder*, London, 1978.

Marshall, T., *Sociology at the Crossroads*, London, 1964.

Martin, S., *Breaking and Entering*, Berkeley, Calif., 1980.

Martins, H., 'Time and Theory in Sociology', in J. Rex (ed.), *Approaches to Sociology*, London, 1974.

Martinson, R., 'What Works? Questions and Answers about Penal Reform', *Public Interest*, 35 (1974).

Marx, G., 'The New Police Undercover Work', *Urban Life*, 8 no. 4 (1980).

—— 'Notes on the Discovery, Collection, and Assessment of Hidden and Dirty Data', in J. Schneider and J. Kitsuse (eds), *Studies in the Sociology of Social Problems*, Norwood, NJ, 1984.

—— *Under Cover: Police Surveillance in America*, Berkeley, 1988.

Mathiesen, T., *The Politics of Abolition*, London, 1974.

Matthews, R., *Policing Prostitution: A Multi-Agency Approach*, Enfield, Middlesex, 1986.

—— and Young, J. (eds), *Confronting Crime*, London, 1986.

—— 'Replacing 'Broken Windows': Crime, Incivilities and Urban Change', in R. Matthews and J. Young (eds), *Issues in Realist Criminology*, London, 1992.

—— 'Reflections on Realism', in J. Young and R. Matthews (eds), *Rethinking Criminology: The Realist Debate*, London, 1992.

Mattravers, A., 'Justifying the Unjustifiable: Stories of Women Sex Offenders', Ph.D. dissertation, University of Cambridge, 2000.

Matza, D., 'Subterranean Traditions of Youth', *Annals of the American Academy of Political and Social Science*, 338 (1961).

—— *Delinquency and Drift*, New York, 1964.

—— *Becoming Deviant*, Englewood Cliffs, NJ, 1969.

—— and Morgan P., 'Controlling Drug Use: the Great Prohibition' in T. Blomberg and S. Cohen (eds) *Punishment and Social Control: Essays in Honor of Sheldon L. Messinger*, New York, 1995.

—— and Sykes, G., 'Delinquency and Subterranean Values', *American Sociological Review*, 26 (1961).

Maurer, D., *Whiz Mob: A Correlation of the Technical Argot of Pickpockets with their Behaviour Pattern*, New Haven, Conn., 1964.

—— 'Prostitutes and Criminal Argots', *American Journal of Sociology*, 44, no. 4 (1939): 546–50.

Mawby, R., 'Kiosk Vandalism', *British Journal of Criminology*, 17 (1977).

—— 'Crime and Law: Enforcement in Different Residential Areas of the City of Sheffield', Ph.D. thesis, University of Sheffield, 1979.

—— (ed.), *Policing the City*, Brookfield, Vermont, 1979.

Maxfield, M., *Fear of Crime in England and Wales*, London, 1984.

Mayhew, H., *London Labour and the London Poor*, London, 1862.

Mayhew, P., 'Displacement and Vehicle Theft: An Attempt to Reconcile Some Recent Contradictory Evidence', *Security Journal*, 2 (1991).

—— *Residential Burglary: A Comparison of the United States, Canada and England and Wales*, Washington DC, n.d.

—— et al., *Crime as Opportunity*, Home Office Research Study No. 34, London, 1976.

—— Clarke, R., and Elliott, D., 'Motorcycle Theft, Helmet Legislation and Displacement', *The Howard Journal*, 28 (1989).

—— and Maung, N., *Surveying Crime: Findings from the 1992 British Crime Survey*, Research Findings No. 2, London: Home Office Research and Statistics Dept., 1992.

—— and Mirrlees-Black, C., *The 1992 British Crime Survey*, London, 1993.

Maynard, D., 'Language, Interaction, and Social Problems', *Social Problems*, 35, no. 4 (1988): 311–34.

Mays, J., *Growing Up in the City*, Liverpool, 1954.

—— *On the Threshold of Delinquency*, Liverpool, 1959.

—— *Crime and the Social Structure*, London, 1964.

Mead, G., 'The Psychology of Punitive Justice', *American Journal of Sociology*, 23 (1918).

—— 'The Philosophy of John Dewey', *International Journal of Ethics*, 46, 1 (1935).

—— *The Philosophy of the Act*, Chicago, 1938.

Melly, G., *Revolt into Style*, London, 1972.

Meltzer, B. et al., *Symbolic Interactionism*, London, 1975.

Merton, R.,

—— 'Social Structure and Anomie', *American Sociological Review*, 3 (1938). Revised and enlarged in successive editions of his *Social Theory and Social Structure*.

—— *Social Theory and Social Structure*, New York, 1949 and 1957.

—— 'Anomie, Anomia, and Social Interaction: Contexts of Deviant Bbehaviour', in M. Clinard, *Anomie and Deviant Behavior*, New York, 1964.

—— *On the Shoulders of Giants*, Chicago, 1993.

—— 'The Emergence of a Sociological Concept', in F. Adler and W. Laufer (eds), *The Legacy of Anomie Theory*, New Brunswick, NJ, 1995.

—— and Nisbet, R. (eds), *Contemporary Social Problems*, New York, 1961.

Miller, D., *George Herbert Mead*, Austin, Texas, 1973.

Miller, E., *Street Woman*, Philadelphia, 1986.

Miller, J., 'Systems of Control and the Serious Youth Offender', in Y. Bakal and H. Polsky (eds), *Reforming Corrections for Juvenile Offenders*, Lexington, Mass., 1979.

—— *Search and Destroy: African-American Males in the Criminal Justice System*, Cambridge, 1996.

Miller, W., *Cops and Bobbies*, Chicago, 1973.

Miller, W.B., 'Lower Class Culture as a Generating Milieu of Gang Delinquency', *Journal of Social Issues*, 14 (1958).

—— et al., 'Aggression in a Boys' Street-Corner Group', *Psychiatry*, 24 (1961).

Mills, C., 'Situated Actions and Vocabularies of Motive', *American Sociological Review*, 5, no. 4 (1940).

—— *The Power Élite*, New York, 1956.

—— *The Sociological Imagination*, New York, 1959.

—— *Sociology and Pragmatism*, New York, 1964.

Mizruchi, F., *Success and Opportunity: A Study of Anomie*, New York, 1964.

Mobilization for Youth, *A Proposal for the Prevention of Delinquency by the Expansion of Opportunities*, New York, 1960.

Morgan, P., *Child Care: Sense and Fable*, London, 1975.

—— *Delinquent Fantasies*, London, 1978.

—— Henderson, P., *Remand Decisions and Offending on Bail*, London, 1999.

Morris, A., *Women, Crime and Criminal Justice*, Oxford, 1987.

Morris, N. and Hawkins, G., *The Honest Politician's Guide to Crime Control*, Chicago, 1970.

Morris, P., *Prisoners and their Families*, London, 1965.

Morris, R., 'Female Delinquency and Relational Problems', *Social Forces*, 43 (1964).

—— 'Attitudes Towards Delinquency by Delinquents, Non-delinquents and Their Friends', *British Journal of Criminology*, 5 (1965).

Morris, T., *The Criminal Area*, London, 1957.

—— and Morris, P., *Pentonville*, London, 1963.

Morrison, W., *Theoretical Criminology: From Modernity to Postmodernism*, London, 1995.

Morse, M., *The Unattached*, Harmondsworth, 1965.

Morson, G., *Narrative and Freedom: The Shadows of Time*, New Haven, 1994.

Moynihan, D., *Maximum Feasible Misunderstanding*, New York, 1969.

Muncie, J., *Youth and Crime: A Critical Introduction*, London 1999

Murdock, G. and McCron, R., 'Youth and Class: The Career of a Confusion', in G. Mungham and G. Pearson (eds), *Working Class Youth Cultures*, London, 1976.

Murphy, E., *The Black Candle*, Toronto, 1922.

Murray, C., *Losing Ground: American Social Policy, 1950–80*, New York, 1984.

—— *The Emerging British Underclass*, London, 1990.

—— *Underclass: The Crisis Deepens*, London, 1994.

Myers, T., and Sangster, J., 'Retorts, Runaways and Riots: Patterns of Resistance in Canadian Reform Schools for Girls, 1930–60', *Journal of Social History*, 34, no. 3 (2001): 669–97.

Nadel, J., *Sara Thornton: The Story of a Woman Who Killed*, London, 1993.

Naffine, N., 'The Masculinity-Femininity Hypothesis: A Consideration of Gender-based Personality Theories of Female Crime', *British Journal of Criminology*, 25 (1985).

Nagel, I., 'Sex Differences in the Processing of Criminal Defendants', in D. Weisberg (ed.), *Women and the Law*, New York, 1980.

National Association for the Care and Resettlement of Offenders (Nacro), *Crime and Social Policy*, London, 1995.

National Research Council, *Understanding and Preventing Violence*, Washington, 1993.

Nelken, D., (ed.), *The Futures of Criminology*, London, 1994.

—— 'Comparing Criminal Justice' in M. Maguire, R. Morgan and R. Reiner (eds) *The Oxford Handbook of Criminology*, 3rd. edn, Oxford, 2002.

Nellis, M., review of R. Reiner and M. Cross (eds), *Beyond Law and Order*, *Howard Journal*, 31 (1992).

Nettler, G., 'Antisocial Sentiment and Criminality', *American Sociological Review*, 24 (1959).

—— *Explaining Crime*, New York, 1978.

Newburn, T., 'The Long-Term Impact of Criminal Victimization', *Home Office Research and Statistics Department Research Bulletin*, London, 1993.

—— and Stanko, E., (eds), *Just Boys Doing Business? Men, Masculinities and Crime*, London, 1994.

Newman, O., *Defensible Space: People and Design in the Violent City*, London, 1972.
—— *Community of Interest*, Garden City, NJ, 1981.
Newson, J. and Newson, E., *Seven Years Old in the Home Environment*, London, 1976.
New York City Youth Board, *Reaching the Fighting Gang*, New York, 1960.
Norris, C. and Armstrong, G., *The Maximum Surveillance Society: The Rise of CCTV*, Oxford, 1999.
Nourse, T, *Campania Foelix*, London, 1700.
Nye, F. and Short, J., 'Scaling Delinquent Behavior', *American Sociological Review*, 22 (1957).
O'Malley, P., 'War and Suicide', *British Journal of Criminology*, 15 (1975).
—— 'Risk, Power and Crime Prevention', *Economy and Society*, 21 (1992).
O'Reilly-Fleming, T., *Post-Critical Criminology*, Toronto, 1996.
Obrist, Hans Ulric, 'Interview with Howard Becker', accessed at http://home.earthlink.net/~hsbecker/obrist.htm.
Osborne, J., 'Juvenile Justice Policy in Canada', *Canadian Journal of Family Law*, 2 (1979).
Ormerod, P., *The Death of Economics*, London, 1994.
Packer, H., *Limits of the Criminal Sanction,* California, 1968.
Pahl, R., *Whose City?* London, 1970.
—— '"Collective Consumption" and the State in Capitalist and State Socialist Societies', in R. Scase (ed.), *Industrial Society: Class, Cleavage and Control*, London, 1977.
—— 'Stratification: The Relation between States and Urban and Regional Development', *International Journal of Urban and Regional Research*, 1, no. 1 (1977).
Pailthorpe, G., *Studies in the Psychology of Delinquency*, London, HMSO, 1932.
Painter, K., *Crime Prevention and Public Lighting with Special Focus on Women and Elderly People*, Enfield, Middlesex, 1989.
—— *Lighting and Crime Prevention for Public Safety*, Enfield, Middlesex, 1989.
Palmer, J., 'Thrillers: The Deviant Behind the Consensus', in I. Taylor and L. Taylor (eds), *Politics and Deviance*, Harmondsworth, 1973.
Park, R., 'The City: Suggestions for the Investigation of Human Behavior in the City Environment', *American Journal of Sociology*, 20 (1915). Reprinted in R. Park and E. Burgess (eds), *The City*, Chicago, 1925.
—— *The Crowd and the Public*, Chicago, 1921.
—— *The Immigrant Press and its Control*, New York, 1922.
—— 'Community Organization and Juvenile Delinquency', in R. Park and E. Burgess (eds), *The City*, Chicago, 1925.
—— 'The City as a Social Laboratory', in T. Smith and L. White (eds), *Chicago: An Experiment in Social Science Research*, Chicago, 1929.
—— and Burgess, E. (eds), *The City*, Chicago, 1925.
Parker, H., *The View From the Boys*, Newton Abbot, 1974.
—— Bakx, K., and Newcombe, R., *Living with Heroin*, Milton Keynes, 1988.
Parker, T. and Allerton, R., *The Courage of His Convictions*, London, 1964.
Parkin, F., *Marxism and Class Theory: A Bourgeois Critique*, London, 1979.
Parsons, T., *The Social System*, New York, 1951.
Patrick, J., *A Glasgow Gang Observed*, London, 1973.
Pavlich, G., 'Critical Genres and Radical Criminology in Britain', *The British Journal of Criminology*, 41 (2001).
Paxton, P., 'Is Social Capital Declining in the United States? A Multiple Indicator Assessment' *American Journal of Sociology*, 105 (1999): 88–127.
Pearce, F., *Crimes of the Powerful*, London, 1976.

Pearson, G., *The Deviant Imagination*, London, 1975.

—— '"Paki-Bashing" in a North East Lancashire Cotton Town: A Case Study and its History', in G. Mungham and G. Pearson (eds), *Working Class Youth Culture*, London, 1976.

—— *Hooligan: A History of Respectable Fears*, London, 1983.

—— *The New Heroin Users*, Oxford, 1987.

Petersilia, J., et al., *Criminal Careers of Habitual Felons*, Washington, 1978.

Phillipson, M., *Sociological Aspects of Crime and Delinquency*, London, 1971.

Phillipson, M., 'Thinking Out of Deviance', unpublished paper, 1974.

—— and Roche, M., 'Phenomenology, Sociology and the Study of Deviance', in P. Rock and M. McIntosh (eds), *Deviance and Social Control*, London, 1974.

Pike, L., *A History of Crime in England*, London, 1876.

Piliavin, I. and Briar, S., 'Police Encounters with Juveniles', *American Journal of Sociology*, 70 (1964).

Pitts, J., and Hope, T., 'The Local Politics of Inclusion—The State and Community Safety', *Social Policy and Administration*, 31, no. 5 (1997): 37–58.

Piven, F. and Cloward, R., *Regulating the Poor*, New York, 1971.

Pizzey, E., *Scream Quietly or the Neighbours will Hear*, Harmondsworth, 1974.

Platt, A., review of *The New Criminology*, *Sociological Quarterly*, 14 (1973).

—— '"Street Crime": A View From the Left'. *Crime and Social Justice*, 9 (1978).

—— *The Child Savers: The Invention of Delinquency*, Chicago, 1969 and 1975.

Player, E., 'Women and Crime in the City', in D. Downes (ed.), *Crime and the City*, London, 1989.

Plummer, K., *Sexual Stigma: An Interactionist Account*, London, 1975.

—— 'Misunderstanding Labelling Perspectives', in D. Downes and P. Rock (eds), *Deviant Interpretations*, Oxford, 1979.

—— *Documents of Life*, London, 1983.

—— (ed.), *Modern Homosexualities: Fragments of Lesbian and Gay Experience*, London, 1992.

—— *Telling Sexual Stories: Power, Change, and Social Worlds*, London, 1995.

Police Review (UK), 3 August 1963.

Pollak, O., *The Criminality of Women*, New York, 1950.

Polk, K., *When Men Kill: Scenarios of Masculine Violence*, Cambridge, 1994.

Polsky, N., *Hustlers, Beats and Others*, Chicago, 1967.

Polvi, N. et al., 'The Time Course of Repeat Burglary Victimization', *British Journal of Criminology*, 31 (1991).

Popper, K., *Conjectures and Refutations*, London, 1963.

Porterfield, A., *Youth in Trouble*, Fort Worth, Texas, 1946.

Poulantzas, N., *Classes in Contemporary Capitalism*, London, 1975.

Power, A., 'How to Rescue Council Housing', *New Society*, 4 June 1981.

—— and Tunstall, R., *Dangerous Disorder: Riots and Violent Disturbances in Thirteen Areas of Britain, 1991–92*, York, UK, 1997.

Poyner, B., *Design against Crime*, London, 1983.

—— Helson, P., and Webb, B., *Layout of Residential Areas and its Influence on Crime*, London, 1985.

Pratt, M., *Mugging as a Social Problem*, London, 1981.

President's Commission on Law Enforcement and Administration of Justice, *Crime and Its Impact: An Assessment*, Washington, DC, 1967.

Probyn, W., *Angel Face*, London, 1977.

Pryce, K., *Endless Pressure: A Study of West Indian Life-Styles in Bristol*, Harmondsworth, 1979.

Punch, M., *Policing the Inner City*, London, 1979.

—— 'Officers and Men: Occupational Culture, Interrank Antagonism and the Investigation of Corruption', unpublished paper, 1980.

—— *Dirty Business: Exploring Corporate Misconduct*, London, 1996.

Putnam, R., *Bowling Alone: The Collapse and Revival of American Community*, New York, 2000.

Quetelet, A., *Essai de Physique Sociale*, Brussels, 1869.

Quinn, J., 'The Burgess Zonal Hypothesis and its Critics', *American Sociological Review*, 5, no. 2 (1940): 210–18.

——. 'Angels, Bandidos, Outlaws, and Pagans: The Evolution of Organized Crime among the Big Four 1% Motorcycle Clubs', *Deviant Behaviour*, 22 (2001): 379–99.

Quinney, R., *The Social Reality of Crime*, Boston, Mass., 1970.

—— 'Crime Control in Capitalist Society', in I. Taylor, P. Walton, and J. Young (eds), *Critical Criminology*, London, 1975.

Rains, P., *Becoming an Unwed Mother*, Chicago, 1971.

Rainwater, L., *Behind Ghetto Walls*, Chicago, 1970.

Raitz, K., 'Ethnic Maps of North America', *Geographical Review*, 68, no. 3 (1978): 335–50.

Ratner, S., "Pioneering Critical Criminologies in Canada", Canadian Journal of Criminology and Criminal Justice, 9, no. 1 (2006).

Raushenbush, W., *Robert Park: Biography of a Sociologist*, Durham, NC, 1979.

Raw, C., Hodgson, G., and Page, B., *Do You Sincerely Want to Be Rich? Bernard Cornfeld and IOS: An International Swindle*, London, 1971.

Rawsthorne, T., 'The Objectives and Content of Policy-Oriented Research', *Home Office Research Unit Research Bulletin*, 6 (1978).

Reckless, W., 'The Distribution of Commercialized Vice in the City', in Burgess, E. (ed.), *The Urban Community*, Chicago, 1926.

—— *Vice in Chicago*, Chicago, 1933.

—— 'The Good Boy in a High Delinquency Area', *Journal of Criminal Law, Criminology and Police Science*, 48, no.1 (1957).

—— *The Crime Problem*, New York, 1967.

—— Dinitz, S., and Murray, E., 'Self-Concept as an Insulator against Delinquency', *American Sociological Review*, 21 (1956).

—— 'A Sociological Case Study of a Foster Child', *Journal of Educational Sociology*, 2, no. 10 (1929): 567–84.

—— 'Juvenile Delinquency and Behavior Patterning', *Journal of Educational Sociology*, 10 no. 8 (1937): 493–505.

—— 'Suggestions for the Sociological Study of Problem Children*'*, *Journal of Educational Sociology*, 2, no. 3 (1928): 156–71.

Reed, Myer S. Jr., Jerry Burnette, and Richard R. Troiden, 'Wayward Cops: The functions of deviance in groups reconsidered', *Social Problems*, 24, no. 5 (1977): 565–75.

Reiman, J., *The Rich Get Richer and the Poor Get Prison: Ideology, Class, and Criminal Justice*, New York, 1990.

—— and Headlee, S., 'Marxism and Criminal Justice Policy', *Crime and Delinquency*, 27, 1 (1981).

Reiner, R. and Cross, M. (eds), *Beyond Law and Order: Criminal Justice Policy and Politics into the 1990s*, London, 1991.

Reiss, A., 'The Social Integration of Queers and Peers', *Social Problems*, 9 (1961).

—— 'Inappropriate Theories and Inadequate Methods as Policy Plagues: Self-Reported Delinquency and the Law', in Demerath, N. et al., *Social Policy and Sociology*, New York, 1975.

—— and Rhodes, A., 'The Distribution of Juvenile Delinquency in the Social Class Structure', *American Sociological Review*, 26 (1961).

—— and Tonry, M. (eds), *Communities and Crime*, Chicago, 1986.

Reuter, P., *Disorganized Crime*, Cambridge, Mass., 1983.

Review Symposium, *British Journal of Criminology*, 24 (1984).

Rex, J., *Key Problems of Sociological Theory*, London, 1961.

—— *Discovering Sociology*, London, 1973.

—— and Moore, R., *Race, Community and Conflict*, London, 1967.

Reynolds, F., *The Problem Estate*, Hants, 1986.

Riele, K., 'Youth "at Risk": Further Marginalizing the Marginalized?', *Journal of Education Policy*, 21, no. 2 (2006): 129—45.

Riesman, D., *The Lonely Crowd*, Yale, 1950.

Riley, D. and Shaw, M., *Parental Supervision and Juvenile Delinquency*, London, 1985.

Robertson, R. and Taylor, L., *Deviance, Crime and Socio-Legal Control*, Oxford, 1973.

Robins, D., *We Hate Humans*, London, 1984.

—— *Tarnished Vision*, Oxford, 1992.

Rock, P., *Deviant Behaviour*, London, 1973.

—— *Making People Pay*, London, 1973.

—— Review of Smart, C., 'Women, Crime and Criminology', *British Journal of Criminology*, 17 (1977).

—— *The Making of Symbolic Interactionism*, London, 1979.

—— and Downes, D., (eds), *Deviant Interpretations: Problems in Criminological Theory*, New York, 1979.

—— 'Has Deviance a Future?', in H. Blalock (ed.), *Sociological Theory and Research*, New York, 1981.

—— *A View From the Shadows*, Oxford, 1986.

—— *Helping Victims of Crime: The Home Office and the Rise of Victim Support in England and Wales*, Oxford, 1990.

—— Foreword to J. Lowman, and B. MacLean (eds), *Realist Criminology: Crime Control and Policing in the 1990s*, Toronto, 1993.

—— 'Rules, Boundaries and the Courts', *British Journal of Sociology*, 49 (1998).

—— 'The Social Organization of British Criminology', in M. Maguire, et al. (eds), *The Oxford Handbook of Criminology*, Oxford, 1994.

—— *Reconstructing a Women's Prison*, Oxford, 1996.

—— 'Holloway' in N. Rafter (ed.), *Encyclopedia of Women and Crime*, Phoenix, 2000.

—— and Cohen, S., 'The Teddy Boy', in V. Bogdanor and R. Skidelsky (eds), *The Age of Affluence*, London, 1970.

—— and McIntosh, M. (eds), *Deviance and Social Control*, London, 1974.

Rorty, R., *Objectivity, Relativism and Truth*, Cambridge, UK, 1991.

Rose, A. (ed.), *Human Behavior and Social Processes*, New York, 1962.

Rosenbaum, D., 'A Critical Eye on Neighbourhood Watch: Does It Reduce Crime and Fear?', in T. Hope and M. Shaw (eds), *Communities and Crime Reduction*, London, 1988.

Rosenhan, D., 'On Being Sane in Insane Places', *Science*, 179 (1973).

Rosenhan, K., 'Female Deviance and the Female Sex Role', *British Journal of Sociology*, 26 (1973).

Roth, J. and Eddy, E., *Rehabilitation for the Unwanted*, New York, 1967.

Rubington, E. and Weinberg, M. (eds), *Deviance*, New York, 1968.

Rubinstein, J., *City Police*, New York, 1973.

Rudé, G., *The Crowd in History*, New York, 1964.

Ruggiero, V., *Organised and Corporate Crime in Europe*, Aldershot, 1996.

—— *Crime and Markets*, Oxford, 2000.

Runciman, W., *Relative Deprivation and Social Justice*, London, 1966.

Rusche, G. and Kirchheimer, O., *Punishment and Social Structure*, New York, 1939.

Rutter, M., *Maternal Deprivation Reassessed* (2nd edn), Harmondsworth, 1981.

—— and Smith, D., *Psychosocial Disorders in Young People*, Chichester, 1995.

Sacks, H., 'Notes on Police Assessment of Moral Character', in D. Sudnow (ed.), *Studies in Social Interaction*, New York, 1972.

Sainsbury, P., 'The Epidemiology of Suicide', in A. Roy (ed.), *Suicide*, Baltimore, Williams and Wilkins, 1986.

—— 'Suicide Trends in Europe: An International Epidemiological Study', unpublished paper.

Sampson, A., *Lessons from a Victim Support Crime Prevention Project*, London, 1991.

—— et al., 'Crime, Localities and the Multi-Agency Approach', *British Journal of Criminology*, 28 (1988).

—— and Laub, *Crime in the Making: Pathways and Turning Points through Life*, Cambridge, Mass., 1993.

—— and Laub, *Shared Beginnings, Divergent Lives*, Cambridge, Mass., 2003.

Sampson, R. and Raudenbush, S., 'Systematic Social Observation of Public Spaces: A New Look at Disorder in Urban Neighborhoods', *American Journal of Sociology*, 105 (1999).

—— 'Disorder in Urban Neighbourhoods—Does It Lead to Crime?', Research in Brief, US National Institute of Justice, Washington, 2001.

—— and Woolredge, J., 'Linking the Micro and Macro Levels of Lifestyle-Routine Activity and Opportunity Models of Predatory Victimization', *Journal of Quantitative Criminology*, 3 (1987).

Samuel, R. (ed.), *Ruskin College, History Workshop Pamphlets*, Oxford, 1970.

Sangster, J., 'Incarcerating 'Bad Girls': The Regulation of Sexuality through the Female Refuges Act in Ontario, 1920–1945', *Journal of the History of Sexuality*, 7, no. 2 (1996): 239–75.

—— 'Criminalizing the Colonized: Ontario Native Women Confront the Criminal Justice System, 1920–60', *Canadian Historical Review*, 80, no. 1 (1999): 32–60.

—— 'Girls in Conflict with the Law: Exploring the Construction of Female 'Delinquency' in Ontario, 1940–60', *Canadian Journal of Women and the Law*, 12, no. 1 (2000).

—— *Girl Trouble: Female Delinquency in English Canada*, Toronto, 2002

Scheff, T., *Being Mentally Ill*, London, 1966.

—— (ed.), *Mental Illness and Social Processes*, New York, 1967.

—— 'Negotiating Reality: Notes on Power in the Assessment of Responsibility', *Social Problems*, 16, no. 1 (1968).

Schichor, D., 'Crime Patterns and Socio-economic Development: A Cross-National Analysis', *Criminal Justice Review*, 15 (1990).

Schur, E., *Narcotic Addiction in Britain and America*, London, 1963.

—— *Crimes without Victims: Deviant Behavior and Public Policy*, Englewood Cliffs, NJ, 1965.

—— *Radical Non-Intervention: Rethinking the Delinquency Problem*, Englewood Cliffs, NJ, 1973.

Schutz, A., 'Common Sense and Scientific Interpretation of Human Action', in M. Natanson (ed.), *Collected Papers*, I, The Hague, 1964.

—— 'The Social World and the Theory of Social Action', in A. Broderson (ed.), *Collected Papers*, II, The Hague, 1964.

—— *The Structures of the Life-World*, London, 1974.

Schneider, E., and E. Young, 'Ecological Interrelationships of Juvenile Delinquency, Dependency, and Population Mobility: A Cartographic Analysis of Data from Long Beach, California', *American Journal of Sociology*, 41, no. 5 (1936): 598–610.

Scott, M. and Lyman, S., 'Accounts, Deviance and Social Order', in J. Douglas (ed.), *Deviance and Respectability*, New York, 1970.

Scott, R., *The Making of Blind Men*, New York, 1969.

—— 'A Proposed Framework for Analyzing Deviance as a Property of Social Order', in R. Scott and J. Douglas, (eds), *Theoretical Perspectives on Deviance*, New York, 1972.

—— *Why Sociology Does Not Apply*, New York, 1979.

—— and Douglas, J. (eds), *Theoretical Perspectives on Deviance*, New York, 1972.

Scottish Office Central Research Unit, *The Effect of Closed Circuit Television on Recorded Crime Rates and Public Concern about Crime in Glasgow*, Edinburgh, 1999.

Scull, A., 'Mad-Doctors and Magistrates', *Archives of European Sociology*, 15 (1976).

—— *Decarceration: Community Treatment and the Deviant: A Radical View*, Englewood Cliffs, NJ, 1977.

Sellin, T., 'The Negro Criminal', *Annals of the American Academy of Political and Social Science*, 1928.

—— *Culture Conflict and Crime*, New York, 1938, in M. Wolfgang et al. (eds), *The Sociology of Crime and Delinquency*, New York, 1962.

—— 'The Significance of Records of Crime', in M. Wolfgang, et al. (eds), *The Sociology of Crime and Delinquency*, New York, 1962.

Semple, J., *Bentham's Prison: A Study of the Panopticon Penitentiary*, Oxford, 1993.

Sennett, R., *The Corrosion of Character: The Personal Consequences of Work in the New Capitalism*, New York, 1998.

—— *Respect in a World of Inequality*, New York, (2003).

Sereny, G., *Albert Speer: His Battle with Truth*, Basingstoke, 1995.

Shapland, J. and Vagg, J., *Policing by the Public*, Oxford, 1988.

Sharrock, W., 'Ethnomethodology and British Sociology: Some Problems of Incorporation', paper, delivered to the British Sociological Association Conference, Lancaster University, 1980.

Shaw, C., *The Jackroller*, Chicago, 1930.

—— *The Natural History of a Delinquent Career*, Chicago, 1931.

—— 'Male Juvenile Delinquency and Group Behavior', in J. Short (ed.), *The Social Fabric of the Metropolis*, Chicago, 1971.

—— and McKay, H., *Juvenile Delinquency and Urban Areas*, Chicago, 1942.

Shearing, C. and Stenning, P., 'From the Panopticon to Disney World', in A. Doob and E. Greenspan (eds), *Perspectives in Criminal Law*, Aurora, Ont., 1985.

Shelley, L., *Crime and Modernization*, Carbondale, Ill., 1981.

Sherman, L. and Berk, R., *The Minneapolis Domestic Violence Experiment*, Washington, 1984.

Shibutani, T., *The Derelicts of Company K*, Berkeley, Calif., 1978.

Shils, E., *The Present State of American Sociology*, Glencoe, Ill., 1948.

—— 'Tradition, Ecology and Institution in the History of Sociology', *Daedalus*, 9 (1970).

Shoham, S., *The Mark of Cain*, Jerusalem, 1970.

Shore, M., 'Carl Dawson and the Research Ideal: The Evolution of a Canadian Sociologist', *Historical Papers*, 1985.

Short, E. and Ditton, J., 'Seen and Now Heard: Talking to the Targets of Open Street CCTVs' *British Journal of Criminology*, 38 (1998).

Short, J. (ed.), *The Social Fabric of the Metropolis: Contributions of the Chicago School of Urban Sociology*, Chicago, 1971.

—— 'The Natural History of an Applied Theory: Differential Opportunity and Mobilization for Youth', in N. Demerath et al. (eds), *Social Policy and Sociology*, New York, 1975.

—— and Strodtbeck, F., *Group Process and Gang Delinquency*, Chicago, 1967.

Shover, N., *Aging Criminals*, California, 1985.

—— *Great Pretenders*, Boulder, Co., 1996.

Simmel, G., *Conflict and the Web of Group Affiliations*, New York, 1955.

Simon, J., 'The Emergence of a Risk Society: Insurance, Law, and the State', *Socialist Review* (1987).

—— 'The Ideological Effects of Actuarial Practices', *Law and Society Review*, 22 (1988).

—— *Punishment and Social Control*, New York, 1995.

—— 'Governing through Crime' in L. M. Friedman and G. Fisher (eds), *The Crime Conundrum: Essays in Criminal Justice*, Boulder, Colo. 1997.

Simon, R., *Women and Crime*, Lexington, 1975.

Simpkin, M., *Trapped Within Welfare: Surviving Social Work*, London, 1979.

Simpson, S., 'Feminist Theory, Crime and Justice', *Criminology*, 27 (1989).

Sklair, L., 'The Fate of the 'Functional Requisites' in Parsonian Sociology', *British Journal of Sociology*, 21 (1970).

Skolnick, J., *Justice without Trial*, New York, 1966.

Small, A., 'Fifty Years of Sociology in the United States', *American Journal of Sociology*, 21 (1916).

Smandych, R., Lincoln, R., and Wilson, P., 'Toward a Cross-Cultural Theory of Aboriginal Crime: a Comparative Study of the Problem of Aboriginal Overrepresentation in the Criminal Justice Systems of Canada and Australia', *International Criminal Justice Review*, 3, no. 1 (1993).

Smart, C., *Women, Crime and Criminology*, London, 1977. Published by Routledge and Kegan Paul Ltd.

—— *Feminism and the Power of Law*, London, 1989.

—— 'Feminist Approaches to Criminology, or Postmodern Woman Meets Atavistic Man', in L. Gelsthorpe and A. Morris (eds), *Feminist Perspectives in Criminology*, London, 1990.

Smigel, E. and Ross, H., *Crimes against Bureaucracy*, New York, 1970.

Smith, A., *Women in Prison: A Study in Penal Methods*, London, 1962.

Smith D., 'Youth Crime and Conduct Disorders', in D. Smith and M. Rutter (eds), *Psychosocial Disorders in Young People: Time Trends and Their Causes*, Chichester, 1995.

—— 'Less Crime without More Punishment', *Edinburgh Law Review*, 3(1999): 294–316.

—— 'Changing Situations and Changing People', in von A. Hirsch, D. Garland and A. Wakefield (eds), *Ethical and Social Perspectives on Situational Crime Prevention*, Oxford, 2000.

—— and Gray, J., *Police and People in London*, London, 1983.

Smith, S., *Crime, Space and Society*, London, 1987.

—— and Razzell, P., *The Pools Winners*, London, 1975.

Snider, L., 'The Sociology of Corporate Crime: An Obituary', *Theoretical Criminology*, 4, no. 2 (2000).

Snodgrass, J., 'Clifford R. Shaw and Henry D. McKay: Chicago Criminologists', *British Journal of Criminology*, 16, no. 1 (1976).

Solomon, P., *Soviet Criminologists and Criminal Policy*, London, 1978.

South, N., 'Drugs, Alcohol and Crime' in M. Maguire, R. Morgan and R. Reiner (eds), *The Oxford Handbook of Criminology*, Oxford, 2002.

Sparks, R. et al., *Surveying Victims*, Chichester, 1977.

Spergel, I., *Racketville, Slumtown, Haulburg*, Chicago, 1964.

Spiegel, J., 'Problems of Access to Target Populations', in R. Conant and M. Levin M. (eds), *Problems in Research on Community Violence*, New York, 1969.

Spierenburg, P., *The Spectacle of Suffering: Executions and the Evolution of Repression*, Cambridge, 1984.

Sprott, J., 'Understanding Public Views of Youth Crime and the Youth Justice System', *Canadian Journal of Criminology*, 38 (1996).

—— and Doob, A., 'Fear, Victimization, and Attitudes to Sentencing, the Courts, and the Police', *Canadian Journal of Criminology*, 39, no. 3 (1997): 297–91.

Srole, L., 'Social Integration and Certain Corollaries: An Exploratory Study', *American Sociological Review*, 21 (1956).

Stander, J., et al., 'Markov Chain Analysis and Specialization in Criminal Careers', *British Journal of Criminology*, 29 (1989).

Stanko, E., 'Typical Violence, Normal Precaution: Men, Women, and Interpersonal Violence in England, Wales, Scotland and the USA', in J. Hanmer and M. Maynard (eds), *Women, Violence and Social Control*, London, 1987.

Stanko, E., 'Women, Crime, and Fear', *Annals of the American Academy of Political and Social Association*, 539 (1995).

Stebbins, R., *Deviance: Tolerable Differences*, Toronto, 1988.

Steiner, G., *Language and Silence: Essays and Notes 1958–1966*, London, 1967.

Stenson, K. and Brearley, N., 'Left Realism in Criminology and the Return to Consensus Theory', in R. Reiner and M. Cross, *Beyond Law and Order: Criminal Justice Policy and Politics into the 1990s*, London, 1991.

Stephens, J., *Loners, Losers and Lovers*, Seattle, 1976.

Stinchcombe, A., 'Institutions of Privacy in the Determination of Police Administrative Practice', *American Journal of Sociology*, 69 (1963).

—— *Rebellion in a High School*, Chicago, 1964.

—— *Constructing Social Theories*, New York, 1968.

Stone, L., *The Family, Sex and Marriage in England, 1500–1800*, Harmondsworth, 1979.

Sudnow, D., 'Normal Crimes: Sociological Features of the Penal Code', *Social Problems*, 12 (1965).

Sullivan, M., '*Getting Paid*': *Youth Crime and Work in the Inner City*, Ithaca, NY, 1989.

Sumner, C., 'Marxism and Deviancy Theory', in P. Wiles (ed.), *The Sociology of Crime and Delinquency in Britain*, ii. *The New Criminologies*, London, 1976.

—— *Reading Ideologies: An Investigation into the Marxist Theory of Ideology and Law*, London, 1979.

—— 'Race, Crime and Hegemony: A Review Essay', *Contemporary Crises*, 5 (1981).

—— (ed.), *Crime, Justice and Underdevelopment*, London, 1982.

—— *The Sociology of Deviance: An Obituary*, Buckingham, 1994.

Sundholm, C. 'The Pornographic Arcade', *Urban Life and Culture*, 2, no. 1 (1974).

Sutherland, E., *Principles of Criminology*, Chicago, 1924. Extensively revised as Sutherland, E. and Cressey, D., *Criminology*, New York, 1979.

—— *White Collar Crime*, New York, 1949.

—— *The Professional Thief*, Chicago, 1956.

—— and Cressey, D., *Principles of Criminology* (5th edn), Chicago and New York, 1955.

Suttles, G., *The Social Order of the Slum*, Chicago, 1968.

—— *The Social Construction of Communities*, Chicago, 1972.

Sutton, M., 'Supply by Theft: Does the Market for Second-Hand Goods Play a Role in Keeping Crime Figures High?' *British Journal of Criminology*, 35, no. 3 (1995).

Sykes, G., 'Men, Merchants, and Toughs: A Study of Reactions to Imprisonment', *Social Problems*, 4, no. 2 (1956): 130–8.

—— *The Society of Captives*, Princeton, 1958.

—— and Matza, D., 'Techniques of Neutralization', *American Sociological Review*, 22 (1957).

Szasz, T., *The Manufacture of Madness*, New York, 1970.

—— 'On Not Admitting Error', 21–2. Available at Cybercenter for Liberty and Responsibility, http://www.szasz.com/freeman19.html. Reprinted with permission, *The Freeman: Ideas on Liberty*, published by the Foundation for Economic Education. All rights reserved.

Tannenbaum, F., *Crime and the Community*, New York, 1938.

Tanner, D., *The Lesbian Couple*, Lexington, Mass., 1978.

Tanner, J., 'Youth Culture and the Canadian High School: An Empirical Analysis', *Canadian Journal of Sociology*, 3, no. 1 (1978): 89–102.

Taylor, A., *Women Drug Users*, Oxford, 1993.

Taylor, H., 'Forging the Job: A Crisis of "Modernization" or Redundancy for the Police in England and Wales, 1900–39', *British Journal of Criminology*, 39 (1999).

Taylor, I., 'Client Refusal', *Case Conference*, 7 (1972).

—— 'Left Realist Criminology and the Free Market Experiment in Britain', in J. Young and R. Matthews (eds), *Rethinking Criminology: The Realist Debate, London, 1992*.

—— *Crime in Context: A Critical Criminology of Market Societies*, Cambridge, 1999.

—— and Taylor, L. (eds), *Politics and Deviance*, Harmondsworth, 1973.

—— (eds), *Critical Criminology*, London, 1975.

—— Walton, P., and Young, J. *The New Criminology*, London, 1973.

Taylor, L., *Deviance and Society*, London, 1971.

—— 'The Significance and Interpretation of Replies to Motivational Questions', *Sociology*, 6 no. 1 (1972).

Taylor, R. and Gottfredson, S., 'Environmental Design, Crime, and Prevention: An Examination of Community Dynamics', in A. Reiss and M. Tonry (eds), *Communities and Crime*, Chicago, 1986.

Teevan, J., and Dryburgh, H., 'First Person Accounts and Sociological Explanations of Delinquency', *Canadian Review of Sociology and Anthropology*, 37, no. 1 (2000): 77–93.

Teilmann, K. and Klein, M., 'Juvenile Justice Legislation: A Framework for Evaluation', in D. Shichor and D. Kelly (eds), *Critical Issues in Juvenile Delinquency*, Lexington, Mass., 1980.

Temkin, J., *Rape and the Criminal Justice System*, Aldershot, 1993.

Thomas, K., *Man and the Natural World: Changing Attitudes in England 1500–1800*, Harmondsworth, 1984.

Thomas, W. I., *The Unadjusted Girl*, Boston, 1923.

—— and Znaniecki, F., *The Polish Peasant in Europe and America*, New York, 1927.

Thompson, E., 'The Moral Economy of the English Crowd in the Eighteenth Century', *Past and Present*, 50 (1971).

—— *Whigs and Hunters: The Origin of the Black Act*, London, 1975.

Thompson, H., *Hell's Angels*, New York, 1966.

Thrasher, F., *The Gang: A Study of 1,313 Gangs in Chicago*, Chicago, 1927.

—— 'Social Backgrounds and Education', *Journal of Educational Sociology* 1, no. 2 (1927): 69–76.

—— 'Social Backgrounds and Social Problems', *Journal of Educational Sociology*, 1, no. 3 (1927): 121–30.

—— 'The Study of the Total Situation', *Journal of Educational Sociology*, 1, no. 8 (1928): 477–90.

—— 'How to Study the Boys' Gang in the Open', *Journal of Educational Sociology*, 1, no. 5 (1928): 244–54.

Tierney, J., *Criminology: Theory and Context*, Hemel Hempstead, 1996.

Tilley, N., *Understanding Car Parks, Crime and CCTV: Evaluation Lessons from Safer Cities*, London, 1993.

Titmuss, R., *Commitment to Welfare*, London, 1968.

Toby, J., 'Social Disorganization and Stake in Conformity: Complementary Factors in the Predatory Behaviour of Hoodlums', *Journal of Criminal Law, Criminology and Police Science*, 48 (1957).

—— 'An Evaluation of Early Identification and Intensive Treatment Programs for Pre-Delinquents', *Social Problems*, 13 (1965).

Tonry, M., *Malign Neglect, Race, Crime, and Punishment in America*, Oxford, 1995.

Townsend, P., *The Last Refuge*, London, 1963.

—— 'Area Deprivation Policies', *New Statesman*, 6 Aug. 1976.

Trasler, G., *The Explanation of Criminality*, London, 1962.

—— 'Situational Crime Control and Rational Choice: A Critique', in K. Heal and G. Laycock (eds), *Situational Crime Prevention*, London, 1986.

Traver, H., 'Crime Trends', in H. Traver and J. Vagg (eds), *Crime and Justice in Hong Kong*, Hong Kong, 1991.

Tunstall, J., *Media Sociology*, London, 1970.

Turk, A., *Criminality and the Legal Order*, Chicago, 1969.

Turnbull, C., *The Mountain People*, London, 1973.

Turner, R., 'Role-Taking: Process versus Conformity', in A. Rose (ed.), *Human Behavior and Social Processes*, New York, 1962.

—— *Ethnomethodology*, Harmondsworth, 1975.

Tyler, G., 'The Great Electrical Conspiracy', in Wolfgang, M. et al. (eds), *The Sociology of Crime and Delinquency*, New York, 1962.

Uggen, C. and Manza, J., 'Democratic Contraction? The Political Consequences of Felon Disenfranchisement in the United States', *American Sociological Review*, 68 (2003).

Valentine, C., *Culture and Poverty*, Chicago, 1968.

Valverde, M., 'Feminist Perspectives on Criminology', in J. Gladstone, R. Ericson and C. Shearing (eds), *Criminology: A Reader's Guide*, Toronto, 1991.

van Creveld, M., *The Transformation of War*, New York, 1991.

van Swaaningen, R. *Critical Criminology: Visions from Europe*, London, 1997.

Von Hirsch, A. (ed.), *Doing Justice*, New York, 1976.

Wacquant, L., 'Deadly Symbiosis: When Ghetto and Prison Meet and Mesh', in D. Garland (ed.), *Mass Imprisonment: Social Causes and Consequences*, London, 2001.

Wade, M., 'Sociological Study of the Dependent Child', MA thesis, McGill University, 1931.

Wadsworth, M., *Roots of Delinquency: Infancy, Adolescence and Crime*, London, 1979.

Waddington, P., 'Mugging as a Moral Panic', *British Journal of Sociology*, 37 (1986).

Walby, S., and Myhill, A., 'New Survey Methodologies in Researching Violence against Women', *British Journal of Criminology*, 41 (2001).

Walker, N., *Behaviour and Misbehaviour: Explanations and Non-explanations*, Oxford, 1977.

Wallerstein, J. and Wyle, C., 'Our Law-Abiding Law-Breakers', *Federal Probation*, 25 (1947).

Walsh, D., *Break-Ins*, London, 1980.

—— *Heavy Business*, London, 1985.

Ward, D. and Kassebaum, G., *Women's Prison*, London, 1966.

Warren, C., 'Mental Illness in the Family: A Comparison of Husbands' and Wives' Definitions', *Journal of Family Issues*, 4, no. 4–(1983): 533–58.

Wasserman, M., 'Rape: Breaking the Silence', *The Progressive*, November 1973.

Webber, C., 'Revaluating Relative Deprivation Theory', *Theoretical Criminology*, 11, no. 1– (2007): 97–120.

Weis, J., 'Dialogue with Matza', *Issues in Criminology*, 6, no. 1 (1971).

Wells, J., 'Crime and Unemployment', in Coates, K. (ed.), *The Right to Work*, Nottingham, 1995.

Welsh, S., 'The Manufacture of Excitement in Police–Juvenile Encounters', *British Journal of Criminology*, 21 (1981).

Werthman, C. and Piliavin, I., 'Gang Members and the Police', in D. Bordau (ed.), *The Police: Six Sociological Essays*, New York, 1967.

West, D., *Present Conduct and Future Delinquency*, London, 1969.

—— and Farrington, D., *Who Becomes Delinquent?*, London, 1973.

—— and Farrington, D., *The Delinquent Way of Life*, London, 1977.

—— and D. Farrington, *Delinquency: Its Roots, Careers and Prospects*, London, 1982.

Westergaard, J., 'The Withering Away of Class: A Contemporary Myth', in P. Anderson and R. Blackburn (eds), *Towards Socialism*, London, 1965.

Western, B. and Beckett, K., *How Unregulated is the U.S. Labor Market? The Penal System as a Labor Market Institution*, American Journal of Sociology, 104 (1999).

Westervelt, S., *Shifting the Blame: How Victimization Became a Criminal Defense*, New Brunswick: 1998.

Westley, W., 'Violence and the Police', *American Journal of Sociology*, 59 (1953).

Whyte, W. F., *Street Corner Society*, Chicago, 1965.

——'In Defense of Street Corner Society', *Journal of Contemporary Ethnography*, 21, no. 1 (1992).

Whyte, W.H., *The Organization Man*, New York, 1956.

Wilkins, L., *Social Deviance*, London, 1964.

Wilkinson, R., *Mind the Gap: Hierarchies, Health and Human Evolution*, London, 2000

Willing, J., 'The Profession of Bootlegging', *Annals of the American Academy of Political and Social Science*, May 1926: 40–8.

Willis, P., *Learning to Labour: How Working Class Kids Get Working Class Jobs*, Farnborough, Hants, 1977.

—— *Profane Culture*, London, 1978.

Wilmott, P., *Adolescent Boys in East London*, London, 1966.

Wilson, A., 'Urban Songlines: Subculture and Identity on the Northern Soul Scene, 1970s and After', Ph.D. thesis, London School of Economics, 1999.

Wilson, H., 'Parental Supervision: A Neglected Aspect of Delinquency', *British Journal of Criminology*, 20 (1980).

—— and Herbert, G., *Parents and Children in the Inner City*, London, 1978. Published by Routledge and Kegan Paul Ltd.

—— and Smith, E., 'Chicago Housing Conditions, VIII: Among the Slovacs in the Twentieth Ward', *American Journal of Sociology*, 20, no. 2 (1914): 145–69.

Wilson, J., *Varieties of Police Behavior*, Cambridge, Mass., 1968.

—— *Thinking about Crime*, New York, 1975.

—— and Herrnstein, R., *Crime and Human Nature*, New York, 1985.

—— and Kelling, G., "Broken Windows': The Police and Neighborhood Safety', *Atlantic Monthly* (March 1982).

Wilson, W., *The Truly Disadvantaged: The Inner City, The Underclass and Public Policy*, Chicago, 1987.

—— *When Work Disappears: The World of the New Urban Poor*, New York, 1996.

Wing Lo, T., *Corruption and Politics in Hong Kong and China*, Buckingham, 1993.

Winlow, S., *Badfellas: Crime, Tradition and New Masculinities*, Oxford, 2001

Wirth, L., *The Ghetto*, Chicago, 1928.

—— 'Culture Conflict and Misconduct', in his *On Cities and Social Life*, Chicago, 1964.

—— 'Human Ecology', in his *On Cities and Social Life*, Chicago, 1964.

—— 'Ideological Aspects of Social Disorganization', in his *On Cities and Social Life*, Chicago, 1964.

Wirth, L., 'Urbanism as a Way of Life', *American Journal of Sociology*, 44, no. 1 (1938): 1–24.

Wittke, C., 'Review', *Annals of the American Academy of Political and Social Science*, Nov. (1936): 369–70

Wolf, Daniel R., *The Rebels: A Brotherhood of Outlaw Bikers*, Toronto, 1991.

Wolfe, T., *Radical Chic and Mau-Mauing the Flak-Catchers*, London, 1971.

Wolfgang, M., *Delinquency in a Birth Cohort*, Chicago, 1972.

—— and Ferracutti, F., *The Subculture of Violence*, London, 1964.

—— et al. (eds), *The Sociology of Crime and Delinquency*, New York, 1962.

—— et al., *Evaluating Criminology*, New York, 1978.

Wootton, B., *Social Science and Social Pathology*, London, 1959.

Worsley, P., *The Trumpet Shall Sound*, London, 1957.

Wright, R. and Decker, S., *Armed Robbers in Action: Stickups and Street Culture*, Boston, 1997.

Wrong, D., 'The Oversocialized Conception of Man in Modern Sociology', *American Sociological Review*, 26 (1961).

Yarrow, M. et al., 'The Psychological Meaning of Mental Illness in the Family', in Rubington, E. and Weinberg, M. (eds), *Deviance*, New York, 1968.

Young, A., 'Feminism and the Body of Criminology', unpublished paper, 1991.

Young, J., *The Drugtakers*, London, 1971.

—— 'The Role of the Police as Amplifiers of Deviancy', in S. Cohen (ed.), *Images of Deviance*, Harmondsworth, 1971.

—— 'Working Class Criminology', in I. Taylor, P. Walton, and J. Young (eds), *Critical Criminology*, London, 1975.

—— 'Mass Media, Drugs and Deviance', in P. Rock and M. McIntosh (eds), *Deviance and Social Control*, London, 1974.

—— 'Left Idealism, Reformism and Beyond', in R. Fine, et al. (eds), *Capitalism and the Rule of Law*, London, 1979.

—— 'Incessant Chatter: Recent Paradigms in Criminology', in M. Maguire R. Morgan and R. Reiner (eds), *Oxford Handbook of Criminology*, Oxford, 1994.

—— 'Left Realist Criminology' in M. Maguire, et al. (eds), *The Oxford Handbook of Criminology*, Oxford, 1997.

—— 'From Inclusive to Exclusive Society', in V. Ruggiero, et al. (eds), *The New European Criminology*, London, 1998.

—— *The Exclusive Society*, London, 1999.

Young, P., *The Pilgrims of Russian Town*, Chicago, 1932.

Yousaf, K. et al., *Young Teenagers and Crime*, Glasgow, 1991.

Zander, M., 'What is the Evidence on Law and Order?', *New Society*, 3 Dec. 1979.

Zedner, L., *Women, Crime and Custody in Victorian England*, Oxford, 1991.

—— 'Dangers and Dystopias in Penal Theories', *Oxford Journal of Legal Studies*, 22 (2002).

Zimring, F. and Hawkins, G., 'The Growth of Imprisonment in California', *British Journal of Criminology*, Special Issue 34 (1994).

Zipfel, T., 'Broadwater Farm Estate, Haringey: Background and Information Relating to the Riot on Sunday, 6th October 1985', unpublished paper.

—— 'Hard Work Transforms a Nightmare Estate', *Peptalk*, 2 (1985).

Zorbaugh, H., *The Gold Coast and the Slum*, Chicago, 1929.

Index

Note: Terms that do not appear in the index may be found in the glossary.

Cusson, M., 146, 155

D'Arcy, Stephen, 264
dark figure of crime/deviance, 41, 42, 43, 209, 318, 363
Davies, Christie, 101
Davies, Garth, 347
Davis, Kingsley, 81, 91, 92, 101
Davis, M., 207, 397n13
Davis, Mike, 112; *City of Quartz*, 397n13
Davis, N., 75
Dawkins, R., 403n108; *The Blind Watchmaker*, 403n108
Dawson, Carl, vii, 62, 63, 64
Death of a Salesman (Arthur Miller), 127
Decker, Scott, 251
decriminalization, 331
defensible/indefensible spaces, 236, 338, 357
deinstitutionalization, 285
DeIulio, John, 352
DeKeseredy, W., 305, 306
delinquency, 144, 252, 363; and class conflict theories, 153; evaluating prevention projects, 321; Miller's six focal concerns, 151–2; as mundane, 140, 142, 157–8, 158; specialization, 139–40; subcultures, 139, 140, 144; Wirth's six characteristics, 138
demonstration projects, 325
Dennis, N., 159
Denzin, Norman, 71; study of domestic violence, 212–14
Depression, 114
deregulation, 111, 115
destigmatization/restigmatization, 332
determinism, 149, 281; biological, 289
Detroit, Michigan, economic decline, 159–60
deviance, 5, 18–19, 80, 94, 182, 204, 283–4, 364; action and reaction, 173, 194; in affluent society, 133; alternative moral order, 70, 207; ambiguity, 4; availability of, 65; blurred boundaries, 207–8; and capitalism, 14, 192, 280, 327; categories of, 4, 210; classification systems, 211–12; in classroom, 215–17; elusive quality, 23–9; hidden vs. visible, 26, 29; institutionalization, 132–3; investigating, 22–3, 24; labelling, 173–4; as learned, 73; medicalization of, 329, 366; normalization, 182; part of everyday life, 155–8; and politics of, 8, 10; and the powerful, 256–7, 268–9; primary and secondary, 131, 182, 229, 367; as a process, 148, 187, 188, 189; relativity of, 10–11; residual, 4, 367; resisting surveillance, 27; response to, 179, 183, 184; role of the public, 177–83; and self, 175–6; sexual, 212, 289, 372n43; and social status, 116; and trouble, 203–4; universal character, 86; vocabulary, 191, 218; why people don't commit, 247
deviant adaptations, 115–16
deviant lifestyles, 68

deviantology, viii, 2, 19, 270, 364; development of, 64–5
deviants, 186, 205, 284: and phenomenology, 205; and social bonds, 228, 229
Dewey, John, 57, 70
diachronic comparisons, 11
Dickens, Charles, 268
Dickinson, D., 158
differential association, 73–4, 139, 170, 245, 364
differential magnification, 165
disability, 346
discrimination, 346
Disney World, 244
disorder, 208, 240–1
displacement, 249–50, 338, 339–40, 364; double, 337
Ditton, Jason, 24, 44n1
diversion policy, 331–2
diversity, 65, 91, 258–9
Dobash, R.E., 213
domestic violence, 152, 271, 300; phenomenology and, 212–14; *see also* violence
Doob, Anthony, 47
Dostoevsky, Fyodor, 177
double-decker buses, 236
Douglas, J., 13, 43, 81, 102, 207, 210, 215; on Durkheim, 105, 128–9, 133; evolution of society, 82; *Observations of Deviance*, 215
Douglas, M., 96, 99, 102, 204, 205, 208, 209
Dowd, L., 253
Dowler, Ken, 46
Downes, D., 30, 105, 144, 145
drift, 140, 142, 143, 310, 364
drugs: in Canada, 209, 279–80; control of, 355; legislation, 209, 277, 278, 279–80; and media, 177 prohibition, 11, 180, 355
drug use, 160, 172; abuse, 180
drug users, 32, 176, 185, 188, 209, 279, 331; female, 308; and police harassment, 164
Dryburgh, H., 141
Durkheim, Émile, 12, 38, 82, 85–7, 106, 323; and anomie, 104, 105, 245; and aspirations, 116; and crime, 81, 84, 85–6, 257, 341–2; criticism of, 43–4, 128, 133; deregulation, 115; latent functions, 92; and penal theories, 89; and the sacred, 82; and social facts, 127; and statistics, 210; and suicide rates, 44, 45, 128–9, 133. Works: *The Division of Labour in Society*, 86, 106, 122; *Moral Education*, 89; *Le Suicide*, 38, 43–4, 106, 107, 127
Duster, T., 209, 211
dysfunction, 92

Eagleton, T., 347
Eaton, M., 300
ecological theory, 52, 59–62, 69, 257, 258, 322; criticism of, 76
Economic and Social Research Council (Britain), 46